accelerated development in recent years and the many challenges that have accompanied such rapid growth, especially those of population change and environmental degradation.

The Tar Heel State is enhanced by 194 illustrations.

MILTON READY is professor emeritus of history at the University of North Carolina at Asheville. The author of books on Georgia and North Carolina history, he received the E. Merton Coulter Award for the writing of Georgia history. He holds a Ph.D. in history from the University of Georgia. Ready lives in the mountains of western North Carolina.

Jacket illustrations: (front) pastel by Will Henry Stevens, courtesy of Blue Spiral 1, Asheville, North Carolina; (back, from top) Sir Walter Raleigh; Jane Johnson, a slave released by abolitionists in Philadelphia; Sequoyah, who invented a Cherokee syllabary; Howard W. Odum; University Day at the University of North Carolina at Chapel Hill, 1961, (left to right) Terry Sanford, William C. Friday, John F. Kennedy, and William B. Aycock; courtesy of North Carolina Collection, University of North Carolina at Chapel Hill

THE TAR HEEL STATE

THE TAR HEEL STATE

A History of

NORTH CAROLINA

Milton Ready

University of South Carolina Press

Published in Columbia, South Carolina,
by the University of South Carolina Press

Manufactured in the United States of America

09 08 07 06 05   5 4 3 2 1

Library of Congress Cataloging-in-Publication Data

Ready, Milton, 1938–
     The tar heel state : a history of North Carolina / Milton Ready.
          p. cm.
     Includes bibliographical references and index.
     ISBN 1-57003-591-1 (cloth : alk. paper)
     1. North Carolina—History.   I. Title.
     F254R43 2005
     975.6—dc22

2005009660

Frontispiece: Wright Brothers' flight, 17 December 1903. Library of Congress.

CONTENTS

ILLUSTRATIONS

PREFACE

In 1584, when Arthur Barlowe described the bountiful game, the abundance of wild grapes, and the sea of endless forests he found in the firm land that would be North Carolina, he became the first of many to chronicle the province's rich and vivid history. Writers from John Lawson to William Byrd II have recorded, depicted, and published North Carolina's history. Yet while modern historians such as Robert D. W. Connor, Hugh Lefler, Albert Ray Newsome, and William Powell have conscientiously and thoroughly interpreted the resources left by the state's early chroniclers and settlers, no general history has been attempted in almost two decades. Moreover, the later studies by Lefler and Powell, while careful and meticulous in presentation, seldom venture into the twentieth century with the same detail or certainty given earlier periods of the state's history. Mostly educated and nurtured in their studies before and just after World War II, both Lefler and Powell brought to their works the strengths, preferences, and predispositions of their training. Thus, an appreciation for the scientism and formality of social studies and its attendant fields, especially politics and economics, marked their works, while some of the new histories of minorities, urbanization, and the environment now appropriate to a later generation did not.

This study attempts to build upon the works of traditional historians such as Connor, Lefler, and Powell and to bring a different emphasis and insight to the history of North Carolina. In this way, more consideration has been given, for example, to the period surrounding the American Revolution as well as to the Civil War in North Carolina, both internal and defining conflicts that proved pivotal to the larger outcome of the nation's overall history. In like manner, chapters on slavery, the Cherokees, and urbanization, while topical in nature, emphasize the key role each has played in North Carolina's development. Spread out chronologically within chapters, subjects such as these frequently become transmuted and marginalized within larger histories. Lastly, the western region of the state, often lost from sight in the view from "tobacco road," has been given more consideration in the state's development.

Like that of so many of its sister states, North Carolina's history involves the experiences of many individuals and groups. Their individual telling would consume more time and paper than prudent, becoming instead a listing rather than a narrative of the state's past. As the scientist Carl Sagan once remarked, the history of the universe is not made up of atoms, but of stories about atoms. The same applies to North Carolina. In this narrative, the state's atoms have been rearranged to present a fresh and different story of North Carolina's past.

ACKNOWLEDGMENTS

Anyone who researches or who writes even a particle or portion of the history of North Carolina or, indeed, of any state or region surely must be impressed by the affection and involvement of those who keep and preserve records of the past. In truth, some of the most pleasurable moments in compiling the long and complicated history of this state came not from long nights of writing and editing but from listening to archivists, librarians, and local historians and authors describing what they had found in their work. One of the greatest treasures of this state lies in the Archives and Records section of the Division of Cultural Resources in Raleigh. Time and again, those who had the most knowledge but the least power in the state, collections specialists, archivists, and ordinary clerks and librarians, not only patiently answered questions and queries about individuals and events but also volunteered their knowledge and effort to obtain additional records and pictures. In Chapel Hill, Keith Longiotti and Stephen Fletcher, photographic archivists at Wilson Library, provided a longitudinal pictorial history of North Carolina through thousands of paintings, facsimiles, and photographic reproductions. In Asheville, Jay Gertz, Nancy Hayes, Noel Jones, and Leith Morgan Tate provided valuable technical and specialized services and support so necessary in today's modern, digitalized, and computerized world of research and writing. In like manner, Kathy Joyner and Michael Honeycutt of the University of North Carolina at Asheville Computer Center helped translate and transcribe manuscripts and visuals between computer softwares and systems. My wife, Nita West Ready, constantly encouraged and reassured me during the darkest days of reviews and revisions. Without Linda Burgin's gentle prodding and Judy Wyatt's and Rick Morehead's enthusiasm and reassurance, I would have taken yet another century to complete this history. Lastly, one person, Ben Leonard, should directly be given credit for prompting me to undertake such an arduous task. Years ago as a student in my North Carolina history class, he suggested that I write a history of the state from my own perspective, or, as he put it, "in my own voice." Yet Ben also represents all of my students who, through the years, have provided me with so much encouragement and knowledge.

THE TAR HEEL STATE

The Great Rift

ONE

The Geography and Geology of North Carolina

For North Carolina, as for so many other states, nations, and regions, geography has been a part of its destiny. At first glance, North Carolina seems more a rift, a sliver of land between Virginia and South Carolina, than a natural ordering between the two. Indeed, the state's ill-adapted east-west alignment, the result of political and not geological forces, has constrained not only its economic but its social and political development as well. The great geological rifts that divided the state into three distinct regions (mountains, foothills, and coastal areas) have also separated North Carolina politically, socially, and economically. It all began millions of years ago.

Perhaps billions of years passed before the first humans set foot on present-day North Carolina. Certainly, the big bang of possibly fifteen billion years ago gave us our first geological record and, with it, the beginnings of our solar system and planet. Thus, an enormous tunnel of time connected modern North Carolina to its creation, to its fission-centered origins. If, as Carl Sagan has suggested, those fifteen billion years made up one cosmic calendar year, then all of man's recorded history occupies the last ten seconds of the last day, 31 December, and North Carolina's existence only the last second.

Geologically, North Carolina's history began somewhere around 16 September of that cosmic year. At the end of the Paleozoic era, 15 September, when fish and plants developed and the first amphibians, land plants, and reptiles appeared, North Carolina existed as a minor part of a supercontinent called Pangaea. As the earth's brittle crust gradually cooled, it opened huge fissures and fractures exposing the molten rock, or magma, below. Existing far beneath the breakable surface, hot spots, really old, sunken volcanoes, pushed the magma into the cracks and ruptures along the length of the eastern United States. As new, hot oceanic crust welled up from the earth's interior along the ridges, cooler and older layers returned to the base foundation in a process called subduction, which took place along the deep oceanic trenches as one plate slid beneath another and down into the underlying mantle. The list of the sequelae of plate movements has been endless, continuing even today as Africa collides with Europe underneath the Italian peninsula. In a procedure that took thousands of years, long thin sheets of vertical rock thrust upward producing dikes between relatively flat areas of the supercontinent. Magmas also forced their way between layers of sediment or dirt, forming sills of rock that eventually hardened. Today, ancient sills as large as three hundred feet in thickness can be found in northern Durham County near the town of Butner, while other smaller dikes and sills in the Piedmont and coastal areas are seldom more than four to seven feet thick.

Graveyard fields, Blue Ridge
Parkway, western North Carolina.
Photo courtesy of Lois Lynn Bellemere,
Mars Hill, North Carolina.

The mountains surrounding the long, wide valley of the French Broad River in western North Carolina are as old as time itself. Long before a place such as North Carolina existed, antedating by millions of years man's first appearance on the eastern seaboard, a vast, shallow, warm sea washed over the area. There were no mountains, only a plateau surrounding an enormous ditch, an Appalachian trough stretching from western New York through North Carolina into southern Alabama. To the east and west the land rose gently to form enormous ridges bordering an immense Atlantean inland ocean.

From the almost continuous soft rain that fell three hundred million years ago, huge, sluggish rivers formed to carry sediment into that great Appalachian canal. Three shoreless deltas slowly formed, each more than one hundred miles wide. Today, the French Broad and Tennessee rivers remain as watery ribbons, faint reminders of those ancient waterways. For millions of years thereafter, more than twenty-five thousand feet of limestone, sandstone, shale, and other residue accumulated in the Appalachian depression. Its enormous weight frequently caused the great trough to sink. Gradually it collapsed an incredible six to eight miles into the earth's soft crust. There the original hard rock came into contact with temperatures high enough to liquefy and change the composition of the rock itself.

The resultant melting of many of the lower rock formations caused the earth above to shift and fold, creating a chain of lofty, majestic mountains. They probably towered five miles or more above the present French Broad plain in the western part of the state, not unlike the rugged Himalayas of today's Tibet and China. In a span of perhaps sixty-four to one hundred million years, erosion and nature inexorably wore down the rugged Appalachian peaks to give them their present grandfathered appearance. Combined with the forces of heat, pressure, erosion, and a gradual surface cooling, the earth's crust first began to bulge and, later, to tear apart. From the ancient supercontinent of Pangaea, the puzzle pieces called North America, Europe, and Africa emerged. The great rift between the continents had begun. At one moment, virtually all of the earth's rocks had been assembled together in one gigantic supercontinent. At another, continental blocks scattered across the globe as they are today. In a never-ending process, a piece of land at one of the poles today might be found at the equator tomorrow, geologically speaking.

As Pangaea split apart and North America migrated to the northeast, what would become the Coastal Plain of North Carolina sank below the onrushing sea. As the ocean swept westward over a retreating continental shelf, igneous and metamorphic rocks, eroded by water and ocean currents, became covered by sand, clay, mud, and sediment. Shallow inlets, coves, bays, and swamps dotted that ancient plain. Older deposits, called the Cape Fear Formation, and later ones, labeled the Middendorf Formation, built up huge deltas formed by rivers and streams silting into the new ocean. Kaolin, a unique white clay that produced fine white porcelain, characterized Middendorf Formations now found in Macon County in western North Carolina but which then existed as part of a vast, shallow Pangaean beach.

The Coastal Plain remained flooded for perhaps seventy million years of Cretaceous time, shifting slowly westward and eastward with changing river deposits and ocean tides. Shallow depths, broad wandering streams, sandy-bottomed lagoons, and an almost tropical climate defined that vast delta called the Black Creek Formation of eighty million years ago.

In the steamy mud and swamps of Black Creek time, primeval ancestors of magnolia, maple, sassafras, and pine trees grew in dense, crowded forests. Four miles below Elizabethtown in Bladen County, a bed of clay called Phoebus Landing, North Carolina's own tar pit, contains bone fragments of prehistoric animals that inhabited the Cape Fear delta. Shards of teeth and bone hint at the diversity of flora and fauna of the Black Creek era of eons past. With them, Phoebus Landing gave the jigsaw pieces to the puzzle of life in North Carolina perhaps eighty million years ago.

Ranging from six to thirteen feet in length, myriad prehistoric sharks infested the swamps and tidal rivers in Black Creek time. Mosasaurs, large marine lizards that grew to be almost thirty feet in length, wolfishly devoured the sharks, fish, turtles, and other vertebrates found in the lush lowlands. Fierce sawfish and rhinopterid ray fish also nested in the shallow lagoons. Bone fragments from dinosaurs whose carcasses floated downstream from the highland plateaus also appeared at Phoebus Landing. At least four and perhaps many more kinds of dinosaurs flourished in the high plains and humid deltas of North Carolina seventy to eighty million years ago. *Dryptosaurus,* a medium-sized carnivore, stood about seven feet high with a body almost thirty-three feet long. With a short, thick neck and huge, muscular hind legs, the flesh-eating *Dryptosaurus* ran down its prey and used its sharp teeth and long claws to tear its victims apart.

A duck-billed North Carolina dinosaur called *Hypsibema crassicauda* weighed almost two tons and grew to be almost ten feet tall and perhaps thirty feet long. A smaller *Hypsibema crassicauda* also lived alongside his larger relative in ancient North Carolina. *Ornithomimus,* an ostrichlike creature, towered almost eight feet in height, grew to be a

4

Plants and animals in North Carolina from John Brickell's 1737 Natural History of North Carolina. North Carolina Office of Archives and History, Raleigh.

little less that sixteen feet in length, ran at an incredible ground speed of twenty to thirty miles per hour, and consumed enormous quantities of plants, insects, and smaller reptiles with its hard, flat beak. Lastly, a ferocious dinosaurian crocodile almost forty feet in length, *Deinosuchus rugosus,* grew to be the size of a modern house with a head as large as a contemporary automobile. Additionally, layers of the Black Creek Formation called marls contained countless shells, bone fragments, and bones left behind by smaller, less menacing animals who lived on that muddy plain in North Carolina so long ago.

As sea levels continued to rise and the rift broadened at the end of Cretaceous time, the Black Creek marls became covered with layers of marine deposits that geologists called the Pee Dee Formation. An emerging continental shelf tilted to the west, draining the bays, swamps, and lagoons near the coast. Eastern North America then passed through a slow and steady ice age lasting into the millennia.

Nahyapuw. The Grype almost as bigg as an Eagle.

Drawing of a bald eagle by John White,
North Carolina's first naturalist.
North Carolina Collection, University
of North Carolina at Chapel Hill.

Animals did not flee before the advancing ice and snow. Instead, they moved with the warmth as the colder climate shifted slowly southward into the present southeastern United States. To the mountains of western North Carolina and Virginia there came giant mammoths and mastodons, various kinds of early bison, horses, panthers, lethal saber-toothed tigers, and huge piglike animals with short tusks called peccaries. Along with them came animals similar to those living in the mountains today, notably black bear and deer. In addition, arctic animals akin to the musk ox, mammoth, and walrus migrated as far south as the Carolinas and Florida.

In about 11,000 B.C.E., the ice and snow began to retreat for the last time. Vegetational patterns altered once more. Animals such as the musk ox and the mastodon followed the ice floes northward. Others, such as the bear, bison, and panther, remained behind, the smaller varieties flourishing on the margins of the forests near the cane brakes of the Tennessee and French Broad rivers in western North Carolina.

Reborn after the last ice age, the forests of North Carolina waited several millennia for man to walk and live in them. With more than fifty species, pines flourished everywhere. From the Piedmont inland, a vast, seemingly unbroken forest of pine and summer-green trees stretched to the horizon. Willow, poplar, birch, elm, mulberry, and sassafras could be found, sometimes with climbing bittersweet grape and creeper vines entwined around their trunks. Even the ancestor of the mighty oak, the king of North Carolina's forests today, grew in that phantom forest of long ago.

For the colony's earliest European settlers, these forests stood not as a source of fear and intimidation but for freedom and opportunity, for a limitless resource to be used to produce a civilization based upon wood and leather. On the eastern seaboard, the first settlers

William Bartram (1730–1823),
who traveled through western North
Carolina cataloging the flora and fauna.
North Carolina Collection, University of
North Carolina at Chapel Hill.

in the Albemarle region set about cutting down
trees; fashioning barrels, hogsheads, and hoops;
and turning clearings into sites for small distilleries and
sawmills producing naval stores such as pitch, tar, turpentine, and rosin. Scantling, a form
of crude pine lumber often shipped to other British colonies, especially those in the West
Indies, soon became a staple of the colony. The sight of burning fires from small distilleries and sawmills so characterized colonial North Carolina that travelers frequently labeled
the sometimes ragged and barefoot settlers who worked them as Tar Heels. The name, like
the substance, stuck.

From the cradle to the grave, early Carolinians found uses for the varieties of trees that
surrounded them. Pine, the most disparaged yet useful tree in early North Carolina, out-
fitted entire homes, from boards, shingles, staves, and clapboards to furniture and uten-
sils. Born into a pine barren environment, many early Carolinians also went to their graves
in a makeshift pine box. Hardwoods such as live oak duplicated many of the functions of
today's nuts and bolts, holding parts for mills and machinery together. Wheels to spin flax
and cotton came from maple, and, as an ultimate use, red cedar sometimes lined not only
trunks but caskets as well. Ingenious in similar and other ways, Native Americans also
adapted the bounty of the forests into their own wood and leather civilization.

From Giovanni da Verrazano, an Italian sailing for France in 1524, to Janet Schaw, the
imperious Scotswoman who visited the colony in the 1770s, early travelers to North Carolina recounted the endless emerald forests that stretched from the shore toward the horizon. The bewildering array of soft- and hardwood trees beneath the green canopy that
covered Carolina invited both awe and exploitation. The "faire fields and plains, . . . full
of mightie great woods," delighted Verrazano, while Schaw described majestic trees fit "to
adorn the palaces of kings." Yet Schaw found nobility only in North Carolina's forests, not
in its inhabitants. To naturalists and botanists drawn by the allure of the American wilderness, men such as William Bartram and the Frenchman André Michaux, North Carolina

Red trillium found along the Appalachian Trail near Bald Mountain in western North Carolina.
Photo courtesy of Brenda Whitt, Wolf Laurel, North Carolina.

Above: Flame azalea from western North Carolina.
Photo courtesy of Lois Lynn Belle-mere, Mars Hill, North Carolina.

Bee balm, also known as Oswego tea.
Photo courtesy of Brenda Whitt, Wolf Laurel, North Carolina.

represented the Garden of Eden peopled by Native Americans, exotic and noble savages from a more idyllic time in the past.

Nestled in the heart of the western mountains was an undulating plateau watered by a river of rugged beauty. Cherokees who first lived there called the river Tah-kee-os-tee (racing waters), and they located villages and burial grounds among the hills and towns in the valleys along the stream after it came down from a magical place called Nah-tah-ne-oh (the place where it became warm). Today the river is called the French Broad; the town, Hot Springs.

Between six thousand and eighteen thousand years ago, a series of shallow, egg-shaped depressions formed throughout the Coastal Plain. These Carolina bays were named after the loblolly bay plant, which grew in profusion in the basins. The evergreen leaves frequently stood out in brown winter scenes along the coast. Perhaps as many as three hundred thousand bays of various sizes existed between Maryland and Florida, possibly fifty thousand or more in North Carolina alone. Ranging from shallow, sandy lakes to vegetation-filled swamps, the Carolina bays measured several feet to a few miles across. Thought to have been caused by either a colossal meteor swarm striking the soft Coastal Plain or by a rising seashore that isolated existing natural depressions, the bays helped shape the earliest settlement patterns in North Carolina. The bays made transportation difficult and tended to isolate communities as well as to retard commerce and economic development.

Initially formed almost one million years ago during an ice age when sheets of frozen water overspread Europe and North America, the barrier islands off the coast define North Carolina's geographical uniqueness. A complex system of islands, rivers, sounds, inlets, and ocean, the islands changed continuously as wind, water, and storms swept over them for thousands of years. For example, when Arthur Barlowe and Philip Amadas sailed along the barrier islands on 4 July 1584, they looked at a far different sight than one would see today. When he landed at Bodie Island not far from the present-day Oregon Inlet, Barlowe romantically described a land "so full of grapes as the very beating and surge of the sea overflowed them," a soil so rich that "I think in all the world the like abundance is not to be found." Gone on today's barrier islands are the green hills, grapes, luxuriant vegetation, and white and red cedar forests first encountered by Amadas and Barlowe centuries ago.

Storms, hurricanes, tectonic shifts, and the gradual process of coastal morphology have combined to shift the location and size of the state's barrier islands. Long before the Roanoke colony appeared, Native Americans surely must have noted the hurricanes that slammed into their coastal settlements. Indians in villages such as Secotan and Pomeioc likely painted them on deerskins and orally passed accounts down for posterity in their folklore and myths. No stranger to hurricanes by the sixteenth century, Spanish ships sailing along the Outer Banks logged their appearances. Even the hardy Sir Francis Drake experienced one off Roanoke Island in June 1586. Barely fifty years after the Roanoke colony disappeared, one hurricane battered the coast on 15 August 1635. Others followed in 1638, 1656, 1667, and 1691. Twenty recorded storms swept across the coast in the eighteenth century, and, as technology and detection grew more sophisticated, sixty-eight more were identified in the next century. As observations and documentation continued to improve, still more storms were chronicled. Between 1900 and 1990, records verified more than 172 hurricanes and gales that had struck the barrier islands, and the hurricane season's beginnings were shifted to June.

One particular seventeenth-century storm stood out. Smashing into the islands in the fall of 1693, a hurricane so large and deadly that "it seemed to reverse the order of nature" forever changed the formation of the Outer Banks. Francis Hawks, an early writer of North Carolina history, found that after the mammoth storm "rivers before navigable, were stopped up; and other channels were opened that were never before navigable." A British customs official later verified the impact of the storm. "I am informed," he wrote, "that . . . according to local inhabitants there was an Inlett about 6 or 7 miles to the southward . . . which was the main Inlett of Currituck being considerably deeper than this [one], and was distinguished from this by the name of Miesquetough [Mosquito] Inlett the both were called Currituck Inlett which Inlett is within 30 years quite stopped up with dry sand and people ride over it."

Unlike hurricanes and gales, geomorphological processes occur gradually and less dramatically over time. This interaction between energy and earth, between shifting sands, blowing winds, and changing currents, causes a continual rearrangement of materials from the beach to the sound side of the islands. Because of this overwashing effect, the islands slowly roll themselves over and march relentlessly westward toward the mainland. In this way, the older barrier islands that have run ashore in the past reveal themselves in layers of peat formed from the tree stumps of long-dead forests and in salt marshes first glimpsed by Arthur Barlowe on that summer's day in 1584. Just as Barlowe's "sweet" grapes and white and red cedars have disappeared under the sea, so, too, have the footprints of the island's earliest Roanoke colonists.

West of Cape Hatteras, the barrier islands have moved northward approximately 90 feet a year for centuries. For all the Outer Banks, the drift landward, both westward and northward, has continued at an overall 106 feet per year. In all, the islands have shifted landward from approximately seventeen miles due west of Cape Kenrick to less than a mile near Cape Hatteras. Indeed, only Cape Hatteras, as prominent on maps now as it was centuries ago, seems largely to have escaped the forces of nature. Still, the rates of movement have declined dramatically since World War II. Thus, the greatest shifts in the barrier islands occurred during the earliest years of the eighteenth century, the least during the modern era.

Several former inlets on the coast may be identified by sunken vessels drawn on old maps and charts. Old and New Currituck Inlets, Caffey's Inlet, Colleton Island Inlet, and at least three other ancient channels were closed at one time or another by sand and sediment filling in around sunken obstructions, usually wrecked or abandoned ships. Coastal North Carolina's shifting dunes and sand bars have made it the nemesis of sailors and mariners since 1584. Indeed, Theodor De Bry's famous map of "The Arrival of the Englishmen in Virginia, 1584," taken from Thomas Hariot's "Account of Virginia," shows a wrecked vessel as a marker for every Carolina inlet. Over the centuries, scores of ships, from pirate galleons to stately steamers, have gone to the bottom of North Carolina's Bermuda triangle, a veritable "Hell's Hole" or "Graveyard of the Atlantic" for both mariners and their unlucky vessels.

Geographically, North Carolina's orientation runs from east to west along a distance of 540 miles, or, as the popular saying has it, from Manteo to Murphy. At its widest point, North Carolina stretches nearly 188 miles from north to south. Still, the state's east-west orientation means that its neighbors, Virginia, South Carolina, Tennessee, and Georgia, have not only influenced North Carolina's history and identity from its earliest settlements onward but have also frequently overshadowed it. Along the coast, the almost continual political squabbles between the Albemarle and Cape Fear regions reflect strong geographic and social ties to Virginia and South Carolina and not to each other, while, in the Blue Ridge mountains, the "Greenville to Greenville" axis demonstrates the economic dependence of the west to South Carolina and Tennessee. In at least two instances, the move to create an independent state of Franklin and the Walton War, westerners have shown their reluctance to be a political partner with the Piedmont and the coast. Indeed, for most of North Carolina's history, mountaineers have felt neglected if not entirely ignored by the rest of the state. Western North Carolinians sometimes have expressed this in the sentiment that several other state capitals are not only geographically closer to them than Raleigh is but also more understanding of their region's problems as well.

Although North Carolina has never ranked among the top ten mineral states, it nevertheless has a time-honored history of mineral production. Frequently called "nature's sample case," it contains important mineral deposits that periodically have had both regional and national importance. Indeed, the most remarkable feature of North Carolina's geology, its more than three hundred samples of minerals, has occurred because, geologically speaking, the state's such a mess, a disorderly jumble of rocks and dirt cut off by unnatural political boundaries. Even so, at different times since the colonial era, the state has produced gold, asbestos, clay (kaolin and common), corundum, feldspar, lithium, mica (scrap and sheet), monazite, olivine, phosphate rock, pyrophyllite, sand, gravel, stone, talc, chromite, copper, iron ore, lead, silver, titanium, tungsten, zinc, and even small amounts of coal. From the great stone quarry at Mount Airy to smaller ones throughout the western mountains, the state produces large amounts of granite for uses ranging from churches to countertops. Currently, North Carolina provides the nation more common clay, corundum, feldspar, lithium, mica, olivine, and pyrophyllite than any other state.

If geography and geology contain the seeds of destiny, then the western mountains personify the state as a sample case of minerals. North Carolina falls into three regions: the Coastal Plain, the Piedmont Plateau, and the Blue Ridge. Covering almost 6,200 square miles and ranging from Mount Mitchell, at 6,684 feet the tallest peak east of the Mississippi, to 1,850 feet in the valleys of the Blue Ridge, the mountains of western North Carolina are part of the Appalachian chain stretching from western New York to northern Alabama. Among the oldest in the world, the westernmost section of the Blue Ridge mountains running through North Carolina contains some of the state's richest mineral resources. For example, below the surface at Ore Knob in Ashe County and at Fontana and Hazel Creek in Swain County, small sulfide ore deposits run in belts that extend from southwestern Virginia through Carolina to the Tennessee border. Mined from 1855 to 1962, Ore Knob produced approximately 1.5 million tons of pyrite-pyrrhotite-chalcopyrite, all lustrous yellow and black minerals used in the manufacture of copper ore and sulfuric acid. Frequently, iron pyrite such as that found at Fontana can be mistaken for "fool's gold" instead of the

Map of North Carolina counties. North Carolina Office of Archives and History, Raleigh.

duller versions containing real gold. The Fontana mine operated from 1926 until 1944; the Hazel Creek mine, from 1900 to 1929 and briefly during World War II. When the TVA closed the Fontana dam, the resultant flooding of underground operations closed the mines. Both now lie submerged below the waters of the dam, a permanent part of the Great Smoky Mountains National Park.

Deposits at Ore Knob strikingly resemble the twenty-million-ton Great Gossan Lead diluvian in southwestern Virginia, while the Hazel Creek and Fontana lodes appear to be miniature versions of the world-class 180-million-ton deposit at Ducktown, Tennessee. Had the state's copper, lead, and pyrite deposits been marginally larger instead of just swatches, then the strip-mining, contamination, pollution, and destruction of the ecosystem that occurred in Virginia, West Virginia, and Tennessee might have despoiled the western mountains as well. The same could be said of silver and gold, coal, and uranium. By having samples and not large deposits of key minerals, North Carolina, for the most part, has managed to avoid the large-scale development and exploitation of its resources experienced by its sister states.

Talc mining began just before the Civil War along a belt extending from Cherokee County to the Hiwassee Reservoir. By 1988, North Carolina had produced more than 250,000 tons of high-grade talc. Used both as a powder and lubricant, talc mined near the town of Murphy in Cherokee County comes from underground, the only subsurface mine in the Carolinas that provides talc for pencils.

Along north Harper Creek in Avery County, the Wilson Creek Gneiss, a rock formation of alternating layers, carries a series of paper-thin uranium veins that stretch to the Crossnore complex in the northeast part of the county. Drilled and explored extensively in the 1970s and early 1980s, the deposits at north Harper Creek, like most North Carolina minerals, seem to be limited in scope, and, at present, are not worth the considerable capital expenditure needed for research and development.

Several significant deposits of pegmatite, a coarse granite rock containing quartz, feldspar, and mica, lie within the mountains of western North Carolina. By far the most significant finds exist in Spruce Pine and also near Franklin and Sylva. As part of the pegmatite deposits, large mica-rich layers and rolls crop up. Indeed, pegmatite deposits near

Spruce Pine have supplied much of the nation's scrap and sheet mica, feldspar, kaolin, and quartz since mining began there in 1868. Well over half of the United States' total sheet and scrap mica has come from Spruce Pine and near Sylva; remaining reserves, estimated at more than ten million pounds, should last another century.

North Carolina leads the nation in the production of olivine, a silicate of magnesium and iron existing usually as green crystals and used as a semiprecious stone of green garnet. Magnetite, a mineral called lodestone when magnetic, and chromite, kaolin, nickel, and vermiculite also can be found in limited quantities in western North Carolina.

Seldom influenced by political boundaries or state lines, geologists instead clump mineral resources into districts, belts, and pods that cross provincial and regional boundaries. In this way, the state's numerous deposits of gold, iron, vermiculite, pyrophyllite, tin, and tungsten, much like North Carolina's history, overlap into South Carolina and Virginia.

Volcanic-caused massive sulfide deposits occur in the Carolina slate belt, a region that extends from southern Virginia to northern Georgia. Along much of that stratum in North Carolina lies the Gold Hill fault zone, frequently the source of base metals such as silver and gold. While the number of such formations is large, almost all are relatively small in size, usually comprising less than five hundred thousand tons. The largest and most productive areas, the Cid District in Davidson County and the Gold Hill sections of Rowan, Stanly, and Cabarrus counties, also gave rise to some of the most romantic stories of gold strikes and subsequent "fevers." Mining in these districts began in earnest in the 1830s and continued randomly until the 1920s. In the Gold Hill belt, shafts as deep as 850 feet and drifts of slag taller than 1,500 feet marked the extent of the zeal of early miners to find the elusive mother lode.

Throughout the Carolina and adjacent belts near King's Mountain and Charlotte, quartz veins filled with gold and lesser base metals such as copper and silver tantalizingly cut across older volcanic and metasedimentary rocks. In this same area, Conrad Reed, the young son of John Reed of Cabarrus County, came upon a seventeen-pound nugget in 1799. Similar "lucky strikes" in Mecklenburg, Cabarrus, and Rowan counties usually consisted of thin two- to three-feet-wide veins of gold. Historically, the area from Morganton southward to Rutherfordton contained some of the state's richest placer deposits and gold-quartz lodes.

Valuable iron formations occur in large pods along a zone nearly fifty miles wide from near Gaffney, South Carolina, to the Catawba River in North Carolina. Called the Old Iron District, the deposits were mined extensively from the 1760s to the end of the Civil War. The opening of the Soo Canal near Sault Sainte Marie in eastern Michigan in 1855 and the subsequent discovery of mammoth deposits around Lake Superior ended the importance of the district, yet, for over a century it provided much of the domestic iron production used in the expansion of the southern frontier.

Surprisingly, coastal North Carolina contains more than five hundred million dry tons of fuel-grade peat. A product of large coastal freshwater swamps, river flood plains, Carolina bays, and small freshwater wetlands, peat furnished low-grade heat and energy as well as soil compost for the area's first settlers. Coastal North Carolina also holds significant quantities of clay, and, off the Florida-Hatteras continental slope, submerged slabs of rock that include important metals such as manganese, cobalt, nickel, arsenic, and platinum. In

1979 exploratory wells were drilled off the Atlantic shelf thirty-five miles northeast of Wilmington, sparking a brief interest in oil and gas development, but attention from oil companies dwindled when lease sales ended in 1985 for lack of appropriate bids.

North Carolina's rivers seem to conspire with other geographic elements of its plains, sounds, rolling hills, plateaus, and mountains to produce rifts and divisions within its history as well. Major coastal rivers such as the Tar, Neuse, and Cape Fear generally run from the interior eventually into the Atlantic Ocean, demarcating the Albemarle region from natural trading partners in Virginia and South Carolina. Broad and shallow, coastal rivers produce difficulties in terms of navigation, transportation, and communication. In the Piedmont, large rivers such as the Catawba, Broad, and Yadkin–Pee Dee also flow into the Atlantic, but through South Carolina and not other parts of the state. Not surprisingly, the swift, narrow rivers and streams of the Piedmont, while not suited to travel or navigation for commerce, furnished power sources for the colony and the state's first mills. In the mountains, rivers such as the French Broad, split by the eastern continental divide, flow south to South Carolina and north to Tennessee, offering no connection at all to the Piedmont or coast.

From the ancient supercontinent of Pangaea to the modern world of politics, the present boundaries of North Carolina emerged as North America drifted apart from the older worlds of Europe and Africa. The great geological rift at the end of the Paleozoic age and the political split between the Carolinas millions of years later effectively outlined the new state's resources and development. The state's odd east and west orientation, which cuts across geological and geographical fissures, has caused its economic, political, and social institutions to lag in their growth. Lacking world-class deposits of precious metals such as copper, iron, coal, tin, and even gold and silver, North Carolina has instead offered miniature bonanzas of metals and minerals. In this way, the "Old North State" developed more slowly and diversely than its sister states. With rivers flowing generally southward from and into adjacent states, the Atlantic Ocean to the east, a coastal island barrier offshore, mountain ramparts to the west, poor roads, and lack of a deepwater port, North Carolina has experienced a much more gradual development than its neighboring states. With no Virginia aristocracy or Charleston trading elite, no extensive tobacco, cotton, or indigo plantations, no significant commercial crop, no large cities or even towns, no center of government until almost the end of the colonial period, and no centralizing political, economic, or social forces, North Carolina had a lagging Rip van Winkle appearance in terms of economic and political development. The geographical rift also hindered the maturation of the state's institutions, from politics to education. To many outside writers and observers, North Carolina seemed "backwards" and "afterwards" in its development, as if the state had slept while others pushed ahead. The combination of geography, geology, and politics, however, gave North Carolina smaller, more progressive, and incremental growth bonanzas and discoveries that, although perhaps appearing even slow or dormant in its development, today makes it the envy of other states.

In 1570 the great Dutch cartographer Abraham Ortelius edited and published the Western world's first atlas, *Theatrum orbis terarum*. "Learned persons," he noted, "rightly call 'Geography' (the knowledge of regions and provinces, of the seas, the locations of mountains and valleys, . . . the course of rivers . . .) 'historiae oculus geographia,'" the eye of history. Geography and its handmaiden, geology, allowed history to be visualized. For individuals concerned with maps and atlases, geography was but the context of a continuously unfolding drama of human experience. The Drakes, Whites, Hariots, and De Brys saw the maps, atlases, and reports of this strange land not as reductive readings of history or as static representations of a place and time, but rather as irreducible representations of events occurring in a strange new world. Thus, the maps, reports, and drawings of De Bry, Hariot, and White furnished the dreamers and schemers in England a stage, a theater, for what they considered to be the workings of providence in a new world. To Drake, De Bry, Hariot, and White, individual features such as the barrier islands and the sounds along the coast might be interesting in themselves, but only as part of the scenery, not as determinants of the course of empire. Thus, the earliest explorers and settlers, whether Indians or Europeans, were but the first players on the Carolina stage that "developed" a drama of human experience over the centuries. Geography did not determine their destiny. It only gave a far-reaching glimpse, an eye, into their history. The other eye of history, that of chronology, of the unfolding of human experience, came next.

ADDITIONAL READINGS

American Meteorological Society. *Bibliography on Hurricanes and Severe Storms of the Coastal Plains Region*. Washington, D.C.: Coastal Plains Center for Marine Development Services, 1970.

Barnes, Jay. *North Carolina's Hurricane History*. 3rd ed. Chapel Hill: University of North Carolina Press, 2001.

Batson, Wade T. *Wild Flowers in the Carolinas*. Columbia: University of South Carolina Press, 1987.

Beyer, Fred. *North Carolina, the Years before Man: A Geologic History*. Durham: Carolina Academic Press, 1991.

Carney, Charles B., and Albert V. Hardy. *Weather and Climate in North Carolina*. Raleigh: Agricultural Experiment Station, 1963.

Carter, J. *Fossil Collecting in North Carolina*. Raleigh: North Carolina Department of Natural and Economic Resources, 1988.

Horton, J. Wright, Jr., and Victor A. Zullo. *The Geology of the Carolinas*. Knoxville: University of Tennessee Press, 1991.

Johnson, Douglas Wilson. *Origin of the Carolina Bays*. New York: Columbia University Press, 1942.

Knapp, Richard F., and Brent Glass. *Gold Mining in North Carolina: A Bicentennial History*. Raleigh: Department of Archives and History, 1999.

Lement, Ben Franklin. "Geographic Influences in the History of North Carolina." *North Carolina Historical Review* 12 (October 1935): 297–319.

Ludlum, David McWilliams. *Early American Hurricanes, 1492–1870*. Boston: American Meteorological Society, 1963.

Merrens, Harry Roy. *Colonial North Carolina in the Eighteenth Century*. Chapel Hill: University of North Carolina Press, 1964.

Phillips, Jonathan D. "A Short History of a Flat Place: Three Centuries of Geomorphic Change in the Croatan National Forest." *Annals of the Association of American Geographers* 87 (1997): 197–216.

Potter, Eloise F., James F. Parnell, and Robert P. Teulings. *Birds of the Carolinas*. Chapel Hill: University of North Carolina Press, 1980.

Rights, Douglas L. "Buffalo in North Carolina." *North Carolina Historical Review* 9 (July 1932): 242–49.

Schoenbaum, Thomas J. *Islands, Capes, and Sounds: The North Carolina Coast*. Winston-Salem: John F. Blair, 1982.

Simpson, Marcus B. "Dr. John Brickell's 'Catalogue of American Trees and Shrubs (1739)': A Bibliographic Misadventure." *Archives of Natural History (Great Britain)* 21 (1994): 67–72.

Stephenson, Richard A. "Comparative Cartography and Coastal Processes: Four Hundred Years of Change on the Outer Banks of North Carolina." *Terrae Incognitae* 22 (1990): 29–39.

Stuckey, Jasper L. *North Carolina: Its Geology and Mineral Resources*. Raleigh: North Carolina Department of Conservation and Development, 1965.

Ward, H. Trawick, and R. P. Stephen Davis Jr. *Time before History: The Archaeology of North Carolina*. Chapel Hill: University of North Carolina Press, 1999.

Webb, Paul A., and David S. Leigh "Geomorphological and Archaeological Investigations of a Buried Site on the Yadkin Flood Plain." *Southern Indian Studies* 44 (October 1995): 1–36.

15

A Clash of Cultures

TWO

Amerindians and Europeans in Early North Carolina

On 12 July 1585, John White began his series of famous drawings of the lives of the first Carolinians. Sitting in the Indian village of Pomeioc, a substantial settlement on Pamlico Sound, White carefully and painstakingly painted the village and its inhabitants. For almost a year he and his companion, Thomas Hariot, thoroughly surveyed, explored, examined, and sketched the people and the topography of the region around Roanoke Island. In so doing, they richly chronicled what would become a lost world of North American Woodland Indians just before European settlement changed and ended their civilization forever. Taken together, White's drawings give a cycloramic perspective of the lives of the first Carolinians before European settlement.

To Wingina, the *weroance,* or chief, of some of the villages around Pamlico Sound, the Europeans hardly were unexpected. Indeed, others who spoke strange languages more

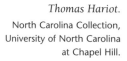

Thomas Hariot.
North Carolina Collection,
University of North Carolina
at Chapel Hill.

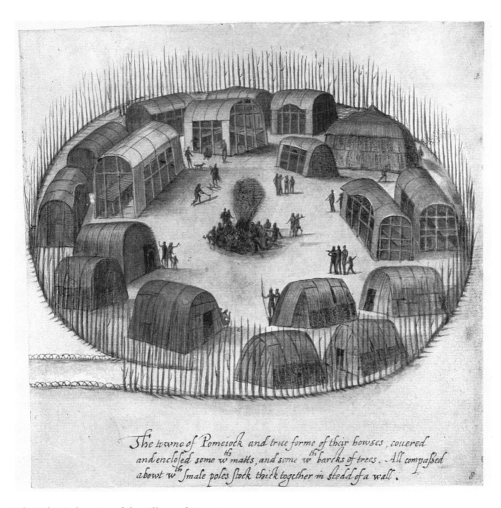

The towne of Pomeiock and true forme of their howses, couered and enclosed some wth matts, and some wth barcks of trees. All compassed abowt wth smale poles stock thick together in stedd of a wall.

John White's drawing of the village of Pomeioc.
North Carolina Collection, University of North Carolina at Chapel Hill.

rapidly and smoothly than the English and whose skins were darker already had visited his settlements. From earlier uninvited Spanish and French guests, his men had traded for, and stolen, metal pots, goblets, live parrots, cloth, and trinkets, some of which remained when White and Hariot arrived. Wingina fully expected the English to behave as the French and Spanish had for the past fifty years. Little did he know that his villages soon would be involved in a vast imperial melodrama between England, France, and Spain, and that his people would never be the same.

Within three decades of Christopher Columbus's discovery of America in 1492, the first European ships appeared along the Carolina coast. Giovanni da Verrazano, a Florentine navigator in the service of the French king Francis I, explored and charted the region from the Cape Fear River along the Outer Banks to the present Kitty Hawk and up to the New England coast in the summer of 1524. Translated into English and published in 1582 in Richard Hakluyt's *Divers Voyages touching the Discoverie of America and the Islands Adjacent,* but known for years among adventurers, explorers, and cartographers, Verrazano's

*Giovanni da Verrazano
(ca. 1485–1527).*
North Carolina Collection, University
of North Carolina at Chapel Hill.

account of an edenic arcadia in the New World became the inspiration for European inter-est in the Carolinas. Sir Walter Raleigh especially liked it so much that he recommended it to Elizabeth, his queen.

Led by Jean Ribaut and René de Laudonnière, the French unsuccessfully tried to estab-lish colonies along the South Carolina and Florida coast in the 1560s only to be frustrated by the more aggressive Spanish. As early as 1526, the Spanish under Luis Vásquez de Ayllón, a swashbuckling conquistador who had his hand in the slave trade and apparently in the Spanish treasury as well, sailed up the "Rio Jordan," probably the Cape Fear River, and set up a sizable colony a few miles inland. Beset by illness, dwindling supplies, and the threat of mutiny, Ayllón abandoned the Rio Jordan and moved farther down the coast into South Carolina. In 1540, the well-traveled and chronicled Hernando de Soto likely crossed the Little Tennessee River into the mountains of western North Carolina. In 1561, Angel de Villafañe set out from Vera Cruz and managed to make his way to Hatteras, only to be "driven to distress" by the inhospitable barriers of the Carolina coast. Villafañe limped southward into Santo Domingo after his cursory exploration. Two other Spaniards, Juan Pardo and Hernando de Boyano, marched inland from along the coast, perhaps all the way to the mountainous barrier of western North Carolina, but, in Pardo's case, assuredly at least to the western foothills. In all this, the interest of the Spanish remained marginal. They found little gold or glory in the Carolinas. Still, their explorations and excursions made the Carolinas a peripheral but pivotal arena in the contest for the domination of the New and Old Worlds.

Enter Sir Walter Raleigh. One of Elizabeth's court favorites, Raleigh, a soldier of fortune, mediocre poet, writer of a history of the world on a grand scale, and unwitting pawn in Elizabeth's international intrigues, soon became a patron of English attempts to

Sir Walter Raleigh (1552–1618).
North Carolina Collection, University
of North Carolina at Chapel Hill.

establish colonies in the New World. When Elizabeth had use of him, she referred to Raleigh as her "dear pug," a sixteenth-century term of endearment for a person and not an animal. When he became a liability, Elizabeth had him tried, convicted, and thrown in the Tower of London. Her successor, James I, eventually had him executed in 1618. A prolific writer and promoter even while held captive, Raleigh, although a failure in his attempts to have England found a permanent colony in the New World, nevertheless firmly planted the idea in the national psyche. On 25 March 1584, he obtained a patent allowing him to have title to any lands "not actually possessed of any Christian prince, nor inhabited by Christian people." To Raleigh, an amateur cartographer who loved maps, especially those by Dutchmen Abraham Ortelius and Gerard Mercator, that meant the Carolina coast, an area far enough away from the Spanish threat at Saint Augustine but still close enough to bedevil the English. Elizabeth approved his plan even as she negotiated with the Spanish. In the summer of 1584, Raleigh sent Philip Amadas and Arthur Barlowe to explore the coast northward from the Spanish at Saint Augustine and to find a suitable site for a settlement. Amadas and Barlowe, both young, impressionable, and seeking Raleigh's favor, brought back not only glowing reports of a Garden of Eden, with the most "fruitful and wholsome" soil "of all the world," but also two noble, innocent savages, Wanchese and Manteo. The two exhibited part of the "goodly people, . . . voide of all guile and treason, . . . such as live after the manner of the golden age," human trophies for Raleigh's consideration. Few propagandists could have done better.

With Barlowe's report as narrative and Wanchese and Manteo as living illustrations, Raleigh had little trouble convincing Elizabeth that a second expedition should immediately set sail. Ever the flatterer, he even suggested that the new country be called Virginia, after the queen, inasmuch as it still had "the virgin purity and plenty of the first creation,

Title page of Sir Walter Raleigh's History of the World.

North Carolina Collection, University of North Carolina at Chapel Hill.

A depiction of one of Raleigh's ships.
North Carolina Collection, University of North Carolina at Chapel Hill.

and the people their innocence of life and manners." Had Raleigh's second expedition under Ralph Lane or the subsequent one begun by John White succeeded, North Carolina would have hosted the first permanent English colony and today would be known as Virginia, instead of the area of the Chesapeake Bay that is. To aid Raleigh in his quest in the New World, and suspicious of his judgment as well, Elizabeth summoned Ralph Lane, a military officer serving in Ireland, to help command and give resolve to the expedition. It proved a tragic mistake.

With a fleet of seven ships "well stocked and manned" by 108 carefully selected voyagers, the second exploratory expedition set sail from Plymouth on 9 April 1585. While Spanish, French, and Portuguese expeditions took along soldiers, priests, and tax collectors, Raleigh's group, typical of the English, had an entirely different cast of characters. The party included Philip Amadas as admiral; Thomas Hariot, Raleigh's tutor in mathematics and a trained scientist; John White, a skillful painter; Thomas Cavendish, a genius at navigation who later sailed around the world; and Ralph Lane, an experienced military officer. Additionally, several apothecaries, a physician, natural scientists, and lawyers also came along. Conspicuously absent were the soldiers, tax collectors, royal officials, and priests sent by the Spanish and French. Interested in finding gold, in acquiring much glory through exploration and discovery, and in pleasing the Crown like the Spanish, French, and Portuguese, the English also clearly wanted to find out as much as they could about

A

DISCOURSE

CONCERNING

WESTERN PLANTING

WRITTEN IN THE YEAR 1584

BY RICHARD HAKLUYT

NOW FIRST PRINTED FROM A CONTEMPORARY MANUSCRIPT

With a Preface and an Introduction

BY LEONARD WOODS, LL.D.

LATE PRESIDENT OF BOWDOIN COLLEGE

EDITED, WITH NOTES IN THE APPENDIX

BY CHARLES DEANE

CAMBRIDGE
PRESS OF JOHN WILSON AND SON
1877

Title page of Richard Hakluyt's
A Discourse Concerning Western Planting Written in the Year 1584.
North Carolina Collection, University of North Carolina at Chapel Hill.

the strange country where they would plant a permanent colony and not just exploit its riches. The curious English intended to stay.

22   The problems that beset the attempt of Ralph Lane and Sir Richard Grenville to plant a colony for England in the New World came on board with them at Plymouth. At the outset, Lane considered the expedition to be military in nature and himself to be the "true commander." He thus resented Grenville's authority and title. When Grenville returned to England for supplies less than six months after the first settlers arrived, Lane took over with a vengeance. He organized the colony as a fort and not a settlement, promulgated a harsh set of laws that were "severely executed," and made himself military commander and overall leader. Interested as much if not more in glory as in geography, Lane sent out parties to look for the fabled passage to the Indies, for better inlets and locations, for exotic and fabulous Indian tribes and their wealth, and for better lands for future settlements. Working for Lane as explorers, soldiers, and servants, the colonists had less interest or incentive to plant crops and to cultivate friendships among local Indians.

Lane, for his part, busied himself not only with planning and sending out expeditions into the interior but also with sending a steady supply of letters to England extolling the virtues of "new Virginia." When Grenville sailed to England for badly needed supplies in September 1585, he carried with him a promotional letter from Lane to Richard Hakluyt the elder describing the lands around the "New Fort in Virginia" as the "goodliest soile" under heaven, "abounding with sweete trees" and an overweening abundance of "wines . . . , oiles . . . , flaxe . . . , currans, sugars . . . and the like," all more plentiful than in any other parts of the world, be they "West or East Indies." Fully understanding England's

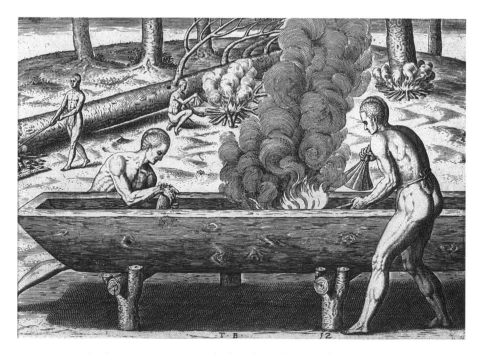

Theodore DeBry engraving of John White's drawing of Indians constructing a canoe.
North Carolina Collection, University of North Carolina at Chapel Hill.

*Theodore DeBry engraving
of John White's drawing of
the village of Secotan.*
North Carolina Collection, University
of North Carolina at Chapel Hill.

emerging mercantile system of trade, Lane hinted that, if the new lands could be claimed and exploited by England, it economically would not have to depend on Spain, Portugal, or France for any of its needs. In Amadas, Barlowe, and Lane, North Carolina had its first boosters and boomers.

Manteo and Wanchese also returned to Roanoke on Grenville's ships, likely bringing with them a new appreciation of white men. While their thoughts on their trip to England always will remain impenetrable, surely they must have been impressed not only by the numbers and power of the English but also by their wealth. Perennially short of supplies and preferring to trade for food than to grow it, the new colonists, busily erecting huts, houses, and palisades, freely entered into commerce with the coastal Indians. Quickly the relative plenty of Lane's colony in terms of trade goods caused friction between settlers and Indians. Wanchese believed the English had an island full of treasure and only needed ships to sail away and to return with it. Why should they be so greedy with their goods? When one of his warriors died at the hands of an angry colonist while trying to steal a silver cup, a wrathful Wanchese prepared to lay waste to the settlement. He never did. Yet similar incidents only increased the hostility and frustration between whites and Indians.

With Grenville and his badly needed supplies overdue from England, with meager prospects for a good crop, and with few friends among the coastal Indians, Lane could hope only for a miracle, which sailed into the Roanoke inlet two weeks later in the form of Sir

Sir Francis Drake.
North Carolina Collection, University
of North Carolina at Chapel Hill.

Francis Drake, one of Raleigh's friends and Queen Elizabeth's infamous sea dogs. Fresh from pirating and looting along the Spanish Main, Drake, heading to England with scores of captured galley slaves and South American Indians, offered to take Lane and his colonists with him. Lane agreed, and Drake hurriedly ushered the Indians and slaves ashore to make room for the colonists. On 19 June 1586, Lane reluctantly abandoned Fort Raleigh and sailed away to England with Drake. In less than two weeks, Grenville, delayed by some of the very storms that pushed Drake toward safety at Roanoke and that helped convince Lane finally to leave, limped into the inlet. After two months of trying in vain to locate Lane and the settlers, Grenville left fifteen men with supplies for two years to hold the site for England, and, like the other expeditions before him, once again caught the tide for England.

Grenville and Lane's failure to set up a permanent colony in the New World contrasted sharply with the success of the propaganda that came from the effort. Thomas Hariot's account of the colony, "a brief and true report of the new found land of Virginia," glossed over the rumors spread by the "malcontents" in Lane's expedition and instead chronicled the richness and bounty of the new land. White's seventy-five paintings not only supported Hariot's view but also gave exciting illustrations of the natives who lived there, replete with ornaments, clothing, tattoos, and "quaint customs and rituals" of cooking, fishing, and worshiping. Even today, White's sketches remain one of the most invaluable portraits of Native Americans as they first came in contact with Europeans.

Because of worsening conditions with Spain and his declining personal fortune, Raleigh eagerly sought to plant "second colonies" in the new land of "Virginia" as quickly as possible. This time, he appointed John White, a popular choice, as governor and sold stocks in his venture to twenty-two London merchants and gentlemen. With 110 settlers, including 17 women and 9 children, on board, the last lost colonists sailed for America on 8 May 1587.

After stopping in the West Indies, White's ships dropped anchor off Cape Hatteras on 22 July 1587, intending only to pick up the men left by Grenville and then proceed to

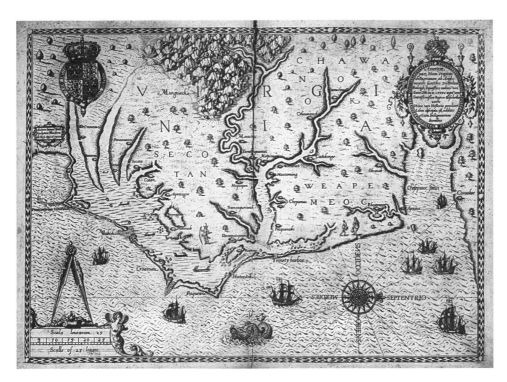

Theodore DeBry engraving of an early map of eastern North Carolina by John White.
North Carolina Collection, University of North Carolina at Chapel Hill.

the deep water of Chesapeake Bay, always the preferred site of English settlement. They never made it. In his account of the expedition, White blamed the pilot, Simon Fernandez, a mysterious figure involved in several earlier colonization attempts, probably a Portuguese Marrano, a Jew who converted to Catholicism to escape persecution, for the fatal decision. Whatever his motives, Fernandez refused to go farther, and White, who apparently disliked confrontations, declined to "contend with him," instead setting the colonists to work refurbishing the fort and repairing the homes left by Lane's men.

Within a month White had christened Manteo, the first recorded Protestant baptism in the New World, and, as per Raleigh's instructions, made him "Lord of Roanoke and Dasamonguepeuk," the first noble title ever granted a Native American. On 18 August, five days later, the small colony continued its good news firsts with the birth of Virginia Dare, White's granddaughter by his daughter, Eleanor White, and her husband, Ananias Dare. Christened Virginia, the first Christian "child . . . borne in Virginia," her birth soon was followed by others.

The first bad news came on the heels of the good. Arriving too late to plant crops, the colonists had only their ship's supplies to sustain them. With few if any of Lane's former colonists with them, White's small contingent had little experience or knowledge of their surroundings. Moreover, few Indians came forward to offer food and provisions in exchange for trade goods. By now, the coastal Algonquins had grown antagonistic, hostile, and increasingly suspicious toward the English. One of White's assistants, George Howe, wandered along the beaches collecting crabs, only to be slain by Indians. Terrified, colonists

Queen Elizabeth I.
North Carolina Collection, University
of North Carolina at Chapel Hill.

seldom ranged far from the fort and town to look for food and provisions. Five weeks after they landed, White's colonists had had enough. Persuaded by the settlers to sail for England and plead on their behalf but reluctant to leave his post and family, White, with only a day's notice, once more prepared to cross the Atlantic to England. Before he left, the colonists told White that if conditions worsened they would move the settlement inland for safety. They assured him that if they did they would leave directions to their location, and if immediate danger threatened they would "carve over the letters or the name a Cross + in this Forme." White sailed for England on 27 August 1587.

After a turbulent and lengthy crossing, White landed in England, smack in the middle of that nation's life-and-death struggle with Spain. He finally met with Raleigh on 20 November, and the two planned to send a small fleet under Sir Richard Grenville to the beleaguered colony as soon as possible. Knowing that Spain planned an invasion that summer, Queen Elizabeth ordered that no ships leave England, instead converting as many as possible to the defense of England's coast and harbors. Once more, Grenville found himself under the command of Sir Francis Drake.

The Spanish Armada finally arrived off the coast of England in late July 1588 and for a month battled England's ships and nature's storms. In his typical eccentric fashion, Sir Francis Drake prepared himself for the coming sixteenth-century Armageddon by going bowling. For Drake and others, it appeared that God himself had come to Elizabeth and England's aid when he "blew with his winds" upon her enemies that summer of 1588. Finally driven into the North Sea by both, the Spanish fleet eventually tried to sail around the coast of Ireland, thought to be Catholic, and allied with them against the English, eventually breaking up on the treacherous western coast. Few ever made it back to Spain. For eighteen months afterward the English navy still battled for control of the waters surrounding Britain, and, in March 1590, an expedition finally left Plymouth to rescue White's colonists.

At long last White reached Roanoke Island on 16 August 1590. There he found the houses "taken down and a high palisade of great trees . . . very Fort-like" erected around them. On one of the large trees at the entrance "was graven CROATOAN . . . in fayre Capitall letters . . . without any crosse or sign of distresse." On another tree, White came across the letters "CRO," again without any designation of danger or disaster. Sailors dug up some chests on the sandy beach, carefully hidden by the departing settlers, containing White's books, notes, pictures, and rusted armor. Clearly, the departing colonists, remembering White's admonition to protect his property, had time to place it in chests and bury them on the beach, there to await his arrival. No human remains were ever discovered.

What happened to the lost colony? For years afterward, White and Raleigh continued to insist that the colonists still remained in America, "lost" but not departed. The legal distinction proved crucial to Raleigh's claim to the new country of "Virginia." With Elizabeth still on the throne and with his colony "planted" somewhere in America yet "lost," Raleigh retained his charter rights to vast lands in the New World. Surrounded by her maritime maps, globes, instruments, and many of White's drawings, Elizabeth died on Thursday, 24 March 1603, and Raleigh's subsequent imprisonment by James I ended the first chartered attempt by the English to settle a colony in America. James I, always chafing at his

Nineteenth-century depiction of John White's return to Roanoke Island finding only the word "Croatoan" carved on a tree.
North Carolina Collection, University of North Carolina at Chapel Hill.

comparison to Elizabeth, wanted to issue patents and charters in his own name. He was content to see Raleigh and Elizabeth's attempts at colonization lost to history.

28   As for the fate of the colonists themselves, like so many early settlements and settlers they passed into history as the stuff of legend, folklore, and myth. Beginning in the 1890s, Hamilton McMillan, a newspaperman, amateur historian, and state legislator, published *Lost Colony Found: An Historical Sketch of the Discovery of the Croatan Indians,* a small treatise maintaining that the Lumbees, a triracial Indian tribe in Pembroke, actually were the descendants of the Croatans and the survivors of the Roanoke colonists. Long before McMillan's book, rumors and stories of blond and blue-eyed Indians along the Virginia and North Carolina border, the result of the intermixing of the lost colonists and Croatans, had persisted for over a century. In the same vein, David Quinn theorized that the Roanoke colonists did indeed move northward after White's departure. In a further twist, Melungeons, another multiracial group living along the mountainous North Carolina–Tennessee border, claimed their ancestry derived from the galley slaves, from the Spanish, Indians, and lost colonists who retreated into the wilderness in the face of European settlements and wars. As in the case of Thomas Jefferson's descendants, DNA eventually might dispel the tales and folklore of the Lumbees and Melungeons, but it will never entirely dissipate the mystery of what happened to the lost colony.

White himself, however, might have given clues as to what happened to the abandoned colonists when he landed at Roanoke in the late summer of 1590. He found little sense of haste, no sign of distress, and even carefully packed chests conveniently buried along the ocean side of the island. Instead of moving inland as they had planned, perhaps the settlers packed their belongings into the small ships available to them and sailed along the coast looking for a better site. To them, all the coastal Indians were Croatans, and, desiring to give clues that they had not moved to the mainland, the settlers used a word that

An 1857 romanticized illustration of Virginia Dare.
North Carolina Collection, University of North Carolina at Chapel Hill.

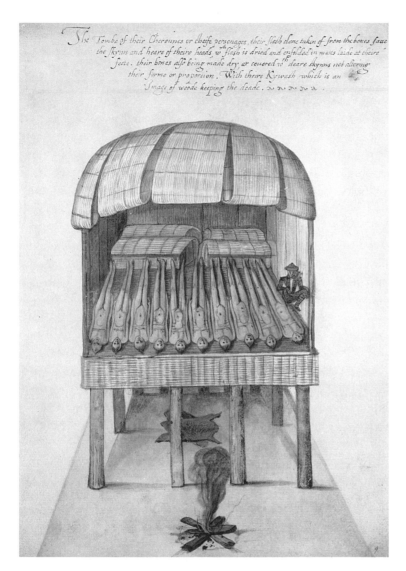

The Tombe of their Cherounes or cheife personages, their flesh clene taken of from the bones saue the skynn and heare of theire heads, w[ch] flesh is dried and enfolded in mate laide at theire feete. their bones also being made dry ar couered wth deare skynns not alterinc their forme or proporcion. With theire Kywash which is an Image of woode keeping the deade.

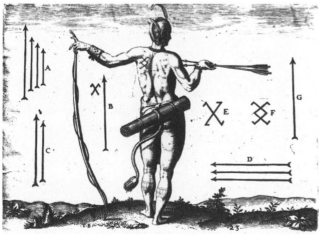

Above: An Indian burial house by John White.
North Carolina Collection, University of North Carolina at Chapel Hill.

Theodore DeBry engraving of John White's drawing of an Indian chieftain with markings.
North Carolina Office of Archives and History, Raleigh.

designated a place as well as a tribe. Like other colonists before them, they might also have attempted a return trip to England across the ocean. Still, their exact fate remains as much a destination on Fortune's wheel now as it did in 1588.

Raleigh's failed attempts at colonizing early Carolina only whetted the appetite of the English for exploration and settlement. The two Richard Hakluyts, the elder and younger, perhaps the most enthusiastic propagandists of that age for the Roanoke colonies, helped convince the Crown to challenge the Spanish monopoly in the New World through their accounts. Thomas Hariot's *A Brief and True Account,* intriguing watercolors by White, and excellent maps, all later published by Theodor De Bry in 1590, made it possible for almost all educated people in England and Europe to discover for themselves the marvels of the New World.

Yet White's drawings of the first Algonquians, whom he met on the islands, excited the most curiosity. White depicted a stable, advanced horticultural Indian civilization of systematic streets and buildings, storage sheds for grains, well-constructed longhouses perhaps seventy-two feet long and thirty-six feet wide, fenced fields, and tall palisades for protection. He portrayed fishermen with well-made canoes casting for fish in an area marked by a weir that runs well out into the water. Group scenes showed "their manner of praying with rattles about the fire." Unfailingly, White presented the Croatans as cheerful, well formed and neatly dressed, healthy, and subsisting upon a simple diet of boiled corn, deer meat, fish and crabs, and some vegetables. In their complicated set of rituals, manners, ceremonies, treatment of the elderly and reverence for the dead, he found a society worthy of admiration and high regard, religious and sober in its everyday life.

Whether romanticized or ritualized, White's watercolors informed as much by what they left out as by what they included. For example, the Croatans and their neighbors along the coast belonged to the Algonquian linguistic family of Indians. Less warlike and politically sophisticated than the Tuscaroras of the inner Coastal Plain, they survived in a chaotic, pell-mell world on the agriculturally poor coast. As it existed at the time of White and Hariot's visit and for perhaps a century afterward, Indian life along the coast reflected this volatile, capricious existence, threatened in the interior by the Tuscaroras and, after 1585, by European settlements. Primary coastal tribes such as the Croatan, Hatteras, Chowan, Weapomeiok, Coranine or Coree, Machapunga, Bay River, Pamlico, Roanoke, Woccon, and Cape Fear Indians had evolved by 1200 C.E. into a culturally sophisticated yet politically unstable society with a relatively meager standard of living that differed from the Tuscarora, Catawba, and Cherokee towns farther west.

With an extensive trade pattern that necessarily extended to the great empires of Mesoamerica northward to Canada, the coastal Indians of North Carolina participated in a cultural explosion after 1000 C.E. that forever changed their relatively stable way of life. Through trade, migration, and intercoastal water travel, the Croatans and Cape Fears, for example, communicated with and traveled widely throughout the other Indian city-states and villages of the Southeast. When John Lawson made his famous journey through Carolina in 1700, he expressed surprise at the extent of the interaction he found between Indian villages and peoples. In the interior of North Carolina he found Congarees living with the Keyauwees, Indian traders from Charleston heading north into Esaw villages, Tutelos and Tuscaroras among the Saponis, and Cheraw traders among the Enos. Almost all European

The aged man in his wynter garment.

Left: Drawing of an old Indian man by John White.
North Carolina Collection, University of North Carolina at Chapel Hill.

Theodore DeBry engraving of John White's illustration of Indians cooking fish.
North Carolina Collection, University of North Carolina at Chapel Hill.

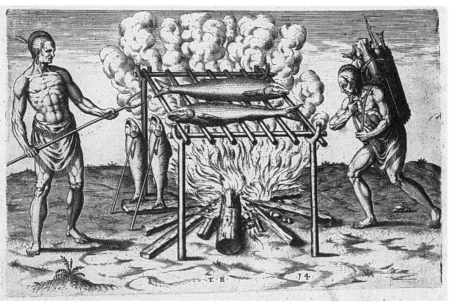

wayfarers cataloged significant numbers of other tribesmen, some friendly but others hostile, living within a given village. Enos, Saponis, Tutelos, and Chowans thus might live within a Tuscarora town or settlement. In fact, Indians freely traveled, traded, lived within each other's villages, and passed on information about other tribes and events long before Europeans came to them as visitors and middlemen. Catawbas knew about Lawson's where-abouts three weeks before he arrived, and Croatans already had stored extra supplies of food and arrows in anticipation of White's landing on Pamlico Sound.

The astonishment in Lawson's journal arose not from the diversity and communication he observed among the Siouan tribes of Carolina's interior, but rather at his nonnotation and lack of mention of coastal Indians by 1700. Most had disappeared or relocated. Because of warfare, migration, disease, and depopulation, small coastal tribes had changed their ethnic identity, frequently merging into larger groups, such as the Chowans. Since the coast had no predominant tribe, a situation noted by White and Ralph Lane, individuals and families naturally gravitated into smaller multitribal groups. Without a common language, customs, or rituals, these weakened composite tribes withdrew into agriculturally marginal lands not coveted by white settlers or larger, more powerful Indian tribes. Over a period of a century and a half, remnants of coastal tribes had amalgamated into triracial groups composed of Indians, escaped slaves, and some whites who later became part of the Tuscarora, Catawba, and Yamassee nations. Most had lost their distinct Indianness.

Further inland, the Cheraws, Occaneechees, Enos, Shakoris, Saxapahaws, Saponis, Tutelos, Keyauwees, Catawbas, and especially the Tuscaroras posed a greater barrier to white settlement. Unlike the coastal tribes, the Tuscaroras and Cherokees belonged to a different language group, the Iroquoians. Centered in the inner Coastal Plain, the largest Tuscarora villages probably pushed down from the northeast at about the same time the Roanokes came to the coast. Two smaller migrations came later. Sandwiched between the Iroquoian Tuscaroras and the Cherokees, a mélange of Siouan tribes such as the Catawba and the Cheraws settled in the drainage area of the Catawba River, west to the Broad River, and south as far as the midlands of South Carolina. Largest of all the Iroquoians, the Cherokees relocated to the southeastern mountains and foothills long before the time of Christ. By their size, stability, isolation, and remoteness from white settlements, the inland tribes formed the most formidable barrier to European expansion.

Known as the Hemp Gatherers for their growth and production of rope and fiber from the tall Asian hemp plant brought to the area thousands of years ago, the Tuscarora had, by 1700, become a settled, prosperous nation of interrelated villages of well-constructed homes, usually of bark and wigwam, and of abundant cornfields and orchards of peach and other fruit trees. Warlike, politically refined, and well organized in a network of villages, the Tuscarora at first did not fear white settlement to the east and north. Yet by 1705 they found themselves threatened by encroaching whites and other Indians. To the east, English settlers pushed ever closer to Tuscarora villages and lands on the Pamlico and Neuse rivers. To the north and south Shawnee and Yamassee war parties raided and took prisoners to Pennsylvania and Charleston to be sold into slavery. Even more troubling, English policy toward the Tuscarora had shifted from a desire to trade with them to a demand for land and removal. In the fall of 1711, after unsuccessfully trying to relocate to Pennsylvania, the Tuscarora turned with a vengeance upon the invading North Carolinians.

*Baron Christoph
von Graffenried (1661–1743).*
North Carolina Collection, University
of North Carolina at Chapel Hill.

Under King Hancock, chief of the gunmen and warriors, the Tuscarora persuaded smaller vassal tribes such as the Coree, Pamlico, Bear River, Mattamuskeet, and Machapunga Indians to join them against the English. While the Tuscaroras and their allies prepared for war, white Carolinians were engaging in a rebellion of their own. Along with Emmanuel Low and Richard Roach, Thomas Cary, a provincial militia leader originally from South Carolina, led an abortive attempt to wrest power in the general assembly from Anglican supporters of the lords proprietors. For two years, from 1708 to 1710, Cary governed the northern part of the Carolina colony.

At New Bern, Cary frightened newly arrived Swiss and German colonists under Baron Christopher von Graffenried by telling them that savage Indians and misguided Carolinians who supported the proprietors schemed to destroy them before they could take up their new lands. To King Hancock, Cary sent emissaries warning that the new government to be sent from England under Edward Hyde planned to give their lands away to the Swiss. In the interim, traders from Charleston, New Bern, Bath, and the Chesapeake region of Virginia, operating in a no-man's-land without law or license, plundered and stole hides, game, and supplies from the Indians. With the English in disarray and fighting among themselves, King Hancock and his allies swooped down upon the Carolina frontier.

The first act of the Tuscarora war opened with the capture of Baron von Graffenried and John Lawson. While sailing up the Neuse River to survey the countryside in early September 1711, the two fell into the hands of a scouting party. To the Indians, Graffenried appeared a curiosity and not a threat, but John Lawson, the official surveyor general of the new government, represented the hated English who wanted the Tuscaroras' land. Wherever Lawson went with his strange instruments and books, English settlers followed. For

Top: Capture of John Lawson and Christoph von Graffenried by Tuscarora Indians.
North Carolina Collection, University of North Carolina at Chapel Hill.

John Lawson and Christoph von Graffenried in captivity.
North Carolina Collection, University of North Carolina at Chapel Hill.

Nineteenth-century depiction of Tuscarora Indians raiding settlements along Albemarle Sound.
North Carolina Collection, University of North Carolina at Chapel Hill.

his part, Lawson did little to help his cause. Because of his extensive travel and knowledge of the Tuscarora, he saw himself as a *weroance* of the English, far superior to the chiefs now before him. His arrogance did little to impress or to persuade his captors.

The Tuscarora held court and tried Lawson for his intrusions upon their land. Graffenried observed that the trial "was conducted . . . in as orderly a manner as could ever be with Christian judges, and I have heard such sensible reasons given by these savages and heathens that I was amazed." Lawson would have none of it. Arrogant and argumentative, he bitterly quarreled with King Hancock and Cor Tom, the Coree king. It cost him his life. Frustrated and angry with the unrepentant and haughty Lawson, the Tuscarora tied him to a stake, stuck scores of lighted splinters of wood into his body, and in a gruesome "petit feu," burned him alive. Knowing the English would retaliate, the Tuscarora decided to act first.

Just before dawn on 22 September 1711, platoons of Tuscaroras, Mattamuskeets, Pamptegos, and Corees struck the farms, plantations, settlements, and towns along the coast in a well-coordinated attack. At Bath, the Indians killed more than forty Englishmen and, at New Bern, more than seventy Swiss and German settlers. For the next six weeks, the Tuscarora and their Indian allies ravaged the Pamlico-Neuse region, ransacking and burning homes and barns, slaughtering and driving away cattle, pigs, and livestock, destroying crops, killing hundreds of settlers, and capturing scores of others. Coming too late to help, Thomas Gale, a major in the North Carolina militia, described the entire region as "totally wasted and ruined," desolate and abandoned.

At Cotechney, King Hancock's chief town, Baron von Graffenried, his life spared but still a prisoner of the Tuscarora, watched the war parties return each day. "A few days after" his capture, he declared, "the robbers came back with their booty. Alas what a sad sight for me to see the women and Children prisoners. It nearly rent my heart . . . I had to remain for six weeks a prisoner in that hateful place . . . always in fear of unutterable dangers and sorrows." With the warriors came scores of slaves, some as prisoners but most as escapees to join the Tuscarora.

As soon as it could be organized and supplied, a relief force from South Carolina under Col. John Barnwell hurriedly left for North Carolina. With him he had thirty whites and more than five hundred Indians. Composed of South Carolina Rangers, Barnwell's own Yamassee company and two groups of "Esaws," a general name for eastern Siouan tribes of the Carolinas who hated the Iroquoian Tuscarora and Shawnee, the expedition marched north expecting help from Virginia as well as North Carolina. One of the Esaw companies took the name of Captain Jack, the mythical chieftain and fighter of the Catawbas, and had in it Santees, Waterees, Congarees, and Catawbas. For his exploits against the Tuscarora, the Yamassee and Catawba warriors referred to Barnwell as Tuscarora Jack, a name that reflected his standing and honor among Indians. Late in January 1712, Barnwell reached the eastern edge of the Saxapahaw villages, now occupied by the Tuscarora.

From 12 January until 17 April 1712, Barnwell and his men ravaged Tuscarora villages. Reaching Narhantes, the first of several fortified Tuscarora strongpoints, Barnwell breached the defenses in less than an hour. So desperate were the beleaguered defenders that "the very Women (were) shooting Arrows, yet they did not yield until most of them were put to the sword." More than a dozen Indian women died inside the fort, and Barnwell counted fifty-two scalps among his soldiers and Yamassees. Still, he regretted that "while we were putting the men to the sword our Indians got all the slaves and plunder, only one girl we got."

On his way to his next prize, King Hancock's fort, Barnwell razed "374 houses wherein there could not be less than 2000 bushels of corn." Approaching Kenta, another Tuscarora town, his men took nine scalps and two prisoners, whom he "ordered immediately to be burnt alive" in full view of the Indian village. Reinforced by North Carolinians, Barnwell reached Hancock's town on Cotechney Creek on 5 March 1712. Impressed by the location and strength of the fortification, the South Carolinians learned that Harry, a runaway slave from Virginia, had helped the Tuscarora in planning the defenses. Undaunted, Barnwell ordered the fort attacked, and after three days the Tuscarora surrendered. In an agreement designed to humiliate the Indians, Barnwell ordered all the remaining white captives, some twenty-two, to be delivered to him along with all the runaway slaves on 19 March. Additionally, the war chiefs and headmen of the Tuscarora also had to confer with him at a later date about a permanent peace.

By the end of March "Tuscarora Jack" Barnwell approached Hancock's Fort, the last Tuscarora stronghold, which he prepared to take under siege. After almost two weeks of indecisive and chaotic fighting, Barnwell once again decided to let the Indians go if they would capitulate. After a mutually agreed-upon surrender, the Tuscarora and their leaders departed, leaving behind "24 Captives children (who) were delivered & 2 negroes, one of wch being a notorious Rogue was cutt to pieces immediately." The war finally ended a year later when another force of Carolinians and Indians under Col. James Moore, this time buttressed by more than 300 Cherokee warriors, broke the last of Tuscarora resistance at Cotechney Creek, the place where it all began. The assault started on 20 March 1713 and ended three days later. Moore lost 22 whites and 35 Indians, while he took 392 prisoners, tallied almost 200 "scolps," burned another 200 to death in the fort, and slaughtered 162 outside after they had laid down their arms. He easily defeated the few remaining bands and villages of Corees and Mattamuskeets, most of whom eventually became slaves or settlement Indians living near white farms, plantations, and towns. The few remaining Tuscarora accompanied Moore's men back to South Carolina, where for a number of years they lived at Port Royal.

In the Albemarle region, the Tuscarora chief, Tom Blount, broke with King Hancock in the South and remained neutral. His actions largely spared the more prosperous and populous part of the colony. After the war, a grateful North Carolina assembly set aside a large tract of land to be reserved for his use. Still, Blount and the Tuscarora could not resist the demands for land from a growing tide of colonists, and in 1802 the last band left to join their brethren in New York and eastern Canada, where some descendants still reside today. With less than a dozen remaining, the Port Royal Tuscarora quit South Carolina to join the Five Nations of the Iroquois Confederation in the North before 1730. By 1810, the Tuscarora in the South had ceased to exist as an identifiable tribe, group, village, or town. They simply disappeared, absorbed like so many others into the multiethnic frontier of southeastern colonial America. Further to the west in the Carolina and Tennessee foothills and mountains, another Iroquoian tribe, the Cherokees, took note of the fate of their Tuscarora kinsmen. With a population of more than twenty thousand spread out in a series of lower, middle, and upper towns, the Cherokees represented the last Indian frontier for North Carolinians.

The Tuscarora war not only ended the power of the Indians, the first Carolinians, along the coast and farther inland, but it also almost extinguished the idea of North Carolina as a colony itself. When Barnwell arrived at Bath on 10 February 1712 with a relief column, he found hundreds of pitiful widows and orphans to the "great incredible wonders and amazement of the poor distressed wretches here, who expressed such extremity of mad joy that it drew tears from most of the men." He suggested that the entire region be abandoned and the remaining settlers be relocated to South Carolina. North Carolina, either as part of the original Carolina grant or as a province unto itself, had almost ceased to exist.

The desolating and debilitating war with the Tuscarora only reaffirmed an earlier decision of the lords proprietors to separate the southern from the northern part of the province. It underscored the weaknesses of governing such a large and diverse colony from London, and, encouraged by the burgeoning success of the settlements around Charleston, the lords proprietors agreed to disconnect the northern province, complete with its few, poor, and rebellious colonists, from the more prosperous and better established south. The official division came in a commission to Edward Hyde, a distant relative of Queen Anne, dated 24 January 1712, naming him as the first governor of the northern part of the Carolina grant. Thus, with Hyde as its first governor, a ravaged and wasted North Carolina became a colony apart from South Carolina. But barely.

ADDITIONAL READINGS

Adair, James. *Adair's History of the American Indians*. New York: Promontory Press, 1974.

Bawlf, Samuel. *The Secret Voyage of Sir Francis Drake*. New York: Allen Lane, Penguin Press, 2004.

Beckerman, Ira C. "Prehistoric Settlement and Subsistence in Piedmont, North Carolina." 2 vols. Ph.D. diss., Pennsylvania State University, 1986.

Beer, Anna. *Bess: The Life of Lady Ralegh, Wife to Sir Walter.* London: Constable, 2004.

Bierer, Bert W. *Indians and Artifacts in the Southeast.* Columbia: Printed by author, 1978.

Binding, Paul. *Imagined Corners: Exploring the World's First Atlas.* London: London Review, 2004.

Black, Jeremy. *Visions of the World: A History of Maps.* London: Mitchell Beazley, 2004.

Blu, Karen I. *Lumbee Problem.* Cambridge: Cambridge University Press, 1980.

Boyce, Douglas W. "Tuscarora Political Organization, Ethnic Identity, and Sociohistorical Demography, 1711–1825." Ph.D. diss., University of North Carolina, 1973.

Brown, Douglas S. *The Catawba Indians: The People of the River.* Columbia: University of South Carolina Press, 1967.

Coe, Joffre L. "The Indian in North Carolina." *North Carolina Historical Review* 56 (April 1979): 158–61.

Coote, Stephen. *Drake: The Life and Legend of an Elizabethan Hero.* New York: Simon and Schuster, 2004.

Dillard, Richard. "Indian Tribes of Eastern North Carolina." *North Carolina Booklet* 6 (July 1906): 3–26.

Dunbar, Gary S. "Hatteras Indians of North Carolina." *Ethnohistory* 7 (Fall 1960): 410–18.

Gilbert, William Harlen, Jr. "Memorandum Concerning the Characteristics of the Larger Mixed-Blood Racial Islands of the Eastern United States." *Social Forces* 24 (May 1946): 438–47.

Harper, Rowan M. "A Statistical Study of the Croatans." *Rural Sociology* 2 (1937): 444–56.

Hazel, Forest. "Occaneechi-Saponi Descendants in the North Carolina Piedmont: The Texas Community." *Southern Indian Studies* 40 (1991): 436–38.

Hudson, Charles M. *Southeastern Indians.* Knoxville: University of Tennessee Press, 1976.

Lawson, John. *New Voyage to Carolina.* Edited and with an introduction by Hugh T. Lefler. Chapel Hill: University of North Carolina Press, 1967.

McMillan, Hamilton. *Lost Colony Found: An Historical Sketch of the Discovery of the Croatan Indians.* Robeson: Robeson Job Printers, 1898.

McPherson, O. M., comp. *Indians of North Carolina.* Washington, D.C.: Government Printing Office, 1915.

Parramore, Thomas C. "Tuscarora Ascendancy." *North Carolina Historical Review* 59 (October 1982): 307–26.

Perdue, Theda. *Native Carolinians: The Indians of North Carolina.* Raleigh: North Carolina Office of Archives and History, 1985.

Rights, Douglas. *American Indians in North Carolina.* 1947. Reprint: Winston-Salem: John F. Blair, 1988.

Sider, Gerald M. *Lumbee Indian Histories: Race, Ethnicity, and Indian Identity in the Southern United States.* Cambridge: Cambridge University Press, 1993.

Speck, Frank G. "Siouan Tribes of the Carolinas." *American Anthropology* 37 (1935): 201–25.

Swanton, John R. *Indians of the Southeastern United States.* Washington, D.C.: Smithsonian, 1979.

Torbert, Benjamin. "Tracing Native American Language History through Consonant Cluster Reduction: The Case of the Lumbee English." *American Speech* 76 (2001): 361–87.

U.S. Department of the Interior. *Indians of North Carolina.* Washington, D.C.: Government Printing Office, 1915.

Watson, Alan D. *Onslow County: A Brief History.* Raleigh: Division of Archives and History, North Carolina Department of Cultural Resources, 1995.

Wetmore, Ruth Y. "Role of the Indian in North Carolina History." *North Carolina Historical Review* 56 (April 1979): 162–76.

Winton, Sanford. "Indian Slavery in the Carolina Region." *Journal of Negro History* 19 (1934): 431–40.

A Chartered Chaos

THREE

North Carolina under the Proprietors

North Carolina experienced several lost and forgotten attempts at colonization before the English effort of 1585–90. From the time the first Native Americans migrated south and east to the coast to the Spanish attempts in the closing decades of the sixteenth century, the region that is now called North Carolina had become a common habitat for an ecological system that increasingly included humans as well as flora and fauna. Within that environment, a successful pattern of settlement had emerged long before the English attempt at Roanoke, one that would continue for decades afterward. From the Croatans to the Tuscaroras to the Virginians, migrations and settlements by land succeeded while attempts by sea failed. When explorer William Hilton's halfhearted proposal to resettle Barbadians and New Englanders fell apart in 1667, North Carolina already had been partially colonized earlier by Virginians without patent or permission from anyone. As historian Herb R. Pascal observed, "After years of grandiose schemes and plans, the job had been done by the farmer pushing out from the Virginia frontier seeking new and richer lands" and not by faraway castle builders across the ocean in London. Scores if not hundreds of Virginians had moved south into the Albemarle region by the late 1650s. The granting of the proprietary charter by Charles II in 1663 only signified a change in governance from the established but distant royal colony of Virginia to the new and ambitious proprietorship of the land now called "Carolina."

The charter for Carolina passed the royal seal on 24 March 1663, and it was given to a powerful coalition of eight lords proprietors. The reasons for establishing a new government south of Virginia coincided with the need to support the "Restoration" of the monarchy in England. The lords proprietors agreed with Charles II that the Crown needed to assert its authority quickly both at home and overseas as well as earn revenues from commerce and trade. A grant to set up colonies in America as rapidly as possible seemed ideal. Thus, instead of having to demand land in America as payment for their loyalty and support of the restoration of the monarchy, the lords proprietors instead found Charles II to be an enthusiastic patron of the plan. In fact, Charles II saw in overseas colonies not only a source of revenue and resources but also a place where English institutions such as religion and government could be liberalized and reformed. Remembering his father's fate, Charles II preferred to try many of his ideas first on faraway colonies. From Carolina to Pennsylvania, he approved charters that granted an unprecedented degree of religious freedom and control of local government to colonists.

The lords proprietors did not intend to set up a medieval English feudal kingdom in America. Although archaic terms, phrases, and references to older laws as well as to new terms of nobility made their way into the language of the Carolina charter, the intention seemed more to align the powers and titles of the proprietors with a prior Catholic colony, Maryland, than to set up a Camelot in a North American setting. Although the Carolina charter gave powers to the proprietors similar to the Muscovy and East India Companies, the precedents for its authority lay more in English common law than in grants to corporations to operate in foreign parts. With limited experience in colonization drawn mainly from Scotland, Ireland, and Wales, the king, acting on the advice of his councilors, included the Bishop of Durham clause. Overall, Charles II's grant to the proprietors came from a more traditional English system of tenure and landholding and took its measure and much of its language from the Heath charter of 1629 and the grant to Lord Baltimore to settle Maryland.

Charles II gave the lords proprietors title to a vast tract of land running from thirty-six degrees north latitude along the southern edge of Albemarle Sound to the south to thirty-one degrees north latitude roughly near the present-day Georgia town of Saint Mary's. In 1665, two years later, the Crown, cognizant of Virginia's trouble with the Albemarle settlements and growing problems with land claims, extended and validated the northern border along its present line, thirty-six degrees thirty minutes, to include Albemarle Sound and extended the southern boundary to twenty-nine degrees, just approximately below Saint Augustine in Spanish-occupied Florida. The colony's westward boundary stretched to the "South Seas," the Pacific Ocean. The colony and state's boundaries became the subject of surveyor's reports, many inaccurate, for the next century and a half. The powerful lords proprietors were Anthony Ashley Cooper, afterward earl of Shaftesbury; Edward Hyde, earl of Clarendon; George Monck, duke of Albemarle; William Craven, earl of Craven; Sir George Carteret of the Isle of Jersey; John Lord Berkeley; Sir John Colleton of Barbados; and Sir William Berkeley, an adventurer and governor of Virginia between 1641 and 1677. At first, Sir William Berkeley and then Sir John Colleton of Barbados dominated the proprietary board, and, after Colleton's death in 1667 and Berkeley's absorption in Virginia's troubles, Cooper, the first earl of Shaftesbury, took the lead until his death in 1683. A commanding personality, Cooper hired a young physician, John Locke, as a member of his personal household and then as secretary to the lords proprietors. Articulate and a skilled clerk and writer, Locke looked to Cooper as a mentor and friend. The collaboration between the two later produced one of the most curious of all the utopian schemes to settle a colony, the Fundamental Constitutions.

The 1663 charter gave to the proprietors well-established rights such as the power to grant titles of nobility different from England's as well as the authority inherent in the Bishop of Durham clause, both common to all colonial proprietary colonies drafted by the attorney general for the Crown's approval. A curiosity to modern readers, the Bishop of Durham clause recognized that Carolina would be a buffer colony against Spain to the south, much as Durham had been against the Scots earlier in English history, and gave to the ruler, to the "bishop," extraordinary autonomy to protect the frontier against the Spanish. In this way, the contest for political power in colonial Carolina centered on the powers of the lords proprietors, the "bishop," and not upon the king or Parliament itself. As was the case with the Maryland charter, the lords proprietors received the widest possible

Anthony Ashley Cooper, the first earl of Shaftesbury (1621–83), one of Carolina's most prominent proprietors.
North Carolina Collection, University of North Carolina at Chapel Hill.

latitude in terms of establishing their authority over the new colony. In this way, the proprietors could establish a political and legal system so long as its laws did not conflict with those of England, make laws with the consent and approval of an elected assembly, institute a judicial system, construct fortifications, organize a militia, and wage war. Most important, the 1663 grant to the lords proprietors "chartered" the idea of representative government in the new colony, a "constitutional right" only enlarged and never forgotten by Carolinians. The words "with the advice, assent, and approbation of the Freemen" in an elected assembly eventually came back to haunt the Crown.

The second charter of 1665 significantly altered the proprietors' rights in two instances. First, the lords proprietors could now "erect, Constitute, and make several Counties, Baronies, and Colonies of and within the said Provinces and territories . . . with several and distinct Jurisdictions, powers, liberties, and privileges." Almost from the first, two and later three separate settlements emerged in Carolina, one at Albemarle Sound, another at Charleston, and, later, a third in the region of Cape Fear. This change provided the legal basis for the ultimate division of the colony into North and South Carolina. With the amended charter of 1665, the proprietors could divide Carolina into several colonies if the need arose. Lastly, with the urging and sensitivity of Charles II, the enlarged charter of 1665 made explicit the measure of religious freedom in the earlier 1663 document by permitting churches other than that of the Anglican faith to be established and maintained in the colony.

The lords proprietors' response to the colonists' requests for change came in the Great Deed of Grant of 1668, which began a series of retreats against their ideas of ever establishing a utopian model of government in Carolina. The deed promised Carolinians that they could now hold lands "upon the same terms and conditions that the Inhabitants of Virginia hold theirs." Settlers looked upon the Great Deed as giving them a straight farthing per acre quit rent while removing the threat of escheat, the reversion or loss of their land to a landgrave, cacique, or manor lord, and of extending the Virginia headright system of fifty acres to all adults—all important to settlers intent on establishing their independence through land ownership. It became a fundamental and revered, if frequently misunderstood, part of Carolinians' perceived constitutional rights to property and participation in government.

The plan for the Grand Model outlined in the Fundamental Constitutions, the most controversial of Carolina's charters, evolved from the utopian thinking of John Locke and the ideals of his mentor, Lord Shaftesbury, the chief exponent of the political philosophy of Grand Whiggery in England. With this philosophy the fundamental principle of government and social organization rested upon the division of wealth and interest according to ownership of land. Thus, while everyone had "interests"—that is, some stake in the outcome of a decision—those who owned the greatest share of productive wealth naturally had the greatest involvement and power. As incorporated into and outlined in the Fundamental Constitutions, really nothing more than a set of laws and ordinances to implement the Grand Model, each province in the colony would be divided into counties where one-fifth of the land would be owned by the proprietors, another fifth by a hereditary nobility called landgraves and caciques (a new title to separate them from English nobility), and the remaining three-fifths by commoners. Tracts allotted to landgraves were called baronies, while commoners' holdings were grouped into colonies and divided into precincts. The three principal organs of government, the proprietors' courts, the Grand Council, and the Parliament, each had checks upon the other and at the same time carefully blended monarchical, aristocratic, and democratic elements. In the scheme of Grand Whiggery, such a balance ensured that no one element would dominate the other.

The lords proprietors first floated the Grand Model in Albemarle in 1670. They hoped the constitutions, or laws, would be implemented gradually in Albemarle and throughout the entire colony, especially the southward settlement at Port Royal, by 1700. When the final draft of the constitutions reached the colonists in 1697, it met only rejection and hostility. Thereafter, the pretense of governing the colony under the Grand Model vanished, and, after 1698, the lords proprietors dropped all mention of it. Elaborate and detailed in its utopian ideals, the Fundamental Constitutions, except in a negative or restraining sense, had little impact upon the social and political development of faraway Carolina.

Instead of a centralized and functioning, if confusing, Whiggish government, for the first thirty-five years the Carolinas had a series of shifting cliques, factions, and personalities that grouped themselves around issues such as taxes, land policies, boundaries, and constitutional prerogatives. The first Carolina settlers in the Albemarle Sound area opposed the idea of compact settlements and relatively small holdings proposed in the Concessions and Agreements of 1665 and in the Fundamental Constitutions. Rather than demographic density based on an English or New England model, the colonists wanted the chance to

Henry Somerset, the duke of Beaufort (1684–1714).
North Carolina Collection, University of North Carolina at Chapel Hill.

accumulate large estates and speculate in land much as had been done in Virginia. More-over, they adamantly opposed large property fees such as the differentially applied rents of the proprietors, and, in lieu of them, pushed for a flat farthing per acre tax like Virginia's.

The dizzying array of men who exercised some measure of control over Albemarle County and the northward parts of Carolina under the proprietors and their chartered dreams exemplified the disarray and disability of government under the proprietorship. Samuel Stephens (1662–64, 1667–70) took his appointment first from the Virginia Coun-cil and later from the lords proprietors; William Drummond drew his authority from the lords proprietors (1664–67); John Jenkins served three terms as governor of Albemarle County (1672–75, 1675–77, and 1678); while Seth Sothel, himself a lord proprietor who could have solved many of the colonists' problems on the spot, proved the worst governor of all. Appointed in 1682 but soon after captured by Algerian pirates, Sothel took up his post early in 1683 after being ransomed. Bitter and arrogant, Sothel began using his war-rant as governor to arrest those who complained against him, to imprison his enemies and critics, to accept bribes for appointments and favors, and to seize land and estates of colonists whether they were living or dead. In his greed and caprice Sothel supposedly stole serving ware and clothing from anyone he visited and threatened them if they pro-tested. Incensed and outraged, the colonists arrested Sothel, tried him in the assembly, and forcibly removed him from the colony in 1689. In 1712 the two Carolinas split. Sothel was governor of South Carlina for a short time but returned to Albemarle, where he died.

Four rebellions by colonial Carolinians pointed to the dissatisfaction they found in government. The first, Culpepper's in 1677, brought to the forefront the factions compet-ing for control of the new colony. A relative newcomer from Charleston to the south, John Culpepper quickly allied himself with John Jenkins, the governor of Albemarle. Described as a mischief maker and rabble-rouser, Culpepper soon found himself in company with

Jenkins and George Durant, who wanted to undermine a faction headed by Thomas East-church and Thomas Miller. Neither group could claim the right to form a legal govern-ment and both acted arbitrarily in the offices they held. Jenkins's authority expired in 1673, and no de jure government existed afterward. The controversy between Eastchurch and Jenkins centered on the enforcement of the Plantation Duty Act of 1673. Eastchurch and Miller conveniently called themselves the Proprietary Party and, with that dubious label, wanted a thorough enforcement of the penny per pound tax on tobacco and of the proprietors' land policy, both unpopular stands in the Albemarle colony.

The struggle climaxed in 1677 when Culpepper and forty followers captured and imprisoned Thomas Miller, seized customs revenues and records, arrested other officials and assemblymen, and issued a call for a "free parliament" for Albemarle. When Miller escaped and went to England to accuse Jenkins and Durant of treason, the rebels sent John Culpepper to plead their case. Disgusted at the self-serving tactics and greed of the Eastchurch-Miller faction and disclaiming any connection they might have had to the pro-prietors, Lord Shaftesbury himself defended Culpepper at the King's Bench. Shaftesbury argued that no settled government existed in the colony and that the colonists had the right "to riot" against the arbitrary excesses of Thomas Miller and Thomas Eastchurch. Pardoned and freed, Culpepper returned to Albemarle a hero. Moreover, the idea that a beleaguered citizenry could "riot" and set up a "free parliament" had taken hold in Carolina.

The second rebellion, led by John Gibbs in 1689, challenged the authority of the newly appointed governor, Philip Ludwell, a Virginian. Gibbs, a cousin of the duke of Albemarle, thought that, as a noble cacique and heir of the duke's proprietorship, he should be gov-ernor and not just a Virginian who sided with the colonists. Recognized briefly as gover-nor, Gibbs, with a few paid supporters, tried to secure his position by force against popular sentiment until Ludwell finally arrived with his official warrants. Denounced by the pro-prietary board in 1690, Gibbs's official claim ended when the Fundamental Constitutions were suspended in 1691. Once more, the colonists' opinions and grievances had helped sway a critical colonial appointment.

Thomas Cary, a Charleston merchant and president of the council, sat as governor until the proprietors named an official representative. From 1708 until 1711 Cary and his followers managed to prevail in the assembly against a series of factions and groups led by William Glover and, at times, John Porter and the Quakers. Fed up with the parade of mal-contents to London and with the obvious chaos in the colony, the proprietors decided to appoint a governor of North Carolina separate from and "independent of the Governor of Carolina." Issued 24 January 1712, the commission of Edward Hyde as the governor of North Carolina marked the official separation of the two colonies. While Hyde met with Baron von Graffenried and newly appointed members of the council, Cary and the mal-contents, in comic-opera fashion, sailed a small ship into Albemarle Sound, plunked two cannonballs onto the roof of the house where the meeting took place, and, while beating a hasty retreat, ran their ship aground. Pyramiding together as they did, Hyde's takeover of government, Cary's burlesque attempt at a coup, and the Tuscarora war almost spelled the end of the fledgling colony.

Yet another test of the quasi-legitimacy of the new colony came sailing down the coast in the summer of 1718. With almost as many aliases as pistols dangling from his person,

Blackbeard and his crew carousing on the Carolina coast.
North Carolina Collection, University of North Carolina at Chapel Hill.

Blackbeard the pirate brought his formidable flotilla of ships and miscreants to Topsail Inlet, now Beaufort Inlet. Known as Edward Teach to Bostonians and as Edward Thatch, Tach, or Thatche to Carolinians, Blackbeard headed straight for Bath, the colony's fledgling capital. There, with the acquiescence of the new governor, Charles Eden, and with the cooperation of Tobias Knight, the colony's secretary and collector of customs, Blackbeard sought a royal pardon under the recently passed Act of Grace. Under the act, even so weakened a government as Eden's could exculpate him. In fact, therein lay North Carolina's appeal.

Legends indicate that for several hogsheads of sugar, some rum, a little gold, and relief from various threats, Governor Eden made Blackbeard and twenty of his hand-picked crew citizens of North Carolina. In short order, the new citizen Blackbeard married the sixteen-year-old daughter of a coastal planter, sailed up and down the coast drunkenly celebrating his good fortune with locals, and, in general, established himself as a good colonial settler. Still, the open sea and the excitement of buccaneering called. After three months, Blackbeard headed for Bermuda with one of his ships, the *Adventure*. Before returning to his nest he had established at Ocracoke Inlet, he looted several English ships and captured a French sloop carrying sugar to the continent. Back in Bath, Governor Eden, for sixty hogsheads of sugar, and Secretary Knight, for just twenty, declared the French ship to be a derelict rescued at sea by Blackbeard, thus giving him salvage rights. Blackbeard then resumed his life as a cheery North Carolina citizen and dubious merchant.

Unhappy with Blackbeard and his ways, some of the colony's merchants and planters, headed by Eden's political enemies, Edward Moseley and Moore, pleaded with Virginia to intervene. Alexander Spotswood, Virginia's governor, needed little urging. Chartering a private navy, Spotswood sent the sloops *Jane* and *Ranger* south to do battle with Blackbeard. Commanded by Robert Maynard, one of the Royal Navy's oldest and most experienced

*The death of Blackbeard at the
hands of Lt. Robert Maynard
of the Royal Navy in 1718.*
North Carolina Collection, University
of North Carolina at Chapel Hill.

serving lieutenants, the small flotilla sailed straight for Ocracoke Inlet. Spotswood deliberately held back the information of his impending attack from North Carolina officials.
Virginia had decided to invade North Carolina.

At daylight on the morning of 23 November 1718, the *Jane* and *Ranger* tacked through
the maze of shallows and sounds outside Ocracoke Inlet looking for Blackbeard and his
ships. Uncannily sensing danger, Blackbeard, on board the *Adventure,* cut his anchor cable
and made for the approaching ships. Suddenly turning and heading back into Ocracoke,
Blackbeard lured the *Jane* and *Ranger* onto a shallow sandbar outside the Inlet. After raking the deck of both helpless ships with deadly canister shot, he prepared to grapple and
board the *Jane.* To his surprise, Maynard had hidden many of his sailors and marines below
deck, protecting them from the murderous fire. Swarming up ladders and holds, Maynard's
men collided with Blackbeard and his pirates head-on in one of the bloodiest sea battles
in North Carolina's history.

Startled but not intimidated, Blackbeard, blazing away with his pistols, rushed straight
for Maynard. Not surprisingly in that century, his shots, even at close range, frequently
missed. Drawing his cutlass, Blackbeard then swung wildly at Maynard, breaking the officer's sword and wounding his hand. Firing a pistol directly at Blackbeard's chest, Maynard
retreated to find another weapon, but he did not need one. Blackbeard fell mortally
wounded at Maynard's feet. With Blackbeard's death, the short and brutal battle ended.

That blustery November morning, Blackbeard lost ten killed, half his crew, while
Maynard suffered twelve dead and twenty-two wounded. Maynard then personally cut off
Blackbeard's head, mounted it on the bowsprit at the front of the captured *Adventure,* and
sailed back to Virginia. For several years afterward, Blackbeard's head and skull, mounted
on a post as a warning to other pirates, greeted ships plying the waters of the Chesapeake.

Ellis Brand, captain of the Royal Navy ship the *Lyme,* then led an overland expedition from Virginia that, in effect, sacked Bath looking for evidence of Blackbeard's piracy. He confiscated eighty hogsheads of sugar from Governor Eden and Secretary Knight, claiming that they had been given as bribes. Brand then rounded up several of Blackbeard's former crew members, now living peacefully around Bath, presumably as proper North Carolinians, and headed back to Virginia, where most eventually were tried and hung.

Despite its gaudy role in historical folklore, the tale of Blackbeard and of piracy in early North Carolina only underscored the feebleness of proprietary control over the colony. So weak was the control of Governor Eden and his council they could only negotiate with and not defend themselves against Blackbeard and his small band of pirates. To Virginia and South Carolina, the entire province seemed less a colony and more a swamp of lawlessness and corruption inhabited by pirates all. North Carolina did not deserve their respect or cooperation in colonial affairs. Although Spotswood later apologized for his illegal invasion of North Carolina, the colony's political troubles did not go unnoticed in England. Something in proprietary North Carolina had gone terribly awry. Only London could attempt to fix it.

The unsettled conditions and uprisings by Carolinians almost from the inception of the colony should be placed not only in a local but also in an American context. When Lord Shaftesbury rose to defend John Culpepper in London, his admission that no settled government existed in Carolina personified the dilemma of well-intentioned but romantic Englishmen who saw in the faraway American colony a place to set up utopias. From the charters of 1663 and 1665 to the Concessions and Agreements and finally to the Fundamental Constitutions, Carolinians consistently opposed the proprietors' land policies, plans for compact settlements, taxes, and proprietary assent to laws passed by the assembly. Until North Carolina became a royal colony in 1729, its institutions of government, except for precinct courts, had shallow roots and only a semblance of control over colonial affairs. Disturbances in the colony tended to center around individuals such as Robert Holden and Seth Sothel and not factions, in spite of one group or another speciously claiming proprietary legitimacy. Yet the daily lives of most early colonists were little affected by these quarrels. In truth, the courts and constables mostly enjoyed broad support in their actions and functioned largely without controversy until the decade leading to the Revolution. Thus, the early political history of North Carolina reflected decades of malfeasance and abuse of colonial offices, corruption, bribery, and outright theft by a series of cliques and rogues at the provincial level but also a striking lack of strife and contention at the most basic unit of all, local government. Small wonder that early North Carolinians developed a coefficient of proximity of government that equated distance with corruption and indifference.

Many of the struggles and rebellions can only be understood by recognizing that they were attempts by opposing individuals and groups to punish opponents unluckily out of office and to settle old political scores. Early government in North Carolina existed both as de jure and de facto in nature, frequently with little distinction between the two. Still, several broad democratic trends emerged early in North Carolina's existence. First, the powers of the legislative body (frequently called the burgess after the Virginia institution because of the large number of settlers from that colony and later labeled a general assembly in the charter of 1665) dramatically exceeded the requirements of the Carolina charters and Fundamental Constitutions. As the colonists pushed for a broader franchise allowing any free, white male, aged twenty-one and over, who had paid a year's tax levy the right to vote, they also incrementally increased the prerogatives of the assembly. While seemingly restrictive by today's standards, the colonial Carolina franchise liberalized voting and office holding at a time when large numbers of new settlers began arriving from Pennsylvania and Virginia. Gradually, the lower house assumed the right to incorporate towns, regulate Indian affairs, approve religious establishments, levy taxes, control and license businesses, issue currency, enact codes for indentured servants and slaves, and install courts and create procedures for them. By the time of the split between North and South Carolina, the lower house had assumed the most essential right of governance, that of collecting, holding, and spending "moneys arising from provincial revenues." As the lower house engrossed more and more legal power and authority, the executive privileges of the governor lessened as did proprietary and, later, royal controls. Much of the shift of power to the general assembly came not because of incompetence, weakness, and abuse of office by governors, although significant, but because local officials like John Jenkins and Samuel Stephens felt they had strong ties to Carolina and not London or they were residents who recognized legitimate local needs. In an American frontier setting, the Bishop of Durham Clause had allowed too much autonomy to colonists at the expense of a centralized government. One agency of government, precinct courts, in many cases functioned as the only significant institution in a colony where there were few towns and a scattered populace.

The weakness of government and the resultant civil disorder and even rebellion in Carolina had practically become a public reality as well as a nascent political philosophy by 1724. Even before the first royal governor set foot in Carolina, settlers already had developed a deep aversion to taxes and government of any kind. In neighboring colonies such as Virginia and Maryland, rebellions led by Nathaniel Bacon in 1676 and John Coode in 1689 mirrored the generalized unrest against government felt by many Carolinians as well. More than seventy years later, South Carolinians would join with their northern brethren in the largest attempt by colonial Americans to "regulate" their affairs. When the Revolution came in 1775, North Carolina, with a history of rebellion and unrest dating from its proprietary past, followed its neighbors as they sought independence for all Americans.

ADDITIONAL READINGS

Albertson, Catherine S. "The First Albemarle Assembly (1665), Hall's Creek near Nixonton." *North Carolina Booklet* 12 (January 1913): 202–7.

Boyd, Julian P. "Sheriff in Colonial North Carolina." *North Carolina Historical Review* 5 (April 1928): 151–80.

Burney, Eugenia. *Colonial North Carolina.* Nashville: T. Nelson, 1975.

Butler, Lindley S. "Governors of Albemarle County, 1663–1689." *North Carolina Historical Review* 46 (July 1969): 281–99.

———. *Pirates, Privateers, and Rebel Raiders of the Carolina Coast.* Chapel Hill: University of North Carolina Press, 2000.

Clark, Walter. "Indian Massacre and Tuscarora War 1711–13." *North Carolina Booklet* 2 (10 July 1902): 1–16.

Cumming, William Petterson. *The Southeast in Early Maps, with an Annotated Check List of Printed and Manuscript Regional and Local Maps of Southeastern North America during the Colonial Period.* Princeton, N.J.: Princeton University Press, 1958. Reprint, Chapel Hill: University of North Carolina Press, 1962.

Fagg, Daniel Webster, Jr. "Sleeping Not with the King's Grant: A Rereading of Some Proprietary Documents, 1663–1667." *North Carolina Historical Review* 48 (April 1971): 171–85.

Faust, Albert B. "Swiss Emigration to the American Colonies in the Eighteenth Century." *American Historical Review* 22 (October 1916): 21–44.

Fraser, Walter J., Jr. *Charleston! Charleston! The History of a Southern City.* Columbia: University of South Carolina Press, 1989.

Hsueh, Vicki. "Giving Orders: Theory and Practice in the Fundamental Constitutions of Carolina." *Journal of the History of Ideas* 63 (2002): 425–46.

Lefler, Hugh Talmage. "Promotional Literature of the Southern Colonies." *Journal of Southern History* 33 (February 1967): 3–25.

Lefler, Hugh Talmage, and William S. Powell. *Colonial North Carolina: A History.* New York: Scribner's, 1973.

McCain, Paul M. "County Court in North Carolina before 1750." *Trinity College Historical Papers Publications* 31 (1954): 1–163.

Parker, Mattie Erma Edwards. "Legal Aspects of Culpepper's Rebellion." *North Carolina Historical Review* 45 (April 1968): 111–27.

Parramore, Thomas. "Tuscarora Ascendancy." *North Carolina Historical Review* 59 (October 1982): 307–26.

Spindel, Donna J. *Crime and Society in North Carolina, 1663–1776.* Baton Rouge: Louisiana State University Press, 1989.

Watson, Alan D. "Ordinaries in Colonial Eastern North Carolina." *North Carolina Historical Review* 45 (January 1968): 67–83.

Wolf, Jacquelyn Hinda. "Patents and Tithables in Proprietary North Carolina, 1663–1729." *North Carolina Historical Review* 56 (July 1979): 263–77.

A Mosaic of Colonial North Carolina

Almost any commentary on life in colonial North Carolina begins and ends with the lament "poor Carolina." Early travelers and writers found in that phrase a description for the pitiable state of the colony's first settlers. Thomas Pollock, an early politician and observer of Carolina, estimated that the population in 1717 numbered around 2,000 tithables, slave and free, and that the overall number of inhabitants, always greater than those taxed, probably exceeded 3,500. A closer look at landholders, heads of households, and average family size yields a more liberal estimate of approximately 14,300 whites and 3,500 slaves in the colony by 1720. When North Carolina became a royal colony in 1729, Hugh Jones, a Virginian, thought the colony to be "vastly inferior" to his own, its trade smaller, and its inhabitants "thinner, and for the most part poorer." Visiting the settlement one year earlier as a boundary commissioner for Virginia, William Byrd II also registered his disgust and disdain for his neighbors. Most Carolinians, he asserted, lived in a state of nature in a vast and untamed wilderness. They recognized no government, paid "no tribute, either to God or Caesar," and had no manners. North Carolinians tolerated his company only so "long as our good liquor lasted" and then departed. To him, North Carolinians could rise no higher than country bumpkins or "homebred" squires. They could never be gentlemen. The colony had neither ports, towns, good roads, nor any semblance or place of government. In fact, it hardly seemed a colony at all. Indeed, North Carolina's settlements, population, and circumstances appeared so meager and undifferentiated in the 1720s that London thought of giving it away to its richer neighbors, Virginia and South Carolina, both of whom probably would have declined the gift altogether.

Yet by 1729 North Carolina had about 36,000 inhabitants living chiefly around Albemarle Sound. Like the fingers of a hand, settlements snaked up the inlets and waterways of Albemarle into the interior. In this northeastern region of the colony, Chowan County had almost 40 percent of the population, and the counties of Currituck, Pasquotank, Perquimans, Tyrrell, and Bertie contained another 40 percent. Southern counties such as Beaufort, Craven, Hyde, and Carteret had few settlers, and New Hanover County in the Cape Fear region still awaited development. As the density of settlement grew from 1691 to 1719, small towns emerged as the focal point of government and commerce. First begun in the 1680s, an area near the mouth of the Little River, while never incorporated, became the earliest seat of government. The "Grand[d] Courthouse," the colony's first significant although not long-standing building, was erected there in 1693 and 1694. Located on the southwest side of the river in Perquimans County, Little River produced some of the colony's most early important figures, such as George Durant, Thomas Blount, and William Glover. John Hecklefield, the village's most substantial citizen, sometimes hosted meetings of the assembly and council in his house. Although it remained a viable community for decades, Little River experienced little growth until after the American Revolution.

Located in Beaufort precinct at the juncture of Old Towne (Bath) and Back creeks, Bath lays claim to being North Carolina's oldest incorporated town. Laid out by the surveyor, John Lawson, along with Simon Alderson Sr. and Joel Martin Sr., from 1704 to 1705, Bath experienced a growth spurt after the assembly first incorporated it in 1705–6. Devastated by the Tuscarora war, Bath grew slowly after 1713 yet remained the meeting place for the precinct court of Beaufort and Hyde counties.

Laid out and incorporated in 1722, Edenton served as North Carolina's capital from 1722 to 1743. First known as the Town of Matecomack Creek and then as the Town on Queen Anne's Creek, Edenton occupied a pivotal position in the colony's early history. Centered as it was in Chowan County, easily the most populous and growing region of Albemarle Sound, Edenton owed its prominence to the construction of a courthouse in 1712 and to its designation as a center for the establishment of the Anglican Church. New Bern's founding resulted from the colonizing efforts of Swiss and German settlers under the leadership of Baron von Graffenried. Since they emigrated from Europe as congregations and as families, the Swiss brought with them a ready-made community. Within a year after its founding in 1710, New Bern boasted more than one hundred inhabitants, a great many of them traders, merchants, craftsmen, and artisans. Hardworking and industrious, New Bern presaged later settlements of Scots and Moravians. As fortunate as Graffenried was in choosing his village at the confluence of the Trent and Neuse rivers, he could not successfully balance the time with the place. Within two years after its founding the powerful Tuscarora fell upon New Bern, killing scores of settlers and imprisoning others. Abandoned by the remaining colonists, New Bern came to life again as a trading center only in 1720.

The Tuscarora war improbably aided the founding of Beaufort in Craven County in 1713. Located across from Topsail Inlet at the mouth of the North River, its location afforded it an outlet to the sea, yet it remained away from any inland trade or contact with the Indians. Still, few settlers bought lots in the town despite its seemingly advantageous situation. Named a port of entry by the proprietors in 1722, Beaufort grew but little during the colonial era.

To any observer of North Carolina history, the lack of large towns, ports, and cities in its early history marks it as somehow culturally and economically undeveloped and unrefined, especially when compared to the city-state of Charleston, South Carolina, and to the pretentious plantation manors and coastal towns of Virginia. Yet the towns and precincts of the colony, however small and rudimentary, served as navels for larger settlement patterns. In Edenton, for example, clusters of settlements radiated out from the town. Indeed, Edenton's importance can be understood not from its number of inhabitants but from the aggregate patents and grants of land around but not in the incorporated area. As the streams and rivers of North Carolina attracted more and more colonists, the frontier and its towns moved south and west from Albemarle Sound and the Chowan River to the Neuse and Pamlico, and, finally, to the lower Cape Fear by 1725. In this way, towns such as New Bern and Bath became jumping-off places for settlers to acquire land and move farther south and eventually westward. Moreover, a great many of the colony's early leaders came from towns and the most densely populated areas around them. Not surprisingly, North Carolina allowed political representation not only from precincts but also from towns, a clear recognition of their economic, political, and social significance.

Still, at some point Carolinians seemed to prefer not to live in towns or in densely settled areas regardless of opportunities for trade, commerce, politics, or socializing. Instead, they elected to live in near isolation in huts and lean-tos in their self-contained wilderness. As property holders on the frontier, they fulfilled Thomas Jefferson's idea of yeoman farmers, yet with less education and fewer aspirations than even he envisioned. William Byrd popularized the life of colonial North Carolinians by describing their existence in what he called "Lubberland." "Surely there is no place in the world," he wrote sarcastically, "where the inhabitants live with less labor than in North Carolina. It approaches nearer to the description of Lubberland than any other, by the great felicity of the climate, the easiness of raising provisions, and the slothfulness of its people."

Janet Schaw, a haughty Englishwoman and reluctant visitor to the Cape Fear region just before the Revolution, thought North Carolinians to be the "most slovenly" and indolent of all Americans, amiably subsisting on "corn and pork" and whiskey. The prolific garden produce of the colonists, an abundant variety of beans, squash, and greens of all kinds as well as a bewildering array of beef, mutton, turkey, wild game, and fish and oysters, somehow escaped the critical notice of this "lady of quality." Certainly, early Carolinians loved to drink "killdevil" and "bombo," two potent rum-punch mixtures, and engage in bouts of fighting, gouging, and wrestling. Janet Schaw's journal, along with the few remaining estate inventories of colonial North Carolina, helps to dispel one of the most enduring myths of the period, that of the self-sufficiency of the first settlers, especially the "hardy" and independent Scots-Irish. From a careful consideration of both records, it appears that early North Carolinians spent a significant proportion of their small disposable income for pottery, iron products, pewter, glass, shot and powder, linen, cloth, rum, tea, and groceries, principally sugar and spices. Most came from abroad, chiefly from England through the Chesapeake and Charleston. Peddlers could be found everywhere.

When Schaw commented on the threadbare appearance of many settlers, it testified to the fact that North Carolinians, like so many colonials, could not make their own clothing despite the fact that they grew flax and some cotton. Although the percentage of spinning wheels consistently increased until, by 1770, an estimated two-thirds of all households had one, their principal function seemed to be to repair and not to make cloth. The manifests of ships from Charleston, such as the *Tryal,* listed "oznaburgs," rough and inexpensive woolen cloth used for slaves, and linens and clothing, because North Carolinians could not make their own. In similar fashion, early settlers did not have neat fields of corn, vegetables, and grain, really a romanticized notion from nineteenth-century farms, but, instead, only a patch or two of upturned earth for smaller produce. Less than 20 percent of North Carolinians had any turned or plowed fields of more than two acres before 1770. It took a revolution before the colonies acquired some independence from England's "woolens acts" and other measures designed to keep them a supplier and not a manufacturer of cloth and also a processor of groceries, notably alcohol and caffeine products.

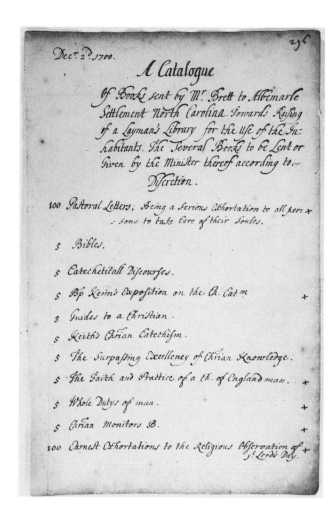

Although North Carolinians never raised as many sheep as did other colonists, they commonly had two or three to a household. Nevertheless, they seldom spun wool into cloth. Weavers conspicuously are absent in colonial North Carolina's inventory of occupations, household or commercial. While in the northern and middle colonies, farms and households had cows and thus milk, cheese, and butter, North Carolinians did not. Indeed, only rarely does a researcher find any mention of the consumption of milk, cheese, or butter in early North Carolina. In reality, North Carolinians, living in semitropical, low-lying coastal areas or in the less humid but nevertheless hot interior, instead drank their milk clabbered, or buttered, if at all, and on rare occasions squeezed the butter from the milk. In the place of butter, they came to love grease, whether from beef, mutton, or pork, even soaking their bread in it and storing cooked-over remains as a larder.

Despite the reproach and scolding from Englishmen, Scots, Virginians, and even South Carolinians concerning their diets, habits, dress, and customs, most of the colony's earliest settlers seemed not only content but also happy with their lives. Given the wide ownership of land, a long growing season, and a mild climate, most settlers did well. While a large majority lived in huts, hovels, and lean-tos built of pine logs with earthen floors, they experienced little poverty or starvation. In 1770 a recent settler in the colony wrote his cousin that North Carolina was "the best poor mans Country I Ever heard of and I have had the opportunity of hearing from south and north." Most early North Carolinians seemed delighted by their chance to have a lubber life of their own, free of the domination and self-importance of a haughty elite personified by the Schaws and Byrds.

Early settlers generally prospered and enjoyed life in early North Carolina. So vast was the land, so temperate the climate, and so negligible the hand of government that the colony attracted immigrants not only from Virginia and South Carolina but also from Pennsylvania, New Jersey, and Maryland. Moreover, Scots-Irish from the Ulster province of northern Ireland, Scots from the highlands and lowlands, ordinary Englishmen from the environs of London and surrounding counties, and Germans from the palatine provinces all found in Carolina the promise of a better social, spiritual, and economic life. After 1729 North Carolina, along with Pennsylvania, generally enjoyed the reputation of being the "best poor man's country" in the colonies.

In early North Carolina, great extremes in wealth, class, and station in life did not exist as they did in other southern colonies. Certainly, the barrier islands and a hostile seacoast did much to insulate and isolate its first settlements. North Carolina was without a great port city such as Charleston or Annapolis and without a staple crop or a well-established plantation system and had few slaves, except in the Cape Fear region. It also lacked a strong established church, such as the Church of England, but did have a large majority of landholders. Thus, North Carolina failed to develop a set of institutions or attitudes that strengthened class distinctions. When observers such as William Byrd decried the lack of "what is called politeness and good-breeding" among North Carolinians, he meant, in eighteenth-century speak, that they deferred to no one and treated everyone alike, if crudely. He found that Carolinians seldom flattered or spoke politely "to their governors but treat them with all the excesses of freedom and familiarity." A contemporary European visitor, Johann Schoepf, expressed amazement at the rudeness of address and the lack of "exterior courtesies" by slaves, yeoman farmers, and planters alike. When he met with the leading inhabitants of New Bern, the Venezuelan aristocrat Francisco de Miranda, traveling in the Carolinas, pointed out that they dressed "carelessly and grossly," and smoked, chewed, and spat tobacco so much that "they could not go to bed and . . . sleep without having a cud" in their mouths. The colony's first royal governor, George Burrington, blamed a lack of deference and social distinctions for the inhabitants' low regard for government. Why, he asked, should North Carolinians respect the decisions of the courts when "there is no difference to be perceived in Dress and Carriage between the Justices, Constables, and Planters that come to Court"? The same held true for militia units since both "Officers and Private men, at a Muster," behaved and dressed the same. North Carolina, he observed, had more "parity" than any other "Country," and it undermined the social and political order. Burrington also pointed to another characteristic of trashy North Carolinians. He thought them to be "not Industrious but subtle and crafty," especially when it came to politics. They always behaved "insolently to their Governours," even throwing some in prison, driving "others out of the Country, at times sett up two or three supported by Men under Arms . . . [and] . . . all the Governors that ever were in this Province lived in fear of the People (except myself) and Dreaded their Assemblys." Early in their history,

Arthur Dobbs (1689–1765), governor of
North Carolina from 1754 until 1765.
North Carolina Collection, University of
North Carolina at Chapel Hill.

poorly dressed and discourteous North Carolinians tended not to defer to but to examine authority.

Haughty aristocrats such as Francisco de Miranda and Janet Schaw undoubtedly thought about Lisbon and London while they wrote about North Carolina. To them, the manners, customs, and dress of North Carolinians seemed somehow rustic and unsophisticated compared to those of the glamorous capitals of Europe that they knew so well. Yet their journals carry praise and no condemnation of the friendliness, hospitality, and hearty nature of North Carolinians, only disapproval of their outward appearance and manners. Francis Vale, another visitor to the Cape Fear region in 1730, found that the lack of formality and proper etiquette did not mean an absence of a system of values. Indeed, he noted that, despite not having a proper clergyman "in the whold government," North Carolinians appeared "religiously inclined," even highly moral. Moreover, the communal custom of North Carolinians living "very lovingly together" and attending "meetings at one anothers houses" struck him as a contrast to class-conscious Europe. Gabriel Johnston, governor after Burrington, from 1734 to 1752, thought North Carolinians to be a "sober," that is, serious, and also a hardworking and "industrious set of people," unlike many he had known in England and Scotland. With few inns and only scattered taverns throughout the province, North Carolinians traditionally took in travelers and strangers, offering them the same plain fare and lodging they worked so hard to acquire. Indeed, the poorly dressed, tobacco-chewing, boisterous, uneducated, and ill-mannered commoners who lived in "poor Carolina" loved their Lubberland as if it were a heavenly home, welcoming the pompous as well as the pathetic to their paradise. William Byrd carried his own Anglican priest with him as he journeyed through the Lubberland of early North Carolina. In a revealing tally,

*Woman taking snuff
in early North Carolina.*
North Carolina Department of
Archives and History, Raleigh.

Byrd noted that no one he met in the colony asked the minister to perform a marriage, but scores wished him to christen their children. To Byrd, that meant that "marriage is reckon'd a lay contract in Carolina" and not a legal one. Yet in early North Carolina lay contracts bound couples "lovingly" together both legally and communally. Informal, affective, consensual marriages flourished in early North Carolina, although lawful wedding ceremonies were often performed by ministers from the Church of England, who were few and far between throughout most of the colonial era. Proper ceremonies did not become the norm until the 1770s, but the practice of common law marriages, named after the English custom, continued until the Civil War. In the towns and communities of colonial North Carolina, most early settlers married by making reciprocal vows, frequently posting them as "banns" in public places but also declaring their intentions and fidelity in front of family and friends. Often marriage followed the birth of a child after a sexual relationship between a man and a woman. Pregnancy and childbirth thus impelled a couple to consider themselves married. When official ministers of the Church of England occasionally made the rounds of the backcountry in North Carolina, they discovered that, while the people openly resented the ministers because of the established status and fees, these deeply religious settlers nevertheless wanted their children christened.

Anglican itinerant Charles Woodmason also found himself baptizing "numbers of Bastard Children," a legal and not necessarily profane term in the eighteenth century. In the few instances where he performed marriage ceremonies, he noted that the woman often "was bigg (with child)," a common state of affairs he soon came to understand. "Thro' want of Ministers to marry and thro' the licentiousness of the People, many hundreds live in Concubinage," he mused, "living in a state of nature, more irregularly and unchastely than the Indians." Not surprisingly, outspoken, brazen, "loose women," and not libertine men attracted his ire as well as his libido. Women annoyed and badgered him as he spoke, frequently suckling their children openly while he implored them to change their ways. Others, "many very pretty," tormented him by coming to hear his sermons dressed provocatively "in their Shifts and a short Pettycoat only, barefooted and Bare legged," with their heads and other parts of their bodies improperly uncovered. Some, he too closely observed, "draw their Shift as tight as possible to the Body, and pin it close, to shew the roundness of their Breasts, and slender Waists." For the service, country women "rubb[ed] themselves and their Hair with Bears Oil and tying it up behind in a Bunch like the Indians—being hardly one degree removed from them," to make themselves more attractive. Woodmason's comments revealed more about himself than the conduct and beauty of North Carolina's ladies and also testified to the influence that women in colonial North Carolina had in church meetings as well as in the governance of households.

The codes and laws that governed marriage in colonial North Carolina never furnished the flexibility or the compliance needed in an expanding frontier society like that of the late seventeenth and eighteenth centuries. The larger community of friends, neighbors, and families exercised a marital jurisdiction over couples that, if anything, proved more enforceable than that of faraway colonial magistrates. Backcountry North Carolinians took up informal marriages, self-divorces, and prenuptial couplings at first with their own consent but, more significantly, with the approval of an entire community and extended family. Throughout the colonial period and well into statehood, courts upheld the practice. In 1827 and again in 1829, the North Carolina Supreme Court ruled that "reputation and cohabitation" or "reputation, cohabitation and the declaration and conduct of the parties" served as adequate evidence that a legal marriage existed. In their own practical manner, these informal marriages proved more durable, more favorable to women and children, and less prone to "divorce" than legal ones centuries later.

If Virginia had its "First Families of Virginia" and South Carolina its Huguenot elite, then North Carolina had only its "First Few Families of no special status." An Englishman visiting the new state in 1800 found that North Carolinians possessed "less intelligence and suavity of manner" than Virginians and less "refinement . . . and the share of polite as well as solid" knowledge and education than South Carolinians. Indeed, early North Carolinians seemed to have had less interest in education than any colonists except those in Georgia. Most members of North Carolina's first families had almost no education at all, and no institution of higher learning existed until 1771, when Presbyterians in Mecklenburg County asked the colonial government to establish a public seminary. While a few children in some wealthier families had private tutors, the practice seemed less widespread than in other colonies. In fact, North Carolinians hardly bothered to attend colleges and institutions of higher learning in other colonies or in England at all. Less than a half dozen went to Harvard; John Ashe in 1746, John Moseley in 1757, and George Pollock in 1758 served as examples, and only Whitmell Hill sat for exams at the College of Philadelphia in 1760. Customarily, leading southern families sent their sons to the Inns of Court in London to study law in colonial America, but North Carolinians preferred other pursuits. Of approximately 139 southerners who presented themselves for instruction at the Inns, only eight were from North Carolina, ranking dead last. South Carolina and Virginia respectively sent 58 and 43, and even fledgling Georgia managed 11 who matriculated. Worse, only one of the North Carolinians who attended the Inns actually ever resided in the colony. The

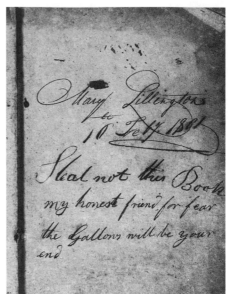

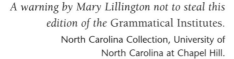

*A warning by Mary Lillington not to steal this
edition of the* Grammatical Institutes.
North Carolina Collection, University of
North Carolina at Chapel Hill.

rest lived in England, happily subsisting on appointments to posts in North Carolina's government as placemen. England's two premier colleges, Oxford and Cambridge, proved no attraction to North Carolinians. Of the approximately 60 southerners who attended Oxford and Cambridge prior to the Revolution, none came from North Carolina. Obviously, formal education had little value for the colony's first families.

The attitude of the colony's leaders toward education permeated all levels of society. Looking backward, critic Elkanah Watson suggested that no colony "had at that period performed so little, to promote the cause of education, science, and the arts, as North Carolina." Indeed, only a few scattered schools could be found in the colony. A disgusted Gabriel Johnston alleged in 1736 that the "legislature has never taken the least care to erect one school, which deserves the name, in this widely extended country." Although the assembly enacted a law in 1743 to build a school in Edenton, nothing ever came of it, and a decade passed before another attempt to fund a public school was made. In 1764 New Bern residents subscribed 120 pounds sterling toward construction of a schoolhouse to teach "children in Such Branches of useful learning as are necessary for several of the Offices & Stations in Life." When Thomas Tomlinson, the New Bern schoolmaster, abruptly left for Rhode Island in the summer of 1772 after disciplining several of the trustees' children, Gov. Josiah Martin fumed because the New Bern residents, "being ignorant and uneducated men," had run off the only learned person in town. At least two early North Carolinians, James Winwright in 1744 and James Innes in 1759, left monies for schools in their wills, but only Innes's in Wilmington was ever built and then only in 1784.

From its beginning in the eighteenth century, education for the general public in North Carolina took on all the qualities of a missionary effort aimed at white heathen. First undertaken by the Society for the Propagation of the Gospel (SPG), a branch of the Anglican Church, the effort proved desultory at best. Yet from the beginning the first schoolteachers in the colony found their zeal to enlighten North Carolinians no match for the indifference of its inhabitants or the frontier state of the province. Charles Griffith, generally recognized as the colony's first teacher, came to Carolina in 1706, opened a school in Pasquotank County, succeeded for a short while, then, as his fellow missionary, James Adams, noted, "fell into the sin of fornication and joined with the Quaker interest." To early Anglicans, Quakers stood second only to original sin. Griffith soon left the colony, preferring to tutor "savage Saponi Indians" in Virginia to devilish North Carolinians.

Until the coming of the American Revolution, Charles Griffith and itinerant teachers like him represented the infrequent and desultory effort to educate North Carolinians. Yet another tendency also emerged early in North Carolina's history: the disparity between the proclamations of public officials to promote education and their subsequent actions. Almost every colonial governor from William Glover to Josiah Martin cried out against the uneducated state of North Carolinians. In 1736 a frustrated Gov. Gabriel Johnston pleaded with the general assembly to do something about the "low state" of education. A prudent assembly responded by lamenting "the want of Divine Publick Worship . . . as well as the general neglect in point of education, the main sources of Disorders and Corruptions," a discreet shift from practical to spiritual matters. The legislators, after duly debating about how to see the twin evils "removed and remedied, are ready to do our parts, toward the reformation of such flagrant and prolifick Evils," promptly did nothing. Even centuries ago, promoting public education made good political sense.

While much of the outlook of North Carolinians toward education can be explained by the colony's slow economic development and frontier condition, an almost anti-intellectual attitude persisted even after material circumstances improved and wealth and capital accumulated. As he traveled about with de Miranda, Henry McCulloh mused that life in North Carolina "may be passed there without too great an exercise of philosophy" or thinking. Always on the lookout for anyone in the colony who dressed and spoke with some degree of refinement, Janet Schaw found only one, a "Gentleman" in Wilmington who was an "excellent Mathematician" who also knew "Physic and Botany," but, alas, the "Gentleman" had discovered only one other man in the Cape Fear region "who had sense enough to understand him."

Unlike their seaboard neighbors, North Carolinians paid less attention to the theater, fine arts, reading, and literature. Indeed, they seemed to take perverse pride in their disregard of intellectual pursuits. The minuscule outpouring of literary works on any subject and the absence of any significant political philosophers reflected an unpretentious, cracker-barrel sensibility that lasted even after North Carolina's wealth and development surpassed that of many other colonies and states. The colony's earliest settlers robed themselves in "poor but proud" habits of life that endured well into the nineteenth century.

Early North Carolinians, like many of their colonial neighbors, had little regard for education beyond literacy or manners beyond facility. Yet in their political and spiritual beliefs they evinced a sophistication that went beyond the facades of Old World castles and cathedrals. Early settlers along the coast of Carolina in the latter part of the seventeenth century, who later spread into the interior, brought with them not only their passionately held beliefs in English constitutionalism but also a cluster of vague but inspirationally held Protestant beliefs. In the amorphous frontier life of early Carolinians, Baptists, Presbyterians, Methodists, and even Lutherans and Reformed Calvinists were all clumped together as "dissenters" in colonial America and were much less clearly delineated than they became after the American Revolution. In reality, pluralism and not conformity, diversity and not orthodoxy, sophistication and not literalism all characterized the place of religion in colonial North Carolina. Indeed, most North Carolinians did not discover their orthodoxy until after the American Revolution.

Beginning as early as 1701, the first attempts by early colonial governors and officials such as Thomas Cary to seek Anglican support and by George Burrington, Arthur Dobbs, and William Tryon to establish Anglicanism as a state religion met with indifference and failure. The absence and inadequacy of Anglican clergymen and the dispersed pattern of settlement made a strong religious life and center difficult if not impossible.

Just as the lords proprietors wanted Carolinians to live in towns and not in the wilderness, they also wanted them to be good Anglicans and not dissenting heathen. The Carolina charters of 1663 and 1665 specifically authorized the setting up of Anglicanism as the official religion, but various acts aimed at establishment either failed in the assembly or else met with disapproval in London. When the assembly passed the Vestry Act of 1741, for example, its end came in London and not in Edenton. The British Privy Council disallowed the law because it permitted vestries, ecclesiastical councils that oversaw church operations, usually made up of a majority of dissenters in North Carolina, to select church representatives such as rectors. When the Vestry Act finally passed in 1765, a century after the colony's founding, only six Anglican priests could be found in the entire province. Never popular or widely supported in North Carolina, the Anglican Church, in the words of a later bishop of the Episcopal Church in America, its American successor, was "helpless, blind, and paralyzed."

Charles Woodmason, the itinerant Anglican minister who traveled widely throughout the colony, found North Carolinians not only annoying but also unchurched, illegally cohabitating together, their homes teeming with bastard children, and their church attendance irregular and irreverent. In other words, they were not good Anglicans. In fact, he noted that they drank during services and brought their dogs to church with them. The depictions of Woodmason and of others of early colonists drinking to excess, spitting tobacco, engaging in fistfights, gouging each others' eyes out, and gambling on cockfights and horses, all the hallmarks of an early frontier society, filled the narratives and reports of colonial travelers and officials. Even to another group, early Native Americans, the seemingly nonspiritual, wicked, and sinful ways of early colonists, so different from their own, must have appeared heathenish and barbaric.

In colonial North Carolina, religious toleration without a formal supporting theory characterized a diverse religious life. Between 1672 and 1740, the colony resembled a checkerboard of dissenting sects of Quakers, Presbyterians, Lutherans, members of the German Reformed Church, Baptists, and, later, Methodists. Indeed, early North Carolina produced its own syncretic Protestant pluralism. In this way, Protestantism in colonial North Carolina would have many faces, and "many are the ways of worship" but only one God. Almost from the beginning, Quakers dominated the religious life of the colony. First appearing in the Albemarle region in 1672 but probably present before the missionary visits of George Fox and William Edmundson that same year, Quakers, formally known as the Society of Friends, wielded the scepter of power in the colony's first assemblies until the Cary rebellion diminished their influence after 1711. As pacifists who followed the doctrine of "the inner light," the presence of God in every person, Quakers did not believe in ordained ministers or in formal church ceremonies and rituals. Democratic and antiauthoritarian for their time, they followed the natural evolution of Reformation theology to its logical end, where every believer became his own priest.

Although their influence and numbers in the Albemarle region declined after 1730, the settlement of the western frontier brought new congregations of Friends to present-day Guilford, Randolph, Chatham, and Alamance counties. Organized in 1754, the New Garden Meeting in Guilford became the seedbed of other monthly meetings throughout the Piedmont. Quakers remained the most important group in colonial North Carolina until the American Revolution, when their pacifist views caused a "time of suffering" as the war made its way into the colony. Their numbers declined rapidly after 1781. Many eventually found their way into the ranks of the swarming Baptist, Presbyterian, and Methodist congregations after the "great revival" of 1805–30. Others left the state for Indiana, Ohio, and Kentucky after their antislavery efforts failed in the 1820s. Despite their declining numbers, the legacy of the Quakers endured in terms of their attempts to reform North Carolina society to make it more egalitarian, civil, and "friendly" to all despite their station in life.

John Brickell, an Irish physician who traveled to the colony in 1737, noted that, "after Quakers, Presbyterians succeed in numbers." Yet despite their plurality, early Presbyterians lacked two elements essential to their practice, the presence of an educated and dedicated clergy and also the discipline of the synod, the ecclesiastical council of the church. Although some individual Presbyterians lived in the Albemarle area before 1700, only two churches, both without pastors, existed near present-day Fayetteville by 1736. Responding to several petitions from "many people of North Carolina," the Synod of Philadelphia sent two ministers, William Robinson and John Thompson, to the colony in 1742 and 1744. Their missionary efforts soon found success, mainly in the Piedmont of North Carolina.

Presbyterian settlement in the Piedmont grew in the 1740s, and within twenty years members of that church correspondingly extended their involvement in local and provincial matters, both in terms of civic and political affairs. Scots-Irish settlers, "Irish Presbyterians" from Pennsylvania and Virginia who came to the Carolinas, brought with them a rich Presbyterian heritage that shaped their community of faith and lives in the frontier backcountry. They remembered economic and religious oppression in Ireland, strongly opposed the Anglican Church because of its affiliation with an English government they disdained, and had come to North Carolina in search of better opportunity for themselves and their families. Largely frustrated in their hopes by corruption and ineptness in local county government and in provincial affairs, many joined the Regulator movement in the 1760s and later went on to become leaders in the Revolution. Henry Patillo, James Hall, David Caldwell, James McGready, and Samuel McCorkle deeply influenced the course of events in the American Revolution in North Carolina, in the writing and ratification of the state and national constitution and in the great revival of 1800–1805. Keenly interested in education, Presbyterians took the lead in the founding and early direction of the University of North Carolina, an institution initially intended to give pastors and leaders of the new republic a classical education within an environment of Christian piety. For Presbyterians, education and religiosity, both appropriately begun in early childhood within the family, congregation, and community, eventually would produce citizens who would maintain America as a land of freedom and opportunity unlike the corrupt older nations of Europe they had known.

Thousands of Scots-Irish swarmed down the Great Wagon Road from Pennsylvania in the 1730s and 1740s as good land in the Virginia and Maryland backcountry became scarcer. Also derisively called the "great bad road," the path began just outside Philadelphia at the Schuylkill River Ferry, wound across the Potomac through the wide valley of Virginia, creating, as it spiraled south, towns such as Winchester and Staunton, thence down through Roanoke, and finally meandered eastward across the Dan River, with Wachovia and Salisbury as its North Carolina destinations. After its establishment by the Moravians, Salem grew into a thriving trading town fed by settlers and supplies from the road. The Great Wagon Road became the backcountry's principal umbilical cord before the Revolution, connecting it more to Pennsylvania and Virginia both physically and ideologically than to its eastern Carolina neighbors.

The chartering of counties—Johnston and Granville in 1746, Orange in 1752, Rowan in 1753, and Mecklenburg in 1763—followed the overflow of the Scots-Irish into North Carolina. Fiercely antiauthoritarian and antiestablishment in their outlook and staunchly congregational and Presbyterian in their religion, they dominated western North Carolina before the Revolution. Marveling at the wheel-to-wheel emigration on the Great Wagon Road, a South Carolinian noted that it led to the "rapid and sudden increase of inhabitants in a back frontier country, . . . that of North Carolina."

Radical in their Protestant beliefs, Baptists came to North Carolina early in the colony's history. As a branch of English reformists and dissenters dating to 1610, they appeared first as clusters or congregations in the southern colonies and were frequently described as "restless," "seekers," "never having enough" religion, "splintering," and "always taking stock" of their religious life. As early as 1695, several Anabaptists, or individual Baptists, probably from nearby Virginia, lived in the Albemarle Sound region. Paul Palmer, the first recorded Baptist minister in the colony, organized a congregation on the banks of the Pasquotank River in Camden County in 1727. A fiery believer in the separation of church and state and also in religious toleration, Palmer appealed his right to preach and to convert under the English Toleration Act. Surprisingly, the governor of the colony, Sir Richard Everard, granted his license. According to Everard, Palmer made hundreds of converts and established several churches within two years.

Early North Carolina Baptists did not relate or connect to each other through ecclesiastical governing bodies like Presbyterian synods or Anglican dioceses. While many local congregations preferred their own independent company and none other, Baptists had the option of associating more widely with other brethren of similar faith. For example, when William Sojourner began the Kehukee Church in 1742 in Halifax County, it had fifty members, large for a gathering so early in the colony's history. In 1769 he formed the Kehukee Association out of congregations in eastern counties such as Edgecombe, Halifax, Beaufort, and Carteret. By 1775 the association included sixty-one churches and more than five thousand members, mostly independent Baptist congregations already in existence for several years who decided to join hands with like-minded others.

The arrival in Randolph County in 1755 of Shubal Stearns, a minister from Boston, signaled a significant shift in Baptist traditions in North Carolina and, eventually, in the South overall. Emphasizing New Light doctrines, Stearns founded the Sandy Creek Church, the first Separate congregation in the colony. Using "protracted meetings," love feasts, the laying on of hands, anointing and blessing of the sick, and feet washing, the Separate Baptists in Randolph and other counties enjoyed instant success in frontier North Carolina. At weekly communions and at camp meetings that revived flagging spirits, perhaps the first of their kind in the colony, the Separatists began a new, less formal, more evangelistic Baptist tradition. George Pope, the minister of the Abbott's Creek congregation, marveled at the "religious epilepsies" and at the "falling down under religious impressions" at the "great meetings" of the Separatists.

The Sandy Creek Church became the "Mother of all Separate Baptists" in the South, and Stearns, along with such figures as John Gano, Isaac Backus, James Manning, Morgan Edwards, and Richard Furman, merited a place among major Baptist figures of the eighteenth century. In 1758 Stearns organized the Sandy Creek Association, the oldest in the state and one of the first in the nation, which soon incorporated other independent congregations into its following. By the beginning of the Revolution, Baptists, whether associated, separated, or individually congregated, had become the most numerous religious group in the colony. Tradition has it that a former North Carolina Baptist minister, John Gano, baptized George Washington by immersion but that Washington, while impressed by Gano's piety and sincerity, did not change denominations. After the Revolution, Baptists, with Gano and Richard Furman of South Carolina leading the way, set up the first national church system in America. It did not last.

In many early Separate Baptist meetings and congregations, whites and blacks worshiped together, referred to each other as brothers and sisters, monitored each other's behavior, and condemned the sins of others. One congregation suspended member Edward Carlile "for the Sin of uncleanness with his Negro wench." They also banished his wife for public drunkenness. In another instance, women members badgered a member of the community, a Mr. Hann, to come forward first to the Anglican and then to the Separate Baptist church to confess he had beaten a young slave girl to death and had taken up with another female slave. In 1766, a "regular" Baptist minister noted with dismay that "the most illiterate among" Separate Baptists "are their Teachers even Negroes speak in their Meetings." The same minister recorded his fear and trembling at the Separates "suffering women to preach in public." They did much more than proclaim and sermonize. Separate Baptist women led public prayers, presided over mass meetings, served as deaconesses and elderesses, organized care for the sick and poor, conducted separate women's meetings, and counseled fellow females throughout the congregation. Eunice Marshall, the sister of Daniel Marshall, a leading Separate Baptist minister, "spread the Word" in nearby Virginia, where she took it "upon herself to exhort and preach Baptist doctrines, was ordered to desist, but not obeying, was (although pregnant at the time) thrown into jail." In the initial democracy of many evangelical Protestant churches in early North Carolina, women played a prominent role not only within congregations but in governance as well.

Methodists came to North Carolina last among the major denominations. First begun by John and Charles Wesley in Georgia in 1737 as a movement, early Methodism had its roots as a reform movement within the Anglican Church. It did not exist as a denomination distinct from Anglicanism until after the American Revolution. Still, several of Wesley's early followers came to North Carolina before the Revolution to set up Methodist societies based upon his ideas and to preach his new revelations. George Whitefield, a major figure of the Great Awakening of 1735–40 and perhaps the greatest orator of his time, who "could make hell so vivid that one could locate it on an atlas," came to North Carolina several times between 1739 and 1765. Joseph Pilmore, a Virginian, preached the first separate and distinct "Methodist sermon" in the colony at Currituck Courthouse on 14 November 1772. Within two years, a Methodist circuit existed that included congregations extending "some distance into North Carolina" with frequent meetings and revivals.

Another radical Protestant group, the Renewed Unity of Brethren, or, more familiarly, the Moravians, came to North Carolina in 1753. Originating in Moravia in the former Czechoslovakia in the fifteenth century, the Unitas Fratrum (United Brethren) suffered persecution and ostracism in eastern Europe for their extremist form of Protestant communalism and piety. Seeking asylum in America under the protection of the English king, George II, the Moravians first came to Georgia and later migrated to Pennsylvania. They subsequently purchased 100,000 acres from the Granville tract in the Piedmont of North Carolina, and, because of its pleasant meadows and streams, supposedly called it Wachau-die-Aue, or Wachovia. Holding their land in trust for the entire community, the Moravians erected a village, Bethabara, in 1753, and another one, Salem, several years later. Closely bound together by their labor and worship, the Moravians did little to proselytize or to convert others. Successful as tradesmen, artisans, craftsmen, merchants, and farmers, the Moravians remained numerically small but influential beyond their numbers. Their religious music, especially their emphasis upon Bach and the use of the organ, as well as their stress on education, set them apart from their neighbors. Salem Academy and College grew out of their effort

Since they came not only to the American colonies but also to the West Indies, Moravians won over some converts there among enslaved Africans. Nevertheless, they did not openly oppose slavery itself. As they settled into life in North Carolina in the 1760s, they began purchasing slaves for use in agricultural, domestic, and craft labor. Yet the Moravians initially did not treat their slaves, many from Africa and the West Indies, as did others in the colony. Moravian slaveholding remained statistically small, perhaps 100 slave owners out of a total population of 1,100. Yet in the separate world of the communalistic Brethren, they became acculturated into a hermetic German society to a degree highly unusual in early America. Creoles, those blacks born in the West Indies and in America, and even some Africans joined the Moravian Church, attended and took part in services, and became incorporated into the cloistered world of the Brethren. Some became skilled artisans, were literate and well educated, played musical instruments, sang in male and female choirs, and even became prominent in the strict labor hierarchy of the Brethren. The majority learned both English and German, and their children attended integrated Moravian schools. Not until 1822, amidst a growing fear of slave revolts and also a crescendo of racial chauvinism, did Moravians segregate Africans and Creoles out of their churches. Even then, the Brethren helped form an all-black congregation, providing them with supplies, funds, and a white minister. The congregation eventually dissolved after the Civil War.

Almost any commentary on life in early North Carolina inevitably centered on the bad roads, poor transportation, difficult travel, and isolation of the early colonists. Whether settled near rivers, swamps, and streams or set in a crossroads village or alone in the seemingly endless pine barrens, North Carolinians had less regard for the quality of their roads, bridges, and ferries than did "foreigners" who came to visit and put in an appearance. Terms such as "poor," "wretched," "miserable," "dismal," and "useless" dotted the descriptions of early travelers. Slowed and stopped often on her way to Wilmington, Janet Schaw maintained that roads in North Carolina meant only that someone had cut away "the trees to the necessary breadth, in as even a line as they can, and where the ground is wet, they make a small ditch on either side." Traveling throughout the province to promote the cause of independence and rebellion, Josiah Quincy of Massachusetts almost drowned while trying to cross "Buffalo Creek" near Albemarle, desperately hanging on to a log while his horse swam alongside him.

Even more than travelers, the general assembly wanted good roads, bridges, and ferries to unite the increasingly settled and far-flung colony and to hasten its development. In 1764 the assembly passed the most comprehensive of myriad road acts dating from as early as 1729. Not surprisingly, the assembly designated county courts, perhaps the only functioning organ of local government, to lay out "Public Roads, and establish and settle Ferries, and to appoint where Bridges shall be built." Additionally, "Overseers of the Highways or Roads" could conscript male taxables from sixteen to sixty to work on roads, bridges, and ferries a set number of days each year, usually six or seven. The 1764 statute also authorized the erection of signs and mileposts and the licensing of ferry keepers who would provide "good and Sufficient Boats." Of all the laws of early North Carolina, the ones requiring the building, maintenance, and regulation of public roads, bridges, and ferries, the most seemingly utilitarian of all, were perhaps the most ignored.

North Carolina nevertheless developed a crude and usable road system by the end of the colonial period. John Collet's 1770 map showed a system of roads, mainly north-south ones leading to Virginia and South Carolina. The primary path led from Brunswick to Wilmington and hence to Bath and Edenton. Another ran from Cross Creek, near Fayetteville, to the north. The Great Trading Path extended from the sound region, intersecting the Upper Creek Path near present-day Concord and then running westward to the mountains. The interior counties were connected more to Virginia, South Carolina, and Georgia than to the western counties; most early roads in the interior counties hugged the west of the sound region. Only the Great Wagon Road from Salisbury and Salem gave the backcountry a principal outlet northward to Virginia, Pennsylvania, and Maryland and southward to South Carolina and Georgia. It would be decades before a system connecting eastern and western counties emerged.

The majority of early North Carolinians doubtless did not think of themselves as poor, either culturally or materially, or as isolated, backward, and uneducated as did their governors, travelers, and uninvited guests. Indeed, most seemed quite content with their lives, families, and friends. The ability to own and to develop land, to worship as they pleased, and to have a say in their governance far outweighed their appearance but not their character. From the first isolated farms and settlements in the Albemarle Sound to the growth of towns in the interior, North Carolinians overspread the eastern counties, moved into the Piedmont, and even began migrating to the far western mountains near Old Fort, Quaker Meadows, and Morganton. Their priorities lay not in education or the fine arts, both overrated in early North Carolina, but in conquering a wilderness, nesting with their growing families, and finding their spiritual selves. In these early influences the institutions of North Carolina, religion, education, family, and government, began to grow and to take shape.

ADDITIONAL READINGS

Anderson, Douglas. "Plotting William Byrd." *William and Mary Quarterly* 56 (1999): 701–22.

Andrews, Charles M. *The Colonial Period of American History.* Vol. 3. New Haven: Yale University Press, 1937.

Berkeley, Edmund, and Dorothy Smith Berkeley, eds. "'The Manner of Living of the North Carolinians,' by Francis Veale, December 19, 1730." *North Carolina Historical Review* 41 (April 1964): 239–45.

Brickell, John. *Natural History of North Carolina.* New York: Johnson Reprint Co., 1969.

Burkitt, Lemuel, and Jesse Reed. *Concise History of the Kehukee Baptist Association.* Halifax: A. Hodge, 1903.

Burney, Eugenia. *Colonial North Carolina.* Nashville: T. Nelson, 1975.

Byrd, William. *Journey to the Land of Eden, and Other Papers.* New York: Macy-Masius, 1928.

Cain, Robert J., ed. *The Colonial Records of North Carolina (Second Series).* Vol. 10, *The Church of England in North Carolina: Documents, 1699–1741.* Raleigh: Department of Archives and History, 1999.

Clark, Thomas D., comp. *Travels in the Old South, a Bibliography.* 3 vols. Norman: University of Oklahoma Press, 1956–59.

Conway, Jill K., with the assistance of Linda Kealey and Janet E. Schulte. *The Female Experience in Eighteenth- and Nineteenth-Century America: A Guide to the History of American Women.* Princeton, N.J.: Princeton University Press, 1985.

Cott, Nancy F. *Public Vows: A History of Marriage and the Nation.* Cambridge: Harvard University Press, 2000.

———, ed. *The Roots of Bitterness: Documents of the Social History of American Women.* New York: E. P. Dutton and Co., 1972.

Crane, Verner W. *Southern Frontier, 1670–1732.* Ann Arbor: University of Michigan Press, 1956.

Craven, Wesley F. *Southern Colonies in the Seventeenth Century, 1607–1689.* Baton Rouge: Louisiana State University Press, 1956.

Daniel, W. Harrison. "North Carolina Moravians and the Negro, 1760–1820." *Virginia Social Science Journal* 12 (April 1977): 23–31.

Duffy, John. "Eighteenth-Century Carolina Health Conditions." *Journal of Southern History* 18 (August 1952): 289–302.

Ekirch, A. Roger. *"Poor Carolina": Politics and Society in Colonial North Carolina, 1729–1776.* Chapel Hill: University of North Carolina Press, 1981.

Fisher, Kirsten. *Suspect Relations: Sex, Race, and Resistance in Colonial North Carolina.* Ithaca: Cornell University Press, 2002.

Freeze, Gary Richard. "Like a House Built upon Sand: The Anglican Church and Establishment in North Carolina, 1765–1776." *Historical Magazine of the Protestant Episcopal Church* 48 (December 1979): 405–32.

Fries, Adelaide Lisetta. "Moravian Contributions to Colonial North Carolina." *North Carolina Historical Review* 7 (January 1930): 1–14.

Greene, Jack P. *Quest for Power: The Lower Houses of Assembly in the Southern Royal Colonies, 1689–1776.* New York: Norton Publishers, 1972.

Hinshaw, Seth Benson. "Friends Culture in Colonial North Carolina, 1672–1789." *Southern Friend* 22 (2000): 3–81.

Huhner, Leon. "The Jews of North Carolina Prior to 1800." *American Jewish Historical Society Publications* 29 (1925): 137–48.

Manning, Susan. "Industry and Idleness in Colonial Virginia: A New Approach to William Byrd II." *Journal of American Studies* (Great Britain) 28 (1994): 169–90.

Powell, William S. *Carolina Charter of 1663, How It Came to North Carolina and Its Place in History, with Biographical Sketches of the Proprietors.* Raleigh: Department of Archives and History, 1954.

Ramsey, Robert Wayne. *Carolina Cradle: Settlement of the Northwest Carolina Frontier, 1747–1762.* Chapel Hill: University of North Carolina Press, 1964.

Rountree, Carlton White. "The Quaker Meeting Near the Narrows of Pasquotank." *Southern Friend* 16 (1994): 64–76.

Salmon, Marylynn. *Women and the Law of Property in Early America.* Chapel Hill: University of North Carolina Press, 1986.

Schaw, Janet. *Journal of a Lady of Quality; Being the Narrative of a Journey from Scotland to the West Indies, North Carolina, and Portugal in the Years 1774 to 1776.* Spartanburg: Reprint Co., 1971.

Shammas, Carole. *A History of Household Government in America.* Charlottesville: University of Virginia Press, 2002.

———. *The Pre-industrial Consumer in England and America.* Oxford: Clarendon Press, 1990.

Shammas, Carole, Marylynn Salmon, and Michel Dahlin. *Inheritance in America: From Colonial Times to the Present.* New Brunswick, N.J.: Rutgers University Press, 1987.

Stephens, Alonso. "Rise of the Presbyterians in Colonial North Carolina." *Quarterly Review of Higher Education among Negroes* 26 (January 1958): 1–14.

Thorp, Daniel. *Moravian Community in North Carolina: Pluralism on the Southern Frontier.* Knoxville: University of Tennessee Press, 1989.

Watson, Alan D. "Anglican Parish in Royal North Carolina, 1729–1775." *Historical Magazine of the Protestant Episcopal Church* 48 (September 1979): 303–19.

———. *Society in Colonial North Carolina.* Raleigh: Department of Archives and History, 1975.

———. *Society in Early North Carolina: A Documentary History.* Raleigh: Department of Archives and History, 2000.

Wood, Bradford J. *This Remote Part of the World: Regional Formation in Lower Cape Fear, North Carolina.* Columbia: University of South Carolina Press, 2004.

Woodmason, Charles. *The Carolina Backcountry on the Eve of the Revolution: The Journal and Other Writings of Charles Woodmason, Anglican Itinerant.* Chapel Hill: University of North Carolina Press, 1969.

Slavery and Servitude
in Early North Carolina

A close study of many of the events in the history of early North Carolina reflects the growth and halting progress of the colony and state's first institutions. From the lost coastal colonies of whites and Indians on Roanoke Island to the furtive attempts at establishing a representative government in the Albemarle Sound and Cape Fear regions, a clear and absorbing story of hardship and overcoming adversity emerges. Yet the narrative largely represents white and not African or Native American history. For example, portrayals of Africans and Creoles who came to early North Carolina, perhaps as much as 20 to 25 percent of the population, must be deduced largely not from their own records but from those of their masters; not from their diaries or accounts but from those of travelers such as Janet Schaw or John Brickell; not from land they owned but from their status as tithables and as property on the land; not from advertisements in newspapers describing wares and goods for sale to them but from notices of slave auctions selling them instead, or of the thousands who voted against their status by running away. While the final passage of the vast majority of white immigrants to North Carolina eventually proceeded from villeinage and servitude to freedom, the assimilation of blacks into the same crudely egalitarian culture only meant harsher and even more rigid forms of bondage.

Unlike Virginia and South Carolina, colonial North Carolina did not become a slave society but rather a culture where slavery became significant but not institutionally dominant. The same factors that affected the colony's early growth and development—especially the presence of the Outer Banks, the lack of a commercial staple crop, the paucity of towns and absence of a large port, and the relative weakness of government at all levels—also made the experience of early black North Carolinians significantly different from that of their white masters and neighbors.

The earliest history of slavery in North Carolina reflected the "provinces within provinces" development of the Albemarle Sound region and of the Lower Cape Fear in relation to the larger and earlier settlements of the Chesapeake and South Carolina. Thus, the first settlers who came to the Albemarle in the 1660s, and in the first decades of the eighteenth century, brought with them blacks who had experience with Europeans. They were Creoles who had either been born in or who had lived a significant portion of their lives in the thriving slave centers of the New World in the Caribbean. Infrequently of mixed European

*Reputed to be a photograph of Haywood Dixon,
a slave carpenter from Greene County, 1860.*
North Carolina Department of Archives
and History, Raleigh.

and African descent and thoroughly knowledgeable of European and American cultures, they easily intermingled with the earliest settlers, sometimes earning their freedom or else gaining an unusual degree of autonomy over their lives as a result. Still, they remained slaves, never fully assimilating or finding acceptance as equals in the rough-and-tumble society of the Albemarle. By 1700, perhaps four hundred lived in the northeastern coast among the scattered settlements of the Albemarle Sound region.

Slavery did not become significant in North Carolina until the 1720s, when the Lower Cape Fear began to develop almost as a province of South Carolina. From a total of almost 1,000 in North Carolina in 1705, the black population grew to 5,500 when the colony reverted to royal control in 1729. Thereafter, it increased exponentially. By 1755, the number of blacks in the colony came to 19,000, and, by the time of the Revolution, it approached 85,000, a number that surpassed traditional slave societies like that of Maryland and equaled that of South Carolina. The census of 1790, the first in the state's history, gave the state's white population as 288,204 and the slave population as 100,572, a little more than 25 percent of the total. Out of a total population of 638,829 in 1820, slaves numbered 172,484, or 27 percent of North Carolinians. On the eve of the Civil War in 1860, North Carolina had a total population of 991,454, of whom 301,056 were slaves and 30,463 were free blacks, the largest percentage of blacks in the state's history. Yet at no time before the Civil War did blacks constitute more than one-third of the colony's population, and, despite majority concentrations in the Lower Cape Fear region, they usually averaged 25–28 percent of those living in the province and later the new state.

Unlike Virginia and South Carolina, North Carolina failed to develop an extensive planter elite or plantation society. Large slaveholdings of twenty or more, standard for a planter class, dominated only the Lower Cape Fear area, and then only after 1755. Before the French and Indian War, only one other region, the Upper Cape Fear, had a significant number of large slaveholders. Thomas Pollock, from Bertie County, owned ten plantations and 75 slaves in 1732, while by 1750 Roger Moore of Orton possessed 250 slaves and Cullen Pollock possessed 154. At the beginning of the Civil War, a southern elite planter class (usually defined as those who owned more than three hundred slaves) of over three hundred families had developed across the entire region, but only four of those came from North Carolina.

The slow rate of development within the colony and the absence of large towns and ports significantly recast the relationship between whites and blacks. Lacking a staple crop such as tobacco, rice, or indigo and with a small population spread over a vast wilderness, North Carolina more resembled a frontier than an established region. In 1767, for example, the Lower Cape Fear counted only 4,500 blacks in an area of almost two thousand square miles, while, in the western counties, only 451 blacks lived in a region of almost twenty thousand square miles. Thus, even in areas such as the Lower Cape Fear, where a significant number of slaves lived, the low population density meant that isolation and not interplay between families and communities marked the lives of most blacks and whites alike.

The early history of slavery in North Carolina consisted of elements of both oppression and autonomy. The first slaves who came to the Albemarle region from Virginia worked beside their masters in subsistence farming and stock raising. Frequent mistreatment meant that slaves could take to the swamps or join Indian bands and groups where they formed triracial Buffalo or Maroon societies. For example, a close reading of the chronicles of the Tuscarora war in 1713 finds accounts of blacks living with Indians, joining their war parties, and suffering execution and reenslavement as well. Unlike in South Carolina, in North Carolina masters, most with fewer than five slaves, worked alongside slaves in the laborious tasks of clearing trees, draining swamps, tilling the land, and planting crops. In the area around Cabarrus, Mecklenburg, and Cleveland counties, slaves also helped their masters in searching for and mining "lucky strikes" of gold. Understandably, close relationships and personal arrangements evolved in such an intimate environment that, while never on an equal footing, became the hallmark of slavery in North Carolina.

Almost all historians of early North Carolina, especially Hugh Rankin and Albert Ray Newsome, believed that the shield of the barrier islands, the absence of a staple crop, and the subsequent slow development of the region meant that slavery "was perhaps milder and more patriarchal" than that of most of the southern colonies and later states. Moreover, to them, the "smaller number of large plantations and slaveholdings" somehow lessened the harshness of the institution in North Carolina. Indeed, the peculiar features of North Carolina's growth during the first century of settlement did mean that the institution of slavery evolved differently than in Virginia or South Carolina, but not necessarily in a benign or more humane fashion. Even the term "paternalism," frequently used to describe slavery in the south, had a more familiar, dysfunctional familial meaning in North Carolina.

The history of slavery in early North Carolina can only be understood as a constant, continuing series of daily interchanges between masters and slaves, mainly in their work lives, not at all on an equal basis. Never part of a unilateral relationship where masters

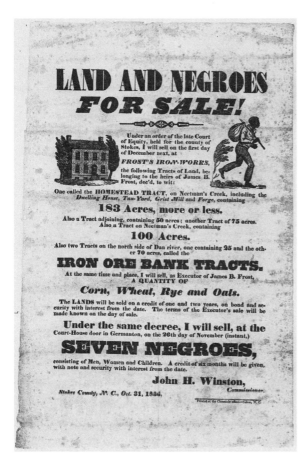

Broadside advertising land and slaves for sale in Stokes County, 31 October 1836.

North Carolina Collection, University of North Carolina at Chapel Hill.

dictated every behavior and movement, slaves in North Carolina were not as wholly subdued as they were in parts of Maryland, Virginia, and South Carolina. More oppressed and with harsher slave codes in colonial South Carolina, for example, slaves on rice and indigo plantations somehow found a way to preserve much of their African culture and still achieve a remarkable degree of individual autonomy. With a population density along the coast more than four times that of North Carolina and with a three- or four-to-one majority of black to white, slaves, many drawn from the same regions in Africa, reconstructed specific West African cultures in a South Carolina low-country plantation setting. That model never applied to North Carolina.

The evolution of slavery in North Carolina, with its small holdings and arbitrary relationships, meant that, unlike in Virginia, Maryland, and South Carolina, blacks sometimes gained an unusual degree of freedom overlaid with only a thin facade of their own African culture. Unlike in South Carolina, the majority of slaves came to the colony not by sea but by land, from Charleston and the Chesapeake area. Because of the barrier islands and the lack of a staple crop and large port, most cargoes that entered through Wilmington or Beaufort contained only a few slaves along with a mixture of trade goods. The earliest mention of slaves imported into the colony came from Bermuda. Always a major destination for early North Carolina shipping, Bermuda shipped ninety slaves, mostly to Virginia, but some to the Albemarle Sound region in 1683. While New York and Jamaica also sent

"Section of a vessel showing the way in which slaves were stowed on board," taken from David Walker's Appeal. North Carolina Office of Archives and History, Raleigh.

slaves to the colony, most came from Charleston, especially after the settlement of the Cape Fear region in the 1720s. In the spring of 1727, the *Phelby,* a small schooner, left Charleston for North Carolina with a cargo of tanned deer hides, twenty-three pairs of "ozenbriggs," a rough cloth used to clothe slaves, and five blacks. Shipping lists of vessels bound for North Carolina usually listed a mixed cargo, seldom with more than one or two slaves. The largest importation, fifty slaves, occurred in 1733 on board the *Tryal,* sailing from Charleston to the Cape Fear River. By both land and sea, the importation of slaves peaked between 1727 and 1755.

Early wills, estate inventories, and land records occasionally give clues as to the origins of slaves listed for purposes of claiming property and land in North Carolina. Names such as Mustafa, Cudjoe, Bobb, Yacknee, Quamino, Quash, Earthina, Keziah, Phoebe, Nan, and Sambo hint at African origins. Moreover, the propensity and repetitiveness of names also locates them within ethnic groups such as the Akan, Ewe, Fanta, Ibo, and Hausa, the dominant bloodlines who came to North Carolina. Slave owners habitually allowed slaves to name their own children but, when recording these names, gave them English equivalents because they often could not comprehend African dialects and languages. Thus, the Ewe names of Adwo and Anani became Adam and Nanny, the Igbo designation of Ulu was heard as Lulu, the Fanta Sisi sounded much like the English Sissy. Adika, the Ewe's distinctive name for a firstborn son, changed into the English Dick, one of the most popular slave names in early North Carolina.

The first or charter population of slaves in North Carolina consisted largely of Creoles, those born in the Americas who had extensive contact with whites and who spoke not only their own native tongues but also some African ones as well. Not surprisingly, Amerindians, a group that had all but disappeared early in the royal period, dotted the rolls and records of early slavery in North Carolina as well. Black slaves came primarily from

Virginia and lived mostly with their yeoman masters on smaller farms and plantations. With the settlement of the Cape Fear region after 1729, the face and features of slavery in North Carolina changed. Slaves now came directly from Africa through Charleston and Bermuda either overland or by sea. A casual look at the slave codes of 1715 and 1741 marks the shift not only from Creoles to Africans but also to a more punitive and obdurate institution. By the time the French and Indian War began in 1756, Africans made up perhaps as many as 70 percent of the colony's slave population, a statistic that reflected the rapid growth of the Cape Fear region. After the war with the French, the migration of blacks from other colonies, primarily Maryland, Virginia, and South Carolina, combined with a rapid natural increase to reduce the proportion of Africans to about 40 percent of the entire slave population by the beginning of the Revolution. In the 1760s, more than 24,000 blacks, both Creoles and Africans, came to North Carolina, the highest number for any British colony in the Americas except Jamaica.

Africans and Creoles who came to North Carolina had only limited access to white culture and institutions. Not allowed to be politically active, they did not frame colonial or state constitutions, nor did they have tea parties decrying British oppression and tyranny. With families and property unrecognized by law, they had difficulties accruing wealth from one generation to another. From so many ethnic groups speaking diverse languages, they invented their own pidgin forms of communication while being forced to speak an English language whose syntax they were not allowed to learn. Slaves saw English forms of religion and worship from afar, almost always being asked to understand them from a slave owner's perspective. Almost overwhelmingly, they worked as field hands, as artisans on farms and plantations, and as domestics in white homes. Less than 4 percent labored in towns and on ships. When they ran away in desperation, it most often meant stepping into another world whose boundaries and mores were but little understood. As a result, blacks who came to North Carolina created their own culture with little of their traditional African support systems in place to comfort them and with inadequate knowledge of white folkways and customs. All this they did with little control over the most basic condition of their existence, their own freedom.

The world that slaves made for themselves in North Carolina came neither from their old homelands in Africa nor from their new ones in America. Instead, Africans and Creoles created a temporary way of understanding their unaccustomed status as slaves by incorporating incomplete elements of both. After the charter generations of the 1680s in Albemarle Sound and of the 1720s in the Cape Fear region, traditional African practices such as sharply filed teeth and cosmetic scarring and mutilation disappeared. Common Guinea and Hausa customs such as paying a price or dowry for brides and polygamy also ceased to exist. In fact, most slaves lived in traditional nuclear families, although the habit of long absences of males from the household persisted. Accustomed to task-oriented work and to a concept of time associated with the seasons and crop production, slaves skillfully adjusted to routines on small farms and even on larger plantations because of their life in Africa. In the attitude of most white Carolinians toward work—that is, long periods of indolence coupled with shorter ones of intense activity—slaves found habits similar to the ones they knew in Africa yet with a key difference. They could not control their working lives like whites.

In the two important areas of religion and communalism, Africans and Creoles altered their view of the world and their place in it to create a new one that marked their final passage into slavery in America. Africans and Creoles were transformed into a new society in America by the traumatic events they endured, beginning with the Africans' capture. From there they were sold to slave traders and transported to factories or ports by way of long ocean voyages. After being routed through the international slave ports of the West Indies, they were finally sold to men in Virginia and South Carolina, where they made a last trek into the wilderness of North Carolina. Permanently separated from mothers, family members, friends, and an entire society that nourished them, slaves in North Carolina built a new community without an institutional framework that had existed for centuries in Africa.

Separated from their African roots and denied the soothing words of their own Fanta or Akan language, the young slaves who came to North Carolina nevertheless created a remarkable community of their own. African rituals, habits, behaviors, and traditions persisted. Without elders, shamans, or sorcerers to transmit an older culture to them and with a new environment to help shape them, slaves remodeled and rethought their place in a new reality. First, older religious beliefs such as voodoo and shamanism, which centered on the belief that humans could manipulate lives and change events by interaction with the supernatural through rites, rituals, and sorcery, survived in the face of attempts by Anglicans and Quakers to eradicate them. In fact, Africans found in Anglican priests and rites similarities to their own sacred medicine men and rituals. To many West Africans, the idea of a sorcerer who came back from the dead and who was deified seemed both logical and likely. Hymns and singing the praise of a great leader or lord also fitted with the idea of a hierarchical order of nature where humans, while important, still did not dominate other animals who also deserved respect for their own special place in the great chain of being.

Believing as they did in the powers of a natural order of being, Africans in North Carolina gave special status to medicine men, or ragmen, and women herbalists and sorcerers. The Yoruban harvest festival of Jonkonnu, or, as it was known in North Carolina, John Koonering or even John Canoe, traditionally began with a ragman leading a parade of dancing, singing, and shouting slaves in a nightlong celebration. Dressed in rags from head to toe with bells and trinkets and his face covered with the skull of a dead animal, the ragman carried a large carved stick as the symbol of his stature and influence. Behind him came the *leman,* the best male dancer, who carried a bag or basket to collect gifts and presents. Forbidden to use drums by their masters for fear of secretly communicating with each other, slaves instead resorted to rhythmic hand clapping, waving scarves, and later to a molo, a stringed instrument that became the banjo. Whites such as Janet Schaw and John Brickell who observed this ceremony knew not to interfere and instead accepted their roles as observers and not as participants or patriarchs.

Africans and Creoles in early North Carolina also kept alive the belief in a connection between the living and the dead, the afterlife and this life. When confronted with unexpected afflictions and illnesses, misfortunes and ruination, even turns of luck, slaves fell back upon their Old World conviction that a malign person had sent or caused the harm to occur. In such cases, a sorcerer, enchanter, or obi doctor would be consulted. Offering counseling as well as advice and action, the voodooist conjured up spells and potions to cast away the misfortune. In a strange happenstance, Africans' beliefs in potions and whites' suspicions that slaves wanted to poison them sometimes combined to produce tragic results. In perhaps one of the best-known cases, Sambo, a noted conjurer in Pasquotank County, gave a potion, or *touck*, to David, a slave, to administer to Mary Nash, his mistress, to change her from a "bad person" and to make her "better to him." Convicted in a slave trial on 2 August 1761 and sentenced to be castrated, Sambo, an elderly Hausa, miraculously survived the sadistic punishment, a sign to his fellow slaves that he indeed was a soothsayer.

When North Carolina split from South Carolina in 1712, the new government began a "Great Revision" of the laws to conform to its changed colonial status. Drafted by John Locke and Anthony Ashley Cooper, the Fundamental Constitutions and Laws of 1669 institutionalized slavery by declaring that "every freeman of Carolina, shall have absolute power and authority over his negro slaves, of what opinion or religion soever." By 1715 an additional consideration, the Tuscarora war and the role runaway slaves played in it, evinced the fear and worry North Carolinians had about their own fledgling province. With growing numbers of slaves and indentured servants in their midst, the colony passed twenty-one ordinances in that year regulating the everyday behavior of slaves and servants. Not surprisingly, five of the laws centered on running away. While servants could not absent themselves from a master's service or leave his property with a firearm in their possession without permission, slaves could not go away without a written pass. Since owners did not want slaves to learn to read or write, little chance of forgery existed. From the revision of 1715, slaves and free blacks were not allowed to serve in militia units or carry weapons without special permission, such as for hunting game.

The 1741 Act Concerning Servants and Slaves intensified legal restrictions and punishments. Alarmed by the Stono Rebellion near Charleston in 1739, the largest slave insurrection in colonial history, North Carolina passed a more comprehensive code aimed at the increasing problem of runaways. Fifty-eight provisions reinforced the legal definition of slaves as chattel or property, while twenty-two dealt with runaways. Slaves and free blacks who lurked about towns and farms could be declared outlaws and hunted for a bounty. Recognizing an increasing problem produced by the intimacy of slavery within a larger society, the 1741 act kept previous fines on interracial marriages and declared them to be "an abominable mixture" whose offspring would be "spurious issue." Yet despite the censure and penalties for interracial marriages and liaisons, they seemed to flourish in early North Carolina. After 1741, an uneasy state of fear, mirrored by an increasingly harsh slave code, existed between whites and blacks.

The 1715 and 1741 acts regulating the behavior of slaves and indentured servants underscored one of the most subtle yet consequential changes in early North Carolina society, that of the shift from white indentured servitude to slavery, from the predominance of whites to blacks on the bottom rung of the labor force. Unlike Virginia's Baconite rebellion in 1676 and Maryland's troubles with John Coode in 1689, North Carolina did not have a landmark white insurrection to mark its passage from indentured servitude to that of slavery. Instead, the mutation occurred more gradually in the decade from 1731 to 1741.

A significant minority if not a majority of the first colonists who came to North Carolina had roots in the Chesapeake, especially in Virginia. They had firsthand experience with indentured servants, primarily white. In a telling indictment, Virginia's exasperated governor, Francis Nicholson, accused the province in 1691 of harboring runaway servants from his colony. Thus, Nathaniel Batts and other Virginians who first settled in the Albemarle region had prior knowledge not only of slavery but also the English concept of villeinage, of a feudal condition including not only restrictions and obligations involving land tenure but also servitude. With the end of feudalism in England and Europe, the notion survived in the form of indenture and bondage, principally by apprentices and servants bound to masters and manors. Many early settlers in the Albemarle Sound region, such as the Pollocks and the Halls, had their roots in these vestiges of white indentured servitude. From this, they voluntarily "bound" themselves either to a ship captain, merchant, broker, or "master" in the New World, served their terms of indenture, obtained their "freedom dues," and moved to the Carolina frontier seeking free land and opportunity. Smaller in number, others "involuntarily" came to the colony as paupers, political exiles, and petty criminals. Most arrived overland from the Chesapeake, but a few arrived by sea directly from England or one of its colonial entrepôts. A large number of Scots-Irish names dotted the early records. In a telling nod to the colony's early composition, the proprietors in 1665 extended eighty acres of land for each adult male servant and half that for any "weaker servant . . . women, children, and slaves." Although Indians are not mentioned so prematurely, a significant few probably worked as servants and laborers.

In spite of frequent mention, the number of indentured servants remains illusory. North Carolina probably did not have as many as Pennsylvania or the Chesapeake colonies. Perhaps the best surmise comes from court records, occasional references to "Christian servants" and runaways, and the Acts of 1715 and 1741. For example, an indication of the prevalence of indentured servants suggests itself in the number of ordinances devoted to them in the Acts of 1715 and 1741. In the first instance, twenty-one statutes dealt with slaves and indentured servants as if they were corporate legal entities, but by 1741 a majority of the laws specifically had to do only with slavery. Persistently lumped together until 1715, white and black indentured servitude, in legal terms, had largely been disconnected by 1741. The later 1741 Act Concerning Servants and Slaves concerned itself mostly with slavery. By 1748 slaves outnumbered white indentured servants in North Carolina. At the end of the French and Indian War in 1763, the ratio increased from five slaves to every one indentured servant. After 1768, white indentured servitude had almost vanished in law if not in fact throughout the colony. In reality, the transition from indentured servitude to slavery throughout the colonies already had started by the time of Carolina's founding. In the Chesapeake region, large numbers of blacks had begun to be imported by the 1660s, replacing white bound labor to a great degree by 1700. Accordingly, the first distinctly "slave" codes appeared in Maryland and Virginia in the 1660s. The settlement of the Carolinas in the 1660s and afterward by Virginians, especially in the Albemarle Sound region, thus represented one of the last residues of white indentured servitude.

Although runaways of both white and black bound servants presented problems to early colonists, those of whites seemed more intractable. In 1716 John Urmston, a minister, noted that "white servants are seldom worth the keeping and never stay out the time indented." Most indentures of "His Majesty's Seven Years' Passengers," who came over on vessels and paid their passage by time worked in North Carolina, served only three or four years. "Seldom worth the keeping" pointed to the high costs of maintaining white servants, both economically and legally. The Act of 1715 ordered masters to teach their servants a trade and also to read and write, all requirements conspicuously absent in later slave codes. Moreover, masters were required to furnish "Dyet, Clothing and Lodging." If punishments exceeded the "Bounds of Moderation," servants could appeal to the nearest magistrate, who then must "bind over such Master or Mistress to Appear & Answer the Complaint the next Precinct Court." Rather severe punishments followed if judged guilty. An invocation and petition to a higher authority than a master doubtlessly alleviated the effects of an unequal power relationship. By 1741 black slaves had a separate court system that had few restraints of English common law and little appeal from arbitrary and unfeeling masters.

At the conclusion of their terms, indentured servants obtained "freedom dues, " usually in the form of a new suit of clothes, a few tools, and some land generally away from their masters. By 1741 only nominal freedom dues, a few pounds sterling and a new suit, remained from the first issues. No land had been granted since 1715, a testament to the declining number of white indentured servants. First and foremost, freed white servants valued land. Without it, they had little to show for their indentures. Two other factors, the rapid settlement of the area around the lower Cape Fear by plantation owners from South Carolina in the 1720s and the subsequent influx of slaves, along with a nascent racism, also contributed to the virtual end of white servitude by the 1760s. Within a short decade, color had supplanted class in terms of indenture and blacks had replaced whites at the bottom of the labor pyramid. In this fashion, whites, largely unnoticed, passed from servitude to freedom while at the same time the vast majority of blacks became part of the same crudely egalitarian society, but in an increasingly more harsh, rigid form of subjugation and bondage—that of slavery.

For all the restraints of institutions, such as courts, community, and religion, white indentured servants in North Carolina nonetheless frequently bore the cross of their time with unrelenting torment and even torture. In perhaps one of the most graphic cases known, Judith, a white indentured servant in the household of John Garzia of Chowan County, a minister for the missionary arm of the Anglican Church, the Society for the Propagation of the Gospel in Foreign Parts (SPG), was beaten for weeks and months until she died. Since Garzia was an Anglican minister, customary visitors to his house publicly cataloged the abuse in a subsequent court investigation. Attending a wedding at the minister's house, Richard Rigby noticed Judith's bruised and limp arm. When asked, Judith replied that "her master had lick't her, & shew'd a bruise from her elbow to her shoulder & down her shoulder as far as [he] could see." Ann Collier, the wife of a local sawyer who worked on the farm, testified that Judith's bruises, discolorations, lumps, and welts came because her master had beaten her with a large, rigid "Mill Stick." Jane McWilliams, who did laundry for the Garzia's throughout the ordeal, told of the increasing savagery of the attacks. At times, she noted, Judith "could not walk upright by reason of such bruises" and that a stumbling and bent-over Judith "would often cry bitterly as she went along." By that time, McWilliams testified, Garzia had taken to beating Judith on her "Groin & Small of her Back," places where "marking her up" would not show. In all this, local artisans and villagers declared that Judith was an ideal servant. Jane McWilliams described her as "good temper'd & never refused . . . to obey her master & mistress's orders." As he rode by the Garzias' one evening in 1735, Rigby "heard the Cry of murder," the screaming of someone in agony and desperation. He thought the voice to be Judith's. When she fell ill and took days to die, the Garzias' finally dragged her "to the Kitchin and laid" her out "on a coarse rug." Judith died two days later, comatose and beaten "senceless." No one knew her last name, nor did the records indicate any. Brought to the courts to see if their treatment of Judith exceeded the "Bounds of Moderation" required by the code, the Garzias, while never convicted, nonetheless found themselves denounced, indicted, and ostracized by the community.

Amended in 1753, 1758, and 1764, the 1741 act remained the basic legal system that governed slavery in early North Carolina. Gradually, the distinctions between punishments for indentured servants and slaves grew apart until, by the end of the Revolution, their legal separateness became practice in the *corpus juris*. As early as 1715 the codes set up a separate court system for slaves, one that effectively denied them due process as well as elements of mercy and compassion found in English common law. Authorized to act summarily without a right to appeal, the courts installed a system of judicial terror applicable only to slaves and not to white indentured servants. Presumed guilty and brought to the local courts, slaves could not call witnesses in their defense, but they could for prosecution against each other. To buttress the slave courts, masters held sway over their own farms and plantations and had authority to mete out private punishments for lesser crimes. In a telling insight on the hardening of the institution, the most severe punishments were reserved for outlawed runaways, murder, rape, and arson. In a century and time noted for brutality to whites, Indians, and blacks, the sentences given to slaves nevertheless seemed especially cruel.

Almost from its beginnings, slavery institutionalized fear and terror. While in 1715 indentured servants and slaves might be whipped and have their "time on the cross" extended for running away, by 1741 the punishments meted out to Africans and Creoles went beyond believable judicial bounds. In a century that did not have prisons but only jails (or gaols) for short internments, hangings and public whippings occurred on a regular basis. While whites and blacks alike could expect to be hung in a town or county seat as part of a public spectacle, only rarely did whites have their heads cut off and displayed on pikes and poles. For slaves, abuse, torture, sadism, and infrequently decapitation unofficially became incorporated into their sentences. In an infamous case in Wilmington, a slave named Will, chained alive in a gallows-like structure called a gibbet and thrashed publicly, took more than a month to die. Convicted of arson and conspiracy, the slave Isaac survived castration only to be hung two weeks later. Between 1741 and 1764, when the law was repealed, at least twenty slaves in North Carolina suffered castration as a punishment. At least three died from the gruesome procedure, usually done by jailers who received twenty shillings, a "middling sum," for the act. Prior to the Revolution, perhaps eight to ten slaves were publicly burned alive, at least thirty hanged, and as many as ten then decapitated and their heads mounted on pikes. Riding through Guilford County in 1781 on his way to battle Charles Cornwallis and the British, a startled Lt. William Feltman discovered the head of a slave mounted on a small sapling on one side of the road, the right side of his torso strapped to a tree on the other. After the Revolution, burnings and decapitations gradually ended while hangings increased.

RANAWAY

FROM the Subscriber near Avery's Ferry, on Cape Fear River, Chatham County, N. C. on the evening of the seventeenth instant, a Mulatto man called WILEY, about twenty-two years of age, and five feet nine or ten inches in height. No particular marks on his person are recollected. He was raised by Mr. Isaac Oliver, on the road from Petersburg, Va. to Halifax, N. C. about twenty miles from the former place, and was sold in Richmond, where I purchased him a fortnight ago. The same fellow escaped from a former owner a few months since, and was apprehended and lodged in Petersburg Jail. A handsome reward will be given to any person who will apprehend and confine him in prison at Raleigh, Warrenton, Petersburg, or Richmond, and give information thereof to Mr. G. W. Denton, or Messrs. E. & A. H. Cosby, Richmond, Va.

W. BARTON.

June 24th, 1829.   81—2t

Newspaper notice of runaway slaves,
Raleigh Register, 24 June 1828.
North Carolina Department of
Archives and History, Raleigh.

In a revealing story, Cato, an outlawed slave from Craven County, "wounded and abused" by his captors, died, like so many others, while in temporary custody awaiting trial. Scores of other runaway and outlawed slaves chose suicide, which some regarded as a form of self-murder, when capture and captivity seemed certain. Surrounded on the edge of the Great Dismal Swamp in December 1770, five outlawed slaves drowned each other rather than be recaptured. Whites never faced castration as punishment, while slaves officially did, some dying during the gruesome procedure. Time and again records reveal the custom of nailing an ear of a habitual runaway to a wooden platform, then cutting it off after a period of several days, to mark him as a felon. Between 1715 and 1785, when the law was repealed, at least eighteen slaves officially and perhaps more privately had one or both ears "Cropt." For stealing "Two Pockets Books and Papers and . . . some ribbons and a pen knife" as well as a stand, slaves Bob and Simon both received fifty lashes a day for three days followed by Simon, thought to be the leader, having both ears nailed to the same whipping post and then amputated. Nor did women escape the scarring punishment. Convicted of coming at her mistress, Judith Boyce, brandishing an ax, the slave Judith had "her right Ear Nailed to the Whipping post . . . to Stand Ten minutes and then to have the Said Ear Cut[away] and then to have forty Lashes well Laid in her Bare Back." Branding and scarring, either on the cheek, shoulder, or forehead of slaves became more widespread after 1748, while white indentured servants and even Indians convicted of habitual crimes could expect only a thumb or finger to be marked. Brands became visible signs of possession and a signature of ownership. The Society for the Propagation of the Gospel routinely marked their slaves by burning in the letters "S-O-C-I-E-T-Y" onto the breasts of both men and women. In some cases, slave owners, especially as the number of Africans increased in the slave population, sought to supercede the "country marks" of cosmetic mutilation that identified certain tribes by burning them out and replacing them instead with their own. A reading of descriptions of runaways in early North Carolina gives ample evidence of the widespread practice of branding.

While only a solitary white ever had a foot, finger, or hand amputated for crimes in early North Carolina, more than a dozen slaves did. Indeed, gender seems to have made only a slight difference in slave punishments. Although males made up more than 90 percent of those convicted, women, usually found guilty of conspiracy and poisoning, faced equally painful penalties. With the aid of several others, Annis, the "house wench" of Henry Ormond, smothered him to death in the summer of 1770. Burned at the stake, Annis reputedly went to her death vowing to follow Ormond into the afterlife and kill him again. Suspected of trying to poison her mistress, Phoebe was chained to a public whipping post, where she received fifty lashes, twenty-five every other day, while her collaborator, Mary, dangled in death from a gallows in front of her. In New Hanover County, Phyllis "died of her Wounds" while being "taken" by a vigilante patrol, and was chained inside a building when a mob burned it.

In a closed system like slavery, where those in bondage found themselves judged and punished daily and privately without appeal or recourse by their masters and mistresses, mistreatment often occurred outside the public's eye. In a particularly horrendous incident, Dr. Matthew Hardy, colonial North Carolina's "evil physician," conducted a *petit feu* in front on his assembled slaves and their families. In Northampton County in 1743, Hardy had Lucy, a young female slave who presumably either refused his advances or who angered him by her actions, tied to a crude triangular ladder. He then made some of her friends whip her, and, in a particularly hateful act, forced her own mother to set fire to the straw gathered at her feet. After a few torturous minutes, Hardy, at gunpoint, ordered another slave to drag Lucy's entire body "through the fire." He then refused supplies and aid to her. She died a few days later from her burns and injuries. Since it was not a felony to kill a slave by the Code of 1741, Hardy appeared in court, offered no explanation for his actions, answered some questions concerning his "breach of the peace," and went back to his rounds as the county's physician, treating the ailments and injuries of both freemen and slaves.

Like many of their countrymen in the southern and middle colonies, North Carolinians seem to have taken many of their punishments for slaves from a long European history of animal husbandry. Indeed, the notion of branding, castration, and cropping of ears derived from the ways in which Europeans customarily managed their livestock, including cattle, pigs, sheep, and other animals. The more grotesque and repellent maltreatments of burning, dismemberment, hanging, and whipping derived from the same concept, although long a practice in Europe. In fact, references in early North Carolina to the way in which masters and mistresses kept many of their slaves either naked or scantily or ill-clothed in all seasons of the year suggested the same regard.

Yet even with the immutable presence of terror and daily reminders of their inferior status as chattel, as disposable personal property, life for Africans and Creoles in North Carolina nonetheless manifested the ambiguities present in all forms of intimate human relationships, even in an oppressive and closed system like that of slavery. Almost echoing an opposition to the increasingly harsh slave codes from 1715 until the Revolution, more and more Africans and Creoles were freed or manumitted by their masters as the years wore on. As early as the 1680s, Virginians looked upon North Carolina as a sanctuary for runaway slaves and free blacks. Both Virginians and South Carolinians fervently believed that North Carolinians concealed runaways and even helped them in their flight. Indeed, a statute passed in 1699 by Governor Walker responded to the charges by Virginians by imposing stiff penalties for harboring or helping runaways and fugitives. The practice seemed

Jane Johnson, a slave of John Hill Wheeler released by abolitionists in Philadelphia in July 1855.
North Carolina Collection, University of North Carolina at Chapel Hill.

widespread enough that in 1715, when the revision of all laws took place, the general assembly not only reaffirmed the two shillings per night fine for harboring and aiding runaways and fugitives but also offered rewards to anyone involved in the apprehension and return of fugitive slaves.

By the time of the Revolution, the Great Dismal Swamp on the border between Virginia and North Carolina had perhaps become the largest sanctuary for runaway and fugitive slaves in the South. Thousands hid in relative safety and seclusion, living there for generations and establishing entire villages of Maroons and mestizos, mixed groups of whites, Indians, and blacks. So well known was the reputation of the swamp for harboring runaways that northern abolitionist poets and writers used it as a literary symbol to plead against "the evil institution." In "The Slave in the Dismal Swamp," Henry Wadsworth Longfellow dramatically portrayed "the hunted Negro," who saw the midnight fires of his pursuers and heard "a bloodhound's distant bay" as he lay in the "dark fens of the Dismal Swamp." Searching for a popular theme to use against slavery, Harriet Beecher Stowe penned *Dred: A Tale of the Great Dismal Swamp,* about a fugitive slave who lived a precarious existence while on the run against "patrollers," before she wrote *Uncle Tom's Cabin,* perhaps the most famous abolitionist book written before the Civil War. Coastal towns such as Wilmington, Edenton, and New Bern attracted scores of runaways and free Africans. By 1770 blacks, both slave and free, made up more than half the population of Wilmington, which, despite passes and patrols, would become a focal point for runaways and fugitives after the Revolution. With access to the sea and with the presence of large tracts of marshy lands and swampy areas around the town, blacks found it relatively easy to hide out and to blend into the population. Moreover, the relatively large free black populations of coastal cities such as Edenton and Wilmington offered security and sanctuary to runaways.

Whites also openly aided runaways. In Chowan County, Catherine Edwards flaunted the law by sheltering as many as five or six fugitives at a time, while in Rockingham

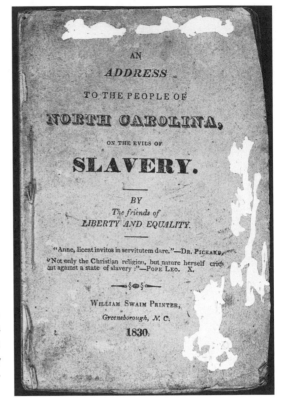

Title page of an abolitionist tract,
An Address to the People of North
Carolina on the Evils of Slavery.
North Carolina Collection, University
of North Carolina at Chapel Hill.

County a public whipping did little to dissuade Meredith Brown from helping blacks escape from slavery. Frequently religious congregations, especially Quakers and Methodists, openly defied the laws and codes relating to slavery and the treatment of blacks. The Standing Committee of the North Carolina Yearly Meeting of Friends, the Quakers, publicly sanctioned manumission for conscience-stricken members and, additionally, encouraged locals to free their slaves. When the general assembly, fearful of freeing slaves during the Revolution, forbade manumission in 1777, Quakers simply labeled their slaves "free members" of households and omitted any reference to manumission. From 1787 on, Quakers set up funds to help runaway slaves find their way north to freedom and sometimes to transport them to Haiti and Liberia and other parts of Africa, out of the reach of American constables and warrants.

Daniel Worth, a Wesleyan Methodist missionary, openly distributed antislavery literature, such as Hinton R. Helper's 1857 *The Impending Crisis of the South: How to Meet It*, and spoke out against the evils of slavery in 1859. Benjamin Hedrick, in the midst of a promising career as a professor at the University of North Carolina, read the abolitionist Theodore Parker's writings against slavery and found himself converted. Parker, an evangelist and congregational minister from Boston, thought slavery to be morally and spiritually wrong, an affront to God's divine plan as revealed in the precepts of the heart. After a lengthy self-examination of his own conscience and principles, Hedrick publicly acknowledged and insisted that slavery contradicted basic American and human concepts of justice and equality laid out in writings from Rousseau to Jefferson to the New Testament.

Left: Hinton Rowan Helper (1829–1909).
North Carolina Collection, University of North Carolina at Chapel Hill.

Title page of Hinton Rowan Helper's The Impending Crisis of the South: How to Meet It, *which became a staple campaign document of the Republican Party in the 1860 election.*
North Carolina Collection, University of North Carolina at Chapel Hill.

THE

IMPENDING CRISIS

OF

THE SOUTH:

HOW TO MEET IT.

BY

HINTON ROWAN HELPER,

OF NORTH CAROLINA.

COUNTRYMEN! I sue for simple justice at your hands,
Naught else I ask, nor less will have ;
Act right, therefore, and yield my claim,
Or, by the great God that made all things,
I'll fight, till from my bones my flesh be hack'd !—*Shakspeare.*

The liberal deviseth liberal things,
And by liberal things shall he stand.—*Isaiah.*

FOURTH THOUSAND.

NEW-YORK:

BURDICK BROTHERS, 8 SPRUCE STREET.

1857.

84

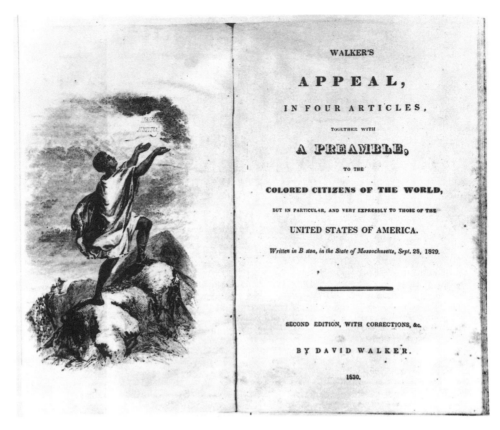

Frontispiece and title page of David Walker's 1830 Appeal in Four Articles to the Colored Citizens of the World. North Carolina Office of Archives and History, Raleigh.

When he announced that he intended to vote for John C. Fremont, the Republican anti-slavery candidate in 1856, public pressure and threats to his life convinced him to abandon Chapel Hill and his career and to leave North Carolina.

The ambivalence and contradictions of slavery in early North Carolina perhaps can be partially understood through the life of David Walker, a free black born in Wilmington in 1785, and also in the life of Harriet Jacobs, born into slavery in Edenton. The son of a preacher, Walker learned to read and write at an early age. After moving to Boston in the midst of an abolitionist sentiment then beginning to sweep the nation, he published an *Appeal to the Colored Citizens of the World in Four Articles* in 1829 calling upon slaves to revolt against their masters. Drawing on the same Christian ideals and biblical context later used so successfully by Martin Luther King Jr., Walker argued that slaves, like the whites who mastered them, had fundamental human rights as Americans and as creatures of God. Recognizing the move to send freed slaves back to Africa as an inappropriate halfway measure, he instead urged slaves to revolt and to take back the land "enriched . . . with our blood and tears."

Walker's *Appeal* alarmed North Carolinians. In 1830 the general assembly hastily passed legislation that banned not only the *Appeal* but any other pamphlets or writings that might "incite insurrection, conspiracy or resistance in the slaves or free negroes" within the state.

Additionally, the law also forbade whites and free blacks to teach slaves to read and write, so fearful were North Carolinians over the growing numbers of free blacks and of the power of the written word. Nat Turner's rebellion in Southampton County, Virginia, in August of 1831, perhaps one of the largest and bloodiest of all slave uprisings in the nation's history, only heightened the tensions felt by many North Carolinians after Walker's *Appeal*. The rebellion occured in Southampton County, a region in Virginia adjacent to North Carolina's border that was heavily populated by both slave and free blacks, white North Carolinians could not help but feel a sense of foreboding over their own peculiar institution. After all, Edenton, Wilmington, New Bern, and almost all the coastal counties, especially the ones around the Lower Cape Fear, looked eerily like Southampton in Virginia. The story of Harriet Jacobs took a different turn. Born into slavery in Edenton around 1813, Jacobs's father, Elijah, had considerable freedom as a carpenter and was "considered so intelligent and skilled in his trade that, when buildings out of the common . . . were to be erected, he was sent for from long distances, to be head workman." Allowed to support himself and manage his own affairs, Elijah Jacobs paid his mistress in Edenton two hundred dollars a year, no small sum in early-nineteenth-century North Carolina, while also managing to save in order to purchase his family's freedom. He never succeeded. Although born a slave, Harriet recalled that "I never knew it till six years of happy childhood had passed away," a testament to the chameleonlike nature of bondage in North Carolina. She and her friends lived in "a comfortable home; and, though we were all slaves, I was so fondly shielded that I never dreamed I was a piece of merchandise." Things changed after 1835. Her new master, James Norcom, a physician, proved not only insufferable but licentious as well. Harriet ran away. Hidden by both white and black sympathizers for seven years, Jacobs, with the aid of Quaker abolitionists operating in North Carolina, made her way first to Brooklyn and finally to Rochester, New York. Befriended by Amy Post, an abolitionist and a participant in the first Woman's Rights Convention in Seneca Falls, New York, in 1848, Harriet soon became one of only a handful of black abolitionists in the 1850s. She wrote "Letter from a Fugitive Slave" for Horace Greeley's *New York Tribune,* and, with Lydia Maria Child's tutelage and encouragement, penned *Incidents in the Life of a Slave Girl,* a first-person account of slave life, especially the sexual abuse of women, in antebellum North Carolina. It richly chronicled the intimacy and inconsistencies of slave life in North Carolina during the crucial decade from 1831 to 1842, particularly the increasingly arbitrary and punitive nature of bondage.

Despite the toughening of slave codes after Nat Turner's rebellion in 1831 and the revocation of many of the rights of free blacks by 1835, the numbers of free and educated blacks continued to grow rapidly even as the institution hardened through time. In Chapel Hill, a free black named George Moses Horton wrote love sonnets for heartsick university students, while in Montgomery County, John, the young slave of David Bruton, ran away to the North, taking with him "a Testament, a Spelling Book, Scott's Lessons, Watts' Hymn Book, and a printed notebook" filled with his writings. The autonomy of David Walker and of many free blacks in North Carolina only perpetuated the torments of slavery for many North Carolinians, both white and black.

Perhaps the greatest achievement of Africans and Creoles who came to be enslaved and even freed in North Carolina lay not in their creation of an autonomous culture overlaid

Example of craftsmanship of Thomas Day, a free black in North Carolina.
North Carolina Department of Archives and History, Raleigh.

with a distinct African identity like that of the South Carolina low country but in their individualistic and even communalistic triumph of humanity. Unlike Africans and Creoles in the Chesapeake and in South Carolina, slaves and free blacks found themselves more divided, both by tribe and by culture, into increasingly smaller groups on farms and plantations, often pitted against each other by their masters and their own traditions. No single African language or dialect survived in North Carolina. Thus, slaves from Albemarle Sound to the Cape Fear put together varying adaptations of Igbo, Hausa, Guinea, Creole, pidgin, and English, with variances in phonology and grammar, unintelligible to masters and to others outside their own region. Forbidden to use drums for fear of signaling and stirring emotions, slaves instead devised elaborate hand claps and banjos that sang to each other. Given rough and scratchy woolen panels for clothing, Africans and Creoles decorated themselves with ornaments and dyed headscarves to counteract the drabness and cheerlessness of their lives. Fiercely clinging to their sense of family and community, slaves insisted on naming their children as their African ancestors did, regardless of how whites referred to them and scribbled down their names for land and tax records. Slaves defied their lot in life by misconstruing daily tasks, breaking tools, feigning illnesses, and hundreds of other oppositional acts each day they were enslaved. Thousands voted for freedom by running away, an act of desperation that frightened slave owners into even harsher and frequently even less effective measures. In the end, whites in North Carolina created freedoms and constitutional protections for themselves at the expense of blacks. Undoubtedly, the initial passage of the majority of North Carolinians from oppression to freedom and self-government simultaneously occurred with the final passage of Africans and Creoles into an increasingly harsher form of slavery from 1663 to 1865.

ADDITIONAL READINGS

Allen, Jeffrey B. "Racial Thought of White North Carolina Opponents of Slavery, 1789–1876." *North Carolina Historical Review* 59 (January 1982): 49–66.

Bassett, John Spencer. *Slavery and Servitude in the Colony of North Carolina.* Baltimore: Johns Hopkins University Press, 1896.

Battle, George Gordon. "The State of North Carolina vs. Negro Will, a slave of James S. Battle, a cause celebre of ante-bellum times." *Virginia Law Review* (April 1920): 515–30.

Bruner, James Howard. "Legislation Designed to Control Slavery in Wilmington and Fayetteville." *North Carolina Historical Review* 30 (April 1953): 155–66.

Chavis, John. "The Influences of John Chavis and Lunsford Lane on the History of North Carolina." Compiled by W. Sherman Savage. *Journal of Negro History* 25 (1940): 14–24.

Cobb, Collier. *American Man of Letters, George Horton, the Negro Poet.* Chapel Hill: n.p., n.d.

Crow, Jeffrey. *Black Experience in Revolutionary North Carolina.* Raleigh: Department of Archives and History, 1977.

———. "Slave Rebelliousness and Social Conflict in North Carolina, 1775 to 1802." *William and Mary Quarterly* 37 (January 1980): 79–102.

Crow, Jeffrey, Paul D. Escott, and Flora J. Hatley. *A History of African Americans in North Carolina.* Raleigh: Department of Archives and History, 1992.

Eaton, Clement. "Dangerous Pamphlet in the Old South." *Journal of Southern History* (August 1936): 323–34.

Egerton, Douglas R. "'Fly Across the River': The Easter Slave Conspiracy of 1802" and "A Rejoinder." *North Carolina Historical Review* 68 (January 1991): 87–110, 122–24.

Elliott, Robert Neal. "Nat Turner Insurrection as Reported in the North Carolina Press." *North Carolina Historical Review* 38 (January 1961): 1–18.

Fenn, Elizabeth. "'Perfect Equality Seemed to Reign': Slave Society and Jonkonna." *North Carolina Historical Review* 65 (April 1988): 127–53.

Franklin, John Hope. *The Free Negro in North Carolina, 1790–1860.* New York: Norton Publishers, 1971.

Gehrke, William H. "Negro Slavery among the Germans in North Carolina." *North Carolina Historical Review* 14 (October 1937): 307–24.

Higginbotham, R. Don, and William S. Price Jr. "Was It Murder for a White Man to Kill a Slave? Chief Justice Martin Howard Condemns the Peculiar Institution in North Carolina." *William and Mary Quarterly* 36 (October 1979): 593–601.

Inscoe, John C. "Carolina Slave Names: An Index to Acculturation." *Journal of Southern History* 49 (November 1983): 527–54.

———. "Generation and Gender as Reflected in Carolina Slave Naming Practices: A Challenge to the Gutman Thesis." *South Carolina Historical Magazine* 94 (1993): 252–63.

Jacobs, Harriet A. *Incidents in the Life of a Slave Girl, Written by Herself.* Edited by Jean Fagan Yellin. Cambridge: Harvard University Press, 1987.

Leaming, Hugo Prosper. *Hidden Americans: Maroons of Virginia and the Carolinas.* New York: Garland Publishing, 1995.

Morgan, Kenneth. "Slave Sales in Colonial Charleston." *English Historical Society* (Great Britain) 113 (1998): 905–27.

Morris, Charles Edward. "Panic and Reprisal: Reaction in North Carolina to the Nat Turner Insurrection, 1831." *North Carolina Historical Review* 62 (January 1985): 29–52.

North Carolina Manumission Society. *Address to the People of North Carolina on the Evils of Slavery.* New York: N. Muller, 1860.

Phifer, Edward William, Jr. "Slavery in Microcosm: Burke County, North Carolina." *Journal of Southern History* 28 (May 1962): 137–65.

Sowle, Patrick. "North Carolina Manumission Society 1816–1834." *North Carolina Historical Review* 42 (January 1965): 47–69.

Taylor, Rosser H. "Slave Conspiracies in North Carolina." *North Carolina Historical Review* 5 (January 1928): 20–34.

Walker, David. *David Walker's Appeal, in Four Articles, Together with a Preamble to the Coloured Citizens of the World.* New York: Hill and Wang, 1965.

Watson, Alan D. "Impulse toward Independence: Resistance and Rebellion among North Carolina Slaves, 1750–1775." *Journal of Negro History* 63 (Fall 1978): 317–38.

———. "North Carolina Slave Courts, 1715–1785." *North Carolina Historical Review* 60 (January 1983): 24–36.

Wood, Bradford J. *This Remote Part of the World: Regional Formation in Lower Cape Fear, North Carolina, 1725–1775.* Columbia: University of South Carolina Press, 2004.

Resistance, Regulators, and the Rhetoric of Rebellion in North Carolina, 1729–1771

The rhetoric of rebellion in North Carolina, never a compliant colony, moved in an unresolved manner from the earlier disruptions of Cary, Gibbs, and Culpepper through the Stamp Act, on to the Regulator movement and, finally, to the Revolution. Indeed, the state's role in the fight for independence and subsequent attempt to build a new nation cannot be understood without a realization that the Regulator rebellion in the western counties in the spring of 1771, the largest mass social uprising in American history, not only determined the course of independence within the state but also in the South as a whole. Three factors, the unrest created by the events from 1764 to 1774, the reaction to them by North Carolinians, and, lastly, the personality of Herman Husband, all served to rekindle Carolinians' frustrations with government since the days of the proprietorship and emboldened them to take up arms against "knaves alike," whether they resided in New Bern or London.

Even before the imperial crisis of the 1760s, North Carolina had, at best, acquired only a veneer of royal government. In many ways, the transition from a proprietary to a royal colony affected North Carolina but little. Instead of a weak succession of governors appointed by the proprietors, the colony now had a stronger selection drawn from a pool of placemen, professional soldiers, administrators, bureaucrats, and officials. Yet that difference proved crucial. Instead of following directives from the proprietary board, governors now drew their instructions from the Crown. By 1729, guidelines for royal governors had been constructed and made systematic to conform to an imperial system grown mature through more than a century of wars and administration. Thus, when George Burrington arrived in Edenton, he saw himself as part of an imperial system that responded to the king and Privy Council, to the Board of Trade, the Treasury Board, War Board, Admiralty Board, customs commissioner, and, later, to the secretary of state for the Southern Department. As a determinant of his role in that far-flung kingdom, Burrington, like all royal governors, thought he must establish the royal prerogative.

A little-used term in modern history, "prerogative" in the eighteenth century meant establishing not only rights and privileges granted to ranks and classes but also those political precedents and priorities imparted to royal authority. In North Carolina, enforcement of that prerogative fell to governors, councilors, and judges largely independent of elected

Map of North Carolina in 1770. North Carolina Office of Archives and History, Raleigh.

general assemblies and legislative bodies. Instead of being dependant upon salaries, fee schedules, and even presents bestowed by popular assemblies, royal governors required regular salaries paid from a permanent fund. Additionally, royal privileges included judges not elected by the vote of the people but serving at the pleasure of the governor and Crown. Moreover, as part of their royal prerogative governors could call elections, summon and end a session of the assembly, dissolve legislatures, decide upon a quorum for any elected assembly, and, when necessary, veto or suspend laws. Lastly, as representatives of the Crown and Board of Trade, royal governors, by fiat, saw to it that trade, commerce, navigation, and other laws of the empire were put into effect. Overlaid and unstated within the concept of prerogative, royal governors also sought to bring a sense of deference, of the natural submission and acceptance not only of the Crown but also of authority in general to the uneducated, uninstructed, unenlightened, and unlearned heathen of North Carolina. If only judges, royal officials, and militia officers would dress and smell better, chew tobacco less in public, and be well mannered, then many governors like Burrington and Arthur Dobbs believed that prerogatives, both social and political, would be fulfilled. Burrington openly despised the rough "country" equality he found among North Carolinians and a corresponding lack of deference to "the better classes."

If North Carolina's newly appointed governors came with an inflexible frame of mind toward the royal prerogative, they found an equally unswayable disposition among the colony's elected representatives toward charter rights, namely that the original instruments setting up the colony not only had granted land titles but also guaranteed the rights of the people. To the majority of North Carolinians, the shift from proprietary to royal control did not mean a corresponding surrender of these rights and privileges, only a change in those who protected them. Moreover, precedent and the interpretation of these rights since 1663 also played a part in their implementation. Having presided over the gradual erosion of both social and political prerogatives of the proprietors and the complementary enhancement of their own in almost continuous squabbles and rebellions since Culpepper's in 1677, the general assembly did not intend to submit to the Crown's interpretation of their "rights." In the following decades, royal governors and elected assemblies clashed in a series of confrontations that had not only philosophical but also unsentimental political consequences. When Grenville's imperial reforms came to North Carolina after 1763, they arrived with the hounds of three decades of suspicion, anxiety, and foreboding nipping at their implications and applications at every step. Three issues, that of the governor's salary, the control of taxation, and the appointment of judges illustrated the battle over prerogatives between the assembly and royal governors from 1729 until the eve of the Revolution. One symbol, that of Tryon Palace in New Bern, embodied the dispute that eventually came to be at the heart of the colony's revolutionary philosophy.

As part of his instructions upon receiving his commission as North Carolina's first royal governor, Burrington had an explicit directive not to accept allowances and allotments from the legislature. Instead, the Privy Council ordered him to obtain "a fixed salary out of a permanent fund without limitation . . . in time," the latter a reference to the annual voting of a fee for the governor by the legislature. Adamant and arrogant, Burrington failed to obtain a salary from the general assembly, as did Gabriel Johnston and Arthur Dobbs. Only William Tryon, perhaps politically and socially the most skilled of all North Carolina's governors, managed to cajole and persuade the general assembly to appropriate funds for his use. Tryon manipulated, influenced, intrigued, and outwitted many in the legislature. At the end of his administration, he had persuaded the general assembly to appropriate 44,844 pounds for his military campaigns against the Regulators and another 15,000 pounds for the construction of his elaborate residence at New Bern. When finally finished, Tryon Palace had pretentious rooms for the council and governor to meet, but no place for the general assembly. It still met wherever it could, frequently in whatever public or private buildings it found convenient. Small wonder that many North Carolinians, especially those in the backcountry, loathed Tryon Palace and the indebtedness it brought to the colony. Nonetheless, the legislature still held to the principle that it had the power to tax and to distribute funds.

In like manner, royal governors and the legislature fought over whether judges should be elected or appointed, what courts should be erected and allowed, and what constituted a quorum for the assembly to meet. In each case, the general assembly fell back upon charter rights, in effect constitutional ones for them, while royal governors insisted upon implementing their instructions from the Crown. To the Crown, a quorum consisted of no less than a proportion of the number required for the House of Commons, fifteen in the case of North Carolina, while the general assembly just as adamantly maintained that the total should be "not less than one full half of the House," thus a majority of the "Representatives of the People." Burrington, Johnston, Dobbs, Tryon, and Josiah Martin understood that, while they might manage to suborn and prevail upon fifteen or twenty members to meet at their call, a majority quorum favored the elected leaders of the assembly. The question of a quorum, really that of representation, was not resolved until North Carolina became a state and had its own constitution in 1776. No room in Tryon Palace could seat a majority of the general assembly, only ten or twelve councilors or perhaps fifteen assemblymen.

Yet in the clash between royal prerogative and legislative constitutional rights, one issue overrode all others. The disputes over the governor's salary, a quorum, the collection and distribution of quitrents, the emission of paper currency, and even poll taxes and land titles had at their core the right to tax. In colonial North Carolina, the right to tax and distribute monies inherently meant the right to govern. Passionate speeches and stubborn insistence by assemblymen and representatives over quaint and archaic issues such as a quorum, quitrents, and prerogatives primarily involved the basic right to govern, that of taxation. Similarly, the assertion and claims made by royal governors from Burrington to Martin as to their rights and privileges converged on the same issue, the right to tax and distribute monies. By 1773, the right to levy taxes and to control purse strings had become an emotional issue that involved the very test of a legitimate government. Small wonder that, in the same year, the assembly declared that "the rules of right and wrong, the limits of the prerogatives of the Crown and the privileges of the people, are . . . well known and ascertained." Then, in a prophetic declaration, the assembly laid down the now accepted view by many North Carolinians that "to exceed . . . them is highly unjustifiable." Yet North Carolina's last royal governor, Josiah Martin, had no intention of giving in to the assembly. With his view from Tryon Palace, he understood that, like his predecessor, William Tryon, he, too, must establish royal prerogatives, if not by reason and persuasion then by force. By 1763, the issue of governance and its legitimacy had been joined.

The chief villain of the drama that occurred after 1763 turned out to be George Grenville, chancellor of the exchequer under George III. Through his program of reorganizing the newly won empire and of easing the tax burden upon England brought about by the French and Indian War, Grenville helped transform the grassroots resentment toward royal prerogative and its "tyrannical" imposition long present in the colony into a more coherent political philosophy of outright rebellion. Although Grenville's measures included the Currency and Sugar Acts, and most significantly the Stamp Act, only two provoked a strong response in North Carolina. In particular, the Sugar Act, the first bill to raise the question of the power of Parliament to tax the colonies for revenue, incited the people and assembly to action to a larger degree than in any other colony except New York. Also known as the Revenue Act, the Sugar Act placed duties on many colonial imports such as sugar, molasses, coffee, wine, silk, and many kinds of cloth. Still, to colonials, the devil lurked in the details.

In spite of the fact that it looked like the older and largely accepted Navigation Acts, the Sugar Act broke with policy and usage. Instead of regulating and channeling trade through England, the new act explicitly aimed at raising revenue, an important right of governance. Moreover, the decree also set up a vice admiralty court in Halifax, Nova Scotia, to try smugglers, again wresting legal power away from local courts and juries. The assembly correctly looked upon the Sugar Act as a direct violation of its hard-won rights over the power to tax. As Gov. Arthur Dobbs observed in 1760, the assembly, mindful of its hard-won rights, thought "themselves entitled to all the Privileges of a British House of Commons and therefore ought not to submit to His Majesty's honble. Privy [Council] . . . or . . . Governor and Council."

Opposition to the Sugar Act, usually in the form of petitions and meetings, centered not only in the assembly but also in towns and along the coastal lowlands, particularly in the Lower Cape Fear region, home to the colony's political and social elite. In the interior, from Anson to Orange to Rowan counties, the counties of origin for a majority of the Regulators, the Sugar Act excited little protest. No one seemed to care.

Yet backcountry men suffered far more anguish over another act than their eastern brethren. Passed in 1764, the Currency Act, prohibiting the issuance of legal tender currency, exacted innumerable hardships upon North Carolina's fledgling economy, especially in the western counties. As population rapidly expanded in the decades after 1730, particularly in the backcountry, a greater need for currency to circulate as a medium of exchange arose. In the past, the shortage had been partially alleviated by the issuance of paper money, a form of provincial script, which, even in depreciated value, served as a useful medium of exchange. When the Currency Act went into effect, approximately 74,800 pounds of paper money still circulated, inadequate even for a population of 200,000. Despite the Currency Act, North Carolina still issued 80,000 pounds of non–legal tender bills from 1764 to 1775, not enough for a colony with a burgeoning population.

The deficit and lack of currency directly contributed to the westerners' grievances against the way they were governed, especially when it came time to pay taxes, a circumstance noted by both Tryon and his successor, Josiah Martin. It helped spur the movement in the backcountry for the "regulation" of their own affairs, especially in terms of representation and taxation. Some counties, especially in the interior, could not get sheriffs to collect taxes after 1764 "because no one would undertake the impossible task . . . where money had virtually disappeared." The currency crisis and the problem of collecting debts also crucially divided the eastern elite of planters, merchants, and lawyers from the small farmers in the backcountry.

Not surprisingly, the Stamp Act, following closely on the heels of the Sugar Act, generated even more opposition. The act itself placed taxes on legal documents, newspapers, almanacs, college diplomas, playing cards, dice, and all customs papers, in effect a form of an eighteenth-century general sales tax. It was passed by Parliament on 1 March 1765 but did not to take effect until 1 November; the eight-month delay gave North Carolinians as well as other colonials precious time to discuss and consider their opinions. By midsummer, small demonstrations had occurred in Cross Creek, Edenton, and New Bern. On 19 October more than five hundred demonstrators gathered at Wilmington in the town square to protest the pernicious new tax and hanged in effigy "a certain *honorable gentleman*," probably Lord Bute, a hated name associated with royal authority but who had little to do with the Stamp Act. The protesters burned a huge bonfire near the courthouse and toasted "LIBERTY, PROPERTY, and no STAMP DUTY." The ranks of the Wilmington mob contained many future Sons of Liberty and Revolutionary leaders such as Cornelius Harnett and John Ashe. A new resistance group provoked mainly by the Stamp Act, the Sons of Liberty was made up chiefly of planters, merchants, and well-to-do farmers from counties in the Lower Cape Fear, such as Brunswick, Bladen, Duplin, and New Hanover, and successfully organized lower classes, mainly dockworkers, artisans, apprentices, and even indentured servants and ordinary citizens, in Wilmington to oppose the act. More important, the Wilmington riot signaled the movement from parliamentary debate to direct action, a quantum step toward rebellion. Notwithstanding the enthusiasm of the Wilmington mob and the coastal towns of New Bern and Edenton, the Stamp Act went largely unnoticed in the western counties. Physically and politically separated and estranged from New Bern, Wilmington, and the coast, westerners took a wait-and-see attitude toward events.

On All Hallows' Eve, the night before the Stamp Act was to go into effect, a second rally took place in Wilmington. Intended to show support for the resolves initiated in Virginia and passed by the Stamp Act Congress in New York and also for displeasure at Governor Tryon's refusal to support delegates from the colony, the Halloween uprising had all the earmarks of a well-planned, purposeful protest. Orchestrated by Sons of Liberty such as Harnett, Ashe, Hugh Waddell, Alexander Lillington, and James and Maurice Moore, the march toward freedom began with the symbolic death of Liberty by Taxation, heralded by a solemn procession through town with her body in a coffin accompanied by doleful drumbeats and an interment in a local churchyard. To no one's surprise, Lady Liberty, her pulse still beating, arose from the dead to inspire the populace. Returning to the town center, the mob "concluded the Evening with great Rejoicings, on finding that LIBERTY had still an Existence in the COLONIES."

On 16 November elements of the same Wilmington throng forced the colony's newly appointed stamp agent, Dr. William Houston of Duplin County, to resign. Sensing the shift of opinion and momentum toward violence and rebellion, William Tryon, perhaps the colony's most skillful governor, subtly sought to bribe the assembly's leaders into compliance with the act. Summoning fifty of the principal citizens from some of the most rebellious counties, including Brunswick, New Hanover, and Bladen, Tryon lavishly feted and fed them on the evening of 18 November. In the pleasantness after dinner, Tryon, persuasive but petulant, insisted that although he personally opposed the Stamp Act and thought it soon would be repealed, North Carolina should accept the law during the few months before its repeal. Moreover, he promised to pay, out of his own pocket, the Stamp Act duties. Further, he would seek for the colony a "favourable indulgence and exemption" from London that would expand its trade while ports in other colonies remained closed. So compelling was Tryon that the rebellious guests, while in his presence, could not refuse his offer. Still, away from the governor and his charm, the delegates, after a good night's sleep and sober reflection, finally rejected the compromise. The issue of liberty versus tyranny now was joined.

The test to determine the will of the populace toward the Stamp Act came ten days later. On 28 November the British sloop *Diligence,* commanded by Capt. Constantine Phipps, sailed into Brunswick harbor to deliver stamps to the colony. Led by John Ashe and Hugh Waddell, a body of armed men, probably local militia and some hangers-on, prevented the delivery of the stamps. Furious, Tryon banned all transactions of the courts, in effect shutting down the daily business of government. Except for a few furtive landings along Cape Hatteras, trade almost ceased. Although the colony seemed "peaceful and quiet," Tryon remained suspicious. "The obstruction of the Stamp Act," he dutifully reported to London on 26 December, "has been as general in this province as in any colony on the continent." That soon changed.

Between 28 January and 7 February, three merchant ships, the *Dobbs,* the *Patience,* and the *Ruby,* entered the Cape Fear River only to be seized by the *Viper,* another British sloop that came to help the *Diligence.* Sensing the mood of the colony, Robert Jones, the attorney general, tried to shift indictments and court proceedings from Cape Fear to Halifax, Nova Scotia, a site more amenable to British authority.

Enraged at the blatant threat to their "liberty," leaders in Duplin, Bladen, New Hanover, and Brunswick counties met at Wilmington on 17 February to form an association to unite and assist each other "to the best of our Power, in preventing the operation of the Stamp Act." Choosing directors such as John Ashe and Alexander Lillington, the association called upon militia Gen. Hugh Waddell to command an armed force of nearly a thousand armed men. On the evening of 19 February, more than eleven hundred marched to Brunswick, seized the customs house, destroyed its records, and demanded that the two impounded ships, the *Patience* and the *Ruby,* be released. The next day, the armed insurgents rounded up the customs collector, controllers, clerks, and any royal officials who were available and forced them to swear an oath that they would not perform any duties involving the stamp tax. In this way, North Carolina, like its sister colonies, entered the mainstream of the coming revolution. Thereafter, an illegal and shadowy association backed by armed militiamen became the de facto government of the colony a decade before the Revolution began. Never again could any royal action be enforced in North Carolina without the approval of the assembly's shadow government. Events on the coast did not go unnoticed in the western counties. If mobs rioted in Wilmington and along the eastern coast, then the backcountry could also resort to violence. Well aware of the developing resistance to British colonial policy, backcountry North Carolinians also understood that provincial leaders such as Ashe and William Hooper posed a threat to their own rights and liberties that was more immediate, menacing, and corrupt than that of the faraway British. An Orange County petition in August 1766 underscored the point. "Whereas . . . great good may come of this . . . designed Evil, the Stamp Law while the Sons of Liberty withstood the Lords in Parliament in behalf of true Liberty let not officers under them carry on unjust Oppression in our own Province." A second protest that same month set forward the same fear. "Take this as a maxim that while men are men . . . though you should see all those Sons of Liberty (who . . . just now redeemed us from tyranny) set in offices and vested with power they would soon corrupt again and oppress [us] if they were not called upon to give an account of their stewardship."

Because of rising unrest in the backcountry, the Townshend Duty Act, passed in June 1767 after Grenville had left office, barely went noticed in North Carolina. Charles Townshend, Grenville's replacement, now persuaded Parliament to tax the lead, paint, paper, glass, and, of symbolic importance, tea that America imported. Concerned less with trade and commerce and more with political stability and economic hardship, the province's leaders saw little in the act that merited their concern. When Speaker of the House John Harvey received the Massachusetts Circular Letter from Sam Adams on 11 April protesting the coming Townshend acts and calling for a nonimportation agreement, he took no action before Tryon dismissed the assembly. Reconvening in November, the House took the letter under consideration, appointing a committee, a sure avenue of neglect, to draft a petition for the colony. Following the example of Virginia, the assembly adopted a set of resolutions nearly identical to those of its northern neighbor and formed several ineffective nonimportation associations. Clearly, the threat from the backcountry concerned provincial leaders more than that from London.

North Carolina's western counties wanted exactly the same rights as their eastern brethren, especially the freedom to have some control over their own affairs and to have equal representation in government. Thus, the rhetoric of resistance put forth by provincial leaders such as John Ashe and Alexander Lillington inadvertently inspired an attempt by the backcountry to manage or to regulate their own local affairs. By 1766 a combination of factors—increased expectations from the repeal of the Stamp Act, a growing dislike of government altogether, and heavier taxation—moved the Regulators toward action. Still, two additional ingredients, a rise in the province's poll tax and the charismatic personality of Herman Husband, sparked the largest mass uprising in colonial American history, the Regulator movement of 1766–71.

Because of large military expenditures approved by the assembly from 1758 to 1763, provincial poll taxes rose from one shilling, eight pence, in 1754, to an average of eight shillings, one pence, by 1763, a sixfold increase. Coupled with a severe shortage of currency in the western counties after 1755 and economic hard times, the tax became the target of Regulators' disaffection. Many westerners, lacking currency or hard money of any kind, were not only reluctant but also unable to pay their taxes. Due to the currency shortage, Regulators wanted commodities, principally tobacco, corn, and wheat, accepted as payment-in-kind for taxes. In addition, the idea of a poll tax, a flat sum for each individual, struck them as overbearing and autocratic. Instead, Regulators wanted an ad valorem tax assessment levied according to an individual's wealth and property.

Herman Husband's personal magnetism and powers of persuasion did much to galvanize discontent in the backcountry. By 1753, Husband, a former Quaker from Annapolis, had moved to the backcountry to be among those he considered to be uncorrupted small freeholders peacefully living in a frontier paradise. Well established and accepted almost as a backcountry Isaiah by 1765, he began the Sandy Creek Association, the first Regulator organization, in 1766. "A firebrand amongst the people," as he was called, Husband, through his eloquence and skills, articulated the major issue of taxation and the power to govern to settlers in the backcountry. Tryon identified Husband as the principal Regulator, while James Hasell, president of the council, recognized him as the chief ringleader. His pamphlet, *An Impartial Relation,* a revolutionary document, set forth the basic grievances and philosophy of the Regulators.

Like Husband, a great many western settlers recently had migrated to North Carolina, principally from Pennsylvania and the Chesapeake region. Overwhelmingly Protestant and anticlerical in spirit, they embraced a religious doctrine where millennialism, the belief in a better world where evil would be banished and peace, prosperity, and happiness would reign on earth, always lurked. In this conviction, prophets like Husband were both expected and welcomed. Anticipating a better life, materially, spiritually, and politically in North

Tryon Palace in New Bern with its cannon mounted for defense.
North Carolina Office of Archives and History, Raleigh.

Carolina, anxious to better their lives in every way, these new emigrants easily embraced Husband's ideas, especially those of economic independence, freeholding, and personal liberty that could be imperiled by a corrupt, centralized government. Husband underscored this fundamental relationship by uniting "Liberty! thou dearest name!" with "Property! thou best of blessings."

What began as a protest in the western counties against corruption and tyrannical power in general quickly became an attack on the colony's whole government when the Regulators learned of the palace. In late 1766 the assembly appropriated five thousand pounds sterling, and in January 1768 another ten thousand, to construct a governor's palace in New Bern. One Regulator remarked, "we want no such house, nor will we pay for it." The Regulators suspected that Tryon, along with Edmund Fanning, whom they viewed as a foe, were "leagued together, knaves alike, to fleece the people that they might build palaces etc." To the Regulators, Tryon Palace symbolized the corruption of government, galvanizing them to organize still more associations.

Events over the next few months propelled the Regulators into open rebellion. In the summer of 1768, Tryon and the council ordered the dissolution of Regulator associations because of the "several outrages in open violation of the Laws of their Country." Militia units from eight coastal counties prepared to march to Orange County. In September 1768 Tryon alerted 1,500 additional militia to protect the courts in Hillsborough from the Regulators. On 20 December 1770, the assembly expelled Herman Husband for libeling Maurice Moore, a superior court justice, and had him arrested to prevent his return to the backcountry. On 15 January 1771 Samuel Johnston, a representative from Edenton, rose in the lower house to propose a "spirited Bill," a riot act that made "outrages" against the government a felony, even treasonous. Rioters now could be tried in any of the province's six superior courts, regardless of where an offense took place, and offenders had sixty days to present themselves for trial. After that, the person could be "deemed Guilty of the offense

Gov. William Tryon (1729–88) confronting the Regulators.
North Carolina Collection, University of North Carolina at Chapel Hill.

and might be killed or destroyed with impunity." Husband's release three weeks later did little to dampen the Regulators' fears. To them, the rhetoric of Johnston and Tryon smacked of that used by Grenville and others to justify their own Sugar and Stamp Acts. All were "knaves alike." Samuel Johnston's riot act confirmed the Regulators' apprehension about a government conspiracy to take away their liberties, threaten their property, and restrict their ancient rights as Englishmen. Additional Regulator enlistments hurriedly came from Halifax and Edgecombe counties. More than ever, the Regulators were convinced that tyrants and despots, whether located in London or Edenton, ruled over Carolina.

Equally persuaded of the Regulators' threat to the colony's stability and public order, Tryon set out on his famous western campaign that would end at a little-known village in Orange County called Alamance. On 14 May 1771 he camped on Great Alamance Creek, just west of Hillsborough, with approximately fourteen hundred militiamen, almost all from eastern counties. Arrayed against him, more than two thousand Regulators, perplexed, frustrated, and angry, determined once more to exercise their rights as Englishmen. On 16 May the Regulators sent Tryon a petition respectfully requesting an audience to air their grievances. Sensing hesitation and division among the Regulators, Tryon haughtily rejected their request, ordering them instead to lay down their arms before he would talk. He further insulted the rebels by giving them one hour to meet his demands. Enraged, the Regulators dared the governor to "fire and be damned," and the battle of Alamance began. After less than two hours of desultory firing, the Regulators, less disciplined and not really caring to fight, left the field. In all, nine militiamen died and sixty-one more were wounded, while the Regulators carried their unknown dead and wounded from the field. On 17 May, the day after the battle, Tryon hanged James Few, a notorious Regulator leader from Hillsborough, and after a court trial six more men met the same fate. Under a lenient amnesty proclamation, more than sixty-four hundred Regulators eventually were pardoned. Lady Liberty, miraculously resurrected from the dead by the Sons of Liberty in Wilmington, expired at Alamance never again to reappear in the backcountry until almost the end of the Revolution.

The Regulators' defeat at Alamance not only changed the course of rebellion in North Carolina; it also later led to a subsequent tragic miscalculation by Gov. Josiah Martin and other British leaders. When British attempts to subdue New England finally failed at Saratoga in 1777, London looked to the South, principally to the backcountry in the Carolinas, for support in reestablishing royal authority in the colonies. The Regulators, so argued Tryon and his successor as governor, Josiah Martin, had suffered countless abuses and, finally, a humiliating defeat at the hands of an assembly dominated by eastern counties. Unscrupulous justices, corrupt and embezzling sheriffs, and, lastly, a paid militia had been utilized by Albemarle and Cape Fear legislators to check the growing power of the west. Every attempt to seek redress and relief for the abuses had met with procrastination, ambivalence, and neglect until, in the end, the assembly had conspired with Tryon to destroy the backcountry farmer's associations by force of arms at Alamance. The very men who controlled the legislature in 1771 now headed the Revolutionary movement, and the Regulators, so Martin reasoned, had no wish to enlarge the power of their old oppressors. If the British moved southward into the Carolinas with sufficient force to protect those whose sympathies lay with the Crown, Martin argued, all the old Regulators, a majority in most western counties, would flock to the king's standard. The general acceptance of this assumption about the backcountry's and the Regulators' views demonstrated not only how much the British were out of touch with their American colonists, but also how desperately they sought a rationale for reestablishing a royal authority that never had much actual power in provinces like the Carolinas.

The counties where the Regulator movement was centered, Anson, Dobbs, Halifax, Rowan, and Orange, produced a great many Loyalists but even more rebels. Although Samuel Johnston thought in 1775 that "the old Regulators are all against us," they were not consequently for the British. Of 883 known Regulators in Orange County, for example, only 34 could be listed as Tories, while the number of Whigs remained unknown. Perhaps the most telling number consisted of the 560 "unknowns" whose allegiance could not be determined. With the Revolution under way in 1775, Governor Martin, with the king's permission, granted full pardons to all the Regulators except, of course, Herman Husband, yet they still did not rally to or wholeheartedly support the royal cause.

From the very beginning, provincial leaders in North Carolina neglected the Regulators' protests in much the same way as they ignored other threats to their newly won authority, whether it came from the governor and council or from London. Just as Dobbs and Tryon represented challenges to the lower house's growing power, so did the underrepresented freeholders in the western counties. In the 1760s, the lower house finally triumphed in its decades-long battle with the governor and council, and, with increased self-confidence, now faced still another menace from the backcountry. When the Regulators threatened to march on New Bern in December 1770, the assembly arrogantly labeled

NORTH CAROLINA
AT THE BEGINNING OF
1775
Showing Approximate County Divisions
within Present State Boundaries
Map by
L. Polk Denmark

North Carolina at the beginning of the Revolution.

the saber-rattling move as a "daring insult . . . to this House" and condemned the association for committing "usurpations of the Power of the Legislature." Clearly, the Regulators, through their use of violence, forewarned the colony's provincial leaders of things to come.

The protests of the Regulators in the backcountry violently underscored the weaknesses of the colony's government. For decades, politics in North Carolina had revolved around such issues as quarrels over land titles, political squabbles between factions from the Albemarle and Cape Fear regions, the perpetual problems of the Granville District, and, in the 1750s and early 1760s, Governor Dobbs's attempts to overhaul an inept, inefficient, and corrupt provincial administration. At times, particularly after the French and Indian War, civil institutions simply ceased functioning. "I must . . . confess," observed Anglican missionary James Reed in 1774, "I am heartily weary of living in this land of perpetual Strife and Contention."

Corruption, self-interest, and loyalty to factions and regions dominated politics in North Carolina prior to the Revolution. While provincial leaders such as Johnston, Harvey, and Ashe sought to reform government by giving more power to the lower house of the assembly, Regulators wanted something else, an entirely new political system. In this, the Regulators' idea of responsible government paralleled more radical plans such as those in Pennsylvania, while North Carolina's more Whiggish leaders from the eastern seaboard looked to Virginia for a more conservative model.

The post-Alamance executions and the banishment of Herman Husband successfully ended the outbreak of violence in the backcountry but in its place left a bitter and simmering resentment of government in general. "Knaves alike" appropriately described the general attitude of many North Carolinians toward those who claimed administration over them, whether their authority came from a parliament, assembly, congress, or crown. All were scoundrels, Pharisees, and abusers of authority, all "knaves alike." By 1771 North Carolinians had developed a disaffection from all authority and government. Backcountry freeholders had become Jeffersonian long before Jefferson in their belief that a government that exercises the least control over its people governs best.

On 12 August 1771, Josiah Martin took the oath of office as royal governor at New Bern, succeeding William Tryon and setting the stage for North Carolina's entry into the Revolution. In faraway western Pennsylvania, Herman Husband arrived in Bedford that fall, estranged from his fellow freeholders in North Carolina but not from their revolutionary ideology of government. The Regulators had failed, but a generalized resentment against "knaves alike," whether in Edenton or in London, persisted. When the Revolution began in North Carolina, backcountry men took a wait-and-see attitude toward both Whigs and Tories. In the end, the Revolution within the new state took on all the aspects of the earlier rebellion by the Regulators, a war within a war, only this time with an increasingly joined political philosophy between the eastern and western counties.

ADDITIONAL READINGS

Adams, George R. "Carolina Regulators: A Note on Changing Interpretations." *North Carolina Historical Review* 49 (October 1972): 345–76.

Booth, Sally Smith. *Seeds of Anger: Revolts in America, 1607–1771.* New York: Hastings House, 1977.

Boyd, William K., ed. "Hermon Husband's 'An Impartial Relation of the First Rise and Cause of the Recent Differences in Public Affairs, Etc. (1770).'" In Boyd's "Some North Carolina Tracts of the Eighteenth Century." *North Carolina Historical Review* 3 (April 1926): 307–62.

Butler, Lindley S. *North Carolina and the Coming of the Revolution, 1763–1776.* Raleigh: Department of Archives and History, 1976.

Caruthers, Eli W. *Sketch of the Life and Character of the Rev. David Caldwell.* Greensboro: Swaim and Sherwood, 1842.

Denson, Andrew C. "Diversity, Religion, and the North Carolina Regulators." *North Carolina Historical Quarterly* 72 (January 1995): 30–53.

Ekirch, A. Roger. "'A New Government of Liberty': Hermon Husband's Vision of Backcountry North Carolina, 1755." *William and Mary Quarterly* 34, 3rd ser., (October 1977): 630–46.

———. "North Carolina Regulators on Liberty and Corruption, 1766–1771." *Perspectives in American History* 11 (1977–78): 199–256.

Kars, Marjoleine. *Breaking Loose Together: The Regulator Rebellion in Pre-Revolutionary North Carolina.* Chapel Hill: University of North Carolina Press, 2002.

Kay, Marvin Lawrence M. "North Carolina Regulation, 1766–1771: A Class Conflict." In *The American Revolution: Explorations in the History of American Radicalism,* ed. Alfred F. Young. De Kalb: Northern Illinois University Press, 1976.

Lee, E. Lawrence, Jr. "Days of Defiance: Resistance to the Stamp Act in the Lower Cape Fear." *North Carolina Historical Review* 43 (April 1966): 186–202.

Nelson, Paul D. *William Tryon and the Course of Empire: A Life in British Imperial Service.* Chapel Hill: University of North Carolina Press, 1990.

Sellers, Charles Grier, Jr. "Making a Revolution: The North Carolina Whigs, 1765–1775." In *Studies in Southern History,* ed. Joseph Carlyle Sitterson. Chapel Hill: University of North Carolina Press, 1957.

Spindel, Donna J. "Law and Disorder: The North Carolina Stamp Act Crisis." *North Carolina Historical Review* 57 (January 1980): 1–16.

Wheeler, Earl M. "Development and Organization of the North Carolina Militia." *North Carolina Historical Review* 41 (July 1964): 307–23.

Whittenburg, James P. "Planters, Merchants, and Lawyers: Social Change and the Origins of the . . . Regulation." *William and Mary Quarterly* 34, 3rd ser. (April 1977): 215–38.

The Beginning of the Revolution in North Carolina

Summers in New Bern are hot. Frequently laced by coastal breezes and surrounded by marshy ground, the flat land around New Bern becomes a spawning ground for hordes of insects, especially mosquitoes and sand flies. Yet to Josiah Martin, the new royal governor, New Bern and North Carolina in 1771 seemed like a Garden of Eden. Born in Dublin either in 1735 or 1737, the son of a prosperous West Indian planter, Martin had spent his childhood in the oppressive, sweltering heat of the island of Antigua. To him, the breezes of New Bern, no matter how hot, seemed almost pleasant.

Initially trained for a legal career, Martin instead became an army officer, serving in that capacity until 1770 when he sold his commission as a lieutenant colonel in the Fourth Regiment of Foot to pursue an occupation in colonial administration. Relying upon his brother's political connections in London, he replaced William Tryon as governor of North Carolina on 12 August 1771.

Lacking any real civil administrative know-how and depending on his army experience as a formula for understanding Britain's imperial policies, Martin frequently hesitated to take risks when problems arose, preferring instead to refer them to England and to await instructions rather than chance criticism of his actions. An ambitious man and an opportunist, he embodied all the virtues and vices of placemen, careerist bureaucrats in the British government who were despised by men such as Herman Husband. Uneasy and intimidated at the prospect of having to replace William Tryon, a skillful politician and forceful manager, Martin lacked the tact, social skills, and charm of his predecessor. Blunt, direct, energetic, stubborn, rash, intelligent, honest, sincere, and fair minded, Martin's personality overall seemed ill suited not only to the enduring problems but also to the new challenges of strife-torn North Carolina.

Martin's initial misjudgment lay in siding with the Regulators against the lower house of the assembly. As he surveyed the political landscape from his new office, Martin knew intuitively that the assembly on prerogative power and privileges had long subjected the powers of the royal governor, who represented London, to encroachment. No royal governor of North Carolina had ever effected a lasting peace with the Albemarle or Cape Fear factions, really clustered groups of representatives who sometimes mirrored the views of Virginians and South Carolinians more than those of the province as a whole. Moreover, none had ever attempted to join forces with the growing western counties to undermine the domination of the east, nor had the coastal counties tried to ally with the Piedmont to control the governor. At best, the 1771 partnership of the eastern legislators, led by Johnston and Ashe, with Governor Tryon, against the Regulators relied on fear and not trust. With Tryon gone and the Regulators subdued, the east coast once again expected the status quo—that is, their ascendancy and control—to be reestablished. Thus, Samuel Johnston and his friends eagerly awaited Martin's arrival. "A very amiable Character," Johnston said of the new governor, certainly not anticipating any uneasiness "at the approaching change" of executives. Unlike Tryon, who gave them a great deal of trouble, Johnston and the assembly thought Martin would be more pliable and manageable.

Martin's first venture into the boggy ground of provincial politics came three days after his arrival. Writing to Secretary of State Lord Hillsborough, his immediate superior, on 15 August, he acknowledged that the lack of currency compounded the colony's economic problems. Like Tryon, he advocated printing more money, "a new Emission of such extent, as may admit the extinction of all former emissions, and supply the present exigencies of the Province and be sufficient medium of circulation in this growing country." By November, in the quicksand of provincial politics, Martin was not so sure of even this initial decision. Within three months, Martin had changed his mind on the currency issue. Writing Hillsborough in November, he explained that his earlier view on "the expedient of a new emission of paper bills" came from Tryon, and, "upon closer examination . . . does not correspond" with his view of reality. Perhaps Hillsborough's well-known opposition to paper currency had at last become evident to Martin.

Meeting on 19 November 1771, two committees of the lower house, both with the same membership of Robert Howe, Cornelius Harnett, and Maurice Moore, all powers in the eastern establishment, prepared petitions to the king. The first protested running a new boundary line with South Carolina; the second called for the repeal of the Currency Act and, with that, the issuance of specie for the colony.

In its initial stages, Martin supported the lower house's request to resurvey the boundary line with South Carolina, but his sympathy soon soured when the Board of Trade rejected the petition and instead asked North Carolina to run a thorough new survey on its own. When the assembly's committee refused to pay for the survey, Martin, acting on his own accord, appointed commissioners to run another boundary to settle the dispute. On 8 July 1772 he showed his disagreement with the committee and contended that "the Association of the House of Assembly that a large body of useful Inhabitants would by such a partition be taken from this Province" by redrawing the boundary "I find . . . to be without foundation." Only "useless and troublesome . . . lawless Bandits" would be lost, and, additionally, land titles and grants then could be cleared, and fees, including his, could be collected. Martin evidently preferred a clear-cut boundary line and the right to collect fees from land grants to having more frontiersmen, "lawless Bandits," as he labeled them, in North Carolina. Martin eventually thought most North Carolinians to be "useless bandits" in their attitude toward his authority, while the assembly regarded them, whether they lived along the coast or in the mountains, as "useful inhabitants."

Piqued at the lower house for opposing him on the currency issue and at having to pay for the expense of the survey, Martin, in an initial attempt to deal sternly with the eastern politicians as a precedent of his new administration, dissolved the assembly on 23

December. To Johnston, Howe, Harnett, and the Moore brothers, the new governor no longer seemed such an "amiable Character."

Determined to redress the balance of power between the royal prerogative and the assembly, Martin moved to ally the executive powers of the governor with the western counties. In March 1772 he asked Hillsborough to arrange for the final disposition of the Granville District, long a source of western grievances, and, a day later, recommended that the Crown appoint county court clerks when the current act allowing the court of pleas, a local authority, to name them ran out. Moreover, he wanted the Crown to name clerks of the inferior courts as well. Overall, "the Influence of Government," royal government to Martin, would "in proportion be extended." By looking to the west for help in passing these and other measures, Martin unintentionally set aside a political maxim that Dobbs and Tryon long had worked to establish, never to commingle provincial and imperial issues. When he toured the Regulator country in 1772, eastern politicians took notice and disapproved.

The Granville District threatened one of the most basic of liberties for North Carolinians, the right to own land in fee simple title and, with that, participation in governance. When the Crown took over the colony in 1729, it gave Lord Carteret, Earl Granville, the only proprietor who refused to sell his original interest, a huge tract of land as compensation for his one-eighth share of the original Carolina. In 1729 the district cut a sixty-mile swath from the Virginia border to Bath, enveloping as it did almost two-thirds of the colony's early population. As a manorial landowner owning the district, Lord Carteret sent agents like Francis Corbin to prepare rolls of those who lived on his land and to collect rents and taxes. For his part, Corbin preferred the comforts of Bath and Edenton to the hard work of riding the marshy pine barrens seeking out Granville's dilatory and troublesome renters. Accordingly, his rolls, collections, and reports netted Granville little in the way of revenue but much in terms of disaffection. Moreover, the vast majority of North Carolinians in the district resented not only the constant threat of the collection of arbitrary rents and fees but also the insecurity of their land titles. Both struck at the very basic functions of governance, and, if the Crown could not guarantee their rights and titles as landowners, then, in the eighteenth century, their entire participation in and allegiance to royal authority was annulled.

The loss of revenues from the Granville District always had nettled and restricted royal governors. For his part, Martin begged London to purchase the entire district, a suggestion also put forward by Dobbs and Tryon. Otherwise, Martin argued, the district crucially divided the colony from royal authority and "fatally embarrassed its policies." The legislature agreed with Martin, but the Crown did nothing. Martin quickly learned that he could control neither imperial policies in London nor provincial ones in North Carolina. His royal authority extended little beyond the flowerbeds and livery stables of Tryon Palace. The coming Revolution and a new American government fittingly resolved the problem of land titles and taxes in the Granville District.

Between 1765 and 1771 issues such as the Sugar Act, Stamp Act, and Townshend duties had set the elected assembly against the appointed governor in a dramatic yet restrained fashion. Petitions, protests, riots, even the excesses of the Sons of Liberty and the extraordinary congress of 1769 called against Tryon never questioned the legitimacy of royal government, only the power of Parliament to tax. In each case, the eastern political establishment exercised direction over the peaceful protests and negotiated with the governor for their resolution. In the backcountry, the lower house held no sway over the Regulators, who considered it to be a part of the problem. While Tryon and the lower house came together to crush the western rebellion in 1771, the specter of another Alamance hung over a conservative eastern establishment. One issue, that of paper currency, threatened to set the west against the east again in yet another bloodbath.

Following Tryon's lead, the assembly voted in December 1771 to discontinue the poll tax because the currency it was designed to "sink," or bring in, had all been recalled and destroyed. Knowing that at least forty-two thousand pounds of paper currency still circulated, Martin, suspecting a trick by the assembly, vetoed the act and ordered the sheriffs to collect the tax nonetheless. Believing the funds were needed to protect public credit and that the eastern establishment only wanted to create mischief and ill-will toward him, Martin stubbornly refused to yield the point. Shrewdly aware of the poll tax's unpopularity and of the governor's inflexible nature, the assembly then ordered the sheriffs not to collect the tax, a position they readily embraced. No poll tax was collected, but Martin's exasperation with the assembly mounted as his popularity declined.

What happened next in North Carolina seemed almost trivial by the events it triggered, yet the court struggle that began in February 1773 inexorably led to a crisis that hastened the revolt against England. The arcane language of the debate over the court bill, quaint phrases and terms such as "oyer" and "terminer," an attachments clause, and inferior and superior courts belied the seriousness of the impasse over who should govern the province.

In February 1773 the assembly sent to Martin a bill continuing but also amending the superior and inferior court laws of 1767 set to expire that year. Knowing that it contained a clause allowing North Carolina courts to attach, or claim, the property of debtors living in England, Martin, acting on instructions from London, disallowed the bill. For its part, the assembly responded by inserting "foreign" for "English," thus emphasizing inclusiveness rather than an exclusiveness that still applied principally to London merchants. The assembly also bypassed bills providing for a temporary court system until the Crown could approve its new actions. At the end of February, Martin and the legislature still could not agree on a bill, and, in an effort to make the members more willing to yield on the attachments clause, he rejected an additional sixteen bills and prorogued the group for three days to give them time to think it over. Instead of returning in a more reflective and submissive mood on 9 March, most of the representatives simply went home. The governor then called for new elections and for a new assembly to meet on 1 May. After the spring of 1773 and the impasse with the assembly, the governor and legislature never again agreed on any laws or issues affecting the colony.

The rift between Martin and the assembly heralded the breakdown of government in general across the province. Without civil or criminal courts, debts could not be collected nor could criminals be punished. In the colony to establish a local committee of correspondence in 1773, Josiah Quincy Jr. of Boston noticed the "great consternation" and widespread discontent caused by the lapse of the court bill. In eastern counties controlled by assembly leaders, the troubles over the court bill solidified a growing anti-British sentiment. In the west, especially in the old Regulator strongholds, citizens blamed both parties but singled out eastern politicians for the greatest reproach. For example, in Halifax, a trading town in the interior, the closing of the courts convinced merchants and landown-ers that easterners only wanted a legal opportunity to escape their debts to British credi-tors through the attachments clause. To them, it seemed too self-serving. The backcountry also wanted some relief for their debts to eastern merchants and planters, an element not provided in the bill.

Far western counties also harbored suspicions about the motives of eastern politicians. Needing courts to protect them from the "licentiousness and Outrage" of ruffians and out-laws who "too soon appeared after the shutting up of [the] Courts of Law," westerners opposed the attachments clause. The regional divisions over the court bill reinforced Mar-tin's misjudgment that a few "mercenary tricking" lawyers from the east had conspired against him and that his best hope of securing and expanding royal government lay in the west. From 1773 until the end of the Revolution, both self-deceptions returned to haunt the British in their attempt to regain control of the southern colonies.

The deadlock over the attachments clause brought North Carolina close to anarchy. Played out in Halifax, New Bern, and London, the battle over the attachments clause and court act brought to a fever pitch a decades-old struggle between the governor and legis-lature over who should rule North Carolina. Leaders in the assembly—including John Harvey, Samuel Johnston, and Joseph Hewes from Albemarle, and Isaac Edwards, Richard Cogdell, Cornelius Harnett, William Dry, Robert Howe, William Hooper, and John Ashe from the Cape Fear area—had by 1773 become resolute opponents of British government and its policies. When Josiah Quincy approached the new assembly in December 1773 about joining the Continental Association, he found them in a receptive mood. Exasper-ated and headstrong, leaders of the legislature welcomed the opportunity to embrace a larger yet sympathetic cause. Responding to Virginia's circular letter and Quincy's request, the lower house appointed a committee of correspondence to align it with the other colonies. With a single act, North Carolina at last had joined the widening Revolutionary movement. After decades of quarreling and squabbling among themselves, the province's leaders, in an insightful moment, changed the course of North Carolina history.

After March 1774, the colony took on many of the appendages of the Revolutionary movement. To a committee of correspondence the assembly appointed nine men, all from the eastern counties, all men of property and standing, all advocates of colonial rights, all experienced veterans of fights against the royal prerogative, and all destined to play promi-nent roles in the Revolutionary struggle. The appointments of John Ashe, Richard Caswell, Cornelius Harnett, Joseph Hewes, John Harvey, William Hooper, Samuel Johnston, Robert Howe, and Edward Vail did more than guarantee many of the future state's place-names. It shaped North Carolina's role in the coming Revolution and in the ensuing constitutional struggle.

Knowing that Martin would not convene the assembly until it proved more concilia-tory, John Harvey, Samuel Johnston, and Edward Buncombe decided instead to call into session a provincial congress, an elected, representative, independent deliberative body. Harvey, the most radical and headstrong of the three, turned to the recently formed com-mittee of correspondence for support, especially seeking out Cornelius Harnett, "the Samuel Adams of North Carolina," and William Hooper, a Harvard graduate, legal expert, and wealthy planter. Hooper proved to be the colony's John Dickinson, the penman of the American Revolution, as a constitutional authority and pamphleteer. The proposed congress never convened, a clear signal that the Revolutionary movement had not yet taken hold in North Carolina. Still, the closing of Boston's port by the British in response to the Tea Party gave radicals like Harvey and Hooper the encouragement they needed to promote the Revolutionary cause.

Virginia's reaction to the harsh Port Act influenced not only the colonies in general, but the actions of radicals in the eastern counties of North Carolina in particular. When Lord Dunmore, the Virginia governor, dissolved the recalcitrant House of Burgess on 25 May 1774, the delegates moved to Raleigh Tavern, where they proceeded to adopt a boycott against British goods, to call for elections to an independent Virginia congress, and, additionally, to endorse a general continental congress for all the colonies. Envisioning themselves more like the Virginia Whigs than Pennsylvania radicals, North Carolina's committee of correspondence quickly met and endorsed Virginia's resolves. Still, Harvey, Hooper, and Harnett, the most outspoken critics of British policy, hesitated to summon a congress. When it came, the call resulted from a mass meeting in Wilmington on 21 July of merchants, planters, and freeholders from six counties in the Cape Fear region. The committee's indecisiveness and an indetermination of the "general sense of the people" became hallmarks of North Carolina's Revolutionary participation.

Martin now felt abandoned and adrift as a royal representative. When he asked the council how best to prevent the provincial congress from meeting, the weak reply it gave, to issue a proclamation against it, did little to allay his fears. Nor did it help in forestalling the inevitable meeting. In fact, when the first provincial congress met on 25 August 1774, all but one of the council members, James Hassell, attended and participated in the sessions. Clearly not even the council sympathized with their governor. Discouraged, heartsick, and feeling ill, Martin left for New York on 4 September 1774, not to return until 9 January 1775. With his departure, what little veneer of government England had established in the colony came apart, never again to be rebuilt.

As a royal governor, Josiah Martin understood England's tenuous hold in North Carolina. Writing that fall to Lord Dartmouth, secretary of state for the colonies, he argued that "Britain must assert and establish her just rights and authority in the Colonies . . . or give up forever all pretensions to dominion over them." By 1775 the critical juncture had come. Not surprisingly, the First Provincial Congress that replaced royal government selected the radical leader John Harvey as its leader, then proceeded to elect William Hooper, Joseph Hewes, and Richard Caswell as delegates to the new Continental Congress. The Provincial Congress then asserted its right to tax and to pass a resolution to support the boycott of British trade until the Coercive Acts were resolved. Local committees, soon to be called committees of safety, were created to enforce the acts of the Provincial Congress. North Carolina's revolutionary infrastructure slowly materialized.

The meeting of the First Provincial Congress inexorably drew North Carolina into the mainstream of the Revolutionary movement. While Governor Martin ostensibly continued to maintain his position and authority, the power of royal government quickly came to an end. In the coming year, local committees of safety, acting on authority from the Provincial Congress, gradually came to control the towns and counties where they existed. To a

*Penelope Pagett Barker (1739?–94), one of
the ladies who led the Edenton tea party.*
North Carolina Division of Archives
and History, Raleigh.

surprising degree, all forms of central government ceased to exist. The commonwealth of freeholders envisioned by Herman Husband three years earlier now seemed to take root in the radical soil of anarchistic North Carolina.

Aside from events in Halifax County in the Piedmont and Rowan County in the west, almost all the action of the committees and revolutionary turmoil took place along the eastern seaboard. While committees of correspondence in towns such as New Bern, Edenton, and Wilmington and in the counties of Halifax, Pitt, Duplin, Chowan, New Hanover, Bute, and Craven began to enforce the resolves and decrees of the Provincial and Continental Congresses, government west of Rowan fell into the hands of locals who did little except wait. Decrees and associations meant to ensure nonimportation and nonconsumption of British goods and to regulate prices of local commodities went unnoticed in the west. Pamphlets and propaganda designed to promote home industries and to discourage extravagant and ostentatious lifestyles and to persuade unenthusiastic citizens had little effect in the interior of the colony. With few generational roots in North Carolina and with the memory of the harsh treatment of the Regulators by eastern militia still fresh, westerners did not trust the Revolutionary rhetoric or actions of the Provincial Congress.

In October 1774 more than thirty-six ladies purported to gather at the home of Mrs. Elizabeth King in Edenton and, over tea and biscuits, agreed to an association to support the Provincial Congress and its work and "to do everything . . . in our power to testify [to] our sincere adherence to the same." Moreover, the Edenton ladies promised to quit "that Pernicious Custom of Drinking Tea" and not to wear English linens "until Parliament repealed the tax on tea." Visiting the region several months later, Janet Schaw, an English "lady of quality," expressed disdain for the ladies and fright at the men who, "inflamed by the fury of an ignorant zeal" for the rebel cause, had exhibited a "natural ferocity" toward anything British. The very "idea of tar and feather" at the hands of an unruly mob sickened her. It had come to that.

When he returned from a visit to New York in early January 1775, Martin brought with him instructions from England on how to deal with the emerging radical element in the colony. Under no circumstances, his orders dictated, should a second provincial congress be allowed to meet nor should delegates to a second continental congress be appointed. With no troops or Loyalists to command, Martin instead resorted to a "war of proclamations," a propaganda campaign aimed at intimidation where he issued public notices against the radicals. When the governor called the assembly to meet in late March, the speaker, John Harvey, countered by summoning the Second Provincial Congress just days afterward. When Congress met on 3 April with sixty-one members present, and the assembly met the next day with forty-eight delegates in attendance, almost all of the members of the Provincial Congress had been reelected to those two bodies. Martin recognized the virtual powerlessness of his position. Harvey, Hooper, and the radicals controlled the political machinery of the colony. Only a military option remained. From Gen. Thomas Gage, he requested arms and ammunition for western Loyalists who, Martin fervently believed, would flock to the Crown. Stepping back from his ineffectual post as governor, Martin also asked to be restored to his former army rank so that he could lead a Loyalist force against the rebels. Contemptuous and frustrated at the weakness of British imperial policies, Martin reverted back to the role of a military commander, to a person who took orders directly and who expected obedience in return.

On 31 May, the safety committee of Mecklenburg County issued its instructions, generally known as the Mecklenburg Resolves, perhaps one of the most freethinking and politically radical documents to come from any southern colony. In it, the radicals denied the authority of Parliament not only to tax but also to govern the colonies altogether. Moreover, North Carolinians, for the first time, rejected outright the sovereignty of the king. The committee declared that "the former civil Constitution of the colonies" would cease to exist after June 1775. A basis for governing the colonies no longer existed, and the united colonies would seek a new basis for governance.

Disturbed at the increasing agitation and at the belligerence of declarations such as that from Mecklenburg, Martin began taking precautions against open insurrection. First he dismantled the ceremonial cannon at the governor's palace, an action that almost immediately set a mob against him, and, afterward, he hurriedly sent his family to safety in New York. Amid rumors that he intended to arm slaves and to lead armed Loyalists against the assembly, Martin decided to leave the unprotected palace for the safer Fort Johnston. Threatened there by a mutinous garrison and roaming mobs, he restlessly awaited the arrival of the HMS *Cruizer,* a small British sloop hastily dispatched to pick him up. On 15 July 1775, Josiah Martin, John Collet, the commander of the fort, and a few loyal men fled to the safety of the *Cruizer.* There Martin watched as the Whigs burned Fort Johnston to the ground four days later. The delightful summer breezes of the Carolina coast that Martin found so pleasing four years earlier when he first came to North Carolina now seemed stifling and ill-omened.

As if somehow drawn into a black hole, Whigs and Loyalists moved to fill the political power vacuum left by the departing governor and British authority. In the summer of 1775, county after county formed military companies and prepared for battle. Watching a review of a fledgling militia group at Wilmington, Janet Schaw, no lover of anything

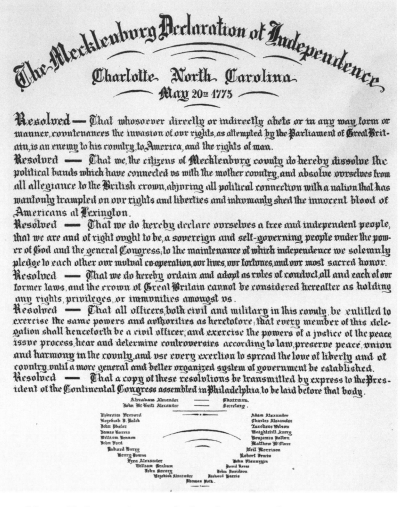

Copy of the Mecklenburg Declaration of Independence. Many do not accept it as genuine.
North Carolina Collection, University of North Carolina at Chapel Hill.

American, howled at the ludicrous display before her: "Good Heavens! What a scene. . . . Their [the militia's] exercise was bush fighting . . . they were heated with rum till capable of committing the most shocking outrages. . . . I must really laugh while I recollect their figure; 2000 men in their shirts and trousers, preceded by a very ill beat-drum and a fiddler . . . who played with all his might." Still, she prophetically observed, while the militiamen looked comical on parade, even the roughest of them could "shoot from behind a bush and kill General Wolfe."

While safely and peacefully floating at anchor on board the HMS *Cruizer,* Martin plotted to regain control of the colony. Stubbornly believing that most North Carolinians still remained loyal to the Crown, he blamed a conspiracy of a few "evil, pernicious, and traitorous" radicals, including John Ashe, Cornelius Harnett, Samuel Johnston, and Robert Howe, for sedition against the government. Issuing a "Fiery Proclamation" on 8 August 1775, the ship-bound and palaceless governor once again appealed to North Carolinians to rally to the royal standard. With such a loyal force, Martin maintained, he could sweep across North and South Carolina, crushing all resistance in his path, and even "hold Virginia and Maryland" in such "awe" that they would be powerless to help. Only a few supplies, arms, and ammunition, he wrote, prevented him from launching such a sure and decisive action. By acting swiftly, Martin resolutely believed, he could crush the rebellion in the South, but only if he received immediate aid from London.

So sure was Martin of the practicability of his scheme that he dispatched Alexander Schaw, Janet's equally charming brother, to London to help persuade Lord Dartmouth. Schaw's blandishments, Martin's overweening confidence in his plan, and the numbing military disasters in Massachusetts helped convince Dartmouth and Lord George Germain, now appointed to quell the growing rebellion, to launch a large-scale offensive against the vulnerable southern colonies. In late October 1775 a large expedition comprising seven infantry regiments and two companies of artillery, convoyed by a "proper naval force," was to be sent to land in late January or early February in the Cape Fear region. There, joined by the thousands of Loyalists that Martin promised to raise, they would subdue the rebels and reestablish royal government. When both North and South Carolina had been overpowered and Loyalists firmly placed in control, so Dartmouth believed, British regular army troops then would march northward through Virginia to join the main army. Sailing from the Chesapeake, the phantom army, now joined by thousands of Loyalists, eventually would land in New York and crush George Washington. Overall command of the southern operation would be in the hands of William Howe, who had recently replaced Gage as commander-in-chief in America.

The Whigs knew all about Martin's plans. With committees of safety strongly in control, patriots watched every road, trail, and inlet that might allow a message to get through to the governor. Almost every Loyalist emissary sent to contact him had been "intercepted coming or going, and searched, detained, abused, and stript of any Papers" he might be carrying. With names of British sympathizers and Martin's plans in hand, Whigs quickly moved to counter his actions. Using threats of physical violence, public censure, and offers of amnesty and reconciliation, Whigs managed to diminish the Tory threat.

On 10 January 1776, assured that regular British troops were on the way, Martin called upon all "His Majesty's subjects" to rally to the royal standard. Issuing orders to Loyalist leaders that same day, the governor directed them to raise militias within their counties, to seize arms and ammunitions for their use, to arrest such "Rebels and Traitors" as they could find, and to march eastward to Brunswick on the coast, there to rendezvous on 15 February with other Loyalists and regular army troops. Martin's peremptory proclamation sparked a sequence of events that began a premature Tory uprising in North Carolina. It also reflected the false premises and subsequent failures of British policy in the South after 1776.

At a called and supposedly secret meeting of Loyalist leaders held near Fayetteville on 5 February, all the Highlander chieftains in the province came, but only four other leaders, three of whom were former Regulators, appeared. Wary and mindful of past abortive uprisings in their sanguine history, the Scots urged a postponement until 1 March so that troops from Britain could surely be available to support them. Remembering past wrongs and injustices at the hands of eastern politicians, old Regulator leaders, especially James Hunter, instead passionately urged immediate action. Swayed by the other leaders and not their own misgivings, the Scots reluctantly agreed, still not confident of the plan yet loyal to their clan leaders. Promised five hundred men already assembled and ready to march with perhaps five thousand more disgruntled backcountry men awaiting only a signal, Capt. Donald McLeod, an experienced British officer and Scot, left to guide them to the designated assembly area at Cross Creek.

When McLeod joined his new command "some sixty miles below Salem," he found their enthusiasm less than that described by James Hunter. For their part, the handful of former Regulators who appeared, visibly disillusioned by the few Scots who came, turned on McLeod. Backcountry North Carolinians had little confidence and even less use for McLeod as their anointed commander, seeing him saw as a foreigner and a less than respected Scotsman and British officer. With rumors circulating that Whig forces were marching against them, the backcountry men, remembering the Alamance event, melted away. In the end, McLeod, lost, stranded, and friendless in a strange land, could not persuade a single person to guide him to Cross Creek. The confused and ineffective Loyalist meeting near Salem presaged events to come.

More a threat to themselves than to the patriot cause, a jumbled kaleidoscope of groups, "loyalists all," rendezvoused at Cross Creek on 15 February 1776. Under the command of Donald MacDonald, a British lieutenant colonel who had seen action at Bunker (Breed's) Hill and who was now appointed by Martin as brigadier general of the militia, the assemblage included over 130 former Regulators under Dr. John Pyle, five hundred Highlanders, and a few "Country born" Loyalists under three leaders, Allen McDonald, Alexander McLeod, and James Cotton. Some five hundred additional Highlanders recruited by Thomas Rutherford and a few curious "volunteers" who randomly came and went rounded out the group. Inexperienced, lacking almost any training, and with only half even having weapons and powder, the ragtag Loyalist army prepared to march to the sea to rally with Martin and the promised British regulars.

News of the Tory uprising reached Wilmington on 9 February, and as rumors spread, Cape Fear militias eagerly swarmed to meet the threat. James Moore, one of a host of new colonels created by revolutionary committees, called out his new and untried North Carolina Continentals. William Purviance also sent out a dozen Paul Reveres to alert his New Hanover County militia to the threat. Two companies of minutemen and eighty additional volunteers under John Ashe, not wanting to be left out of the action, rushed to join Moore at Wilmington. Minutemen from Duplin, Onslow, and Brunswick counties converged on Wilmington, convinced that something exciting surely must happen. With news that the HMS *Cruizer* had slipped away to attack the town, citizens and militiamen hastily erected breastworks and fortified areas around the wharves and main streets. By land and sea, North Carolinians prepared for their own Lexington and Concord. What happened next resembled a hesitant Highland fling between two opposing forces, both stumbling about in the pine-barren low country, both reluctant to fight yet knowing that they somehow must.

Moore marched northward along the Cape Fear River, arriving seven miles south of Cross Creek on 15 February. Soon joined by other militias with five small artillery pieces, Moore had by 19 February over 1,100 men eagerly spoiling for a fight, with more than 800 under Caswell hurrying from New Bern to join him. Knowing that Caswell soon would arrive to reinforce Moore, MacDonald attempted to bluff the North Carolina Continentals by brashly asking Moore to surrender by noon on 20 February and to "repair to the royal standard." Moore courteously refused, and MacDonald reluctantly prepared for battle the next day.

Faced with the certainty of combat and the vagueness of their cause and compatriots, many of the westerners left the Loyalist camp that night. When he awoke the next day, MacDonald found that two companies of Anson County militia had departed, taking their weapons with them. Calling the remaining Loyalists into formation, MacDonald, almost seventy years old but nonetheless an inspiring figure, delivered a fiery address condemning the deserters and called upon others who had doubts about supporting the king to lay down their arms and be gone. In the midst of daunting Highlander cheers, more than twenty additional Anson volunteers nonetheless stepped forward, surrendered their weapons, and left camp. That night, assured that he had his remaining men's loyalty, MacDonald crossed the Cape Fear at Campbell and, adroitly avoiding an engagement with Moore, marched toward the coast to meet with phantom regular British army troops that he thought surely must be at hand.

Instantly realizing MacDonald's intention, Moore hastily broke camp on 21 February and, in furious pursuit, set off to intercept the Tories before they reached the sea. Knowing that he had little time, Moore sent orders to Caswell, who was still on the march, diverting him to "obstruct, harass, and distress" the Tories along their route. Both Caswell and Ashe were ordered to take possession of a key bridge southwest of the Black River on Moore's Creek, a turbulent stream that flowed across MacDonald's line of march and one that he must cross.

When MacDonald arrived at Moore's Creek Bridge on 26 February he found Caswell and Lillington with over 1,100 men on the west side of the stream with the bridge at their back. At a council of war that night, MacDonald, exhausted and ill with a fever, yet still wanting to spare as many lives as possible, counseled against an attack. The Highlanders, confused and embarrassed by their advance from Cross Creek and spoiling for a fight, voted instead to risk everything in a heroic frontal assault. MacDonald first demurred, then agreed with his Highlanders. After midnight, they formed a battle line and charged the patriot camp. Anticipating the Highlander attack, Caswell had left his tents erect with campfires burning nearby while he retreated safely across the bridge, ripping up the planking as he went. When the Tories swept into Caswell's camp, they found it empty and deserted.

Emboldened by their charge and convinced the patriots would not fight, the Highlanders next examined the bridge over Moore's Creek, the quickest path to Caswell's men. A Loyalist patrol led by Alexander McLean found that more than half the flooring had been ripped up, exposing two large sleeper or support logs beneath them. Both had been smeared with wax and soft soap on Caswell's orders, an open challenge for the Highlanders to attack. Forming a company of Highlanders armed only with broadswords, McLean and John Campbell led a headlong dash across the bridge. With the first Highlander yells as a signal, the patriots, having carefully laid their cannon to cover the bridge, opened up on the charging Scots. Two companies of Caswell's militia, his best marksmen among them, raked the bridge with a deadly fusillade to engulf the screaming Highlanders. McLean and Campbell, both fatally wounded, somehow made it across the bridge before dying in a final volley in front of the Whig positions. Almost the entire company of Scots were killed, wounded, or drowned as they fell into the surging creek. The ten or so who survived the deadly bridge died before they reached Caswell's trenches. Moore later estimated the Tory dead and wounded at seventy. The patriots suffered one man dead from his wounds and another slightly injured by covering fire from Tories on the west bank.

The murderous charge by the Highlanders effectively ended the battle at Moore's Creek Bridge and any Loyalist uprising in North Carolina. When patriot musket and cannon fire first rang out, many of the remaining Loyalists from the western counties, realizing the price that now would be exacted for their part in the uprising would be in their blood, deserted the field. The flight soon became wild and disorderly, with men and officers racing to the supply wagons for safety and refuge. Panic stricken and fearful, Loyalists cut horses from their harnesses and, both mounted and on foot, fled into the woods for safety.

By 10 March 1776, Caswell, with the aid of Moore's troops, had rounded up and paroled over 850 militiamen suspected of being Tories. Abandoned by his troops and too ill to move, MacDonald was captured in his tent. More than forty other Tory leaders were jailed in Halifax. Eventually, more than one hundred would be tried before a special committee of safety appointed by the Fourth Provincial Congress "to enquire into the conduct of insurgents and suspected persons." Twenty-six—including MacDonald; his second-in-command, Allen MacDonald; and Farquard Campbell, a "Spy and Confidential Emissary of Governor Martin"—were sent under guard to Philadelphia to be given over to authorities of the Continental Congress. Twenty-seven others, including the four notorious Field brothers, leaders of the backcountry Loyalists, were sent to Maryland and Virginia.

The ferocity of the battle at Moore's Creek and the surprisingly lenient treatment of Tories afterward did much to dampen future uprisings against the Revolutionary government in North Carolina. Surprisingly, harsher penalties, imprisonment and death, were not meted out by North Carolina's Fourth Provincial Congress, which was especially remarkable during wartime, when treason meant survival or death. Admittedly, relocation discomfited individuals and families, but the colony's Provincial Congress, perhaps remembering the grim hangings of Regulators, took pains to see that the convicted insurgents received good treatment, even in exile. Moreover, many of the potential Tories in the western counties, mostly former Regulators, found good reasons after the battle at Moore's Creek Bridge to disassociate themselves from Martin and his Loyalist supporters. To backcountry North Carolinians, the fanaticism of the Highlanders contrasted sharply with the tolerance of the Whigs. In conjunction with that, North Carolinians implicitly realized that most of the Tories and their leaders, from Martin to the MacDonalds, did not come from the province or adjacent colonies and, in a significant way, were strangers in a land that valued close community and family ties. Additionally, the determination of the militias and Continentals under Caswell, Moore, and Lillington, and their willingness to stand and die for a belief as abstract as self-government, impressed less-principled North Carolinians in the western counties. While Martin's and the Loyalists' promises of muskets, lead, powder, uniforms, and the support of the British army and navy failed to materialize, the Whig militias at Moore's Creek appeared well supported, motivated, supplied, and coordinated. The battle at Moore's Creek Bridge, the Concord of North Carolina and the South, effectively ended any immediate British invasion or future Tory uprising and secured control of the Fourth Provincial Congress over the colony. Still, it did not unite North Carolinians in support of the patriot cause. In the long years of fighting that lay ahead, North Carolina, as a new state, only reluctantly supported the forces of independence.

ADDITIONAL READINGS

Alden, John Richard. *The South in the Revolution, 1763–1789.* Baton Rouge: Louisiana State University Press, 1957.

Connor, Robert Digges Wimberly. *Revolutionary Leaders of North Carolina.* Spartanburg: Reprint Co., 1971.

Davidson, Philip G. "Sons of Liberty and Stamp Men." *North Carolina Historical Review* 9 (January 1932): 38–56.

Frech, Laura Page. "Wilmington Committee of Public Safety and the Loyalist Rising of February, 1776." *North Carolina Historical Review* 41 (January 1964): 21–33.

Kerber, Linda K. *Women of the Republic: Intellect and Ideology in Revolutionary America.* Chapel Hill: University of North Carolina Press, 1980.

McEachern, Leora H., and Isabel M. Williams, eds. *Wilmington–New Hanover Safety Committee Minutes, 1774–1776.* Wilmington: Wilmington–New Hanover County American Revolution Bicentennial Committee, 1974.

Morgan, David Taft. "Cornelius Harnett: Revolutionary Leader and Delegate to the Continental Congress." *North Carolina Historical Review* 49 (July 1972): 229–41.

Moss, Bobby G. *Roster of the Loyalists at the Battle of Moores Creek Bridge.* Spartanburg: Scotia-Hibernia Press, 1992.

———. *Roster of the Patriots at the Battle of Moore's Creek Bridge.* Spartanburg: Scotia-Hibernia Press, 1992.

Rankin, Hugh F. "Moore's Creek Bridge Campaign, 1776." *North Carolina Historical Review* 39 (January 1953): 23–60.

Sheridan, Richard B. "West Indian Antecedents of Josiah Martin, Last Royal Governor of North Carolina." *North Carolina Historical Review* 54 (July 1977): 254–70.

Stumpf, Vernon O. *Josiah Martin: The Last Royal Governor of North Carolina.* Durham: Carolina Academic Press for Kellenberger Foundation, 1986.

Taylor, H. Braughn. "Foreign Attachment Law and the Coming of the Revolution in North Carolina." *North Carolina Historical Review* 52 (January 1975): 20–36.

Tryon, William. *Correspondence of William Tryon and Other Selected Papers.* 2 vols. Edited by William S. Powell. Raleigh: Department of Archives and History, 1980–81.

Watson, Alan D., Dennis R. Lawson, and Donald R. Lennon. *Harnett, Hooper and Howe: Revolutionary Leaders of the Lower Cape Fear.* Wilmington: L. T. Moore Memorial Commission and Lower Cape Fear Historical Society, 1979.

Cautious Revolutionaries

North Carolina in the American Revolution, 1776–1780

The Whig victory over the Loyalists at the Battle of Moore's Creek in late February 1776 and the subsequent waning of support for the king meant that for the next four years rebels would control the government of the new state. When Cornwallis, Henry Clinton, and Adm. Peter Parker belatedly landed off the coast near Wilmington in May, they found few to greet them except Josiah Martin and a few diehard Loyalists. Sweeping up Martin and his entourage, the British flotilla sailed southward toward Charleston. There they discovered the almost impregnable palmetto log palisades of the city's defenses too much for their cannon, and, defeated and disappointed once more, the British abandoned the South to the Whigs. It would be four years before they returned.

Freed from the threat of an internal Loyalist uprising and an external British invasion, the new state government set about doing what it did best, dividing into factions and quarreling. The only unanimity came in North Carolina's early decision to separate itself entirely from England. Three months before the colonies officially declared their independence, North Carolina resolved at Halifax to join the others in Congress in declaring their independence from England and in forming a new nation but still "reserving to this Colony the sole and exclusive right of forming a Constitution and laws for this Colony." William Hooper, Joseph Hewes, and John Penn eventually signed the 4 July declaration for North Carolina. Yet independence brought with it a host of problems.

On 14 April 1776, two days after the Halifax Resolves, the Fourth Provincial Congress, North Carolina's only functioning government, set about trying to write a "temporary Civil Constitution" to restore order after the collapse of royal government. The committee charged to write the new constitution dissolved in disarray by the first of May with only a heady outline of ideas but with few concrete proposals. The entire Provincial Congress went home a few days later. For the next five months an experimental body called the council of safety, really a cabal of mostly Cape Fear radicals led by Cornelius Harnett, ruled the state. Authoritarian and despotic in nature, the council governed through six committees of safety, arbitrary bodies with Whiggish views spread throughout the state that censored those who opposed them and raised money to train militias and men to enforce their rule. An interim organization with few pretensions to rule the state permanently, the council called for elections in the fall of 1776. The October campaign for delegates to be elected to the Fifth Provincial Congress, the group that would write a new, permanent constitution for the state, exposed not only divisions among the Whigs, those who had opposed royal government and voted for independence, but also the fragility of sentiment for the patriotic cause.

The fall election in 1776 in North Carolina chartered the evolution of Whiggery, the political theory of opposition to the king and to any central, "tyrannical" government within the state. Led by Samuel Johnston, William Hooper, and James Iredell, names made famous by their Revolutionary zeal, the so-called conservative Whigs, while they wanted independence from England, feared the movement toward popular democracy. They simply wanted the king replaced with a strong executive in America, an independent judiciary appointed and not elected, and they wanted guaranteed protection of their property rights. Johnston feared the weight and meanness of numbers, the masses of people involved in political processes, and wanted qualifications, usually in the form of property and personalty, for voting and holding office. Anticipating the movement of the Revolution toward mobocracy, the conservatives foreshadowed the Federalism that wanted checks and balances upon the power of the people.

Led by Willie Jones, Griffith Rutherford, and Thomas Person, names less noted but equally significant in North Carolina political history, the radical Whigs wanted to follow the natural evolution of Whiggery, from the overthrow of the king to independence and ultimately to a simple democracy. In their judgment, neither North Carolina nor the United States needed a strong executive, whether a king or prime minister, or appointed and arbitrary court judges or placemen. Instead, the radicals favored a strong legislature, especially in the lower house, frequent elections, no ties to any established church or religion, a free press, and religious freedom for everyone. While the radicals believed in broadening the electorate and loosening property qualifications for voting and holding office, they still wanted yeoman farmers to have some small investment in government, either in land or personal property. Their view of government presaged Thomas Jefferson's later Anti-Federalist and more republican ideas.

The elections of 1776, held in relative calm and with independence newly proclaimed, stirred many passions but little overall interest among the state's citizens. Disgusted that North Carolinians did not defer to his class, experience, or position in society, Samuel Johnston, like a great many conservatives, derided the electorate that did not send him to Halifax to draft a new constitution. Wrapping his sarcasm in Latin, he railed that "gentlemen everywhere" were "borne down per ignoble vulgus—by a set of men without reading, experience, or principles to govern them."

When the congress met in Halifax on 12 November 1776, less than one-half of the 169 delegates even came. Slowly, others dribbled in the next few days until 149 finally arrived, yet no more than 100 attended any one session. Almost evenly divided between radicals and conservatives, the delegates sat down to write a new constitution. From the beginning, the radicals from the backcountry, chiefly the old Regulator strongholds of Orange and Mecklenburg counties, wanted a bill of rights added to any new constitution to protect them from the possible new tyranny of the eastern Whigs. By 18 December, within five short weeks, the Halifax convention had agreed upon a new constitution and a bill of rights. By broadly construing their empowerment and without submitting the new documents to the people for approval in a general election or calling for revisions by counties or committees, the delegates adjourned. The new state of North Carolina had its de facto constitution. It would not be revised until 1835, nor would it be replaced until after the Civil War.

North Carolina's Revolutionary constitution reflected the ascendancy of radical Whig-gery, of popular democracy, and of a movement away from the more conservative ideas of men such as William Hooper and Samuel Johnston, the initial leaders of the rebellion against England. Pieced together primarily from earlier state constitutions of Virginia and Maryland, the 1776 document used the language of other bodies of laws to express North Carolina's abhorrence of a strong central government, whether provincial or national, and its reluctant Revolutionary radicalism. The new constitution significantly shifted power away from the executive, the governor, and to the legislature, especially the lower house. So emasculated did the chief executive's office become that William Hooper complained that the only duty retained by the governor was "to sign a receipt for his own salary." North Carolina would continue its policy of rendering its governors harmless but politically in-fluential for the next two centuries. Much of the credit for its writing should be given to Richard Caswell, chairman of the committee that drafted the new constitution, and to Thomas Jones of Edenton, both of whom represented the shift away from more conserva-tive and to increasingly popular forms of democracy. Still fuming over his defeat and that of the conservatives in general, Samuel Johnston called the new document "Mr. Jones' Constitution."

Instead of anachronistically judging the Revolutionary constitution by twenty-first-century standards that usually concentrate on racism, sexism, and a broader concept of suffrage, a fuller and more meaningful understanding might be had by looking at the poli-tical theories and turmoil surrounding the first year of freedom for the new state. The Revolution had few historical precedents. North Carolina and its sister states sought their freedom from England, the first colonies to do so in modern history. Failure seemed cer-tain, success dubious and ill defined. Assuredly, the North Carolina constitution of 1776 should be judged and appreciated as more than an undemocratic product of an antedilu-vian and obsolete political philosophy of eighteenth-century Whiggery. Yet such a glib determination misses the substance and philosophy of an instrument that so many North Carolinians not only cherished but also gave their fortunes and lives to defend.

First, the constitution of 1776 was but the necessary first step in a historical transition to a larger and more meaningful democracy. In twenty-five articles, North Carolina spelled out a bill of rights that became the hallmark of its Revolutionary commitment. It later would become the core of the first ten amendments, an integral part of a new national con-stitution passed in 1787. Early in the Revolution, North Carolina, agreeing with Virginia and Maryland about the establishment of individual political rights, guaranteed its people free and open elections, the supremacy of civil over military authority, the right to bear arms, and the right of assembly, frequent elections, trial by jury, immunity from "cruel and unusual punishment" and excessive bail, as well as freedom of the press and freedom of conscience and religion. Such rights became not only the eventual guarantors of liberty but also the basis for an ever-broadening concept of democracy.

Although the governor had little power, the legislature, that body most representative of the general will of the people, in keeping with the recent experience with the British Crown, had much. North Carolinians keenly remembered their battles with royal gover-nors over prerogative and taxation, fundamental rights they thought guaranteed in initial charters or constitutions. Chosen annually, members of the general assembly, the lower

*Engraving of a North Carolina
Revolutionary War soldier.*
North Carolina Department of
Archives and History, Raleigh.

House of Commons and the Senate, could elect the governor, council of state, attorney general, and other executive officers. Each county could select one senator and two assemblymen to the lower house. In a quaint yet politically important nod to the east, six borough towns were allowed an additional representative in the House of Commons. To be eligible for the Senate, a North Carolinian must be a resident of a county and have a freehold of three hundred acres. For election to the lower house, only residence in the county for one month and the state for one year, and a freehold of fifty acres, was needed. In terms of the suffrage, all freemen, whether white or black, could vote if they met the constitution's qualifications. The judiciary was comprised of "Judges of the Supreme Courts of Law and Equity, . . . of Admiralty, and Attorney General," all appointed by the general assembly. Even local justices of the peace were appointed by the county representatives in the general assembly and were afterward commissioned by the governor to hold office during "good behavior." Clearly, Revolutionary ideologues wanted to give the greatest power to the branch of government closest to and most representative of the people, the legislature.

Not surprisingly, Richard Caswell, the chief architect behind the new constitution, became the state's first governor under it. Amidst great fanfare, Caswell took the oath of office on 10 January 1777. Far from the decisive battlefields of Massachusetts, New York, and Pennsylvania, the new state government seemed content to do as little as possible in the war against England, almost as if, after the Battle of Moore's Creek Bridge, it took its independence for granted. Indeed, the new state had every appearance of conducting the business of war, mostly passing laws to encourage "the militia and Volunteers" to enlist to fight the Cherokees in Griffith Rutherford's 1776 campaign and to enroll in the ten regiments asked for by the Continental Congress, but with little urgency. In the entire conduct of the war, North Carolina sent almost 7,800 soldiers to fight in the Continental army, the smallest per capita contribution of any state. For example, Massachusetts, with relatively the same population as North Carolina, sent 97,000 men to the Continental army, and Virginia, with a larger population, sent more than 98,000 to fight against the British. Nor did North Carolina fare better in enrolling militiamen on state pay. Only 10,200 signed on to fight to preserve its independence, one of the smallest aggregates of any state. Still, the "weight of numbers" that eventually turned the tide in North Carolina and the South came not from those enrolled in the Continental army or on state payrolls but from the partisan bands of minutemen who gathered in meadows, fields, and streams to defeat the threat of Banastre "the Bully" Tarleton and Cornwallis coming not from the North but the South.

On 12 May 1780, Charleston surrendered to the British. Thought impregnable after Sir Henry Clinton's defeat at Fort Moultrie four years earlier, Charleston fell, changing the complexion of the war in the South and sending convulsions through Whig leaders throughout the region. In the largest American military disaster of the war, Benjamin Lincoln, in charge of the southern army at Charleston, surrendered more than 5,300 men, including North Carolina's Continental brigades commanded by Jethro Sumner and James Hogan and 600 state militiamen who could not slip away in time. The new nation's southern army had ceased to exist, and, from Georgia to Virginia, the South lay open to British arms and conquest. In Charleston, an exultant Josiah Martin, convinced that he was right all along about the loyalty of the backcountry to the king, eagerly awaited his vindication. It never came.

Confident that the tide of war had turned, Clinton sailed back to New York, leaving Lord Charles Cornwallis in command in Charleston. To Cornwallis he gave two orders: complete the conquest of South Carolina and Georgia, and, with his communication and supply lines secured by a string of forts and outposts, conquer North Carolina and Virginia. Above all, Clinton warned Cornwallis, do not be adventurous and stray far from your southern strongholds. The British could win the war in the South. With Savannah and Charleston fortified and protected, Cornwallis proceeded to set up outposts near Augusta, the gateway to the frontier, in Ninety-Six, so named because of the miles the British counted to get to it, the communications and storehouse center for the region, and Camden, strategically located between the two Carolinas and a jumping-off place for the campaign into North Carolina. With hundreds of Loyalists swarming to the king's standard and with a string of victories in the last six months, Cornwallis eagerly awaited his chance.

On 25 July 1780 Horatio Gates, still wreathed in the glory of his victory at Saratoga, took over command of the Maryland Division, really the remnant of the Continental army in the South, from its interim leader, Baron de Kalb. Thomas Sumter of South Carolina, now dubbed "the Gamecock" for his tenacity and stubbornness in opposing the British, dashed off a note to Gates that proved not only speculative but also deadly. In estimating British strength in the Carolinas, he listed only seven hundred troops in "Camden and its Vicinity." Eager for action and encouraged by Sumter's figures, Gates immediately set his army into motion on a grim march into South Carolina without waiting for supplies, provisions, or militia units to catch up.

Located 120 miles northwest of Charleston, the town of Camden occupied a key place in the chain of strongpoints that Lord Cornwallis had established in the Carolinas and Georgia. First it was called Fredericksburg and then Pine Tree Hill, after the gentle plateaus and sandy soil that drained the area; the settlers changed the name to honor Lord Camden, a passionate defender of American rights in the Stamp Act crisis. When the Declaratory Act giving Parliament the right to tax the colonies "in all cases whatsoever" passed the House of Lords after the repeal of the Stamp Act by a vote of 125 to 5, one of the four dissidents who supported the young Camden was Earl Cornwallis, one of the conquerors of Charleston and now occupier of the town of Camden.

Francis Lord Rawdon commanded the British garrison at Camden under Cornwallis's direction. Made up mostly of Irishmen from the northern American colonies, Rawdon's Volunteers of Ireland, often called the "Green Coats," had a reputation for cruelty and ruthlessness that matched that of Tarleton; Tarleton's Legion, composed of Loyalist and British troops, flaunted many of the conventions of eighteenth-century warfare, especially those of rendering quarter or mercy to wounded and captured Whig militiamen. Rawdon soon erected stockades that contained scores of Carolinians who refused to serve in Tory units and who hated his northern militia units. In a clear message to his troops and to the local inhabitants, Rawdon offered "ten guineas for the head of any deserter belonging to the Volunteers of Ireland and five guineas only" if brought in alive. Two things worried the young lord, the mosquitoes that swarmed over his redcoats, giving them malaria and episodic fevers, and an even greater affliction farther to the north, a gamecock named Thomas Sumter.

On 1 August, "the Gamecock" struck again, this time at Rocky Mount, a critical juncture on the Catawba River where it changed into the Wateree just twenty-six miles north of Camden. Although driven off by the New York Volunteers, a Loyalist unit, Sumter's raid nevertheless alarmed Rawdon. Five days later Sumter stormed an enemy post at Hanging Rock, just twenty-two miles from Camden. In a bitter three-hour battle that began at daybreak, the rebels killed, wounded, and captured almost three hundred Loyalists. Writing to Gates, Sumter, with his usual disdain, reported that he suffered only "Twenty Kild, forty wounded, Ten Missing." It all seemed too easy.

As he rapidly descended upon Camden, Horatio Gates half expected the British to flee to the safety of Charleston rather than fight his growing and increasingly confident army on its southward march. As Gates crossed the Pee Dee River, a group of over one hundred well-trained, battle-hardened Virginia veterans under Charles Porterfield fell in with his Continentals, with Armand's Legion, and with scores of straggling militiamen, mostly from North Carolina and Virginia, who brought up the rear. As he approached Camden and an increasingly certain battle, a perplexed Gates wondered what had happened to the most crucial part of his army, the North Carolinians under Richard Caswell. He had reason to worry.

Setting out before Gates, Caswell and more than 1,500 North Carolinians had arrived at Big and Little Lynch's creeks a few miles north of Camden, where they suddenly found themselves facing Rawdon's troops. Excited at the prospect of assaulting and defeating the hated British Loyalists by himself, Caswell, the hero of the battle at Moore's Creek Bridge, hurriedly sent a dispatch rider to Gates. An infuriated Gates read Caswell's egoistic note. "I have received information that the enemy intend attacking us with their whole force in a very short time . . . if [he] does, we will endeavor to behave in a becoming manner." Not only had the North Carolinians failed to furnish any information or coordination on their whereabouts, under the impudent Caswell they insisted on acting as if they were a completely separate army and entity. Camden would be no Moore's Creek Bridge. Sensing disaster, Gates ordered the Maryland Division to "march immediately" to Caswell's camp.

Short of provisions and exhausted by lack of sleep from almost continuous forced marches and the suffocating August heat, Gates's men stumbled into Caswell's bivouac near Lynch's creeks. By noon on 7 August, the last Continentals had linked up with the North Carolinians in front of Rawdon's lines. Gates had at his command perhaps three thousand men, fewer than one thousand veteran Continentals from the Maryland and Delaware brigades, along with Armand's Legion. The remaining troops consisted mostly of untested militia from North Carolina. Worlds apart in terms of their training, background, leadership, and commitment to the Whig cause, the two groups had even less in common when they entered into battle.

Self-confident to the point of pretension, Richard Caswell had little use for Gates and his professional Continentals. Active in North Carolina politics for more than a quarter century, he had held every important political office from Speaker of the Assembly under the Crown to governor of the new state. In 1771 he commanded a militia unit against the Regulators at Alamance and in 1775 against the Tories at Moore's Creek Bridge, never tasting defeat or even knowing futility. A major general in charge of the state's militia, Caswell had with him at Camden the last significant military force left to defend North Carolina. At Charleston, three Continental regiments from the state and an additional six hundred militia had surrendered to Cornwallis. Although many North Carolinians served in South Carolina and in Virginia Continental lines and with guerrilla bands like Thomas Sumter's, Caswell's men represented the state's best, last line of defense.

Opposing Gates and Caswell, Cornwallis had assembled 2,239 men, including six batteries of Royal Artillery and two of the finest regiments in the British army, the Twenty-third Foot, or Royal Welsh Fusiliers, Cornwallis's own regiment, and the Thirty-third Foot, or Webster's Own, a first-line unit from Yorkshire that had saved the day at bloody Monmouth to the north. Undefeated and undaunted, the Royal Welsh Fusiliers marched into Camden to the somber cadence of their own proud military history, to their bloody victories in Europe at "Boyne, Blenheim, Minden." They intended to add Camden to their battle flag and to their measured victory march.

In one of history's frequent ironies, North Carolinians at Camden under Caswell's command fought other North Carolinians from the Seventy-first British Loyalists, called Fraser's Highlanders, and those in John Hamilton's Tory regiment. The bloodletting typified the civil war that engulfed the southern colonies after the fall of Charleston. On 15 August, Gates ordered a night assault to surprise the British. Between 10 P.M. and 2 A.M. the next morning, the American army, led by Armand's Legion, moved straight toward Rawdon at Lynch's creek. In the hot and sultry mist that overlay the creeks and swamps of that part of South Carolina, the two armies, like blind moles, burrowed slowly into each other.

Just after 2 A.M., forty of Tarleton's Legion out on patrol blundered headlong into Armand's lead horsemen. With shouts of "Huzza," Tarleton's men, with their usual élan, dashed forward only to be caught in a withering crossfire by Porterfield's Virginians on

British trooper of Tarleton's Legion during the Revolutionary War in the South.
North Carolina Department of Archives and History, Raleigh.

their right flank. Falling back under the pelting musket fire of the Virginians, the legionnaires found safety under the guns of an advancing British light infantry unit. For several minutes the Royal Welsh Fusiliers traded volleys with the Virginians and Caswell's militia, both units stubbornly refusing to give ground until Porterfield, fatally wounded with a shattered and bleeding leg, commanded them to retire. Only thirty minutes had elapsed.

At dawn on the sixteenth, the two armies, now aware of each other's positions, made ready for battle. In textbook fashion, Gates lined up his Americans with the weakest units, the North Carolina and Virginia militias, on his left, and with the strongest, the Second Maryland and Delaware Continentals under Baron de Kalb, on his right. Gates stationed himself behind the center of the line with Smallwood's First Maryland Brigade in reserve. Opposite them, Cornwallis did the same, aligning his fusiliers and Thirty-third Foot opposite the Carolinians and Virginians with the Volunteers of Ireland, infantry from Tarleton's Legion, and the Royal North Carolina Tory Regiment on his left. In reserve he kept three hundred unreliable Tory militia and Tarleton's restless but ruthless cavalry. The battle hinged upon the weakest and not the strongest units in each army. The loser would give way first.

Eager to press the issue and sensing timidity in the Americans, Cornwallis ordered Webster to send the fusiliers and his Thirty-third Foot forward. With a scarlet front more than three hundred yards wide, the British infantry, three to four rows deep, bayonets fixed and drums steadily beating a quick march, tramped relentlessly toward the Virginians and North Carolinians. The sight of hundreds of British redcoats with glistening bayonets stepping machinelike toward them unnerved the Americans as it had Europe's finest armies for centuries. Before them, the militiamen, untrained and expecting an easy victory, turned and ran. In less than fifteen minutes, 1,900 of Gates's men fled the field, most without firing a shot. One North Carolina regiment under Griffith Rutherford, the hero of the campaign against the Cherokee Indians, rallied near the artillery at the center of the line before Rutherford fell wounded. Seeing the oncoming Thirty-third Foot and failing to keep his militia lines intact around him, a North Carolina militia captain called it quits for the day, yelling, "I'll be damned if I'm here to be shot down," as he ran for his life. He would live to fight another day for a cause much closer to home.

The Continentals stood fast, proving "obstinate and unrelenting" in Cornwallis's words. At the center of the fiercest fighting stood Baron de Kalb, resplendent in his flashing gold epaulets and iron helmet and rallying his Continentals against the feared British bayonets. Fifty-nine years old, shot many times, bleeding and bandaged, the old warrior finally collapsed. As full daylight swept over the battlefield, the shooting suddenly stopped.

One hundred and sixty-two Continentals and 64 British soldiers lay dead; more than 300 Americans and 245 British lay wounded. Pursued by a vengeful Tarleton's Legion, hundreds more Americans fled toward Charlotte and safety in North Carolina. Their leaders, Gates and Caswell, led the headlong dash toward the rear. As they stripped the American dead of valuables and boots, Loyalists, awed by de Kalb's glittering uniform and his reputation, dragged the mortally wounded old lion to his feet, propping him over a wagon wheel while they twisted his coat, pants, and boots from his body. Bleeding from eight bayonet and saber wounds as well as three bullets to his chest, the unwrapped and unsheathed de Kalb died an agonizingly slow death. With him, the American army of the South also breathed its last.

After Camden, Cornwallis turned confidently to one of his closest advisers, Josiah Martin, North Carolina's last royal governor, as he prepared to consolidate his gains and to invade the state. A refugee at Charleston, Martin had not changed his bewitching story of southern loyalty since he left Wilmington. To Cornwallis, Martin had become like Circe, the enchantress from Homer's *Odyssey,* spinning irresistible stories of massive Tory uprisings as soon as the victorious British swept into North Carolina. Partially convinced by the conduct of the Seventy-first Loyalist Regiment, which was filled with North Carolinians, and by Hamilton's Tory Regiment, both of whom had fought well at Camden, and also seduced by his own ambition, Cornwallis, with Martin as his siren, prepared for his long-awaited offensive to capture the South for the British. Success awaited him in North Carolina. Or so he thought.

With the disintegration of the last American army in the South, Cornwallis found his path obstructed not by Continentals or militia but by assorted groups of wraiths, banshees, and gamecocks who became the stuff of legend, folklore, and place-names. Instead of professionals like Gates and de Kalb, men such as Francis "the Swamp Fox" Marion, Thomas "the Gamecock" Sumter, Isaac Shelby, John Sevier, William Campbell, William Davie, William Davidson, Andrew Pickens, and Joseph and Charles McDowell now appeared and disappeared to fight the British. Just as the Tories admired de Kalb for his shimmering uniform, dedication, and professionalism, so did Francis Marion's own men praise him when they affectionately called him "an ugly, cross, knock-kneed, hook-nosed son-of-a-bitch" whom they would follow to the death. Hardened by the violence of Indian wars, of frontier life, and of failed Regulator movements, North and South Carolinians who never joined a Continental line or a state militia regiment nonetheless rushed from their Piedmont and mountain homesteads to fight the British. More than historical curiosity demands an answer for their actions. Why did they do it?

First, the "Backwater Men," or barbarians, as Patrick Ferguson called them, had little loyalty to a Whig cause that had few traditions and little history to recommend it. They did not fight the British because of patriotism to a new nation they hardly knew or of an allegiance to an abstract cause such as liberty or independence. Seeing men like Richard Caswell, Cornelius Harnett, and Robert Howe, all hated by the Regulators and mountaineers, emerge as leaders of the new state and nation not at all encouraged upcountry Carolinians to flock to the new American standard. Moreover, the backcountry men suspected the easterners of harboring tyrannical views not dissimilar to those of the British themselves. Like Thomas Sumter, many preferred to sit out the war on their homesteads and farms, fence-riders for years, waiting for one side to emerge as the stronger and more capable of protecting their life and property or to reveal itself as the more tyrannical and despotic.

The glories, trappings, titles, and pretensions of British citizenship and loyalty correspondingly had little value for most backcountry men. Unlike many recent immigrants, such as the Highland Scots, they had somehow become more American than British over the course of time. In this way, British Loyalists and supporters—such as Christian Huck, a New York Loyalist; Patrick Ferguson, well born and of Scottish gentry; Banastre Tarleton, son of a Liverpool mayor; George Hanger, a lover of fine things such as satin coats and London society; and, of course, English aristocrats such as Rawdon and Cornwallis—all struck a majority of backcountry men as somehow being foreign—that is, unlike them in ways that made a difference. They were not country born and bred. While most of the Whig leaders came from their own culture and region, Loyalists and Tories somehow seemed more distant and removed. Certainly news of Tarleton's slaughter of Buford's Virginians at the ensuing Battle of Waxhaws and of other atrocities committed by Loyalists and "men clothed in GREEN" had spread throughout the Carolinians that spring and summer, bringing with it ill-will and a smoldering desire for revenge. While Continental and militia officers generally gave worthless script and paper currency for supplies and confiscated goods, British requisitioners frequently gave nothing yet also asked for complete loyalty in return. Although the British managed to recruit some Loyalists from the backcountry, their commitment to the king's standard seemed less sanguine and spirited than Martin and Cornwallis had hoped.

Perhaps Lord Rawdon best captured the astonishment of the British at the phantom armies that now sprang up to oppose them. "A numerous army," he wrote Cornwallis, "now appeared on the Frontier drawn from Nolachuki and other Settlements beyond the mountains whose very names had been unknown to us." From the Watauga and Holston valleys and from the hills of northern Georgia and South Carolina, from the mountains of Virginia and North Carolina, hundreds of men who had never heard of Thomas Paine's *Common Sense* or of Thomas Jefferson's Declaration of Independence and who cared little about the fall of Charleston and its planter elite came together in great pastures such as Quaker Meadows to fight the British. In part, their wrath seemed almost biblical, a re-enactment of Gideon's people who rose up to smite their oppressors. As they pushed westward and northward, the British found themselves consumed by the fires of civil millennialism and of virulent vengeance in the southern backcountry.

Three weeks after the debacle at Camden, a confident Cornwallis, ignoring Clinton's advice not to be drawn into the interior away from his supply bases, launched his invasion of North Carolina. Confident of victory and anticipating, as Martin had promised, thousands of sympathizers who would flock to his standards, he dared to split his forces. While Cornwallis marched with his elite British regulars straight toward Charlotte and Hillsborough, he sent Patrick Ferguson with 1,200 Tories to protect his western flank from the backcountry men. What happened next foretold the course of the war in the South.

Scorning rumors of yet another "disorganized rabble" like that at Camden coming together to oppose him, the imperious Ferguson sent a paroled prisoner northward across the Blue Ridge with a threatening message. If any backcountry man did not swear allegiance to the Crown or dared oppose him, he would "come over the mountains and put him to death and burn the whole country" before him. After Waxhaws and Camden, few doubted the words of the square-faced Scot. Yet Ferguson's ultimatum had an unintended consequence. Instead of succumbing to fear, awe, and intimidation, great numbers of backcountry men from the Carolinas, Virginia, and Georgia responded by embracing the opportunity to fight the devil himself. If Ferguson's Loyalists wanted a brawl, frontiersmen, remembering how they had fought the Indians in savage encounters, would not wait for them to come into their settlements and burn their farms. Instead, they would take the fight to them over the mountains.

By late September, small groups of Overmountain Men began moving south to meet Ferguson. Along the way, entire congregations as well as lone woodsmen joined them. Strangely enough, this ad hoc army had no commander, only an officer of the day, William Campbell, a six-foot-six Virginian who coordinated movements and supplies. A group of militia officers collectively helped Campbell, but not a single Continental officer joined the group. Indeed, the novelty as well as the riddle of the coming battle at King's Mountain lay in the fact that on the American side not a single professional soldier or unit participated. Unprofessional, untrained, unpaid, and largely undisciplined by European standards, the backcountry men welcomed the oncoming clash as a kind of atavistic Armageddon.

Ferguson soon realized that the onrushing frontiersmen intended to fight, yet he seemed more irritated than alarmed. Turning east, he quickly mapped a route to join Cornwallis at Charlotte. Sending a courier ahead, he asked for "three or four hundred good soldiers, part Dragoons," to join him en route. Only thirty-five miles from Charlotte and thinking that his support was on its way, Ferguson, seeing the open ground before him, coolly placed his well-trained troops atop King's Mountain, the best natural fortress within a hundred miles. He dared the ragtag Americans to attack, bragging that "all the Rebels from hell" could not drive him and his sharpshooters from the mountaintop. One day later, hell's minions did exactly that.

Frontiersmen who faced Ferguson at King's Mountain on 7 October had little in common with the militia units from the Carolinas who panicked and fled at Camden. With no thought of pay, bounties, or provisions, they fought as a result of what they perceived to be a threat to their property, families, communities, and freedoms. Experienced fighters against the British and Indians, their idea of combat perhaps went beyond even Tarleton's infamous "quarter," the eighteenth-century plea for mercy that he so murderously disregarded. As William Davie, the redoubtable commander of many of North Carolina's backcountry men, remarked to a retreating Horatio Gates after Camden, he and his men "were accustomed to Tarleton and did not fear him." Marching hundreds of miles over unmarked roads and trails, sometimes through snow and unrelenting rain, sleeping on the ground and in trees, even riding all night to catch Ferguson before he neared Charlotte, the frontiersmen who dismounted at the base of King's Mountain feared neither the Scot nor his new breech-loading rifles. In four serpentine, circling columns, nine hundred frontiersmen eagerly moved straight up the steep slopes toward the entrenched Loyalists. As they neared the top, William Campbell made himself a conspicuous target by yelling, "Here they are boys! Shout like hell and fight like devils." They did.

Ferguson's death charge at the Battle of King's Mountain.
North Carolina Collection, University of North Carolina at Chapel Hill.

The battle soon looked like a murderous dance of two blooded embracing partners. As the backcountry men ascended, Ferguson's men charged with fixed bayonets, driving the Americans down the slope. Hating the "long knives" of the Loyalists, attacking riflemen took shelter behind pine trees from where they methodically began to pick off Ferguson's men. Soon the battle became one of frontal assault, countercharges with bayonets, and deadly rifle fire from snipers on both sides. One American survivor reported that "an unusual number of the killed were found to have been shot in the head. Riflemen took off riflemen with such exactness, that they killed each other when they were taking sight, so . . . that their eyes remained after they were dead, one shut and the other open, in the usual manner of marksmen." Once again, the outcome hinged upon who would give way first, a contest the British had always won.

Even with an ever-shrinking circle of defenders at the top of the mountain, Ferguson, convinced the Americans ultimately lacked any except initial courage, spurned any thought of surrender. Rallying his men for still another bayonet charge, he screamed that he would never admit defeat "to such damned bandits," and, with a final huzza from his men, he led them straight toward the surging frontiersmen. Shot to pieces by riflemen within seconds, Ferguson fell dead from his white horse, one foot entangled in a stirrup. As Ferguson's horse galloped among the pine trees with his body bobbing up and down like a bloody cork, the Loyalists vainly sought surrender. When Ferguson's men raised white flags, rebel riflemen, shouting "Tarleton's quarter," shot them dead, raking the ranks of the demoralized Loyalists. Already in a vengeful mood made more demonic by the blood of battle, backcountry men fell upon the Tories in a murderous frenzy. One hundred fifty-seven Loyalists died at King's Mountain, more than half cut down after the first white flag went up. An additional 163, so badly wounded that they could not walk or ride, remained on the hill to live or die where they fell, all without help from the Americans. Seven hundred others were marched off to Rutherfordton, but only 130 ever made it to Hillsborough to be tried or imprisoned. Hundreds simply went home, paroled and pardoned by mostly disinterested backwoodsmen. Although some were executed after a hasty drumhead court-martial, the majority of the Tory leaders, paroled by the Americans, eventually made their way to England never to return to America. By contrast, only 28 Americans died, while 62 others suffered wounds. As quickly as it had come together, the phantom army disappeared, melting away into the endless forests and mountains. Still, the foxes, gamecocks, and "old men," an affective term of veneration, who led them, the Sumters, Marions, Davies, and Davidsons, remained at every crossroads, mill, and river, waiting to fight, to harass, and to bleed Cornwallis and his hated Tory legions as they marched into North Carolina.

News of the complete annihilation of Ferguson and his men at King's Mountain and of the savage aftermath unsettled Cornwallis and his commanders. The loss of Ferguson's entire well-trained Loyalist army doomed any hope of thousands of Tories rushing to join the British. Ferguson's troops, the force that Cornwallis hoped would be the military nucleus of a popular uprising against the Whigs, simply had ceased to exist. With it went any expectation of a swift and decisive march northward through the Carolinas and Virginia. Moreover, Cornwallis's western flank now lay exposed, and, all too soon, rebel bands fell upon interior posts such as Georgetown outside Charleston and raided Ninety-Six on his outer line of defenses. Almost two months after the last southern American army had been wiped out at Camden, Cornwallis, wondering what had happened and why, turned and retreated southward toward Winnsboro, halfway between Ninety-Six and Camden. Roads from Camden led only to catastrophe.

As the British retreated southward, Horatio Gates, still in command of the southern army, limped into Charlotte to make a winter's encampment. With him he had, at least briefly, fifteen hundred men, perhaps half survivors of Camden, the rest new recruits to the Continental army, all ill-equipped and "literally naked," without tents and camp equipment. As Gates surveyed his forces and wondered what could happen next, it did. Maj. Gen. Nathanael Greene rode into camp and presented himself as the new commander. A dejected Horatio Gates, without the honor or shame of the resolution of his actions at Camden through a court-martial, bowed out of the Revolution and exited the stage of history for good.

As Greene took stock of his half-starved, poorly armed, and ill-trained troops, he kept two considerations in mind. First, George Washington, his mentor as well as commander, had advised him to pay direct attention to the numerous rivers that crisscrossed the region. On one side would be refuge and safety; on the other, defeat and disaster. When Greene looked at the map depicting his and Cornwallis's positions, he studied not towns and roads but rivers, always rivers. Then, too, Gates had warned him of the fickle militias and irregular bands that swarmed over the South. Explaining the debacle of the North Carolina militia at Camden, Gates commented that "a man may pit a cock, but he can't make him fight." Yet at King's Mountain and at scores of smaller actions such as Ramsour's Mill and Williamson's Plantation, hundreds of frontier riflemen, unpaid and untrained, had marched through driving snow, forded swollen rivers, and climbed steep slopes to be able to kill or be killed by the British. The riddle of the militia perplexed Greene. Still, he understood that while militias might harass and bleed the forces of the Crown they could never decisively defeat them. Only the Continental army could do that, but not without the cooperation of the irregulars. If nothing else, they added the weight of numbers to any campaign. With rivers and militias at the heart of his plan, Greene outlined a scheme to defeat the British in the South.

First, he split his army. Taking the less serviceable, most malnourished troops with him, Greene moved to Cheraw—close enough to Camden to monitor British movements yet out of harm's way. The better equipped and fed half of his army he sent into the northwest corner of the border of the Carolinas. To lead the western wing of his army, Greene rescued a southern legend, Daniel Morgan.

A celebrated Indian fighter from the Virginia mountains, tall with a deep scar across his cheek from a bullet wound, Morgan, like Sumter, had chosen to sit out the war after being passed over for promotion in the Continental army. Faced with the possible invasion and devastation of his beloved mountain homeland by the British and lured by the promise of a general's star as well as an independent command, Morgan came down from the Blue Ridge to help Greene. Affectionately called "Old Man" by his men and mockingly "Scar Face" by the British and their Indian allies, Morgan, only forty-five, seemed much older. He suffered painful and debilitating attacks of arthritis and gout, which made him even more surly and irritable, not a good prognosis for the British.

As the nucleus of Morgan's army, Greene detached the battle-hardened remnants of the Maryland and Delaware Continentals, perhaps three hundred in all, and also eighty cavalrymen under the portly but hard-charging and highly effective William Washington, George's second cousin. More than six hundred militiamen, mostly from North Carolina, surprisingly joined the Continentals on their way west. When reports of Greene's movements reached Cornwallis at Winnsboro, he scarcely could believe the good news. The Americans had presented him with the opportunity he long had sought. With Greene's southern army split apart more than 120 miles, fifteen hundred reinforcements of crack British and Hessian regulars newly arrived, and Banastre Tarleton, the most feared British officer in America, at his disposal, Cornwallis finally had his chance to win the big, big battle of his career and of the Revolution. With victory, he could secure the South for the British and turn the long tide of the war against the Americans. To the north he hurriedly sent Tarleton, with his dreaded legion, now more than five hundred strong, two artillery pieces, and more than six hundred British and Scottish soldiers. Tarleton would be the hammer, pinning down and engaging Morgan, while Cornwallis, moving quickly behind him, would be the anvil that shattered Greene and the American army north of Winnsboro.

Morgan knew of Tarleton's coming, even the numbers and dispositions of his troops. Quickly he retreated northward, putting distance and rivers between his men and Tarleton's flying legion. By mid-January of 1781, Morgan's motley collection of Continentals, militias, and some stray frontiersmen had reached a pleasant, rolling meadow locally known as Hannah's Cowpens. There, with the Broad River at his back, Morgan turned to fight Tarleton, "the bully." While the taciturn Morgan did not fear Tarleton, often referring to him derisively as "Benny," he understood the shortcomings of his own men in battle. Watching the groups of militiamen come and go, he observed that "it is beyond the art of man to keep [them] from straggling."

Fully expecting to lose or be displaced and forced to retreat, Morgan arranged his forces in one of the most inventive and resourceful dispositions of the war. With the river at his back and militiamen to his front, he layered his troops in three lines, the first consisting of 150 of his finest marksmen, the second of untested militiamen from the Carolinas, and the third of his veteran Maryland and Delaware Continentals. To the rear of the Continentals he detached William Washington and his cavalry, a mobile reserve force that could be used as the situation warranted. Morgan asked the first sharpshooters to hide behind trees and mounds of earth and to "shoot . . . the epaulets" off the British officers when they came into range, a decidedly undignified and barbarous breach of etiquette in eighteenth-century combat. After picking off as many officers as possible, the sharpshooters then would fall back to give backbone to the inexperienced militiamen from the Carolinas. For their part, Morgan asked the militia to do two things. First, no one would fire until the buttons on the uniforms of the advancing British clearly could be seen. Second, when the insignia on the buttons could be made out, Morgan told the Carolinians, "hold up your heads, boys, three fires [shots], and you are free" to run away for home and wives. Knowing the advantage that hundreds of muskets might give him, even temporarily, Morgan wanted a volume of fire for a minute or two, then he gave permission for the backcountry men to turn and run and "the girls [will] kiss you for your gallant conduct." The day then would be won or lost by the Continentals and by Washington's small force of dragoons waiting on the hillside.

As the brash Banastre Tarleton approached the peaceful, undulating meadow at sunrise the next morning, he saw clumps of rebel soldiers standing by trees and embankments in an open field, almost inviting him to attack by their lassitude. "America," he thought, seldom produced "more suitable" battlefields for him than the lovely Cowpens. Recalling how hundreds of rebels had broken and run before just a few of his hard-charging legionnaires scores of times, Tarleton quickly dispatched fifty of his green coats to scatter the Americans clustered before him. Within two minutes, astonished, he watched fifteen of his men fall from their saddles under an accurate and blistering American fire while the others whirled and dashed back to the safety of the trees. Enraged, Tarleton ordered his best infantrymen to drop their packs and to attack the Americans from the right. With gleaming bayonets and shouts of huzzah, the British foot soldiers advanced in what one awed North Carolinian described as "the most beautiful line I ever saw." Beauty and death heightened the drama of Cowpens. As planned, the sharpshooters quickly retreated to the waiting line of Carolina militia.

For Morgan and for American fortunes in the South, the moment of truth had come. If the militia broke and ran before firing their weapons as planned, Morgan and Greene had little chance of defeating the British in a decisive battle. Morgan's dependence on rivers and irregulars would be as misplaced as Gates's on militiamen and on marshes at Camden. Riding among the restless frontiersmen, Morgan did his Presbyterian best to reassure them. To their front, a parade line of green and red jackets with glistening bayonets and poised sabers came straight at the nervous militiamen.

At just under one hundred yards the militiamen unleashed a raking fire at the advancing British line. Of the 110 British men and 39 officers killed along with the 229 wounded at Cowpens, almost all fell in that first withering blast. Stunned, the British hesitated while the militia turned and ran, some firing two, three, even several more shots as they left the battlefield. At Cowpens, well-trained and -disciplined British recruits to the Seventh Foot, not raw rebel militiamen, panicked and fired as they retreated out of musket range.

With his infantry decimated and disorganized and the Americans running to cover, "Bully" Tarleton, as he had done so often before, sent his cavalry galloping to chop down the retreating rebels. Watching closely from a hillock with his Continentals, Daniel Morgan had anticipated just such a move from the brash "Benny." He quickly sent William Washington, now reinforced by forty-five eager southerners on fresh horses, boiling over the hilltop, catching the British by surprise. Shocked at having to fight mounted horsemen in superior numbers, the British cavalry uncharacteristically turned and galloped out of the battle and away from victory.

As his infantry recovered and moved up the hill toward the Continentals, Tarleton decided to play his last card. To flank the Americans, he sent in two hundred kilted Highlanders from North Carolina along with his last one hundred cavalry. Unexpectedly, the Continentals abandoned the top of the hill as the British approached and fell back on the reverse slope. As the Seventh Foot, Scots, British Legion, and cavalry saw the Americans disappearing over the hill, they broke ranks, and, in moblike fashion, stumbled over the hill to fall onto the escaping rebels.

As the British rushed pell-mell over the hill, the Continentals, retreating in good order, on Morgan's command, suddenly turned like clockwork and fired almost point-blank on their pursuers. Fixing bayonets, the Americans then charged the broken British units. To the right, the Highlanders advanced, seeking to envelop the American flank only to encounter a stinging fire from militiamen who, rallying around Andrew Pickens, had decided to stay and fight and fire more than three shots. As the "green coats" of the British Legion charged toward the Americans, William Washington, cherubic, oval-faced, portly, and spoiling for a fight, met them with a fierceness worthy of an avenging angel. Within a few minutes, the legion's horsemen had had enough, turning and galloping to the rear.

By now all seemed lost for the British. Troops from the Seventh Infantry Regiment dropped their muskets and "fell upon their faces" in surrender. Infantrymen from the British Legion, mostly Tories from the north, took to their heels. The Seventy-first North Carolina Highlanders, soon swamped by the Continentals, reluctantly surrendered. Frantically calling for his remaining two hundred cavalry to return to the battle, Tarleton's pleas abruptly ended when his horse suddenly dropped dead beneath him, shot by an American bullet. Sensing disaster, his remaining horsemen quickly cantered away to safety. Only the blue-coated Royal Artillery continued to fight, firing and defending two small "grasshoppers" captured from the Americans at Camden. Refusing to surrender, every artilleryman died or fell wounded by their guns. Humiliated and crushed, Tarleton, joined by fifty others, at last left the battlefield. Terrified that they might be hacked to pieces or shot by Americans eager to settle old scores, the British prisoners knew that they now faced Tarleton's Quarter from the backcountry men.

Yet Old Man Morgan had other ideas. He later swore that "not a man was killed, wounded, or even insulted" after the surrender. Morgan had more pressing matters at hand than exacting revenge. Less than a day's ride away, Cornwallis marched doggedly toward him. Drained by battle and tormented by arthritis made almost unbearable by the dank January cold, Morgan turned and, with his army dwindling as he marched, headed eastward toward Greene. He hoped Cornwallis would follow him in "a merry country dance" into the North Carolina wilderness, there to be defeated by nature and Greene.

ADDITIONAL READINGS

132

Allen, William C. "Whigs and Tories." *North Carolina Booklet* 2 (September 1902): 1–24.

Boyd, William Kenneth. "The Battle of King's Mountain." *North Carolina Booklet* 8 (April 1909): 299–315.

Bradford, Samuel S. *Liberty's Road: A Guide to Revolutionary War Sites.* Vol. 2. New York: McGraw-Hill, 1976.

Brown, Wallace. *King's Friends.* Rhode Island: Brown University Press, 1965.

Calhoon, Robert M. *Loyalists in Revolutionary America, 1760–1781.* New York: Harcourt Brave Jovanovich, 1973.

Chidsey, Donald Barr. *War in the South: The Carolinas and Georgia in the American Revolution.* New York: Crown Publishers, 1969.

Crow, Jeffrey. *Chronicle of North Carolina during the American Revolution.* Raleigh: Department of Archives and History, 1975.

Dann, John C., ed. *The Revolution Remembered: Eyewitness Accounts of the War for Independence.* Chicago: University of Chicago Press, 1980.

Davis, Burke. *Cowpens-Guilford Courthouse Campaign.* Philadelphia: Lippincott Co., 1962.

Davis, Sallie. "North Carolina's Part in the Revolution." *South Atlantic Quarterly* 2 (1903): 314–24; 3 (1904): 27–38, 154–65.

DeMond, Robert O. *Loyalists in North Carolina during the Revolution.* Baltimore: Genealogical Publishing Co., 1979.

Ganyard, Robert L. "Threat from the West: North Carolina and the Cherokee, 1776–1778." *North Carolina Historical Review* 45 (January 1968): 47–66.

Hoffman, Ronald, Thad W. Tate, and Peter J. Albert, eds. *The Uncivil War: The Southern Backcountry during the American Revolution.* Charlottesville: University Press of Virginia, 1985.

King, Clyde L. "Military Organizations of North Carolina during the American Revolution." *North Carolina Booklet* 8 (July 1908): 43–55.

Kyte, George W. "Victory in the South: An Appraisal of General Greene's Strategy in the Carolinas." *North Carolina Historical Review* 37 (July 1960): 321–47.

Lazenby, Mary Ellen, comp. *Catawba Frontier, 1775–1781; Memoirs of Pensioners.* Washington, D.C.: n.p., 1950.

Messick, Hank. *King's Mountain: The Epic of the Blue Ridge "Mountain Men" in the American Revolution.* Boston: Little, Brown, 1976.

Moss, Bobby G. *Patriots at King's Mountain.* Blacksburg: Scotia-Hibernia Press, 1990.

O'Donnell, James H., III. *Southern Indians in the American Revolution.* Knoxville: University of Tennessee Press, 1973.

Peckham, Howard Henry, ed. *Toll of Independence: Engagements and Battle Casualties of the American Revolution.* Chicago: University of Chicago Press, 1974.

Quarles, Benjamin. The *Negro in the American Revolution.* Chapel Hill: University of North Carolina Press, 1961.

Rankin, Hugh Franklin. "Cowpens: Prelude to Yorktown." *North Carolina Historical Review* 31 (July 1954): 336–69.

———. *North Carolina Continentals.* Chapel Hill: University of North Carolina Press, 1971.

Tarleton, Sir Banastre. *History of the Campaigns of 1780 and 1781 in the Southern Province of North America.* Spartanburg: Reprint Co., 1967.

Washburn, George C. "Cornwallis in the Carolinas, 1780, from a Contemporary British Account." *Journal of American History* 24 (April 1960): 107–13.

A Country Dance

NINE

Cornwallis's March through North Carolina

At Ramsour's Mill, eleven miles south of the Catawba River, Charles Cornwallis paused in the last bitter days of January 1781 before he entered the North Carolina wilderness. To Lord Rawdon in Camden he confessed, "My situation is most critical. I see infinite danger in proceeding . . . certain ruin in retreating. I am therefore determined to go on." Nothing would stop Cornwallis in his relentless pursuit of the last remaining American army in the South and, with it, the chimera of an ultimate victory in the Revolution. Just before daybreak the next morning after writing Rawdon, the earl ineluctably committed himself and his men to his quest for a final southern victory. In front of a huge bonfire, Cornwallis threw his books, tent, and all his personal baggage into the symbolic flames. He then asked his men to do the same. Every officer and soldier then followed his lead, some hesitantly, and soon casks of rum, empty wagons, tents, and extra baggage were added to the flames. Then each man received an issue of extra leather for fresh soles for his boots for the heavy

Charles Cornwallis (1738–1805), whose visage belied his ambition and determination.

North Carolina Collection, University of North Carolina at Chapel Hill.

marches that lay ahead. While undoubtedly dismaying to ordinary soldiers, this act under-
lined Cornwallis's commitment to push into the vast Carolina labyrinth. To the north

stretched the forests, rivers, and wilderness of North Carolina and, somewhere within, a
will-o'-the-wisp American army under Nathanael Greene. This time, Cornwallis would not
retreat, nor would he be driven southward again.

Setting off only two hours after his victory at Cowpens, Daniel Morgan managed to
cross above Ramsour's Mill just in front of Cornwallis's troops, moving northeast to join
up with Greene, who still did not know of Morgan's enormous defeat of the British. When
news of Morgan's victory arrived at Greene's camp at Cheraw six days after the battle, an
exuberant Greene ordered a round of rum for his overworked troops and an even more
potent "Cherry Bounce" for his officers. With little sleep, Greene arose the next morning,
and, with an aide and two dragoons, dashed more than a hundred miles through dangerous countryside to meet Morgan on the Catawba. After almost six years of war, Nathanael
Greene, like Cornwallis, believed that the end had come.

When Greene reached Morgan's camp at Sherrill's Ford on 30 January, he found Cornwallis camped on the other side of the river. Only a swollen stream and the lack of bridges
for fording separated the two. Ever true to his Virginia roots, an unwell and ailing Morgan
urged Greene to turn westward into the vastness of the Blue Ridge mountains, where
friendly settlements and fresh supplies awaited. Hearing that Cornwallis had burned his
baggage trains and had received reinforcements from General Alexander Leslie, Greene,
after listening to Morgan, carefully studied his maps and decided otherwise. To an amazed
Morgan, he instead pointed north. If Cornwallis would follow the Americans into North
Carolina, Greene announced, "He is ours." The race through North Carolina had begun,
from its southern border all the way to the Dan River in Virginia and eventually to victory.

Greene understood that with two to three times the men and with superior training and
equipment, Cornwallis easily could have defeated and destroyed both parts of his southern American army, either separately or together. Still, after a long march that pulled the
British away from their bases on the coast and with militia reinforcements and renegade
bands to help, Greene believed the outcome might be different. Until time, nature, and the
weight of numbers took their toll, Greene knew he must be chased but never caught.

Not everyone in Cornwallis's command shared his commitment to pursuing elusive
rebels through the wilds of North Carolina. Charles O'Hara, a brigadier who had joined
Cornwallis with Leslie's men from New York, shuddered at the prospect. A seasoned veteran who had served with Cornwallis at the Battle of Minden in Europe and who had commanded a British outpost in Senegal manned by deserters and felons serving for life, the
intrepid O'Hara somehow dreaded the idea of chasing Greene through an uninviting
wilderness. "In this situation," he lamented, "without baggage, necessaries, or provisions
of any sort for the officer or soldier, in the most barren, inhospitable, unhealthy part of
North America, opposed by the most savage, inveterate, perfidious, cruel enemy, with zeal
and bayonets only, it was resolved to follow Greene's army to the end of the world." The
first few days made clear what a cross-country pursuit would entail and, additionally, that
O'Hara's misgivings would smack of clairvoyance.

Within two days the Catawba River fell, allowing Cornwallis to cross, yet Morgan's men
already had decamped, leaving behind William Davidson and five hundred North Carolina

Depiction of Elizabeth Steele at her tavern in Salisbury consoling and giving money
to Nathanael Greene during the darkest days of the American Revolution.
North Carolina Collection, University of North Carolina at Chapel Hill.

militia to delay and harass the British at every crossing. Since the Catawba could be easily forded at a number of shallow locations and Davidson did not know which the British would select, he split his North Carolinians into groups of thirty to fifty to cover individual crossings while he kept three hundred others as a ready reserve. Beatties and Tucka-seegee fords on the main road to Charlotte seemed likely choices, yet Tool's and Cowan's (also called McCowan's) fords on the way to Salisbury had to be watched as well. Knowing the Charlotte crossings would be heavily guarded, Cornwallis sent Col. James Webster and two hundred troops to threaten and feint a crossing at Beattie's Ford while he led the main body across at Cowan's Ford. While a small occurrence in the southern campaign, Cornwallis's crossing of the Catawba made O'Hara's warning seem prophetic.

Starting at 2 A.M. on the morning of 1 February 1781, Cornwallis's troops, slogging through the mud and numbing cold, began their torturous march toward Cowan's Ford. Just before dawn, at the head of his brigade, O'Hara reached the crossing. Even to O'Hara and to the hardy and disciplined regulars, the surging stream looked fearsome. Although below flood stage, the Catawba's level still was well above normal, and, to add to the difficulty, more than five hundred yards had to be crossed in a swift and frigid current. The three British generals, Cornwallis, O'Hara, and Leslie, plunged in first. Behind them came hundreds of elite infantrymen, guardsmen, and fusiliers, "up to their breasts in a rapid stream, their knapsacks on their backs and sixty or seventy rounds of powder and ball in each pouch tied at their necks, their firelocks with bayonets fixed on their shoulders." As the water deepened, Leslie's horse lost its footing, unseating the general and disappearing downstream in the current. O'Hara's own mount fell, but he managed to keep the reins. Cornwallis then had his horse shot by an alert American picket, but he continued toward

The crucial crossing of Cowan's Ford on the Catawba River by Cornwallis in 1781.
North Carolina Collection, University of North Carolina at Chapel Hill.

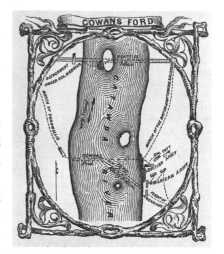

shore on his wounded animal. As the water heightened, desperate British soldiers held their muskets above their heads as they inched ahead straight into the Americans.

On the American side of the river, darkness and the roar of the river camouflaged the British crossing until only one hundred yards remained. Awakened by the sound of horses whinnying and men splashing and cursing, North Carolinians on the opposite shore began a ragged fire. Robert Henry, a schoolboy wounded by a bayonet at King's Mountain, stared in disbelief at the magic lantern scene before him on the river. Unable to fire, the British troops, led by officers on horseback, lined up as silhouette targets for the Americans. A Tory who rode with the British chronicled the grotesque scene. Looking at the guards, he "saw 'em hollering and a snortin' and a drownin'—the river was full of them . . . a hollerin' and a drownin'." With the discipline born of countless drills, the British slowly emerged from the river, knelt down, and delivered their first volley. Shot in the chest, William Davidson fell from his horse, probably dead before he hit the ground. As the British volleyed and fixed bayonets, preparing to charge, the North Carolinians prudently withdrew. Cornwallis was across the river.

British records gave the dead at only three but with thirty-six wounded. Yet certainly more perished in the stream. Carolinians who lived along the Catawba reported that it "stunk with carcasses" for days, and more than two hundred British soldiers disappeared from Cornwallis's rolls in that week, all reported as "missing," either dead or deserted. Only one river had been crossed, at enormous cost, and Cornwallis still had made up precious little time in overtaking Morgan and Greene.

The country dance through North Carolina between the British and Americans inevitably centered on fords, crossings, mills, taverns, towns, and courthouses. In the vast emerald wilderness of the backcountry, they represented points of civilization, supply, and rest. While Morgan and Greene's men knew the country and had long since adapted and acclimated to its vagaries, the vastness of the forest and woods and the unfamiliar terrain presented an additional obstacle to the British. Even with a full supply of provisions, rum, uniforms, weapons and powder, tents, and camp supplies, America's wilderness still proved harder for the British to negotiate. Without these aids and comforts, more intimate and necessary than ever in the eighteenth century, nature debilitated Cornwallis's forces far more than Greene's. When the British marched into Guilford Courthouse some six weeks later, they, and not the Americans, needed new shoes and uniforms. Faded, torn, and patched, their redcoats looked almost pink, their white trousers, blackened by mud and dirt, mirrored their ashen, gray spirits. For two days before the battle at Guilford, the Royal Welsh Fusiliers had only turnips to eat. On the morning of battle, 15 March 1781, the entire British army marched to Guilford without breakfast or any ration at all. Weak, pale, and fatigued, his shattered hand in a sling, Banastre Tarleton could barely stay in his saddle. Desperate for food, forage, and supplies, Cornwallis's men succeeded in alienating what support they had in North Carolina by confiscating supplies and looting and burning farms, homes, and mills, frequently failing to distinguish friend from foe. To their credit, the bone-weary and hungry British army displayed the tenacity, discipline, and lionheartedness at Guilford that won them battles and empires around the world. Although outnumbered two to one by the Americans, they still managed a victory, albeit a Pyrrhic one.

By 11 March the hunted had become the hunter. Rested, refreshed, and now with new recruits from a three-week stay just across the Dan River in Virginia, Greene's army had swollen to between four and five thousand men. On 10 March, John Butler and Thomas Eaton had arrived with almost one thousand North Carolina militiamen and a freshly raised regiment of Continentals. From Virginia, William Campbell once again appeared with more than four hundred Overmountain Men, soon to be joined by two hundred more under Thomas Lynch, already notorious for his summary trials and hangings of Loyalists. Two days before the battle, Saint George Tucker, an American line officer, wrote to his wife, "We

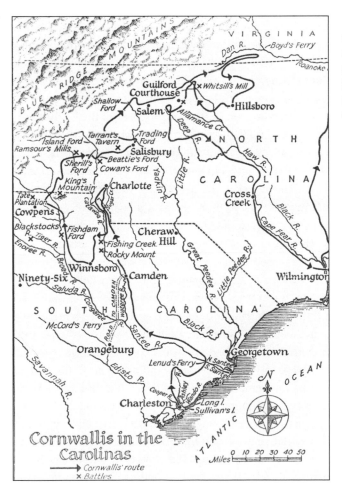

Cornwallis's march through the Carolinas. Note the numerous smaller battles before Guilford Courthouse.
North Carolina Office of Archives and History, Raleigh.

marched yesterday to look for Lord Cornwallis . . . We are now strong enough to cope with him to advantage." North Carolinians and the American army in the South at last wanted a fight.

Like those at King's Mountain and Cowpens, the battle around Guilford Courthouse depended, at least in Greene's thinking, on the militia, especially the North Carolinians. Bedridden and weak, Daniel Morgan nevertheless influenced the battle. Writing to Greene, he strongly urged him to use the three-line, three-shot tactic that had worked so well at Cowpens. For his part, Cornwallis stuck with the same plan of attack he had used so successfully at Camden. To his left he placed the bloodied veterans of the Thirty-third and Twenty-third with light infantry and Hessian Jagers on the flank. The right wing included the reconstituted Seventy-first Highlanders, again with many North Carolinians in its ranks, and another German regiment, the Bose. Between the two, Cornwallis positioned his two artillery pieces, not as crucial on the battlefield as they would be in another century. Tarleton's green coats, now almost faded olive, and some battalions of guards made up the reserve. The two armies met at Guilford Courthouse, the heart of Quaker country in colonial North Carolina.

With superb discipline and courage, the red, green, and blue regiments of the British and Germans deployed and marched straight toward the waiting muskets and rifles of the North Carolinians poised along fences near the courthouse. Roger Lamb, a sergeant in the Royal Welsh Fusiliers and an astute diarist as well, wryly considered the aim of the Americans as he advanced toward them. "Within forty yards . . . it was perceived that their whole force had their arms presented and resting on a fence rail. . . . They were taking aim with the nicest kind of precision." Lamb's musket, or fusil, could reach the militiamen, but their long rifles would exact a toll for each step he took. With two volleys from the North Carolinians, "one half the Highlanders dropped on that spot," Dugald Stuart of the Seventy-first noted, and, as he surveyed the carnage, "the part of the British line at which they [the Americans] aimed looked like the scattering stalks in a wheat field when the harvest man had passed over it with his scythe." The center of the North Carolinian line then turned and ran, leaving the field to the British.

Made up of Virginians, the second American line exacted still another heavy payment from the lines of the advancing Thirty-third and Jägers. The Virginians finally gave way when their commander, Stevens, had to be carried from the field with a shattered thigh. When the British and their best commander, Lt. Col. James Webster, rushed toward the retreating militiamen, they charged straight into the waiting ranks of the First Maryland Continentals, the southern army's best unit. Holding their fire until Webster's men came within thirty yards, the Marylanders unleashed a deadly volley, and, with fixed bayonets, fell on the stunned redcoats. Staggered and confused, the British broke and ran.

Nathanael Greene probably could have won the battle at Guilford Courthouse had he chosen to risk an all-out attack at that moment. Still, he hesitated. Unlike modern warfare, eighteenth-century strategy and tactics sought to minimize casualties and keep units intact rather than win at any cost. Instead, Greene sought to punish Cornwallis by inflicting as many casualties as possible rather than risking the existence of the last American army in the South. Although Cornwallis justifiably could claim victory at Guilford, he knew the war could never be won at such a price. His superiors, both military and political,

The British cavalry charge at the Battle of Guilford Courthouse.
North Carolina Collection, University of North Carolina at Chapel Hill.

understood that maxim as well. When the victory at Guilford Courthouse became known in London, Charles James Fox, a leader of the opposition to the British war in America, sarcastically observed that "another such victory would ruin the British Army." Horace Walpole, one of England's most influential politicians, also knew that Guilford, although a victory, "was productive of all the consequences of defeat." Although the Royal Welsh Fusiliers and Brigade of Guards marched to victory after victory in the years after the Revolution, they never attached a Guilford pennant to any of their battle flags.

Of the almost 2,000 British soldiers at Guilford, 93 died in battle while 413 were wounded and 26 went missing. Almost 25 percent of Cornwallis's elite, irreplaceable regulars who faced Greene that day never fought again. Fifty of the more seriously wounded died during the night, and the British could do little for those seriously injured who survived that frightful first twenty-four hours. Deep in hostile territory, lacking proper rations, tents, and especially medical supplies, Cornwallis, desperate to help the scores of wounded, piled them into seventeen wagons and sent them southward to the tender mercies of the Quakers at New Garden. The next day, Sunday, 18 March, after a brief service, British and German soldiers dug long trenches at the nearby Hoskins house and tossed scores of dead into the fresh pits. Running low on time and with some soldiers too weak to dig, the British burned their remaining dead in a surreal funeral pyre that smoldered and stank for days afterward and marched out of the "Court House of the dead."

After Guilford, Cornwallis considered three options for his forces. First, he could pursue Greene, an unlikely choice considering his weakened army, or else he could march back to South Carolina and to the protection of Lord Rawdon's forces at Camden. Lastly, he could stay in North Carolina, moving to Wilmington, on the coast, where a British squadron now resided and where the Royal Navy could bring reinforcements and supplies to him. The problems that had plagued him since Charleston, especially those of the dependability and support of the Loyalists and the Royal Navy along the coast, once again tormented him in the tangled disorder of his march through North Carolina.

Cornwallis barely hesitated. To return to South Carolina would be an admission of defeat and also would bring Greene, Pickens, Davie, and a host of rebel groups swarming back into pacified territory. Moreover, he no longer had the strength to chase Greene through the wilds of North Carolina. Explaining his decision to Clinton, his superior, the earl spelled out his reasons for turning toward Wilmington. Owing to the "great fatigue of the troops, the number of wounded, [and] the want of provisions," he could no longer pursue the enemy. Instead, he planned to turn northward into Virginia.

Nathanael Greene somehow sensed that the battle at Guilford Courthouse had changed the course of the war in the South. When he first realized that the obsessed earl would follow him into North Carolina and eventually into Virginia, he remarked, "Then he is ours. I am not without hopes of ruining Lord Cornwallis," especially "if he persists in his mad scheme of pushing through the country" of North Carolina. Still, he "never felt an easy moment" after the British crossed the Catawba until "the defeat of the 15th" at Guilford. With the earl's army "ruined," Greene thought that the British would retire and leave North Carolina to the rebels. In any other course, he prepared to hound the British hares through the southern wilderness.

Loyalists in North Carolina apparently agreed with Greene. To succeed in his drive northward, Cornwallis desperately needed the sort of help from the Loyalists that Whig militiamen had given to the Americans at King's Mountain, Cowpens, and at Guilford. American militia and irregulars had exacted a heavy toll in casualties and supplies, so much so that, by the spring of 1781, a final British victory in the South seemed even more remote than ever. Any thought that Cornwallis still harbored of conquering the Carolinas and Virginia inevitably returned to the same question. Where were all the loyal subjects in the South promised by former royal governors such as Josiah Martin and James Wright? With victory after victory, why had they never rallied to the king's standard in substantial numbers? Without Loyalist support, victories such as the one at Guilford Courthouse meant little.

The strange case of Dr. John Pyle illustrated the enigma of Loyalist support in North Carolina and throughout the South. A passionate supporter of the Crown, Pyle had, since the debacle at Moore's Creek Bridge, patiently awaited the arrival of the British army in strength. When he learned of Cornwallis's approach in February 1781, Pyle persuaded three hundred to four hundred of his neighbors to join His Majesty's forces along with him. Recalling his experiences in South Carolina, where little protection had been given Loyalists, Cornwallis hastily dispatched Tarleton's tattered legion to escort Pyle's men into the safety of his encampment. He clearly understood that if he could not protect Pyle and his band of diehard Loyalists, few others would join his ranks.

Caught up in the excitement of the apparent approach of British troops and eagerly anticipating revenge upon the Whigs in the region, Pyle's men "thought it fit to pay visits to their kindred and acquaintances before they repaired to the British camp." They raided, stole, and pillaged from their Whig neighbors. A wild, drunken shivaree with their Loyalist supporters fatally delayed their departure. Finally on the road by 25 February, Pyle's band encountered the expected column of green-coated cavalry led not by Tarleton and the British but by Light Horse Harry Lee of Virginia. Americans from Virginia also dressed in green. Supported by South Carolina troops under Pickens, Lee's dragoons cut down the surprised Loyalists with muskets and sabers at point-blank range. Lee reported that "the conflict was quickly decided and bloody. . . . Ninety of the royalists were killed and most of the survivors wounded . . . . in some parts of the line the cry for mercy was heard" but seldom given. Not a single Revolutionary died and only three suffered wounds. Greene gleefully wrote that Pyle's disaster "so happily timed . . . in all probability will be productive of such happy consequences." They occurred sooner than expected. Two days later Tarleton's Legion blundered into a local militia company, and, wary of Continentals in the vicinity, charged them with their usual ferocity and determination only to discover that they were Loyalists, not rebels, on their way to Cornwallis's camp. Along with British insistence that Loyalists enlist for eighteen months, incidents such as Pyle's effectively ruled out the possibility that Cornwallis could strengthen his army with Loyalist militias.

Still, Cornwallis persisted in his belief that Loyalists would rise up and join the Crown against the rebels. His success increasingly depended on it. On 18 March, the earl asked Josiah Martin to issue a proclamation calling upon "all loyal subjects to stand forth and take an active part in restoring good order and government." Cornwallis's disappointment only deepened afterward. "Some of them [Loyalists] indeed came within the lines," he revealed, "but they remained only a few days." As soon as Greene turned to go after Cornwallis, what few Loyalists remained, "warm friends" of the Crown, soon abandoned the British camp and went home. Dejectedly, Cornwallis wrote Clinton that "our experience has shown that their [Loyalist] numbers were not so great as had been represented and that their friendship was only passive." Three weeks later, Cornwallis, by sheer determination and spirit, dragged his pitifully small army into Wilmington. He was safe at last.

Greene had no intention of following Cornwallis to Wilmington. To him, Wilmington would imprison the British and save the Americans the trouble. On 5 April, he turned south toward Rawdon and the British outposts in South Carolina. He had driven Cornwallis into a snare by the sea, a point he drove home to his mentor, George Washington, and, while the British licked their wounds and wondered what to do, he headed toward Camden and Charleston. Greene knew his enemy well. Ever since the fall of Charleston in 1780, Charles Cornwallis had looked north, always north toward North Carolina and Virginia, never to the south. Greene thought that the earl would abandon Lord Rawdon and the British in the Carolinas while he made his way toward Virginia, still in search of his final, decisive victory. He was right. After arriving in Wilmington, the impatient Cornwallis headed north toward Virginia and his final battle at Yorktown. His self-deception had remained intact despite his increasingly perilous position. Writing Clinton in New York, Cornwallis theorized that "the Chesapeake may become the seat of war, even (if necessary) at the cost of abandoning New York. Until Virginia is . . . subdued, our hold of the Carolinas must be difficult, if not precarious." On his own initiative, Cornwallis planned to mount a decisive campaign in Virginia, forcing the passive, defensive-minded but patient Clinton to send troops to his aid. On 25 April 1781, Cornwallis headed north into Virginia, still hoping for one last supreme battle that would decide the fate of a continent. No one, he concluded, could have won in North Carolina. He had done his best. Now Virginia and Yorktown awaited him.

ADDITIONAL READINGS

Alden, John Richard. *The South in the Revolution.* Baton Rouge: Louisiana State University Press, 1957.

Boyd, William K. "The Battle of King's Mountain." *North Carolina Booklet* 8 (April 1909): 299–315.

Dann, John C., ed. *The Revolution Remembered: Eyewitness Accounts of the War for Independence.* Chicago: University of Chicago Press, 1980.

Davis, Burke. *Cowpens-Guilford Courthouse Campaign.* Philadelphia: Lippincott, Co., 1962.

Dickson, William. "A Picture of the Last Days of the Revolutionary War in North Carolina." *North Carolina Booklet* 21 (1922): 59–67.

Gibson, George H. "Twenty-Seven Tickets." *North Carolina Historical Review* 37 (October 1960): 477–87.

Graham, William A. "Battle of Cowan's Ford—The Passage of the Catawba River by Lord Cornwallis, February 1, 1781." *North Carolina Booklet* 5 (April 1906): 232–46.

———. "The Battle of Ramsaur's Mill, June 20, 1780." *North Carolina Booklet* 4 (June 1904): 5–23.

Hatch, Charles E., Jr. *Battle of Guilford Courthouse.* Washington, D.C.: National Park Service, 1971.

Higginbotham, R. Don. *War and Society in Revolutionary America: The Wider Dimensions of Conflict.* Columbia: University of South Carolina Press, 1988.

Massey, Gregory de Van. "British Expedition to Wilmington, January–November 1781." *North Carolina Historical Review* 66 (October 1989): 387–411.

Newsome, Albert Ray, ed. "British Orderly Book, 1780–1781." *North Carolina Historical Review* 9 (January 1932): 57–78; (April): 163–86; (July): 273–307; (October): 366–92.

Paden, John. "A Study of Southern Loyalism: The Politics of Thomas MacKnight." *Southern Historian* 15 (Spring 1994): 78–86.

Rankin, Hugh Franklin. *Greene and Cornwallis: The Campaign in the Carolinas.* Raleigh: Department of Archives and History, 1976.

Robinson, Blackwell P., ed. *Revolutionary War Sketches of William R. Davie.* Raleigh: Department of Archives and History, 1976.

Rodman, Lida T. "Patriotic Women of North Carolina in the Revolution." *Daughters of the American Revolution Magazine* 45 (August 1914): 145–52.

Troxler, George Wesley. *Pyle's Massacre, February 23, 1781.* Burlington: Alamance County Historical Association, 1973.

Wood, William J. *Battles of the Revolutionary War, 1775–1781.* Chapel Hill: Algonquin Books of Chapel Hill, 1990.

A Jeffersonian State

North Carolina had become a Jeffersonian state long before Thomas Jefferson's political and social philosophy took shape and helped launch the new nation's dialogue on what it should become. In fact, government of any sort, whether Caswellian or Jeffersonian, existed only peripherally during the Revolution itself. A great many North Carolinians liked it that way. As it emerged in the next decade, Jefferson's philosophy of simplicity, frugality, and a government that left people free "to regulate their own pursuits of industry and improvement" satisfied North Carolina's post-Revolutionary needs. His belief that states and not a central government were "the most competent administrators for our domestic needs" became the hallmark of North Carolina's increasingly narrow political philosophy for almost a century. In fact, North Carolina adapted Jefferson's philosophy to their parochial beliefs to such an extent that it eventually assumed a new form that many thought superior to Jefferson's. In North Carolina, the parricide inherent in Jefferson's or anyone's political philosophy came full circle.

From the Battle of Guilford Courthouse in March 1781 until the British commander, Maj. James Craig, evacuated Wilmington on 18 November 1781, North Carolina had little effective functioning government at all. Tory raiders under the notorious David Fanning had captured its governor, Thomas Burke, at Hillsborough in 1781, and, for all practical purposes, the state had existed in a state of constant crisis and often anarchy throughout much of the latter part of the Revolution. A native of Virginia who grew up in Johnston County, Fanning, bound on an indenture to a prosperous eastern merchant, found in the Revolution not only the right set of circumstances to redress old grievances from his harsh treatment as an apprentice but also a golden opportunity for advancement. Recruiting Loyalists chiefly from the old Regulator counties around Orange, he received a colonel's commission from James Craig. Fanning needed little else. After the Battle of Guilford Courthouse, Fanning, always an opportunist, sensed Cornwallis's predicament, left him, and began pillaging the backcountry. At Pittsboro in July 1781 he dashed into a rump court-martial for some of his Loyalist friends, freed them, and, in the confusion, captured more than fifty prisoners, at least three assemblymen among them. A raid on Hillsborough came next.

For more than a year after Guilford Courthouse, Fanning conducted his own bitter war against personal enemies and Whigs of all persuasions in the backcountry. Exiled to Canada after the Revolution along with some of his Loyalist and Scottish friends from North Carolina, Fanning, forever a social outcast, an undesirable, and a ruffian, eventually found

Map of North Carolina in 1795. North Carolina Collection, University of North Carolina at Chapel Hill.

himself indicted for serious crimes by the British Canadians who harbored him. No one better personified the exploitative anarchy in North Carolina during the latter stages of the Revolution more than David Fanning.

From Cornwallis's entry into the state in September 1780 until Fanning galloped from the state to end the Tory war in May 1782, North Carolinians enjoyed a temporary hiatus from organized government, royal or rebel, of any sort. Freed yet frustrated at his impotence as governor, Burke told a reconvened general assembly in 1782 that "Neglect of Duty, Abuses of power, Disobedience of Laws, Your monies unaccounted for, and public credit almost sunk" meant that the state needed to establish its "authority and correction" to the chaos of the Revolutionary years. Yet most North Carolinians, despite the sporadic partisan warfare that affected some of them, enjoyed the default of taxes and responsibilities, the absence of a multitude of laws, and the lack of power, usually exerted by sheriffs and tax collectors, that came with a functioning and able state government.

The Revolution and its end had a different effect on women in North Carolina. When fifty-one met in Edenton to endorse the nonimportation agreement in 1774, Arthur Iredell, then in England, wrote to his relative in North Carolina, James Iredell, asking, "Is there a Female Congress in Edenton, too? I hope not, for we Englishmen are afraid of the Male Congress, but if the ladies, who have ever, since, the Amazonian Era, been esteemed the most formidable Enemies, if they, I say, should attack us, the most fatal consequences is to be dreaded." Although mocking in its tone, Iredell's observation nonetheless pointed out the crucial role played by women during the Revolution.

First, the Edenton congress indicated the keen interest women had in politics, not only in ideological but in practical terms. Seemingly an elite group who met over tea to protest Britain's policies, women in North Carolina, with a great deal of say in the governance of households, in essence dictated whether an economic boycott worked or not. Along with that of other caffeinated drinks, the consumption of imported tea from England permeated all levels of society, not just the wealthy few. Its rejection required the acquiescence of large segments of the population. While equally as dedicated to the Whig cause as their husbands, brothers, and sons, women in North Carolina nevertheless found the conflict to be more civil and less sanguinary. In fact, they sometimes determined that men took the idea of warfare too far, becoming far too petty and mean-minded in the process.

When a desperate Cornwallis occupied Wilmington just before heading to Virginia, he expelled twenty-one prominent patriot women. When Americans retook the town in 1782, they likewise forced out wives and children of absent Loyalists. The Americans' own wives objected. A petition of many of the patriotic women initially driven out by Cornwallis asked that the Loyalist women and children be allowed to return. Why? As Anne Hooper, whose husband signed the Declaration of Independence, explained, the Loyalists' wives had done nothing wrong. Indeed, their situation affected "the helpless and innocent" of the town as a whole. When Hooper and other patriot women had been cast out, Loyalist women had "expressed the greatest indignation at it, and with all their power strove to mitigate our sufferings." A strong sense of sisterhood underlay their appeal.

In the petition, Anne Hooper and others claimed a privilege earned through patriotism to the American cause. "We shall hold it as a very signal mark of your respect for us," she steadfastly maintained, "if you will condescend to suffer to remain amongst us our old friends and acquaintances whose husbands, though estranged from us in political opinions, have left wives and children much endeared to us. . . . The safety of this State . . . is now secured beyond the most powerful exertions of our Enemies, and it would be a system of abject weakness to fear the feeble efforts of women and children." William Hooper and the Whigs listened to their wives, sisters, and mothers. The women had supported, suffered, and nursed them through the long years of the Revolution. Indeed, much of the medical care and many of the hospitals during the Revolution like the one established by the Continental army at Hillsborough were run entirely by women by 1781. In 1784, the new state of North Carolina officially guaranteed widows not only the traditional one-third of any estate "in dower" but also an equal share of personal property such as stocks, bonds, money, and, more important, slaves.

In North Carolina, the Whigs, those who had opposed the king and who had supported rebellion and independence, found that it was easier to get rid of the old government than to fashion a new one. Almost immediately after the Battle of Moore's Creek Bridge in February 1776, a great many Whigs slowly came to the realization that it was a political fallacy to think that a better government automatically replaced a worse one. In fact, backcountry men who had fought Tryon and his militias in the Regulator war only a decade before now recognized many of the same names and faces of their old enemies in government, the same lawyers, merchants, large landowners and slaveholders, land speculators, and

*North Carolina's first
state constitution in 1776.*
North Carolina Collection, University
of North Carolina at Chapel Hill.

placemen, now all fellow Whigs who clamored for more control and government as a worse "set of knaves." Drawn chiefly from the east coast and from towns and commercial centers, old Regulator adversaries such as Samuel Johnston, William Hooper, and John Penn now had emerged as leaders in the rebellion against the British. Still conservative in their social and political outlook, they now wanted to bring North Carolina out of the "chaos and disorder" caused by the Revolution itself. Yet others in the backcountry and some even along the coast embraced the brief anarchy created by rebellion. They were the David Fannings who had been on the winning side. "Chaos and disorder" suited them just fine.

This more radical group of Whigs, less fearful of new ideas and distinguished in class and status, saw in the simple conception of Jefferson's Declaration of Independence not chaos, confusion, and clamor, but genuine change and a chance for a new beginning. Ideas are never responsible for those who follow them, and those of Jefferson and Paine set out in a few short but widely distributed pamphlets prior to 1781 found formative fields in North Carolina's social and political wilderness. If the conservative Whigs despised chaos and disorder, disdained the mobocracy of the majority, and insisted that credit and debtor laws rigidly be enforced through the courts, then radical Whigs wanted the opposite. Largely poor subsistence farmers, frequently in debt and marginally educated, they embraced a more instinctive proto-Jeffersonian ideology throughout the decade of the 1770s and 1780s. The vast majority of North Carolinians who made up this group wanted such things as an inflated paper currency that would, for all practical purposes, reduce or eliminate their debts. For them, the confiscation of Tory property meant redistributing the assets and wealth of neighbors who turned against them in the Revolution. While conservative Whigs supported court decisions that protected confiscation of Tory estates under the rhetoric of securing "property rights," such specious judgments made little sense to poor North Carolinians who had little property themselves. When Elizabeth Bayard, the daughter of the Tory merchant Samuel Cornell of New Bern, sued for the return of her property confiscated and sold to the Whig Spyers Singleton in 1787, the judges, largely conservative and led by Samuel Ashe and John Williams, agreed and returned her holdings. To historians such as Hugh Lefler and William Powell, the *Bayard v. Singleton* case marked the first time that a court exercised its authority to declare a legislative act unconstitutional, a precursor to John Marshall's sweeping 1803 *Marbury v. Madison* decision that institutionalized judicial review of written constitutions. Yet to the radical Whigs, the case symbolized the arbitrary power of an appointed judiciary, largely conservative and predisposed to protect property rights. They opposed it. Radicals similarly wanted debts to British merchants contracted before the Revolution vacated and lands to the west toward Tennessee opened for settlement. For the common people, free land and freedom from debts embodied Jefferson's idea of liberty in its most basic form. Having fought to dispose of an overweening royal governor such as Josiah Martin and an arbitrary king in London like George III, radicals had no wish to have placemen as judges and a strong state executive in North Carolina. They preferred to elect their governors every year, their judges almost as quickly, and their assemblymen every two years.

Most of all, the great divide between the conservative and radical Whigs manifested itself in one simple idea. How far should the ideals of the Revolution go in making the new state more democratic? Conservatives such as William Hooper and Samuel Johnston feared that the theory put forth in Jefferson's Declaration of Independence went too far, threatening to replace the tyranny of the king with that of the mob. Clearly, conservatives distrusted an amorphous "will of the people." William Hooper openly doubted the abilities of "the common people," who were so easily swayed that even a "drink of toddy" could buy their vote. Growing increasingly bitter as his election losses mounted, Samuel Johnston called the radicals "a set of unprincipled men" who sacrificed political ideals for a common, vulgar "popularity." Led by Willie Jones, who nettled the conservatives by emphasizing his preferred pronunciation of his name as "Wily," the radicals did not so much manipulate the masses as they did make manifest a latent distrust of government among quite ordinary North Carolinians. Along with Thomas Person, Matthew Locke, and Samuel Spencer, "Wily" Jones and the radicals increasingly controlled the general assembly after 1780.

When the constitutional convention met at Philadelphia in the summer of 1787, North Carolina found in the debate swirling around the adoption of the new constitution a new set of political names, now Americanized, for their older views of Whiggery and government. Strongly supporting the new constitution, the conservatives now called themselves Federalists. Radicals opposed the Federalists, initially preferring to be designated as Anti-Federalists, later disdaining the "anti" characterization and moving toward an American form of nationalism by labeling themselves as Jeffersonian Republicans, and, by 1816, even calling themselves Jeffersonian nationalists. Yet despite the new designations, the politics of the two groups remained the same. No matter whether they were stamped as conservative Whigs or Federalists, the idea of a strong central government, both in the nation and in the state, that could protect property rights, enforce debt payments, stimulate and encourage trade, and even promote "dignity and respect" for the state and nation in foreign matters remained the hallmark of planters, merchants, large landowners, and the "Federalist few."

Federalist support centered along the eastern coast, largely in towns and commercial centers. Federalists feared mobocracy and argued for a stronger "Union" as well as a system of checks and balances between the three branches of government, the executive, legislative, and judiciary. The radical Whigs, whether called Anti-Federalists, republicans, Jeffersonians, or Jeffersonian nationalists, still held to the conviction that that government that governs best governs least, that only states' rights prevented the return to the tyranny of a king or despot, whether called a king or a president, and that the greater threat to liberty came not from the weakness of government but from its coercive strength. Anti-Federalists wanted the legislature strengthened, the judiciary elected, and the executive diminished. Located primarily in the backcountry and in the expanding western counties, the Anti-Federalists came to reflect North Carolina's long distrust of government and its chief function, that of taxation.

North Carolina sent lukewarm conservatives William R. Davie, Richard Dobbs Spaight, Richard Caswell, Alexander Martin, and the equally passionate radical Willie Jones to the Grand Convention in Philadelphia. Suspicious of the politics of the majority of the Philadelphia conventioneers and of their agenda, "Wily" Jones soon bowed out. Hugh Williamson replaced him. In ill health, Caswell, then governor, appointed William Blount in his place. None represented the proto-Jeffersonian sentiments of the small farmers and common laborers who formed the vast majority of the state's population. Except for Martin, all came from the eastern counties. Of North Carolina's delegates, none made any significant impact on the work of the convention. Hugh Williamson, warming to his latent Federalist sentiments in a convention of the likeminded, made seventy-three speeches and proposed twenty-three motions, mostly secondary in nature. Williamson led the group that originated the idea of six-year terms for senators. Spaight first proposed that senators be elected by state legislatures and that the president be allowed to make minor appointments when Congress was not in session, both conservative Whig ideas that fit in well with their mistrust of the common man. In all, North Carolina's delegation reflected its conservatism and distrust of the will of the majority of the populace. Eventually Williamson, Spaight, and a reluctant Blount signed the new constitution for North Carolina.

North Carolina's refusal to ratify the Constitution established two post-Revolutionary trends, the first of which was how much the conservatives were out of touch with the majority of the state's voters; the second, how much North Carolina had distanced itself politically from Virginia, always North Carolina's preceptor, and the rest of the nation. Even before the finished constitution had been published in the *State Gazette of North Carolina* in October of 1787, Williamson and Davie had urged voters to select capable, virtuous, and dedicated men to the general assembly—that is, Federalists—and not the "blind, stupid set that wish Damnation to their Country"—namely, the Anti-Federalists. Indeed, Federalists saw in the fight over the ratification of the new constitution an issue that would return them to power, to their rightful place as the state's leaders. James Iredell, perhaps the most skillful at promoting both the new constitution and himself, argued that it offered

William Richardson Davie (1756–1820),
governor of North Carolina, 1798–99.
North Carolina Collection, University of
North Carolina at Chapel Hill.

"popular representation of the people" as well as opportunities to amend and change it, especially in incorporating a "set of rights" to protect against abuses by the central government. Without personal liberties and rights "billed" into the original document, Iredell and many Federalists knew that North Carolinians would not accept it.

The arguments of the Anti-Federalists, seldom as reasonable or as intricate as those of the Federalists, usually ignored political theories of checks and balances, of rights of amendment and of impeachment, or of a larger and more powerful union of the states, and, instead, simply echoed older emotional pleas that smacked of Regulator rhetoric. That struck a chord among North Carolina's voters. Lemuel Burkitt, a fiery Baptist preacher and advocate of states' rights, decried the "new Caesars" who would govern the nation from a walled capital city, unleashing their "legions" to crush "the liberties of the people." Thomas Person thought the whole idea "impracticable and dangerous," especially so since it called for balancing groups, factions, and the interests of so many states over such a large geographic region. Willie Jones, along with many Anti-Federalists, looked upon George Washington and James Madison as "scoundrels," knaves, and even traitors to the Revolutionary generation, sentiments he later denied publicly, but he privately apologized.

In the end, Anti-Federalists won a resounding victory by electing 184 delegates to the convention called to ratify the Constitution to only 83 for the Federalists. Despite the appeals of Federalists to elect able and qualified men to the convention, relatively unknown and unheard-of commoners defeated famous framers and signers such as William Hooper and Richard Caswell. When the convention met at Hillsborough on 21 July 1788, Willie Jones asked that they vote on the first day, have a drink, and then go home because "all the delegates knew how they were going to vote" and "public money" should not be "lavished" on the convention. He was right. North Carolina rejected the Constitution by a vote of 184 to 83, but the debate and formalities nonetheless took until the first of August to finish.

Except to North Carolinians, the rejection of the Constitution meant little. The document already had been adopted by the requisite number of states, nine, and, when the state convention met at Hillsborough to consider ratification, only North Carolina and Rhode Island still remained outside the national union. Yet within eighteen months the state had reversed its position, the Federalists temporarily had won elections in the summer of 1789, and North Carolina reluctantly had agreed to join the union. Although Federalists and historians took heart and meaning from the fact that North Carolinians had come to their senses and at last had ratified the Constitution for purposes both practical, prudent, and political, it also seemed that the state saw little danger in ratification in 1789. Why?

First, the question of the Bill of Rights, whose absence unsettled the delegates at Hillsborough, substantially did not affect ratification at the subsequent Fayetteville convention in 1789. North Carolina joined the Union well before the amendments had been added to the Constitution, even as fellow southerners such as James Madison and George Washington assured their passage. Even with the bill of rights attached, North Carolinians still had misgivings about whether a strong central government with a dictatorial "president" and an appointed judiciary would enforce them. Although many in the state did not like comparisons with the only other state still outside the Union, Rhode Island, a province notorious for its "rogues," radicalism, and chaotic issues of paper money, most North Carolinians found such contrasts and measurements meaningless if not vacuous. Although farmers and merchants generally credited the new Federalist government in New York with helping reverse the lingering depression of the 1780s and returning the state to economic prosperity, they nevertheless benefited little from the suspension of tonnage duties and of tariffs, two key elements in the recovery. North Carolina had few vessels, and most of its shipping went through Virginia and South Carolina, both firmly admitted to the Union. In the end, North Carolina joined the other states in ratifying the Constitution out of indifference and apathy, not out of defiance and principle.

In the initial debates over the adoption of the Constitution, North Carolinians had displayed considerable ardor and excitement. For example, an impassioned James Iredell had painted the choice in Manichean terms in 1788. To accept the Constitution, he declared, would mean that "we shall truly be a union, happy in ourselves and respected by the rest." To reject it meant that the United States would continue to be "an irreconcilable scattered people," forever "doomed to feel the curse of all human discontent." William Hooper fought for the ratification with his fists as well as his reputation, proudly proclaiming that he had his "eyes blacked" but not put out by a rough and tumble Anti-Federalist. Willie Jones, who lambasted the "Grand, Pretentious Conventioneers" of Philadelphia, had nothing to say only a year later. Lemuel Burkitt, one of a number of Baptist and Methodist ministers who led revival-like meetings against ratification in 1788, found few "Romanites" to rail against in 1789. Instead, few within the state even bothered to vote for delegates to the ratification convention, and, North Carolina, with no other course of action available, defaulted its way into the Union in 1789. Still, finally having joined the Union, North Carolina then spent the first decades of the nineteenth century as if it did not exist.

North Carolina's delegation to the new Congress barely had seated itself when it began to discover how Jeffersonian it really was. When Alexander Hamilton, the Federalist Prometheus, issued his first report to Congress in 1790, North Carolinians saw in his ideas the embodiment of their fears of a strong central government. Hamilton proposed that the national government fund the Revolutionary debt at face value, that it also assume existing state debts, and, lastly, that it charter a national bank for twenty years to bring credit and order to the economy. Hugh Williamson, now a congressman, saw in Hamilton's proposals the diminution of states' rights and the promotion of the national government's power. For example, funding the Revolutionary war debt at face value, while laudably patriotic, also assured the nation an unnecessary and burdensome indebtedness, and, accordingly, its gradual reduction and abolition by new taxes levied by a bloated central government. Moreover, if the states let the central government assume their Revolutionary debts as well as those of private individuals and corporations, they would also give up their right to tax, and, with it, to govern. Together with this, the idea of a national bank also meant that a "money power" might be institutionalized along with a tyrannical political one. Except on the issue of the national bank, North Carolina's delegation voted against Hamilton's measures, including his infamous excise tax on whiskey. Both senators voted for the bank, and, in the House, Williamson, Ashe, and Timothy Bloodworth, all ardent Jeffersonians, opposed the act.

In the years after Hamilton's policies won approval, North Carolina conversely moved toward Jefferson's views on government and away from the Federalists' views. Of all North Carolina's governors for the next two decades, only William Davie consistently called himself a Federalist. Although it did not issue its death rattle until 1815, by 1800 Federalism in North Carolina effectively had ended. With Federalists weakened and barely surviving election after election, Jeffersonians subsequently dominated state politics for almost three decades. Two issues, education and the location of the capital for the new state, exemplified North Carolina's drift toward a more cocooned form of Jeffersonianism after 1800. Unlike most colonies, North Carolina had never settled upon a permanent site for its government, which met variously at large homes and buildings in the Albemarle region and, later, at Bath, Edenton, and New Bern until 1778. In 1766 the general assembly passed "An Act for Erecting a Convenient Building within the Town of New Bern," in reality a measure to give the colony a permanent capital. In 1767, John Hawks, a talented and artistic architect brought over by then Lt. Gov. William Tryon, set out erecting a building that would be a meeting place for the royal governor, the council, and an impressive number of officials, including Tryon's secretary and, for the first time, a tax collector. Built of brick, surrounded by impressive gardens, stables, and dependencies, trimmed with marble, and featuring a mahogany staircase, Tryon Palace, as the new structure was derisively called by the majority of North Carolinians, survived as one of the most tasteful public buildings in colonial America. Yet in a telling detail, the building did not include a place for the general assembly to meet. Instead, the legislature convened somewhere else in New Bern, in a church or in a large home, but never in the convenient building erected as a seat of government.

Tryon's pretentious palace held the key to early North Carolina's aversion to government in general, to the transition from colony to statehood in particular, and to its steady relocation to Jeffersonianism in its overall political philosophy. In August 1768 the citizens of Orange County in the backcountry protested the imposition of a per capita assessment, a poll tax, to pay for the governor's palace. "We are determined not to pay the Tax for the next three years," the petition for relief explained, "for the Edifice or Governor's House. We want no such House, nor will we pay for it." Instead, backcountry men, tired of the arbitrary taxation and lack of representation for their counties, wanted to "regulate" their own affairs, to govern themselves far removed from New Bern. Less than three years later, Gov. William Tryon, equally frustrated that his sheriffs could not collect taxes to pay for his "Edifice" of government or for any of its functions, led his eastern militias into the rebellious counties of Orange, Anson, Granville, and Halifax, eventually hanging seven Regulators and restoring order to the colony in 1771. New Bern remained the capital until 1778. For over a decade, the general assembly, governor, upper house, and state officials trudged willy-nilly to Hillsborough, Halifax, Smithfield, Fayetteville, New Bern, Tarboro, and to the courthouse at Wake, sometimes even meeting in private homes, churches, and briefly outdoors during the summer of 1780. Tryon Palace, perhaps the finest structure in colonial North Carolina, burned and fell into ruin in 1798. No one cared.

The Hillsborough Convention of 1788, called upon by the assembly to vote on the new U.S. Constitution, also decided that if North Carolina did not join the new federal union it should at least have its own separate capital. At last North Carolina had become serious about locating a permanent seat of government. In Jefferson-like fashion, the assembly, after duly considering the Hillsborough resolution for a new capital, proceeded in snail-like fashion to decide upon a location. The assembly eventually endorsed the convention's suggestion that the new location should be within ten miles of Isaac Hunter's tavern in Wake County, centrally located and also within riding distance to a favorite watering hole. Once again, the radicals, now looking more and more like Jeffersonian Republicans, deliberately bypassed large towns such as Fayetteville, the favorite of easterners, and two contenders from the backcountry, Tarboro and Hillsborough. The proposal to purchase Joel Lane's plantation of one thousand acres and to erect a new seat of government in Wake County brought howls of protest from conservative easterners. Why not Fayetteville, they maintained, centrally located in 1790 and also "at the head of the best navigation in the State." As the new capital, Fayetteville "would have a great and instantaneous effect upon the decayed commerce of this country," while Lane's plantation, situated in the middle of nowhere, "was inconvenient with commerce" and would never "rise above the degree of a village." Jeering easterners noted that Hunter's tavern, very near the new site and a frequent meeting place for Hillsborough conventioneers, served a potent rum punch popular with backcountry representatives. Caring little for commerce with others and for pretentious towns filled with conservative merchants and lawyers, the assembly voted for Lane's plantation, just ten miles from the Wake County courthouse. Named "Raleigh" after the ill-fated "Cittie of Raleigh," the abandoned scheme for a colonial capital, North Carolina's first permanent center of government took four years to be ready. It was completed in 1796. Richard Dobbs Spaight became the first governor to reside in Raleigh even as construction continued around him. In a telling tribute, the state, on the advice of an aging Thomas Jefferson, hired Antonio Canova, a noted Italian sculptor, to fashion a marble statute of George Washington to stand in the rotunda of the statehouse. The building, described as "the most precious work of art in the country," replaced Tryon's pretentious palace as the state's "Edifice" to government.

North Carolina's disinterest in education as a colony continued into statehood in the new nation, only to be enmeshed within the same political struggle between the radical and conservative Whigs when it became an issue in 1789. Taking advantage of the wave

Joseph Caldwell (1773–1835), first president of the University of North Carolina in 1804.
North Carolina Collection, University of North Carolina at Chapel Hill.

of optimism following the adoption of the Constitution, conservative Whigs, now labeled Federalists for their support of a stronger central government, managed in 1789 to push through a bill chartering the University of North Carolina, the first state-supported college in the nation. Priding themselves on thinking continentally and not provincially, they hoped that the university would provide North Carolina with a cadre of well-educated men who would use their talents to preserve the new American nation's ideals. On a more emotional level, Federalists also wanted to use the university's early chartering to blunt the image of North Carolina as a cultural and intellectual wilderness. Even though Federalists championed the establishment of the university, no real consensus emerged among them on how a state university should be run. At first, advocates of the university wanted to make it a voice for traditional Christianity as well as a place for teaching a classical curriculum. In its early history, the university was neither.

The first trustees of the university faced other problems as well. Difficulties such as administering a university, finding and keeping a qualified faculty, securing an adequate source of funds, and, most disturbing of all, quelling frequent student rebellions and combating indifference to education filled the minutes of early meetings. In its first two decades, the university enrolled, either officially or informally, between twenty-five and forty students. By 1835, only eighty students attended Chapel Hill, the number rising dramatically to four hundred by the Civil War. Within a decade, the Federalists, squabbling with Jeffersonians over the mission of the university, lost control of the board of trustees. In 1804, the new board appointed Joseph Caldwell, a staunch Jeffersonian, as the university's first president, a move that brought stability and stature to the school. Now dominated by Jeffersonians, the general assembly thought the university aimed to be too elite, "a school for the rich," especially wealthy Federalists, and, after 1804, they elected trustees themselves instead of letting an independent board select its own.

Caldwell busied himself by hiring two noted educators, Denison Olmsted in chemistry and Elisha Mitchell in mathematics, by building a library, and by broadening the curriculum to include more than religion, philosophy, and ethics. An avid supporter of public

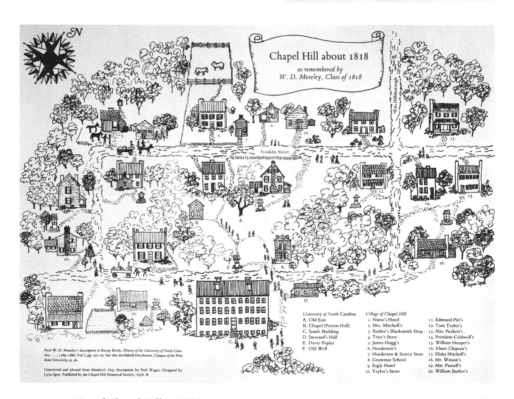

Denison Olmsted (1791–1859), whose appointment to the University of North Carolina in chemistry did much to establish its early academic reputation. Olmsted published the first geological survey of the state in 1824. North Carolina Collection, University of North Carolina at Chapel Hill.

Chapel Hill about 1818

as remembered by
W. D. Moseley, Class of 1818

Franklin Street

to Hillsborough

University of North Carolina
A. Old East
B. Chapel (Person Hall)
C. South Building
D. Steward's Hall
E. Davie Poplar
F. Old Well

Village of Chapel Hill
1. Nunn's Hotel
2. Mrs. Mitchell's
3. Barbee's Blacksmith Shop
4. Trice's Store
5. James Hogg's
6. Henderson's
7. Henderson & Searcy Store
8. Grammar School
9. Eagle Hotel
10. Taylor's Store
11. Edmund Pitt's
12. Tom Taylor's
13. Mrs. Puckett's
14. President Caldwell's
15. William Hooper's
16. Abner Clopton's
17. Elisha Mitchell's
18. Mr. Watson's
19. Mrs. Parnell's
20. William Barbee's

Find W. D. Moseley's description in Kemp Battle, *History of the University of North Carolina . . . , 1789–1868,* Vol. I, pp. 271–73. See also Archibald Henderson, *Campus of the First State University,* p. 36.

Conceived and plotted from Moseley's 1853 description by Paul Wager. Designed by Lynn Igoe. Published by the Chapel Hill Historical Society, 1976. ©

Map of Chapel Hill in 1818. North Carolina Collection, University of North Carolina at Chapel Hill.

Elisha Mitchell (1793–1857). Along with Olmsted's, Mitchell's appointment to the University of North Carolina faculty as a mathematics professor did much to help establish its early academic reputation. Mitchell published a second geological survey of the state in 1827, noting that North Carolina had the highest mountains in the East.
North Carolina Collection, University of North Carolina at Chapel Hill.

education, after his idol, Thomas Jefferson, Caldwell went on to publish two influential pamphlets, the *Numbers of Carlton* (1828) and *Letters on Popular Education* (1832), both of which did much to win support not only for the university but for education in general. In the early months of 1812, Robert Hett Chapman succeeded Caldwell as president of the university. Chapman lacked Caldwell's literary talent, managerial ability, and magnetism. Moreover, his opposition to the War of 1812 and the eagerness of young students to fight England, the "old tyrant," soon led to still another student uprising. Chapman's administration collapsed in late 1816, and, once again, Caldwell accepted the presidency, again intensifying his efforts to make the university a significant institution within the state.

The rising tide of evangelicalism within the state in the early nineteenth century led to a quandary over the role of religion at the university. Portraying themselves as nonpartisan patrons of the university, Federalists wanted the school to turn out well-rounded young men who would take as their religion the American republic and the commerce by which it stood. They looked to Benjamin Franklin and his practical University of Pennsylvania as a model. Jeffersonians, who effectively controlled the university by 1804, followed a more Enlightenment-based approach at odds with traditional ideas about learning and religion. Embodied by Caldwell and Chapman, the views of the Jeffersonians dominated, and the university gradually became a typical classical college emphasizing philosophy, Greek, Latin, history, mathematics, and, as the decades wore on, the natural sciences. While evangelicals failed to establish religion as the chief mission of the university, they did infuse rituals such as chapel and prayer into the students' lives. Still, legislators harbored deep-seated populist suspicions that the university promoted radicalism and agnosticism among its students and faculty. Frequent student rebellions and outspoken faculty members only added to the general assembly's misgivings about what was taught at the school.

By the 1820s, the university had become what Jeffersonians wanted it to be, an important vehicle for socializing the young men of the state. It had taken North Carolinians from all sections and all walks of life within the state and, through a common pattern of education, experience, and ideas, prepared them to lead the state into a future that replicated a conservative society based upon the enormous inequality that they had known. In a parricide of ideals, the university's initial Jeffersonian radicalism had become more conservative, even reactionary, by the 1830s. It had also become politically as well as educationally institutionalized. Between 1814 and 1972, thirty-one of North Carolina's forty-eight governors had studied at Chapel Hill. In this way, the University of North Carolina, like Jefferson's own University of Virginia and similar state institutions in Georgia and South Carolina, succeeded in helping transform North Carolina from a benighted wilderness into a state much like the others in the nineteenth-century South.

Yet perhaps the greatest impact of Jefferson's ideas came in religion and the freedom attained through it. The end of the American Revolution transformed the religious world of North Carolina, striking down the Anglican Church, changing Baptists, Methodists, and Presbyterians from dissenters into rivals while also infusing a new freedom into forms of worship. Competition for the newfound religious enthusiasm of the unchurched majority of North Carolinians forced denominations to experiment and change, testing the tactics of their rivals and setting the stage for the South's great revival of 1800–1805. Yet North Carolina's Presbyterians, Baptists, and Methodists, now free to proselytize with the state's approval, only intensified their efforts to distinguish themselves from each other and to present clear religious alternatives to prospective converts. In their zeal, they redefined religious life and identity in Jeffersonian North Carolina.

In the end, the great revivals that swept over North Carolina and the South from 1800 to 1805, and later in the 1830s, homogenized religious values and life, separated white and

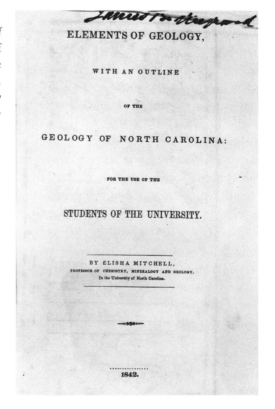

Title page to Elisha Mitchell's 1842 edition of Elements of Geology with an Outline of the Geology of North Carolina: For the Use of the Students of the University. North Carolina Collection, University of North Carolina at Chapel Hill.

ELEMENTS OF GEOLOGY,

WITH AN OUTLINE

OF THE

GEOLOGY OF NORTH CAROLINA:

FOR THE USE OF THE

STUDENTS OF THE UNIVERSITY.

BY ELISHA MITCHELL,
PROFESSOR OF CHEMISTRY, MINERALOGY AND GEOLOGY.
In the University of North Carolina.

1842.

black churchgoers, and created a folk culture without an attendant sense of responsibility to a wider community. Within two generations, evangelical religion had, to an unusual degree, come to shape the outlook of North Carolinians of all classes, from rich merchants and landowners to ordinary subsistence and even poor scratch farmers. Instead of a larger, coherent religious community like that the older Anglican Church tried to establish, evangelicals succeeded, by 1830, in creating a religious culture based on localism and scattered congregations. In so doing, they moved from the diversity sought by Jefferson to an orthodoxy feared by him, from a powerful dissenting force in southern life to one that merely supported the status quo.

At first, Presbyterians, Baptists, and Methodists had little attraction for well-to-do farmers, landowners, merchants, and the small minority of slaveholders in the new state. Pietistic, appealing to the rustic and simple in life, otherworldly in their outlook, emotional in their attempts to convert, evangelicals seemed the very antithesis of the rational, calculating, worldly, ostentatious, even arrogant members of North Carolina's elite, men such as Samuel Johnston and Richard Caswell. Still, as memories of the Revolution faded and as converts multiplied, Presbyterian, Baptist, and particularly Methodist revivals attracted not only the poor from the tidewater backcountry but also an increasing number of the middling sort of North Carolinians from everywhere. Instead of being on the outside, finding fault with an established church such as the Anglican and preaching religious freedom, evangelicals managed to establish their own values and denominations as the dominant ones by Jefferson's death in 1826. By embracing Jefferson's idea of religious freedom, North Carolinians had created a Protestant evangelical folk identity more orthodox and influential than that of the earlier Anglican Church.

As the years wore on, North Carolina moved even further from Jefferson's beliefs in minimal governance. After 1789, the state produced its own version of Jefferson, a crusty tobacco planter from Warren County named Nathaniel Macon who out-Jeffersoned the famous Virginian in matters of economy of government and disdaining foreign involvements, as well as in his demand for frequent elections of officials and in supporting common folks. Born in 1758 and a veteran of the Revolution, Macon, like Jefferson, strongly endorsed a strict interpretation of the Constitution and of states' rights. Worldly and well educated at the College of New Jersey (now Princeton), Macon seldom strayed from his roots in North Carolina. As a prosperous planter, he eschewed trappings of wealth and display of any kind, instead leading a frugal and sometimes even a parsimonious life. When the bill to construct a tomb for Washington came before the House of Representatives, Macon, then a congressman from North Carolina, spoke at length against the monument mania sweeping the nation that cost precious public monies. For Macon, the push to erect monuments reminded him of the idolatry of ancient Rome. He even went so far as to vote against furnishing the newly constructed White House, instead suggesting that presidents should bring their own furniture with them. He reminded his fellow congressmen that he had "no splendid luxury or extravagance," nor did any other "Poor North Carolinians." Macon served in the House of Representatives from 1791 until 1815, as Speaker and one of the most powerful men in the nation from 1801 to 1807, and as a member of the Senate from 1815 until 1828.

In a schism that closely corresponded to North Carolina's own political alienation, Macon split from Jefferson when the Virginian became president in 1801. As Jefferson struggled between his vision of an empire of liberty that required an active president and his belief in minimal government, Macon found himself increasingly at odds with the Virginian who in the end turned into a political pragmatist. Macon vowed never to abandon principle for politics or practicality. As early as 1803, when Jefferson went beyond any president before him to purchase Louisiana without congressional knowledge or permission, Macon, then Speaker of the House, turned against him. In the following years, Macon joined John Randoph, another Virginian, but one who believed that Jefferson also had betrayed his strict constructionist beliefs, to form the Quids, a small but vocal faction within the ruling Republican Party who questioned anything that Jefferson and the "regular republicans" did. To Macon and Randolph, *quid*, from the Latin, always meant asking "what and why" to justify any political action.

Macon lost his position as Speaker of the House in the fight over Jefferson's Embargo Act of 1807. The act followed Jefferson's long struggle to keep the nation out of the European war between Napoleon and England by a policy of "peaceable coercion," thus forcing both France and England to recognize America's neutral rights by threatening to withhold trade if one or the other refused. It failed. By 1807 Jefferson, almost desperate to keep the new nation out of Europe's troubles, asked Congress to forbid American ships to leave for European destinations. As leader of the largest neutral trading nation, Jefferson hoped to use the leverage of American commerce to force England and France to recognize American shipping rights. Macon and the Quids saw the action as self-inflicted punishment, even dishonorable and unnecessary. Afterward, Macon and the Quids found themselves opposing almost all the actions of Jefferson and his successor, James Madison.

The nadir of Jeffersonian republicanism in North Carolina came with the War of 1812. Never enthusiastic about the possibility of foreign entanglements and involvement, North Carolinians had even less ardor for the "new nationalism" of the war hawks who came to power in 1810. Led by Henry Clay from Kentucky and John C. Calhoun from South Carolina, the new coalition of westerners and southerners clamored for war with England to assuage national pride and also to annex Canada, a prize piece of the puzzle of Jefferson's "agrarian imperialism." When the British warship *Leopard* fired on and boarded the American naval vessel the *Chesapeake* in American territorial waters in 1807, the war hawks found the issue that eventually set aside Jefferson's policy of peaceable coercion, that of national honor and pride. As the British continued to seize scores of American vessels after 1807 and also to press ordinary American seamen into the British navy, the clamor for war, largely from the West and the South, increased. On 18 June 1812, Congress, with a bare majority in the House and a slightly larger one in the Senate, declared war on Great Britain.

No war hawks came from North Carolina. Indeed, two antiwar Jeffersonian Republicans, William Kennedy and Richard Stanford, took their seats in the 1812 election after campaigning against the war, joining fellow congressmen Thomas Person and Archibald McBryde in voting against "Mr. Jefferson's War." Running on a similar antiwar campaign, William Gaston, more populist than Federalist on the issues, joined his congressional colleagues by labeling the war declaration "unwise . . . and unnecessary." Only North Carolina's two senators, both lukewarm in their approval, voted for the war resolution.

The first battleship North Carolina. *A caption describes "the squadron under Commodore Rogers leaving Port Mahon, 1825 . . . with the 74-gun Ship-of-the-Line North Carolina."*
North Carolina Collection, University of North Carolina at Chapel Hill.

The limitations of Jefferson's theory of minimal government and of an aversion to a large standing army became apparent as the nation drifted into war with England. Because Jefferson and Macon had collaborated to reduce the federal budget, especially military expenditures, the regular army numbered less than seven thousand in 1812. Many of its top-ranking officers had seen only limited and even dubious service in the Revolution and had spent most of their time away from their units afterward. Dubbed "the mosquito fleet" because of its lack of firepower, the navy had less than two hundred vessels, most of them gunboats with outdated ordnance and with crews of only a dozen or so. Only sixteen could operate outside coastal waters with any degree of force and protection.

In parallel fashion, North Carolina had less than ten thousand ill-trained militiamen and five Federal gunboats to protect its largely defenseless coast, a fact jarringly brought home when, on 12 June 1813, one year after the declaration of war, the British, under Rear Admiral George Cockburn, arrived off the coast of North Carolina with a flotilla of over one hundred vessels and several thousand troops, a force effectively larger than the entire American army and navy. The next day, the British landed on Ocracoke Island and proceeded to occupy the "pretty little town" of Portsmouth. Searching for more important objectives farther up the coast toward Baltimore and Washington, the British left four days later. Suddenly, many North Carolinians sounded more like Federalists than Jeffersonians, demanding protection from the central government.

With a long history of pirates, privateers, and freebooters, North Carolina responded to the War of 1812 by loosing the legendary Otway Burns and Johnston Blakeley upon the British. An Irishman who likened himself to John Paul Jones, Blakeley had moved to North Carolina, briefly attended the university, and in 1806 enlisted in the navy to seek his fame and fortune, in this case to fight the Barbary pirates. When war came in 1812, he commanded the *Enterprise* and later the *Wasp,* two medium-sized sloops having less than thirty guns and two hundred men. Although almost always outgunned, Blakeley sought battle with heavier British ships such as the *Fly, Reindeer,* and *Avon,* eventually defeating them all. After sinking and disabling over twenty ships, primarily in the English Channel, Blakeley and the pernicious *Wasp* sailed off into a setting sun, toward America, only to disappear forever over war's horizon, presumably sunk by a British ship somewhere in the Atlantic.

From Beaufort, Otway Burns refitted and commissioned his own ship, beguilingly named the *Snap Dragon,* and, with a license as a privateer, he sailed from North Carolina to Newfoundland and then southward to the Caribbean in search of British prizes. In the next two years, Burns captured scores of merchant vessels, sold them for prizes, and, as a result, made a small fortune. From Stokes County, Benjamin Forsyth joined the army, rose to the rank of lieutenant colonel, and died at the battle of Odelltown when the Americans invaded Canada. In the War of 1812, fewer than fourteen thousand North Carolinians served in the army, navy, and militia, almost all seeing little action. Andrew Jackson, a former North Carolinian who had opened a law office first in Salisbury and then at Guilford Courthouse, closed his law books and offices in his newly adopted state of Tennessee and, taking a motley collection of regular army units, militiamen, and volunteers, won the epic Battle of New Orleans for the Americans in January 1815. When the British burned Washington, D.C., in August 1814, Dolley Madison from North Carolina, the diminutive wife of President James Madison, hurriedly helped her husband leave not only a warm dinner, to be eaten by the British, but also the executive mansion to be burned almost intact by them as well. To cover the charred facade, the building was painted with a whitewash and thereafter became known as the White House. Unhappy about entering the war, North Carolinians had even more criticism for its ending. Along with Macon, William Gaston and David Stone denounced the Treaty of Ghent, which ended the war. Gaston lamented in a sibylic burst of eloquence that it only concluded a war where "the visionary hope of planting the 'star spangled banner' in Quebec had yielded to the necessity of self-defense." Nothing had been gained from the British in recognizing American rights such as freedom of the seas, nor had London agreed to pull its troops out of the old northwest territories, where they supported Indian raids against American settlers. For North Carolinians, the lessons learned from abandoning Jeffersonian principles and meddling in European affairs seemed clear. The state should increasingly isolate itself from not only foreign but also national concerns. The state should become more like Macon, a trusted native son, and less like Jefferson and Madison, even though both came from Virginia, a state much emulated and envied by North Carolina.

By embracing Jeffersonianism in all its rudimentary forms, North Carolinians had, by 1826, created a yeoman's paradise without progress. Afraid of granting the general assembly power to tax or to regulate, North Carolinians could not even decide on a place where it could deliberate or meet for nearly a decade after the end of the Revolution. In education, North Carolina established the nation's first state-supported university, then let it languish for years. Led by Nathaniel Macon, an easterner who thought Jefferson too radical in his views of government and the Constitution, North Carolina made a vice of frugality and of economy in all its affairs. Briefly stirred by the War of 1812, North Carolina soon returned to its languid contentment with itself after 1815. Only in religion did the state "revive" itself in the two decades after the Revolution. While its sister southern states, Virginia, Georgia, and South Carolina, preached Jeffersonianism and practiced a southern brand of Hamiltonianism, North Carolina instead disdained even Jefferson himself as a false prophet, turning to the most narrow interpretation of his writings by Macon and his followers.

Macon managed to be more self-effacing than Jefferson even in death. Meticulously arranging his own unpretentious funeral, Jefferson carefully planned to be buried at Monticello with a modest epitaph on his tombstone that declared his greatest achievements, conspicuously leaving out his political offices. For his part, Macon prescribed an even simpler service. Buried outside his presentable but plain Buck Spring plantation in Warren County, Macon asked that each of his friends place a rock on his grave and afterward have a good meal and some grog. The marker at the grave site further explained "His wish . . . that no grief be expressed at his funeral." He asked only to be remembered as an unpretentious, ordinary North Carolinian.

ADDITIONAL READINGS

Best, James Arthur. "Adoption of the Federal Constitution by North Carolina." *Trinity College Historical Papers Publications* 5 (1905): 12–30.

Boyd, Julian P. "North Carolina Citizen on the Federal Constitution, 1788." *North Carolina Historical Review* 16 (January 1939): 36–53.

Boyd, William K. "Methodist Expansion in North Carolina after the Revolution." *Trinity College Historical Papers Publications* 12 (1916): 37–55.

———. "Nathaniel Macon in National Legislation." *Trinity College Historical Papers Publications* 3 (1900): 72–88.

Broussard, James H. "North Carolina Federalists, 1800–1816." *North Carolina Historical Review* 55 (January 1978): 18–41.

———. *Southern Federalists, 1800–1816.* Baton Rouge: Louisiana State University Press, 1978.

Butler, Lindley S., ed. *Narrative of Col. David Fanning.* Davidson, N.C.: Briarpatch Press, 1981.

Caldwell, Joseph. *Letters on Popular Education, Addressed to the People of North Carolina.* Hillsborough, N.C.: Dennis Heartt, 1832.

Cavanagh, John C. *Decision at Fayetteville: The North Carolina Ratification Convention and the General Assembly of 1789.* Raleigh: Department of Archives and History, 1989.

Connor, Robert Digges Wimberly, comp. *Documentary History of the University of North Carolina, 1776–1799.* 2 vols. Chapel Hill: University of North Carolina Press, 1953.

Cunningham, Noble E., Jr. "Nathaniel Macon and the Southern Protest against National Consolidation." *North Carolina Historical Review* 32 (July 1955): 376–84.

Drake, William Earle. *Higher Education in North Carolina before 1860.* New York: Carlton Press, 1964.

Eaton, Clement. "Ebb of the Great Revival." *North Carolina Historical Review* 23 (January 1946): 1–12.

Gillespie, Michael Allen, ed. *Ratifying the Constitution.* Lawrence: University Press of Kansas, 1989.

Gilpatrick, Delbert Howard. *Jeffersonian Democracy in North Carolina, 1789–1816.* New York: Octagon Books, 1967.

Green, Fletcher Melvin. *Constitutional Development in the South Atlantic States, 1776–1860.* New York: DaCapo Press, 1971.

Hoffman, William Stephany. *Andrew Jackson and North Carolina Politics.* Gloucester, Mass.: Peter Smith, 1971.

Jackson, Harvey H. "Prophecy and Community: Hugh Bryan, George Whitefield, and the Stoney Creek Independent Presbyterian Church." *American Presbyterians* 69 (1991): 11–20.

Johnson, Guion Griffis. "Camp Meeting in Ante-Bellum North Carolina." *North Carolina Historical Review* 10 (April 1933): 95–110.

Kerber, Linda K. *Women of the Republic: Intellect and Ideology in Revolutionary America.* Chapel Hill: University of North Carolina Press, 1980.

Lemmon, Sarah McCulloch. *Frustrated Patriots: North Carolina and the War of 1812.* Chapel Hill: University of North Carolina Press, 1973.

Lycan, Gilbert L. "Alexander Hamilton and the North Carolina Federalists." *North Carolina Historical Review* 25 (October 1948): 442–65.

Mathews, Donald G. *Religion in the Old South.* Chicago: University of Chicago Press, 1977.

McPherson, Elizabeth Gregory, ed. "Letters from Nathaniel Macon to John Randolph of Roanoke." *North Carolina Historical Review* 39 (April 1962): 195–211.

Newsome, Albert Ray. "North Carolina's Ratification of the Federal Constitution." *North Carolina Historical Review* 17 (October 1940): 287–301.

Parramore, Thomas C. "Conspiracy and Revivalism in 1802: A Direful Symbiosis." *Negro History Bulletin* 43 (April–June 1980): 28–31.

Pelt, Michael R. *A History of Original Free Will Baptists.* Mount Olive, N.C.: Mount Olive College Press, 1996.

Perkins, David, ed. *The News and Observer's Raleigh: A Living History of North Carolina's Capital.* Winston Salem: John F. Blair, 1995.

Pratt, Walter F. "Oral and Written Cultures: North Carolina and the Constitution, 1787–1791." In *The South's Role in the Creation of the Bill of Rights,* ed. Robert J. Haws, 77–99. Jackson: University Press of Mississippi, 1991.

Price, William S., Jr. "Nathaniel Macon, Planter." *North Carolina Historical Review* 78 (April 2001): 187–214.

Remini, Robert V., and Robert O. Rupp, comps. *Andrew Jackson: A Bibliography.* Westport: Meckler, 1991.

Rohrer, S. Scott. "Evangelism and Acculturation in the Backcountry: The Case of Wachovia, North Carolina, 1753–1830." *Journal of the Early Republic* 21 (2001): 199–229.

Shammas, Carole, Marylynn Slamon, and Michel Dahlin. *Inheritance in America: From Colonial Times to the Present.* New Brunswick, N.J.: Rutgers University Press, 1987.

Snider, William D. *Light on the Hill: A History of the University of North Carolina at Chapel Hill.* Chapel Hill: University of North Carolina Press, 1992.

Stokes, Durward Turrentine. "North Carolina and the Great Revival of 1800." *North Carolina Historical Review* 43 (October 1966): 401–12.

Wagstaff, Henry M. *Federalism in North Carolina.* Chapel Hill: University of North Carolina Press, 1910.

Antebellum North Carolina

Unless a determinate event such as a revolution, a civil war, or the assassination of a president occurs, history seldom divides itself neatly into epochs, periods, or ages. Instead, historians frequently describe eras in terms of the evolution of political structures and parties, the transition between philosophical systems such as the Enlightenment and Romanticism, or as struggles between groups and classes such as serfs and nobility, slaves and freedmen, even men and women. Yet in North Carolina in 1835 such an epochal event occurred that clearly defined the state in terms of its past, present, and future. The constitutional convention of that year served as a vehicle that moved North Carolina from the older republicanism of Thomas Jefferson in national affairs and the fierce individualism of Nathaniel Macon in local politics to the newer democracy of Andrew Jackson then sweeping the nation. It also solidified the rise of the second party system within the state. The 1835 constitutional convention neatly divided antebellum North Carolina from its Jeffersonian past and its Whiggish future. One person, William Gaston, delivered perhaps the most celebrated speech in the state's history at the 1835 convention, an oration so eloquent that it both defined and mirrored the promises and limitations of that age. It all started with a frustrated neo-Federalist, Archibald DeBow Murphey.

From the end of the War of 1812 until 1835, North Carolina somehow seemed "a state asleep" to both contemporaries and critics, and, much later, to historians. Archibald DeBow Murphey tried to awaken North Carolina from its Jeffersonian slumber by a series of reports he filed with the state senate from 1815 until 1819. Thwarted by the party politics of Jeffersonian North Carolina, by his own unrequited Federalist agenda, and by the refusal of the "better sort of people" to listen to him, Murphey's recounting of the ills of North Carolina after the War of 1812 seemed somehow not only apparent in its indictment but also prophetic in its suggestions.

Murphey, who always considered himself to be a Federalist—that is, someone who thought continentally and not provincially—seized upon the wave of nationalism that swept the country belatedly at the end of the War of 1812 to promote his program. To him, it seemed a golden opportunity. The end of the conflict meant "the admittance of liberal," non-Jeffersonian ideas, and Murphey did not intend for North Carolina to be left out of the "mania for change." For his reports, he depended not only upon information from census, county, and official state summaries, but also from questionnaires sent by independent agencies to counties throughout the state. In 1810, for example, Thomas Henderson, editor of Raleigh's newspaper the *Star,* sent out surveys to leading citizens, who were mostly

Archibald DeBow Murphey (1777–1832).
North Carolina Collection, University of
North Carolina at Chapel Hill.

sympathetic to the *Star*'s views, asking them a series of questions about economic, educational, and social conditions in their counties. Since it tended to act as an agent in favor of change, the *Star*'s survey naturally produced intended results. Bartlett Yancey, for example, noted that Henderson County had a large number of people who lacked any sort of education or ambition. Absent were the "spreeing Irishmen, revolutionizing Frenchmen, or speculating Scotchmen" who brought fresh ideas, enterprise, and energy for change with them. In their stead, Henderson County had a large group certainly "entitled to the rank of mediocrity." Overall, the reports, both from counties and newspapers, revealed how much North Carolina by 1815 had become the Lubberland described by William Byrd a century before.

Murphey's reports also showed how North Carolina had become a state unto itself, separate even from its southern neighbors. It had few towns, little industry, limited capital, only three banks, and an inadequate system of public and private education. In Caswell County, less than half the population could read and write. Beginning in 1819 and continuing until 1835, the state senate committee on education reported that "nearly one-half of every family . . . received no education and . . . are as yet unprovided with the means of learning to read and write." Not until the census of 1840 did the percentage of illiterate adults drop to less than one-third. Yet to Murphey, internal improvements, the system of roads, canals, ferries, and, in the 1820s, railroads, seemed to be the most pressing problem.

From its founding through its role in the new nation, North Carolina always had been known for its few and bad roads, its sluggish rivers that emptied into the Atlantic, its lack of adequate ports, harbors, and towns. Internal improvements, the idea of interconnecting roads, turnpikes, rivers, canals, ferries, and railroads that would knit the state together and provide arteries for commerce, crops, industry, and also access to markets, came to be the universal solution for all North Carolina's problems. As envisioned by Archibald Murphey, who appointed himself the spokesman and prophet for internal improvements, it would usher in a golden age of progress, affluence, and education. Towns would grow where none

Above: Ferries like this one in Wilmington formed a crucial link in transportation in early North Carolina.

North Carolina Collection, University of North Carolina at Chapel Hill.

An advertisement for coach services between Morganton and Asheville, 30 July 1831.

North Carolina Collection, University of North Carolina at Chapel Hill.

RUTHERFORDTON, SATURDAY EVENING, J

4 HORSE POST COACH,
FROM MORGANTON TO ASHEVILLE.
J. H. & R. W. TATE,

HAVING become contractors of this Line of Mail Stages, inform the travelling public that they run once a week and back, from Morganton to Asheville, a distance of sixty miles, in two days, a line of four horse Post Coaches, which leave Morganton on every Saturday morning at 4 o'clock A. M. and arrive at Asheville at 6 o'clock, P. M. of the same day; and leave Asheville at 4 o'clock, the following morning, (Sunday) and arrive at Morganton at 8 o'clock, P. M. This line immediately intersects with the line from Salem to Greenville at Morganton and also with the great Western line at Asheville. The accommodation in this Line are excellent—having good coaches, able horses and experienced drivers. This is the speediest and shortest route for those who are travelling either westwardly or eastwardly, as it harmonizes with the Salem, N. C. and Greenville line, which runs 50 or 60 miles per day. ☞FARE—6¼ cents per mile.

N. B. All possible care will be taken of baggage, bundles, &c.; yet the contractors will not be responsible for losses.

Morganton, May 12, 1831. 13tf

SALEM AND GREENVILLE LINE OF
POST-COACHES.

THIS LINE is run through a distance of 196 miles in three days and a half, by way of Huntsville, Statesville, Morganton, Brindletown, Bedfordsville, and Rutherfordton to Greenville S. C. The contractors have good horses and excellent drivers; they have made their stands with a view to

Richmond Mumford Pearson (1805–78), perhaps North Carolina's greatest jurist before the Civil War.
North Carolina Collection, University of North Carolina at Chapel Hill.

existed before, agriculture would be transformed, North Carolina would have access to markets worldwide, and an economic revolution would reawaken the state from its post-Revolutionary swoon. Or so he thought.

Yet Murphey also understood that nothing would be done about internal improvements or even education until North Carolina abandoned the Jeffersonian belief in a minimal, passive role for government. From the end of the American Revolution until Jefferson became president, for example, not a single bill addressing public education was introduced into the general assembly. Revolutionary in its declaration, the provision for public education in the 1776 constitution proved unprogressive in its application. Section 41 of that constitution mandated that "a School or Schools shall be established by the Legislature for the convenient Instruction of Youth, with such Salaries to the Masters paid by the Public, as may enable them to instruct at low prices." Only the University of North Carolina, largely a Federalist idea, grew out of that clause. North Carolina continued its fervid inaction toward education for more than forty years.

Between 1776 and 1825, the general assembly rejected every bill to set up any system of public schools or to furnish significant aid to the University of North Carolina. In that year it established the Literary Fund, more wishful thinking than a realistic plan to bring education to the people of the state. At best, the fund depended upon discretionary monies from restricted state income, dividends from state-owned stock left over after providing for internal improvements, state-owned stock in a few navigational and canal companies that more often than not went bankrupt, occasional legislative appropriations, and, in the most useless of all funding sources, the sales of vacant swamplands. In the decade from 1825 to 1836, the fund accumulated $243,000 and spent $239,000, less than 20 percent of which was for public schools. Riddled by graft and corruption, chiefly from John Haywood, the state treasurer, the Literary Fund represented North Carolina's first attempt to set up a system of public schools since it became a state. In 1828, the general assembly's education committee, calculating that it had a better chance through prayer and fasting to promote public education than by forwarding more bills to the legislature, appealed to "God

David Lowry Swain (1801–68),
governor from 1832 to 1835.
North Carolina Collection, University
of North Carolina at Chapel Hill.

Almighty" to help educate North Carolina's children because the state would not. The Literary Fund existed until after the Civil War, when it went bankrupt due to yet another bad investment, this time in Confederate bonds. To Murphey and his followers, North Carolina's government needed to become more active in promoting the overall welfare of the state's citizens. As much as anything, the 1776 constitution had to be amended and overhauled to allow a more ambitious government to function.

Murphey's call for a more active government found a sympathetic audience largely in the western counties. In the east, neo-Federalists such as Edward Dudley and William Gaston echoed Murphey's appeal for a revitalized government, but, in the west, he found his greatest support. David L. Swain, John Motley Morehead, William A. Graham, and Joseph Caldwell, some of whom had studied law with Murphey, saw in his reports a way out of the political and sectional gridlock that had curtailed the representation of western counties for over three decades.

Running along the Atlantic coast in three tiers, eastern counties, small but proportionally populated, contained much of the state's taxable wealth but less and less comparatively, because of a growing population. Until 1800, large but sparsely inhabited western counties had reasonable representation in the assembly but not in appointed offices. The situation worsened under Jeffersonian, largely eastern political control. Between 1776 and 1833, eighteen new western and fifteen new eastern counties came into being, but, increasingly, slavery and diminishing free land in the east meant fewer people in ever-smaller, chopped-up counties, while in the west abundant land and the relative absence of slavery meant increased opportunities for settlement in ever-larger counties. Moreover, western counties resented the borough franchise, the practice of giving additional representatives to older, established eastern towns that tended to overrepresent eastern counties while underrepresenting newer, western ones. By 1825, an imaginary line dividing east and west politically, socially, and economically ran through Granville, Wake, Cumberland, and Robeson counties.

After the War of 1812, western politicians began to push the issue of representational reform. Through newspapers, pamphlets, mass meetings, and heated debates in the general assembly, westerners sought to set themselves apart from the east and to achieve some sort of legislative parity. In Salisbury, the newspaper *Carolina Watchman* became the voice of western discontent. Murphey's reports only intensified the west's belief in the need for political reform. In 1823 a caucus of western legislators called for a special convention, an old Federalist idea, to amend the 1776 constitution and to seek more equitable representation. Although a failure, the proposal for an extralegal convention nonetheless held an appeal for politicians from all sections of the state as a way to get around the cumbersome political logjam of one-party Jeffersonianism that dammed the legislative process and prevented reform in several areas.

The issues raised by Murphey and his supporters, those of education, internal improvements, equitable representation, and a generalized desire to amend the 1776 constitution came to a head with the rise of a new national political party and its leader, Andrew Jackson. No sooner had the 1823 convention failed than the state turned its attention to the first truly new national party in decades, the Democrats. In 1824, the one-party facade of Jeffersonian republicanism crumbled under the impact of the epic battle between Andrew Jackson, Henry Clay, William H. Crawford, and John Quincy Adams. In its ashes, a new two-party system emerged in North Carolina. Predictably, in 1824 the eastern counties, the very heart of Jeffersonian North Carolina, supported the selection of the "official" Republican caucus, William Crawford of Georgia, while the west, with a youthful, reinvigorated leadership headed by men such as Charles Fisher and David Swain "attained a unanimity for Jackson" equal to its zeal for constitutional reform. Yet by 1828 the west had all but abandoned Andrew Jackson and his new democracy. To western representatives, it all smacked of an older Jeffersonianism practiced by Nathaniel Macon and the eastern elite.

For the nation, Jacksonian democracy had come to mean the expansion of the franchise—that is, the right to vote—and the removal of many of the property qualifications for holding office. At the same time, Democrats emphasized a loyalty and party discipline that older Jeffersonians admired. Under Martin Van Buren and Andrew Jackson, the Democrats also adopted platforms that neatly embraced programs of proposed action while they excluded others. For Charles Fisher, David Swain, and John Motley Morehead, Andrew Jackson's democracy tended to favor the interests of the older planter elite of the east and not the expanding west. The west desperately needed roads and representation. When the Republican Party settled into a nationalism that promoted leaders from the northeast, such as John Quincy Adams from Massachusetts, North Carolina's Republicans suddenly discovered that they were Jacksonian Democrats after all. Four years later, in 1828, North Carolinians found that, overall, they preferred Jackson to his presidential opponent, John Quincy Adams, no friend to the South, and temporarily jumped on the popular Tennessean's bandwagon. Elected president in 1828, Jackson became the folk hero for eastern politicians and the bane of the west. When Jackson appointed John Branch of Halifax to his cabinet as secretary of the navy, a minor post, and vetoed the Maysville road bill, an act that literally would have paved the way for the federal government to help with internal improvements, western politicians such as John Motley Morehead and David Swain found themselves once more without a party or an advocate.

The mania for Jackson died in western North Carolina and was reborn in the east. When Jackson killed the Bank of the United States with his veto, westerners found they

William Gaston (1778–1844), one of North Carolina's leading figures before the Civil War.
North Carolina Collection, University of North Carolina at Chapel Hill.

had some allies in the eastern counties who, representing commercial interests, wanted easier access to credit and capital. James Iredell from Chowan, governor from 1827 to 1828 and an astute observer of state politics, wryly opined that more banks certainly would not hurt North Carolina's economy. North Carolina had only three, the Bank of New Bern, the State Bank in Raleigh, and, the largest, the Bank of Cape Fear in Wilmington, all small state banks inadequate to its needs. Some old Federalists such as William Gaston of Craven County and Edward Stanly of Beaufort, uneasy with the narrow Republicanism of Jefferson and Macon, became equally disenchanted with Jackson's churlish, pinchpenny politics as president. By 1832 politicians in the far eastern and western counties had formed the Whig Party, an instrument to express their common dislike of Andrew Jackson and also a means to reform the outdated constitution of 1776. In North Carolina, Archibald DeBow Murphey helped to end the one-party system that had dominated state politics since the Revolution and to create the new Whig Party. Those who opposed Murphey's reforms found their leader in Andrew Jackson and his concept of a limited democracy. In Whiggery, the opposition to arbitrary policies made by absolute rulers such as "King" Andrew Jackson, politicians from eastern and western counties, who seldom shared issues and interests, came together in the convention of 1835. Ironically, Jackson, with strong ties to North Carolina and an advocate of the common man, served as a lighting rod for the state's warring political factions to come together and emerge in a new party, the Whigs. The convention of 1835 further served as a stage to display North Carolina's second national party system, the Whigs and the Democrats. The two dominated state politics until the Civil War.

Two other events, both within the state, promoted a sense of urgency, of an impending crisis that led to the calling of a constitutional convention. First, the state capitol accidentally caught fire and burned to the ground in the summer of 1831, and the ensuing debate over its rebuilding spurred new animosity and factionalism between the east and west. William Gaston, an enormously popular figure but a Catholic legally disbarred by Article 32 of the 1776 constitution that allowed only Protestants to hold public office, received an appointment to the state supreme court. Gaston's nomination called into question the antiquated features of North Carolina's constitution and government. After the capitol burned, Fayetteville and its eastern supporters, sensing the weakness and drift in state affairs, organized a petition to have the capital moved from Raleigh to there. For two years the general assembly battled over funds to rebuild or relocate the state capitol, frequently meeting within sight of the charred ruins of the old state offices. Fayetteville and its supporters, many from the east, eventually lost, but, in the complicated debates and debacles that followed, found that they had supporters from the west who would like to see the capital relocated. In the abortive convention of 1823, westerners passionately called for the revocation of Article 32 of the 1776 constitution, the unpopular "test" clause aimed at excluding atheists, Jews, Catholics, and even pacifists such as Quakers and Moravians, from public office. Seldom enforced, the article pointed to the inadequacies of an outdated eighteenth-century constitution that limited state government in an era of new nationalism.

In the post-Jacksonian general assembly of 1830, disgruntled representatives elected as governor Montford Stokes, a prominent reformer from Wilkes County, and two years later David Swain of Buncombe County, both avid supporters of a constitutional convention. In 1831, both westerners and their supporters in the east threatened to hold up the rebuilding of the state capitol and postpone Gaston's appointment until the people voted on the "convention question." In the 1834 assembly, the Convention Act narrowly passed both in the lower house and in the senate. Later that same year, the act, in a popular referendum, passed by 5,856 votes. North Carolina could now reform itself.

On 4 June 1835, the delegates met in Raleigh. Of the 130 who came, 76 represented eastern counties, 54 western. Sixty-three came from the newly formed Whig Party, 38 labeled themselves as Democrats, and 29 preferred to be called Independents. More important, 44 actively had been involved in the movement for internal improvements, while at least 23 others had supported measures to improve roads, bridges, ferries, and public education. Nathaniel Macon, the elected president of the convention and the éminence grise of North Carolina politics, hovered over the deliberations more as a patriarch than a participant. Recalling their constitutional forefathers who had met in Philadelphia in 1787, several delegates, led by Jesse Spaight, a former Speaker of the House from Greene County, objected to the oath that would force the convention to abide by the restrictions and limitations set by the act. Instead, argued Spaight, they should revise the constitution in the name of the majority of the people who voted in the election, not by the dictates of the assembly. Easily sweeping aside the broader interpretation of the act, William Gaston led a majority who agreed that the oath legally bound them. Otherwise, counseled Gaston, "we are not the Convention called by the people, but a self-constituted body." Gaston's speech demonstrated his key position within the convention while also pacifying reformers and conservatives from both parties. The issues addressed by the 1835 convention—the elimination of the borough franchise, the modification of Article 32, the process of amending the constitution, the method of representation in the assembly and of electing the governor, and the scrapping of the vote for free blacks—all mirrored the aspirations and limitations of Jacksonian democracy in North Carolina.

The borough franchise, an ancient English custom kept by North Carolina's revolutionary founders that allowed older eastern towns to have representatives as well as the counties where they were located, had as its defenders prominent delegates such as William Gaston of New Bern, while the attack against the vote for towns came from James Smith of Orange County and Jesse Wilson of Perquimans County. Although a quaint and archaic issue that demands little attention today, the borough franchise debate took several days of the convention's work in 1835, the most of any issue. The subject matter, that of representation by the people or the boroughs, plunged into the thinking of what democracy meant to nineteenth-century North Carolinians and called forth more passions and rhetoric than any other issue. Gaston maintained that representatives from towns such as New Bern and Edenton gave an urban perspective to debates, that towns paid a large share of the state's taxes and should be entitled to special representation, that legislation related to commercial activities required the advice of legislators who were merchants, and that towns or boroughs essentially had a unique voice in the state's matters that balanced an overwhelmingly rural interest. The same political rhetoric would surface again 150 years later when North Carolina largely had become an urban and not a rural state. In opposition, James Smith pointed to the undemocratic nature of the borough franchise, left over, he asserted, from "the British Monarchical Government, but . . . not suited to our Republican system. " The delegates never strayed from that central point.

Jesse Wilson, in a point-by-point retort to Gaston's speech, underscored the autocratic, arbitrary nature of the franchise. "With what semblance of justice," he mockingly asked

50

The proscriptive denunciation contained in this article—whether it could or could not be enforced—never has been enforced. The question before us is one, not of practical convenience, but of fundamental principles. He who would sacrifice such principles to the passion or caprice or excitement of the moment, may be called a politician, but he is no statesman. We are now examining into the soundness of the foundation of our institutions. If we rest the fabric of the constitution upon the prejudices—unreasoning and mutable prejudices—we build upon the sand. But let us lay it on the broad and firm basis of natural right, equal justice and universal freedom—freedom of opinion—freedom, civil and religious—freedom, as approved by the wise, and sanctioned by the good—and then may we hope that it shall stand against the storms of faction, violence and injustice, for *then* we shall have founded it upon a ROCK.

NOTE.—The amendment proposed by the committee, substituting the word *Christian* for "Protestant," was decided by the following vote of the Convention, viz.

For the Amendment, . . . 74
Against it, ... 51

Majority, ... 23

THE END.

William Gaston's speech in the 1835 convention against the use of the word "Protestant" in the 1776 constitution that forbade Catholics and Jews to serve in state government.

North Carolina Collection, University of North Carolina at Chapel Hill.

the delegates, "was a member to be allowed to the towns of Fayetteville, New Bern, and Wilmington, whilst Washington, Plymouth, and Elizabeth City are to be debarred that privilege?" If merchants needed representation, then why did New Bern and Wilmington send "Lawyers or Doctors" while other, more rural counties elected merchants and tradesmen to voice their concerns? Moreover, maintained Wilson, almost every single town in the state that had more than five hundred people had elected a delegate to the convention itself. Lastly, he upheld the Jacksonian ideal that "the people are honest and discerning," and, as such, would elect "their men of intelligence, whether living in town or country." The towns had nothing to fear in popular, democratic elections. The vote to retain the borough franchise failed.

The convention then turned to the central problem that dominated all others, equitable representation. The act authorizing the convention called for senators to be elected by districts based on taxation while the House of Commons would have its representatives selected on the basis of the federal census. The convention also could choose the number of senators, a minimum of 34 to a maximum of 50, and of representatives, from 90 to one 120. The problem of representation really had been decided when the 1834 assembly authorized the convention to decide the question. Thus, the arguments took little time, the maximum number of senators and representatives having already been decided. Still, Jesse Wilson of Perquimans County and Jesse Spaight from Greene County nonetheless contested the inevitable outcome. The west, they contended, wanted "power in their hands, not because Lincoln, Orange . . . were unequally represented . . . but because they wanted to construct railroads, canals . . . to give them an outlet to the ocean." The arguments from smaller counties such as Perquimans fell on deaf ears. He was right. Of course, the west as well as many of the other counties in the state wanted internal improvements. That meant control of the government, and the obvious point did little to persuade the delegates already committed to that outcome. William Gaston's address assured the end result.

The concern over the transfer of power to the west, Gaston contended, had its roots in sectionalism, an age-old problem that plagued North Carolina and kept it from a natural progress that its people and resources implied. Instead, the west wanted the same things as the east, internal improvements and systems of roads, canals, and railroads that would bind the state together and undo the animus of sectional animosity. Sounding much like an old Federalist, Gaston argued the larger question of nationalism and all but ignored the sectionalist issues. "Who but must wish," he declared, "that her disconnected fragments were brought together by those facilities of communication which might make them feel and act as one people in interest and affection?" Reapportionment in the House of Commons of the general assembly would come after the censuses of 1840 and 1850.

In quick succession the convention put into force other pillars of Jacksonian democracy. The assembly would meet every two years, not annually, and the people, not the members of the assembly, would elect the governor. Moreover, the governor would serve for two years instead of one but not for more than two terms or four years altogether. The attorney general, instead of serving indefinitely "for good behavior," would have only four years in office. The poll tax on each head, whether free or slave, would be the same. In a move to remove everyday ordinances and business from the affairs of the assembly, the convention voted to provide general laws for divorce and alimony, the changing of names, and the legitimization of children born out of wedlock, all personal and petty business that consumed much of the time and business of the assembly. For many women, the removal of domestic issues such as divorce and alimony from the agenda of the assembly meant good news. Additionally, public officials at last could be impeached through a process similar to that in the national Constitution, where the House of Commons would prosecute and the senate would convict for individual crimes and misdemeanors. Two processes and not one would allow for any future amendments to the new constitution. The assembly could call a special constitutional convention or else the legislature could, by a three-fifths vote at consecutive sessions, recommend amendments to the public. For approval, the people could decide upon the appropriateness of amendments at a special election called for that purpose.

Two additional questions defined the scope of Jacksonian democracy in North Carolina and, in so doing, took up much of the convention's time. The religious test, Article 32 of the 1776 constitution, stirred so much passion that delegates too ill to walk asked to be carried on litters to hear the debates. At the heart of the issue lay the ancient animosity between Protestants and Catholics. James Smith of Orange County, appropriately named for William of Orange, "the defender of the faith," asked that the test be retained but used only "when necessary to defeat some deep laid scheme of ambition." From Martin County, Jesse Cooper, a fiery legislator and part-time preacher, testified that "the Roman Catholic is the very offspring of a despot," espousing a "dangerous doctrine," and "should be excluded from holding office." Reluctant to be branded bigots, many delegates silently agreed with Cooper but still had qualms about enforcing the ban. Sensing the moment, William Gaston, the only Catholic member of the convention, rose to rebut Smith and Cooper and to defend the principle of religious liberty. Notable for its reasoned thought and its clarity, Gaston's speech defined the limited democracy of its age. Religious freedom would be debated intensely yet slavery would not. First, Gaston agreed with many of the points made by Cooper and Smith, thus making it more difficult to differ with him. True, he ruminated, the test oath, by a "purely . . . legal exposition," did not specifically disbar Catholics from office, mostly because the idea of denying the truth of Protestantism defied any sort of logical definition. As a Catholic, Gaston found he could affirm the general truth of Protestantism since both religions had similar origins. Moreover, no one, not even Jews such as Jacob Henry, who had been seated in the House of Commons in 1808, of course with Gaston's support, need be excluded by their own religious beliefs. As early as 1823 Gaston had spoken against the article as "hostile to the Principles of Religious freedom and unworthy of the liberality of the age," words that resonated in his 1835 speech. Although the article was not actually enforced, Gaston maintained that it did not necessarily follow "that no practical evil has arisen from it." By distancing any citizen from an attachment to the "institutions of his country, by causing him to feel that a stigma was cast . . . if it has swelled the arrogance or embittered the malice of sectarian bigotry" then vast had been its "practical mischief." After a long history of the progression of religious liberty in the colonies and new nation, Gaston closed with a declaration of his loyalties. "I owe NO ALLEGIANCE to any man or set of men," he avowed, "save only to the State of North Carolina, and, so far as she has parted with her sovereignty, to the United States of America." One delegate recalled the "great deliberation" of Gaston's speech, received "amid breathless silence, for two days" that "riveted the attention of all present," an oration "unequaled in our memory." Gaston then insisted that the word "Christian" be substituted for "Protestant," an amendment that easily passed. Yet still bowing to precedent and prejudice, the revised clause nonetheless excluded Jews, atheists, and pacifists, an excommunication more in principle than in practice.

174

If the debate and passion elicited by the issue of a religious test and its propriety mirrored the liberality of Jacksonian democracy, then the issue of the enfranchised black person laid bare its racial divide. James Iredell and William Gaston, two of North Carolina's most renowned politicians of the era, had long advocated the abolition of slavery. In 1832, Gaston delivered a stirring oration at the University of North Carolina urging an end to the "vile institution." By 1858 his address had run through five editions and had become a staple of abolitionist literature throughout the South and the nation. As early as 1815, the state had organized manumission societies that, with the ending of the slave trade in 1808, hoped to persuade North Carolinians and southerners in general to free their slaves through wills or paid labor. Between 1823 and 1826, the American Colonization Society, using North Carolina as a model, proudly announced that the "Old North State" had freed more than two thousand slaves. By 1830, the North Carolina Manumission Society, with thirty chapters located mainly in the Piedmont counties, had more than 1,200 members. Yet when the convention met in 1835, manumission had substantially ended and sentiment

William Gaston's
"Old North State."
North Carolina Collection,
University of North Carolina
at Chapel Hill.

had turned against freed slaves and increasingly favored severe restrictions, even deportation, from the state.

Events between 1819 and 1835 made the free Negro in North Carolina the scapegoat for Jacksonian democracy. The acrimonious 1819 debate over the entrance of Missouri into the Union as a slave state, and thereafter of Maine into the Union as a free state, upset North Carolinians as well as other southerners. The Missouri Compromise hardly modified their fears over the future of slavery. Thomas Jefferson remarked that the attack upon the South and its "peculiar institution" by the North in the debate over Missouri's petition for statehood in 1819 "awakened him like a fire bell in the night," and it also sounded the alarm over slavery in North Carolina. Aroused by the fiery rhetoric of northern congressmen, North Carolinians began to defend the "peculiar institution" of slavery along with Jefferson and John C. Calhoun of South Carolina, both southern neighbors. In the 1820s, the fear of a slave rebellion increased when eighty slaves from Onslow County left en masse to join other runaways in the Great Dismal Swamp. Two events in 1831 further heightened North Carolinians' fears. First, Nat Turner led a rebellion in rural Southampton County, Virginia, that turned into perhaps one of the bloodiest and most costly of all slave insurrections. A scant few miles away in bordering Northampton County, North Carolinians joined their Virginia neighbors in the vengeful search for Turner and his followers.

In January 1831, William Lloyd Garrison began publication of the *Liberator,* a newspaper that called for the immediate, not gradual, end of slavery. Uncompromising in his stern manner, Garrison proclaimed that in ending slavery "I do not wish to think, or speak, or write with moderation. . . . I will not equivocate—I will not excuse—I will not retreat a single inch—AND I WILL BE HEARD!" Denouncing manumission, colonization, and gradual emancipation, he dismissed the idea that southern slave owners should receive some form of compensation for freeing their slaves. The morality, the righteousness of the cause, Garrison insisted, was payment enough. That same year a free African American convention in Boston also dismissed manumission and colonization to Africa as proslavery and antiblack. "This is our home . . . our country," a delegate avowed, "Beneath its sod lie the bones of our fathers; for it some of them fought, bled, and died. Here we were born, and here we will die." After 1831 North Carolina, along with many southern states, found itself defending slavery instead of working to abolish it.

Almost from its founding, North Carolina always had a significant free black population and seemed less restrictive in its black codes on those held in bondage. In Chatham County, George Moses Horton lived on his master's farm but, with a great deal of freedom and trust, frequently visited the University of North Carolina at Chapel Hill to sell fruits and vegetables for discretionary monies. Encouraged by Caroline Hentz and also by several students, Horton wrote love poems, which he sold to eager students, penned tracts, and in 1837 published the first of three volumes of poetry, *The Hope of Liberty*. David Walker, a free black and son of a minister, instead left the state for the North, where in 1829 he distributed his *Appeal to the Colored Citizens of the World*, an incendiary tract that urged slaves to rise up against their masters. Free black women fared even worse than men after 1835. Always vulnerable because they had even more limited occupational choices than free black men or poor whites had, they risked their children being taken from them and sold into slavery. Having less protection within the community, free black women found themselves ostracized, disinherited, and all too often at the mercy of a legal system that now considered them in a different light. Local authorities jailed Fanny Mason, a black woman freed for over twenty years, mostly because her presence irritated them. On legally questionable grounds they imprisoned her because "she has nothing to show that she is free and from her appearance we think she must be a slave." The mood in North Carolina after 1835 effectively reversed the state's historical laissez-faire attitude toward free and enslaved Africans at the same time it opened up the state to the "more liberal ideas" of Murphey and Gaston.

The older state constitution of 1776 did not mention race in relation to suffrage or holding office. Freed blacks who could meet the state's property qualifications could and did vote for assemblymen in both houses for four decades. Still, the numbers, varying as they did from a few score to several hundred, proved negligible, seldom influencing any election. Yet the proposition to eliminate "free persons of color" from voting in the 1835 convention called forth little of the passion and rhetoric of the debate over Article 32 and the principle of religious liberty and equitable representation. From the introduction of the initial resolution until the final vote, the general mood and consensus, conditioned as it had been by the events from 1831, dampened the deliberations both from the Whigs and the Democrats. Nonetheless, James Bryon of Carteret County, in the only substantial speech on the subject, advocated the elimination of the free black vote not because of incapacity but inasmuch as "in the hands of designing and ambitious demagogue(s)" it would be abused. A moderate argument, the same rationale had emerged countless times in past constitutional conventions whenever the "better class" wanted to do away with the votes of "lesser classes," whether poor farmers, white trash, propertyless city dwellers, or free black people. Jesse Wilson, strongly Jacksonian and passionate in his attack upon the borough franchise as autocratic and undemocratic, not only wanted the free black vote eliminated but also defended slavery as an attempt to give "debased Africans" a better life. Hugh McQueen, soon to be the state's attorney general and just as quickly a hero of the Texas revolution against Mexico, thought that "no sort of polish which education or circumstance" could give black people would ever "reconcile the whites to an extension of the right of suffrage." Two other arguments used history as precedent. Since free blacks had not voted before the present state and nation had been formed, their current exercise of the privilege seemed accidental, "coeval with the Constitution," certainly not planned by the founders. The weight of numbers of free Negroes voting in predominantly black counties and towns such as New Bern, if the franchise remained and more slaves were manumitted, meant that one day they could form a majority and elect their own sheriffs, councilmen, and representatives, an ominous warning of the end of slavery or the extension of the franchise to freedmen.

Throughout the proceedings westerners such as David Swain remained silent, preferring to let easterners settle what they believed to be their problem. Moreover, it would not have served the western interests of equitable representation, internal improvements, and easier ways to amend the constitution to have intervened, no matter what their views. William Gaston and John Branch of Halifax, a former governor, senator, and secretary of the navy, spoke in favor of keeping the free black vote but with a property qualification. Joseph Daniel and John Toomer also supported Branch and Gaston's stand but with seemingly little passion or advocacy. By a vote of sixty-six to sixty-one, assuredly not an overwhelming

Eng and Chang Bunker (1811–74),
the original Siamese twins, who settled in
Mount Airy in 1839, married sisters, and
lived amicably with their neighbors.
North Carolina Collection, University
of North Carolina at Chapel Hill.

majority, the convention voted to end the right of free black people to vote. Only five votes, less than 3 percent of those cast, separated North Carolina from its racial destiny as a southern state. Had Gaston, Branch, and others such as Macon and Iredell campaigned as hard for the free black vote as they had for extending religious liberty by amending Article 32, North Carolina would have stood alone among its southern and many of its northern sisters in allowing free black people the right to vote. Yet in 1835 the state instead decided to become more southern.

After the convention of 1835 the Whigs became the dominant party in North Carolina, standing for internal improvements, progress, increased expenditures on education, a more active state and local government, and the interests of merchants and planters. The period also saw the strengthening of black codes, those petty local and state ordinances designed to restrict the ability of slaves and free blacks to move within communities, associate with others, intermarry with whites, bear arms, be licensed to trade and engage in commerce, pursue an education, and be emancipated or, if freed, remain in the state. In 1835, the same year he spoke so eloquently on Article 32 in the convention and so ungenerously on the issue of slavery and the free black vote, William Gaston, using his new status and security as a state supreme court judge, ruled in the case of *State vs. Will* that slaves had a right to defend themselves against the unlawful and arbitrary attempt of masters to kill or injure them, a reversal of several prior court decisions. Thus, through the courts, Gaston sought to protect both slaves and free men from an increasingly hostile environment. In 1838, Gaston held that in *State vs. Manuel* a free black man had the same constitutional protections of government as did anyone. Still, in antebellum North Carolina the acquiescence of the 1835 convention in eliminating the free Negro vote was the price of state solidarity, of bringing the sections together, and, in the eyes of Gaston and others, a necessary device for building a modern southern state and awakening North Carolina from its post-Revolutionary slumber. After 1835, North Carolina became more like its antebellum southern neighbors.

Although assuredly patriarchal and hierarchical before 1835, North Carolina seemed to become more so in the years leading to the Civil War. With harsher attitudes toward free blacks and slaves made into law and with an increasingly orthodox evangelical Protestantism dominating the state's folk culture, subordination to male authority permeated all classes. When the 1835 convention moved divorce laws from the whims of the general assembly to common law, the practice tended to favor women of means and standing in the community. In fact, most women who left their husbands or who filed for divorce in antebellum North Carolina often received reprimands from their churches, fathers, families, communities, and from other women as well. Only with rare exceptions, usually that of overt abuse, like that of Mrs. Westley Rhodes, did male patriarchy assert itself in a woman's favor. One night in 1823 Westley beat his wife "in a most cruel manner." Because he had "indulged himself in the habits of intemperance and abuse to his wife for years," she "fled to her father's house for protection." Angered, her mother marched to Westley's house and, supported by her husband and Mrs. Rhodes's grandfather, "reprimanded him for his conduct," in the end striking him repeatedly "with a tobacco stem which she had picked up on the road." A fight ensued between Westley and Mrs. Rhodes's grandfather, ending with the censure of the entire community against the errant husband.

Today, incidents such as these smack of sexism and patriarchy, but in nineteenth-century North Carolina they pointed to another bias that trumped almost all others, that of class. Almost forgotten alongside contemporary obsessions with racism, ageism, sexism, and sexual preferences, the idea of class, of belonging to a socially designated group on the "great chain of being," ordered eighteenth- and nineteenth-century society. Ameliorated by the Revolution, the conceptualization reemerged in antebellum North Carolina, particularly after 1835, when the state became more like its southern sisters. The idea of class clearly divided both male and female North Carolinians into wealthy planters and merchants, free white yeoman farmers, free blacks and slaves, and even large, mostly landless varieties of "white trash." Yet it also allowed the existence of marginal groups, made up mostly of women, that did not fit any suitable category. By antebellum standards, most led precarious, dubious, uncertain, and, not surprisingly, vulnerable lives. While ideas of purity and chastity might have dominated perceptions of wives of the slaveholding elite and a "cult of domesticity" for the middle class, those women on the bottom rungs of society, free whites, free blacks, and slaves, increasingly found themselves with little security and not many constraints in a male-dominated antebellum North Carolina. Poverty and few occupational options for free black women, for example, meant that they lived a precarious existence on the fringes of North Carolina society, frequently with equally disadvantaged white men and women. Those women who either withdrew from "respectable society" or suffered ostracism and isolation because of sexual liaisons or pregnancy formed part of an increasingly larger biracial grouping in the years leading to the Civil War. Living and traveling alone, supporting themselves frequently through menial jobs and questionable romances, congregating around taverns and "liquor houses," brashly and openly speaking their minds, and sometimes even engaging in brawls and gouging matches with both men and women, they took up with men who provided them with even a small measure of security and substance. In antebellum North Carolina, such women, both white and black, worked at backbreaking labor, drank, gamed, swapped, bartered, bargained, and

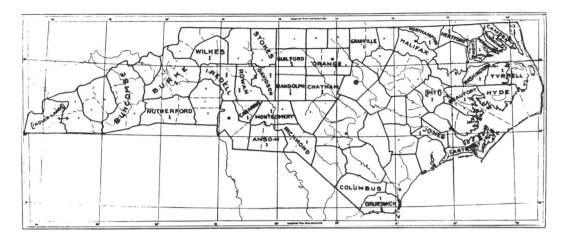

A map of North Carolina in 1836.
North Carolina Office of Archives and History, Raleigh.

embraced each other across color lines. Court records, not diaries or memoirs, chronicled their lives. More often than not, their behavior did not aim at openly defying or even confronting the conventions of the majority of North Carolinians. Instead, their conduct normed the standards of a largely unrecognized, broadening group of the poor whom they lived with and depended upon for survival.

From 1835 until 1850, the newly formed Whig Party, triumphant not only in the state but nationally as well, sought mightily to implement the reforms sought by Murphey and his allies. The linchpin to all the Whigs' visions of what North Carolina should be after 1835 lay in one scheme, that of bringing a railroad system to the state. Plans for railroads had existed in North Carolina for almost a decade prior to the Whig ascendancy to power in 1836, but they never went beyond neat tracks laid on paper. As early as 1828, scores of farmers in the western counties of Orange, Chatham, and Guilford had met to consider how to bring a railroad to the center of the state to allow them access to markets in Virginia and South Carolina. In a series of newspaper articles published earlier in 1827 that came to be called *The Numbers of Carlton,* Joseph Caldwell, as president of the University of North Carolina, dismissed Murphey's earlier insistence upon canals, turnpikes, ferries, and roads and instead endorsed railroads as the only form of internal improvement needed by the state. Caldwell even went further than Murphey. He wanted the state not only to charter a railroad but also to invest public monies in it through taxes, a revolutionary idea for an antebellum Jeffersonian state. Except for authorizing funds to survey railroad routes and issuing charters for private companies, the state had spent nothing on railroads prior to 1835. When the capitol burned in 1831, a construction company in Raleigh laid down a 1.25 mile experimental railroad to haul quarry stones in horse-drawn cars, a curiosity that appealed to locals fascinated by the rails and iron wheels. Yet except for meetings, surveys, largely inactive charters, and novelty rides, railroads never got on track in North Carolina until after 1833.

Late in the summer of 1833, the Petersburg Railroad, operating from Virginia, extended its lines nine miles into North Carolina, stopping near Halifax at the new town of Blakeley.

From there, North Carolinians sent their tobacco and farm products into Virginia, thence northward to be connected to the Baltimore and Ohio, and eventually to be marketed to all the seaboard and northeastern states. In Raleigh, the impact of the new line upon North Carolina's commerce and industry was not lost upon the latest internal improvements convention, which was meeting there in 1833. With the coming of the Petersburg Railroad, railroad fever had at last struck North Carolina. Every town had to have one. Within three years, Wilmington, Raleigh, Weldon, Gaston, Goldsboro, and the Roanoke River region began to plan their own lines.

In Wilmington, Edward Dudley, a prominent businessman soon to be more celebrated as the state's first Whig governor, promoted the Wilmington and Raleigh Railroad Company by helping to raise $1.5 million in capital, no small sum in antebellum North Carolina. Upset when the good citizens of Raleigh failed to subscribe their share of stock and suspecting that they anticipated the line would come to Raleigh anyway, Dudley changed the route to pass forty miles east of Raleigh through Goldsboro and on to Weldon in the Roanoke River valley. There the line ended suspiciously close to the Petersburg Railroad terminus in Blakeley. A traveler in 1849 noted that when traveling south toward Wilmington, "passengers for Raleigh leave this train about midnight, right in the woods," while those bound for Wilmington arrived in comfort at a spacious facility on the Cape Fear River. Completed in 1840, the Wilmington and Weldon Railroad spanned the coast into the Piedmont; at 161 miles, it was the longest continuous railroad in the world at that time.

When Dudley's railroad from Wilmington left Raleigh in a cul-de-sac, the unsubscribed citizens petitioned the legislature for an interstate line to be built in cooperation with the Petersburg Railroad from Greenville County, Virginia, to a southern point at Wilkins Ferry just across the border in Northampton County at a juncture appropriately called Gaston. It later would be extended to Weldon. From there it ran to Raleigh. Built with the cooperation of Virginians in Petersburg and Richmond, the new Raleigh and Gaston Railroad provided access from the Piedmont to the mid-Atlantic states. For over a decade the Raleigh and Gaston lost money until, in 1845, the state took over the failing line for a sum of $363,000. The precedent had been set. The state of North Carolina now was in the railroad business.

Elected governor in 1841 from Guilford County, John Motley Morehead, "the railroad governor," championed a state railroad system to connect the coast to not only Raleigh but also the interior. The landlocked and growing western counties, led by Whig representatives such as David Swain and Charles Manly, cried out for railroads. In a stirring address to the general assembly in 1842, Morehead maintained that west of Greensboro North Carolina ceased to exist. "Cheraw, Camden, Columbia . . . Greenville, . . . Augusta, and Charleston are much more familiarly known than . . . Fayetteville and Raleigh." To unify the state politically and to become more economically independent of Virginia, South Carolina, Georgia, and Tennessee, North Carolina needed railroads that ran from the east to the west as well as from the north to the south. Even distant Buncombe County in the far west had caught the fever by 1841.

The idea of a railroad bill for a state-owned railroad that connected earlier lines and ran to western towns such as Charlotte, Salisbury, and even Greensboro persisted in the general assembly for over a decade. Finally, in 1849 W. S. Ashe of New Hanover County managed to introduce a bill that despite bitter partisan bickering from established railroad

*John Motley Morehead (1796–1866),
governor from 1841 to 1845.*
North Carolina Collection, University
of North Carolina at Chapel Hill.

companies and entrenched private interests passed by a single vote, that of Calvin Graves, Speaker of the Senate from Caswell County. A Democrat, Graves went against his own party and that of the interests of the eastern seaboard to cast his vote. In so doing, he helped promote "North Carolina's declaration of economic independence" from its southern neighbors, unify the three sections of the state, and end his own political career.

Not surprisingly, Morehead took the lead as president of the new North Carolina Railroad. A tireless booster and promoter, he managed to raise more than $1 million in stock from private sources to match the $2 million from the state. When Calvin Graves symbolically helped lay the first rails from Greensboro two years later, work already had begun in Goldsboro, the eastern terminus. Five years later, North Carolina at last had its own railroad, a system more than 223 miles in length that passed through Hillsborough, Salisbury, Concord, Charlotte, and Greensboro in a politically gerrymandered half-moon route that eventually ended in Goldsboro. Because of railroads and politics, Goldsboro and Weldon as well as Raleigh and Charlotte became new bustling centers of commerce and industry. Connected at last to its southern neighbors and also to its western siblings, North Carolina boasted one of the best interior railroad systems in the South just prior to the Civil War, a fact not lost upon the original Petersburg Railroad and its confederated investors in Richmond. Yet at times North Carolina's growth prior to the Civil War seemed more accidental than incremental.

With the coming of the railroad, North Carolina seemed to strike economic gold after 1835. In 1799, according to legend, Conrad Reed, the son of John Reed, made a lucky strike on his father's plantation in Cabarrus County that truly uncovered gold. Conrad found a seventeen-pound nugget in the bed of a small stream called Meadow Creek. Taken to nearby Concord, the nugget, when finally smelted, purportedly produced a solid gold bar more than eight inches long. Between 1803 and 1831, numerous interlopers and the Reeds found scores of nuggets within a mile of the initial discovery. Rich flint and quartz veins nearby led to the nation's first gold rush that slowly panned out when gold was discovered in the north Georgia mountains in the late 1820s and in California in 1848. In 1840 John

Grist mills like this one in Guilford County dotted antebellum North Carolina.
North Carolina Collection, University of North Carolina at Chapel Hill.

Wheeler, superintendent of the newly opened Charlotte mint, reported that North Caro-lina produced $500,00 worth of gold and $35,000 worth from the Cabarrus mines. Not to be outdone, Christian Bechtler, a German jeweler, assayer, and entrepreneur, set up his own mint in Rutherfordton in 1831. The only private mint ever to operate in the United States prior to the Civil War, Bechtler's firm continued to produce coins until 1857. Today, his coins, graded higher than the U.S. Mint's in Philadelphia and Charlotte because of a greater gold content, have considerable value on the numismatic market. Prospectors fol-lowed the "golden creek" to the north and west after 1824, looking for the mother lode in the mountains of western North Carolina and Georgia.

By 1828 gold diggers in Burke and McDowell counties to the north began to trace the veins southwestward into the region around Dahlonega, Georgia. In an area of over two hundred square miles extending from the first and second Broad rivers along the South Carolina border, thence from Muddy Creek and Silver Creek into the mountains of the Carolinas and Georgia, miners fanned out in search of the mythical Cherokee mine that contained a mother lode of almost pure gold. They never found it. Not until the discov-ery of gold in California in 1848 did prospectors and diggers abandon the idea of finding either a secret Indian mine or more gold and silver in the northwest mountains. By 1850 more than fifty-three mines still operated throughout the state, chief among them the Reed, Gold Hill, Phoenix, and Barnhardt mines in Cabarrus County; the Davis, Pfifer, and Pewter mines in Union County; the Hearne in Stanly County; King's Mountain in Gaston County; Rhymer and Fisher Hills mines in Rowan County; the Rudisil mine in Mecklenburg County; and the Conrad Hill and Silver mines in Davidson County. Although most of the mines shut down during the Civil War, North Carolina continued to produce significant amounts of gold until 1916.

Although the origins of gold leaf, lemon leaf, or, as it came to be called, bright leaf tobacco remain unclear, it emerged as a staple crop in the two decades prior to the Civil

War. According to myth and tradition, Stephen, the blacksmith slave of Abisha and Elisa Slade in Caswell County, either accidentally added charcoal from his forge to the wood used to cure tobacco or else fell asleep and allowed a barn of curing tobacco to burn, thus producing higher temperatures and a new "cure" for tobacco. Years later, agricultural agents from North Carolina State University discovered that chemicals in the porous soil along the Virginia border produced the bright yellow and more mellow form of the "noxious weed," not higher temperatures. From less than five million pounds in 1830, North Carolina's tobacco production, aided by access to markets by the coming of the railroad, jumped to twelve million pounds in 1850 and to thirty-three million in 1860. North Carolina had almost replaced Virginia as the tobacco capital of the nation by the Civil War.

By lowering freight rates, decreasing the time it took to get crops to markets, and furnishing lines to the state's three regions, the railroad spurred a small economic boom after 1835. Between 1840 and 1860, cotton production more than quadrupled, from 34,617 bales, each weighing approximately 500 pounds, to 148,000 bales by the coming of the Civil War. Located almost exclusively in Brunswick County, rice production topped more than 800,000 pounds by 1860. Wheat more than doubled, from 2 million pounds in 1850 to almost 5 million pounds by 1861. Corn remained the staple crop, its uses ranging from fodder for horses, mules, pigs, poultry, and cattle to roughage for humans such as hoecakes, cornbread, mush, hominy, and roasted ears. Lastly, consumption of "cracked corn" or corn whiskey, produced throughout the state, continued unabated as a staple of trade and of social gatherings.

Although North Carolinians had been derisively referred to as Tar Heels for their small distilleries of turpentine, pitch, and tar before the American Revolution, the period from 1824 to 1860 stamped that image indelibly upon the state's history. By the Civil War, North Carolina had more than 1,600 turpentine distilleries. Two-thirds of the nation's turpentine came from North Carolina; one-half from two counties, Bladen and New Hanover. With the new railroad from Wilmington bringing factors and merchants to the state from all over the world, the nation saw firsthand the crude distilleries, usually run by small gangs of

*Processing turpentine
in early North Carolina.*
North Carolina Office of
Archives and History,
Raleigh.

The turpentine industry in North Carolina.
North Carolina Collection, University of North Carolina at Chapel Hill.

barefoot, poorly dressed whites and blacks. Turpentine, pitch, and tar made up the only manufacturing industry in the state carried on mainly for export prior to the Civil War. After 1824, North Carolina became the nation's leading producer of naval stores, thus stamping its Tar Heel perception across the country.

In a seedbed scattered along streams and in counties throughout the Piedmont, antebellum North Carolina planted a textile industry that eventually made it the economic engine of the South. On Great Alamance Creek, Edwin M. Holt, a successful planter and merchant, in 1837 constructed a large water wheel, spinning mill, and cotton mill that produced "Alamance plaids," large sheetings of colored cotton cloth marketed throughout the South. At Rocky Mount, the Battle family began manufacturing cotton textiles, as did Francis Fries in Salem. By 1860 the state ranked first in the South with thirty-nine cotton

*Dipping crude turpentine in
Sampson County.*
North Carolina Collection, University
of North Carolina at Chapel Hill.

mills. Early North Carolina mill owners such as the Battles, Holts, Hokes, Fries, and Hanes emerged after the Civil War as the homegrown capitalists and entrepreneurs of a New South.

Things also changed in education after 1835. In 1839 the state adopted a publicly supported plan for free common schools for white children, and the next year the first public schools opened. Still, the system, which was the product of Whig politicians and Democratic allies, languished for over a decade until another Murphey-like missionary, Calvin H. Wiley, took it over. A young lawyer, indefatigable writer, excellent administrator, and inexhaustible circuit rider, Wiley, the father of public education in North Carolina, quickly brought order and purpose to a position he created and defined, that of state superintendent of schools. He served in that capacity until the end of the Civil War. Wiley wrote the state's first instructional handbook, the *North Carolina Reader* (1851), put in place examinations and licensing procedures for teachers, set up county institutes to train teachers, founded and edited the *North Carolina Journal of Education,* and single-handedly organized the Educational Association of North Carolina. Given a free pass by the state, Wiley took advantage of the new railroad system, frequently getting off at the end of the line and continuing by horse and carriage to outlying counties to carry the "good news" of the state's schools.

Almost magically, schools seemed to mushroom overnight where Wiley trod, so great had been the state's need for education. From fewer than 315 schools in 1835 to more than 3,050 in 1850 with 118,000 students, North Carolina sprinted to catch up with the rest of the South and the nation. Within a decade the state justifiably could boast the South's leading educator in Wiley and even the best-run and supported public school system, no small praise in a region that was the last in the nation to institutionalize public education. It

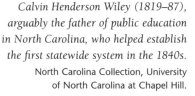

Calvin Henderson Wiley (1819–87),
arguably the father of public education
in North Carolina, who helped establish
the first statewide system in the 1840s.
North Carolina Collection, University
of North Carolina at Chapel Hill.

would be a century after the Civil War before North Carolina regained the educational prominence it had under Wiley. Yet despite the fact that North Carolina had more than 3,000 public schools and 500 private academies and "old field," or subscription, schools by 1850, illiteracy, the product of generations of neglect, persisted. In the South, only Virginia had more illiterates by the beginning of the Civil War. As many as 40 percent of the entire adult population, mostly slaves and lower-class whites, could not read or write.

With a new, active state government, North Carolina found itself open to many of the reforms that already had swept over the Northeast and to the liberal ideas promoted by Archibald Murphey. Famous for helping the mentally ill in Boston and New York, Dorothea Dix at last turned her attention to the South in 1848. Visiting North Carolina, she unsurprisingly found a need for the state to care for the insane. Rebuffed by the general assembly after a passionate address to its members, Dix turned her persuasive and magnetic skills upon individual members, particularly John Ellis and James Dobbins. Dobbins's wife, incurably ill, responded to the empathy and appeal of Dix, and, on her deathbed, made her husband promise to sponsor the bill. In a lengthy and poignant speech, Dobbins implored the Democrats to lay aside their differences with the Whigs and to vote for a state mental hospital. The bill passed, and in 1853 construction began on a hospital at a site appropriately if unofficially called Dix Hill. Completed in 1856, the hospital housed up to 150 patients. Spurred by the actions of William D. Cooke, head of the Virginia Institute for the Deaf and Dumb, North Carolina moved to establish a similar institute. Opened in 1856, the institute, also superintended by Cooke, housed twenty-three students. Murphey's belief that liberal ideas would wake the state from its Jeffersonian hibernation seemed to be coming to pass.

The year of 1835 divided North Carolina in other, more subtle ways. The discovery of gold in the foothills and mountains of western North Carolina opened up vast new lands for settlement. Forced to leave on the long Trail of Tears, Cherokee Indians abandoned foothill and lower towns, leaving almost unharmed their fields, crops, farmhouses, and orchards. Although the Quallas, the eastern band, remained almost intact, they, too, retreated deeper into the balsams and the "smoking" mountains of their original homeland, well out of the path of onrushing settlers. Frontiersmen moved into counties named after figures such as John Haywood, Bartlett Yancey, President Andrew Jackson, and even Indians who had just been removed, such as the Cherokees and the Watauga. With the opening up of the West, new leaders, including David Swain and Bartlett Yancey, desperately needing new roads, whether by plank, turnpike, or rail, emerged as leaders in the state for the first time, bringing with them a fresh perspective on state affairs that required Raleigh to be more active and energetic.

The great revivals that swept over North Carolina and the South in the 1830s forever moved religion onto the center stage of the state, socially, culturally, and even politically. As much as the coming of the railroad, more equitable representation for western counties, a functioning system of education, and the increasing prosperity that came after 1835, religious schisms changed North Carolina. Between 1830 and 1860, the end of religious revivalism served to homogenize evangelical religious values throughout society, to separate white and black churchgoers more rigidly than ever, and, by the Civil War, to create a folk culture without an attendant sense of responsibility to a wider national community. Within the lifetime of Nathaniel Macon, evangelical religion had, to an unusual degree, come to shape the outlook of North Carolinians of all classes, from rich merchants and landowners to ordinary subsistence and even poor "scratch" farmers. Instead of a larger religious community such as that established by the older Anglican Church, evangelicals succeeded, by the 1840s, in creating a religious culture based on localism and scattered, independent congregations that only associated together. In so doing, they moved from a powerful, dissenting force in southern and North Carolina life to one that merely supported the status quo. North Carolina became antebellum in religion as well as in politics.

After the Revolution, Presbyterians, Baptists, and Methodists had little attraction for well-to-do farmers, landowners, merchants, and the small minority of slave owners in the new state. Pietistic, appealing to the rustic and to the simple in life, otherworldly in their outlook, emotional in their attempts to convert, evangelicals seemed the very antithesis of the rational, calculating, worldly, status-seeking, even arrogant members of North Carolina's emerging elite. Still, as the memories of the Revolution faded and as converts multiplied, Presbyterian, Baptist, and Methodist revivals attracted not only the poor from the tidewater and the backcountry but also an increasing number of the middling sort of North Carolinians. Instead of being on the outside, finding fault with an established church such as the Anglicans, evangelicals by 1830 had established their own values and denominations as the dominant ones. In the constitutional convention of 1835, so secure did mainline denominations feel that they little opposed the removal of Article 32 of the old 1776 constitution excluding from public office anyone who denied the "being of God or the truth of the Protestant religion." With so few Catholics and Jews in the state, Baptists, Presbyterians, Methodists, and Episcopalians could afford to be liberal.

Within the state, evangelical religion became the standard for orthodoxy in the 1830s. Baptists, Methodists, Presbyterians, and Episcopalians all separated spiritually if not physically from their northern brethren and formed southern associations instead. In North Carolina, early Baptists had convened with their northern neighbors to help found Rhode Island College, now Brown University, in 1764. Largely dependent upon southern support for its survival in its early years, Brown incorporated northern and southern Baptists into a cooperative effort on behalf of missions and education. In 1826 the Triennial Convention of Baptists, meeting in Philadelphia, voted down southerners Richard Furman and Luther Rice, the founder of Columbia College, now George Washington University, and moved its headquarters farther north to Boston. In effect, the Triennial Convention disenfranchised southerners, causing them to found not only their own colleges but also, by 1845, their own branch of American Baptists, the Southern Baptist Convention. In North Carolina, Primitive Baptists, or First Baptists, split with the older Separate Baptists, or, as they came to be known, Missionary Baptists, over the problem of having an educated ministry. To primitive Baptists, who harkened to the "original" and literal meaning of the Bible, clergy needed only to be divinely called and not educated to the ministry. The mainstream Baptist Convention, composed mainly of Separate and Missionary congregations, asked the state to charter a Baptist state school. Located in Wake County, and begun by North Carolina Baptists, the Baptist Literary Institute, now known as Wake Forest University, in 1834 had twenty-five students.

Between 1816 and 1844, Methodists not only split into northern and southern branches but also many of their black congregations formally separated by forming the African Methodist Episcopal Church (AME), the African Methodist Episcopal Zion Church (AME Zion), and the Colored Methodist Church in America (CME), renamed the Christian Methodist Episcopal Church in 1954. In 1830 Methodists could claim 180,000 black members, principally in the South, but only 78,000 by the end of the Civil War. Similar divisions occurred among Episcopalians and Presbyterians.

The explanation for the great divide in religion after 1835 between evangelical denominations and their mother churches in the North lay in a single issue that increasingly dominated North Carolina society, that of slavery. When the great revivals of the 1830s swept over the North and the West, southerners felt passed over and left out. While northern evangelicals such as Charles G. Finney and Theodore Weld talked of perfecting society through the abolition of slavery and the formation of utopian, classless communities, North Carolinians instead turned inward to defend their culture and institutions. In Rochester, thousands gathered to hear Finney speak out against slavery while, in North Carolina, equally large crowds met outdoors under arbors and trees along the Yadkin and Neuse rivers to hear local preachers such as William Winams exhort them to defend slavery based on the same "Christian principles." For Benjamin Palmer, a Presbyterian minister, the poverty, inequities, injustices, and oppressions of this world mattered less than sin, salvation, and the conversion of lost souls. In bondage to their own inadequacies and eking out a marginal living, Tar Heels, who were frequently poor and in "reduced straits," saw in this evangelical message a renunciation of their own physical and social limitations and, in their place, a promise of a better life in the hereafter. While northerners might be richer and better off than they, North Carolinians could at least feel morally superior in their religion and pietism.

With the Nat Turner slave revolt, the publication of William Lloyd Garrison's polemical newspaper, the *Liberator,* in 1831, and the final split between Baptists and Methodists from their northern brethren by 1845, North Carolina adopted a rigid and orthodox religious life in place of one that had been more mutable and open, and accepted an increasingly segregated religious experience in lieu of a biracial one. As long as the majority of Baptists,

Methodists, and Presbyterians lay outside the mainstream of southern life and practiced dissenting and warmly democratic ideals and fellowship, they welcomed blacks and, to an extent, women, with open arms. Before 1835 blacks and whites frequently sat together during church services (although blacks commonly occupied back pews and balconies, heard the same sermons) took communion together, and, on rare occasions, participated in church governance and became deacons and elders. In death as in life, blacks and whites frequently found their final rest, their last communion together, in the same graveyards if in separate sections. To a remarkable degree, North Carolina had fewer slave cemeteries than other southern states. Not until after 1831 did "God's acre" commonly become two half acres, one for each race. In the charters founding scores of Baptist and Methodist churches in early North Carolina, both whites and blacks signed the rolls, often only with an "X."

Because of the intimate religious interaction between whites and blacks before 1835, North Carolina's early evangelical churches included features derived from Africans and Creoles. Almost all African societies believed in "God as One," monotheism, and sorcerers with magical powers who could come back from the dead. Thus, African ideas of a supreme being and a conjurer who could raise the dead and cast spells found a parallel in evangelical Christianity. Moreover, members of tribes such as the Igbo, Yoruba, and Hausa, a great many of whom came to North Carolina, also embraced the idea of God as omniscient and omnipresent, "He Who knows all and sees all," and "He Who is everywhere and nowhere." Yet Africans and Creoles also brought with them the ideas of communal openness, a closer relationship to life through nature, a more emotional rather than rational relationship to God, lengthy and protracted meetings, spontaneous musical worship, and a minister who tended to his community as well as to his congregation in everyday life. In sum, many of the evangelical elements that pervaded the protodenominations of North Carolina before the 1830s had their roots in not only the dissenting sects from England and Europe but also a folk culture deeply influenced by Africans and Creoles.

Despite the religious interactions between whites and blacks in antebellum North Carolina, the vast majority of Africans and Creoles as well as free blacks largely resisted the efforts of their masters and dominant white churches to proselytize them. By 1800 in the South, perhaps as few as 5 percent of Christians, fifty thousand out of a million, listed themselves as colored. The number increased only to seventy-five thousand by 1830. Yet in 1860 the number had risen to 12 percent. The first known black Baptist church in the South began in Silver Bluff in South Carolina, in 1774, but doubtless others took root in North Carolina as well. By and large, most black churches and congregations remained unnoticed during slavery, outside the boundaries and the sight of record keepers and of mainline denominations.

Because of their invisibility, African American churches in North Carolina took on a different mission than that of their white counterparts. First, while their African roots gave them similar conceptions of God and of right and wrong, their religious leaders also had to give their worshipers a basis to survive slavery and to reconcile the faith of whites with their oppressive conduct. Thus, the idea of "a better day a coming," of a "New Canaan," of the moral uplift of suffering and sacrifice, and of a dream of freedom long deferred dominated the thought of despairing blacks for more than two centuries of slavery. When mainline denominations such as the Baptists, Methodists, Presbyterians, and Episcopalians came to support the status quo more and more after 1831, blacks increasingly turned away from them and toward their own invisible churches.

African Americans also rejected the perceived spiritual hollowness, the quietness, the lack of celebration and fellowship, the orderliness, and the rituals of many antebellum white churches as they grew more conservative and less evangelical and radical in the 1830s. Additionally, music, always an integral part of African worship, became even more indispensable as a tool to celebrate life and to discover what many believed to be part of "the true Gospel." In the face of a white majority that disdained, diminished, and dehumanized their everyday lives, African Americans and their preachers instead turned to another message, that of the underlying truths that lay beneath the false goodness of white churches and of the necessity of benevolence and self-help through their own. Invisible but omnipresent, black ministers and their communities sustained the intertwined ideas of hope and heaven during the long night of slavery until a better day surely would come. It did not come until 1865. Then, the invisible churches and congregations of African Americans emerged, phoenix-like, to become the unhidden rock on which an entire, separate society had existed for centuries.

The image of North Carolina as a state that had awakened from its slumber and come to life in the decades prior to the Civil War, seemed, on the surface, to have merit. With more than six hundred miles of railroads, a burgeoning textile industry, a tripling of tobacco and cotton production, a liberalized and certainly more democratic constitution, a brand new capitol in Raleigh, the opening of the western mountain counties to settlement, a new and invigorated Whiggish and businesslike state government, and a rash of new governors from the west, North Carolina increasingly looked like its southern neighbors. With harsher slave codes, more and more restrictions upon free blacks, and also less social interaction between the races, North Carolina also seemed more in line with Georgia, South Carolina, and Virginia in its hardening attitudes toward race. Yet the embodiment of antebellum North Carolina lay not in railroads or in bustling industries and manufactures but rather in the proliferation of its distilleries that processed pitch, tar, and turpentine. Tar products remained the chief export prior to the Civil War. Tar Heels and not Tara, poverty and not plantations, illiteracy and not scholarship, Weldon and not Richmond, and Wilmington and not Charleston typified the growth of North Carolina until the Civil War. Known to other southerners as Tar Heels, the nickname, with its limited vision of progress and stubborn backwardness, defined the state in 1860 more than Lubberland did a century before. It has stuck ever since.

ADDITIONAL READINGS

Barfield, Rodney, and Keith Strawn. *Bechtlers and Their Coinage.* Raleigh: Department of Archives and History, 1980.

Boyd, William K. "Antecedents of the North Carolina Convention of 1835." *South Atlantic Quarterly* (January–April 1910): 1–29.

———. "Federal Politics in North Carolina, 1824–1836." *South Atlantic Quarterly* 18 (January–April 1949): 41–51, 167–74.

———. "The Finances of the North Carolina Literary Fund." *South Atlantic Quarterly* 13 (July 1914): 361–70.

Bynum, Victoria E. *Unruly Women: The Politics of Social and Sexual Control in the Old South.* Chapel Hill: University Press of North Carolina, 1992.

Cecil-Fronsman, Bill. *Common Whites: Class and Culture in Antebellum North Carolina.* Lexington: University Press of Kentucky, 1992.

Connor, Henry G. "Convention of 1835." *North Carolina Booklet* 8 (October 1935): 89–110.

Connor, Robert Digges Wimberly. *Ante-bellum Builders of North Carolina.* Spartanburg: Reprint Co., 1971.

Counihan, Harold J. "North Carolina's Constitutional Convention of 1835: A Study in Jacksonian Democracy." *North Carolina Historical Review* 46 (October 1969): 335–64.

Ford, Paul M. "Calvin H. Wiley and the Common Schools of North Carolina, 1850–1869." Ph.D. diss., Harvard University, 1960.

Franklin, John Hope. *The Free Negro in North Carolina.* New York: Norton and Co., 1971.

———. "Free Negro in the Economic Life of Ante-Bellum North Carolina." *North Carolina Historical Review* 19 (July 1942): 239–59; (October 1942): 359–75.

Gaston, William. *Speech of the Hon. Judge Gaston Delivered in the Recent State Convention of North Carolina Assembled for the Purpose of Revising the Constitution.* Baltimore: Lucas Co., 1835.

Green, Fletcher M. *Constitutional Development in the South Atlantic States, 1776–1860.* New York: DaCapo Press, 1971.

———. "Gold Mining: A Forgotten Industry of Ante-Bellum North Carolina." *North Carolina Historical Review* 14 (January 1937): 1–19; (April 1937): 135–55.

Hoffman, William Stephany. "Downfall of the Democrats: The Reaction of North Carolinians to Jacksonian Land Policy." *North Carolina Historical Review* 33 (April 1956): 166–82.

Hoyt, William Henry, ed. *Papers of Archibald D. Murphey.* 2 vols. Raleigh: North Carolina Historical Commission, 1914.

Hubbard, Fordyce Mitchell. *North Carolina Reader, Number 1, Prepared with Special Wants and Interests of North Carolina, under the Auspices of the Superintendent of Common Schools.* Fayetteville: E. J. Hale and Son; Raleigh: W. L. Pomeroy, 1856.

Knapp, Richard F. *Golden Promise in the Piedmont: The Story of John Reed's Mine.* Raleigh: Department of Archives and History, 1975.

Malone, Henry T. *Cherokees of the Old South: A People in Transition.* Athens: University Press of Georgia, 1956.

McCormick, Richard P. *Second American Party System: Party Formation in the Jacksonian Era.* Chapel Hill: University of North Carolina Press, 1966.

McLoughlin, William G. *Cherokee Renaissance in the New Republic.* Princeton, N.J.: Princeton University Press, 1986.

McMillen, Sally G. *Motherhood in the Old South: Pregnancy, Childbirth, and Childrearing.* Baton Rouge: Louisiana State University Press, 1990.

Morris, Charles E. "Panic and Reprisal: Reaction in North Carolina to the Nat Turner Insurrection, 1831." *North Carolina Historical Review* 62 (January 1985): 29–52.

Nash, Francis. "Borough Towns of North Carolina." *North Carolina Booklet* 6 (October 1906): 82–102.

North Carolina Constitutional Convention of 1835. *Journal of the Convention, Called by the Freemen of North-Carolina, to Amend the Constitution of the State.* Raleigh: Gales and Sons, 1836.

Perry, Percival. "Naval Stores Industry in the Old South, 1790–1860." *Journal of Southern History* 34 (November 1968): 509–26.

Purdie, Samuel A., and Thomas D. Hamm, eds. "Quakerism in Dixie." *Southern Friend* 21 (1999): 43–63.

Schauinger, Joseph Herman. "William Gaston and the Supreme Court of North Carolina." *North Carolina Historical Review* 21 (April 1944): 97–117.

Shirley, Michael. "Yeoman Culture and Millworkers' Protest in Antebellum Salem, North Carolina." *Journal of Southern History* 57 (1991): 427–52.

Sommerville, Diane Miller. "The Rape Myth in the Old South Reconsidered." *Journal of Southern History* 61 (1995): 481–518.

Strickland, John Scott. "Great Revival and Insurrectionary Fears in North Carolina: An Examination of Antebellum Southern Society and Slave Revolt Panics." In *Class, Conflict, and Consensus,* ed. O. V. Burton and R. C. McMath Jr., 57–95. Westport, Conn.: Greenwood Press, 1982.

Turner, Herbert Snipes. *The Dreamer, Archibald De Bow Murphey, 1777–1832.* Verona, Va.: McClure Press, 1971.

Vogt, Peter. "William Cornelius Reichel (1824–1876): Nineteenth Century American-Moravian Educator and Historian." *Transactions of the Moravian Historical Society* 30 (1998): 55–74.

The Cherokees

"In the beginning the Creator made the heaven and earth and everything on and above it. To protect the people he gave them the gift of fire. Smoke from the fire carried prayers back to the Creator from his people. At first all was water. Animals and everything else lived in Heaven, which became very crowded. The Creator sent countless beetles to push up the earth and make suitable land for them. Then He made a Great Buzzard fly over to find dry land for His Principal People. Tiring from his efforts, the Great Buzzard flew low to the ground in the place that came to be known as the place of the Cherokee. When his great wings struck the soft earth, valleys formed. As he lifted upward, the wind beneath his gigantic wings caused mountains to be made. To this day, the land of the emerald valleys and smoky mountains remains the home of His Principal People, the Cherokee" (Cherokee Myth of Creation).

The Principal People, the Cherokees, probably came to the mountains of western North Carolina, Tennessee, and Georgia from the north perhaps a thousand years ago. Possibly three hundred years before the first whites set foot in North America, the Cherokee population peaked at perhaps twenty thousand. By the time of the American Revolution, between twelve and thirteen thousand lived in forty villages and small towns scattered throughout the region. Called by Europeans the Lower, Middle, Valley, and Overhill settlements because of their geographic location, they contained one of the largest concentrations of Indians east of the Mississippi River who shared a common culture, traditions, and language. Characterized as vigorous and industrious by European travelers and traders such as James Adair and William Bartram, Cherokees presented the most formidable barrier to the expansion of the Carolinas and Georgia well into the nineteenth century.

Cherokees of the Lower Towns lived along the banks of the Keowee and Tugaloo rivers, which flowed southward into the Savannah River and thence through Georgia and South Carolina. In the very western tip of present-day North Carolina, the Middle Towns sprawled across the Tuckaseegee and headwaters of the Tennessee rivers, just as the Great Buzzard had prepared for the Principal People. In eastern Tennessee, the Valley Towns followed the course of the Hiwassee River through large, treeless mountain meadows and plains. The Overhill Towns clustered along the banks of the Little Tennessee and Nolichucky rivers in eastern Tennessee. The influence of the Cherokees extended farther east to the Broad and Kanawha rivers, reaching north to the Ohio, southward into the Piedmont of Georgia and Alabama, and westward past the Tennessee River. Adaptable, energetic, independent, and sharing a common history and culture, Cherokees watched as white settlements crept closer in the middle decades of the eighteenth century.

At first, whites only wanted to trade with Cherokees, not to take their land. Existing as they had for hundreds of years before European settlement, Cherokees initially regarded white traders and, later, settlers, with curiosity and apprehension rather than fear or anxiety. The idea of exchanging and bartering goods had been a part of Cherokee life hundreds of years before whites came to the towns of the Principal People. To the north ran the upper trail, a trading route that connected the overmountain settlements to the broad valleys of Virginia and Tennessee. To the south, a lower path cut through Keowee and linked Cherokees to the Tuscarora, Creek, and Catawba nations. In the 1630s white traders from a new place called Virginia followed the well-trod footpaths into the sanctuary of the Principal People. Fifty years later more "Virginians," as Cherokees called all white men, came from another settlement called Charleston. They offered strange goods unlike any the Principal People had ever known, items such as iron kettles that lasted longer than the porous pottery made by Cherokees; planting sticks, made of the same hard metal and not of stone, that dug deeply into the ground; guns that allowed one to kill animals from a longer distance; pigs that tasted better than venison; and horses that easily traveled vast distances into other tribal hunting grounds. Along with disease and settlement, trade thus became part of a toxic triangle that poisoned and forever changed the traditional ways of the Principal People.

For almost fifty years Cherokees successfully integrated the new technologies and goods of the Virginians and Carolinians into their ways of life. The iron hoe, for example, quickly became a staple of the trade, frequently appearing on inventories to the nation from Charleston. The iron hoe proved more efficient and productive than the sharp-ended digging stick or the heavier stone hoe. Along with an increased demand for deerskins and medicinal herbs, the iron hoe subtly led to a transformation of Cherokee culture and life.

For centuries the Cherokees' system of agriculture had evolved into a delicate yet sustainable balance between their needs and the capacity of the land to produce. From the heartland of the towns on the Little Tennessee River to the scattered settlements along the Tugaloo and Oconee rivers, clusters of villages nestled along the rich fingers of valleys and meadows. With a clear preference for a riparian pattern of settlement, the Principal People successfully adapted an intensive cultivation of corn to their towns along the region's rivers. Limited by the amount of fertile bottomland and also by the forest itself, Cherokees developed a pattern of life built around the cultivation of corn that sustained not only their bodies but also their most cherished institutions for centuries.

First, agriculture in Cherokee towns dictated their social structure. Cherokees held land communally and not individually. In settlements along rivers, dwellings and public gathering places alternated with cultivated land, fallow fields, and trees, giving the overall appearance of a multicolored green and gold tartan. As he rode through the town of Echota in the lower settlements, William Bartram, an appreciative botanist, observed that "the road carried me winding about through . . . little plantations of Corn, Beans, etc., and up to their council house. . . . All before me and on every side appeared . . . young Corn, and Beans divided from each other by narrow strips or borders of grass which marked the bounds of each one's [clan's] property, their habitation standing in the midst." Largely

Ostenaco, principal chief of the Cherokee Nation, 1762.
North Carolina Collection, University of North Carolina at
Chapel Hill.

confined to the rich bottomland of rivers, Cherokee settlements, almost always permanent, sustained populations of a few score to seven hundred. Designed for the production of corn as their main staple crop, Cherokee villages, over the course of centuries, developed an efficient and seasonal division of labor for planting, cultivating, and harvesting. Within a radius of ten to twenty miles, an area adjacent to each town provided grounds for hunting and foraging, all interconnected to other settlements for defense and socializing. When the first whites arrived in the 1630s, the Cherokee population had peaked at perhaps twenty thousand. Within a century it would be half that number.

Clearly, Old World diseases unknown or else suppressed centuries ago decimated Cherokees, but epidemics such as those of smallpox, which struck the settlements in 1738 and 1759, had a more deadly, viral, long-term effect. Trade already had weakened the Principal People. Complexes of flulike infections such as tuberculosis, measles, influenza, and smallpox took a constant and frequently epidemic toll upon Cherokees. Aided not only by the relative absence of those diseases for hundreds of years but also by a society no longer self-sufficient or self-supporting, epidemics ravaged Cherokee villages. In their system of agriculture and reliance upon corn production supplemented by hunting and fishing, the Principal People had set an internal clock that governed reproduction and age groupings for hundreds if not thousands of years. A birthrate centered around having children upon a four- and not a two-year cycle, an unevenness of age groups where children marginally outnumbered adults, and a system of clans and kinship patterns all allowed Cherokees to optimize their population in relation to the resources provided by their riparian settlements. Trade with Charleston and Virginia signaled the beginning of a depopulation that would ravage the settlements for two centuries.

At first, white traders wanted only deerskins, some medicinal plants, and, occasionally, corn from Cherokees. Accustomed to trading with other tribes, Cherokees initially dominated the exchanges, acting as middlemen and buying and selling on favorable terms. As commerce with whites grew in volume and persisted over time, it gradually pervaded and altered Cherokee society, making it vulnerable not only to disease and chronic warfare but also to the fragile ecosystem that had sustained it for centuries. By the beginning of the eighteenth century, Cherokees could no longer grow enough corn for food or clothe themselves. At one time in the 1750s, Cherokees, praying to the protective spirits that dwelled in Soco Valley, asked that Carolinians send a blacksmith to their towns to help repair and maintain their farming tools and iron implements, so dependent had they become upon European trade and implements. By the time of the French and Indian War, Cherokees, to a large extent, existed as a trading fief of Charleston. Weakened by malnutrition, hunger, famine, and shortages of blankets and goods, an already strained social structure fell prey to diseases and epidemics.

As a people with a strong culture, Cherokees understood, adapted, protested, and even warred against the maelstrom of change sweeping over them. With a steady decline in their population and the gradual reduction of a land base for their agriculture, Cherokees had been reduced almost to half their prediscovery population, around twelve thousand, by 1750. A trader reported that, on a trip to the nation in 1752, he saw only three thousand gunmen, but in his earlier visits he remembered "six thousand stout men in it." In eighteenth-century terms, whites calculated Indian populations by multiplying the number of gunmen by four, a ratio considered appropriate to the support needed to produce one warrior or gunman. Riding through abandoned towns near Keowee in 1774, the same William Bartram who earlier recalled the pristine settlements of the Cherokees now came across only "feeble remains . . . the vestiges of the ancient dwellings . . . yet visible on the feet of the hills bordering and fronting on the vale, such as posts or pillars" of their homes. The long-term effects of trade had caused the removal of many Cherokees as well as the diminution of their culture even before the new American nation had been born.

The Cherokee system of self-sufficiency built around the production of corn depended upon three uses of the land along the riverbanks. After planting an area for four or five years, new fields were "tickled" by planting sticks and stone hoes to bring them under production. Older fields lay fallow for an additional five to seven years to restore and preserve their nutrients. Within a given settlement, fields, fallow and fertile, intertwined with trees and habitations and extended radially along the river. The size of the population of each town, typically no more than a few score or hundred, depended upon the resources provided mainly by farming and hunting. As the territory needed by each town for sustenance extended in any direction, the time required for cultivation and production also increased, finally reaching a point where the entire system became inefficient and socially disorderly. Built around an agricultural system worked out over time, the Cherokees' social system remained intact, stable, communal, and traditional for centuries. The introduction of the iron hoe and farming tools from the whites permitted Cherokees to dig more deeply into the soil, release more nutrients, and increase production, and it allowed a greater shift of labor toward hunting and the deerskin trade. In the short run, the Principal People found that trade with Virginia and Charleston greatly benefited them. They sold corn to white traders and nearby Indian settlements, quickly became horse traders and stockmen par excellence, and, in general, enjoyed greater wealth and power than before. Yet the increased benefits came at a price.

First, participation in the South Carolina and Virginia trading system and in an international mercantilistic economy meant that more deerskins and medicinal herbs would be needed for trade and barter and that more men must hunt instead of cultivate cornfields. Coupled with a declining population brought on by European diseases and contact, men abandoned the fields and took to hunting further afield, frequently encroaching upon grounds reserved for other towns, groups, and tribes. An internecine warfare soon followed.

Farming territory declined significantly, and fields closer to towns and villages lay fallow for less time. At first, yields increased, but, with more intensive and deeper cultivation, soils soon became exhausted. With fewer men for labor, fewer new sites could be cleared and fields opened. Soon, Cherokees found themselves buying corn instead of selling it to the whites and to other Indians. By the 1760s, intermittent famine in the Lower Towns warned of the declining self-sufficiency of the Cherokees. In like manner, the introduction of animals such as pigs, cows, and horses significantly altered traditional Cherokee lifestyles and rituals of labor. Pigs and horses placed additional demands upon a decreasing area of cleared land. Because Cherokees did not traditionally fence their fields, pigs had to be penned and fed during the growing and harvesting season, a task that took even more effort by a declining labor force decimated by disease and malnutrition. By the 1740s, horses also had become part of the Cherokee pattern of life. Moreover, the Cherokees took to the horse with an enthusiasm not found in other woodland tribes. James Adair, visiting the lower towns on a trade commission, observed that "almost every one [of the Cherokees] hath horses, from two to a dozen." With horses, Cherokee bands ranged further into other hunting grounds, bringing back with them more hides and also additional intrusions and raids by other Indians. They also became an important source of packhorses for traders and other Indians. The pressure of grazing and herding large numbers of horses and cows kept near towns and settlements helped undermine the older, traditional agricultural economy of the Cherokees.

In addition, trade and new technologies from whites also affected the roles and status of women in Cherokee society. Membership in one of the traditional clans such as the Turtle, Bear, or Bird descended from the mother, not the father, and women enjoyed heightened status in Cherokee life because of that singular influence. Kinship through clan ties cut across all other tribal loyalties and obligations, including those of the home and field. In those spheres, women not only ruled but also owned and decided. They also seem to have enjoyed a modicum of sexual freedom and also a say in diplomatic and military decisions, roles unfamiliar to most Europeans. Acknowledging this, Adair, writing about Cherokees but thinking like a European, derided them for being ruled by a "petticoat government." Cherokee women also played an active role in the deerskin trade and in collecting botanical plants for food and medicine. By the 1740s, the demand for deerskins and for three plants, Indian pink (*Spigelia marlandica*), Virginia snakeroot (*Aristolochia serpentaria*), and ginseng (*Panax quinquefolius*), effectively changed their role in Cherokee life.

The eighteenth century saw the gradual diminution of women's status and roles in Cherokee society. As Cherokees changed and as the Principal People increasingly became acculturated through Anglo-American institutions, women's political influence declined. Nonetheless, as pressure for removal mounted in the early nineteenth century, Cherokee women strongly spoke out against it. In two remarkable petitions in 1817 and 1818, the Women's Councils to the Cherokee Nation expressed their strong opposition not only to removal but also to land cession and relocation somewhere "over the Mississippi." Led by Nancy Ward, the matriarch of the council and a "war woman" since the 1750s, the Women's Councils urged their "beloved chiefs" not to give up the land where "we have raised all of you . . . which God gave us to inhabit and raise provisions." Nancy Ward also spoke to "her children." "Warriors," she beseeched the assembled chiefs, "take pity and listen to the

197

talks of your sisters. Although I am very old yet cannot but pity the situation in which you will hear of their minds. I have great many grand children which [I] wish . . . to do well on our land." Yet Cherokee men listened but little to their women in war and diplomacy in the nineteenth century, much like their white counterparts.

The work of planting, caring for, and harvesting corn, the backbone of Cherokee agriculture, customarily entailed the labor of the entire community. Nonetheless, women and children still furnished the majority of the workforce. The growing season began in early spring and ended with harvests in late fall. Accompanying the springtime rituals of clearing and sowing fields, women also collected wild plants in May and June from nearby woods and uncultivated fields. Between 1760 and 1773, the amount of pinkroot and snakeroot shipped from Charleston more than quadrupled, varying from two to seventeen hogsheads of dried plants annually. At the same time, Charleston sent more than 170,000 deerskins abroad each year, both figures suggesting that Cherokee trade now had become important on the world market. As incipient capitalists swept up in an international system of trade, the Principal People now applied most of their energies to hunting, curing, tanning, and packing hides as well as to the collection and drying of botanical plants. With fewer men to hunt and work in the fields, women now hurriedly cured hides, always marginal work in traditional Cherokee life, packed them, and devoted greater time and energy to gathering increasingly scarce plants far afield. Not surprisingly, with fewer women and men in the fields and fewer hands in the spring and fall, not as many fields came under cultivation, more fallow ones were replanted too quickly, and cows, hogs, and other European barnyard animals marauded the unpenned fields.

In addition to their changed roles in trade and agriculture, Indian women emerged as diplomats and as peace chiefs by the 1690s, an indication that Cherokees were anxious to maintain the flow of European goods such as kettles, axes, knives, needles, and iron tools of all kinds. Intermarriage between white traders and Cherokee women proved indispensable to the cementing of good trading relations. In the Lower Towns along the South Carolina and Georgia border and in the Overhill Towns of Tennessee, the children of mixed marriages such as the Rosses and Ridges frequently acquired positions of power and authority. Only in the more isolated Oconaluftee or Qualla Indian communities in the North Carolina mountains did a more traditional culture persist. The Qualla towns, the purest of the Principal People and the most clannish, eventually became the Eastern Band of the Cherokee after removal in 1838.

Inextricably, the Principal People, through trade and diplomacy, found themselves caught up in the undercurrent of wars whose surges washed over colonial America and Europe in the eighteenth century. Beginning in the 1690s and continuing until the American Revolution, Cherokee towns and bands tried to decide for themselves whether to support the French, English, and, in the end, all white colonials. To the English and French, the Cherokee way of government, dependent upon local chiefs and clans who led only until their decisions proved unwise, seemed both arcane and puzzling. In a society without a nucleus, each individual unit made its own choices, chiefs came and went, and treaties, boundaries, and finality seemed ephemeral to Europeans. Sir Alexander Cuming, an eccentric English trader and gadfly, declared a single person to be chief of the Principal People, an amazed Indian named Moytoy, who was selected more in frustration than in

Early depiction of chiefs of the Cherokees.
North Carolina Division of Archives and History, Raleigh.

authority. In 1730 Cuming brought a hand-picked Cherokee delegation of "chiefs" to England for an audience with King George II. Afterward, the English usually recognized and tried to deal with an appointed chief in each town and group, but the Principal People blithely ignored British and French "chiefs," except when it suited them, and instead went about their usual communalistic and clannish ways.

In the French and Indian War of 1756–63, the Principal People demonstrated their changeableness. At first strong supporters of the British, Cherokees turned on their English trading partners and fell upon the British garrison at Fort Loudon near the Overhill town of Chota. After the garrison's surrender, they helped massacre many of the prisoners. In retaliation, the British laid waste to more than twenty Cherokee villages, not discriminating as to who had or had not participated in the carnage at Fort Loudon. In the decade between the end of the French and Indian War and the beginning of the American Revolution, the Principal People firmly allied themselves to the British camp. To them, the British, with their new southern Indian superintendent, John Stuart of Charleston, wished to trade with the Principal People and not take their land as the "Virginians" or Carolinians wanted. The distinction proved crucial.

When the colonies rebelled against the British in 1775 and declared their independence a year later, the Principal People, sensing a weakness among the frontiersmen and encouraged by their English trading allies, fell upon backcountry settlements with a vengeance. Yet promises of British troops and aid proved empty, and in 1776 frontier militiamen under Griffith Rutherford of North Carolina moved against them, decimating towns and villages from New Echota to Quallatown. For a decade, raids and punitive expeditions continued, much like the incessant "revenge" forays of clans and villages and the clannish fighting between Tories and Whigs, until by 1785 Cherokees signed their first treaty with the new American government at Hopewell, South Carolina. By then, the Principal People had abandoned their Eden-like settlements sprawled along the rivers and valleys of up-country South Carolina, their sacred Echota homeland, and retreated west and southward into North Carolina, Georgia, southeastern Tennessee, and, lastly, the hill country of northern Alabama. Successful as farmers, hunters, and traders, Cherokees now had to find a way to deal with the Americans, a new and an increasingly larger and more determined

Left: Nathan Kirkland (ca. 1760–1860), a Cherokee from Graham County.
North Carolina Office of Archives and History, Raleigh.

Cherokee chief Chuta Sotee, who died in 1879.
North Carolina Collection, University of North Carolina at Chapel Hill.

white tribe who wanted their farming and hunting grounds. Not surprisingly, the Principal People, blessed by the Creator and shown the way by the Great Buzzard, found still another path to come to terms with the American threat.

Initially the new American tribe looked very much like the Iroquois confederacy of nations in the North, from whom the Principal People had removed themselves centuries ago. From thirteen states, or hunting grounds, the Americans allied themselves in a similar loose confederation of articles and, instead of a chief called king, almost always George, their leader took the name of president, but his name still remained George. Unlike King George, who sent redcoats, the new chief, "President George," sent warriors dressed in bluecoats and commissioners without gifts to negotiate treaties not for trade goods, routes, and fair prices, but for land. Moreover, the new chief president spoke of "civilizing" the Principal People, an unusual concept in the Cherokee view since they first settled the land and certainly were less savage than the whites, who burned and killed not for revenge but to wipe out entire clans and villages. To the Principal People, they would have to deal with the dangerous new tribe, even accommodate it, but somehow use the skills given them by the Creator when they first came to this enchanted land of emerald valleys and smoky mountains.

First, the commissioners from the United Tribes insisted that Cherokees give up the chase, their nomadic way of life, and instead live on small plots of land and settle down to farming. To incredulous Cherokees, the idea of settling down in villages and fields and returning to a traditionalist culture after decades of turbulence and change brought about by the demands of trade and treating with so many different Europeans seemed a benediction given by the Creator. Moreover, the Americans wanted the Principal People to be educated, to adopt a strange set of laws and ordinances, and, lastly, to allow missionaries such as George Barber Davis and Humphrey Posey to come into the territory and tell them even more about the Creator. The idea of education, of learning more about the white tribe's language, customs, and ways did not threaten Cherokees so long as it took place in their own clans, villages, and towns. Somehow, the idea of a written language like that of the whites' appealed to the Principal People in its simplicity and power, and, from the first, their wisest medicine men and elders sought a way to express their own ideas in a similar form. Within one generation they succeeded. Sequoyah, their own genie, gave them a syllabary that magically ran across paper just like the whites' letters, only with the Cherokees' subtle intonations and speech patterns. Strongly entrenched in a traditionalist culture dating back thousands of years, medicine men understood that they easily could adapt to white missionaries and religion, even converting many of them, like Evan Jones, to Cherokee ideas and turning them against the very whites who sent them. Change and new ideas did not threaten the Principal People. In the next few decades, they prospered only too much in dealing with the new United White Tribes.

By the 1820s the Principal People had grown to almost seventeen thousand strong and were spread unevenly over Georgia, North Carolina, Tennessee, and, increasingly, northern Alabama. They owned sixteen hundred slaves overall but only forty in North

201

Sequoyah, who invented a syllabary that allowed the Cherokee language to be written.

North Carolina Collection, University of North Carolina at Chapel Hill.

Carolina. The slave-owning distinction proved crucial. Mixed-blood elites such as the Boudinots, Ridges, and Rosses lived in Georgia, Tennessee, and Alabama; tended small and moderate-sized farms and even owned larger plantations, like whites did, in Georgia and Tennessee; and lived in prosperous clans, villages, and towns or else owned substantial huts, even frame and brick homes, in the countryside. For example, John Ross, a prominent chieftain, was seven-eights Scottish. His mother, Mollie MacDonald, came from Inverness in Scotland. Some Cherokees owned mills, helped with trading stores to smaller communities, operated ferries, and sold hides, foodstuffs, and herbs to nearby whites. With Protestant missionaries and schools in their midst, many nominally converted to Christianity.

Better known as Sequoyah, George Gist invented a syllabary, a phonetic alphabet, that brought instant and widespread literacy to the Cherokees. Elias Boudinot, who made it a point to understand the whites and their legal system, soon published a tribal newspaper, the *Cherokee Phoenix,* which printed laws and issues affecting the Principal People. Born Buck Watie, Boudinot, a prominent orator, writer, and editor, took his name from that of a New Jersey benefactor and subsequently sued the U.S. government on behalf of the Cherokees. His brother, Stand Watie, took a different warpath and fought against the federal government, eventually becoming a Confederate general, the last to surrender in 1865. By 1828 Cherokees had set up a nation within a nation, carving its edifice from that of the United States, complete with an Indian court system, constitution, and legislature. At New Echota, the bustling capital in north Georgia, John Ross, the principal chief, set about protecting the remaining Cherokee heartland from further encroachment. The Principal People, with their own internal economy and polity, prospered under the peace afforded them by the whites' insistence upon civilization.

Living almost exclusively in North Carolina along the Nantahala, "the river of the noonday sun," Soco Creek, and the Oconaluftee River, the Qualla Cherokee in large part remained outside and distinct from the nation. Almost 3,600 strong by 1830, the Lufty Indians considered themselves citizens of North Carolina by virtue of treaties made in 1817 and 1819, took no subsidy from either the state or federal government, had the highest percentage of pure-bloods, owned less than forty slaves, and, in general, only wanted to be left alone to continue their centuries-old lifestyle. Their chiefs had names like Yonaguska, Junaluska, Salola, and, in a rare case, Wil-Usdi, William Holland Thomas, the only white ever to be named a full chief of the Quallas. When removal came, they resisted most, and those who hid in the mountains and coves and successfully eluded Gen. Winfield Scott's troops became the heart and soul of the Eastern Band of Cherokees, in their minds and spirit the true remnants of the Principal People.

Two events precipitated the removal of Cherokees in 1838. First, the discovery of gold in the north Georgia mountains in 1828 and, coincidentally, the election of Andrew Jackson that same year all but brought about the extinction of the new Cherokee civilization that had flourished in the Southeast since 1783. When Georgia ceded its western land claims to the federal government in 1802, one of the last states to do so, it stipulated that Washington try to persuade Cherokees and Creeks to give up their land claims and move westward. After the War of 1812, only Cherokees remained in significant numbers, and they, too, had begun to move to Oklahoma. Called the Old Settlers, hundreds left the

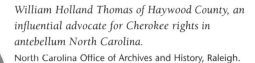

William Holland Thomas of Haywood County, an influential advocate for Cherokee rights in antebellum North Carolina.
North Carolina Office of Archives and History, Raleigh.

nation and made the trek beyond the Mississippi by 1828. Still, thousands more remained, flourished under the protection of the federal government, and, with John Ross leading the way, began to fight through the court system to retain their lands. All this and the discovery of gold proved too much for the expansive Georgians.

With the imminent election of Andrew Jackson in 1828, North Carolina, historically lukewarm not only about the Cherokees but also the western counties in general, informed Congress that "the red men are not within the pale of civilization" and were "disagreeable and dangerous neighbors" as well. Such insults, seldom backed by action, did little to threaten the Principal People, secure in their Qualla towns and villages. Moreover, the North Carolina Cherokees had a remarkable new leader, William Holland Thomas, who had powerful friends in Raleigh.

Born in Haywood County in 1805, Thomas began working as a youth in Felix Walker's trading store with its many Cherokee customers. Yonaguska, a frequent buyer of goods and whiskey at Walker's store, soon regarded the young Thomas with favor, and, with his mother's reluctant permission, adopted him as a son and called him Wil-Usdi, "Little Will." In the communalistic and closely knit society of the Cherokees, Wil-Usdi found a place where he was understood, tolerated, and loved. Loyally and willingly, Thomas devoted himself to the Cherokees and, realizing his unique position, immersed himself in a study of the law, hoping to protect his people from the onrush of white civilization.

Thomas matured both physically and intellectually at the exact time that Cherokees found themselves threatened with the greatest crisis of all, removal to a land not sought by the Great Buzzard, a place far beyond the great waters of the Mississippi, a place flat and without the emerald valleys of the beloved smoking mountains. Understanding the politics of the federal government, North Carolina, and his adoptive people, Thomas determined that only one solution would ever protect Cherokees. They must become full citizens of the state of North Carolina.

In one of history's many ironies, the original inhabitants of the region now sought to be accepted as citizens of a new state called North Carolina. Unless citizenship status was bestowed, the Principal People forever would be victims of vacillating policies of states such as Georgia, of presidents elected on promises to civilize or to remove them, and of lower federal courts and the Supreme Court that perhaps would interpret the many differing treaties in ways not always beneficial to Cherokees. Whoever promised protection and citizenship, whether the state or the federal government, would find strong allies in the Principal People and in their most effective spokesman, Wil-Usdi. In 1828, Thomas looked warily at Washington and at Andrew Jackson, the newly elected president. The words of Junaluska, the war chief who led Cherokee warriors under Jackson in the campaigns against the Creeks, resonated within his doubts. "Do not trust the Wooden General. He has no friends." On 29 December 1835, Elias Boudinot, John and Major Ridge, and other Cherokee "chiefs" signed the infamous Treaty of New Echota that called for the removal of the nation to the west within two years. Soon afterward, Maj. Gen. Winfield Scott's blue-coated soldiers moved into the mountains of western North Carolina to prepare for removal.

Scott's assembly, caging, and ejection of the Principal People and their long trek on the Trail of Tears westward across the Mississippi became the central theme of a modern Cherokee myth of re-creation. Moving throughout the nation, soldiers rounded up thousands of Indians, frequently giving them only minutes to pack what few things they could, and herded them into stockades, where they awaited transshipment west. Of the approximately 12,000 sent westward on the trail, perhaps 3,500 died, an appalling statistic even by nineteenth-century standards. In North Carolina, Brig. John Wool, assessing the attitude and geography of the Qualla Indians in the Smoky Mountains, thought his task all but impossible. He was right. North Carolina Cherokees provided more resistance than expected and in a surprising form.

Every year thousands of visitors to the town of Cherokee come to watch *Unto These Hills,* an outdoor drama depicting the heroic role of Tsali, a North Carolina Cherokee who sacrificed his life so that his people, the Qualla Cherokees, could survive and remain in their beloved emerald valleys and smoking mountains. As the story has it, because of Tsali and the intransigence of others such as Hog Bite, a hermit reputed to be more than one hundred years old, the Lufty Indians remained, eventually becoming the Eastern Band of the Cherokees. Tsali's story exemplified not only the resistance of the Principal People to removal but, more important, the divisions within the "official" Cherokee Nation and separate bands such as the Qualla Indians of North Carolina. Universally opposed to removal,

Trail of Tears. From Ora Blackman's *History of Western North Carolina to 1880.*

the Quallatown Cherokees of North Carolina never faced the massive roundup and removal endured by the thousands who belonged to the nation outside the mountains, nor, except for a few families, did they participate in the Trail of Tears. Instead, they remained apart from the larger Cherokee Nation of mixed- and full-bloods, a traditionalist, clan-centered, and communalistic group altogether different from their brethren in the nation. Largely with the cooperation of state and federal officials and using their own initiative, they remained in the rugged mountains of North Carolina. Instead of being indegted to Tsali, the Eastern Band of Cherokees owed its survival to Wil-Usdi.

In the fall of 1836, the young Thomas, already regarded as a chief by the Cherokees, called all the Qualla Indians together to discuss the question of removal. In the meeting, he asked those who wanted to stay in North Carolina to pass between two sentinels, symbolically representing gatekeepers, and those who wanted to go west with their brothers to remain where they were. Heeding the advice of Yonaguska, now old but still venerated, and Thomas, the only white they trusted, all the Lufty Indians arose and quietly walked between the two defenders. From that moment, Thomas understood that, at all costs, he must keep his beloved brothers in their sacred mountains and valleys, even if it meant betraying other Indians and cooperating with the whites.

Thomas's determination to disassociate the Qualla Indians of North Carolina from their brethren in the nation led to perhaps the most unnecessarily overly romanticized episode in Cherokee history, the legend of Tsali, also called Charlie by whites and Zollie by blacks. An old, illiterate full-blood, Tsali lived with his family near the headwaters of the Nantahala River in 1835. As the story goes, Tsali, enraged by the brutal treatment of his wife by white soldiers, pulled a hatchet from his robe and killed a soldier. Gathering up his wife and sons, he escaped to the rugged mountains, where, along with hundreds of other Lufty Indians, he hid from the marauding soldiers of Winfield Scott. Only when Scott agreed to let the other Indians remain did Tsali turn himself in to the waiting soldiers. To humiliate him and to make the point that resistance was futile, Scott forced other Cherokees to execute Tsali, his two sons, and his brother. Because of his bravery and sacrifice, as the saga continued, the Lufty Indians remained in North Carolina while their brothers in the nation endured removal and the Trail of Tears.

The facts of Tsali's story radically differ from those of its oral tradition, yet the subsequent cloak of heroic resistance and sacrifice spread over removal embodied by the legend eventually served all factions of the Cherokees well. First, the pedestrian efforts of William Holland Thomas and not Tsali's exciting flight and fight against the soldiers largely saved the Quallatown Indians from removal. Tsali became the central figure in the drama only when his part in the murder of two soldiers under Lt. Andrew Jackson Smith of the First U.S. Dragoons threatened the uneasy peace between Scott and the Lufty Indians. On 5 November, Smith wrote his official report to his immediate superior, Lt. C. H. Larned, and the document mentioning Tsali became part of federal records. From John Ross of the nation to Thomas, Cherokees universally condemned the killings and, from that, the murders became part of the continuing internecine strife between Indian clans and groups. When Scott issued orders to shoot down "the Individuals guilty of this unprovoked outrage" and "to collect all, or as many as practicable, of the fugitives (other than the murderers) for

Reunion of Cherokee Indian veterans of the Confederate army, Companies A and B, North Carolina State Troops, Thomas's Legion. North Carolina Office of Archives and History, Raleigh.

emigration," Thomas panicked. To him, the Oconaluftee Indians stood apart from the fugitives and should not suffer their fate. He also suspected that white soldiers would not be meticulous in distinguishing between Indians of the nation and of the Luftys. Although Scott understood and sympathized with Thomas's offer of help in the form of scouts and warriors, he thought it "against the honor of the United States to employ, in hostilities, one part of a tribe against another." Thomas's quick intervention and use of Quallatown warriors soon overcame Scott's conceptions of honor, and afterward the War Department routinely used Indians as runners, scouts, and units to fight against other hostiles, principally in the West.

Setting out ahead of Col. William S. Foster and his sluggish companies trudging into the mountains, Thomas arrived at Quallatown in early November 1838. There he dispatched a band under Euchella (or Oochella or Utsalah), a fugitive himself, and also some of his more trusted Lufty warriors. Within a week, Foster excitedly wrote Scott that he had "captured (through the exertions of Mr. Thomas, the O. co ne lufty Indians, and Euchella's band, headed by himself) two of the murderers," Tsali's oldest son, Nantayalee Jake, and Nantayalee, also called Big George. Foster's account made them the "principal actors in the murder," not Tsali, who had only been present. On 24 November, Foster reported that "three adult males had been punished yesterday morning by the Cherokees themselves." All three had been tried and found guilty by a military and Cherokee court, and, as an obligation under the "ancient custom" of the Principal People, they were shot to death by members of Euchella's band. Foster spared Tsali's son, Wasituna (Washington) because of his youth. For Thomas and the Quallatown Cherokees, as well as for Foster and Scott, the executions effectively ended the incident, and the soldiers of the Fourth Infantry headed back to their camps. Later that same day, some of Euchella's warriors under Wachucha

Cherokee Indians in western North Carolina.
North Carolina Collection, University of North Carolina at Chapel Hill.

captured Tsali, and the next day they executed him. Except as a postscript, nothing in the official accounts or records mentioned Tsali as anything other than a minor figure in the entire incident. As Thomas noted, Cherokees had accomplished in less than two weeks what would have taken Scott's troops "months, and probably years."

By the first month of December 1838 Scott had concluded that the Quallatown Indians posed no threat to white settlements, and one month later the commissioners for Indian removal permitted Euchella's small band to stay with the Lufty Indians and not be removed to the West. In 1843, a white settler and tracker who originally went with Euchella's band, Jonas Jenkins, maintained that he had witnessed old Tsali's execution, and that, unlike the three shot the day before, Tsali faced his brothers and executioners with calm courage, pleading with them to take care of his aging wife and children. The story grew to epic proportions and came to embody many of the stoic yet virtuous characteristics of "noble savages" portrayed by James Fenimore Cooper in his romantic "last of the Indians" tales. In Tsali's case, the fusion of fact and fiction occurred simultaneously with the disappearance of all but a few Indians from east of the Mississippi and grew in proportion to the absence of a once populous Principal People. The Quallatown Indians were all but forgotten for decades, allowed to live in the vastness of the mountains of western North Carolina and to carry on their more traditional way of life. Buried in the past, the parts played by Thomas, Euchella, and the Lufty Indians in the drama of removal, revenge, and betrayal became more enigmatic as the legend of Tsali grew. For his part, William Holland Thomas worked tirelessly to purchase thousands of acres for his beloved Luftys and to make them permanent citizens of North Carolina. Only then would they be safe to continue their centuries-old way of life. As the Great Buzzard had foretold a thousand years before, the destiny of the Principal People, no matter how convoluted, had to be played out "unto these hills."

ADDITIONAL READINGS

208   Alden, John R. *John Stuart and the Southern Colonial Frontier . . . 1754–1775.* New York: Gordian Press, 1966.

Anderson, William L. *Cherokee Removal Before and After.* Athens: University of Georgia Press, 1991.

Bartram, William. "Observations on the Creek and Cherokee Indians." *Transactions of the American Ethnological Society* 3, pt. 1 (1853): 1–81.

Bloom, Leonard. "Acculturation of the Eastern Cherokee: Historical Aspects." *North Carolina Historical Review* 19 (October 1942): 323–58.

Cherokee Nation. *Laws of the Cherokee Nation, Adopted by the Council at Various Periods (1808–1835).* Wilmington, Del.: Scholarly Resources, 1993.

Conser, Walter H., Jr. "John Ross and the Southern Resistance Campaign, 1833–1838." *Journal of Southern History* 44 (May 1978): 191–212.

Corkran, David H. *Cherokee Frontier: Conflict and Survival, 1740–62.* Norman: University of Oklahoma Press, 1962.

———. "Cherokee Pre-History." *North Carolina Historical Review* 34 (October 1957): 455–66.

Crow, Vernon H. *Storm in the Mountains: Thomas' Confederate Legion of Cherokee Indians and Mountaineers.* Cherokee, N.C.: Press of the Museum of the Cherokee Indian, 1982.

Ehle, John. *Trail of Tears: The Rise and Fall of the Cherokee Nation.* New York: Doubleday and Co., 1988.

Finger, John R. *Eastern Band of Cherokees, 1819–1900.* Knoxville: University of Tennessee Press, 1984.

———. "Saga of Tsali." *North Carolina Historical Review* 56 (January 1979): 1–18.

Fogelson, Raymond D., comp. *Cherokees, a Critical Bibliography.* Bloomington: Indiana University Press for Newberry Library, 1978.

Ganyard, Robert L. "Threat from the West: North Carolina and the Cherokee, 1776–1778." *North Carolina Historical Review* 45 (January 1968): 47–66.

Godbold, E. Stanly, Jr. *Confederate Colonel and Cherokee Chief: The Life of William Holland Thomas.* Knoxville: University of Tennessee Press, 1990.

Halliburton, R., Jr. *Red Over Black: Black Slavery among the Cherokee Indians.* Westport, Conn.: Greenwood Press, 1977.

Harmon, George D. "North Carolina Cherokees and the New Echota Treaty of 1835." *North Carolina Historical Review* 6 (July 1929): 237–53.

Hill, Sarah H. "Cherokee Patterns: Interweaving Women and Baskets in History." Ph.D. diss., Emory University, 1991.

Jahoda, Gloria. *Trail of Tears.* New York: Holt, Rinehart and Winston, 1975.

King, Duane H. *The Cherokee Indian Nation: A Troubled History.* Knoxville: University of Tennessee Press, 1979.

Landau, Elaine. *The Cherokees.* New York: Franklin Watts, 1992.

McLoughlin, William Gerald. *Cherokee Renascence in the New Republic.* Princeton, N.J.: Princeton University Press, 1986.

Malone, Henry T. *Cherokees of the Old South, a People in Transition.* Athens: University of Georgia Press, 1956.

———. "Cherokee-White Relations on the Southern Frontier in the Early Nineteenth Century." *North Carolina Historical Review* 34 (January 1957): 1–14.

Neely, Sharlotte. *Snowbird Cherokees: People of Persistence.* Athens: University of Georgia Press, 1991.

Perdue, Theda. *The Cherokee.* New York: Chelsea House, 1989.

———. *Slavery and the Evolution of Cherokee Society, 1540–1866.* Knoxville: University of Tennessee Press, 1979.

Reid, John Phillip. *A Better Kind of Hatchet: Law, Trade, and Diplomacy in the Cherokee Nation*. University Park: Pennsylvania State University Press, 1976.

———. *Law of Blood: The Primitive Law of the Cherokee Nation*. New York: New York University Press, 1970.

Russell, Mattie U. "Devil in the Smokies . . . . " *South Atlantic Quarterly* 73 (Winter 1973): 53–69.

Thornton, Russell. *Cherokees: A Population History*. Lincoln: University of Nebraska Press, 1990.

Woloch, Nancy. *Early American Women: A Documentary History, 1600–1900*. New York: McGraw-Hill, 1997.

Woodward, Grace S. *Cherokees*. Norman: University of Oklahoma Press, 1963.

A State of Indecision

THIRTEEN

North Carolina Enters the Civil War

Like many leaders before and after him, whether presidents or prime ministers, John Ellis thought he knew what was best for the people he served. Newly elected as the state's governor in 1858, the dynamic young man from Rowan County addressed his concerns to the general assembly at his inauguration on 1 January 1859. He had much to trouble him. The Old Union he had learned to revere in his legal studies with Richmond Mumford Pearson in Yadkin County, perhaps one of North Carolina's finest legal minds of the nineteenth century, seemed to be falling apart. The specter of bleeding Kansas meant that congressional compromises no longer worked; the Dred Scott decision by the Supreme Court was sure to be disregarded in the North; President James Buchanan was indecisive and feared that any action on his part would ignite a civil war; and the caning of Sen. Charles Sumner of Massachusetts by Congressman Preston S. Brooks of South Carolina signaled the breakdown of the entire democratic process. Reasonable men could no longer debate or deliberate rationally on the issue of slavery. Neither Congress, the Supreme Court, nor the president could solve the problems then facing the nation. Ellis understood that North Carolina faced an uncertain future in 1859, a darkling time that would try men's souls every bit as much as 1776. He looked forward to the challenge.

Yet despite the seemingly imminent collapse of the Union, Ellis had no idea of what would replace it. "Grievous as are all these causes of discontent," he cautioned, "we are

John Ellis (1820–61), governor in 1861.
North Carolina Collection, University of North Carolina at Chapel Hill.

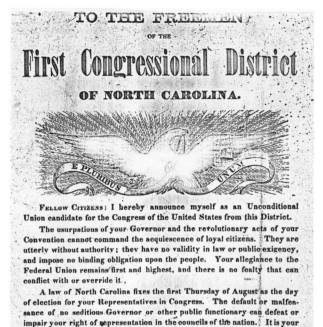

not prepared for the acknowledgement that we cannot enjoy all our constitutional rights in the Union." Therein lay North Carolina's dilemma. For Unionists throughout the state, loyalties were located not within the new interpretation of the Constitution given by the Radical Republicans but rather in an older one that had been endorsed and written by southern slaveholders like James Madison and George Washington. Unwilling to cast aside the Old Union, North Carolinians feared the new one dominated by the Republicans emerging in the West and Northeast. Although the state felt itself increasingly pushed from its comfortable place within the nation before 1859, nothing as yet had materialized to pull it from the Union. That quickly changed.

In June 1859 President James Buchanan visited the state, ostensibly to give the commencement address at the University of North Carolina but also to rally and reassure a key border state. Tall and heavyset with a Jackson-like mane of flowing white hair, exceptionally courteous as perhaps only southerners of that time cherished, Buchanan's remarks were meant to inspire confidence not only in Ellis but also in many other North Carolinians as well. With a career in public service that included twenty years in the House and Senate, as well as serving as secretary of state under a favorite son, James K. Polk, Buchanan hoped to strike just the right chord for an unsettled Ellis. Preserve the Union and follow the Constitution, he challenged the graduates and their families, but, most of all, see the crisis through. Struck by the honorableness and sincerity of Buchanan's remarks, one North Carolinian who heard his speech, George Washington Duke, an Old Unionist, named his son after the deferential and charming president.

Buchanan's visit did little to allay Ellis's fears. Up until now, the governor and general assembly, indeed, all the appendages of state government, stood together in a correspondingly cautious attitude. The council of state, playing apostle to Ellis's political necromancy, resolved that, if North Carolina could not "hold our slave property and at the same time enjoy repose and tranquility in the Union, we will be constrained, in justice to ourselves and our posterity, to establish new forms." Yet no new political forms had limned the nation's increasingly surrealistic picture in 1859. In the next year, North Carolina existed as a state of debate. Lincoln's election in 1860 changed that.

For Ellis and for so many other southerners, Lincoln's ascension to the presidency could only mean the eventual end of slavery as a legal entity protected by the Constitution, and, from that, of a southern way of life. The Old South under the Old Union would cease to exist. The heart and head of the new nation established under the Constitution, the South would be only a "peculiar appendage" after 1860. Addressing the general assembly on 16 November 1860, just after Lincoln's triumph, Ellis warned that if Lincoln moved against slavery through "an effort to employ the military power of the general Government against one of the southern states," it would inevitably "involve the whole country in civil war."

Reelected in 1860, Ellis's second inaugural speech fell on a quorumless, wary, and hesitant general assembly. In the short space of two years, Ellis had become a passionate states' rights advocate while the majority of North Carolinians, following William Holden's advice to watch and wait, had adopted a prudent, go-slow attitude. In the two years between his inauguration speeches, John Ellis, unlike most fearful North Carolinians, at last had decided on whether or not to leave the Union. In the face of the great issue of secession, Ellis had come to believe that the state's future lay outside the Constitution, aside from a gathering Republican strength in the North and the West and protected from an increasing abolitionist sentiment throughout the nation. Still, one caveat remained. North Carolina had no new forms of union to which to attach itself, no alternative to the Old Union so beloved by many in the state. Ellis took it upon himself to provide a direction for the state.

After his reelection in 1860, Ellis had asked the general assembly to take the lead in calling for a general conference of all southern states, to summon a state convention to consider the question of secession, and to begin to take military preparations to defend North Carolina from northern aggression. In a telling vote, the legislature decided not to act on Ellis's recommendations. To the largely Democratic general assembly, the question of leaving the Union seemed not only premature but also uncalled for. A disappointed Ellis, convinced of the urgency of the moment and frustrated by the general assembly's restraint, wondered what it would take for North Carolina to leave the Union. Events outside North Carolina gave the answer.

In the two years between Ellis's elections as governor in 1858 and 1860, party labels, platforms, and loyalties in the state simply disintegrated. The second two-party system between Whigs and Democrats imploded into swirling factions whose only difference lay in how they viewed "constitutionality" and, from that, limits on states' rights. Initially a Henry Clay Whig who favored internal improvements, public schools, and measures such as a sound currency and banks, Ellis had by 1860 emerged as a radical Democrat, a states' rights advocate who urged immediate secession from the Union. If Whigs behaved like Democrats between 1858 and 1860, then Democrats functioned as if they were without a party at all. Captained by Ellis's mentor and now his political rival, William Holden, North Carolina's delegation to the Democratic Party's convention in Charleston in 1860 sat firmly on their hands as eight southern states, led by South Carolina, walked out in protest over the adoption of a northern plank on slavery in the western territories.

In the subsequent Baltimore convention, the state's delegates, indignant at the nomination for the presidency of Stephen A. Douglas, the favorite of northern Democrats, just as decisively bolted the ranks of their Democratic brethren. They joined their fellow southerners who had initially left the Charleston convention, and a rump group met in Richmond to nominate John C. Breckenridge of Kentucky, ostensibly still a Democrat, on a platform supporting a federal slave code that would protect the South's most essential institution. The last major national party, the Democrats, finally had pulled itself to pieces. To underscore the breakdown of the Democratic Party process instituted by Jackson, John C. Bell of Tennessee emerged as the candidate of the Constitutional Union Party, a title descriptive of its more conservative southern stance. For their part, the Republicans nominated Abraham Lincoln in a bid to capture Illinois and other doubtful states the party had lost in 1856.

The key to North Carolina's indecisive sentiment just prior to the outbreak of the Civil War lay in its voting pattern in the 1860 election. Breckinridge, the official Democratic candidate in the South, swept the state's entire electoral vote but by the narrowest of margins, 48,539 to 44,990 for Bell, the Unionist candidate. Douglas received a scant 2,701 votes. As in many southern states, Lincoln did not even appear as an option on any ballot. In sum, North Carolinians, while they vacillated on secession, never considered staying in a union run by men such as Lincoln and Douglas as a viable alternative. By the end of 1860, North Carolinians already had made up their minds about the Republicans and about Lincoln and Douglas. No abstract notion of nationalism and loyalty under the Constitution underlay their Unionist feeling. First and foremost, they thought of themselves as southerners, even as they watched and waited to see what Lincoln would do as president. To be a Unionist in North Carolina did not imply an unconditional loyalty to a central government under the Constitution, nor did it infer a disloyalty or disaffection from the South. The election of 1860 finally had pushed North Carolina into action.

The winter of 1861 only heightened North Carolina's discontent. In Congress, Sen. John Crittenden of Kentucky introduced a series of resolutions that would lead to the amending of the Constitution and allow the old Missouri Compromise line of 36°30' to extend all the way to California, in effect dividing slavery north and south. Additionally, he proposed an "unamendable amendment" that would forever protect and preserve slavery in the states where it already existed. Uninterested in making concessions that would have allowed Crittenden's resolutions to be passed, both the Republicans and southern secessionists in effect killed the compromise. "The argument is exhausted," declared southern representatives, as indeed it was in 1861.

Many southern states did not even wait for Congress to act. On 20 December 1860, just after Lincoln's election, South Carolina unanimously passed a resolution in a special convention called to consider the secession issue. That January the rest of the states in the Deep South, stretching in an arc from South Carolina to Texas, followed South Carolina's lead. Born on 7 February 1861, the new Confederate States of America elected Jefferson

Davis as president and just as quickly sent representatives to North Carolina, Kentucky, Virginia, and Maryland, hoping to convince them to join the new union. North Carolina now had the method, a specially called convention, and the means, new forms of government through the alliance of southern states, that would allow it to leave the Union.

Still, the pull of secession failed to convince many in the state to leave the Union. In January 1861, the general assembly had voted to consider a convention in a statewide referendum. Despite the fact that the weeks-long campaign produced a decided majority of pro-Unionist candidates, the people of North Carolina, fearful that even a convention might lead to secession, voted it down by the narrowest of margins, 47,323 to 46,672, almost a replica of the presidential vote of 1860.

After the failure of the initial referendum on a secession convention, Unionists found themselves without a cause. In effect, the defeat of the Crittenden resolutions and Lincoln's insistence that he and the Republicans would not "surrender to those we have beaten," in this case, southern slaveholders, meant that only disunion existed. Taken with the formation of the new Confederacy, zealots and extremists now had the upper hand. The issue of secession became more emotional and less analytical, a boon to extremists and fanatics. North Carolina nonetheless sent delegations to Montgomery, Alabama, in February 1861 to work for a fraternal compromise of the widening sectional dispute among the new Confederate states but found little sympathy among radical secessionists. In the same way, the state also sent representatives to a last-ditch peace conference in Washington called by Virginia in February 1861, attended by twenty-one states. When Lincoln and the new U.S. Senate made known their opposition to the Peace Conference and to the arrangements it proposed, North Carolina found itself caught between opposing, unyielding, uncompromising forces. It had to make a choice.

On his first day in office, 5 March 1861, Abraham Lincoln received a dispatch from the War Department asking that Maj. Robert Anderson, commander of the Federal garrison at Fort Sumter, snugly surrounded by eleven artillery batteries in the port of Charleston, South Carolina, be resupplied with food and provisions. Without such aid, Anderson informed Washington, he could last for only a few weeks at best. Remembering his inaugural address, given only hours before, in which he had promised to "hold, occupy, and possess" Federal property and to sustain a "perpetual Union . . . of these states," Lincoln determined to send a relief expedition to Fort Sumter. For his part, Jefferson Davis, understanding that if the United States held property and maintained military forces within the Confederacy, the latter had no legitimate claim to independence, ordered South Carolina forces to demand Anderson's surrender. When Anderson, acting on orders from Lincoln, declined the offer, Confederate batteries began shelling exposed, helpless Fort Sumter before dawn on 12 April 1861. The Civil War had begun.

In response to Fort Sumter's ensuing surrender, Lincoln called for 75,000 volunteers to put down the rebellion, with two regiments to be raised from North Carolina. His summons became an ultimate litmus test for loyalty to the Union. Governor Ellis, replying to Lincoln's request, followed Virginia's lead in declaring that "you can get no troops from North Carolina." When he heard the reports from Raleigh and Charleston, Zebulon Vance of Buncombe County, a passionate Unionist, recounted that he "was pleading for the Union with hand upraised when news came of Fort Sumter and Lincoln's call for troops. When

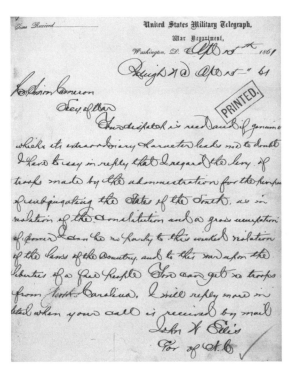

Gov. John Ellis's reply to the federal government's request to supply two regiments of North Carolina troops to quell the rebellion in South Carolina. North Carolina Collection, University of North Carolina at Chapel Hill.

my hand came down from that impassioned gesticulation, it fell slowly and sadly by the side of a Secessionist." Vance's experience paralleled that of the majority of North Carolinians, indecisive no longer. John A. Gilmer, an unwavering Unionist, asserted that North Carolinians were "all one now."

In the vastness of the western mountains, the Eastern Band of the Cherokees looked to their beloved white chief, Wil-Usdi (William Holland Thomas), for insight into the quarreling white factions. Few owned slaves, and the arguments over the Constitution and states' rights seemed not only irrelevant but sophistic to the Qualla Indians. Still, they, too, had a stake in the state's future. Wil-Usdi reminded them of the federal government's attempt only a generation ago to remove their fathers and mothers from their beloved smoking mountains. Moreover, he pointed out, Zeb Vance, Thomas Clingman, and David Swain had befriended them. They had prospered as de facto citizens of North Carolina. Echoing Vance's plea, Thomas thought it better to shed Northern blood in a tribal feud between warring white clans and not that of their neighbors in North Carolina. When Vance asserted that arguments had ceased and "the sword being drawn, all classes in the South united as if by magic," the Eastern Band of Cherokees also found out that they, too, were North Carolinians and would fight with their white kindred in the mountains against Northern aggressors.

With plans already in place, John Ellis ordered almost all the Federal properties in North Carolina, small outposts at Caswell and Johnston on the Cape Fear River, the arsenal in Fayetteville, and the mint in Charlotte, to be taken over by state troops. He also called a special session of the legislature to meet and to authorize the election of delegates to a convention to meet in Raleigh on 20 May to consider secession, a moot point so late that spring. Not surprisingly, the secession convention unanimously adopted an ordinance

Pvt. Thomas D. Royster, Company D, Twelfth
North Carolina State Troops in the Civil War.
North Carolina Collection, University of
North Carolina at Chapel Hill.

Pvt. William James McCuiston, Company A,
Fifty-fourth Regiment, North Carolina State Troops.
North Carolina Office of Archives and History, Raleigh.

of secession. Events outside the state at last had moved North Carolina to action. Its decision had been made outside its borders.

Yet even at that time, North Carolina equivocated. Delegates at the secession convention differed on how the state should leave the Union. Old Unionists such as George E. Badger looked to the Revolution and wanted to base secession on the right of revolution against an illegitimate and oppressive government. Representing radical secessionists, Burton Craige instead wanted a simple declaration that secession was a right of any state, and, from that, could dissolve "the union now subsisting between the state of North Carolina and the other states." Craige's resolution passed unanimously after a sharp but intense debate. In the end, North Carolina invoked the doctrine of states' rights to protect the institution of slavery and a way of life it felt was threatened. Still, North Carolina's sudden ardor for secession never transmuted into an equal fervor for the Confederacy, a point not lost on Jefferson Davis.

North Carolina hesitantly had joined the new union in 1789 and just as haltingly left it in 1861 for an even newer union of the Confederate States of America. Yet the state's enthusiasm once it embraced the Civil War did not mirror its indecision in entering the conflict. In fact, North Carolina, really the last Southern state to secede in spite of Tennessee's equivocation, bled more than any of its Southern neighbors in the slaughterhouse called the Civil War. Beginning with Henry Lawson Wyatt of Edgecombe County, purportedly the first Confederate to die, at the battle of Big Bethel in Virginia on 10 June 1861,

North Carolina's senators and representatives in the Confederate Congress, 1861–65.
North Carolina Collection, University of North Carolina at Chapel Hill.

and continuing to the skirmish at little Bethel in western North Carolina on 26 April 1865, North Carolinians suffered more deaths by disease and combat than Southerners from any other state. Indeed, the high-water mark of the Confederate cause, Gen. George Pickett's charge at Gettysburg, was inspired not by the sons and grandsons of the Virginia aristocracy but rather by the sons and grandsons of Carolina yeoman farmers, most of whom had never owned slaves. Of 128,889 men between the ages of twenty and sixty living in the state in 1860, perhaps 125,000, almost 97 percent, served in Confederate armies, militias, and home guards, all but 19,000 as volunteers. North Carolina's total loss during the Civil War, 40,275, of whom 19,673 died in battle, represented the greatest bloodletting suffered by any Confederate state. At Gettysburg, Tar Heels, commanded mostly by Virginians, accounted for more than 25 percent of Confederate casualties. Although the vast majority of those who died were white, the lists of those who fell also included Cherokees and, perhaps surprisingly, some blacks as well. At its core, the Civil War in North Carolina swept all elements of the state's dysfunctional southern family into its maelstrom. Some deserted. In the chaotic world of Civil War enlistments and volunteerism, perhaps as many as 24,000 North Carolinians deserted or absented themselves without official leave, yet, of that number, more than 8,000 rejoined their units.

Although North Carolina furnished the Confederacy two lieutenant generals, T. H. Holmes and D. H. Hill, eight major generals, and twenty-six brigadier generals, they had little influence upon the overall conduct of the war. Indeed, most North Carolina troops fell upon the great battlefields of Virginia and Pennsylvania, commanded and led not by

*James Iredell Waddell (1824–86), commander
of the Confederate cruiser* Shenandoah.
North Carolina Collection, University of
North Carolina at Chapel Hill.

the Holmeses, Hokes, and Hills from their home state but by the Lees, Jacksons, Johnstons, and Longstreets from other Southern states, especially Virginia. Much of North Carolina's lack of influence and position within the Confederate government could be explained by the untimely death of John Ellis, an early advocate of secession, by the state's absence at the birth of the Confederacy in Montgomery, by its indecision bordering on faithlessness to the new Confederacy, by its relative lack of development, and, additionally, by its few leaders of national prominence just prior to the Civil War. Nonetheless, those factors seemed less applicable as the war continued into its second year. Incensed by the continuing refusal of the Confederacy and Jefferson Davis to promote North Carolinians within the army and the bureaucracy, particularly to important cabinet positions, Zebulon Baird Vance, at first a colonel of the newly formed Twenty-sixth Regiment from western North Carolina, eventually carried on his own civil war with the Confederacy after he became governor of the state in 1862.

With a tradition of pirates, privateers, pitch, turpentine, and Tar Heels along the coast, North Carolinians showed an unusual dash and daring at sea throughout the war. James Iredell Waddell, commander of the cruiser *Shenandoah,* sailed around the world disrupting Union shipping from October 1864 to November 1865, an unrepentant southerner who never surrendered to the Union but who defiantly gathered in the Confederate flag and walked away from the late enemy in Liverpool, England, seven months after the war had ended. John Newland Maffitt resigned his commission in the U.S. Navy and for a brief time commanded the Confederate ironclad *Albemarle,* built on the lower reaches of the Roanoke River. Yet he wreaked the greatest havoc among Union shipping as captain of the Confederate cruiser *Florida.* The Rhett Butler of blockade-runners, Maffitt regularly made daring trips from Wilmington to Nassau in the Bahamas to bring in much-needed medical and war supplies. At the end of the war, Maffitt sailed the aptly named blockade runner *Owl* into Liverpool rather than surrender to Federal authorities. For more than two years, he commanded merchant ships bound for South America, returning to North Carolina only at the end of Reconstruction, when he felt it was safe to do so.

On 1 May 1861, even before secession but in anticipation of the oncoming war, the general assembly authorized ten regiments, or almost seven thousand men, to be raised for three years or the duration of the war. James G. Martin, a West Point graduate then on duty at Fort Riley, Kansas, hurried home to equip, train, and lead the new troops as the state's adjutant general. Training camps sprang up throughout the state, usually close to rail lines. Factories at Jamestown, Wilmington, Asheville, and Greensboro soon began to produce armaments for the new units. At Lincolnton in the west, A. S. Piggott quickly turned his personal laboratory into a larger one producing pharmaceutical supplies, while Charles Johnston, appointed as surgeon general for the new troops, opened hospitals in Raleigh, Weldon, Tarboro, Goldsboro, Salisbury, and Charlotte. Anticipating joining his sister states yet still bold and self-willed, Ellis wanted the state to be self-sufficient whether part of the Confederacy or not. Occurring almost simultaneously, Ellis's death and the state's subsequent secession left North Carolina in turmoil and uniquely vulnerable to the appeal of Southern extremists.

On 20 May 1861 North Carolina seceded from the Union and joined its fortune with that of its southern sister states. In the Civil War, geography and demography, two of history's handmaidens, determined the state's destiny. At the outset of fighting, the North decided upon an immediate invasion of Virginia and the capture of the new Confederate capital at Richmond in hopes of quickly ending the conflict. On a long-term basis, Lincoln wanted to split the South by taking control of the Mississippi River at New Orleans and at Vicksburg while also blockading the coast wherever possible. North Carolina's entry into the fray posed an additional problem for the North. In order to defeat Virginia, the key to Confederate survival, North Carolina, a chief supplier of men, supplies, and munitions for the Army of Northern Virginia, had to be neutralized. Then, too, North Carolina's coastline, "the most dangerous stretch of shore in the whole Confederacy," posed the greatest threat to Union shipping. Almost every vessel traveling along the coast had to skirt Cape Hatteras and the barrier islands because they jutted so far out into the Atlantic, a fact clearly recognized by Ellis. Writing to Jefferson Davis on 27 April 1861, he pointed out that

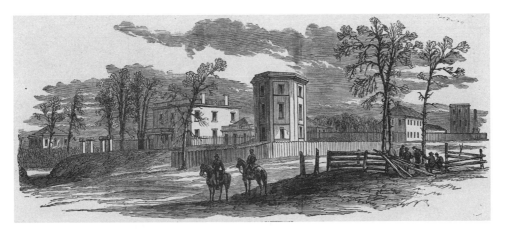

U.S. armory at Fayetteville taken over by the state during the Civil War.
North Carolina Collection, University of North Carolina at Chapel Hill.

"the Enemy's commerce between N. York and all the West Indies and South American ports could be cut off by privateers" operating off Roanoke Island and Cape Hatteras. A few "bold and Skillful Seamen" like the North Carolina pirates and buccaneers of the last century could disrupt the Union's plans for the war. Ellis proved to be a prophet for North Carolina's role in the war.

The Union early in the war decided that the coast of North Carolina not only threatened its shipping but also offered an opportunity for a quick and easy application of naval power along the southern coast. In 1861, to enforce a blockade of over four thousand miles of coastline, Lincoln could muster only three modern ships out of a navy of over ninety vessels, most of them in dry dock for repairs or overseas on duty. Understanding this, North Carolina and Confederate officials thought the state's coastline fairly safe and so devoted few first-line troops and ordnance to its defense. The taking of the nation's capital in Washington seemed more important and appealing. On the morning of 27 August 1861, a telegraph message reached Raleigh that electrified and shocked state officials, sending them scurrying for help. A national fleet of Union ships had passed Norfolk and steered straight for Cape Hatteras and the North Carolina coast. Two of the four most advanced ships in the Union navy, the steam frigates *Minnesota* and *Wabash,* the older sloop *Cumberland,* and a gaggle of converted civilian ships and transports numbering more than 150 with the Ninth and Twentieth New York regiments on board, the largest naval expedition in American history to that time, headed straight for the lightly defended Carolina coast. The next morning, guided by the Cape Hatteras lighthouse, the flotilla appeared off Hatteras Island and began landing troops on the side away from the Confederate fort on the island. Lincoln had decided to risk most of his dry-docked navy in a daring raid on North Carolina's coast. A little more than three months after it seceded, North Carolina faced invasion from the sea. Without waiting, the Civil War had come ashore all too soon for the state and its troops.

As he counted the masts of the Union ships appearing across the island and realized that they outnumbered the troops of the Seventh North Carolina under his command at Fort Clark, Col. William F. Martin decided that resistance would serve no purpose. A steady bombardment from Union ships that began that same midmorning only underscored his predicament. Hastily firing all his ammunition stores in the general vicinity of the Federal ships amidst wild cheering, Martin prepared to evacuate his men from the first of the coastal forts, Fort Clark. At noon, some 350 men of the Twentieth New York landed on the beach, nauseous, seasick, and unfit even to stand on their own legs. As the cheering Rebels straggled away from the fort toward Fort Hatteras, Col. Max Weber and his sickly invalids from the Twentieth New York staggered into the smoldering ruins. Like Raleigh almost three hundred years before, the Union now laid its claim to North Carolina.

On an unpredictably smooth sea the next morning, the Federals began their fusillade against the stronger Fort Hatteras. In three hours Union ships peppered the fort with more than three thousand rounds, sometimes hurling twenty to thirty shells at once against the mud-packed walls. Within a few hours the inexperienced Confederates had had enough. They ran up the white flag just to stop the battering and abuse. They quit before lunch on 29 August 1861. More than six hundred Confederates surrendered on Hatteras, the first large-scale capitulation of the war. Hatteras Island and with it a base to interdict inland waterways supplying Virginia and seal off coastal privateers and raiders, now fell into Union hands, all without the loss of a single man. As a jubilant North celebrated its first significant victory, the heart of coastal Carolina now lay open and vulnerable to Union attacks and invasion. What would be next?

North of Hatteras lay Roanoke Island, the last barrier before Albemarle Sound, and historically the very genesis of North Carolina. If the taking of Hatteras had all the elements of a comic opera—incessant and frequently harmless barrages, steaming and misdirected warships, seasick troops from New York who spoke only German crawling ashore to assault a deserted Fort Clark, and the frantic bombardment of a herd of wild horses mistaken for Confederate cavalry—then the next chapter of the conquest of the North Carolina coast, the attempt to establish a first Reconstruction government in a Southern state, took on all the aspects of political burlesque.

Col. Rush Hawkins, the flamboyant new Federal commander of Hatteras Island, firmly believed that North Carolinians, so late to join the Confederacy, still harbored loyalist sympathies for the Old Union. They would be eager to rejoin and to disassociate themselves from Southern nationalists and the new Confederacy. This delusion seemed to be shared by a number of Federal commanders—from Benjamin Butler to Ambrose Burnside —whose careers washed ashore along the southern coast, wrecked by the siren call of reconstruction and reunion. Indeed, from Hawkins to Burnside to Adm. Samuel DuPont, letters and reports abounded listing the possibilities of reestablishing a loyal government along the coast. Not surprisingly, two North Carolina sand mites, Marble Nash Taylor and Charles Henry Foster, both opportunists and "sunshine patriots," emerged from the obscurity of the barrier islands with just such a plan, one easily embraced by Hawkins and his superiors.

On 18 November 1861, Taylor and Foster presided over the Hatteras Convention, an assemblage of a few curious villagers and hangers-on who promptly passed a set of impractical and inconceivable resolutions setting aside the elected government in Raleigh, reinstating the federal constitution, and, lastly, declaring Taylor a provisional governor until new and proper elections could be held. For his part, Foster had himself been elected to Congress by a few hundred votes, mostly fraudulent, and then attempted to take a seat in Congress as the state's duly elected congressman. Recognizing the fallacy of establishing a loyalist government with the help of such knaves, Congress and Lincoln disavowed the two as scalawags and the Hatteras Convention as bogus. Thereafter, Taylor and Foster scurried back to their burrows in the sand, waiting to emerge once again when another opportunity arose. It never did. Still, the attempt to reestablish and rebuild Union sentiment through provisional governments in the South resonated within Lincoln's war aims. Further to the south, Admiral DuPont found more support that same November when he and his forces landed at Port Royal in South Carolina for yet another rehearsal for reconstruction.

George McClellan loved maps. Replacing the ancient Winfield Scott as commander of Union forces, McClellan found in maps the organization, guidelines, and predetermination he needed to chart the course of the war. Without them, he was lost. By looking at the relative positions of cities like Richmond, Raleigh, Goldsboro, Knoxville, Savannah, New Orleans, and Vicksburg, and at the railroad lines and rivers that crisscrossed his

Landing of Union troops from Burnside's expedition at Roanoke Island in 1862.
North Carolina Collection, University of North Carolina at Chapel Hill.

topographical charts, he understood what he must do to defeat the South. Maps brought clarity and predictability to his planning and strategy. They gave clues to the impact of new technologies such as railroads and rifled cannon on the course of battle and to the importance of combined arms operations between the army and navy along the southern coast. Instead of massed land battles à la Napoleon in Europe, vast Southern armies could be defeated and Richmond taken by destroying key centers of communication such as rail junctions, bridges, canal locks, telegraph lines, railroad stations, and industrial centers like Fayetteville and Norfolk. The deaths of scores of thousands could be averted by proper planning, training, and organization. A master strategist and schemer, McClellan brought overall planning and organization to Union war aims. He gave Lincoln a detailed map as to how to win the Civil War even though he lacked the energy and decisiveness to see it through to the end. His battle atlas of the United States contained two maps and several plans that included the barrier islands and eastern coast of North Carolina. He chose to entrust his blueprints and plans for winning the war in North Carolina and Virginia to an old friend, Maj. Gen. Ambrose Burnside.

Burnside commanded the newly formed amphibious division of the Union army envisioned by McClellan and strangely anticipatory of today's modern Marine Corps. The unit contained troops from Rhode Island, New York, and Massachusetts who knew how to operate from boats and to use them tactically. Supported by the navy yet trained by the army, the troops would strike at vulnerable points along the southern coast. Moreover, he already had a strategic foothold on the Outer Banks. The North Carolina towns of Beaufort and New Bern on the mainland stood out on McClellan's maps. Using them as bases, the Wilmington and Weldon Railroad could be attacked and interdicted at Goldsboro.

Charge of Col. Rush Hawkins's Zouaves at Roanoke Island.
North Carolina Collection, University of North Carolina at Chapel Hill.

From there, only a short distance remained before a vital link with Unionists in eastern Tennessee and western Virginia could be effected. Virginia then would be isolated and cut off from its supply lines to the Carolinas and the war would soon be over. Maps made it all seem so easy and predictable.

As he approached the North Carolina coast on 5 February 1862, Ambrose Burnside prepared to hurl his nearly 120 ships and 13,000 well-drilled infantrymen at Roanoke Island, a spit of land twelve miles long and three miles wide that sat as a bottle stopper to coastal shipping. Opposing him on the northwest coast of Roanoke Island the Confederates had erected three forts, Huger, Blanchard, and Bartow, but only the latter's guns could be maneuvered to fire at the Federals. In command of the 1,400 Rebels on Roanoke, Gen. Henry Wise, ill with a fever and flulike symptoms, like many of his troops, knew he had little chance to defeat Burnside. While the Federals had a well-armed flotilla, Wise could count on only a few old tugboats, steamers, and barges that made up North Carolina's hasty contribution to the Confederate navy, aptly dubbed the Mosquito Fleet. Moreover, Wise and his Confederates could expect no help from Richmond. They were on their own.

Using Hatteras as a springboard, Gen. Ambrose Burnside launched one of the largest amphibious operations in American history, sending surfboats and ferries loaded with 7,500 troops churning ashore at Roanoke Island on 7 February 1862. The battle for Roanoke Island lasted two days and ended in a complete victory for the Union. Starting with a mammoth bombardment by the massed Union fleet, Burnside sent 4,000 men storming up the only road to the fort. When met by stiff resistance from Col. H. M. Shaw and more than 400 entrenched Confederates, Union troops, in a charge led by Rush Hawkins, the theatrical colonel of the Ninth New York Zouaves, flanked the Rebel positions. Shaw quickly yielded. In less than two days, Burnside, "Old Sideburns" to his troops, had taken the island that functioned as a barrier between Virginia and North Carolina shipping. He had suffered only 37 men killed and more than 214 wounded, while, incredibly, the Roanoke defenders lost 23 killed, 58 wounded, and a great many who meekly surrendered, most without firing a shot. With their capitulation, a large part of northeastern North Carolina lay open to Union seizure and occupation. The messenger of death had come early to North Carolina—and would stay for four long years. Yet the state's humiliation had only begun.

Realizing that the Federals would turn toward Elizabeth City after capturing Roanoke, Com. William F. Lynch, commander of the pitiful Mosquito Fleet, moved his remaining vessels to defend that port. As if on cue, Comdr. Stephen Rowan and Union ships appeared off Cobb's Point near Elizabeth City on 10 February 1862. Awaiting them, Lynch's futile fleet valiantly lined up for battle, first with the *Black Warrior,* then the *Seabird, Ellis, Appomattox, Beaufort,* and a captured Union ship, the *Fanny.* With the others either blown out of the water or else scuttled, only the *Beaufort* among all the Confederate ships escaped to fight another day. Coastal Carolina, except for the area commanded by the guns of Fort Fisher, now belonged to the Union. Supplies from blockade-runners could enter only under the guns of Fort Fisher after April 1862. The job of the Union navy blockading the North Carolina and southern coast now became immeasurably easier.

By April 1862 Burnside and his forces had captured more than twenty North Carolina towns, and more than 2.5 million acres had fallen under Union control. In a series of disasters at New Bern, Plymouth, Winton, Morehead City, Edenton, Beaufort, Elizabeth City, and Washington, North Carolina's troops had put up only token resistance or else fled the scene altogether. The loss of New Bern, the most important coastal city besides Wilmington, consolidated the Union's control of eastern North Carolina. To the Virginians and Georgians who fought with the North Carolinians along the coast, "Tar Heel" had come to mean soldiers mistaken for jellyfish and crabbers, always finding a way to trap themselves or fleeing first and fighting later at the first surge of a tide of Union soldiers. In conquering the coast, Burnside had lost few men and supplies. Nature and the unpredictable weather turned out to be his greatest enemies. Still, the battles along the Carolina coast gave the state its first war hero, Zebulon Baird Vance of Asheville.

Inexplicably, Burnside stopped to consolidate his gains, rest his eager troops, and consider his options. Should he push on to Goldsboro and Raleigh while destroying the Wilmington and Weldon Railroad, the chief supply line for Lee's Army of Northern Virginia, or reduce and occupy Fort Macon, the only Confederate stronghold left in North Carolina? Cautious and wary, he chose to attack Fort Macon. A masonry fort whose emplaced guns could fire only in a straight trajectory and thus could not harm tunneling infantrymen, Macon, hardly a formidable obstacle, fell by 26 April.

To the north, George McClellan, Burnside's old friend from their days with the Illinois Central Railroad, prepared to attack Richmond, and, if successful, to move from there to Raleigh to meet up with the coastal division. To aid him, he enlisted Old Sideburns and seven thousand of his men, significantly weakening his capacity to mount attacks against Goldsboro and Raleigh and to disrupt the Wilmington and Weldon Railroad. Instead, Union troops staged a series of not altogether successful raids against smaller prizes such

Occupation of New Bern by the Forty-fifth Regiment of Massachusetts.
North Carolina Collection, University of North Carolina at Chapel Hill.

as South Mills and Tratner's Creek. For their part, Confederate officials in Richmond, realizing what North Carolina meant to the Army of Northern Virginia and to the Confederacy, moved to strengthen the state's defenses. Several detachments of state troops, bloodied veterans of First Manassas, Big Bethel, and now the brutal Peninsular campaign, entrained for Raleigh and Goldsboro. More than thirteen thousand new Enfield rifles, freshly smuggled from England, gave the regiments more firepower. Talented and enthusiastic amateur officers such as Vance and Richard Gatlin were replaced by Samuel French and Robert Ransom, professional and seasoned officers of Indian wars and foreign service. In a happenstance of fate and pluck, an incident occurred on 10 March 1862 that made Burnside and McClellan hesitate in their advance southward.

Unsuspected and unanticipated, a Confederate ironclad, the *Virginia,* formerly the *Merrimac,* sailed toward Union ships at Hampton Roads to challenge Lincoln's blockade. Without a seagoing navy, the Confederacy had found a way to neutralize the Union blockade along the shallow waters of the coast. As he regarded the attack of the *Virginia* and surveyed the myriad streams and sounds along the North Carolina coast, Ambrose Burnside perhaps envisioned an endless stream of ironclad barges and tugboats, all with torpedoes and enormous rams, steaming straight at his helpless ships. Not more than thirty miles from Elizabeth City, an eighteen-year-old named Gilbert Elliott imagined the same thing. He set about building a turtle-shaped ironclad called the *Albemarle* to make Burnside's nightmare a reality. Although it took more than two years to finish, long after Burnside had left North Carolina, the bulky *Albemarle,* North Carolina's best-kept secret, eventually would rise from the murky Roanoke River mud and panic Union blockaders.

In the spring of 1862 Burnside introduced a new governor for a reconstructed North Carolina, Edward Stanly, a native Tar Heel, lukewarm Unionist, antebellum Whig, and passionate opponent of the "Secesh," secessionists who supported the Confederacy. Exiled in California for more than a decade, Stanly soon learned that what the Federals had told him and expected of him differed from what he found along the coast. First, Unionist sentiment never manifested the levels described by Burnside. The Union flags flown by

North Carolinians over Washington and Winton as the Federals approached might have indicated compliance but never enthusiasm for the Union cause. Moreover, the burning of Winton and the pillaging and depredations of Union troops appalled even their most ardent champions. Then, too, Stanly himself appeared as an early carpetbagger to North Carolinians or, at worst, a traitor. Even Burnside held him in low esteem. Lastly, Stanly, at heart, could never support the emancipation of slaves, even though he personally did a great deal to help freedmen under Union authority. By January 1863, his shadow government, by mutual assent, simply ceased functioning.

On 28 June 1862, Ambrose Burnside received the marching orders he long had anticipated. At Lincoln's urging, he left with two divisions, more than seven thousand men, to join McClellan on the great battlefields of Virginia for a decisive clash with Robert E. Lee. There and not in North Carolina would he find the recognition and honor denied him in the backwaters and swamps of the coast. There he would also meet Robert E. Lee, the nemesis of Union generals and a suitable opponent.

The new commander of the Carolina coast, Gen. John Gray Foster, proved a capable replacement. A master engineer, West Point graduate, and student of harbor defenses, Foster carefully fortified New Bern and Washington, arranging his strongpoints so that they could be supported by gunboats and naval vessels. Understanding his new role now with fewer men than the Confederates, he went over to the defensive, conducting harassing raids against railroads and towns to tie down Richmond's troops so they could not reinforce Lee in Virginia. For the next year, from the fall of 1862 until late in the summer of 1863, Confederate forces in North Carolina went on the offensive, hoping to recapture or at least pin Union forces in strongpoints along the coast. Still, the Federal occupation of much of northeastern North Carolina provided an appropriate set of circumstances for the Union to reconstruct its thinking about the conduct of the war.

By the time Lee surrendered at Appomattox Courthouse, almost 180,000 African Americans had served in the Union army, thousands from North Carolina. Of the first thirty regiments to be formed, four came from within the state. With Burnside's seizure of a large portion of coastal and eastern North Carolina, hundreds of plantation owners and farmers had been displaced, leaving thousands of slaves and free blacks to fend for themselves. By the time Burnside landed on Roanoke Island, Maj. Gen. David Hunter, the new commander of the Department of the South, already had organized a black regiment in the Sea Islands of South Carolina. In faraway Kansas, Brig. Gen. James Lane had enlisted two regiments of blacks to fight bushwhackers from Kansas and Missouri. In New Orleans, Maj. Gen. Benjamin Butler, an opportunist always operating outside his orders, welcomed a regiment of freed blacks and mulattoes who only recently had fought for the Confederacy. Anticipating the emancipation of slaves by Lincoln, Gen. Rufus Saxton, Hunter's replacement as commander of the Department of the South, received permission from the War Department to recruit and train black regiments in South Carolina not to exceed five thousand troops. By the fall of 1862, just as the Union consolidated its control over a large portion of slaveholding North Carolina, the recruitment and training of African Americans for the Union army had begun in earnest.

Lincoln's Emancipation Proclamation of 1 January 1863 directly paved the way for the recruitment of North Carolina blacks into the Union army. In unique fashion, the political

Freed slaves entering New Bern in 1863 after the Emancipation Proclamation.
North Carolina Collection, University of North Carolina at Chapel Hill.

aims of Abraham Lincoln, the availability of recently freed blacks around New Bern and Washington, and the missionary zeal of Massachusetts abolitionists all came together to produce one of North Carolina's almost forgotten tales of the Civil War. Much of the story began in Massachusetts.

Careful and cautious in its new policy of raising colored regiments, the War Department authorized only a few officials and organizations to recruit African Americans for Union service. One of these, Gov. John Andrew of Massachusetts, asked Francis Gould Shaw of Boston, an abolitionist and longtime enemy of slavery, if his son, Robert Gould, would command a black unit. As prototypes, the Fifty-fourth and Fifty-fifth Regiments of Massachusetts Colored Volunteers would be the model for other units in the Union army. On 17 July 1863 at Fort Wagner outside Charleston, Robert Gould Shaw led the Fifty-fourth in its charge to glory against the well-entrenched Confederates. Shaw, most of his officers, and over 40 percent of the more than 630 men in the regiment died in the ferocious but futile charge. After Fort Wagner, African Americans, proud of the bravery and courage under fire shown by the Fifty-fourth, rushed to join the Union standard.

Led by John Andrew and a Massachusetts delegation of antislavery supporters and abolitionists, Northerners pushed the War Department to turn its attention to the areas in North and South Carolina occupied by Union forces. Federal commanders in the South such as Vincent Collyer estimated that more than 7,500 black refugees lived in the area around New Bern and more than 10,000 others in the coastal region controlled by Burnside's troops. A soldier in the Twenty-third Massachusetts Regiment stationed in New Bern called it the "Mecca of a thousand aspirations" of newly freed slaves, at least some of which included taking up arms against their former masters. Governor Andrew of Massachusetts even proposed sending elements of the Fifty-fourth Massachusetts to North Carolina to be the "nest egg of a brigade" of locally recruited units. Failing in that, Andrew produced a roster of zealous officers, mostly with abolitionist sentiments, who wished to go to North Carolina and form black regiments. Edward A. Wild headed the list.

228

Wild cemented the Massachusetts connection. In April 1863, even as his old unit turned southward toward Charleston and the slaughterhouse at Fort Wagner, Wild arrived at New Bern to raise "a brigade (of four regiments) of North Carolina volunteer infantry, to be recruited in that state, and to serve for three years" or the duration of the war. A fervent abolitionist from Brookline, Massachusetts, Wild had served as a colonel with the Thirty-fifth Massachusetts at Antietam. Wounded and with his left arm amputated, he returned to Massachusetts, where, with his friend Robert Gould Shaw, he helped recruit and train the Fifty-fourth.

To command his regiments, Wild, now a brigadier general, chose experienced veterans but, more significantly, abolitionists whose ardor and zeal rivaled his own. For the First North Carolina Colored Volunteers, he selected James Beecher, half brother to Harriet Beecher Stowe, as colonel and commander. As a lieutenant colonel, Wild appointed William N. Reed from New York, a graduate of a German military school in Kiel and very likely a mulatto who became the highest ranking African American soldier in the Civil War. John V. DeGrasse, an African American physician from Boston who previously had practiced in France, became the regimental surgeon. With the help of Abraham Galloway from New Bern, a helpful spy and informant for Union forces, Wild and his northern abolitionists soon mustered one thousand into the First North Carolina Colored Volunteers. The new unit entered service on 30 June 1863.

Distribution of captured Confederate clothing to freed slaves in New Bern.
North Carolina Collection, University of North Carolina at Chapel Hill.

**ATTENTION!
CONSCRIPTS!
RECRUITS WANTED!**

$100 *Bounty and* **$25** *per month pay.*

The subscriber and others have been ordered by Maj. Gen. G. W. Smith to receive recruits for the defence of North Carolina. The Conscription law has been partially suspended for the benefit of Conscripts. A favorable opportunity is now extended to Conscripts to volunteer, and thus secure both State and Confederate bounty. By joining my Company the recruit will receive **One Hundred Dollars** bounty, in addition to **Twenty-five Dollars** per month pay. Ours is the most healthy and desirable branch of the service. **NOW IS THE TIME TO VOLUNTEER!** North Carolina is invaded. It is the duty of her sons to defend her. To the rescue, sons of the "Old North State"! Your brethren in arms have had hard work to do in the battles before Goldsborough. They call upon you to help them drive back the vile invaders of our soil. Apply to me in Fayetteville, or to R. W. Hardie, Esq. at the Court House.

ARCH'D McFADYEN,

Lieut. Co. A, 63d Reg't N. C. T.

A recruiting poster for North Carolina troops during the Civil War.
North Carolina Collection, University of North Carolina at Chapel Hill.

As the men of the First North Carolina Colored Volunteers marched off to Florida for their first taste of combat, they found that they, too, had to affirm the ability and resolve of African Americans to fight and die not only for the Union but for themselves as well. In the summer of 1863, "colored" units found themselves engaged in widespread combat throughout the South and, in terms of civic acceptance, throughout the North as well. Battles at Port Hudson, Milliken's Bend, and Fort Wagner evinced not only their valor but also their constitutional right to full citizenship.

Still, the First North Carolina Colored Volunteers represented a new element in the struggle for recognition and acceptance. Consisting mainly of ex-slaves, the troops from North and South Carolina, unlike the Massachusetts, Louisiana, and Missouri troops drawn mostly from dispersed free black populations, had never faced their former masters in combat. Would they fight, flee, or freeze in the heat of combat? To the Massachusetts abolitionists and to the War Department, the First North Carolina Colored Volunteers' fate embodied the "thousand aspirations" held by millions of slaves and their supporters throughout the nation.

In Florida, the First North Carolina Colored Volunteers first had to fight through all the tedious fatigue, pioneer, and patrol duties usually assigned to new troops, especially African Americans, before they ever saw a Confederate soldier. Still, their baptism of fire came on 20 March 1864 at a small town named Olustee sitting astride the Confederate rail line leading into Georgia. In one of the nastiest and bloodiest small battles of the war, the Federals lost 1,355 out of a total of 5,115 men. Of the First North Carolina Colored Volunteers, 230 soldiers fell on the battlefield. Out of 550 men from the Eighth United States Colored Troops from South Carolina, less than 250 survived. One eyewitness to the carnage observed that, often without even a day's drill in loading and firing their weapons, many "black men stood to be killed" and wounded at Olustee. Now renamed the Thirty-fifth United States Colored Troops, the North Carolinians received orders to move to Georgia for a raid on the railroad line above Savannah. At the brushy top of a slope ironically called Honey Hill, twenty miles from Augusta, black North Carolinians stormed the Confederate defenses only to be thrown back with heavy losses. The battle at Honey Hill would be the last for the Thirty-fifth. Remaining in the South Carolina low country until hostilities ended, the Thirty-fifth, in yet another of history's incongruities, occupied Charleston after the war ended, taking up quarters in the old citadel not far from the slave

230 market where South Carolinians had begun the "unfortunate conflict" four years earlier. In June 1866, at the end of their enlistments, the Thirty-fifth solemnly marched through the streets of Charleston and at a mustering-out ceremony received their honorable discharges. Most never returned to North Carolina.

ADDITIONAL READINGS

Auman, William T. "Neighbor Against Neighbor: The Inner Civil War in the Randolph County Area." *North Carolina Historical Review* 61 (January 1984): 59–92.

Auman, William Thomas, and David D. Scarboro. "Heroes of America in Civil War North Carolina." *North Carolina Historical Review* 58 (October 1981): 327–63.

Baker, Robin E. "Class Conflict and Political Upheaval: The Transformation of North Carolina Politics during the Civil War." *North Carolina Historical Review* 69 (April 1992): 148–78.

Bardolph, Richard. "Confederate Dilemma: North Carolina Troops and the Deserter Problem." *North Carolina Historical Review* 66 (January 1989): 61–86; (April 1989): 179–210.

———. "Inconstant Rebels: Desertion of North Carolina Troops in the Civil War." *North Carolina Historical Review* 41 (April 1964): 163–89.

Barrett, John G. *Civil War in North Carolina.* Chapel Hill: University of North Carolina Press, 1963.

Beers, Henry P., comp. *The Confederacy: A Guide to the Archives of the Government of the Confederate States.* Washington, D.C.: National Archives and Records Administration, 1986.

Black, Wilfred W., ed. "Civil War Letters of E. N. Boots from New Bern and Plymouth." *North Carolina Historical Review* 36 (April 1959): 205–23.

Bridges, Leonard H. *Lee's Maverick General, Daniel Harvey Hill.* Lincoln: University of Nebraska Press, 1991.

Brown, Norman D. "Union Election in Civil War North Carolina." *North Carolina Historical Review* 43 (October 1966): 381–400.

Butler, Lindley S. *Pirates, Privateers, and Rebel Raiders of the Carolina Coast.* Chapel Hill: University of North Carolina Press, 2000.

Casstevens, Frances H. *The Civil War and Yadkin County, North Carolina: A History.* Jefferson, N.C.: McFarland, 1997.

Clark, Walter, ed. *Histories of the Several Regiments and Battalions from North Carolina, in the Great War 1861–65.* 5 vols. Raleigh: E. M. Uzzell; Goldsboro: Nash Brothers, 1901–5.

Coker, Charles Frederick William, ed. *North Carolina Civil War Records: An Introduction to Printed and Manuscript Sources.* Raleigh: Department of Archives and History, 1977.

Colyer, Vincent. *Report of the Services Rendered by the Freed People to the United States Army, in North Carolina, in the Spring of 1862, after the Battle of Newbern.* New York: Vincent Colyer, 1864.

Davidson, Roger A., Jr. "'They Have Never Been Known to Falter': The First United States Colored Infantry in Virginia and North Carolina." *Civil War Regiments* 6 (1998): 1–26.

Delaney, Norman C. "Charles Henry Foster and the Unionists of Eastern North Carolina." *North Carolina Historical Review* 37 (July 1960): 348–66.

Dix, Mary Seaton, ed. "'And Three Rousing Cheers for the Privates': A Diary of the 1862 Roanoke Island Expedition." *North Carolina Historical Review* 71 (January 1994): 62–84.

Dornbusch, Charles Emil, comp. *Military Bibliography of the Civil War.* New York: New York Public Library, 1971.

Edwards, Laura F. *Scarlett Doesn't Live Here Anymore: Southern Women in the Civil War Era.* Urbana: University of Illinois Press, 2000.

Goff, Jerry C. "Geographic Origins of North Carolina Enlistments during the War between the States." Master's thesis, University of North Carolina, 1987.

Graham, Matthew J. *Ninth Regiment, New York Volunteers (Hawkins Zouaves)*. New York: E. P. Coby and Co., 1900.

Guide to Civil War Records in the North Carolina State Archives. Raleigh: Department of Archives and History, 1966.

Harris, William C. "Lincoln and Wartime Reconstruction in North Carolina, 1861–1863." *North Carolina Historical Review* 63 (April 1986): 149–68.

Honey, Michael K. "War within the Confederacy: White Unionists of North Carolina." *Prologue* 18 (Summer 1986): 74–93.

Jernigan, J. A. "'Making Soldiers of Slaves': Pat Cleburne, North Carolina, and the Price of Southern Independence." Honors essay, University of North Carolina, 1980.

Jordan, Weymouth T., and John D. Chapla. "'O What a Turbill Affair': Alexander W. Reynolds and His North Carolina–Virginia Brigade at Missionary Ridge, Tennessee, November 25, 1863." *North Carolina Historical Review* 77 (July 2000): 312–36.

Kirwan, Thomas. *Soldiering in North Carolina; Being the Experiences of a "Typo" in the Pines, Swamps, Fields, Sandy Roads, Towns, Cities, and among the Fleas, Wood-ticks, "Gray backs," Mosquitoes, Blue-tail Flies, Moccasin Snakes, Lizards, Scorpions, Rebels, and Other Reptiles, Pests and Vermin of the "Old North State."* Boston: T. Kirwan, 1864.

Massey, Mary E. "Confederate Refugees in North Carolina." *North Carolina Historical Review* 40 (April 1963): 158–82.

McCaslin, Richard B. *Portraits of Conflict: A Photographic History of North Carolina in the Civil War.* Fayetteville: University of Arkansas Press, 1997.

McKinney, Gordon B., and Richard McMurray, eds. *Guide to the Microfilm Edition of the Papers of Zebulon Vance.* Frederick, Md.: University Publications of America, 1987.

Parker, Francis Marion, and Michael W. Taylor. *To Drive the Enemy from Southern Soil: The Letters of Col. Francis Marion Parker and the History of the 30th Regiment North Carolina Troops.* Dayton, Ohio: Morningside Press, 1998.

Parramore, Thomas C. "Burning of Winton in 1862." *North Carolina Historical Review* 39 (January 1962): 18–31.

Poore, Benjamin P. *Life and Public Services of Ambrose E. Burnside, Soldier, Citizen, Statesman.* Providence, R.I.: Reid and Co., 1882.

Quarles, Benjamin. *The Negro in the Civil War.* Boston: Little, Brown, 1953.

Reid, Richard M. "Protest and Dissent in Civil War North Carolina." Ph.D. diss., University of Toronto, 1976.

Sauers, Richard A. "General Ambrose Burnside's 1862 North Carolina Campaign: A Thesis in History." Ph.D. diss., Pennsylvania State University, 1987.

Smith, Steven D. "History and Archaeology: General Edward Wild's African Brigade in the Siege of Charleston, South Carolina." *Civil War Regiments* 5 (1996): 20–70.

Trotter, William R. *Silk Flags and Cold Steel: The Civil War in North Carolina.* Vol. 1: *The Piedmont.* Greensboro: Signal Research, 1988.

Wellman, Manly W. *Rebel Boast: First at Bethel—Last at Appomattox.* Westport, Conn.: Greenwood Press, 1974.

Yates, Richard E. *The Confederacy and Zeb Vance.* Tuscaloosa, Ala.: Confederate Publishing, 1958.

Ebb Tide of the Confederacy

In April 1862 the Confederate Congress, hoping to bolster sagging enthusiasm and depleted armies, passed the Conscription Act, drafting all males between the ages of eighteen and thirty-five into the army. Bitterly resented throughout the state, the act set many North Carolinians against the Confederacy. Zebulon Vance, an ex-Confederate colonel from Buncombe County who was elected governor in September 1862, bristled at Richmond's conscription of North Carolinians. After all, the state voluntarily had furnished more troops than any other with little voice in their use. As North Carolina's wartime governor, Vance took aim at Richmond and Jefferson Davis, the Confederate president. First, Vance determined to fight the Unionists and peace advocates who sought to betray the state; additionally, he would uphold North Carolina's rights within the Confederacy, even if it meant arresting Richmond's officials who sought to enforce unpopular laws such as the Conscription Act or the tax-in-kind levied on poor farmers. In the fall of 1862, North Carolina's own internal civil war began in earnest with Zebulon Vance as its reflection.

From the fetid swamps along the coast to the caves of the Piedmont to the vastness of the mountain wilderness in the west, groups of bushwhackers, deserters, Unionists, common outlaws and bandits, runaway slaves, and peace men sprang up to harry Confederate supply points, rob and loot helpless women and children, and, in general, oppose the policies of Richmond and Raleigh. Called bushwhackers in the mountains and Buffaloes along

Zebulon Baird Vance, North Carolina's governor during the Civil War. North Carolina Department of Archives and History, Raleigh.

Soldiers of the Forty-fifth Massachusetts stealing pigs in eastern North Carolina. North Carolina Collection, University of North Carolina at Chapel Hill.

the coast, they lived by robbing and stealing in the no-man's-lands on the fringes of the war, retreating at night to hideouts deep in the swamps and to the caves and woods in the Piedmont and mountains where weakened Confederate home guards dared not follow. In Hertford County an elderly runaway slave named "Old Gil" led a mixed group of Buffaloes, runaway slaves, uniformed Unionists, and illiterate whites until he died in a shootout in 1863. By the spring of that same year the area around New Bern had been reduced to a wasteland dotted by burned farm buildings, abandoned homes and towns, rotted crops, and skeletal outlines of dead animals. As the war wore on and desertions increased, parts of North Carolina, especially along the coast and in the adjacent Piedmont, sank into chaos and anarchy, with Confederate troops resorting to sweeps and raids against bushwhackers and Buffaloes in an attempt to maintain some veneer of authority.

In February 1863 Governor Vance saw Richmond agree to one of his demands. A North Carolina general, D. H. Hill, assumed command of the state's troops under Major General Longstreet of the Virginia and North Carolina district. With a reputation as a fighter and a man of action, Hill immediately sought to reclaim the coast for the Confederacy. Having Longstreet's approval, he planned a diversionary attack on New Bern while his troops stormed and took Washington and regained control of the Pamlico River and Beaufort.

The high-water mark of the Confederacy was from February until July 1863. With victories at Chancellorsville and around Richmond and with the advent of the Emancipation Proclamation, Confederate opposition not only stiffened but also threatened the North with a second invasion of Pennsylvania. In planning for his assault upon the North, Lee needed supplies and troops from North Carolina more than ever. Thus, Hill's attempt to regain control of the Carolina coast played a significant strategic role in Lee's daring plan to end the war. Understanding this, Hill eagerly assumed command of the more than 14,500 troops facing the Union forces at New Bern and Washington.

North Carolinians welcomed Hill's take-charge attitude. In Raleigh, a newspaper mirrored the state's resentment of past Confederate generalship in the state. "We have had vastly too much strategy, too much science, and too much digging and ditching in North

*Stephen D. Ramseur (1837–64), one of
North Carolina's youngest and ablest
generals during the Civil War.*
North Carolina Collection, University of
North Carolina at Chapel Hill.

Carolina," the editor proclaimed. Hill promised action. With Hill's appointment, North Carolinians expected "a change in management," specifically more fighting and victory. Still, Hill's words as he took command betrayed his weaknesses. For his cavalry officers and men, he had nothing but disdain and sarcasm. Of J. J. Pettigrew he asked, "Can you help me? . . . I have been torturing my brain to devise a system by which our cavalry can be got under fire." On another occasion he mused that, as he toured battlefields, he futilely tried to find dead soldiers with spurs. At a crucial moment, when Henry Burgwyn and his well-trained Twenty-sixth North Carolina strained to charge and reduce the Union strongpoint at Fort Anderson, the key fort just across the Neuse River from New Bern, first Pettigrew and then Hill wavered, afraid of the horrific casualties that would come with the assault. Instead, Burgwyn's troops died in driblets as the siege against New Bern and Washington wore on. Still, Hill claimed success against the Federals. While his troops bombarded Union troops and gunboats with shells, yells, and insults, Confederate wagons and quartermasters fanned out along the coast, collecting corn, pigs, wheat, cotton, and anything else they could lay their hands on for Lee's starving troops. By May 1863 Confederate troops withdrew from New Bern and Washington. Lee needed all the men he could get for his invasion of Pennsylvania. Once again, Wilmington, Fort Fisher, Raleigh, Goldsboro, and the Piedmont counties lay open to attacks from the Federals, outlaws, Buffaloes, and outlier bands who conducted their own civil war against North Carolina's "Secesh." North Carolina's proximity to the great battlefields of Virginia and Pennsylvania and its interior system of railroads combined to give the state one of the South's most notorious prisons. Less than two months after North Carolina left the Union in May 1861 Confederate and state officials already had singled out the old Maxwell Chambers factory building, built in 1839, in the town of Salisbury as a prison site. The surroundings included sixteen acres in the town of Salisbury as well as "the principal factory building, about ninety by fifty feet, three stories high with an engine house at one end about sixteen by eighty feet, constructed of good brick." Sixteen buildings, used mostly for factory workers and, later, students, surrounded the old factory. By November, 1861, the first Confederate guards arrived, and, in December, the first contingent of prisoners.

Soldiers from General Wild's First North Carolina Colored Volunteers liberating slaves in eastern North Carolina in January 1864. North Carolina Collection, University of North Carolina at Chapel Hill.

After the first battles at Big Bethel and Bull Run (First Manassas), Union prisoners by the hundreds crowded into the tobacco warehouses of Richmond and Raleigh. Faced with having to form a government, raise an army and navy, write a constitution and manufacture an instant government, build infrastructures, and create whole new bureaucracies, Richmond, already strained in its capacities, looked to the states for help in housing prisoners. Because of its strategic position and also the willingness of Raleigh to cooperate, Salisbury, deep in the heart of North Carolina, quickly became an important prison center.

From August 1861 until November 1864 conditions at Salisbury seemed tolerable for a nineteenth-century prison, originally built to house a few hundred prisoners. The numbers swelled, especially after the bloodbaths of 1863, to more than two thousand. At the end of the war, more than fifteen thousand had been imprisoned at Salisbury at one time or another, mostly ordinary servicemen from the Union army but also several hundred Confederate soldiers serving out terms from courts-martial, some Union deserters, several score political prisoners, and perhaps two to three hundred ex-slaves and freedmen. Although the numbers cannot be known for certain from incomplete records, perhaps as many as four thousand died there, more than 26 percent in all, making Salisbury one of the most infamous prison camps of the war, in terms of its mortality rates. Overburdened by the breakdown of prisoner exchanges after 1863, Salisbury, like many southern prisons, could not cope with increasingly overcrowded conditions. Death came not from abuse by guards and starvation but from the poor conditions of so many massed into such a small space.

As the war progressed, more and more attention focused on Wilmington, the state's finest deepwater port. With Beaufort occupied and Charleston, Savannah, Mobile, and New Orleans either blockaded or captured, Wilmington, some 28 miles upstream from the

Slave labor helping to construct Fort Fisher. North Carolina Division of Archives and History, Raleigh.

Blockade-runner Wando *near Fort Fisher.* North Carolina Office of Archives and History, Raleigh.

mouth of the Cape Fear River, became the favored port of entry for much of the Confederate's badly needed supplies. This time, geography favored the Confederates. Some 674 miles from Bermuda and 575 miles from Nassau in the Bahamas, Wilmington, almost halfway down the southern coast, had railroad connections to Charleston, Columbia, and, intermittently, to the Wilmington and Weldon Railroad into Virginia. Guarded by Fort Fisher and its famous Flying Battery of Whitworth rifles, as well as four large-rifled cannon that could heave rounds five miles with almost pinpoint accuracy, blockade-runners could enter under the safety of Col. William Lamb's guns by either the Old or New Inlets to the ocean.

Wilmington became the new "smugglers' den" of North Carolina. Beginning in the spring of 1862 and climaxing in the summer of 1863, more than 585 steamers ran the blockade into Wilmington. In 1863 alone, perhaps two or three runners entered and left daily. Clyde steamers, named after coastal ships that plied the Clyde and Mersey rivers in England, came to dominate the trade. Riding low in the water with almost no superstructure, tapered like an arrow and drafting little water, the steamers, with high-powered engines, simply outran and outmaneuvered the slower Federal gunboats and vessels.

The crews of the runners reflected the motley makeup of the new breed of Civil War sea dogs and privateers. Licensed by the Confederate government out of Richmond, official runners usually had Southern officers as captains, with ordinary soldiers and ex-merchantmen as crew. Private companies such as the Anglo-Confederate Trading Company frequently preferred pensioned Royal Navy officers, captains who had experience sailing southern waters, and tough English and Irish sailors for their vessels. In the fall of 1862 still another player entered the high-stakes game of blockade running, North Carolina's own freebooter and free spirit, Gov. Zebulon Vance.

The philosophy behind blockade-running perfectly fitted North Carolina's bold, brash new governor. Simmering with resentment against Richmond's neglect of the Carolina coast and the state as a whole, fed up with Union invasions and with the intermittent looting and burning of towns, plantations, and farms, Vance found in the plan a way to get even with the North, to show his independence from Richmond, and to make North Carolina militarily self-sufficient. If the state could run the blockade with its own ships, no North Carolina troops would lack shoes, good clothes, enough food, or efficient rifles and powder ever again.

As his agent abroad, Vance chose John White, a clever Scottish schemer from Warrenton. Sent to England, White purchased a Clyde steamer using more than $190,000 of state money with only Vance's knowledge and approval. Renamed the *Ad-Vance,* the state's ship became one of the most successful of all the blockade-runners. From the spring of 1863 to February 1864, the sleek runner made more than a dozen voyages, mostly to Bermuda, bringing in much-needed ammunition and medical supplies, 40,000 blankets, an equal number of shoes, and more than 150 tons of bacon and pork. More than 120,000 cotton cards, small, hand-held paddles that allowed cotton to be converted into yarn, helped North Carolinians clothe themselves and their soldiers at the front. Still, Wilmington depended upon Fort Fisher, the "Gibraltar of the south," and young Lamb's makeshift Flying Battery of Whitworth guns.

In the spring of 1864, Richmond sent yet another general, Robert F. Hoke, to try to loosen the Union's stranglehold upon the state's northeastern coast. From Lincolnton in western North Carolina, Hoke had fought in every major campaign in Virginia, been severely wounded at Fredericksburg while fighting with Jubal Early, and won a promotion to brigadier general in January 1863. A brilliant and veteran campaigner at twenty-seven, Hoke planned to sweep the Federals from the coastline like a Hatteras hurricane. Hoke had learned his lessons from studying Burnside's campaign. To retake the coast, he planned a combined arms operation using the ingenuity of an even younger confederate, Gilbert Elliott, and his monstrous creation, the CSS *Albemarle.* Instead of attacking New Bern, Hoke chose a lesser defended yet strategic town, Plymouth. Guarded by a ragtag brigade of over 3,200 troops that included more than 120 Unionist volunteers from the coastal counties, Plymouth, even with its intricate complex of redoubts and strongpoints, presented an easier target than New Bern or Beaufort. In the Roanoke River, Union comdr. Charles W. Flusser's gunboat squadron of the *Miami, Whitehead, Ceres,* and *Southfield* anchored Plymouth's water defenses. Hoke counted on surprise and the *Albemarle.*

The Union's Sassacus *ramming the Confederate ram* Albemarle.
North Carolina Collection, University of North Carolina at Chapel Hill.

On 18 April, Hoke launched his assault against Plymouth, hurling Matt Ramson's brigade against Fort Williams, one of the town's strongpoints, while he concentrated on Fort Wessells, an emplacement whose guns commanded half the town itself. By noon the Yankees had abandoned Wessells, and, with his own thirty-two-pounders in place, Hoke now could sweep the town with his guns. Still, on the placid Roanoke River as yet undisturbed by the battle, one of the major dramas of the war unveiled itself.

Guided by Elliott, its teenaged designer, the *Albemarle* had maneuvered through Union obstacles and wooden piles on the night of 18 April until, cloaked by the night, it charged straight at the *Southfield* and *Miami*. Bound together by heavy chains and spars, the two Union ships hoped to entangle the oncoming *Albemarle* in a spider's web of metal and wood while their guns blew it out of the water. Instead, the alligator-shaped *Albemarle* rammed the *Southfield,* sending her to the bottom of the Roanoke. Closing with the *Albemarle,* Flusser, on board the yet unscathed *Miami,* tried to board and disable the behemoth. At point-blank range, Flusser fired a massive ten-inch hundred-pound Parrott rifle at the *Albemarle,* only to watch incredulously as the huge shell bounced off the ironclad, and, in a seemingly impossible arc, landed at his feet. A monstrous explosion shredded Flusser and badly damaged the *Miami.* Once again the Roanoke River belonged to the *Albemarle* and North Carolina. In all the havoc and destruction it caused that April night, the *Albemarle* also sealed her own fate. Thereafter, the vessel became marked prey for the Union navy until one of its most daring officers, William Cushing, a close friend of Flusser's and Abraham Lincoln's favorite commando, hunted it down and torpedoed it six months later. Even though Confederate forces managed to occupy Plymouth for six months, the assault upon it and Union forces in the region ultimately failed. Much of northeastern North Carolina remained in Federal hands until the end of the war.

Away from the coast, North Carolina's own civil war took on a renewed intensity with the coming of more Confederate troops. Late in the summer of 1862, groups of outlier bands of militant Unionists who still wanted an affiliation with Washington and not Richmond, together with draft dodgers and deserters, began to raid the central counties, paticularly Randolph, Chatham, Yadkin, Moore, and Wilkes counties. A secret group of Unionists called the Heroes of America organized support for renegade bands that included safe hiding places, food, supplies, and early warning signals of Confederate troops in the vicinity. Upon his inauguration in September 1862, Governor Vance vowed to hunt down and prosecute all crimes of desertion, draft dodging, and disloyalty from Wilmington to Franklin. Knowing Vance's determination meant little chance of amnesty and parole, outlier bands instead turned to more pitiless and inhumane acts. North Carolina's own inner civil war raged unabated until Joseph Johnston's surrender on 22 April 1865.

The greatest plunder and ravaging took place in the central counties of the state. There, in Randolph, Guilford, Wilkes, Yadkin, Chatham, Montgomery, Forsyth, and Moore counties, disaffection from the Confederate cause and "Secesh" leaders seemed greatest. Quakers, Moravians, old-line Wesleyan Methodists, and even a few German Reformed members and Lutherans tacitly and openly criticized the Confederacy and its supporters. There antisecession sentiment found its greatest expression and the peace movement its most passionate adherents. Late in 1863 and again in August 1864, large uprisings of dissident bands required the efforts of hundreds of regular Confederate troops, militia, and Home Guards sent to keep the peace. By the spring of 1865, when the war ended, as many as two hundred, perhaps even three hundred, had been killed in the central counties, while scores of homes and barns had been burned or destroyed.

A single incident in the winter of 1863 gave all-too-human qualities to North Carolina's internal civil war. In January of that year, a group of men from several pro-Unionist families in Laurel Valley raided Marshall, the seat of Madison County and the center of Confederate loyalty in the mountainous west. As they left the town, the "Tories," as they were dubbed for their disloyalty, robbed and sacked the home of L. M. Allen, a local merchant but also a colonel in the Sixty-fourth North Carolina regiment. In a tangled skein of motives that included family feuds, old political rivalries, and Confederate and Unionist sympathies, J. A. Keith, a lieutenant colonel in the Sixty-fourth with family ties to Allen, rounded up and cold-bloodedly murdered thirteen old men and young boys from Shelton Laurel, who had little to do with the raid on Marshall. Horrified at the massacre, Governor Vance, a neighbor of some of those slain, demanded an investigation, which ultimately led to Keith's resignation. Still, resentments over raids from outlier bands, Buffaloes, and bushwhackers haunted North Carolina for decades after the war ended.

The buffeting of calamitous defeats at Vicksburg and at Gettysburg in July 1863, along with the lengthening rolls of North Carolina's dead and wounded, aroused latent Unionists within the state. At scores of meetings in over forty counties, critics of Confederate policies openly attacked Richmond's conduct of the war, petitioned for Jefferson Davis to call a halt to the fighting, and pleaded with him to appeal to Lincoln for a peace agreement. In Raleigh, Vance watched as his old adviser, William H. Holden, published the proceedings in his *North Carolina Standard* with a suspicious paraphrasing. Instantly recognizing Holden's hand in promoting the movement, Vance broke with him, accusing him of promoting "submission, reconstruction, or anything else" that would put him "back under Lincoln and stop the war." In the gubernatorial election of 1864, Vance, vowing to "fight

Running the Blockade, a popular board game during the Civil War in North Carolina.
North Carolina Collection, University of North Carolina at Chapel Hill.

the Yankees and fuss with the Confederacy," overwhelmingly defeated Holden and the "peace party" by a vote of 44,856 to 12,647. North Carolinians had no wish to secede again. Within the state, the theory of secession died even before the outcome of the war decided its fate nationally. In 1863, North Carolina had no place to go.

In 1864, the war came to North Carolina with a renewed vigor and vengeance. After the summer of 1863 and the disastrous defeats at Vicksburg and Gettysburg, the Confederate cause seemed somehow more quixotic. Although Richmond and Lee still held the Yankees to the north, control of the Mississippi and the Gulf fell to the Union. Increasingly, the lifeline of the Confederacy depended upon the port of Wilmington and upon an extravagant sandcastle guarding it, Fort Fisher. Inappropriately called the "Gibraltar of the south," Fort Fisher consisted not of rock and stone but rather of a continuous series of interwoven earthen works largely constructed by William Lamb and Gen. William Henry Chase Whiting that, for the 1860s, became one of the largest man-made structures on earth. To a faraway alien, Fort Fisher and its surrounding earthen trenches must have seemed like Mars's mysterious canals. Col. William Lamb, the young genius behind the massive project, presided over the fort's defenses from an elevated strategic summit known as "the Pulpit," giving him a commanding view in any direction. He would need it.

For more than two years the Navy Department had wanted to take the pesky Fort Fisher and Wilmington. In the summer of 1864, Ulysses S. Grant authorized an expedition against Fort Fisher to be led by Gen. Benjamin Butler, the hero of the assault upon Forts Hatteras and Clark, and Rear Adm. David Porter, a veteran naval officer who commanded the Mississippi squadron. Altogether, more than twelve thousand troops and fifty-seven naval vessels, the largest armada of that time, made up the force that would attack Fort Fisher late that fall.

When William Lamb spotted the forest of Porter's masts at dawn on Christmas Eve, 1864, he knew his time had come. With fewer than one thousand men and a dwindling stockpile of ammunition for his guns, Lamb could not match the Union ships and troops round for round or man for man. Instead, he ordered his guns to fire only twice each hour, hoping to hold out until the final assault or until Confederate forces in Wilmington reinforced him. They never came. For more than nine hours the Union ships blasted away at Fort Fisher, sometimes firing more than 115 rounds per minute. Late that afternoon Porter broke off the engagement and withdrew to a safe anchorage several miles offshore. Convinced by the sporadic and erratic return fire of the Confederate batteries that his bombardment had silenced most of their guns, Porter buoyed up a wavering Benjamin Butler's confidence about the attack by land the next day. The battered Confederates would offer little resistance, he reassured Butler.

On Christmas Day, Porter's lines of ships once more blazed away at Fort Fisher and its supporting batteries. Reinforced that night by William Kirkland's battle-hardened Confederate brigade of more than twelve hundred men, Lamb now had more troops to defend against an attack from land. Led by Brig. Gen. Newton Curtis, Butler sent two New York regiments to establish a beachhead some five miles north of the fort. Within two hours, more than twenty-five hundred troops had positioned themselves for the attack, waiting only for Butler's final order. It never came. By five o'clock that afternoon Curtis's skirmishers and sharpshooters had come within a few yards of Lamb's sandcastle. There they encountered an enormous cul-de-sac made of log and sand looming more than seventeen feet high. Remembering the senseless slaughter at Fort Wagner, another earthen Confederate fort guarding Charleston made famous in the movie *Glory,* Federal commanders, fearing more butchery and the loss of their reputations so late in the war, indecisively hesitated. Soon, night and an approaching gale made an all-out attack impossible. Within two days, all the Union troops had managed to make it back to the safety of Porter's fleet,

First bombardment of Fort Fisher in December 1864. North Carolina Office of Archives and History, Raleigh.

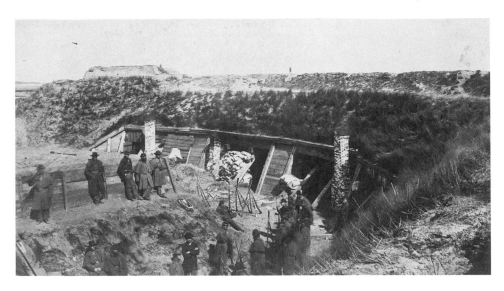

Fort Fisher after its capture. North Carolina Collection, University of North Carolina at Chapel Hill.

which soon pulled up anchor and sailed away. The South's last major port remained open. But not for long.

Three weeks later, an even denser forest of Union ships' masts once more appeared off Cape Fear. This time, Butler had been replaced by a Union general who would fight, Maj. Gen. Alfred Terry, and by an additional two thousand African American troops eager for battle. Disquieted at the sudden appearance of the Union fleet so soon after the first attack, Lamb knew that without the help of Braxton Bragg's newly arrived Confederate forces in the Wilmington area, Fort Fisher had little chance. With fewer than fifteen hundred men available and a scant twenty-four hundred rounds of shot left, Lamb could not endure a long siege and attack. Inexplicably, Bragg wavered, almost ignoring Lamb's pleas for help.

For four days, the Federal warships subjected Fort Fisher to a drumbeat bombardment, destroying most of its log palisades and plowing up sand into small hills. In a combined army and naval operation, Union forces launched their final assault on the morning of 15 January. After fierce hand-to-hand combat for more than twelve hours, Fort Fisher, with Lamb wounded and incapacitated, surrendered at 10 P.M. In all, Lamb, in a desperate last stand, had lost more than four hundred killed and wounded, while Union forces suffered more than twelve hundred casualties.

The fall of Fort Fisher, the Gibraltar of the South, inevitably doomed the Confederacy. As the last major port still in Southern hands, Wilmington furnished essential supplies for Lee's Army of Northern Virginia. With Fort Fisher in Union hands, Wilmington, all but defenseless, surrendered on 22 February, and, five weeks later, the Union's Twenty-third Army Corps, commanded by Gen. John Schofield, marched into Goldsboro. With Goldsboro, the main Wilmington-to-Richmond railroad terminus, under Union control, Schofield began to amass supplies as he waited for Sherman's oncoming army.

After laying waste to much of Georgia and South Carolina, William Tecumseh Sherman had turned from Columbia to march into North Carolina. On 17 March, Gen. Joseph E. Johnston, the new commander of Confederate forces in North Carolina, learned that

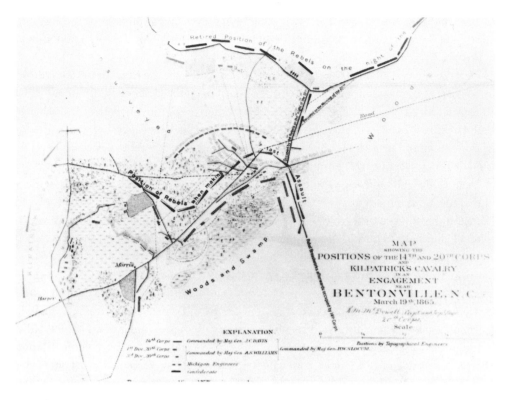

Map of the Battle of Bentonville, the last major engagement of the Civil War.
North Carolina Office of Archives and History, Raleigh.

Sherman, his army split into two columns totaling more than sixty thousand men, intended to head for Goldsboro and afterward take Raleigh. With fewer than twenty thousand men, mostly fragments of shattered divisions, brigades, regiments, and companies composed of weary veterans and also some adolescent junior reservists from North Carolina, "the seed corn of the Confederacy," as Vance described them, and lacking any significant artillery support, Johnston had little with which to fight. His only chance to keep the Federals from Goldsboro lay in a hasty attack upon one of Sherman's columns, hoping to surprise and defeat part of the Union army before the whole could respond. His chance came at the small village of Bentonville in southeastern North Carolina.

After sharp but short skirmishes at Kinston on 15 March and at Averasboro on 16 March, Johnston's forces fell upon the leading division of Sherman's left column on 19 March at Bentonville. In a three-hour attack, the Confederates almost succeeded in flanking and smashing through Sherman's vanguard regiments. Only the timely arrival of Union reinforcements and the main weight of the right wing of Sherman's army kept Hoke and Hill's men at bay. In a series of desperate charges that rivaled Pickett's at Gettysburg, long grey lines of ragged Confederates threw themselves upon the Union breastworks. "What a truly beautiful sight," wrote one Confederate soldier, yet also "a painful sight to see how close their battle flags were together, regiments being scarcely larger than companies and a division not much larger than a regiment." When he learned that Schofield had taken Goldsboro, Johnston, with little direction from Richmond and no overall objective except to keep fighting, abandoned Bentonville and stole away in the middle of the night to Smithfield. In all, Union forces suffered 1,520 casualties while Johnston lost 2,600, a great

many of whom surrendered.

After Bentonville, North Carolina became the backdrop for the Confederacy's last death throes east of the Mississippi. One week after Johnston attacked Sherman, Grant launched a massive offensive against Lee, and by 5 April rumors began to circulate in Raleigh that Richmond had fallen. On the night of 10 April, Sherman learned of Lee's surrender at Appomattox, and in a congratulatory message to Grant he vowed to concede the same "magnanimous and liberal" terms to Johnston if he would do the same. On the morning of 12 April, Joseph Johnston went to Greensboro to meet with Jefferson Davis, the retreating Confederate president, who, instead of asking for peace terms, told an astonished Johnston that "in two or three weeks he would have a larger army in the field" with which to repel Sherman. To save itself from being burned like Columbia, Raleigh surrendered on 13 April, but not before a stubborn Zeb Vance shipped thousands of bushels of corn, enormous quantities of clothing and medical supplies, and thousands of rifles to Greensboro and Salisbury to prepare for a last stand in the western part of the state. With little confidence in a delusional Jefferson Davis and limited power to resist, Johnston asked Sherman for a suspension of hostilities and also for a meeting of the two somewhere on the Hillsborough road equidistant from Durham and Hillsborough. When the two met on 14 April, Sherman, wanting to talk privately, asked where they could sit down and work out terms. Remembering a farmhouse he had just passed, Johnston suggested it, and the two generals and their aides made their way to the small, unpretentious farmhouse of James Bennett.

Jeff Davis and the remnants of the Confederate government leaving North Carolina
by crossing the Pee Dee River after the fall of Richmond in April 1865.
North Carolina Collection, University of North Carolina at Chapel Hill.

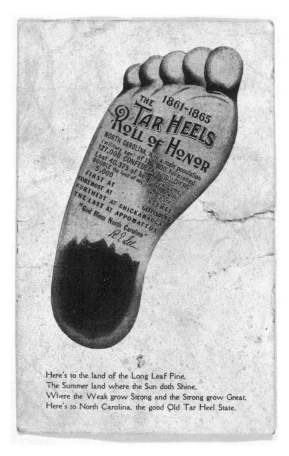

Here's to the land of the Long Leaf Pine,
The Summer land where the Sun doth Shine,
Where the Weak grow Strong and the Strong grow Great,
Here's to North Carolina, the good Old Tar Heel State.

A popular postcard depicting North Carolina's "Tar Heel Roll of Honor" during the Civil War.
North Carolina Collection, University of North Carolina at Chapel Hill.

Although Johnston and Sherman reached a fraternal yet idealistic agreement in two days that went beyond even Grant's generous terms to Lee, the interference of Jefferson Davis, still stubbornly clinging to the chimera of the Confederacy, and the assassination of Abraham Lincoln complicated its ratification. The final accord, signed on 26 April, nonetheless demonstrated Sherman's regard for his beaten foe. The last Confederate army would hold its final muster in Greensboro, where ordnance pieces would be turned over to the Union army and the men paroled to their homes. Both officers and enlisted men would be allowed to keep their private property and horses, and Union quartermasters would furnish rations for ten days, as well as transportation home. For his part, Johnston agreed to announce the cessation of hostilities and the end of the war to all the governors of seceded Southern states and to any remaining Confederate troops still under arms in the field.

Yet sporadic fighting continued in the mountains of western North Carolina into early May. While Sherman invaded North Carolina from the east, Gen. George Stoneman marched into the western part of the state with seven thousand men from his Army of the Tennessee. After occupying and burning much of Salisbury and its hated prison on 12 April, Stoneman turned westward toward the mountains. If Sherman had proved unexpectedly lenient in his march through eastern North Carolina, then Stoneman upheld his maxim that "war is hell" in the west. In two weeks, he laid waste much of western North Carolina from Wilkesboro to Asheville, burning railroads, depots, bridges, factories, buildings, and any military supplies he could find. On 25 April, Col. George Kirk took Asheville, the last remaining Confederate bastion in the west, and, in occasional skirmishes, fought one ending battle against Col. William Thomas's Legion, a Confederate unit that contained two companies of Cherokee Indians. Two days later, the final Confederate general to surrender would be Stand Watie, a Cherokee in faraway Oklahoma who was the brother of Elias Boudinot. On 13 May, Zeb Vance's birthday, a squad of Confederate cavalrymen rode into Asheville, raced around the public square shouting, "Hurrah for the southern Confederacy," and, accompanied by wild Rebel yells, fired their weapons into the air and sprinted out of town as quickly as they had come. It was the last hurrah for the South's lost cause in North Carolina. One of the final states to leave the Union, North Carolina also had been one of the last to lay down its arms for the Confederacy. Only in the trans-Mississippi West, in Texas, did General Kirby finally surrender later that June. The Civil War ended in a sputter and not a spasm.

ADDITIONAL READINGS

Ashe, Samuel A. "Charge at Gettysburg." *North Carolina Booklet* 1 (March 1902): 1–28.

Ballard, Michael B. *Long Shadow: Jefferson Davis and the Final Days of the Confederacy.* Jackson: University Press of Mississippi, 1986.

Barrett, John G. "General William T. Sherman's March through North Carolina." *North Carolina Historical Review* 42 (April 1965): 192–207.

———. *Sherman's March through the Carolinas.* Chapel Hill: University of North Carolina Press, 1956.

Bradlee, Francis Boardman Crowninshield. *Blockade Running during the Civil War and the Effect of Land and Water Transportation on the Confederacy.* Salem, Mass.: Essex Institute, 1925.

Bright, Leslie S., William H. Rowland, and James C. Bardon. *C.S.S. Neuse: A Question of Iron and Time.* Raleigh: Department of Archives and History, 1981.

Brown, Louis A. *Salisbury Prison: A Case Study of Confederate Military Prisons, 1861–1865.* Wilmington, N.C.: Broadfoot Publishing Co., 1992.

Catton, Bruce. "Gallant Men in Deeds of Glory." *Life* 50 (6 January 1961): 48–64, 66–70.

Cochran, Hamilton. *Blockade Runners of the Confederacy.* Indianapolis: Bobbs-Merrill, 1958.

Crawford, Martin. *Ashe County's Civil War: Community and Society in the Appalachian South.* Charlottesville: University Press of Virginia, 2001.

Davis, Burke. *Long Surrender.* New York: Random House, 1985.

Donnelly, Ralph W. "Charlotte, North Carolina, Navy Yard, C.S.N." *Civil War History* 5 (March 1959): 72–79.

Earnhart, Hugh G., ed. "Aboard a Blockade Runner: Some Civil War Experiences of Jerome Du Shane." *North Carolina Historical Review* 44 (October 1967): 392–99.

Eaton, Clement, ed. "Diary of an Officer in Sherman's Army Marching through the Carolinas." *Journal of Southern History* 9 (May 1943): 238–54.

Edwards, Laura F. *Scarlett Doesn't Live Here Anymore: Southern Women in the Civil War Era.* Urbana: University of Illinois Press, 2000.

Elliott, Gilbert. "Career of the Confederate Ram 'Albemarle'; Her Construction and Service." *Century Magazine* (July 1888): 420 ff.

Fore, Cornie G. "Cabinet Meeting in Charlotte." *Southern Historical Society Papers* 41 (1916): 61–7.

Gragg, Rod. *Confederate Goliath: The Battle of Fort Fischer.* New York: Harper Collins, 1991.

Hicks, Glenda. "Forgotten Sons: North Carolinians in the Union Army." Master's thesis, University of North Carolina, 1974.

Horn, Stanley F. *Gallant Rebel, the Fabulous Cruise of the C.S.S. Shenandoah.* New Brunswick, N.J.: Rutgers University Press, 1947.

Horner, Dave. *Blockade-Runners: True Tales of Running the Yankee Blockade of the Confederate Coast.* New York: Dodd, Mead, 1968.

Jones, Catherine M. *When Sherman Came: Southern Women and the "Great March."* Indianapolis: Bobbs-Merrill, 1964.

Massey, Mary. "Confederate Refugees in North Carolina." *North Carolina Historical Review* 40 (April 1963): 158–82.

McLean, Alexander T. "Fort Fisher and the Wilmington Campaign, 1864–1865." Master's thesis, University of North Carolina, 1970.

Melton, Maurice. *Confederate Ironclads.* South Brunswick, N.J.: T. Yooseloff, 1968.

Merrill, James M. "Fort Fisher and Wilmington Campaign: Letters from Rear Admiral David M. Porter." *North Carolina Historical Review* 35 (October 1958): 461–75.

Nichols, Roy G., ed. "Fighting in North Carolina Waters." *North Carolina Historical Review* 40 (January 1963): 75–84.

Official Records of the Union and Confederate Navies in the War of the Rebellion. 27 vols., 1st ser.; 3 vols., 2nd ser. Washington, D.C.: Government Printing Office, 1894–1922.

Paludan, Phillip S. *Victims: A True Story of the Civil War.* Knoxville: University of Tennessee Press, 1981.

Pierce, Thomas L. "Their Last Battle: Fight at Bentonville, N.C., between Sherman and Johnston." *Southern Historical Society Papers* 29 (1901): 215–22.

Price, Charles L., and Claude C. Sturgill. "Shock and Assault in the First Battle of Fort Fisher." *North Carolina Historical Review* 47 (January 1970): 24–39.

Robinson, Kenneth W. "North Carolina's Blockade Running Partnership: An Effort Toward Self-Sufficiency." Master's thesis, North Carolina State University, 1974.

Roske, Ralph J., and Charles Van Doren. *Lincoln's Commando: The Biography of Commander W. B. Cushing, U.S.N.* New York: Harper and Co., 1957.

Soley, James R. *The Blockade and the Cruisers.* New York: Scribner's Sons, 1883.

Trotter, William R. *The Civil War in North Carolina.* 3 vols. Greensboro: Signal Research, 1988–89.

———. *Ironclads and Columbiads: The Civil War in North Carolina along the Coast.* Winston-Salem: John F. Blair, 1989.

Tucker, Glenn. "Some Aspects of North Carolina's Participation in the Civil War." *North Carolina Historical Review* 35 (April 1958): 191–212.

U.S. Naval History Division. *Civil War Chronology, 1861–1865.* 6 vols. Washington, D.C.: Navy Department, 1971.

Van Noppen, Ina W. "Significance of Stoneman's Last Raid." *North Carolina Historical Review* 38 (January 1961): 19–44; (April 1961): 141–72; (July 1961): 341–61; (October 1961): 500–526.

Wheeler, Richard. *Sherman's March.* New York: T. Y. Crowell, 1978.

Wise, Stephen R. *Lifeline of the Confederacy: Blockade Running during the Civil War.* Columbia: University of South Carolina Press, 1988.

Wood, Richard E. "Port Town at War: Wilmington, North Carolina, 1860–1865." Ph.D. diss., Florida State University, 1976.

Deconstruction and Reconstruction in North Carolina

Before North Carolina could look forward to reunion and reconstruction after the devastation of the Civil War, it first had to look backward to understand its own recent antebellum transformation into a southern state. First, the old political theories of secession and states' rights had died along with so many thousands on the fields of battle. Yet the politicians who argued as Whigs and as Democrats for decades before the war still remained afterward, chiefly Zebulon Vance and William Woods Holden, only now they belonged to new parties and factions that grew out of the Civil War and Reconstruction. Out of the Union for four years, a defeated yet still defiant North Carolina now faced an uncertain future, a time where its exact status stood somewhere between reconciliation and full statehood within a triumphant Union. Devoid of any representation in Congress or the courts, North Carolinians now found themselves depending more and more on freedmen, scalawags, and carpetbaggers to influence a Republican government in Washington to have any say at all in national affairs.

Albion W. Tourgée of Ohio (1838–1905), reviled as a carpetbagger by conservatives in North Carolina.
North Carolina Collection, University of North Carolina at Chapel Hill.

A caricature of Albion W. Tourgée from the Patriot and Times *newspaper from Greensboro in 1868.*
North Carolina Collection, University of North Carolina at Chapel Hill.

*Horace James (1818–75), superintendent
of the Freedmen's Bureau in North Carolina.*
North Carolina Collection, University of North
Carolina at Chapel Hill.

The very terms used in Reconstruction, words such as "freedmen," "scalawags," "carpetbaggers," and "conservatives," did not exist as such previously, only in the historic melodrama and mythology of Reconstruction. A derisive expression during and even after Reconstruction, a scalawag, from its original meaning as worthless, bony, inbred ponies from the Scottish island of Scalloway, came to mean someone from North Carolina or the South, hence inborn, who was worthless in the eyes of his fellow southerners because he had sold out his heritage—that is, his roots—for an opportunity with an illegitimate government supported only by occupying troops. Before the Civil War, "scalawag" simply might mean a maverick pony or person, someone mischievous and playful who set themselves apart from the herd of society. In its reconstructed form, it mocked its past usage. If anything, the label "carpetbagger" had a more contemptible implication: outsiders and interlopers who came to the South carrying only a carpetbag and leaving in a few years with train cars and wagons filled with riches fleeced from a prostrated, helpless South. Before the Civil War, many North Carolinians as well as fellow southerners considered carpetbaggers to be somewhat harmless, much like innocuous traveling salesmen, flimflam men trying to sell goods who easily could be brushed away. Before the Civil War, the term "freedmen" existed hardly at all. After 1865 and the passage of the Thirteenth Amendment, it came to mean mainly a black male "freed" by the infamous bureau set up by the Republicans and persuaded by them that they actually could govern and exercise control over whites without any prior experience or education. Traditionally, someone opposed to change and even reactionary, a Conservative in a Reconstruction sense, instead served as a glowing code word for those who wanted to go back to the Old South and the Old Union without the burden of slavery. Although creating a distorted and biased view of history as well as overwrought and melodramatic stereotypes, these words and terms, coined mostly by ex-Confederates, came to define the period of Reconstruction in the South. They had been deconstructed from the past to shape a new interpretation of southern history immediately after the Civil War.

With the abolition of slavery and the renunciation of Confederate war debts, North Carolinians recognized that they had little money or capital to begin rebuilding the state.

With thousands of returning Confederate war veterans, many maimed, wounded, and destitute yet still bitter, the state had few resources to aid them and, further, feared their pent-up anger and hostility. With more than 350,000 newly freed slaves, North Carolina now had to adjust to an expanded concept of citizenship and civil rights that challenged older prejudicial beliefs and values that had been a part of a folk culture for centuries. Not surprisingly, the state looked back to its past to prepare for an uncertain future.

After Lincoln's death, Andrew Johnson, a native North Carolinian but a senator from Tennessee who remained with the Union in 1861, became president. On 29 May 1865 he appointed William Woods Holden of Raleigh as provisional governor, thus beginning the process of deconstructing and reconstructing the state. Under Johnson's vague plan, only three requirements, those of repeal and renunciation of the ordnance of secession, ratification and approval of the Thirteenth Amendment abolishing slavery, and cancellation of the Confederate war debt, had to be met before North Carolina could rejoin the Union. Still, even those mild conditions perturbed those who looked to North Carolina's past to heal the breach caused by the Civil War, a group now calling themselves "the conservatives."

Composed of a loose coalition of mainly Democrats who had supported secession, prewar Whigs and Unionists, the conservatives believed that only a return to "first principles," namely, the original concept of government in the Constitution, the due process of law, and the hallowed customs and traditions of the past, could rekindle that love of Union held by North Carolinians before the war. Led by prewar Unionists and ex-Confederates such as Zebulon Vance, David L. Swain, Augustus B. Merrimon, Nathaniel Boyden, William A. Graham, and Thomas Ruffin, the conservatives embraced Lincoln's position that the southern states had never left the Union and that the victory of Union armies had made it legally impossible for them to do so. The convenience and conciliation of the argument suited their political purposes.

To the conservatives, North Carolina had never left the Union and therefore did not need to be reconstructed. Thus, for them the failure of the rebellion had de facto "restored" the state to its "legitimate and original position within the Union." Because of this, North Carolina only needed to reconvene its legislature, call a constitutional convention to overhaul its antiquated constitution, do away with slavery, repudiate the Confederate war debt, and, as soon as federal troops left, the state rightfully would resume control over local affairs. North Carolina could reconstruct itself without outside help, especially from northern, carpetbagger Republicans.

Holden's appointment as provisional governor by President Andrew Johnson, a turncoat southerner to many North Carolinians, infuriated the conservatives. William Graham, for example, thought Holden to be an opportunist, a changeling who first supported Vance and the Confederacy and then became a lukewarm Unionist, a peace advocate, and, at the end of the war, a scalawag who did not represent traditional, pro-Unionist sentiment or leadership in the nation or the state. By appointing Holden and ignoring older leaders such as Vance, Swain, and Graham, Johnson's policy, at least to the conservatives, ensured continued disharmony, distrust, and division.

The state elections in the fall of 1865 simply revived older Civil War factions. William Holden, the perpetual candidate of prevalent causes, ran against Jonathan Worth, the pick of the Democrats and remaining Whigs. A former wartime state treasurer under Governor Vance, Worth clearly had the backing of "the Confederate party," the conservatives. In November, Worth received 31,643 votes to Holden's 25,704. In the elections to Congress, only one representative could "eligibly" take the proposed "iron clad" test oath renouncing voluntary Confederate service while another, Josiah Turner, never received a presidential pardon for his war efforts. To Radical Republicans in Congress, the 1865 elections in North Carolina reflected the state's unrepentant and defiant attitude. Elated at their success, Democrats and former secessionists in North Carolina eagerly anticipated the forthcoming elections as a chance once again to take over control of state affairs. Their jubilation proved ephemeral.

The delegates to the 1865 constitutional convention, called before the November elections, seemed more concerned with looking over their shoulders trying to win the approval of a majority of white North Carolinians and to outwit the Republicans in Congress than with accepting even a moderate set of terms from the victors. The delegates quickly moved to repeal the ordinance of secession but balked at the insistence of Johnson that it constitutionally had been illegal from the beginning. By their own first principles, Democrats and Whigs adhered to a prewar interpretation that allowed states the right to secede. North Carolinians still did not fully understand that the older concept of states' rights had died with the rebellion. A majority bowed to the inevitable and abolished slavery yet refused to repudiate the Confederate war debt, in part because it would impoverish the state but also inasmuch as it represented their commitment to a just but lost cause. Many North Carolinians still sought to avoid the truth about the war and their subsequent defeat. Only Johnson's angry intervention convinced the delegates that they must cancel the debt and look elsewhere for revenues.

By March 1866 political tensions in the state worsened. Sensing the shift to a more radical and punitive stand by congressional Republicans, Holden and his considerable supporters in the state legislature followed along, suggesting that "enemies of the Union" should be put in their place, namely, under "Unionist feet." Conservatives publicly disdained "test oath men," those North Carolinians who would swear that they had not voluntarily helped or aided the Confederacy, and looked to their past conduct for present guidance. To them, ex-Confederates should not be required to take such an oath, nor should they take blame for or feel guilty about the war. Expressed in Vance's declaration of sentiments in 1865, conservative North Carolinians felt that responsibility for the war should be placed elsewhere, most often in Lincoln's White House, and that a harsh settlement was unwarranted. In December 1865 Governor Worth reminded Washington of the state's enduring loyalty to the Union and cautioned that if pushed further, North Carolina "can scarcely hope to do anything which will be held satisfactory." Threats, not reconciliation, marked the end of 1865.

Tensions heightened during the summer and fall of 1866. When President Johnson objected to the Civil Rights Bill of 1866, Congress overrode his veto. Clearly, power in reconstructing the Union had shifted from the White House to Congress, from a moderate to a more radical and intransigent position. In North Carolina, David Swain sensed the danger to the state. Recalling his visit to the North three months after the end of the war, he warned that reasonable men there looked upon southerners as not only "in the wrong, but without the semblance" of any excuse for the war. Lumped together with Lincoln's murder by John Wilkes Booth, a Marylander who acted like a Virginian, with Johnson's ill-considered veto, and with the return of unreconstructed and unpardoned southerners to state and national office, the shift of power to more radical Republicans in the Congressional elections of 1866 meant North Carolina could expect harsher terms for its reentry into the Union. Accept Johnson's plan both in fact and in spirit, Swain urged, and quickly. Otherwise, the process might worsen and take years to complete. He proved to be a prophet.

Dominated by conservatives, the general assembly, seemingly oblivious to radical actions in Congress, passed the Black Code of 1866. The first state to pass a comprehensive set of laws governing freedmen, Mississippi, had incurred the wrath of northerners who saw in the regulations an attempt to reestablish slavery and thus do away with the verdict of the war. Wary of the scorn heaped upon Mississippi even though the initial codes were never implemented, Governor Worth explained that North Carolina's measures sought only to "prevent pauperism, vagrancy, idleness, and their consequent crimes" in order to regulate public safety. No attempt would be made to deny freedmen "any of the essentials of civil or religious freedom." To Worth, some laws needed to be enacted to recognize the new social relationship between freedmen and whites, but they should not go as far as Mississippi's. If they did so, the "odious" Freedmen's Bureau, a temporary federal agency established to assist freed slaves and much despised by the conservatives for its work, would usurp state authority and remain indefinitely in North Carolina.

The resultant code, mild compared to those passed in Mississippi and South Carolina, became a barometer of how far North Carolina would go in granting rights to freedmen. Of the nine proposed laws, only one, that barring interracial marriages, specifically referred to blacks. By implication, the others aimed at restoring some sort of social relationship with freedmen on white terms. At least five of the new provisions, the vagrancy laws that limited freedom of movement, the measure prohibiting blacks from carrying firearms unless licensed, an ordinance making the intent to rape a white woman punishable by death for a black but only two years imprisonment and a public whipping for a white, the apprentice law, and limitations on blacks testifying against whites in the courts, clearly discriminated against freedmen. Laws aimed at legitimizing marriages, both white and black, and also at theft, crime, and extending the right to a trial by jury affected whites, mostly poor, and blacks alike. Only at the urging of Governor Worth did the general assembly change the measure and allow blacks to testify in all cases. As one observer noted, the right to testify had little impact since, with all-white judges and juries, the testimony of blacks would "be taken for just its value," thus counting for little. Reviewing the code, Clinton Cilley, an official of the Freedmen's Bureau, thought that it revealed precisely how far white North Carolinians would go "to impress it thoroughly on the blacks that they are inferior, and must be so kept by law." North Carolinians could not look forward to emancipation without remembering slavery in their past.

Coupled with an increasing level of violence against freedmen, the black code represented a last conservative attempt to define race relations in the absence of slavery, the only social order known to generations of North Carolinians. As early as August 1865, before congressional intervention, Maj. Gen. Thomas Ruger, military commander of North

Carolina, had expressed concern for the physical safety of freedmen. "Acts of unlawful violence against freedmen are becoming more frequent," he reported, and state courts and juries consistently refused to convict whites for abusing blacks. Later incidents only underscored Ruger's caution.

In Pittsboro in Chatham County, a fight between an intemperate ex-Confederate and a freedman resulted in the arrest of the former slave. Afraid of a lynch mob, the local sheriff prescribed the traditional thirty-nine lashes used in slavery, but in this case the punishment would be administered in three separate and less lethal doses while the victim hung suspended by his thumbs, his toes not quite touching the ground. Angered at the seemingly mild sentence, the ex-Confederate tried to pistol-whip the shackled victim, only to be restrained by deputies afraid he would kill the man. A two-month investigation by the Freedmen's Bureau failed to turn up the name of the assailant, even though he resided in the county. Locals would not help the bureau. In Beaufort County four Confederate veterans on a rampage wounded several freedmen and brutally murdered another. Turning themselves in to the local police, the four suspiciously escaped less than twenty-four hours later, never to be heard from again. Still, as the bureau noted, the four voted in a town election one month later and left undetected and unmolested. Just as it had in antebellum North Carolina, local law enforcement remained in the hands of whites. After the Civil War, almost all the local militias and police forces replicated Confederate units, some even with the same commanding officers as during the war.

Yet in the face of such brutal incidents, the Freedmen's Bureau reported that as of January 1866 an overwhelming majority of landowning whites who employed freedmen treated them honestly if discourteously. Violence between the former large farmers and landowners and freedmen took the form of insults, face-slapping, and cuffs about the ears and head, "slave fashion," as one worker remembered. Few criminal and property assaults on former slaves occurred. Only after the implementation of civil rights, especially that of the privilege of voting, did a greater, more systematic class rage emerge against freedmen in the form of the Ku Klux Klan (KKK).

The KKK came relatively late to North Carolina. First organized in middle Tennessee in 1866 and in north Georgia in 1867 by ex-Confederates, the Klan seems to have emerged in North Carolina in 1867 in response to the Reconstruction acts of that year and also to black suffrage. It did not assume any real importance until the elections of 1868. Also called the Invisible Empire, the White Brotherhood, and, in North Carolina, the Constitutional Union Guard, Klan members at first did little except dress in white sheets, with "mysterious inscriptions" on their hats, and parade around courthouses and squares in county seats. To many, notices of Klan meetings proclaiming, "Attention! First Hour! In the Mist! At the Flash! Come! Come! Come!" looked like the work of an excited bumpkin who loved exclamation points. At the Klan's beginning, locals seemed to regard it as a curiosity and not a threat. Initially appearing in mountain counties such as Yancey, Rutherford, and Alleghany, their rallies and marches stirred more mirth than fear. After the elections of 1868 and the subsequent rise to power of the Republicans, Klan membership quickly grew. Ridicule and disdain soon changed to terror and dread.

Although Klan membership in North Carolina eventually reached almost forty thousand during Reconstruction and embraced all classes and regions, the Klan's center of

254

Plato Durham, a Conservative member of the 1868 constitutional convention and a notorious Klan leader from Cleveland County.
North Carolina Collection, University of North Carolina at Chapel Hill.

power radiated from the Piedmont outward, especially in Orange and surrounding counties. Smaller organizations also existed in Lenoir and Jones counties on the coast. One of the most notorious of all Klan leaders, Plato Durham, came from Cleveland County. After a surge of activity near Wilmington, the Klan, with few night riders and even fewer acts of violence, almost disappeared, perhaps dissuaded by armed bands of freedmen and black militias that patrolled the Lower Cape Fear at night. In general, the Reconstruction Klan functioned best in those counties where blacks represented a swing vote, where a few votes made a significant difference. Thus, in clumps of coastal counties like New Hanover and Craven, where blacks constituted a majority of voters and residents, the Klan existed marginally if at all.

David Schenck, a den leader who recanted his loyalty to the Invisible Empire, told a senate committee investigating the Klan that it began as "a secret political organization" that sought to overthrow William Holden and the Republicans. "A great many ignorant men were attracted" to the Klan, he maintained, and it grew "up as a counteracting movement" to the Union Leagues, Heroes of America, and Red Strings, all of which initially sought to enlist adherents to the Republican Party and support Radical Reconstruction.

Although the motives of Klansmen varied widely, it seems as if two fears, one of Republican and black control of the polity through the vote and the other of widespread crime and anarchy, combined to produce one of the state's most reactionary organizations. In one of the worst applications of southern codes of chivalry and honor, Klansmen vowed "to protect the weak, the innocent, and the defenseless" and to uphold the true United States Constitution—that is, the one before the Thirteenth and Fourteenth Amendments, the 1787 instrument that validated states' rights and slavery for unreconstructed Rebels. Nonwhites, Union veterans, members of the Union League, Republicans, and those who did not believe in "southern rights" and a "White man's government" could not be members. In the case of the KKK, exclusion, not inclusion, reflected its true goals.

The emergence of the Klan in North Carolina coincided with two political realities of Reconstruction. First, the older, backward-looking antebellum leaders of the state, concentrated mostly in the conservative faction, had supported Andrew Johnson's and not Congress's plan to reunite the nation. Thus, most men of "wealth and intelligence" adamantly opposed the Radical Republicans' and particularly William Holden's right to rule. Moreover, the Republicans, with the backing of federal troops and legally questionable pieces of legislation, always confronted the problem of their own legitimacy. With the votes of freedmen and the backing of scalawags and carpetbaggers, Republicans faced the almost impossible task of building trust among rank-and-file North Carolinians reluctant to change or admit defeat. With the traditions and institutions of more than two centuries now called into question by the end of the war and Reconstruction, North Carolinians, facing an uncertain future, looked to the past for guidance. In the Klan, they found an organization that, at first, looked to honor that past while disguised as a mutual protection association like the old militias and patrollers. Moreover, it also assailed a Republican rule it perceived to be illegitimate.

The rhetoric of the conservatives, emphasizing as it did after 1867 the subversion of Republican rule and also the dangers of freedmen voting, came to be understood by many North Carolinians as an appeal for a white man's government, much like that from the days before the Civil War. While conservatives such as Worth, Graham, and Vance stressed the importance of "civil and political rights" for all North Carolinians, including blacks, Klan members instead heard in the same rhetoric an appeal for action against a Republican government that had little popular support. While conservatives tried to promote their own interests both politically and socially, the Klan, with less enthusiasm for legalities and sophistry as well as for conservative leaders, simply wanted to do away with the newly perceived threat of black suffrage and equality as well as the Republican Party. To them, the propaganda of the conservatives justified any means necessary, whether illegal, violent, unsanctioned, or unconstitutional.

The Klan little affected the elections of 1868. Instead, the results of the vote spurred the Klan to action. In the next two years the Klan, buoyed by both active and passive support, launched a campaign of violence and terror that included at least twenty outright murders and scores of whippings, clubbings, and beatings. In February 1870 Wyatt Outlaw, a spirited black Republican stalwart and active Union Leaguer from Alamance County, was hanged at the county courthouse in Graham while scores watched from the safety of their homes in the flickering torchlight. John W. Stephens, dubbed "Chicken" by the conservative newspaper the *Raleigh Sentinel*, represented Caswell County as a state senator in the new Republican assembly. Bitterly opposed to the Klan, Stephens, a Holden supporter, state senator, and Union League leader, found himself convicted by a rump Klan jury operating outside the law and subsequently stabbed to death in Yanceyville. In May 1870 Samuel Allen, an avid Republican who also lived in Caswell County, had his house attacked twice in one week by a group of "outriders." Instead of running or pleading with the Klan, Allen fought back with an old army sword, reputedly skewering and killing one Klansman and injuring several more in the second attack. As the level of violence escalated, many prominent conservatives privately deplored the Klan's "outrages" and disassociated themselves from the Invisible Empire. For them, the Klan represented not only lawlessness and disorder but also a rougher class of southerners they disdained. Only with the intervention of the federal government in 1871 did the Klan's activities lessen and eventually end.

The atrocities and acts of violence by the Klan, especially against Stephens, Holden's personal agent, spurred him to action. To him, local authorities, both courts and courthouses, either ignored the Klan's conduct or else refused to take action. Holden firmly believed this do-nothingism threatened the fragile political coalition between the Union League, those who supported Reconstruction policies, and freedmen. Convinced of a conspiracy and collusion against him and his Republican colleagues, he determined to take action. Using his new authority under the Militia Act, he placed two counties, Caswell and Alamance, under martial law. To command the militia, he named George W. Kirk, generally disregarded as a turncoat because of his invasion of western North Carolina at the end of the Civil War at the head of a regiment of North Carolina volunteers in the Union army. For his part, Kirk, never a formalist or a harsh disciplinarian, allowed the ill-trained militia to "forage" for supplies and "necessities," usually against the homes and stores of those who had opposed Holden and the Union League. Together with that, he used his broad military powers to arrest scores of citizens, whether conservatives or not, and to hold them without benefit of a writ of habeas corpus. Many conservatives and ordinary North Carolinians considered Kirk and Holden's actions to be still another civil war against the state, one they could win this time. Kirk's undoing, and, eventually that of Holden, came when he refused to honor writs issued by some of North Carolina's most prominent judges, William A. Graham, Augustus Merrimon, and, in the end, the most venerated of all nineteenth-century magistrates, Chief Justice Richmond Mumford Pearson. His arrogant reply, "such papers are played out," clearly set him against not only Pearson, his old mentor, but ultimately federal courts as well. For his part, Holden, thinking he had President Grant's approval, advised Pearson that "the public interest requires that these military prisoners shall not be delivered up to the civil power." Pearson, incensed and exasperated by Holden's reply as governor, decided to teach his former apprentice a lesson in jurisprudence. He immediately turned to Grant and the power of the chief executive. "The power of the judiciary" in North Carolina "is exhausted," he announced, and now "the responsibility must rest with the Executive."

Ignoring pleas not to go further in his efforts, Holden, always egocentric and a self-pleaser, ordered Kirk to arrest Josiah Turner Jr., one of his most vocal critics, at Hillsborough in Orange County and to jail him at Yanceyville, the seat of Caswell County, away from his friends. Clearly, Holden no longer only sought to preserve the public order and to break up "secret societies" like the Klan but instead used his authority to suppress political opposition. Finally, George W. Brooks, a federal judge in Salisbury, ordered the prisoners freed on a writ of habeas corpus and brought before his court. Holden thereupon telegraphed Grant, asking that Kirk be allowed to ignore the judge's order on the basis that it constituted an illegal intrusion into the implementation of the militia law. Grant, never one for legal dilemmas, instead turned to his attorney general who, not surprisingly, supported Brooks. Now on firm ground as a commander-in-chief, Grant ordered Holden to obey Brooks's writ. It would not be the last time Grant abandoned Republicans in the South to violence and mistreatment. Realizing that he had little support either in Washington or in Raleigh, Holden declared the anarchy and civil disorder at an end and ordered Kirk to turn over the prisoners and to dismiss his troops. The Kirk-Holden war abruptly had ended, but the disaffection and even venomousness against Holden had only gathered more sail.

On 15 January 1868, the constitutional convention began its business of radically reorganizing North Carolina's antiquated, antebellum constitution and government. Dominated by seventy-four scalawags, eighteen carpetbaggers, and fifteen freedmen, the convention, opposed at every step by a spiteful minority of thirteen conservative delegates, proceeded to draft one of the most forward-looking and progressive documents in the state's history, one that, except for minor changes, would last for more than a century.

The establishment of manhood suffrage for everyone, black or white, represented the most momentous, historic change of all. In a mood of tolerance and amnesty, the convention agreed that no one could be disqualified for public office because of participation in the war for the North or the South. Looking backward to the old county court system of appointed justices of the peace and of Supreme Court justices, the new constitution made those offices elective, responsible to the people and not to political patronage. Yet perhaps the most significant changes occurred in the assumption that government, for the first time, had a collective responsibility for the overall welfare of the citizens of North Carolina. Physical punishments for crimes such as public beatings and hangings ended, replaced instead by a system of penitentiaries designed to confine yet rehabilitate criminals at the same time. A Board of Public Charities helped provide for the "poor, the unfortunate and the orphan[s]" of the state. In perhaps the most far-reaching enactment of all, the convention enshrined the idea that "the people have a right to the privilege of education" and that the legislature must "provide by taxation . . . a general and uniform system" of free, public education. For the first time, North Carolina had new elective offices, those of lieutenant governor, superintendent of public works, auditor, and superintendent of public instruction. In themselves, the new posts signaled the intent of North Carolina's government to be more involved in the everyday lives of its citizens.

While the constitutional convention of 1868 set about the business of liberalizing the state's laws and customs, another group met on 5 February determined to keep the status quo antebellum. Over three hundred delegates, rallied by a call to action by the *Raleigh Sentinel,* came together determined to undermine Radical Reconstruction and to return the state to its traditional leadership. Led by former governors such as Worth, Vance, Charles Manly, and Thomas Bragg, ex-senators such as Bedford Brown and Weldon Edwards, president of the secession convention in 1861, the gathering represented a coalition of Whigs, conservatives, and Democrats who, while they disagreed over specific points such as taxation and internal improvements, found a single political issue that united them all, the desire to return North Carolina to a "white man's government" as it was before the Civil War.

In a speech made more remarkable by its misplaced indignation as well as by its rhetoric, former Gov. William Graham asserted that Radical Reconstruction had brought into question "the very existence of civilized society" in North Carolina and the nation. North Carolina had no quarrel with the federal government, he insisted. Rather, it only wanted to preserve its people's basic rights as American citizens against a government forced upon them by vengeful, partisan Republicans in Congress. In his appeal to rights and to a government founded upon reason and the consent of the governed, Graham echoed the older Unionist sentiment of many North Carolinians before the Civil War.

Then he added his own misconstruction of Radical Republican policy. By allowing more than seventy thousand ignorant and politically naive blacks to vote and by denying many whites the same rights, Graham argued, the new Republican government had concocted a recipe for political and social disaster. Unless whites united in a single party, "exhibit[ed] their power, and assert[ed] the dignity and rights of the race," a violent social cataclysm would surely follow. Swept up in the latent racist legacy of slavery, the old Whig governor then asked if North Carolinians could afford to carry "the dead weight of the bar-

A political cartoon celebrating the "burial of radicalism" in North Carolina.
North Carolina Collection, University of North Carolina at Chapel Hill.

baric race of Africa" now that they were freed. Graham's long-stated position that Reconstruction should follow constitutional principles quickly gave way to a new, more incendiary issue, that of race.

In the statewide elections of April 1868, North Carolinians soundly rejected the racial appeal of the conservatives and Democrats. In an electorate swollen by freedmen and by resurgent white voters, 56 percent voted not only for William Holden and the Republicans but also for the new, more liberal constitution. Eighty-five percent of those eligible voted, and Republicans completely dominated the general assembly and most local governments. Still, conservatives and Democrats managed to make headway against the Republican majority, not so much because of the race card but because the Republicans, never with strong local roots and party traditions, faced a united and determined opposition for the first time. Nonetheless, Radical Reconstruction had at last come to North Carolina.

Although Radical Republicans only fully controlled the state for barely two years between 1865 and 1876, conservatives nevertheless manipulated events so that radical rule, no matter how brief, came to be seen as unendingly corrupt, profligate and wastrel in its financial policies, ruled over by a ring of "outsiders," carpetbaggers, scalawags, and naive and inexperienced freedmen. Wrapping themselves in the rhetoric of the "glorious lost cause," the conservatives claimed they only wanted to redeem North Carolina, to deliver the state from its present anarchy, and to return it to its antebellum roots and to its rightful place in the nation under the Constitution. They quickly set about to undermine the Republican victory.

On balance, radical rule, in its brevity, seemed more exploratory, untried, and under an 259 overly harsh conservative microscope instead of dishonorable, crooked, and criminal in nature. In its session of 115 days, the Republican-dominated legislature of 1868–69 passed 282 statutes and 63 public resolutions. In trying to modernize the state and make government more active in the lives of most North Carolinians, Republicans concentrated upon internal improvements, principally the building of railroads, the repeal of antiquated stay laws for debtors, public education with separate schools for the two races, and increased taxation to pay for these changes. Recognizing the threat posed by the Klan, the legislature made it a felony to go masked or disguised upon any public thoroughfare with the intention of terrifying or intimidating citizens. Under the new militia act, the governor could send state troops into any county to put down any illegal or unauthorized assemblies, particularly those of secret societies such as the Klan. Forty-nine acts authorized county commissioners to enact special taxes to alleviate local economic conditions. Sixteen provided for state aid for the building of railroads and turnpikes, both sorely needed in a state long hindered by a lack of transportation. At the end of February 1869 the legislature had authorized the spending of almost $18 million, unheard of by a historically ungenerous state and a populace who had come to regard any form of taxation as constitutionally unwarranted. Small wonder that the conservatives fell upon the liberal legislation of the Republicans with a vengeance. Using charges of corruption, fraud, and indebtedness, the conservatives had, by 1870, successfully undermined the fragile Republican coalition of freedmen and their white supporters. In the elections of that year, only Holden returned as governor of the state. The legislature fell into the hands of the conservatives, and Holden's reelection was by a slim margin.

One week after the 1870 elections, conservative newspapers such as the *Tarboro Southerner, Raleigh Daily Sentinel,* and *Greensboro Patriot* began a long drumroll that ended with the impeachment of William Holden, the Antichrist to old guard conservatives. The Kirk-Holden war had all but made the governor defenseless and open to attack. Recognizing the forces now arrayed against him both in the legislature and in the courts, Holden, in his inaugural address, appealed to those conservatives who had distanced themselves from the Klan's lawlessness and violence, arguing that he had called out the militia only to "aid in bringing offenders to justice and restoring peace and order" to the state. Understanding Holden to be more of a threat than the Klan, conservatives swept aside his rhetoric and moved to rid the state of their old nemesis. They moved to impeach him.

The heart of the conservatives' indictment of Holden rested upon his formation of a private militia to stop the Klan's violence against Republicans and freedmen, the much-hated Kirk-Holden war. To conservatives, no insurrection existed. As William A. Graham, one of the prosecutors whose hostility toward Holden knew few bounds, argued, the mere existence of organizations such as the Klan, the Constitutional Union Guard, the White Brotherhood, and the Invisible Empire did not, per se, give rise to "some overt resistance to the government" that would be required to justify a proclamation of insurrection and rebellion against the state. Then the prosecutors, or, as they were called, house managers, proceeded to call witness after witness who insisted that the Klan did not exist at all.

The house managers, Augustus Merrimon from Buncombe County, Thomas Bragg, a former governor and long-time enemy of Holden, and Graham, the old Whig governor who loathed all Republicans, centered their attack on the person Holden had chosen to head the militia, George Kirk. In the eyes of many ex-Confederates, such as Merrimon, Vance, and Bragg, Kirk, with Holden's urging, had conducted a war of vengeance against ex-Confederates and "Secesh Democrats" in Alamance and Caswell counties, all under the pretense of insurrection by an invisible enemy that existed only in their minds. To many conservatives, the Kirk-Holden war itself constituted grounds for removal.

In a largely partisan vote, the senate convicted Holden of "high crimes and misdemeanors" while in office, finding him guilty on six of eight counts. Yet any explanation of Holden's impeachment would be insufficient without consideration of the bitterness many in the state, especially Merrimon, Graham, and Pearson, had toward him. Indeed, much of the dislike toward Holden came from decades of accumulated grudges against him, all heightened by the personal intimacy of state politics. Conservative whites throughout the state hailed the governor's removal as the end of radical rule, an event that would cause Republicans to "die an infamous death." David Schenck spoke for many North Carolinians when he observed that Holden deserved impeachment and disgrace since he had "betrayed his race and color [and] . .. the Confederacy" and made war on "innocent men in time of peace." For his part, William Holden spent the rest of his life defending his actions and denying his wrongdoing and indictment. After a stroke partially incapacitated him in 1889, the old Republican warrior painstakingly set down his memoirs, judiciously transcribed by his daughter, always maintaining that his old enemies should be blamed more than his mistakes in judgment while governor. He never repented.

Holden's removal effectively ended Radical Reconstruction in North Carolina. Although the state formally rejoined the Union in 1870, it had never been out of the control of the old gang of politicians, now called conservatives, for more than two years. Yet even this brief period showed North Carolinians a different view of government, one that they would recall when the old ways returned in the 1880s. The role of government effectively had been reconstructed in their thinking after only two years. Still, conservatives managed to associate all the shortcomings and failures of Reconstruction with radical rule, no matter how brief and transitory. Under Holden, Republicans sought to encourage industry by providing subsidies and loans through state sponsorship. Republicans promoted the rebuilding of North Carolina's railroad system, often corrupting themselves and plunging the state into debt in the process. Little investment came into the state from outside sources; thus taxation and bonds became methods of replacing lost capital and rebuilding the state's infrastructure after the devastation of the war. The expansion of government, particularly in education and social services, and the traditional relationship between business and mercantile interests often offered irresistible temptations for fraud and corruption. By 1872, North Carolina's public indebtedness had increased sixfold from its 1860 base. While fraud and corruption undoubtedly contributed to the debt in North Carolina, most of the dramatic increases came from rebuilding a devastated state after the war.

Yet Reconstruction allowed the state the opportunity to liberalize, however briefly, its concept of government and its role in the lives of most North Carolinians, especially African Americans. Before the war, government had provided little in the way of education

By late 1865, cotton once more had become one of the state's principal crops.
North Carolina Collection, University of North Carolina at Chapel Hill.

or aid to its citizens. Looking backward to the vision of Archibald Murphey and David Swain, the new state government for the first time constructed a public school system that benefited everyone, white and black alike. Even more pressing, the newly reconstructed government had to deal with the changed legal and social status of thousands of freedmen who, by virtue of the Thirteenth, Fourteenth, and Fifteenth Amendments, became full citizens with concomitant civil and political rights.

Reborn as North Carolinians and U.S. citizens after the Civil War, ex-slaves sought first not the right to vote, hold office, serve on juries, or own property, but the freedom to bind their families together, both legally and traditionally. Their search for families split apart by slavery revealed one of the most poignant yet hidden private and personal costs of bondage. Undertaken during the New Deal, narratives of former North Carolina slaves recorded by the Federal Writers' Project of the early 1930s indicated that perhaps 20 to 25 percent had had their families separated. One elderly ex-slave, Ben Johnson, recalled that he knew "nothin' 'bout my mammy an' daddy, but I had a brother Jim who was sold . . . I sat dar an' I cry . . . I ain't neber hyar from Jim since an' I wonder now sometimes if 'en he's still livin.'" Another ex-slave, Charlie Barbour, remembered what it meant to be free. "I wuz glad ter be free, case I knows den dat I won't wake up some mornin' ter fin' dat my mommy or some ob de rest of my family am done sold."

After emancipation, North Carolina's freedmen and freedwomen sought to reconstitute family bonds that had been broken under slavery. The vagrancy and "aimless wandering" of ex-slaves reported by many white observers frequently only had as its purpose the re-establishment of families, the search for wives, husbands, parents, children, brothers, and sisters separated under slavery. Charles Dickens, a former slave, told how his father, who lived in Franklin County, walked all the way to adjacent Wake County, where his wife and children lived, and "carried us to Franklin County" and to freedom. Temple Herndon Durham thought back to emancipation as the happiest day of her life. The mother of nine children, Temple knew that "after we was free . . . den me an' Exter could be together all the time 'stead of Saturday an' Sunday." When Owen Smaw and his wife, Celia, came to register with the Freedmen's Bureau in 1866, Celia collapsed when she found that her first husband, John Bryan, long thought to be dead, had been seeking her through the bureau. "At the request of all parties," Celia left Owen Smaw once again to be with first husband,

John Bryan, a wrenching personal decision that now she and not an institution could make.

Ex-slaves enthusiastically accepted North Carolina's order to register all continuing marriages by the fall of 1866. Negro Cohabitation Certificates, records of African Americans who came forward to register, existed in seventeen of eighty-six counties. Almost nineteen thousand blacks quickly complied with the law, nearly 15 percent of the state's entire slave population in 1860. Many who had "jumped the broom" in informal but recognized marriages now wanted their affection and devotion to be formally accepted and legitimized publicly within a larger society. Several older African Americans interviewed in the Federal Writer's Project recalled being present when their parents finally heard the words never said to slaves, "Whom God hath joined together, let NO MAN put asunder." For many freedmen, basic human rights took precedence over civil ones. Freedom and the abolition of slavery reinforced the separation between blacks and whites. Once freed, African Americans migrated to areas around Wilmington, New Bern, Durham, and Greensboro, where substantial black communities already existed. There they founded new institutions and continued or changed older ones. Ties to white churches established under slavery largely ended; in their place, freedmen organized new congregations incorporating their own beliefs and values. For the first time, education, at best haphazard and casual under slavery, became institutionalized as a part of black culture and life.

Under slavery, blacks and whites who worshiped together or separately heard different messages from Christianity. Masters generally agreed that baptism and communion conferred spiritual but not physical freedom upon slaves. Indeed, many whites, following passages in Genesis and Jeremiah, believed that, in the Bible, God divinely ordained blacks to be inferior, either as slaves or servants, and that as masters they must look out for their well-being. For their part, slaves mistrusted the injunction of their masters to be obedient and meek, holding instead to the conviction that the idea of agape, of universal love, and of equality before God did not mean enslavement. In their own prayer meetings and ceremonies, freedmen gradually formulated a newer, more emotional and, for them, spiritual set of ideas about Christianity rooted in the Old Testament and in their ideas about Jesus. Freedom gave them the opportunity to formalize these beliefs.

After 1865, churches quickly became the most segregated part of life for North Carolinians. Unwilling to abolish separate seating and to allow blacks a voice in governance for their black members, many white churches saw the wholesale withdrawal of freedmen from their congregations. Southern Presbyterians initially tried to keep their black members, asserting that "the ecclesiastical separation of the races would threaten evil to both races, especially to the colored." The meaning of "especially to the colored" affirmed the belief among many freedmen that white congregations, even if allowing them membership, still believed them to be inferior. The State Baptist Convention took an opposite approach, encouraging blacks to form their own separate Baptist churches and associations while providing "such aid and encouragement . . . as may be compatible with the interests and duties" of Baptists everywhere. Indeed, funds and aid were set aside to help freedmen form their own Baptist churches and groups. Not surprisingly, freedmen soon set up the Orange

Street Baptist Church in Wilmington and the Raleigh First Baptist Church, Colored, as well as scores of other churches throughout the state. Methodists soon followed suit, and, by 1868, churches had become the first truly separate and segregated institution under Reconstruction.

Education did not follow the same course. At first it seemed to offer the best chance of the two races interrelating. At the end of the war, the old school Literary Fund, valued at $2 million in 1861, had almost ceased to exist. Invested in banks and subsequently in Confederate bonds, the monies evaporated with the fortunes of the South. With the occupation of the Outer Banks in 1862, many northern aid and benevolent societies sent not only goods and supplies but also teachers and books to North Carolina, principally to educate freed slaves. By the end of 1864, the American Missionary Association, the New England Freedmen's Aid Society, and the National Freedmen's Relief Association had set up more than fifteen schools and had sent more than sixty-six teachers to North Carolina, fifty-six of whom were women. Other New Englanders such as Jennie Bell and Eliza Perkins came to the Outer Banks on their own, and, using their own funds or donations, worked independently to teach freedmen.

In September 1864 Secretary of War Edwin Stanton authorized the Freedmen's Bureau to appoint officers to establish schools for blacks. Thereafter, the aid associations cooperated in recruiting, training, and paying teachers' salaries while the federal government, either through the bureau or more directly the army, furnished subsistence, supplies, and buildings. By March 1867, 156 schools with an enrollment of 13,039 African Americans had been organized throughout the state. At the end of the war, religious organizations such as the Friends Society (Quakers), Presbyterian Church, and the Episcopal Commission quickly moved into the Piedmont and western part of the state to inaugurate schools both for whites and blacks.

Despite the support of only a small number of Republicans, the convention of 1868 offered an early if tentative hope of setting up an integrated public school system in the South. Dominated by radicals frequently enthused by northern idealism and zeal, the convention's committee on education within a year remarkably had provided for the organization of a statewide system of public education overseen by a board of education supervised by the state. Seventy-five percent of the poll tax levied by each county went to public education, while the state set aside $100,000, no small sum then, to assist in the establishment of schools. Both in 1868 and 1869 amendments to the committee's report and to the funding of the system provided for the separation of whites and blacks in schools. Both times the amendments failed. Clearly, a few Republicans on the committee sought to "mix" the races in public schools. S. S. Ashley, elected first state superintendent, came from Massachusetts and publicly favored whites and blacks going to the same schools. As his assistant, Ashley selected J. W. Hood, an African American, to show his determination to have mixed schools. Dubbed "Pilgrim" by the conservatives for his nobleness, incorruptibility, and missionary zeal, Ashley nonetheless had to settle for having each county decide if it wanted integrated schools or not. Not surprisingly, almost all chose separate schools. Still, by preserving the element of choice, however small, Ashley and the radicals sought to promote the idea of integrated schools rather than have conservatives deny them at the outset by amendments to bills and reports.

From 1864 until the 1880s, North Carolina did not operate under a strict de jure or de facto system of segregation in education or, indeed, in much of public life. In fact, attempts to have both races attend schools together as well as engage in agricultural, mercantile, and political life demonstrated more a laissez-faire attitude toward race relations that persisted in the state for nearly two decades. Blacks and whites came together, if not on an equal basis at least with an altered sense of their place in society, in the marketplace, in schools, in politics, in penal institutions, even in public transportation. In a dramatic deconstruction of the past, North Carolinians increasingly segregated themselves privately but not publicly after 1877. Yet the long shadow of slavery and racism in the end stalked even these halcyon days of racial adjustment in North Carolina. In the end, the lasting legacy of Reconstruction in North Carolina lay not in the charges of corruption and wantonness of carpetbagger government, in the rise of the KKK, in the Kirk-Holden war, or in the false melodrama of the impeachment of Gov. William Holden, so beloved by many of the state's historians and writers. Instead, the new, liberalized state constitution of 1868 more appropriately represented the impact of Reconstruction upon the state. More than the limited democracy of Jacksonianism, the new constitution, for the first time, enshrined universal manhood suffrage, did away with remaining property qualifications for holding office, and provided for the election of court justices. Equally important, North Carolina established agencies for providing for the poor, the orphaned, and the imprisoned by setting up statewide institutions through boards and commissions. Archaic and barbaric punishments such as public hangings and beatings ended.

For the first time, the state mandated universal public education and, equally significant, provided necessary and essential funding for its establishment. The new constitution propelled North Carolina into providing valuable social services for its citizens, both black and white. To pay for the new and expanded role of a government that increasingly cared for its citizens, North Carolina levied new taxes, the surest sign of legitimacy in governance yet a move resisted by old-line conservative, reactionary politicians such as Graham and Vance. After 1868, the state of North Carolina became more and more a booster and promoter for industry, especially railroads, thus paving the way for boomlets in textiles, tobacco, and furniture. Above all, the constitution of 1868 helped modernize the state in an attempt to bring it into line not with its southern neighbors but with the nation in general. Not astonishingly, the radical changes supported by the new constitution met not only public disapproval but also violence from masked groups such as the KKK. Even so, the vast majority of North Carolinians benefited from the deconstruction and the reconstruction of the state from 1865 to 1875. For a brief period, the state even seemed to enter a honeymoon period of race relations where both blacks and whites experimented with new ways of civic and political cooperation, in a laissez-faire time of racial adjustment before voluntary segregation became de jure banishment. Socially, the two races institutionally remained apart. For over a century, no political party sought to do away with the 1868 constitution, a testament to its legacy and to that of Reconstruction within North Carolina.

ADDITIONAL READINGS

Alexander, Roberta S. "Hostility and Hope: Black Education in North Carolina during Presidential Reconstruction, 1865–1867." *North Carolina Historical Review* 53 (April 1976): 113–32.

————. *North Carolina Faces the Freedmen: Race Relations during Presidential Reconstruction, 1865–67*. Durham: Duke University Press, 1985.

Balanoff, Elizabeth. "Negro Legislators in the North Carolina General Assembly, July, 1868–February, 1872." *North Carolina Historical Review* 49 (January 1972): 22–55.

Battle, William H. *Report on the Proceedings in the Habeas Corpus Cases on the Petitions of Adolphus G. Moore and Others . . . from the County of Caswell*. Raleigh: Nichols and Gorman, 1870.

Bellamy, Donnie D. "Black Education in Onslow County, North Carolina: A Brief History 1868–1966." *Journal of the Georgia Association of Historians* 19 (1998): 258–78.

Bernstein, Leonard. "The Participation of Negro Delegates in the Constitutional Convention of 1868." *Journal of Negro History* 34 (October 1949): 391–409.

Bogue, Jesse P. "Violence and Oppression in North Carolina during Reconstruction, 1865–1873." Ph.D. diss., University of Maryland, 1973.

Currey, Craig J. "Role of the Army in North Carolina Reconstruction, 1865–1877." Master's thesis, University of North Carolina, 1991.

DeMuro, Arthur. "'We are Men'—Black Reconstruction in North Carolina, 1865–1870." Master's thesis, University of North Carolina, 1979.

Edwards, Laura. *Gendered Strife and Confusion: The Political Culture of Reconstruction*. Urbana: University of Illinois Press, 1997.

Hamilton, Joseph G. D., "The Freedmen's Bureau in North Carolina." *South Atlantic Quarterly* 8, pts. 1, 2 (1909): 53–67, 154–63.

————. "The Union League in North Carolina." *Sewanee Review* 20 (October 1912): 143–52.

Heyman, Max L., Jr. "'Great Reconstructor': General E. R. S. Canby and the Second Military District." *North Carolina Historical Review* 32 (January 1955): 52–80.

Holt, Sharon Ann. "Making Freedom Pay: Freedpeople Working for Themselves, North Carolina, 1865–1900." *Journal of Southern History* 60 (1994): 229–62.

Jones, Bobby F. "Opportunity Lost: North Carolina Race Relations during Presidential Reconstruction." Master's thesis, University of North Carolina, 1961.

Miller, Robert D. "Of Freedom and Freedmen: Racial Attitudes of White Elites in North Carolina during Reconstruction." Ph.D. diss., University of North Carolina, 1976.

Mobley, Joe. *James City: A Black Community in North Carolina, 1863–1900*. Raleigh: Department of Archives and History, 1981.

Morrill, James Roy, III. "North Carolina and the Administration of Brevet Major General Sickles." *North Carolina Historical Review* 42 (July 1965): 291–305.

Olsen, Otto H. "Ku Klux Klan: A Study in Reconstruction Politics and Propaganda." *North Carolina Historical Review* 39 (July 1962): 340–62.

Trelease, Allen W. *White Terror: The Ku Klux Klan Conspiracy and Southern Reconstruction*. Westport, Conn.: Greenwood Press, 1979.

Troxler, Carol Watterson. "'To Look More Closely at the Man': Wyatt Outlaw, a Nexus of National, Local, and Personal History." *North Carolina Historical Review* 77 (October 2000): 403–33.

Wade, Wyn C. *Fiery Cross: The Ku Klux Klan in America*. New York: Simon and Schuster, 1987.

Walker, Jacqueline B. "Blacks in North Carolina during Reconstruction." Ph.D. diss., Duke University, 1979.

Woodward, C. Vann. *The Strange Career of Jim Crow*. New York: Oxford University Press, 1955.

Zipf, Karin L. "'The Whites Shall Rule the Land or Die': Gender, Race, and Class in North Carolina Reconstruction Politics." *Journal of Southern History* 65 (1999): 499–534.

Zuber, Richard L. *North Carolina during Reconstruction*. Raleigh: Department of Archives and History, 1969.

Trains, Towns, Textiles, and Tobacco

SIXTEEN

North Carolina's Vision of a New South

In 1886 Henry Woodfin Grady, who traced his ancestry both to Georgia and to western North Carolina, spoke to the prestigious New England Club of New York, the first southerner to do so after the Civil War, on the topic of the New South that had emerged after Appomattox. The South, he maintained, had changed and risen anew from its Civil War ashes. It had "fallen in love with work," "established thrift in city and country," and soon would "out Yankee the Yankee." Of course, Grady insisted, it first must rid itself of the myths of the Old South, those of slave labor, large plantations, and a privileged elite. Paying homage to the noble cause of the South during the Civil War, a necessity for any southern spokesman after 1865, Grady dismissed it through eloquent praise. The New South would achieve "a fuller independence . . . than that which our fathers sought to win in the [political] forum by their eloquence or compel in the field by their swords." Nor would the New South seek to reenslave blacks but instead would strive to incorporate them into the newer, freer, more educated labor force needed for industrialization and diversification. It was exactly what New Englanders wanted to hear.

Daniel A. Tompkins, another New South evangelist, echoed Grady's words but with a North Carolina twist. As memories of the Civil War receded and a new century loomed, Tompkins insisted that his generation looked forward to a changed South, to a place of

Henry Woodfin Grady, spokesman for the New South in the 1890s.
North Carolina Department of Archives and History, Raleigh.

Daniel A. Tompkins, who helped found textile mills throughout the Carolina Piedmont.
North Carolina Office of Archives and History, Raleigh.

"unlimited raw material from which products required by the whole world may be produced." In the Piedmont of the Carolinas he saw "cotton factories springing up quietly but with a rapidity equaled nowhere in the United States in any industry," even in the mushrooming iron mills of Alabama and Tennessee. The Old South had been betrayed by cotton and slavery, Tompkins maintained, so much so that, while "the industrial progress of the Piedmont Carolinas should have been parallel with that of Pennsylvania," the Carolinas "practically stood still . . . wealth fell into the hands of fewer people, general development ceased, . . . [and] resources were neglected." His message resonated in the foothills and Piedmont of the Carolinas and Georgia.

Tompkins saw the advantages of industrialization from the vantage point of his education in the North. A South Carolinian by birth, he obtained a civil engineer's degree in 1873 from Rensselaer Polytechnic Institute in Troy, New York. As a representative of the newly electrified Westinghouse Machine Company of Pittsburgh, Tompkins helped build several score of cotton mills in a wide swath extending from Texas to Virginia. Eventually, he acquired ownership of mills in Charlotte and High Shoals, North Carolina, and also in Edgefield, South Carolina. In 1891 he acquired the *Charlotte Chronicle,* renamed it the *Daily Observer,* and made it a principal advocate of "the gospel of salvation through manufacturing" for the New South. By 1880, more than fifty cotton mills dotted North Carolina, located mainly in the same Piedmont counties that today form the Interstate 85 corridor. By 1900, the number had grown to more than two hundred with perhaps 67 percent owned by the same families as before the Civil War.

A way of life centered around mill villages had replaced much of the older agriculture of the state. Between 1900 and 1921, for example, Charles "Charlie" Cannon expanded his holdings in Cannon Mills from four plants employing 6,700 workers to twelve mills with more than 20,000. Charlotte author Harry Golden described him as "the last of the feudal barons in the twentieth century," holding for his own use the town of Kannapolis, a classic Greek rendering of the Cannon family name, "in the same way that William Faulkner owns the imaginary town of Jefferson, Yoknapatawpha." He did indeed.

Above: Housing for textile workers along Pine Street in Kannapolis. The young girl in the left foreground is getting water from the community well.
North Carolina Collection, University of North Carolina at Chapel Hill.

Young girl working in textile mill.
North Carolina Division of Archives and History, Raleigh.

One of the ironies of New South leaders, such as William S. Battle in textiles, lay in the fact that many of them had laid the foundations for a newer industrial South long before the drumbeat rhetoric of the secessionists drowned them out. Like so many others during Reconstruction, Battle, using cash reserves carefully built up and nurtured here and abroad, quietly bought new machinery and repaired old in the creditless, capital-starved decades after the end of the Civil War. Along with the Battles and the F. W. Dawsons, names of older antebellum mill owners such as the Moreheads, Schencks, Frieses, Holts, and Odells, all owners of cotton mills in the emerging New South, soon came to dominate not only commerce and manufacturing but also cultural life in North Carolina well into the twentieth century.

Left: Kemp Plummer Battle (1831–1919).
North Carolina Collection, University of North Carolina at Chapel Hill.

James Buchanan Duke (1856–1925). North Carolina Collection, University of North Carolina at Chapel Hill.

A common folk story that circulated among North Carolinians after the Civil War had it that when Joseph Johnston surrendered to William Tecumseh Sherman on 14 April 1865, the "Old North State" took its revenge among the occupying Yankees by plying them with a more addictive, flue-cured, bright leaf tobacco. If they could not shoot them, at least the Yankees might spend a good bit of money in the long run. The first tobacco factory opened in Winston in 1871, manufacturing mainly chewing tobacco. Three years later P. H. Hanes, Hamilton Scales, and Richard J. Reynolds also established factories in Winston. In Durham, Green and Blackwell began advertising their brand of Bull Durham. That same year, in North Carolina, Washington Duke and his sons opened their first factory.

In 1876, a young eighteen-year-old Virginian, James Bonsack, made a crude machine that rolled cut-up tobacco leaves and paper together to make cigarettes. Washington Duke and his son, James Buchanan Duke, spent months adapting Bonsack's primitive roller, at first small and hand held, so that it would produce more cigarettes than even the fastest skilled workers. With Bonsack's machine, imported Jewish labor from Europe, and a growing urban market in the North, the Dukes launched their tobacco empire. Within two decades, their American Tobacco Company largely controlled the tobacco industry throughout the nation.

From the end of the Civil War until the turn of the century, consumption of tobacco products quadrupled. Easy to carry, "quick and potent," slim, and aesthetically almost an extension of the hand, cigarettes suited the new urban market of the Northeast. Immigrants from Europe soon took up the habit. In the South, especially in North Carolina, men and even women shunned the new cigarettes as "sissylike," preferring instead the older, supposedly more masculine, frontier habits of "smokeless" tobacco, chewing, dipping, snuffing, and spitting. By 1900, Americans spent more on tobacco than clothes or

George Washington Duke standing at the doorway of the barn that served as his first tobacco factory near Durham.
North Carolina Office of Archives and History, Raleigh

An advertisement for Duke's high grade smoking tobacco mixture in 1912.
North Carolina Office of Archives and History, Raleigh.

toiletries. "Buck" Duke instinctively understood the addictive qualities of his products and just as intuitively knew that advertising and marketing, concentrated, coordinated, and aimed at a national audience, would help him obtain the monopoly he wanted. Using promotional tools such as collectible picture cards and free "safety" matches, Duke set out to overwhelm and buy out his competitors. He succeeded. Before he died, his American Tobacco Company held all the playing cards, both literally, figuratively, and collectively of the industry, and, in a rare instance, North Carolina came to dominate a national market. Duke and other tobacco kingpins reinvested their profits in North Carolina and Virginia, helping to transform sleepy towns like Winston into bustling small cities. With a rakish smile, southern charm, and utilization of the region's natural resources, Buck Duke and a New South business elite, at least in tobacco and textiles, had "out Yankeed the Yankees." North Carolina began to produce its own "brand" of robber barons, only with a southern drawl to go along with some back-slapping, down-home charm.

After the Civil War, railroads and their construction had come to be the spellbinding terminus of the New South's philosophy. With railroads, North Carolina and the South could compete with the North and West. Without them, they would remain rural, agricultural,

Top: Cigarettes rolled by hand in a Durham cigarette factory.
North Carolina Collection, University of North Carolina at Chapel Hill.

The Duke residence and the Duke Tobacco Company in Durham, 1895.
North Carolina Collection, University of North Carolina at Chapel Hill.

backward, and underdeveloped. Pinning all their hopes on the construction and comple-
tion of new lines, North Carolinians began an almost paniclike building of new railroads
after 1870. In the summer of 1865, with the Civil War over, North Carolina's twisted rails,
disintegrating and washed away roadbeds, worn-out rolling stock, and destroyed or abandoned depots meant that the state had little with which to build or to initiate reconstruction. North Carolina began its railroad frenzy by abandoning not only many of the older
lines but also its former policy of limited state aid to railroads. After 1870, the general
assembly turned over the task of developing a railroad system to private investors, but
with assurances that the state would invest heavily in and guarantee the results of the
effort. This time, railroads would not end in new southern cities such as Charlotte and in
small towns like Weldon but would run through them to connect the whole of North
Carolina to the rest of the South and the nation.

Four trends typified the state's frenzy to build railroads after the Civil War: continuation, consolidation, corruption, and control. Even before the war, portions of the lines from Wilmington to Rutherfordton and from Salisbury to Asheville and thence to the Tennessee line remained unfinished. If ever the state were to realize its dream of being the linchpin of a newly industrialized and diversified South, the western region of the state would have to be connected to the Piedmont and coast, a dream long anticipated by David Swain, William A. Graham, Zebulon Vance, and especially John Motley Morehead. Gradually and with state help, the Western North Carolina Railroad, facing heavy grading and ballooning construction costs as it pushed into the mountainous west, inched ever closer to Asheville, the only town of any size in the western part of the state. Reaching Old Fort, at the bottom of the Blue Ridge, in 1869, the road stopped, even as much of the roadbed construction and grading advanced toward Asheville. In the next eight years, the schemes and attempts to build a railroad to Asheville and beyond were so numerous that the state failed to appropriate funds even to maintain existing turnpikes and roads. Infuriated because railroad schemers in Raleigh ignored the western part of the state, Buncombe County commissioners in 1871 presented the Western Division of the Western North Carolina Railroad a bill to pay for the "bad condition . . . of the Turnpike." That same year work stopped altogether on the line.

In 1871, state officials painfully discovered that George W. Swepson and Milton Littlefield, two of Western's highest ranking officials, had made off with all the company's funds. Bankrupt and sold at auction in 1875, the Western North Carolina Railroad was purchased by the state for $825,000 to protect its heavy investment in the project. Work resumed in 1879 when the state sold its interest in the line to William Best, James Fish, J. Nelson Tappan, and William Grace, partners in a New York syndicate, for the $850,000 debt plus $600,000 for its outlay since 1875. Best agreed to finish the line by 1 July 1881. The Western line finally reached Asheville in 1880 and Murphy in the far west in 1885. Soon afterward, the Richmond and Danville Railroad purchased the Western North Carolina, only to become part of the Southern Railway system in 1894.

Bear hunters at Highlands in western North Carolina in the 1890s.
North Carolina Collection, University of North Carolina at Chapel Hill.

A group of construction workers on the Tallulah Falls Railway, built in Macon County in western North Carolina in 1904. North Carolina Collection, University of North Carolina at Chapel Hill.

One line, the Richmond to Atlanta route, occupied much of the state's attention. In 1871 North Carolina consigned the task of completing the line through the state's textile and tobacco districts, the "Tobacco Road" route, to Virginia, New York and Ohio capitalists who hoped first to acquire the Richmond and Danville Railroad, then the Piedmont Railroad, and, finally, the North Carolina Railroad from Greensboro to Charlotte. Over 70 percent of the state's freight and transshipments went north and south through Greensboro and Charlotte, the key part of the line, and the state's prosperity depended upon developing the towns as well as tobacco and textile industries along the route. The towns along the route, Charlotte, Concord, High Point, Greensboro, Durham, and Raleigh held the key to the state's development. Therefore, the Tobacco Road route attracted the interest of many of the nation's most notorious and well-known schemers and capitalists. Two of them, John Inman and J. P. Morgan, soon began to notice the development of North Carolina railroads. The association of their names with lines within the state coincided not only with the passing of control from regional to national markets just before the turn of the century but also with the consolidation of the numerous railroad companies into larger, better-financed business organizations.

In Virginia, the Richmond Terminal, a titanic railroad holding company by 1891, had a controlling interest in more than one hundred railroad lines and owned more than 8,500 miles of track throughout the South and the mid-Atlantic states. Twenty-seven steering committees presided over the terminal, and from 1880 to 1894 it made and lost several fortunes. When the company finally sank in 1894, it owed more than $12 million in debts. In that same year, J. P. Morgan, the nation's richest and foremost banker, took over the Richmond Terminal, renamed it the Southern Railway, and immediately recapitalized the

*A North Carolina mountain woman
smoking a pipe in the 1890s.*
North Carolina Collection, University
of North Carolina at Chapel Hill.

company with $375 million in funds. Soon Morgan's company acquired rights to tracks from Greensboro to Charlotte and to a line from Tarboro southward to Alabama and northward to Norfolk. Through Morgan's empire, North Carolina now had connections from New York to New Orleans and from Jacksonville to Memphis.

By 1900 North Carolina's railroad system largely had been completed. From less than 1,600 miles in 1880 the state now had more than 3,380 miles completed. More significantly, North Carolina now had access to regional, national, and even international markets. Soon Englishmen and Egyptians would be smoking Buck Duke's cigarettes and perhaps even laboring in shirts woven in Tompkins's textile mills. Railroads carried North Carolinians into a worldwide network of companies and markets—and also into a cosmos of uncertainty and risk where New Southerners found the stakes to be much higher and riskier than in the Old South.

The North Carolina that emerged after the Civil War once more saw its forests spawn a new generation of Tar Heels, not only on its east coast but also in the rugged western mountains. For more than two centuries, farmers had made tar from pine trees and distilled turpentine on the side. Tickled by slashing soft conifers and then trapped, resin, once burned and recovered, yielded tar used in medicines, both patent and prescriptive, and in harsh soaps. After the Civil War, North Carolina lost its tar pitting role first to South Carolina and then to Florida. Nonetheless, the forests along the eastern seaboard remained largely intact, no longer producing naval stores but now being logged chiefly for their soft pine and scantling lumber for the Northeast.

The coming of the railroad and the emergence of new markets once more opened up the state's forests for exploitation. This time the loggers moved not only into the conifer forests along the east coast but, for the first time, into the dense hardwood forests in the western part of the state. They came not in the form of small sawmills and distilleries as they had on the east coast, but in huge logging camps financed by large companies that dotted the virtually untouched timber stands in the rugged mountains. Only marginally logged because of the inaccessibility and high costs of bringing the lumber down from the high peaks, western North Carolina's forest bonanza now lured industrialists and entrepreneurs alike. Chauncey Mitchell Depew, a prominent New York Republican and officer of the Vanderbilt railway system, urged Yankees to "Go south, young man," and bring lumber and timber products back to the North and Midwest. One of Vanderbilt's sons, George

Above: Workmen at a lumber camp near Double Spring Gap in Haywood County.
North Carolina Collection, University of North Carolina at Chapel Hill.

A lumber camp in western North Carolina in 1910.
North Carolina Collection, University of North Carolina at Chapel Hill.

Washington Vanderbilt, took Depew's advice but resolved to save the forests instead, eventually purchasing more than 125,000 acres in western North Carolina.

Peter G. Thomson of Hamilton, Ohio, followed Depew's suggestion and looked toward North Carolina instead of Maine to expand the operations of his Champion Coated Paper Company. Since beginning his operations in Ohio in the late 1880s, Thomson had purchased the pulp for his mills on the open market, frequently suffering shortages and damaging price fluctuations. Like John D. Rockefeller in the oil industry, he wanted to control the entire papermaking process from cutting the trees to distributing the finished product to wholesalers and brokers. The enormous spruce and balsam forests of Western North Carolina and the increasing shortage and long hauling distances of northern timber made him look south to North Carolina, Tennessee, and Georgia.

In the late nineteenth century, spruce dominated paper woods, the basic ingredient for books, newspapers, and "fine papers of all kinds." Only two substantial spruce forests remained east of the Mississippi by 1890, one a narrow ribbon that crisscrossed the U.S. and Canadian border from Maine to Minnesota, the other stretching in a two-hundred-mile girdle across the southern Appalachian Mountains from Tennessee through North Carolina and on into Georgia. When the Southern Railway reached Murphy in 1890, Thomson had all the ingredients needed to establish his pulp mill operation in western North Carolina and access to affordable transportation as well as a plentiful supply of cheap timber, water, and labor. Within a decade his Champion Paper Company had established itself as one of the largest industries in the western counties. Lumber companies and railroads followed companies like Champion Paper not only into towns like Canton and Spruce Pine but also up mountains and across streams throughout the western counties. Highly mobile, dispersed across the northern and western tier of counties, notoriously wasteful in their brush and clear-cutting methods, lumber companies off-loaded trailers for their employees from rail lines even before the tracks had been completed. Housed in these early mobile homes, thousands of workers laid track, often at precarious angles, up onto the mountains, cutting timber along the right-of-way as they went. Instant communities and towns such as that of Sunburst in Haywood County sprang up overnight, almost always centered around a cafeteria and community center. They soon disappeared as quickly as the forests around them, eventually becoming part of local folklore even as they vanished from the landscape. Vast stretches of denuded land extended in an arc from Murphy to Boone as the loggers cut their way through the mountains. By 1916, only a few pockets of virgin forests remained, chiefly in the balsams of western North Carolina.

In an effort to save many of the forests in the western part of the state, George Washington Vanderbilt, who came to Asheville in the late 1880s to build Biltmore House, the finest castle in America, brought in forestry experts with the same care as he did masons and artisans. Carl Schenck, a professionally trained forester from Germany, and Gifford Pinchot applied the principles of scientific forestry at the Biltmore Forest School, one of the first efforts of its kind in the United States. Intent on demonstrating that the forester and lumberman had the same interests, Pinchot wanted to manage the forests efficiently, thus producing the best money results for everyone. At the Columbian Exposition in 1893, perhaps the greatest industrial exhibition of the century, Pinchot touted his efficient management of North Carolina's forests. One visitor to Chicago, Theodore Roosevelt, seemed especially impressed by Pinchot's efforts. A decade later, Roosevelt, now president of the United States, appointed him the nation's first chief forester. Even as North Carolina's trees fell under the onslaught of timber companies at the end of the century, Asheville and the forests of western North Carolina become a southern ashram for devotees of preservation and scientific management.

High Point, with some of the finest timber in North America surrounding it and with railroads connecting it to Danville and other growing markets in America and abroad, soon became the center of the state's expanding furniture industry. Before the Civil War, High Point, along with Thomasville, Hickory, Lexington, and a host of Piedmont towns, had a well-established cottage and craft industry in the production of beds, sideboards, and chairs. Selling only to local markets, furniture manufactures remained a small but viable industry before 1860. In 1881 William E. White opened a factory to manufacture wooden spindles, chiefly for textiles, and, using the same equipment, he gradually began to produce furniture as well. In that same year, Ernest Ansel Snow from High Point first began to ship partially finished lumber to Baltimore to be reassembled into furniture. Like Grady in Georgia, Snow wondered why North Carolina, with perhaps the finest hardwood forests in the nation, had to send its products northward to be processed. The son of a Union veteran who had moved to High Point in 1871, he began planning his own New South industry in North Carolina. Snow's years of delay in opening a furniture factory reflected the lag time in the state's industrial development largely produced by a lack of capital. Not until 1889 did Snow convince some local merchants, John H. Tate and Thomas F. and M. J. Wrenn, to invest their life savings in his venture, the High Point Furniture Manufacturing Company. It worked.

Within two years the company had sales in excess of $150,000. Wagons hauled loads of furniture, towering like piles of hay, to the new rail lines to be shipped across the nation. So much furniture left High Point in the first few years that a surprised Thomas Wrenn "thought surely the whole world would soon be supplied . . . and the forests of North Carolina . . . completely destroyed." With the fusion of old craft practices long resident in the region and new industrial and machining technologies, High Point and North Carolina quickly became known not only for its Sears and Roebuck line of home furniture but also for the quality of its products. Drexel, Tomlinson, and White soon competed with older, highly regarded furniture lines in Virginia, Pennsylvania, and New York. By 1900, the area immediately around High Point had replaced Danville as the furniture capital of the nation.

In North Carolina, Henry Grady's New South attitude did not produce large industrial cities such as Lowell, Massachusetts, and Pittsburgh, Pennsylvania, but compact villages, bustling mill towns, and a few smaller cities such as Charlotte, Asheville, Raleigh, Winston, and Greensboro that in their newness still reflected older southern traditions of space and landscaping, principally large lawns and gardening. Urbanization on a scale that had swept over the North would wait still another fifty years in North Carolina. There cotton and tobacco mills shaped the organic demographic patterns of the New South, a proliferation of crossroads and towns along with some small- and medium-sized cities that became the nucleus for ever larger ones. North Carolina would not have anything like an Atlanta or a Richmond until after World War II. Moreover, textiles, tobacco, and furniture

*Women selling flowers to tourists
in Hot Springs in the 1890s.*
North Carolina Collection, University
of North Carolina at Chapel Hill.

manufacturing also led to a shift in economic activities and in population from the coast to the Piedmont.

As North Carolina's railways expanded from 1870 until 1910, clusters of small towns, mills, and cities sprang up along a new network from Raleigh to Gastonia. Town and urban growth occurred predominantly in the interior of the Piedmont, in towns like Durham, Greensboro, and Charlotte, and on a smaller scale along the seacoast and in the mountains. Tobacco in Durham and Winston, furniture in High Point, and cotton mills in Greensboro, Charlotte, and Gastonia soon came to dominate local economies. These growing urban areas quickly outstripped smaller towns that traditionally had served banking, commercial, legal, and transportation needs.

Unlike railroads, tobacco, cotton, and furniture manufacturing depended mainly upon local money for capitalization, usually from well-to-do merchants, landowners, bankers, and successful farmers. The relatively small size of the mills and their operations facilitated a paternalistic relationship between owners, managers, and workers. Owners provided jobs for rural workers who faced chronic indebtedness and tenancy, thus assuring themselves of a steady supply of semiskilled laborers. Most work in cotton mills required tending machines, usually spindles, a skill easily learned by young women and children. Until after 1900, women made up the majority of workers in textile mills in North Carolina, with one-fourth younger than sixteen. Most employees came from a tightly knit group of families cloistered in a mill village. For them, the family-wage system meant an increased sense of well-being and a more optimistic outlook about the future despite the fact that most mill jobs offered only limited chances for promotion. Reporting on record profits from textile mills in 1881, the *Wilmington Daily Review* wryly asked, "will philanthropy pay better?" Not in North Carolina.

When he spoke to the New England Club in New York in 1886, Henry Grady's most elaborate point concerned not industrialization or the newly acquired "Yankee habits" of work and thrift, but the place of the black person in the South after the Civil War. "Have we solved the problem he presents or progressed in honor and equity toward a solution?" Answering his own question, Grady went on to assert that newly freed blacks had prospered

A brochure advertising the gold fields of North Carolina in 1891.
North Carolina Collection, University of North Carolina at Chapel Hill.

as a working class, at least as much as whites, in the New South. Moreover, he continued, they "share our school fund" and have "the fullest protection of our laws and the interest of our people. Self-interest, as well as honor, demand that he should have this. Our future, our very existence depend upon our working out this problem in full and exact justice."

To many writers and historians of the past, Grady's words smacked of insincerity and false goodness, of lip service to a cause he knew Yankees held dear but southerners did not. Worse still, it masked an increasingly segregated society. Yet Grady, like so many southerners and North Carolinians after 1877, genuinely sought to incorporate blacks into the movement to industrialize and to change the South in fundamental ways. The same sentiment that reviled the old planter class and a backward economy based upon agriculture also disdained slavery as a labor system that exploited both whites and blacks alike. "The old south rested everything on slavery and agriculture," Grady sermonized, "unconscious that these could neither give nor maintain healthy growth. The New South presents a perfect democracy . . . a social system compact and closely knitted . . . and a diversified industry that meets the complex need of this complex age." The New South movement sought to incorporate blacks into a new vision for the region, and North Carolina led the way. In so doing, it pointed the way to a forgotten alternative in race relations, to a system that, before it fossilized into legal segregation, allowed whites and blacks a brief racial intermission.

The towns, trains, and tobacco mills that attracted white North Carolinians enticed its black citizens as well. Even "cotton mill" fever proved color blind and irresistible. In 1896, Warren Clay Coleman, an African American entrepreneur in Concord, intent upon building a cotton mill with a group of black associates, proudly proclaimed that North Carolina, "the foremost of the States" at the World's Fair in Chicago and at the Atlanta Exposition, would be the first in the entire nation to have a cotton mill to be owned and operated "principally by the colored people." Sounding like Henry Grady, Coleman the entrepreneur, mirroring the spirit of the age, asked his fellow African Americans if they would "catch the spark of the new industrial life and take advantage of this unprecedented opportunity to engage in the enterprise that would prove to the world our ability as operatives in the mills." His enterprise failed, and blacks soon found themselves relegated to menial cleaning and maintenance jobs in an almost all-white labor force.

African Americans also climbed aboard the new railway systems that crisscrossed North Carolina. At the end of Reconstruction, North Carolina blacks, buttressed by the Civil Rights Act of 1875 that forbade racial discrimination in all public accommodations, transportation, places of amusement, and juries, scrambled aboard steamboats and railroads, freely attended musicals and plays at theaters, stayed at hotels with white guests, and mingled with whites at parks and public gatherings. James O'Hara, a future African American congressman, easily persuaded a steamer captain from Greenville to Tarboro to accept black passengers as well as give them the same facilities as whites. T. McCants Stewart, an African American from Boston who had not visited his home in South Carolina since Reconstruction, found an unexpected degree of tolerance and acceptance as he made his way through the former Confederate states. Aboard a steamboat headed toward Wilmington he complained because a colored waiter had seated him at a separate table, even though in the same dining room, with whites and other blacks. At Wilmington, he ate with whites and observed that in dining rooms and train cars whites often and easily entered into conversations with him for no other reason except "to pass the time of day." "I think," he mused, that "the whites of the south are really less afraid to [have] contact with colored people than the whites of the north." Stewart's impressions, observably accurate and correct, proved to be as superficial and fleeting as his trip southward.

In North Carolina, the end of Reconstruction did not mean the reenslavement or immediate segregation of blacks. Indeed, what happened after 1870 might be characterized as a period of laissez-faire race relations, a live-and-let-live policy where whites and blacks chose to be integrated publicly yet privately segregated themselves. Older conservative attempts at restriction and reenslavement through black codes and night riders from the Ku Klux Klan gave way to a more permissive alternative in race relations. When Henry Grady and other New Southerners spoke of the "problem of the Negro," they were referring more to education and the integration of blacks into a newer, more skilled workforce than to race and politics. Indeed, the sentiment for agricultural and technical education embraced both blacks and whites alike in North Carolina. When ex-Confederate Gen. Daniel Harvey Hill passionately spoke out in 1866 against the "old plan of education in the palmy days of the south," he envisioned a "New south" which had "a practical acquaintance with the ax, the plane, the saw, the anvil, the loom, the plow," all vastly more useful than "the everlasting twaddle" about politics and philosophy. When Walter Hines Page of the Watauga Club in Raleigh and Leonidas L. Polk, editor of the *Progressive Farmer* and an early Populist leader, spoke of the need for trained workers, they included blacks as well as whites. With the aid of the federal Morrill Act, also known as the Land Grant College Act, the state legislature established in 1877 the Fayetteville Colored Normal School, the first black school to train teachers in the South, and in 1891 the Elizabeth City Colored Normal and the North Carolina Agricultural and Mechanical College for the Colored Race in Greensboro. Not surprisingly, the era also saw the establishment of a State Agricultural and Mechanical College in Raleigh for whites in 1887 and a State Normal and Industrial School for white women in Greensboro in 1891. All came from the same basic New South philosophy.

"It is amazing," Kemp Battle wrote from Raleigh in 1886, "how quietly our people take negro juries, or rather negroes on juries." A writer in the staunchly conservative *Raleigh Standard* noted that "the two races now eat together at the same table, sit together in the same room, visit and hold debating societies together" in political conventions. In Rutherfordton, Randolph Shotwell, a notorious Klan sympathizer who once went to prison rather than reveal the names of members of the Invisible Empire, professed his disgust at seeing long lines of farmers "entering the village by the various roads mounted and afoot, whites and blacks marching together, and in frequent instances arm-in-arm, a sight to disgust a decent negro" or white. Shotwell's aversion took on a more visible and ominous form as relations between the races deteriorated in less than a decade.

In his study of what happened to blacks in South Carolina after slavery, the historian Joel Williamson maintained that in order to escape the saturated "constant, physical intimacy" of slavery, African Americans after emancipation instead voluntarily moved to separate themselves privately but not publicly from whites. As early as 1870, he asserted, "separation had crystallized into a comprehensive pattern which . . . remained unaltered until" after the *Brown v. Board of Education* decision in 1954. While whites and blacks might socialize and walk arm in arm down public roads, bargain and contract for goods and services in competitive markets, vote and debate together in elections, and even dine and travel together on railroads and steamboats, they also segregated themselves in schools, churches, jails, hospitals, and asylums, perhaps in an attempt to break from the cloying intimacy of slavery. Thus, a new pattern of race relations began to emerge after the Civil War. The more formal, harsher legal system would come to dominate North Carolina after 1912. Thus, at first, there was an enlargement of opportunities for blacks.

As evangelists and as visionaries, New South boosters such as Henry Grady and D. A. Tompkins succeeded in elaborating a new role for the South and for North Carolina. Not surprisingly, their dream failed to transform North Carolina or the South into an industrialized, urbanized region smacking of Yankee values and ambitions. Despite the declaration of the *News and Observer* in June 1885 that "everywhere signs of improvement are becoming visible," North Carolina remained stubbornly rural and backward. From 1870 to 1900, the number of towns of more than 10,000 increased from only one, Wilmington, to six, Wilmington, Charlotte, Asheville, Winston, Raleigh, and Greensboro; those from 5,000 to 10,000, from two to six; and those from 1,000 to 5,000, from fourteen to fifty-two. In 1880, 55,000 people lived in cities, yet more than 1,345,000 remained in the countryside. By 1900, the urban population stood at 187,000, but the rural population also increased to 1,707,000. While the state remained small-townish and doggedly rural, a new, wealthier urban class whose money lay in tobacco, textiles, and furniture gradually had begun to take center stage both politically and socially. The growth of the New South corridor from Raleigh to Charlotte moved the political and economic focus of the state inexorably westward from the coast to the Piedmont.

The railroad, textiles, tobacco, lumber, and furniture industries that grew up after 1875 not only gave North Carolina a new economic base but also did away with the pessimism that followed the end of Reconstruction. Perhaps the enduring legacy of New Southerners lay not in the textiles, trains, and towns they founded but more properly in the renewed spirit of optimism and progress that they engendered. The small islands of industrialization that grew up around Concord, Charlotte, Greensboro, Winston, Durham, Hickory, and Raleigh became the visible manifestations of a civic crusade to change the state that lasted well into the twentieth century. Boosters, boards of trade and commerce, and newspaper editors such as Tompkins at times sounded more like Bible-thumping evangelists for a new vision for the future, for a new way of salvation for North Carolina and the South, than they did hardheaded "Yankeeized" businessman. Their lasting contribution lay not in the trains, towns, tobacco, and textile mills that dotted the Piedmont after 1900 but in their expectation that North Carolina and the South could transform itself using its own resources and ingenuity.

ADDITIONAL READINGS

Abrams, William H., Jr. "Western North Carolina Railroad, 1855–1894." Master's thesis, Western Carolina University, 1976.

Ayers, Edward L. *Promise of the New South: Life after Reconstruction.* New York: Oxford University Press, 1992.

Barefoot, Pamela, and Burt Kornegay. *Mules and Memories: A Photo Documentary of the Tobacco Farmer.* Winston-Salem: John F. Blair, 1978.

Billings, Dwight B. *Planters and the Making of a "New South"; Class, Politics, and Development in North Carolina, 1865–1900.* Chapel Hill: University of North Carolina Press, 1979.

Boggs, Wade H., III. "State-Supported Higher Education of Blacks in North Carolina, 1877–1945." Ph.D. diss., Duke University, 1972.

Brown, Cecil K. "History of the Piedmont Railroad Company." *North Carolina Historical Review* 3 (April 1926): 198–222.

Burgess, Allen E. "Tar Heel Blacks and the New South Dream: The Coleman Manufacturing Company, 1896–1904." Ph.D. diss., Duke University, 1977.

Davidson, Elizabeth H. "Child Labor Problem in North Carolina, 1883–1903." *North Carolina Historical Review* 13 (April 1936): 105–21.

Ebert, Charles H. "Furniture Making in High Point." *North Carolina Historical Review* 36 (July 1959): 330–39.

Eller, Ronald D. *Miners, Millhands, and Mountaineers: Industrialization of the Appalachian South.* Knoxville: University of Tennessee Press, 1982.

Ferguson, Maxwell. *State Regulation of Railroads in the South.* New York: Columbia University Press, 1916.

Freeze, Gary R. "Model Mill Men of the New South: Paternalism and Methodism in the Odell Cotton Mills of North Carolina, 1877–1908." Ph.D. diss., University of North Carolina, 1988.

———. "Roots, Barks, Berries, and Jews: The Herb Trade in Gilded-Age North Carolina." *Essays in Economic and Business History* 13 (1995): 107–27.

Glass, Brent D. *The Textile Industry in North Carolina: A History.* Raleigh: Division of Archives and History, 1992.

Griffin, Richard W. "Reconstruction of the North Carolina Textile Industry, 1865–1885." *North Carolina Historical Review* 41 (January 1964): 34–53.

Hall, Jacquelyn Dowd, James Leloudis, Robert Korstad, Mary Murphy, Lu Ann Jones, and Christopher B. Daly. *Like a Family: The Making of a Southern Cotton Mill World.* Chapel Hill: University of North Carolina Press, 1987.

Hearden, Patrick J. *Independence and Empire: The New South's Cotton Mill Campaign, 1865–1901.* De Kalb: University of Northern Illinois Press, 1982.

Janiewski, Dolores E. *Sisterhood Denied: Race, Gender, and Class in a New South Community.* Philadelphia: Temple University Press, 1985.

Kane, Nancy F. *Textiles in Transition: Technology, Wages, and Industry Relocation in the U.S. Textile Industry, 1880–1930.* Westport, Conn.: Greenwood Press, 1988.

Pinkett, Harold T. "Gifford Pinchot at Biltmore." *North Carolina Historical Review* 34 (July 1957): 346–57.

Porter, Patrick G. "Advertising in the Early Cigarette Industry: W. Duke, Sons and Company of Durham." *North Carolina Historical Review* 48 (January 1971): 31–43.

Price, Charles L. "Railroads and Reconstruction in North Carolina, 1865–1871." Ph.D. diss., Duke University, 1959.

Roberts, Bennett W. C., and Richard F. Knapp. "Paving the Way for the Tobacco Trust: From Hand Rolling to Mechanized Cigarette Production by W. Duke, Sons, and Company." *North Carolina Historical Review* 69 (July 1992): 257–81.

Rouse, Jordan K. *Noble Experiment of Warren G. Coleman.* Charlotte, N.C.: Crabtree Press, 1972.

Simon, Bryant. "'I Believed in the Strongest Kind of Religion': James Evans and Working-Class Protest in the New South." *Labor's Heritage* 4 (1992): 60–77.

Sitterson, Joseph C. "Business Leaders in Post–Civil War North Carolina." In *Studies in Southern History,* ed. Joseph C. Sitterson, 111–21. Chapel Hill: University of North Carolina, 1957.

Stover, John F. *The Railroads of the South, 1865–1900: A Study in Finance and Control.* Chapel Hill: University of North Carolina Press, 1955.

Taylor, Stephen Wallace. *The New South's New Frontier: A Social History of Economic Development in Southwestern North Carolina.* Gainesville: University Press of Florida, 2001.

Thomas, David N. "Early History of the North Carolina Furniture Industry, 1880–1921." Ph.D. diss., University of North Carolina, 1964.

Tilley, Nannie M. *The Bright-Tobacco Industry, 1860–1929.* Chapel Hill: University of North Carolina Press, 1948.

Trelease, Allen W. *The North Carolina Railroad, 1849–1871, and the Modernization of North Carolina.* Chapel Hill: University of North Carolina Press, 1991.

Tuttle, Marcia L. "Location of North Carolina's Nineteenth Century Cotton Products Industry." Master's thesis, University of North Carolina, 1974.

Weare, Walter. *Black Business in the New South.* Urbana: University of Illinois Press, 1973.

Woodward, C. Vann. *Origins of the New South, 1877–1913.* Baton Rouge: Louisiana State University Press, 1971.

283

The Farmer's Last Stand

"We meet in the midst of a nation brought to the verge of moral, political, and material ruin. Corruption dominates the ballot box, the legislatures, the Congress, and touches even the ermine of the bench. The People are demoralized; most of the States have been compelled to isolate the voters at the polling-place to prevent universal intimidation or bribery. The newspapers are largely subsidized or muzzled; public opinion silenced; labor impoverished; and the land concentrating in the hands of the capitalists. . . . The fruits of toil of millions are boldly stolen to build up colossal fortunes for a few, unprecedented in the history of mankind; and the possessions of these, in turn, . . . endanger liberty. From the same prolific womb of governmental injustice we breed the two great classes—tramps and millionaires" (Preamble to the 1892 platform of the national Populist Party).

By 1892, most North Carolinians, at least the vast rural majority who were farmers, suddenly found themselves outcasts, tramps in a rapidly industrializing society they once had dominated in Jefferson's agricultural empire of liberty. Once thought of as the backbone of society, farmers by the 1880s had come to be considered hicks, hayseeds, and wool hatters, ignorant country bumpkins left out of a modern, rapidly industrializing society. In Henry Grady's New South that overswept North Carolina in the 1880s with its bustling mills and towns, farmers had little place. Something had gone terribly wrong for them.

Conditions for farmers had deteriorated for almost two decades since the panic of 1873, usually referred to as the "Great Crime" for its effect on their lives. In that year, one of the nation's major banking houses, Jay Cooke and Company, failed to meet its financial obligations, and, with its closure, much of the late-nineteenth-century industrial house of cards collapsed. A substantial portion of Cooke's money had been placed in railroads, especially in the Northern Pacific, and, in the ensuing panic, a great deal of blame turned to railroads, their management, and their political influence. After all, Jay Cooke had been a chief financier of the Civil War for the North and had also helped lobby and promote extensive Republican subsidies to railroads and corporations. By 1876, perhaps 15 to 20 percent of all laborers suffered underemployment or unemployment. Farmers had been bitterly introduced to the first of many boom and bust cycles that typified an increasingly industrialized nation.

The administration of Ulysses S. Grant did little to help alleviate the problems of the first economic downturn after the Civil War. In fact, to many suffering farmers and industrial workers, politicians at all levels, whether Republican or Democrat, seemed unresponsive and even indifferent. Heavily in debt from oppressive mortgages and high interest rates,

A black sharecropper's family in Henderson County in 1884.
North Carolina Collection, University of North Carolina at Chapel Hill.

and with rapidly falling prices for their crops, farmers turned to one determinate solution they thought would bring them relief. They cried out for more paper money in circulation. Forced to repay debts with dollars whose value increased as the number in circulation decreased, farmers desperately sought to have the federal government increase the supply of greenbacks, paper money available for use as legal tender. In a stunning development, Grant vetoed such a greenback bill in 1874, thus fueling farmers' belief that government, controlled by a mysterious money power of capitalists like the Cookes and J. P. Morgans, served only the interests of big business and corporations. While a surge in farm prices blunted the effects of the panic by 1878, it did little to dull the resentments of farmers for the way government had ignored their pleas.

The briefness of the recovery after 1880 also gave farmers an insight into the boom and bust cycles brought about by industrialization and into their role in the new economy. Within the thirty years from 1865 to 1895, prices for farm goods fell by one-half. Caught up in a deflationary spiral with few respites, they intuitively if not rationally began to examine the new forces that now governed their lives. On both a practical and a judicious level, farmers understood that their failure to organize against increasingly impersonal and ever larger businesses, banks, railroads, corporations, and even government had left them more vulnerable and isolated in the New South than they had ever been in the Old South.

A small farmer in Macon County tending his land.
North Carolina Collection, University of North Carolina at Chapel Hill.

Two trends from 1880 to 1890—tenancy and increased farm ownership—mirrored the dilemma of farmers in North Carolina. First, the breakup of plantations and large farms after the Civil War and the end of slavery led to the evolution of sharecropping, tenancy, and farm ownership. In North Carolina, they seemed a natural adjustment to the problem of what to do with large numbers of landless, relatively unskilled, and poor people, both black and white. At first, sharecropping and tenancy provided a practical and necessary experience for farm ownership, but as the decades wore on they turned into dead-end work for scores of thousands of North Carolinians. In 1888 the *Progressive Farmer* called tenancy "a worse curse to North Carolina than droughts, floods, cyclones, storms, . . . caterpillars, and every other evil that attends the farmer."

Tenancy, sharecropping, crop liens, and "furnish" soon became staples of rural life in North Carolina after 1870. Local merchants and well-off landowners allowed tenants to occupy housing and "furnished" them provisions, supplies, equipment, even work animals, food, and clothing in return for their labor in bringing in a crop, usually tobacco or cotton. Part of the proceeds of the sale of the crop, a share, went to the indebted farmer who then had to pay off his crop lien for goods and supplies to the local merchant, often at usurious and arbitrary interest rates. Typically a crossroads merchant or a larger, more prosperous farmer, the furnisher who held the lien against the crop usually received one-third, while the farmer garnered the rest. Yet with inflated prices of furnish and extortionist charges, merchants and larger farmers frequently collected much more. In this way, declining prices for crops, especially staples such as tobacco and cotton, meant more and more indebtedness for sharecroppers, tenants, and farmers in general. When railroads penetrated all regions of the state by 1880 and brought North Carolina farmers into contact with distant markets, pressure increased to turn to profitable staples such as tobacco and cotton and away from subsistence farming overall. Tenants, sharecroppers, and small farmers resorted to local merchants and large landowners for monthly draws, or rations, for food, clothing, fertilizers, and seed. In a crucial way after 1870, North Carolina farmers failed to diversify, bought food that their parents had produced for themselves, and grew more cotton and tobacco than they could sell in a volatile and frequently declining market. In the absence of banks in rural areas, crossroads merchants, a new professional class in North Carolina after 1870, controlled local credit as well as politics. Linked by railroads to burgeoning centers of commerce and trade in Richmond, Charlotte, Nashville, and Atlanta, merchants and country stores spread the values of consumerism, modernization, and industrialization into rural North Carolina. "Merchants," groaned Leonidas Polk, the state's first commissioner of agriculture in 1877, had replaced "former masters and had made peons of them and their former slaves." Beset by declining prices, controlling merchants, and larger and larger indebtedness, many farmers did not understand the changing world in which they now lived. Few did, and politicians seemed to comprehend least of all.

Between 1880 and 1890, the number of farm owners in the state increased from 157,609 to 193,500, yet the average acreage plummeted from 142 to just over 100 acres per farm. Tenants occupied one-third of farms owned by someone else in 1880, a number that had risen to almost 40 percent by 1890. Sharecropping and farm tenancy typically remained high among the eastern coastal counties and well into the Piedmont, areas where cotton and tobacco flourished and where prices for land rose. Between 1870 and 1900, white tenants and sharecroppers always outnumbered blacks, but, in terms of percentages, more black farmers drifted into tenancy and out of outright ownership of farms.

Although depressed prices, indebtedness, tenancy, and sharecropping lay at the core of their problems, North Carolina farmers also had other grievances. Railroads that came to small towns and crossroads to bring glittering new products from afar and to take away local products charged rates that, to farmers, seemed excessive and discriminatory. Operating as individuals in the marketplace, farmers found that favorable rates went to larger wholesalers, middlemen, mills, corporations, and points such as Charlotte, Raleigh, and Gastonia, where goods could be centrally stored in depots and silos. No one regulated railroad rates, and, in spite of appeals and petitions, small farmers, an increasing majority throughout the state, came to understand that no one seemed to listen or care.

Farmers looked to Raleigh for help in creating a railroad commission to check for discriminatory rates and practices, but the Bourbon Democrats did little to respond. More and more farmers came to suspect that Democratic politicians had conspired with money men, capitalists, bankers, manufacturers, mill owners, and railroad barons to exploit their labor and production. If the Democrats would not create a railroad commission or enact legislation to regulate rates, then farmers must move into politics. At the state Farmers' Alliance meeting in 1887 in Raleigh, a delegate told representatives that "we don't advise bringing politics into . . . farmer's organizations, but we do advise taking . . . agricultural questions into politics." Within five years, farmers had all but abandoned an earlier alliance model of influencing politics and now wanted to control them directly. Increasingly angry

Leonidas Lafayette Polk (1837–92), leader of the Farmers' Alliance, in his Confederate uniform.
North Carolina Collection, University of North Carolina at Chapel Hill.

and frustrated with the decades-long political dance between Democrats and Republicans, farmers wanted to form their own party and initiate their own legislation. In lieu of having a state agency oversee and regulate railroads, farmers wanted North Carolina to own railroads outright and to run them for the greater interests of the people and not just for fat cats and plutocrats.

Three prophets, Leonidas L. Polk, Marion Butler, and Harry Skinner, two apostolic and one sidereal, emerged in North Carolina to articulate farmers' grievances. In their revelations and preachings, they mirrored not only the state's response to the farmers' malaise but also the nation's as a whole. Moreover, the dissonance of their approaches and solutions exposed the weaknesses in the farmers' revolt of the 1880s and 1890s and ultimately help explain why the People's Party, or the Populists, failed not only in North Carolina but throughout the nation as well. The two most influential, Polk and Butler, neatly fell on either side of the national election of 1892, the dividing line between Alliances and Populists.

Born on a farm in Anson County in 1837, Leonidas L. Polk knew only hardship and rough times as a youth. Orphaned at fourteen, he obtained only a common field school education, but he steadily became an avid reader of any books and pamphlets he could find. At the age of twenty-three, already a well-known orator and speaker, he ran for the general assembly. Elected in 1860, he had barely taken his seat when the vote for secession from the Union occurred. A cautious man, Polk hesitantly cast his ballot for secession, then resigned from the house and enlisted in the Confederate army as a private. Service in the Civil War only sharpened his leadership skills. After 1865, as an army man and a colonel, he again was elected to the general assembly, and, despite that body's absorption with carpetbag issues and reconstructing the state, his own interest increasingly turned to the problems besetting agriculture.

Disappointed with the persistent lack of concern over agricultural problems in the general assembly, Polk, in 1886, began publishing the weekly *Progressive Farmer,* the state's most important agricultural journal. As North Carolina's first agricultural commissioner, Polk used that office to promote several of his pet projects, namely the establishment of a state department of agriculture, a statewide farmer's organization, and an agricultural college to provide both education and technical assistance to farmers. Largely because of his advocacy, the North Carolina College of Agriculture and Mechanic Arts, now North Carolina State University, opened in the fall of 1889. Polk insisted that the college be set up near Raleigh so that politicians would not overlook it or its farmer-students.

Polk took his big idea of organizing farmers from two men, Oliver Hudson Kelley, the founder of the National Grange of the Patrons of Husbandry, and C. W. Macune, the all-purpose doctor from Texas and the father of the Farmers' Alliance. After the Civil War, Kelley, at the request of President Andrew Johnson, traveled throughout the Carolinas and Virginia to report on agricultural conditions in the former Confederate states. His report, a classic on the devastated rural slum that existed in the South just after the Civil War, predicted the coming of tenancy, indebtedness, sharecropping, and the monetary deflation that existed within a decade of the end of the war. Farmers, Kelley observed, overwhelmed by war and with little capital, would soon become "the lien law slave of the merchant." Kelley's solution? A national organization of farmers, fraternal and educational in nature, that would embrace the South, West, and North and draw the sections together to overcome the hatred and resentment that lingered from the war. He envisioned farmers coming together like "the Mississippi and its tributaries," all flowing into a common confluence, into "a national organization and its subordinates."

Kelley first called his new organization the League of Husbandry but soon settled on "Patrons" instead of the more formal "League." Inspired by a novel he had read on English plowmen, he designated individual lodges as granges. He planned a secret order, patterned after the Masons, but with only four degrees, one for each of the seasons. Unlike the speculative Masons, however, he wanted a practical meeting each month where members always could carry away something of use. Officers had titles such as master overseer, chaplain, steward, gatekeeper, and secretary. No treasurer existed to tithe members. Kelley's insistence upon progressive learning and a land-grant college for farmers and mechanical arts in every state gave substance to Polk's thinking. Even Kelley's vision of a statewide agricultural fair held every fall—with prizes and awards given to men, women, and children for produce and exhibits and the proceeds donated to the poor—appealed to the stoic and practical Polk.

Kelley's emphasis upon the fraternal and educational to the exclusion of the political, however, did not address one of Polk's concerns: how to bring the farmhouse into the statehouse. Kelley, ever the utopian visionary, thought that the Patrons of Husbandry, like the mighty Mississippi, would prove irresistible to politicians because of its size and overweening presence. With members in the millions, it would be a constant reminder, a standing pressure group that would lobby for millions of dollars in farm aid, bring about the creation of a national department of agriculture, push the federal government to gather data on farmers and their problems, and send out farm agents with scientific knowledge to lecture to farmers throughout the nation. In Polk's eyes, Kelley, while Moses-like in his appeal, did not have the appropriate commandments for farmers in his writings and revelations. Instead, Polk soon found himself fascinated with another "Moses" of rural democracy, the alliance's C. W. Macune.

A self-educated lawyer, physician, veterinarian, and progressive farmer, Macune found in the growing farmer's cooperatives in the West and the South—alliances, as they soon came to be called—the perfect vehicle for his aspirations and talents. Resembling more an Irish bartender from New York than a Texas farmer, Macune, with his quick wit, "hail fellow well met" personality, and enormous personal charm, rose quickly in the farmers' groups to become executive secretary of the Southern Alliance by 1886. At a convention in Shreveport, Louisiana, in October 1887, C. W. Macune first met the sedate, serious, black-bearded, and determined Leonidas Polk. By April 1887 Polk, along with Sydenham B.

Alexander, an equally important and well-known farmers' spokesman in North Carolina, had organized the Ash Pole Alliance, the first in the state, at Rockingham, east of Charlotte in Richmond County. Within a year the ever spreading alliance movement counted over forty-two thousand members in its wheels, or chapters, throughout the state. Polk and Alexander went to Shreveport to represent North Carolina at the alliance convention that fall.

If Polk found in the portly, mustached, and charismatic Macune the prophet he ardently sought, then Macune also encountered the perfect apostle in Polk, a serious thinker, artful writer, and Lincoln-like speaker. Unlike the Patrons of Husbandry, the alliance had no organizational blueprint, no rituals, ceremonies, practices, observances, celebrations, or even secret handshakes to give it roots and a foundation. Growing out of farmer's grievances and needs in remote corners of the South and the West, it instead spread like a version of modern-day kudzu, soon covering fifteen states and numbering in the millions. Macune needed men like Polk to give the organization form and substance. At Shreveport, Macune made Polk vice president of "the great alliance."

The amorphous nature of alliances perfectly suited Polk. Watching the movement swallow farmer's wheels, mutual aid associations, Brothers of Freedom chapters, even embryonic labor unions as it went from state to state, Macune the visionary warned that the coalition would "burst both political parties into atoms and scatter them like a star dust throughout the universe." Although the alliance formally disdained forming a political party, it suggested that exact probability should the Democrats and Republicans ignore its teachings. Attacked by the press in the Midwest and Northeast because it at first included the word "white" in its title, the Southern Alliance dropped the adjective from its description and deliberately changed its eligibility clause to include "Colored." Moreover, both white and black wheels frequently met in Georgia, Arkansas, Texas, and North Carolina. To Polk, the alliance, by including colored wheels, suggested a harmony of interests that he had found missing since Reconstruction.

Macune believed in alliance exchanges, cooperatives where farmers, by eliminating middlemen and merchants, could market their products, purchase supplies and equipment at reduced prices, and deal with railroads and businesses on a more equitable basis. In Arkansas, Kentucky, and Missouri, alliances had set up cooperative stores, tobacco warehouses, and equipment outlets, sometimes with state aid, that saved farmers thousands of dollars and allowed them to market their produce at better prices. To Polk, Macune's preachings went beyond those of Kelley's National Grange, offering North Carolinians more than just socializing, lectures, and high spirits.

By 1890, the Southern Alliance had 2,147 wheels and more than 90,000 members in North Carolina. Polk moved his publication, the *Progressive Farmer,* from Winston to Raleigh, where it became a vehicle for the dissemination of alliance ideas. The turning point for the alliance movement came in Saint Louis in December 1889. There, Polk, succeeding Macune as national president of the alliance, sat on the Committee of Monetary Systems, an innocent-sounding name for an advisory group that, because of its emphasis upon money as the key reform of the decade, inadvertently guided the fate of farmers' movements in the 1890s. Thoughtful and focused, Polk explained a plan given to him by Harry Skinner, a Greenville attorney, that, in its simplicity and directness, appeared to solve most of the farmers' problems. Skinner wanted the state or federal government to create a system of warehouses in large agricultural counties where farmers could store their produce when prices dropped. He reasoned that since farmers sold their crops in late summer, the time when the market was glutted, why should not they, like businesses, wait for the market to rise and then sell when demand was higher? The federal government could issue farmers greenbacks at 80 percent of a crop's current value to settle their yearly debts. When the market improved, farmers would get a bonus from the sale of their warehoused surpluses, thus seeing them through hard times. If prices declined, then farmers still had a guaranteed income that allowed them a limited means to overcome their chronic indebtedness. Skinner's idea solved a problem Macune had pondered for over a decade: how to bring immediate relief to farmers when prices fell. Fascinated by the scheme, Macune called the warehouses "subtreasuries," a more appealing epithet that implied they stored money as well as crops. The convention easily endorsed the idea, and the subtreasury plan dominated alliance and Populist thinking for over a decade.

Spurred on by Polk and the alliance, North Carolina elected a farmers' legislature in 1891 that enacted an impressive number of reforms. For the first time, North Carolina created a railroad commission to regulate and monitor rates and practices. Not only did Polk have his wish for agricultural colleges for white men in Raleigh and black men in Greensboro, but the state also founded a normal college for white women in Greensboro and another for black and white women in Elizabeth City. The state also created an agency to help farmers in purchasing farm equipment, seed, fertilizers, supplies, even food for the home. By 1892, the agency had saved farmers perhaps $500,000, a significant sum.

By the spring of 1892, Leonidas Polk, with his successes in North Carolina and the Farmers' Alliance, had achieved national prominence and recognition. In 1889, with the failure of alliances at the Saint Louis convention to form a political party and to agree upon a common set of goals, attention had turned to still another grassroots movement, the People's Party, more commonly known as the Populists. Recognizing the weaknesses of the alliances, Polk shifted his interest to the Populists; by 1892 he had positioned himself as a leading presidential candidate for the most important new political party since the Civil War. Polk's death in June 1892 opened the door for James B. Weaver of Iowa to become the first Populist presidential candidate. He polled over one million votes and won an impressive twenty-two electoral votes. Suddenly, the nation had a viable third party to challenge the Democrats and Republicans

In North Carolina, Marion Butler emerged not only as Polk's successor but also as a Pauline interpreter of Populism and a person who helped guide farmers to the one issue that defined their revolt. Born on a farm in Sampson County, Butler graduated from the University of North Carolina in 1885 and looked forward to a satisfying career in Raleigh as a lawyer and politician. However, he quickly moved back to Sampson County in late 1885 when his father died, taking over his family's farm and founding a small academy to educate his younger relatives and neighbors' children. When the alliance movement swept over southeastern North Carolina in 1887, Butler joined, almost immediately becoming head of the Sampson County wheel. At twenty-seven, his fellow farmers sent him to Raleigh in 1890 as an alliance Democrat in the state senate. An admirer of Polk and Macune, Butler became a key figure in helping pass legislation in the 1891 farmers' legislature. Chosen head of the state Farmers' Alliance that same year, he became first vice president of the

John C. Dancy, a black leader in the 1890s who initially opposed the alliance of Republicans with the Populists.
North Carolina Collection, University of North Carolina at Chapel Hill.

National Alliance in 1892 and, after Polk's death, president of the entire organization in 1893. Rarely had someone so young and obscure risen with such rapidity in state and national affairs. Cometlike, he would also quickly disappear.

The election of 1892 changed not only Butler's thinking but also the state's political geography. Increasingly, Butler grew disheartened with the tactics of the Democrats and his role within the party. By the summer of 1892, when the national party nominated Grover Cleveland of New York, a strong enemy of inflating the currency through the coinage of silver, Butler found himself drawn to the Populists, whose inflationary stand on silver, sixteen to one, he favored. Butler had come to believe that more money in circulation meant less misery for farmers, yet he saw little chance that conservative Democrats would ever champion such a radical idea. Moreover, the rigidity of North Carolina Democrats and of their party frustrated him. In 1892, Butler and many alliance Democrats wanted to vote for Weaver in the presidential election yet run on the Democratic slate locally. Democratic Party pols insisted that Butler and alliance men could not split the ticket between the state and nation, that loyalty counted above all. Still, Weaver's surprising success helped convince Butler and other alliance Democrats that the Populists had created a viable third party that embraced their views, and in 1893 they walked out of the "white man's party" of the Democrats that had redeemed North Carolina from the "evils of Reconstruction" and had ruled the state in an increasingly rigid fashion ever since. The withdrawal of Butler and of many alliance men from the Democratic Party set in motion a chain of events that, in the end, meant the last stand in the nineteenth century not only for farmers in the state but also for blacks. For two decades, African Americans in North Carolina had watched as Democrats slowly eroded their civil and civic rights. Two trends especially bothered black leaders such as Henry Plummer Cheatham, John C. Dancy, and James H. Young. First, the Democrats promoted themselves as "the white man's party," and, in a series of laws and practices, gradually had relegated African Americans, almost all of whom still belonged to the Republican Party, to the margin of North Carolina politics. Young especially resented a series of tricky and more often than not dishonest election laws that presaged the onerous grandfather and literacy tests yet to come. To get around the preponderance of black voters in eastern counties, Democrats further centralized political power in Raleigh, and, through the use of patronage, monopolized local county offices through appointments. As Young observed, blacks could not elect a black coroner even in Craven County, where a majority of the births and deaths were African American.

A more ominous drift bothered Cheatham and Dancy. Between 1876 and 1892 the number of lynchings had increased each year. Segregated in their own communities and with little protection from police or other law enforcement agencies, African Americans, although not defenseless, increasingly had become scapegoats for the ills that beset post-Reconstruction society. Terrorist raids led by gangs of Red Shirts, local paramilitary groups, and a resurgence of the Ku Klux Klan only intensified the fears of African Americans. Black leaders sensed a growing disaffection from the white majority throughout the state, and to them night rides and lynchings underscored an increasing distance and hostility between the two races.

Butler correctly understood that as a brand new political party the Populists needed help either from sympathetic Democrats or else blacks in the Republican Party to succeed. As head of the National Farmers' Alliance, Butler advocated a policy that came to be known as "fusion," a word he coined that forever entered North Carolina's political glossary. Its success in North Carolina and elsewhere vaulted him into power as the national chairman of the People's Party and one of the most influential Populists of the 1890s. Fusion would allow two political parties in a state to blend their platforms and candidates. In the West, Democrats and Populists, both favoring an increased coinage of silver, could cooperate by selecting slightly different slates but agreeing on only one set of issues. In southern states, history and race played a more significant role. Fusion occured between Populists and Republicans, not Democrats. Republicans would agree with Populists on key issues, perhaps even allow them to help in choosing a gubernatorial candidate, and, in return, Populists, most of whom came from the Democratic Party, would vote Republican. In the meantime, the Populists kept their party alive in presidential elections and gradually built grassroots organizations and support among Democrats and Republicans at the state level. To Butler, the swing vote of Populists and an increased participation by blacks would ensure election in states like North Carolina, where only a few thousand votes made a difference in winning and losing.

Fusion created confusion among blacks in North Carolina. First, many African American leaders such as Dancy and Cheatham mistrusted the "white trash" and "hayseeds" who made up the bulk of the People's Party. To them, lynchers and the mob that terrified black communities came from the same farmer class, although of a meaner sort who once oversaw slaves and were patrollers on the lookout for runaways before the Civil War. Moreover, a great many black Republican leaders carefully had nurtured open and amicable ties with white businessmen, politicians, and merchants that would be endangered by fusion with farmers. Beneath those relationships with the white upper class lay a basic belief by conservative black leaders that the interests of African Americans would be best served by an alignment with "plutocrats," "aristocrats," and "fat cats," and not with their "croppers and tenants." Well-educated and thoughtful African Americans like John Dancy, a professional tradesman, editor, and collector of customs at Wilmington under the Republican president Benjamin Harrison from 1889 to 1893, had prospered from Republican ties and Democratic tolerance, and they did not want to risk such limited successes by a temporary interracial adventure with farmers.

Other black leaders opposed Dancy and Cheatham. James H. Young from Wake County and George H. White from Edgecombe County saw in Populism and fusion not a threat to the gains won by blacks since Reconstruction but a unique opportunity to promote and perhaps even liberate African Americans from that same status quo. Editor of the *Raleigh*

Gazette, perhaps the leading journal of a growing and influential black press, Young, elected to the state assembly as a Republican, instead came to believe in the ideas of Polk, Butler, and free silver as a panacea for the ills that beset black communities, especially sharecroppers and tenants. Young also distrusted the "lily white" leadership of the Republican Party that all but ignored blacks in governance and in leadership roles and only counted their votes during elections. A graduate of Howard University, an attorney and member of both the state house and senate in the 1880s, White saw in fusion with Populists increased political opportunities for blacks and an alternative to the Old Guard politics of the Republicans.

Marion Butler's Populists and the Republicans joined together in 1894 to forge an alliance that swept to an astonishing victory in North Carolina, taking over both houses of the legislature by substantial majorities. Butler and the Republicans had shocked Tar Heel Democrats with their first statewide defeat since Reconstruction, and politics as usual, at least for the old Bourbons, had ended. Butler, the Populists, and their new allies, the Republicans, immediately set about to turn their reforms into reality. To black leaders such as Young, Cheatham, and Dancy, the promises and talk of the fusion farmers would now be measured by their actions. They were not disappointed. Within six months, the general assembly had restored self-government to counties, taking it away from Raleigh and allowing local elections for office. Voters could now elect justices of the peace and county commissioners as well as local officers such as registers of deeds and sheriffs. New election laws that set up voter registration lists along with oversight by election officials from both parties helped ensure more honest elections.

The 1895 legislature also addressed two additional issues that troubled African Americans: more aid to public schools and equal protection under the law. Statewide property taxes for education increased, with larger appropriations going to universities, both white and black, and to county commissioners for local schools. Recognizing that appointed county school superintendents and boards of education had created perpetual hierarchies that often worked against public education, the general assembly abolished them and instead turned local school affairs over to elected county commissioners, a move that opened up education but also made it less professional in its implementation. By allowing more control by counties and cities over local affairs, the assembly also assured that eastern counties with a majority of blacks could elect sheriffs, appoint deputies, and supervise police affairs through county commissions and city councils. Smarting against usurious rates charged by merchants and creditors, the assembly also capped interest rates at 6 percent. The legislature then rewarded the leaders of the fusion movement, Marion Butler from the east and Jeter C. Pritchard from the west, by electing them to the senate, common constitutional practice in statehouses before the Seventeenth Amendment changed the method of election to a direct popular vote. Buoyed by the successes of 1894, Marion Butler looked forward to a bright future for the Populists not only in North Carolina but in the nation, as a whole. Looking ahead, he saw the Populists emerging as a major political party in the nation with the Democrats gradually disappearing, as had other major political parties in the past.

For Populists and Republicans, farmers and blacks, the national election of 1896, both locally and nationally, came to be a Pyrrhic victory. The Republican national convention assembled on 16 June, came out unreservedly for sound money, and named William McKinley of Ohio, a high-tariff man who read prepared speeches from his front porch to friendly reporters on the virtues of gold and monetary standards. Silver-backed Republicans from the western states, many of whom, like Sen. Henry Teller of Colorado and Sen. Richard Pettigrew of South Dakota, had fused with the Populists locally, promptly bolted the party, and looked to Butler and the Populists for leadership in their upcoming convention.

The Democrats convened at Chicago the first week of July and were expected by Butler and the Populists in every respect to follow a similar course. Grover Cleveland, the incumbent president and leader of the eastern wing of the party, counted upon the delegates endorsing William C. Whitney, his former secretary of the navy, multimillionaire adviser, and designated successor. Butler understood the dynamics of both parties and conventions, and he expected a split over the silver issue. He also believed that, in the end, disaffected Republicans and Democrats would flock to the Populists. Anticipating and planning for the election in 1896, Butler accordingly scheduled the Populist nominating convention for 22 July in Saint Louis, just after both parties had selected their candidates. Yet something went terribly wrong at the Democratic convention in Chicago the second week of July.

In a stunning development, the Democrats cast aside the conservatives and Grover Cleveland, along with his handpicked successor, the millionaire William Whitney. Ignoring the threat of a split party and Whitney's trains—filled with supporters, cigars, and drink—the delegates veered left. In one defining moment, William Jennings Bryan, the "boy orator" from Nebraska and a political phenomenon, took the delegate's political breath away with his "cross of gold" speech. A passionate advocate of free silver, Bryan, preeminently a missionary and an evangelist for issues, cloaked free silver in biblical terms in his speech. "You shall not press down upon the brow of labor this cross of thorns," the gold standard, he thundered, "you shall not crucify mankind on a cross of gold." A consummate politician as well as an inspirational speaker, Bryan quietly had built up delegate support largely from the gathering movement toward silver in the six months before the convention. He also distanced himself from politicians from both parties and from traditional politicking and deal-making during the convention. The "cross of gold" speech turned the convention and also the election of 1896 into a national crusade for silver.

Bryan's nomination both shocked and perplexed Butler. It meant that the Democrats had preempted the silver-first strategy of the Populists and most of its platform as well. Butler had done much to promote reforms while a senator, bringing up the free silver issue in the senate, advocating an income tax, attacking Cleveland's administration, and making an inflated currency "the one overshadowing issue in the next great struggle between the classes and the masses." Moreover, Butler had long spoken for "putting principle above party," mostly because he wanted to recruit Populists from the Democrats and Republicans, both of whom seemed to have few morals and mandates except that of reelection. Now the Populists had to decide upon the principle of free silver or the very existence of their own political party.

Bryan's past history also seemed to make him more a Populist than a Democrat. Nebraska Populists had written both James Weaver and Butler that everything Bryan stood for made him "practically a Populist, except in name." As a thirty-two-year-old congressman from Nebraska, he vehemently advocated free silver, yet somehow as a thirty-four-year-old

Elias Carr (1839–1900), governor from 1893 to 1897.
North Carolina Collection, University of North Carolina at Chapel Hill.

senator from North Carolina, Butler had lost sight of Bryan in his own ardor for the same issue. For his part, the Nebraskan had not overlooked Butler and the possibilities raised by fusion. At Chicago, he believed that his nomination resulted more from "the friendly relations existing between Democrats, Populists, and silver Republicans than to any other one cause" and not to his stirring speech. If Butler brought the South into the Democratic fold, then Bryan, unlike a Populist, could carry the South as well as his native West, and, with that, the nation. The Democrats knew that in 1896 they "must have the solid south" to offset McKinley's strength in the East, and they looked to the Populists for support.

The thought of incorporation by the Democrats in the 1896 election appalled Marion Butler and a great many southern Populists. No matter what the "great principles" of free silver or the logic of fusion with the Democrats necessitated, sectional and state requirements demanded the existence of a separate and distinct Populist Party. In North Carolina, the very political lives of farmers such as Butler and of Republicans such as Daniel Russell and George White depended upon the preservation of a Populist Party. Still, the split between the pro-Bryan Populists from the West and the "midroaders" from the South, who only demurely endorsed him, presaged the death of the Populists after 1896. The Saint Louis convention reluctantly endorsed Bryan as the Populist candidate but chose Tom Watson from Georgia as its vice presidential candidate in a last flurry of independent defiance.

The twilight of the farmer's last stand in North Carolina came during the 1896 elections. Bitter and confused by Bryan's national campaign and its subsequent failure, state Populist and Republican leaders nonetheless came together to support local tickets for legislative, congressional, and lesser state offices. Daniel Russell, the Republican candidate, won the governor's race in a record turnout. In all, he polled 153,787 votes to the Democrat

Cyrus Watson's 145,266. Defiant to the end, Populists, although implicitly agreeing to support Russell, still cast 16,000 votes for their candidate, William A. Guthrie, and carried only Sampson County, Butler's home seat. The key difference in the election lay in the increased turnout of Republicans, 59,000 more than had voted in 1892, and in the efforts of black Republicans, especially James Young and George White, who had promoted greater participation through the series of election reform laws passed earlier by "fused" legislatures. State Democratic Party leaders noted both facts and began planning not only to marginalize the "redneck vote" but also to eliminate "the Negro problem" altogether from North Carolina politics.

As governor from 1897 to 1901, Daniel Russell appointed more than three hundred black magistrates to office. In cities such as Wilmington and in predominantly black counties such as Craven, Warren, and New Hanover, record numbers of African Americans, in cooperation with local Populist, Republican, and business leaders, became mayors, council members, registers of deeds, deputy sheriffs, coroners, and county commissioners. For example, between 1897 and 1901, New Hanover County and the city of Wilmington had more than forty elected and appointed black officials. The rolls of outstanding African Americans elected to the general assembly certainly would include Henry Eppes, a Methodist minister from Halifax who eventually served ten years in the state senate, and William P. Mabson, a former school teacher and leader of the Republican Party in Edgecombe County. North Carolina also elected three black congressmen during the farmers' revolt—J. E. O'Hara (1883–87), Henry P. Cheatham (1889–93), and George H. White (1897–1901)—to go to Washington. White would be the last black North Carolina congressman for almost a century, the last from the South for more than half a century, and the last nationwide for over a quarter of a century. After White, North Carolina did not elect blacks to Congress until Eva Clayton and Mel Watt in 1992. Moreover, Jeter Pritchard and Marion Butler would be the last Republicans and Populists to serve in the senate until the last decades of the twentieth century as well. A multitude of lasts followed the failure of the Populists to take root in North Carolina politics.

The farmers' revolt ended in the confusion created by fusion with the Republicans and with the failure of the charismatic Bryan to win the presidential election. Between 1896 and 1900, other unforeseen national and international events combined to bring about the gradual dissolution of the Populists. To many farmers, more money meant less misery, and, after 1897 more currency and an inflated economy lessened their plight. Primarily because of discoveries of gold in Alaska and South Africa, the world's gold output doubled that of 1880, and by 1900 it had more than tripled. When the Republicans pushed through the Gold Standard Act in 1900, few protested or hardly noticed. There was no need. Free silver had lost its temporal appeal. With more money in circulation and with increased prosperity, farmers felt that they at last had found a place for themselves in an international, increasingly industrialized society. Additionally, the Spanish-American War in 1898 turned attention to international affairs. As Tom Watson of Georgia noted, "The blare of the bugle drowned the voice of the Reformer." North Carolina sent both white and African American regiments to fight in the war.

Yet the dynamism of Populist reform and the ensuing farmers' revolt in North Carolina met another fate, different from that of its southern neighbors. Its last stand little resembled that in Georgia and South Carolina. In Georgia, an embittered Tom Watson turned upon blacks, Jews, and Catholics, blaming them for the failure of Populism and using them as political scapegoats. In South Carolina, "Pitchfork" Ben Tillman became a demagogue, appealing to the racial fears of southern whites and to their reactionary impulses against change and reform. As Populism fell apart in some southern and western states, it retrogressed into its always-present baser elements of race and class prejudice. In modern political rhetoric, Populism came to stand for demagoguery, hatemongering, and provincialism and not for its ambitious attempt to reform and stabilize a new industrial order.

In North Carolina, Marion Butler kept his principles even as his party disintegrated. After Bryan's last hurrah in the presidential election of 1900, Butler even became a Republican rather than return to the "white man's party" of the Democrats. Always a reformer who continued to campaign for the direct election of senators as well as a progressive income tax even after 1900, he refused to embrace the racism and prejudice that permeated North Carolina after 1898. A close reading of his letters and papers reveals no bias toward Jews or Catholics, only the intention of giving them equal rights in society. Like so many Populists in North Carolina, Butler echoed the sentiments of the farmer who wrote him in 1900 maintaining that he was "not in favour of the negro but I do beleave in giving the pore negro his dues." So did Marion Butler. Led by Furnifold Simmons, North Carolina Democrats set out vengefully to redeem North Carolina for a second time in 1898 and to end once and for all any further attempts by blacks, farmers, and Republicans to reconstruct the state.

The legacy of the farmers' last stand lay not in a failure to understand the world or to react to the complicated issues of the 1890s, but in the fundamental issues in state and national politics. Because of farmers and fusion, all North Carolinians benefited from more appropriations for public education and from the expansion of higher education for women, blacks, and those in the agricultural trades in general. Caps on interest rates and the efforts of the railroad commission to regulate rates, while ineffective or even bypassed, planted the idea that the state should and could proactively intervene to redress many of the inequities of industrialization. Moreover, the state now had an agricultural commissioner, and farmers at last had a permanent voice in state government. Yet the greatest legacy of the farmers' revolt lay in the bright promise it brought of changing society as a whole, and in the excitement it gave to North Carolina politics, however brief and flawed. In 1892, a total of 280,203 North Carolinians voted, a significant increase over 1888. Four years later, the total climbed to 330,254, the largest number of North Carolinians to vote for the next forty years. Regardless of the quaintness of the silver issue today, scores of thousands in the latter part of the nineteenth century understood that it had become, in Butler's words, "the one overshadowing issue in the great struggle . . . between the classes." When asked if anyone understood the monetary issue, James A. Garfield, a congressman from Ohio in 1880, jokingly replied that, yes, one person in Congress did, and he was mad. No one quite comprehended silver and gold as issues in the great monetary struggles during the last decades of the nineteenth century, but almost everyone grasped their decisiveness in determining the nation's fate. Marion Butler and the Populists should not be dismissed as mere farmers reacting to an increasingly more complex and industrialized society by longing for a Jeffersonian past. Indeed, most of the farmers' reforms eventually made their way into the fabric of state and national society. As she watched the successes of the Progressives some twenty years later, Florence Faison Butler, Marion's wife and also a shrewd strategist, pointed out that, when the Populists advocated the same reforms "that the whole country is now, we were called 'long-haired cranks.' Does it not seem funny how soon people forget, or, rather, I might say, how long it takes them to learn?" North Carolina learned from the Populists long after they were forgotten.

More than politics, race, and reform, the farmers' last stand in North Carolina meant the end of a way of life that had defined and delineated them as Tar Heels for more than two centuries. In reality, the "culture" in "agriculture" stood for a timeless attachment to the land; a seasonal pattern of labor; a daily set of routines; a shared labor among men, women, and children; a traditional and hierarchical social order bound by deference and formality; and a series of smaller rituals, customs, protocols, and practices that had characterized and explained life in North Carolina since 1663. No longer. Oliver Hudson Kelley and the Granger movement had hit upon something vital to farmers when they emphasized not politics but community, family, high spirits, and the enjoyment of the culture of farming as a way of life. Small wonder that granges symbolically survived but politics and Populism did not. In the twenty-first century, of a farm culture that had defined North Carolina for centuries, only nostalgia and sentiment, both wrapped in commercial convenience, remain.

ADDITIONAL READINGS

Bromberg, Alan B. "'Worst Muddle Ever Seen in N.C. Politics': The Farmers' Alliance, the Subtreasury, and Zeb Vance." *North Carolina Historical Review* 56 (January 1979): 19–40.

Carroll, Grady L. E. *Leonidas Lafayette Polk and Samuel A'Court Ashe: Faithful Public Servants.* Raleigh: Published by author, 1981.

Crow, Jeffrey J. "'Fusion, Confusion, and Negroism': Schisms among Negro Republicans in the North Carolina Election of 1896." *North Carolina Historical Review* (October 1976): 364–84.

Durden, Robert F. "Battle of the Standards in 1896 and North Carolina's Place in the Mainstream." *South Atlantic Quarterly* 63 (Summer 1964): 336–50.

Edmonds, Helen G. *The Negro and Fusion Politics in North Carolina 1894–1901.* New York: Russell and Russell, 1973.

Faulkner, Ronnie W. "North Carolina Democrats and Silver Fusion Politics, 1892–1896." *North Carolina Historical Review* 59 (July 1982): 230–51.

Goodwyn, Lawrence. *Democratic Promise: A Short History of the Agrarian Revolt in America.* New York: Oxford University Press, 1978.

Hicks, John D. "Farmers' Alliance in North Carolina." *North Carolina Historical Review* 2 (April 1925): 162–87.

Hunt, James L. "The Making of a Populist: Marion Butler, 1863–1895." *North Carolina Historical Review* (January 1985): 53–77; (April 1985): 179–202; (July 1985): 317–43.

Kimmel, Bruce I. "Political Sociology of Third Parties in the United States: A Comparative Study of the People's Party in North Carolina, Georgia and Minnesota." Ph.D. diss., Columbia University, 1981.

Kretschmann, James F. "North Carolina Department of Agriculture, 1877–1900." Master's thesis, University of North Carolina, 1955.

Mabry, William A. *Negro in North Carolina Politics since Reconstruction.* New York: AMS Press, 1970.

McMath, Robert C., Jr. "Agrarian Protest in the Forks of the Creek: Three Subordinate Farmers' Alliances in North Carolina." *North Carolina Historical Review* 51 (January 1974): 41–63.

————. *Populist Vanguard: A History of the Southern Farmers' Alliance.* New York: Norton and Co., 1977.

Muller, Philip R. "New South Populism: North Carolina, 1884–1920." Ph.D. diss., University of North Carolina, 1971.

Noblin, Stuart. *Leonidas LaFayette Polk, Agrarian Crusader.* Chapel Hill: University of North Carolina Press, 1949.

Noblin, Stuart, and Bill Humphries. *Hold High the Torch: The Grange in North Carolina, 1929–1989.* Greensboro: North Carolina State Grange, 1990.

Paoli, Donna J. "Marion Butler's View of the Negro, 1889–1901." Master's thesis, University of North Carolina, 1969.

Redding, Kent T. "Failed Populism: Movement-Party Disjuncture in North Carolina, 1890 to 1900." *American Sociological Review* 57 (June 1992): 340–52.

Schulup, Leonard. "Adlai E. Stevenson and the 1892 Campaign in North Carolina: A Bourbon Response to Southern Populism." *Southern Studies* 2 (Summer 1991): 131–50.

Schwartz, Michael. *Radical Protest and Social Structure: The Southern Farmers' Alliance and Cotton Tenancy, 1880–1890.* New York: Academic Press, 1976.

Smith, Robert W. "Rhetorical Analysis of the Populist Movement in North Carolina, 1892–1896." Ph.D. diss., University of Wisconsin, 1957.

Steelman, Joseph F. "Republican Party Strategists and the Issue of Fusion with Populists in North Carolina, 1893–1894." *North Carolina Historical Review* 47 (July 1970): 244–69.

Sumner, Jim L. "'Let us Have a Big Fair': The North Carolina Exposition of 1884." *North Carolina Historical Review* 69 (January 1992): 57–81.

Trelease, Allen W. "Fusion Legislatures of 1895 and 1897: A Roll-Call Analysis of the State House of Representatives." *North Carolina Historical Review* 57 (July 1980): 280–309.

Weaver, Philip J. "The Gubernatorial Election of 1896 in North Carolina." Master's thesis, University of North Carolina, 1937.

Whitener, Daniel J. "The Republican Party and Public Education in North Carolina, 1867–1900." *North Carolina Historical Review* 37 (July 1960): 382–96.

Wilson, Jeanette Ouren. "One Hundred and One Years: Solomon Isaac Blair's School, the High Point Normal and Industrial Institute, and William Penn High School." *Southern Friend* 44 (October 1995): 22–31.

A Progressive State

Between the end of the farmers' revolt in the 1890s and the beginning of World War I, an amorphous, loosely organized reform movement called Progressivism swept over the South and the nation. At first glance, Progressive reformers seemed to reflect a mood, a need to address the ills of industrialization and urbanization, rather than a coherent movement advocating a specific agenda for change. Progressivism itself became part of a broad process of adjustment to a new industrial order. It took different forms in cities and states and in the West, East, and especially the South. In Mississippi, James K. Vardaman personified the often inconsistent motives and agenda of southern Progressives. The very image of an antebellum planter in his long, flowing white coat with a tangled mass of hair wildly cascading to his shoulders, Vardaman relentlessly campaigned for the "hillbilly" vote, all the while deliberately challenging entrenched business interests and attacking lynching as a "vile crime." In North Carolina, Charles B. Aycock, the youngest of ten children of a small farmer and politician in Wayne County, earnestly supported education for both whites and blacks while still endorsing the concept of segregation. Although regionally divided, all reflected the unstructured, frequently formless yet passionate attempt to reform the nation at the turn of the century.

Fletcher Watson Waynick and one of his early automobiles made in Rockingham County.
North Carolina Collection, University of North Carolina at Chapel Hill.

Wright Brothers' flight,
17 December 1903.
North Carolina Collection,
University of North
Carolina at Chapel Hill.

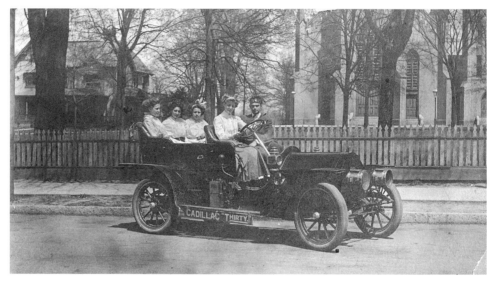

A 1907 Cadillac in front of the First Presbyterian Church on West Trade Street in Charlotte.
North Carolina Collection, University of North Carolina at Chapel Hill.

The roots of Progressivism lay in the chaos and uncertainty of industrialization and urbanization that swept the country in the 1880s. In the South, the philosophy of Henry Grady and New Southerners who wanted to "out Yankee the Yankee" created a profound societal disequilibrium as it sought to promote change. As textile, tobacco, and furniture mills and towns replaced farms and smaller communities, southerners, firmly planted in traditions and institutions both politically and socially, now found themselves suddenly displaced, rootless, and facing an uncertain future. Writing from Nashville in 1909, a Vanderbilt University faculty member noted that "the most capable business men, lawyers, doctors, and preachers are practically all leaving the country for the city and town." New cities such as Atlanta, Birmingham, and Charlotte became "the great centers of life . . . influence, and authority," dominating southern culture and politics. Yet the hurried growth of towns and urban centers also intensified an inbred southern need for order and stability, creating, as it did, new classes of merchants, entrepreneurs, service workers, public planners, administrators, and public health officials who entered a rapidly growing middle class. Indeed, the new professionals of the South led the Progressive movement, especially in North Carolina.

The arrival of the railroad and the utilization of the telephone in North Carolina helped spur the growth of the middle class and their organizations. Towns, cities, and even farm communities found themselves less isolated and even more interconnected in terms of vocations and specializations. Bankers, merchants, chambers of commerce, social workers, and traditional professions such as medicine and the law came together voluntarily and by association. Not surprisingly, women increasingly formed interest groups after 1890 that centered around issues such as suffrage, Prohibition, and child welfare. The organizational impulse that moved through the nation between 1890 and 1920 drew much of its southern stimulus from North Carolina, where women such as Gertrude Weil used clubs as a base to combat many of the ills of New South society. Some groups, such as the National Tuberculosis Society, focused on a specific problem, while others, such as the General Federation of Women's Clubs, promoted more inclusive causes. Others, such as the Band of Hope, a temperance organization founded by blacks in Raleigh in the 1870s, reflected common concerns over the regulation of community morality and "race improvement." In almost every case, Progressivism gave an opportunity for these diverse groups to promote their separate, sometimes conflicting agendas within the public sphere.

In North Carolina, a series of events and circumstances set in motion a succession of reform attempts among these various groups and interests. The first, the panic of 1893, exposed the weakness of the state's still largely agricultural economy. The downward spiral of farm prices from 1893 to 1895 threatened North Carolina's farms and smaller towns with still more mortgage indebtedness and peonage. Between 1885 and 1890 the price of wheat dropped two-thirds from $1.10 per pound to $.37 per pound. Temporarily buoyed by the demand of textile mills, cotton prices, which had risen to $.20 per pound as early as 1871, declined to half that by 1893. Railroads, largely sponsored by state funds and bonds, added to the general economic malaise by discrimination through rates and carriers. The moribund Democratic Party paid little attention to the economic ills besetting the majority of North Carolinians, concentrating instead on promoting new industries and mills.

The second factor centered around the sudden rise and equally rapid decline of the Populist Party and the farmers' revolt of the 1890s. The successful fusion of the Populist and Republican parties after 1894 only underscored the weakening of traditional political parties within the state, especially the Democrats. Moreover, the alliance of Populists and Republicans spurred a second reconstruction of North Carolina, one that brought marginal voters, especially blacks, back into the electorate in substantial numbers. Their participation democratized the matrix of issues in Raleigh. Indeed, many of the rhetorical impulses of Populism, emphasizing as they did such issues as the state's ownership of railroads and the direct election of senators, continued well into the twentieth century and influenced a middle-class progressive impulse. Lastly, the success of the farmers' revolt exposed North Carolina's enduring political frailty and gave an opportunity for organized

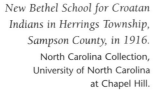

*New Bethel School for Croatan
Indians in Herrings Township,
Sampson County, in 1916.*
North Carolina Collection,
University of North Carolina
at Chapel Hill.

groups, whether farmers, women, or professionals, to influence public policy, a lesson not lost on the Progressives.

A third factor, that of race, emerged dramatically with the Wilmington riot of 1898, perhaps the most savage in the state's long history of civil disorder. On 10 November 1898, just after the general election, a large mob of some four hundred whites descended upon the offices of Alexander Manly, editor of the *Daily Record,* a black newspaper in Wilmington, and, after wrecking much of his equipment, burned the entire building. In the ensuing chaos, the throng, now grown to over six hundred, killed eleven blacks and wounded at least twenty-five more. Three white men suffered minor wounds. Two days later local militia units marched in and regained control of the city.

On the surface, the outburst seemed aimed at Manly, an outspoken defendant of African Americans, and at his 18 August editorial. In that article, Manly noted that, instead of whites always looking at black men making overtures toward white women, many should question why white women sometimes paid too much attention to black men who wanted few of their advances. The vagaries of whether whites or blacks had been too forward in their regard for each other sexually had less to do with the riot than the politics of the election that year. Sensing victory and incensed at the fusion alliance between Populists and Republicans, many of whose voters were black, that had deposed them in 1894 and again in 1896, Democrats played the race card in 1898. At that time, the political race card intimated that blacks, purportedly because of the arrogance given them by their newly elected "profligate politicians," had taken indecent liberties with white women. In 1898, sexuality and miscegenation defined racial boundaries within an increasingly segregated North Carolina society.

Because of its long association with Republicans and Reconstruction politics, Wilmington's "black rule" especially irritated Democrats such as Alfred Waddell, a local white businessman and politico. The fact that Wilmington had a white mayor, Silas Wright, and that whites easily made up the majority of officeholders and elected officials did little to assuage Waddell and his followers. Still, facts and truths such as these had less bearing on the riot

A cartoon depicting the fear of a race war in 1900.
North Carolina Collection, University of North Carolina at Chapel Hill.

than politics and perceptions. Backed by a coalition of businessmen and Red Shirts, a notorious paramilitary organization described as "redneck ruffians," Waddell began to plot to take over city government from the Republican-backed alliance. Manly's editorial, only one of many deemed offensive by Waddell and the Democrats in the year preceding the election, formed a convenient pretext to cloak Waddell's declared intent to take over city government. When Manly and hundreds of blacks fled after the murderous anarchy of 10 November, whites, almost all with Waddell's blessing, took over most city offices. In reality, the Wilmington race riot unmasked and highlighted the determination of white supremacists after 1898 to take over local and state government either legally or by a coup d'état.

"Bloody Wilmington" terrorized both blacks and whites. It brought into the open the ancient haunting specter of a race war while it also focused attention on the newer problem that had emerged since Reconstruction and fusion politics. What should be done with the black vote, the newest factor in North Carolina politics? To a growing middle class of white professionals and also to many African Americans who saw their hard-won political and social gains suddenly threatened, the chaos and anarchy portended by Wilmington sounded an alarm bell that signaled a larger conflagration just ahead. Scrambling for answers in a weakened political framework within the state, many Progressives eventually came to two solutions that seemed to them to be both pragmatic and prudent: segregation and disfranchisement. One removed African Americans from social contact with whites while the other got them out of the dirty business of "white politics." To a surprising degree, a great many enlightened, Progressive thinkers, white and black, embraced both ideas as reforms that would help both communities. Thus, in North Carolina, legal segregation and disfranchisement of African Americans ironically emerged as Progressive reforms alongside humanitarian impulses like those intended to help working children and end corruption in politics.

The symbiotic relationship between Progressivism and the ostracism, segregation, and disfranchisement of blacks manifested itself in the state's new governor, Charles B. Aycock. Nominated by a standing ovation in the Democratic Party's state convention in 1900, the popular Aycock promoted a platform that included better care for the insane, a direct primary for state elections, a minimum school year of four months, and also the endorsement

*An engraving depicting the exodus of blacks
from North Carolina during the height of
lynching and discrimination in the 1890s.*
North Carolina Collection, University
of North Carolina at Chapel Hill.

of the inappropriately named "suffrage amendment" that sought to get rid of the black vote. A spellbinding orator who abhorred the actions of the KKK and Red Shirts, likening them to "a pestilence" that stalked the state, he nonetheless agreed that eliminating the votes of blacks would help "clean up" North Carolina politics by doing away with the manipulation of elections and the fraud he associated with the introduction of black suffrage in 1868.

Once again following Mississippi's lead, the general assembly in 1899 had introduced a proposed amendment requiring that anyone registering to vote must pay a poll tax and also be able to read and write any section of the state constitution, a prerequisite that doubtless would have excluded all but a few of the representatives themselves. Yet if any person had qualified to vote before 1867, the year before black suffrage, the amendment continued, or if his lineal descendant failed to meet the new "literacy" requirement, they nonetheless could be grandfathered in if they registered to vote before 1 December 1908. By allowing many illiterate whites an additional opportunity to qualify, the amendment thus enfranchised them and extended the suffrage in North Carolina, at least on paper. The proposed amendment deceived no one. Although Aycock easily carried the state in 1900, the suffrage amendment, in a bitterly contested vote, passed by a much lesser margin, 182,217 to 128,285.

Lastly, the advent of Progressivism in North Carolina coincided with a historical happenstance that enshrouded and mistranslated reformist impulses, the passing of the Civil War generation. From Zebulon Vance to Leonidas Polk, almost all the prominent political figures who shaped state Democratic, Populist, and frequently even Republican parties had ties to the Confederacy. One wag commented that, in the 1880s, if you entered a Raleigh dining room and asked for "the colonel," half the gentlemen stood. Yet as the end of the century approached, Civil War veterans began dying daily by the scores. Reunions became smaller as monuments and commemorations grew larger. Almost every depiction of a

North Carolina delegates to the United Daughters of the Confederacy meeting in Richmond in 1925.
North Carolina Collection, University of North Carolina at Chapel Hill.

Fourth of July parade or an important event during the period included an increasingly smaller group of ex-Confederates at its head. By the end of World War I, few remained.

As Civil War veterans grew older, they turned to the legacy they would leave not only to the state but also to future generations. State holidays honored not only the birthday of Robert E. Lee but also a Confederate memorial day when the rebel battle flag would be flown in Raleigh. Scores of towns and cities rushed to erect monuments to the thousands who fell during the war. From Asheville to Wilmington, Confederate veterans' reunions served to romanticize and to remind the public of the South's heroic but lost cause. Yet perhaps the greatest shrine lay not in memorial days and in monuments but in the founding of commemorative societies such as the United Daughters of the Confederacy and the Sons of Confederate Veterans. To their sons, daughters, relatives, and future generations, dying Confederates institutionalized their legacy in these organizations. In fact, many of the Progressives, especially women, belonged not only to clubs seeking to change the state but also to organizations such as the United Daughters of the Confederacy, the largest woman's association in North Carolina at the turn of the century. In this way, the Old South's legacy of patriarchy, hierarchy, and racism underlay the Progressive impulse for change and order.

As the century drew to a close, these events, the depression of 1893, the revolt of the farmers in the mid-1890s, the Wilmington race riot of 1898, and the desire of a dying Civil War generation to institutionalize and preserve their legacy not only severely altered the state's political system but also shaped the Progressivist impulse within it. First, the political base, the electorate, drastically shrank from 1894 to 1914, from the height of the Populist revolt and fusionism to the gradual institutionalization of segregation. Disfranchisement laws, political ostracism, literacy tests, and restrictive election laws not only deprived most black North Carolinians of the ballot but also sharply restricted the participation of thousands of poor, illiterate, marginal whites as well. The suffrage amendment had worked only too well. In 1892, with Democrats in control, 280,203 North Carolinians voted. Four years later, with Republicans and Populists fused, participation increased to 330,254, a phenomenal 18 percent jump. In the election of 1912, only 148,105 North Carolinians voted. By 1914, the political participation of more than 125,000 blacks and 325,000 whites effectively had been eliminated.

The constriction of the electorate changed not only the complexion but also the class of participants in North Carolina politics. Between 1868 and 1900, 101 African Americans had been elected to the general assembly, 26 to the senate and 76 to the lower house. Since Reconstruction, voting and office holding by blacks, while they waxed and waned with the political fortunes of the Republican Party, had become commonplace throughout the state. Throughout their careers, blacks who served in Raleigh and Washington from Reconstruction until the turn of the century reflected a broad array of interests and concerns that afterward all but disappeared from North Carolina politics. First, Stewart Ellison of Raleigh, a city alderman for eight years, also oversaw the state penitentiary for four years, a position crucial to blacks and to Progressives, who saw the penal system as a corrupt, vicious institution that must be reformed. With African Americans largely absent in North Carolina's penal and criminal justice system as Progressivism wore on, chain gangs and convict labor, largely composed of blacks as well as poor whites, soon dotted the state's landscape. Another African American, James H. Harris of Wake County, spent four years as director of the Deaf, Dumb, and Blind School working to extend its social services to poor whites and blacks. While some historians have seen these posts as minor and as proof that African Americans did not have political clout during the period, in another view they accurately reflected the Progressives' belief that the extension of social services benefited everyone alike, whether white or black. Still, without political and social representation, African Americans increasingly found these state institutions less responsive to their needs and concerns.

The contraction of the electorate also eliminated a class of whites who elected Populist representatives like Charles Aycock, who, although they frequently professed racist views, also worked hard to improve public roads and education, increase local school taxes, enlarge the power of state commissions to regulate railroads and utilities, reform election laws, do away with child labor, extend social services, and democratize state institutions such as the judiciary and the penal system. This strange amalgam of views toward race and reform came together in the move by the Democrats to do away with the black vote in North Carolina politics without violating the Fifteenth Amendment to the Constitution or eliminating a vast number of illiterate white voters through the suffrage amendment. In so doing, the Progressives, with their middle-class mind-set, did not shrink from making the lowest classes of voters, whether white or black, marginal to the democratic process.

As he reflected on the election of 1898, certainly one of the most crucial in the state's history, the new Democratic senator, Furnifold Simmons, no friend to Progressives or blacks, pointed to the double helix that both limited and promoted turn-of-the-century reforms in North Carolina. "We were determined," he mused, "to change the constitution of the State in such a manner as to disfranchise the Negroes without depriving any of the whites of their right to vote." The presence of blacks in politics, Simmons and others

*Courting in the mountains
of western North Carolina
in the 1890s.*
North Carolina Collection,
University of North Carolina
at Chapel Hill.

believed, only confused matters, preventing any progress on the "really vital issues" necessary for progress. Race must be eliminated from politics.

What, then, made up the "really vital issues" that Simmons and other Democrats thought needed to be addressed before North Carolina could move forward into the new century? First, the shifting agenda included better educational facilities for both races and also for women, antitrust legislation, a guarantee of bank deposits for all, relief for children and women working in textile, furniture, and tobacco mills, Prohibition, better public health and welfare programs, and, not surprisingly, better race relations as a result of all these reforms. Still, the changes would be on white terms. Yet many in North Carolina like Simmons and Charles Aycock believed that by 1908, a decade after educational reforms had taken hold, blacks once more would vote and hold office. In this way, a statewide move toward a more open, participatory government through primaries and the direct election of senators and away from corrupt machine politics filtered through Progressive thinking. Not surprisingly, many reformists in North Carolina embraced woman suffrage by stressing what they saw as pragmatic results, namely reducing political corruption by introducing purer elements into the process, increasing the base of the electorate, bringing a higher level of moral sensibility into politics, and alleviating social conditions that they thought would destroy homes and families. Yet Progressivism, like many reform movements, also contained elements of political parricide within its ideals that, in the maelstrom of politics in North Carolina, had tragic results.

Regardless of the outcome of these reforms, Progressives wanted, through them, an expanded concept of the state's responsibilities toward its citizens. They sought to move away from the older regulation-and-restraint mode of governing to a more positivistic, active style. The idea of a powerful government engaged with more of the state's problems and increasingly influenced by an emerging middle class lay at the heart of Progressive thinking in North Carolina. Yet gradually both reformers and their attempts at change became mired in the same increasingly factionalized politics of the Democratic Party until, by 1920, Progressivism emerged as a right-wing reactionary impulse where temperance

A woman washing her clothes on Bear Wallow Mountain in Henderson County in western North Carolina in 1910. North Carolina Collection, University of North Carolina at Chapel Hill.

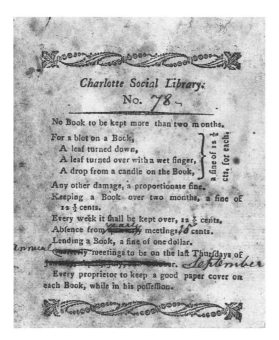

Thrice accursed CARDS and DICE!
You have been my ruin!

Left: Regulations of the Charlotte Social Library, ca. 1907.
North Carolina Collection, University of North Carolina at Chapel Hill.

An early pamphlet depicting the evils of gambling and drinking.
North Carolina Collection, University of North Carolina at Chapel Hill.

became Prohibition, primaries became exclusive and white, racial separation for social stability became de jure segregation, and the fight over the right to vote for women pulled to pieces the concept of sisterhood in North Carolina.

For the first time in public life, Progressivism in North Carolina attracted a great many women seeking an expanded role, a larger life outside the domestic sphere of the home. From the beginning of the first religious revival that swept over North Carolina from 1800 to 1805, women had found in the limited democracy of newly formed churches an outlet for their concerns. Coming together in prayer groups, Sunday schools, and in teaching circles, women in Methodist, Presbyterian, and Quaker congregations created a world separate from that of men. Indeed, women in Methodist and Quaker churches began to take the lead in promoting not only church activities but also community ones as well. Not surprisingly, women from Quaker and Methodist societies in the Piedmont helped promote and pioneer Progressivism in North Carolina.

After 1890, women increasingly formed interest groups that focused on concerns outside their more traditional spheres of home, church, and family. For women in North Carolina, both black and white, bringing up children, processing and preparing food, keeping house, and taking care of others now involved decisions that entered the public sphere of larger communities and groups beyond typical nineteenth-century meetings of Methodist, Quaker, Baptist, and Presbyterian church groups.

That new vision of women's roles came thumping into Greensboro in November 1883, in the form of Frances Willard, national president of the Woman's Christian Temperance Union since 1879. Despite the fact that North Carolina women had organized temperance societies as early as 1879 in Asheville and Greensboro, they soon disbanded after a disastrous defeat in 1881 at the hands of the "wets," those who disdained any form of the state's regulation of alcohol. In a statewide referendum on 4 August 1881, North Carolinians, by a vote of 166,325 to 48,370, easily defeated a bill passed by the general assembly to ban the manufacture of "spirituous and malt liquors" and also the sale of alcohol except for medical, chemical, or mechanical purposes. Realizing that a womanless electorate would not pass a referendum prohibiting "spirituous . . . liquors," the state's legislators easily bypassed the thorny issue by a "refer-en-dum," as it was called, that effectively squelched the matter. So devastating had been the collapse afterward that, by 1883, the national Woman's Christian Temperance Union (WCTU) listed North Carolina as only one of two states without a local chapter.

Exhorting her followers to do everything and to do it nationwide, Willard determined to revive the moribund temperance movement in North Carolina before the tenth anniversary of the national WCTU's founding. Within a year after her provocative visit, North Carolina had enrolled 458 members in twelve chapters. By the turn of the century, brigades of women wearing the WCTU's white ribbons had not only marched into saloons singing hymns for the lost and strayed but also had tramped into the halls of the legislature and governor's mansion demanding changes in the state's way of doing things, especially exhorting it also to do everything for the state's progress.

Willard's urging of the WCTU to do everything introduced women in North Carolina to a wider range of issues, many of which might otherwise have been ignored. Although the WCTU and other women's groups continued to work for legal Prohibition and individual

Pepsi-Cola and Grape-Ola, both products of North Carolina, at a Raleigh plant in 1928.
North Carolina Collection, University of North Carolina at Chapel Hill.

abstinence, they also became involved in larger social and political problems that had little to do with alcohol. For over two decades, white ribboners in North Carolina turned their interests to prison reform, education, safer working conditions in industrial factories and mills for women and children, public sanitation, and, ultimately, women's suffrage.

Although women's clubs and groups eventually embraced and spread to all regions of the state, the seeding of the movement began in Greensboro. There, in the Quaker community around Guilford, organizations such as the WCTU, League of Women Voters, and North Carolina Federation of Women's Clubs (NCFWC) found fertile soil in the New Garden tradition of education and activism among women. From 1883, when Frances Willard came to Greensboro, until 1908, when the reform movement largely lost its impetus, more than fifteen women associated with the New Garden Boarding School for Boys and Girls or Guilford College held statewide offices in the WCTU and NCFWC. Three Quaker women, Mary Mendenhall Hobbs, Mary Chawner Woody, and Laura Annie Winston, embraced not only the insistence of southern Progressives concerning Prohibition but also Willard's charge to do everything. Within that appeal, white-ribboners found their greatest confirmation and rebuff.

African American women also organized their own branches of the WCTU with the aid of their white sisters. By 1885, Rosa Steele, in charge of "Colored Work" for the state WCTU, noted that one chapter for black women had been organized in Greensboro, along with seventeen youth groups throughout the state. For several years, African American temperance unions sent delegates to the state convention. In Steele's absence in 1886, Florence Garrett, president of Greensboro's black WCTU, delivered a report on the progress of work among African Americans to the annual WCTU convention, probably the first black woman to address a predominantly white audience in North Carolina.

Suspicious of white efforts to organize them for temperance and other reforms, many of which seemed pretentious to African Americans, black women held a meeting on 15

Above: Sallie Southall Cotten, known as Mother Cotten for her work with women's clubs in North Carolina.
North Carolina Office of Archives and History, Raleigh.

Bayard Wooten of New Bern, one of North Carolina's finest photographers in the early twentieth century. Wooten designed the Pepsi-Cola logo.
North Carolina Collection, University of North Carolina at Chapel Hill.

July 1890 at Saint Matthew's Church in Greensboro to form their own separate union. With Frances Willard and Mary Woody in attendance, the newly formed state organization, with Mrs. J. M. O'Connell as president, called themselves WCTU Number 2, cautiously avoiding using the word "colored," because, as O'Connell explained, "that would exclude any white sisters who wished to work with us; in other words, we wanted it distinctly understood that we had no race prejudice, for we believe all men are equal." WCTU Number 2 thus became the first state temperance organization for black women in the nation. By 1891 it had more than four hundred enrolled members in nineteen local unions. While interested in temperance and Prohibition because alcohol devastated their communities and families, WCTU Number 2's in North Carolina had less enthusiasm for women's suffrage. Increasingly, they instead sought to protect the diminishing right of their men to vote.

Although North Carolina came late to the club movement already well under way nationally by the 1870s, a plethora of joining swept the state after Willard's visit. The sudden surge surprised leaders like Sallie Southall Cotten, "Mother Cotton." Earlier, she had found that "clubs were few and unpopular—were considered unwomanly and existed solely for mental culture." Yet by 1902 Cotten had become vice president of the newly formed North Carolina Federation of Women's Clubs when seven groups met at Salem College. Within three years the NCFWC included twenty-nine clubs with more than 550 members. By 1924 the Federation represented more than 50,000 women in thirty-five organizations spread across the state. Sisterhood had at last come to North Carolina, and it sought more than just mental culture and social stimulation.

1909 meeting of the North Carolina Federation of Women's Clubs in Raleigh.
North Carolina Collection, University of North Carolina at Chapel Hill.

The fortunes of the WCTU in North Carolina waxed and waned according to its chief issue, Prohibition. In 1903 the union claimed nearly three thousand members in sixty-five chapters, but, when North Carolina adopted statewide Prohibition in 1908, the numbers had fallen to less than one thousand white-ribboners in fifty affiliates. Fewer than twenty unions survived the Great Depression. Other white women's organizations such as the Colonial Dames, United Daughters of the Confederacy, and King's Daughters, a nondenominational charitable society seeking to promote a "Sisterhood of Silent Service," grew dramatically during the period, a reflection of the nostalgia for a passing generation of Confederates.

Just as Sallie Cotten and other North Carolina delegates had been invigorated by their attendance at the ladies exhibit at the Columbian Exposition in 1893, African American women found a similar incentive in their exclusion from participation in the exposition and in their attempts to join the General Federation of Women's Clubs. Even the sisterhood of issues espoused by the WCTU appeared only skin deep to many African American women. In 1909 they came together to form the North Carolina Federation of Colored Women's Clubs (NCFCWC) in Charlotte. Marie Clay Clinton, wife of a bishop in the African Methodist Episcopal Zion Church, became its first president. Her successor, Charlotte Hawkins Brown, went on to become a nationally recognized leader of African Americans and one of the state's most remarkable women.

Born in Henderson in 1883, Brown moved to Cambridge, Massachusetts, as a child. There, as a public school student, she met Alice Freeman Palmer, president of Wellesley College. The two formed a lifelong friendship. After graduating from Salem Normal College in Massachusetts, Brown moved back to North Carolina to teach. With the help of Charles Duncan McIver, president of the new normal college for women in Greensboro, and Charles Eliot, Harvard's president, she opened the Palmer Memorial Institute, named after her benefactor and friend. Palmer Memorial went on to become one of the state's leading liberal arts and industrial schools, a tribute not only to Brown but to the black Progressive insistence upon equal educational opportunity.

Along with clubwomen like Mary Woody and Sue Tomlinson Hollowell, Charlotte Hawkins Brown continuously tried to promote interracial cooperation at a time when white supremacy and segregation became institutionalized throughout North Carolina society. In early October 1920, Brown, along with Fanny Yarborough Bickett, Mrs. Harvey Boney, Gabrielle deRosset Waddell, and Mrs. F. L. Siler, attended a conference at the Young Men's Christian Association in Memphis, Tennessee. There, she helped launch the Woman's Committee on Interracial Cooperation. Afterward, she promoted woman's committees on interracial cooperation, with white and black members, operating throughout the state. For her part, Sue Hollowell used the WCTU to organize black women and children for temperance in the 1880s, and, after suffering through the white supremacy campaigns of 1898 and 1900, once again enlisted both races for a Woman's Association for the Betterment of Public Schoolhouses (WABPS) in Granville County. Little recognized and acknowledged, WABPS did much to promote better educational facilities for both blacks and whites. A lifelong Quaker activist, Mary Chawner Woody moved to North Carolina in 1880 when her husband, John Woody, joined the faculty at New Garden. Elected president of the state WCTU in 1884, she held that position for a decade until she and her husband moved to California. The Woodys returned to North Carolina when John became president of the Slater Industrial and Normal School, an institution for African Americans that developed into Winston-Salem State University. An untiring champion of racial cooperation and outreach, Mary once again took up her work with the WCTU, this time as superintendent of evangelical work from 1899 until 1917.

Perhaps no issue defined the promises and problems of women in North Carolina or of the politics of Progressivism more than that of suffrage. In November 1894, Helen Morris Lewis began a series of meetings of men and women in Asheville at the home of

Charlotte Hawkins Brown in her wedding dress, 1912.
North Carolina Division of Archives and History, Raleigh.

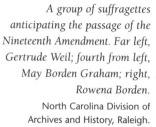

*A group of suffragettes
anticipating the passage of the
Nineteenth Amendment. Far left,
Gertrude Weil; fourth from left,
May Borden Graham; right,
Rowena Borden.*
North Carolina Division of
Archives and History, Raleigh.

Thomas Patton that evolved into the state's first equal suffrage movement. With Lewis as its flashpoint, some of the nation's most well-known suffragists, such as Willard and Laura Clay of Kentucky, came to North Carolina to promote the cause. Anticipating a more open and flexible political system, Lewis and the first equal suffrage association found themselves increasingly detoured by the race question after 1898. By 1900 the association disbanded. Lewis soon after returned to her native Charleston.

The limitations of influencing public policy and of shaping legislation through clubs and betterment societies quickly became apparent in the battle over school board membership, perhaps the most important precursor to outright suffrage. As one of its first initiatives, Lewis's equal suffrage association had called for female representation on school boards, and, "as a result of the suffrage meeting held in Asheville," the general assembly began debate on a bill to grant the request. Lillie Devereaux Blake, a noted writer and suffragist from New York but a native of Raleigh, passionately addressed the bickering legislature on its behalf. On a pedestrian level, the request hardly seemed seditious or insubordinate. After all, women traditionally had been interested and involved in public and private education for decades, a natural outgrowth of their concern for children. Yet the bill conjured up two iconoclastic ideas in the minds of the men in the general assembly. First, it marked the emergence of women not as those who indirectly influenced but who now forthrightly made public policy. Education, the core of new reformist ideas for Democrats, Republicans, and Populists alike, seemed but the beginning of a host of attempts to change the state into one with a more activist and responsible government, one not relished by many hidebound legislators. Moreover, many in the general assembly distrusted the idea of equal suffrage, as a friar's lantern that signaled changes too deeply into North Carolina's well-ordered, hierarchical, paternalistic society. After a spirited and "hot discussion," the bill failed to pass. Patriarchy cast a long shadow from North Carolina's Civil War past.

After 1900 the majority of women's organizations in North Carolina embraced the cause of equal suffrage. The WCTU, WABPS, and state Teacher's Assembly took up the

*Walter Clark (1846–1924), as chief justice of
the North Carolina Supreme Court in 1909.*
North Carolina Collection, University of
North Carolina at Chapel Hill.

cause, soon to be joined by Sallie Cotten and the NCFWC in 1911. After a meeting with the state's attorney general, Thomas Walter Bickett, in May 1912, Cotten emerged with the understanding that because they could not vote and thus hold office, women could not serve on school boards. Soberly, Cotten wondered if all women "must . . . become suffragists" in order to move ahead. Although he turned down her request for a favorable ruling, Bickett would remember Cotten's plea years later on another crucial vote for women.

While most men in the state either openly or "mysteriously" opposed woman suffrage, Walter Clark, chief justice of the state supreme court, steadfastly endorsed the idea even as he ran for the U.S. Senate in 1912. Clark surprisingly found not only men but also many women opposed to the idea. After addressing the Raleigh Woman's Club in 1913 on the less radical idea of women voting in municipal and not state or national elections, "the women heard with pleasure, gave him a vote of thanks, and voted unanimously not to take it up." Noting that North Carolina women preferred standing on their political skirts until conditions changed and men freely admitted them into the arena, Clark asserted that, if that were the case, they might never get the vote. In 1913 North Carolina women decided to organize once more to promote suffrage, long after the issue had reached the national stage. Still, they chose to affiliate with the more moderate Equal Suffrage Association (ESA), a wing of the National American Woman Suffrage Association, and not with Alice Paul's more radical Congressional Union. The decision spoke volumes about sisterhood in North Carolina just after the turn of the century.

Attention once more focused on North Carolina with the passage of the Nineteenth Amendment by the House of Representatives in January 1918 and by the Senate on 4 June 1919. In order for it formally to become part of the Constitution, three-fourths of the states, thirty-six of the forty-eight in 1919, had to approve the "Susan B. Anthony Amendment," as it was called. One year later, thirty-five states had accepted it, and, in the rush to ratify in time for the upcoming fall elections in 1920, all eyes turned to two southern states, North Carolina and Tennessee, for the thirty-sixth and final vote. North Carolina's Progressive moment had arrived.

North Carolina and Tennessee scheduled special legislative sessions in August just to consider the amendment, and, buoyed by the rising tide of approval, state suffragists like Cotten confidently predicted that the "Old North State" would "stand up for women" and cast the deciding vote. Since 1912, support for suffrage once more had grown, and, by 1920, the ESA had more than twenty-four chapters. Backing had come from a broader base of support, from college students, prominent state officials such as the Speaker of the House and lieutenant governor, a great many state representatives, and, although reluctantly, the ruling Democratic Party, urged on by President Woodrow Wilson, from Virginia. Even

Thomas Bickett, now governor, came out for passage of the amendment, although unenthusiastically.

On 17 August, amidst tumultuous and passionate "scenes which had not been witnessed since the days of the Civil War," the state senate effectively killed the amendment by narrowly voting twenty-five to twenty-three to postpone action until the next regular session in 1921 so that they would have more time to consider such an emotionally charged yet critical decision. With the Senate vote as a shield, the House defeated the resolution, and, with it, the issue of woman suffrage died in North Carolina. Across the state line in Tennessee, their lower house, cognizant of what had happened in North Carolina, decided to ratify the Nineteenth Amendment on 18 August, one day after the senate in Raleigh had acted. Carrie Chapman Catt eagerly wired a disillusioned Gertrude Weil in Raleigh that, despite North Carolina's actions, "the thirty-sixth state is won." The nation had at last allowed women the right to vote.

The long battle over woman suffrage exposed the ambiguity of Progressive reform in North Carolina. Alarmed at the social changes brought about by industrialization, urbanization, and the coming of the railroads, Progressives sought to use a more active government to improve the conditions of the majority of the people of the state. An expanding middle-class of professionals and managers and, increasingly, voluntary organizations of men and women saw the weakness of state government as the problem. To them, the decay and decline of the old Bourbon Democrats presented an opportunity to expand their role in public policy making. Progressives believed that better education, good roads, improved social services, better working conditions for women and children, and a more open electoral process would benefit everyone in North Carolina no matter what race or gender.

A cartoon playing the race card against Judge Francis Winston in the election of 1904.
North Carolina Collection, University of North Carolina at Chapel Hill.

Still, the Wilmington race riot of 1898, perhaps the most unsettling event of the period, had endangered the entire social order with instability and chaos, frightening prospects to an emerging middle class with few historical roots. Thus, reform and racism became intertwined, as did changing ideas of gender and traditional roles of men and women. Not surprisingly, the initial attempt at equal suffrage died along with the disfranchisement and segregation of African Americans at the turn of the century. It would not surface again for a decade, only to be vetoed once again. Suffrage for women threatened to undermine one of the most basic divisions of southern society, that of gender, and increasingly the arguments of the antisuffragists focused on how the franchise for women would blur the boundaries between masculine and feminine spheres. If women could speak and vote for themselves, it would do away with perhaps one of the most significant privileges still remaining to southern men, the separation of themselves from women and African Americans, both politically and socially.

Other Progressive issues had similar outcomes. As early as 1902, reformers had petitioned the general assembly to enact the Australian, or secret, ballot. By 1923, only North Carolina and six other states had refused to adopt some form of privately marking ballots. The state would continue to hold out until 1929. Realizing that the Bourbon Democrats based their politics upon the denial of popular democracy, loosely organized party machines built around personalities such as Furnifold Simmons, and the inclusion of business interests, especially railroads, Progressives wanted new initiatives such as the direct primary, initiative, referendum, state utility commissions, and the direct election of senators. Walter Clark, the advocate of equal suffrage, attracted strong national attention when he demanded that senators as well as other appointive officials be elected by popular vote and not be selected by the general assembly or governor. Clark's untiring and radical reform views, at least in the eyes of most North Carolinians, assured him of a rousing defeat when he ran for the senate in 1912.

A similar lack of enthusiasm by Democratic members of the legislature meant that many Progressive reforms such as the direct primary came late to North Carolina. As early as 1899, Thomas J. Jarvis had led a campaign to move away from backroom caucuses and toward primaries, but the general assembly evaded the issue and only agreed to a piecemeal plan in 1914. Yet Progressivism, while a failure overall, nonetheless had changed the thinking of many North Carolinians. Within two decades the state had embraced much of the agenda of Progressive reforms, including better educational facilities, a secret ballot, the election of many state officials, especially court judges, an improved system of roads, the regulation of child labor, and hours limiting labor in industrial plants to forty-eight for women and fifty-five for men; in so doing, the state became more actively engaged in the daily lives of North Carolinians. The Bourbon Democrats, who, except for the brief revolt by farmers and fusionists in the 1890s, had run the state since the end of Reconstruction, now came to be known as progressive plutocrats, a term that suggested that they had learned from the past but were still reluctant to embrace change. Nonetheless, despite party labels and descriptive terms like Bourbon Democrats, progressive plutocrats, or suffragettes, the trappings of reform did little to alter North Carolinians' attitude toward change. They embraced it only hesitantly and tardily. In part, Progressivism met with less success in North Carolina because of the reemergence of old ideals in a changing, increasingly industrialized, and chaotic society. Walter Hines Page, who left the state only to become one of its chief critics and writers, observed in his *Mummy Letters* that "ghosts," principally the legions of Confederate dead, religious orthodoxy, and the "Negro problem," haunted North Carolina's past and retarded its progress. Certainly, Page's "ghosts" burdened North Carolina's middle-class Progressives as they attempted to reform the state. In their zeal for social order and stability, they embraced de jure segregation. In their quest to temper the evils of alcohol, they welcomed Prohibition as a natural outgrowth of their conservative, even evangelical, Protestantism. Yet over all this hovered the legacy of the Old South and the lost cause of the Confederacy. In 1908, one writer expressed this frame of mind by suggesting that everything had to conform to "the Democratic platform, the Daughters of the Confederacy, old General So-and-So, and the Presbyterian creed." Lost in the rush to memorialize a dying generation of Confederates, another offspring of the Old South, slaves freed after 1865, also began to vanish, only without monuments, societies, or parades to honor their legacy of struggle and endurance. Their children, freed along with their parents or else born after 1865, battled to keep alive a new inheritance, their just claims to limited political, social, and economic rights despite the menace from mobs of lynchers and clubs of moderate white Progressives.

Caught between trying to create a more active and involved state government and a suddenly enshrined legacy of Old South ideals, reform issues in North Carolina found lukewarm support among the general populace. The end of World War I and the collapse of Woodrow Wilson's administration coincided with and reinforced the crumbling of the Progressive impulse in North Carolina. Seldom united on any one issue, reformers no longer had a common idea of what further social programs should be initiated. The coming of equal suffrage for women and of national Prohibition had removed much of the energy and ambition of many reformers, and, after World War I, the task shifted instead to educating North Carolinians in their new civic duties, particularly that of voting. Yet in its own hesitant way, North Carolina had come to view itself as a progressive southern state.

ADDITIONAL READINGS

Anderson, Eric. *Race and Politics in North Carolina, 1872–1901: The Black Second.* Baton Rouge: Louisiana State University Press, 1981.

Aydlett, A. Laurence. "North Carolina State Board of Public Welfare." *North Carolina Historical Review* 24 (January 1947): 1–33.

Birmingham, Stephen. *Certain People: America's Black Elite.* Boston: Little, Brown, 1977.

Brooks, James T., Jr. "Rhetorical Study of the Campaign Speaking of Selected Southern Reform Governors during the Progressive Era." Ph.D. diss., University of Florida, 1974.

Brown, Charlotte Hawkins. *The Correct Thing: To Do, to Say, to Wear.* Sedalia, N.C.: Charlotte Hawkins Brown Historical Foundation, 1990.

Connor, Henry G., Jr. "Shall This General Assembly of North Carolina Ratify the 19th Amendment?" *North Carolina Booklet* 19 (April–July 1920): 121–32.

Cott, Nancy F., ed. *No Small Courage: A History of Women in the United States.* Oxford: Oxford University Press, 2000.

———, ed. *The Roots of Bitterness: Documents of the Social History of American Women.* New York: E. P. Dutton and Co., 1972.

Cotten, Sallie Southall. *History of the North Carolina Federation of Women's Clubs, 1901–1925.* Raleigh: Edwards and Broughton Publishers, 1925.

Gay, Dorothy A. "Crisis of Identity: The Negro Community of Raleigh, 1890–1900." *North Carolina Historical Review* 50 (April 1973): 121–40.

Gilmore, Glenda E. "Gender and Jim Crow: Sarah Dudley Pettey's Vision of the New South." *North Carolina Historical Review* 68 (July 1991): 261–85.

Green, Elna C. "Those Opposed: The Antisuffragists in North Carolina, 1900–1920." *North Carolina Historical Review* 67 (July 1990): 315–33.

Hodges, Alexander W. "Josephus Daniels: Precipitator of the Wilmington Race Riot of 1898." Honors essay, University of North Carolina, 1990.

Huggins, Kay H. "City Planning in North Carolina, 1900–1929." *North Carolina Historical Review* 46 (October 1969): 277–97.

Janiewski, Dolores E. *Sisterhood Denied: Race, Gender, and Class in a New South Community.* Philadelphia: Temple University Press, 1985.

Keith, Benjamin F. *Memories: "Truth and Honesty Will Conquer."* Raleigh: Bynum Printing Co., 1922.

Link, Arthur S. "Progressive Movement in the South, 1870–1914." *North Carolina Historical Review* 23 (April 1946): 172–95.

Logan, Frenise A. "Movement in North Carolina to Establish a State Supported College for Negroes." *North Carolina Historical Review* 35 (April 1958): 167–80.

Mabry, William A. "'White Supremacy' and the North Carolina Suffrage Amendment." *North Carolina Historical Review* 13 (January 1936): 1–24.

Marteena, Constance H. *Lengthening Shadow of a Woman: A Biography of Charlotte Hawkins Brown.* Hicksville, N.Y.: Exposition Press, 1977.

Nasstrom, Kathryn L. "'More Was Expected of Us': The North Carolina League of Women Voters and the Feminist Movement in the 1920s." *North Carolina Historical Review* 68 (July 1991): 307–19.

Perman, Michael. *Struggle for Mastery: Disfranchisement in the South.* Chapel Hill: University of North Carolina Press, 2003.

Prather, Henry L., Sr. "Red Shirt Movement in North Carolina, 1898–1900." *Journal of Negro History* 62 (April 1977): 174–84.

———. *We Have Taken a City: Wilmington Racial Massacre and Coup of 1898.* Rutherford, N.J.: Fairleigh Dickinson University Press, 1984.

Redding, Kent. *Making Race, Making Power: North Carolina's Road to Disfranchisement.* Urbana: University of Illinois Press, 2003.

Roller, David C. "Republican Factionalism in North Carolina, 1904–1906." *North Carolina Historical Review* 41 (January 1964): 62–73.

Sims, Anastasia. "Feminism and Femininity in the New South: White Women's Organizations in North Carolina, 1883–1890." Ph.D. diss., University of North Carolina, 1985.

———. "Sallie Southall Cotten and the North Carolina Federation of Women's Clubs." Master's thesis, University of North Carolina, 1976.

———. "'The Sword of the Spirit': The WCTU and Moral Reform in North Carolina, 1883–1933." *North Carolina Historical Review* 64 (October 1987): 394–415.

Smith, Margaret Supplee, and Emily Wilson. *North Carolina Women: Making History.* Chapel Hill: University of North Carolina Press, 1999.

Stambler, Errol H. "Struggle over Disfranchisement in North Carolina, 1898–1901." Master's thesis, University of North Carolina, 1971.

Steelman, Joseph F. "Edward J. Justice: Profile of a Progressive Legislator, 1899–1913." *North Carolina Historical Review* 48 (April 1971): 147–60.

————. "The Progressive Era in North Carolina, 1884–1917." Ph.D. diss., University of North Carolina, 1955.

Stephenson, Wendell H. "The Negro in the Thinking and Writing of John Spencer Bassett." *North Carolina Historical Review* 25 (October 1948): 427–41.

Taylor, A. Elizabeth. "Woman Suffrage Movement in North Carolina." *North Carolina Historical Review* 38 (January 1961): 45–62; (April 1961): 173–89.

Waddington, Charles W., and Richard F. Knapp. *Charlotte Hawkins Brown and Palmer Memorial Institute.* Chapel Hill: University of North Carolina Press, 1999.

Walsher, Richard G. *Watauga Club.* Raleigh: Wolf's Head Press, 1980.

Watson, Richard L., Jr. "Furnifold M. Simmons: 'Jehovah of the Tar Heels'?" *North Carolina Historical Review* 44 (April 1967): 166–87.

Webster, Irene F., ed. *Seventy-Five Years of Service: History of the National Society of the Daughters of the American Revolution in North Carolina.* New Bern, N.C.: Owen G. Dunn, 1975.

Wheeler, Marjorie S. "New Women of the New South: The Leaders of the Woman Suffrage Movement in the Southern States." Ph.D. diss., University of Virginia, 1990.

Wheeler, William B. "The Challenge of Progressivism: The North Carolina Democratic Senatorial Primary of 1912." Master's thesis, University of North Carolina, 1963.

Whitener, Daniel J. "North Carolina Prohibition Election of 1881 and Its Aftermath." *North Carolina Historical Review* 11 (April 1934): 71–93.

Wilkerson-Freeman, Sarah. "Emerging Political Consciousness of Gertrude Weil: Education and Women's Clubs, 1879–1914." Master's thesis, University of North Carolina, 1986.

Williams, Charlotte B. Grimes. *History of the North Carolina Division of the United Daughters of the Confederacy, 1895 to 1934.* Raleigh: United Daughters of the Confederacy, 1934.

Wooley, Robert H. "Race and Politics: The White Supremacy Campaign of 1898 in North Carolina." Ph.D. diss., University of North Carolina, 1977.

The 1930s

NINETEEN

New Deals and Old Politics in North Carolina

On 5 July 1938, the day after the nation celebrated its 162nd birthday, Franklin D. Roosevelt, now president for more than five years, declared that the South still remained "the Nation's No. 1 economic problem—the Nation's problem, not merely the south's." In North Carolina, the "No.1 problem," at least as far as Raleigh was concerned, was not the economy but "that damned liberal Democrat in the White House," Franklin Roosevelt, and his "socialist" New Deal policies. After the 1932 election, Democrats had become the liberal party nationwide but not in the South. Although Roosevelt swept the state in 1932 and again in 1936, conservatives in the state, led principally by Governors O. Max Gardner and John C. B. Ehringhaus, along with Sen. Josiah Bailey, fought the Roosevelt administration and its New Deal. Yet Josephus Daniels, once considered a racist as a Progressive but now viewed as a liberal editor of the *Raleigh News and Observer,* and Clarence Poe, editor of the *Progressive Farmer* and an advocate for poor farmers, strongly supported Roosevelt's relief measures and argued for the state's continued participation in New Deal programs. Still, North Carolina's two governors during the early 1930s, Gardner and Ehringhaus, and its two senators, Josiah Bailey and Robert Reynolds, best exemplified the state's mixed response to the New Deal. Mirrored through them, the New Deal, while undoubtedly successful in North Carolina, had an additive effect, not a transformational one as it did in other southern states. In North Carolina, the New Deal filtered through the state's old politics.

Perhaps the phrase "progressive plutocracy," referring to the political hegemony of politicians and textile, tobacco, and furniture giants who had effectively governed the state for more than two decades and who considered themselves enlightened and open to limited change, best described North Carolina as it entered the Great Depression. By the mid-1920s it had established itself as the leading industrial state of the New South. Sixteen percent of all southern wage earners lived in North Carolina. Only Texas and Georgia, with 30–40 percent fewer workers, rivaled the Tar Heel State. In terms of every index of industrial development, such as the number of establishments, capital investment, and production, North Carolina ranked first. When the Great Depression first sifted through the state in 1929, North Carolina produced half the nation's cotton yarn with only one-fourth its textile mills. Sprinkled throughout the Piedmont and mountains, these mills also turned out significant quantities of hosiery, blankets, denim, and underwear.

By 1930, one-half of the country's cigarettes and two-thirds of its smokeless tobacco came from the Piedmont of North Carolina. In times of scarcity and with infrequent

A trio of North Carolina governors. Left to right: Locke Craig, Cameron Morrison, and Thomas Bickett.
North Carolina Collection, University of North Carolina at Chapel Hill.

malnutrition during the Depression, many in the nation smoked more. As the price of tobacco declined, profits nonetheless increased, and tobacco companies throughout the state fared well while others faltered and failed. Between 1927 and 1932, profits increased by 30 percent, from $115 million to $145 million. The furniture industry did not make out as well as textiles and tobacco. By 1925, North Carolina led the nation in the manufacture of wooden furniture, yet the demand for large-ticket household furnishings and furniture declined from 1929 until the end of World War II.

The progressive plutocracy that dominated the Democratic Party in the 1920s reacted to the Great Depression as it had to other crises, conservatively yet positively. For Governors Gardner and Ehringhaus and industrial "busycrats," North Carolina, with the most balanced economy of any southern state, would survive the temporary downturn as it had others in the past. Even when the stock market crashed in 1929 and prices, wages, salaries, and businesses spiraled downward for the next four years, state officials nevertheless remained optimistic. Between 1929 and 1931, manufactures declined from $603,000,000 to $384,000,000; retail trade dwindled from $1,155,000,000 in 1928 to $878,000,000 by 1931; and banks failed at the rate of two a week from 1930 to 1933. Still, a more telling barometer of the impact of the Depression on North Carolina lay in another statistic: farm incomes. The Great Depression hit farmers the hardest. Between 1928 and 1932, their income plummeted from $283,000,000 to $97,000,000. Three-fourths of North Carolinians in 1930 lived outside towns and cities, half actually residing on working farms. In 1925, North Carolina placed second in the nation in the number of farms and forty-eighth in the number of cultivated acres per farm. Small, inefficient, family-owned farms formed the basic structure for agriculture and gave the state its continuing rural nature. Tobacco, cotton, and corn easily fit the subsistence and marginal economies of small farms, usually worked by family labor and a tenant or two. Yet in 1929, North Carolina ranked forty-fifth in per capita income, ninth overall in the South, traditionally the poorest region of the

Oliver Max Gardner (1882–1947), governor of North Carolina from 1929 to 1933.
North Carolina Collection, University of North Carolina at Chapel Hill.

nation. Although 25 percent of North Carolinians lived in urban areas, no city had a population of more than 100,000.

North Carolina's reaction to New Deal policies mirrored its hesitantly progressive predisposition. When Roosevelt announced the first National Industrial Recovery Act in 1933, representatives of cotton textile mills quickly moved to cooperate with the National Recovery Administration, the act's operational engine, to set up the nation's first industrywide codes. Tobacco and furniture manufacturers reacted with an equally calculated indecisiveness. At the same time, the codes also gave impetus to the organization of labor throughout the state, a side effect stringently opposed by mill owners. When Congress introduced the LaFollette-Costigan bill in 1931 to give direct federal grants to states for unemployment relief, North Carolina's delegation also voiced a similar ambivalence. Sen. Josiah Bailey, echoing conservative sentiment throughout state officialdom, confided to Gov. O. Max Gardner that he opposed "the dole" because "once you're on it, you'll never want to get off it," and he vowed that he would only vote for direct relief, a dole in his thinking, to prevent a revolution. Still, North Carolina nominally supported initial help from the federal government while voicing suspicion of its overall impact.

At first, North Carolina sought to help itself without depending upon federal aid. Gardner, governor from 1929 to 1933, responded to the deepening depression with a program of relief, consolidation of state bureaus, retrenchment of services, and a reevaluation of tax policies and burdens. The state had its own version of Franklin Roosevelt and a New Deal in Gardner and his plan. As North Carolina faced the worsening economic crisis from 1929 to 1931, it had to deal with a crushing tax burden left over from the expansive 1920s. In the decade of the 1920s, the state's tax burden ballooned from $13 million to $178 million. Only Florida had a higher per capita state debt. As the Depression continued into 1930, Gardner, realizing that the emergency of a recession had broadened into a catastrophic depression that had no end in sight, asked the Brookings Institute for help in reorganizing North Carolina's government to make it more efficient while at the same time reducing expenditures and taxes, an efficiently progressive response. Using the Brookings study as a guide, he gave to the general assembly in 1931 his first reaction to the darkening depression. Maintaining that North Carolina must "put its house in order to survive the economic storm," Gardner recommended that state salaries be cut 10 percent across the board, that several smaller counties, principally in the east, be consolidated, that the state university system be centralized, and that state government be reorganized. Clearly, the time for more public spending and taxation, a hallmark of the 1920s, had passed. Now North Carolinians needed relief from taxes, especially those on real property. So great had tax delinquency grown that, by the end of 1932, one-third of all counties together with seventy-four towns had defaulted on repaying their debts. In the future, Raleigh would not trust unrestrained local authorities to tax or to manage their debts.

The general assembly responded to Gardner's program by enacting most of his proposals, with the notable exceptions of the consolidation of counties and the short ballot, both of which would have significantly increased the executive's power while diminishing that of the legislature. With his eyes cast toward Washington and FDR, Gardner set about selling his "Brookings Plan" to the people of North Carolina. Using the "newfangled radio" for a forum, he carefully explained his program to the people, all the while praising the legislature for its speedy response to the crisis. To encourage more self-sufficiency, he also inaugurated a "Live at Home" campaign to urge people to grow and to process their own food, skills that largely had been declining for decades. In a *Saturday Evening Post* article published at the end of his administration, Gardner pointed to the four 1931 acts of legislation as "revolutionary, each . . . designed to meet the situation prevailing under changed economic conditions." North Carolina was "not afraid to stand by itself . . . . it pioneered in road legislation, in public-school legislation, in legislation for control of public debt, and in university consolidation." North Carolina, he proudly proclaimed, had "cleaned house," saving $5–$7 million in just two years. Gardner went on to become a successful attorney and lobbyist in Washington, undersecretary of the Treasury, and, eventually, ambassador to England.

His successor, John C. B. Ehringhaus, followed Gardner's Depression policies, promising a "program of progress," a balanced budget, and a "strict but sane economy," a swipe at the liberal spending policies of the 1920s and at what he considered to be the socialist policies of the New Deal. Noting the expectations stirred among industrial workers, blacks, and the poor by some of Roosevelt's programs, he cautioned that material progress must come before social change, a traditionally pragmatic, go-slow, conservative approach. Active in state politics since 1905, Ehringhaus came from Elizabeth City and in 1932 had a reputation as a tireless campaigner and loyalist for the Democrats. Sen. Josiah Bailey became the most vocal of North Carolina's New Deal critics, lukewarm on the National Recovery Administration (NRA) and openly hostile to relief efforts such as the Federal Emergency Relief Administration (FERA) and the Agricultural Adjustment Administration (AAA). Yet in 1932 North Carolina produced its own version of Huey Long, the famed Kingfish of Louisiana politics, in the guise of Robert Reynolds, who served as a courtier and a counter to Bailey and Ehringhaus.

From Asheville, in the western part of the state, "Our Bob," as he referred to himself during the senatorial campaign of 1932, seemed more a showman, an orator, and a flim-flam man than a politician. A perennial candidate for various offices ranging from lieutenant governor to congressperson to U.S. senator, Our Bob had not even come close to winning a major campaign until the New Deal came along. An outsider in his own party, scandalized by four marriages and a reputation as a ladies' man, a notorious wet in a Prohibition-bound state, a known shirker who did not serve in World War I, Reynolds, with little money and no statewide organization, seemed at best an amusing diversion in the 1932 Senate race. His opponent, Cameron Morrison, appeared to be a shoo-in. As a popular governor in the 1920s and also as the appointee to fill the senatorial seat vacated by the death of Senator Overman in 1930, Morrison had promoted good roads and good schools, all the while consolidating his position with good works within the Democratic Party. Yet Reynolds's Populist appeal found an audience among North Carolinians resentful of the politics of tobacco, textiles, and "good ol' rich boys" in general.

In the depths of the Depression of the early 1930s, Our Bob attacked the wealthy, and in Cam "the Million Dollar Man" Morrison, he had a perfect target. With his declamatory style and bombastic rhetoric, Reynolds portrayed Morrison as a "Duke Power man" con-

trolled by big business interests, especially tobacco, all the while ridiculing his fancy limousine and his ritzy Mayflower apartment in Washington as well as his high-class airs. As he waved a Mayflower Hotel menu in front of crowds throughout the state, Reynolds scoffed at Morrison's preference for caviar, Russian fish eggs, instead of good old North Carolina hen eggs. It became the theme of his campaign. Portraying himself as a man of the people, Our Bob told of his need, because of poverty, to borrow money, beg for stamps for his mailings and cars for his travels, and stay with friends in their homes. A rich man himself, Reynolds had spent much of the year traveling around the world, sending postcards to voters in North Carolina on his stops; in the campaign itself he often traveled on a private plane. He liked to pose dressed in khaki, as if he were on safari in Africa. Still, voters chose not to look behind his false front. His Populist rhetoric and a widening distrust of plutocrats appealed to many North Carolinians eager for a change.

Yet the issues framed by Reynolds's campaign smacked more of genius than of buffoonery. Anticipating repeal of the Prohibition amendment and sensing its increasing unpopularity among many of the meaner sort of North Carolinians, he called not only for its end but also for government control and taxation of liquor, an understandable alternative to many throughout the state. Railing against big tobacco and textiles, he wanted to soak the rich by taxing corporations and relieving the tax burden of the poor. Lastly, he urged payment of the soldier's bonus from World War I, a sore point in a patriotic state, and, anticipating action from Washington, he wanted bank deposits guaranteed by the federal government. In a nod toward responsibility, he called for a balanced budget at both the state and federal level. Still, some darker issues resided in Reynolds's Populist rhetoric. He also favored restricting immigration, especially by radicals from Europe, a view that eventually included stopping the flow of Jewish refugees from an increasingly repressive Germany. Notwithstanding his political and social peccadilloes, Reynolds, as a senator, eventually set fewer conditions for receiving New Deal programs within the state than did Joseph Bailey.

In the first two years of the Depression, North Carolina huffed and puffed along with little assistance from the federal government. Indeed, Raleigh and not Washington shone as the center of the early Depression political universe, aiming to ease the worsening crisis without outside aid. Nonetheless, even Gardner's modest program of retrenchment, reduction in property taxes, and relief for counties by taking over expensive tax outlays like road building made little impact upon growing unemployment rolls and declining crop prices. By July 1932 more than 175,000 North Carolinians had applied for relief. Although North Carolina had cleaned house in state government, encouraged people to live at home with their traditional self-sufficiency and expediency, asked churches and volunteer organizations to step up their activities, and even trumpeted its own revolutionary approach to the Depression, the worldwide economic downturn and not the state's distinctive economic and political condition brought Washington onto center stage. In 1932 Roosevelt easily swept the state, and federal aid came to North Carolina, whether it wanted it or not.

At first, North Carolinians liked at least one of the new ideas from Washington, the National Industrial Recovery Act (NIRA). The NIRA aimed at increasing total national purchasing power as well as restoring jobs by raising wages, reducing shift hours, doing away with unfair competition, and encouraging collective bargaining between management and employees. For the first time in the state's history, a branch of government, in this instance Congress, had intervened and sided with labor and actively encouraged its bargaining. Moreover, the National Labor Relations Board, created in 1935, gave limited protection to the right to organize. Still, code-makers under the act, big textile, furniture, and tobacco officials, instantly recognizing the possibility of unionization, moved to form in-house company associations, called "sweetheart unions" or "kiss me clubs" by the outside Union of Textile Workers.

As the leading industrial state in the South, North Carolina keenly felt the economic reversal of the 1930s. Although only 7 percent of the state's population worked in industry, the value to the state's economy in 1933 exceeded that of agriculture by four to one. By far the largest segment, 158,504, worked in textiles, perhaps 40 percent of whom were women. By 1933, their real wages had declined by a third while working conditions had worsened. Because textile workers and plants largely outnumbered tobacco and furniture manufactures, mills could be found almost anywhere throughout the state. Textiles dominated the state's industry. If the NIRA's operational engine, the National Recovery Administration (NRA), could help textiles recover their dominant position, North Carolina's economy would also be revitalized. Thus, cotton textiles led the way in initial cooperation with the NRA and also the New Deal. Even so, it proved to be a mixed blessing.

When textiles first fell on hard times in the 1920s, industry officials reacted by setting up the Cotton Textile Institute (CTI), a trade association that attempted to limit production and competition, especially from the northeastern states. Textile owners also wanted to end price cutting from one company to another. The industry responded positively to the institute, and by 1930 80 percent of cotton manufacturers voluntarily limited production. Located in Charlotte, the CTI looked upon the New Deal's NRA as simply an extension of what it had already been doing. On a national scale, it held out the promise of predictability in terms of costs, marketing, production, employment, and wages for cotton textiles and goods. The CTI quickly moved not only to endorse the idea of codes but also to formulate them in accordance with the CTI system.

George A. Sloan, head of the CTI, chaired the original NRA code committee for the textile industry. With one-fourth of the nation's cotton goods establishments located within the state, five of the twenty code members came from or else had close ties to North Carolina, more than any other state. T. M. Marchant, president of the American Cotton Manufacturing Association, headquartered in Charlotte, and prominent mill owners such as Charles Cannon, Ben Gossett, and Stuart Cramer helped frame the initial codes. Moreover, former governor Gardner, now a lobbyist and an attorney based in Washington, exerted considerable influence with Roosevelt's advisers who formulated the NRA during the first hundred days. Instead of voluntarism, always capricious, the CTI could use the power and resources of the federal government to further the purposes of the textiles' trade association. Still, the codes came with a price, that of trade unionism.

Before the New Deal, North Carolina had a long history of labor unrest and union failures. In the 1880s, the Knights of Labor, an idealistic all-inclusive union, tried to organize textile workers, but the decline of the Knights after the Haymarket Square riot in 1886 and

Children of Ella May Wiggins photographed in 1929.
Left to right: Albert, 3; Myrtle, 11; Chalady, 13 months;
Clyde, 8; and Millie, 6.
North Carolina Collection, University of North Carolina
at Chapel Hill.

Ella May Wiggins (ca. 1900–1929), killed in the 1929 Gastonia union strike.
North Carolina Collection, University of North Carolina at Chapel Hill.

the depression of 1893 meant their efforts in North Carolina had little result. Between 1898 and 1902, the American Federation of Labor formed the United Textile Workers, and, immediately after World War I, the workers recruited thousands into their ranks. By 1919, it had thirty thousand members in forty-three locals throughout the state. With a demand for shorter hours and safer working conditions, the United Textile Workers launched successful strikes at Kannapolis, Concord, and Charlotte. Still, unrest peaked between 1928 and 1932 with the Marion and Gastonia strikes, two of the most violent and bloodiest in the South.

At Gastonia, mill officials brought in an outside efficiency expert who immediately cut workers and wages by having fewer employees oversee more looms, thus increasing productivity. Incensed at the "stretch out" of their labor, workers responded to the appeal of Fred Beal, a representative for the National Textile Workers Union, a new organization strongly influenced by the workers' paradise of an emerging socialist Russia. After five mill workers lost their jobs for being members of the Communist Party, a called strike by Beal soon spread to five mills and eventually included one thousand workers. Panicked by the possibility of mass unrest and anarchy, mill owners asked the governor to call out the National Guard. Soon five companies of the North Carolina National Guard marched into Gastonia. In an ensuing fracas between the workers and the National Guard, firing broke out and the Gastonia police chief was shot dead. Found guilty of conspiracy to murder, Beal fled North Carolina for Russia, only eventually to return and serve four years of the sentence. A subsequent strike at Marion also ended in death and violence.

In Greensboro, more than four thousand workers asked for help with unionization, and, with flying squadrons of workers rolling from community to community in trucks and cars, the walkout spread to High Point, Kernersville, Lexington, Jamestown, and Thomasville. In the summer of 1932, the American Federation of Labor, using its roaming truckloads of workers and sympathizers and encouraged by the new NIRA, managed to shut down 150 factories with sixteen thousand workers. In the brief kingdom of the NIRA from 1933 to 1935, labor unions prospered in North Carolina for the first time. When the second New Deal began in 1935, an estimated 35 percent of textile workers had joined a union.

Nonetheless, the peculiarity of the textile industry eventually undermined North Carolina's brief honeymoon with unionism. Scattered among dozens of mainly small mills spread throughout the state, mostly unskilled, and poorly educated, textile workers frequently worked closely with foremen, bosses, and middle management. Some even enjoyed personal relationships with mill owners. Second and third generations of families grew up in mill villages whose close-knit communities undercut the leverage of unionism. Highly individualistic yet deferential in a folksy way to authority, southern workers did not easily take to outside agitators and union organizers who came into their towns and lives. The paternalism of an older, agrarian way of life had found new roots in mill villages and towns.

Yet the New Deal temporarily breathed new life into the textile industry. Less than a year after the codes went into effect, cotton mills reported more than $13 million in net profits, an increase of more than 4 percent in terms of net worth. Employment also soared. From March 1933 to April 1934, 142,000 new workers joined the industry, the largest single yearly increase in history. When a series of strikes and outages struck cotton textiles in 1934, workers averaged $11.54 for thirty-six hours of work per week, well above the southern scale of $9.70 for similar conditions. By the fall of 1934, NRA officials in Washington concluded that cotton textiles had experienced a more dramatic upward adjustment because of the codes than most other industries. Still, the basic problems of cotton textiles—low consumption, high production, poor wages, and harsh working conditions—remained to haunt the industry decades later.

A North Carolina cotton field in 1936.
North Carolina Collection, University of North Carolina at Chapel Hill.

Looping tobacco in Granville County in 1930.
North Carolina Collection, University of North Carolina at Chapel Hill.

Tobacco corporations in North Carolina disdained the NRA altogether. Depression-proof and foolproof, the industry flourished during the economic crisis of the 1930s. Annual cigarette production grew from 8.6 billion in 1910 to 112 billion in 1933. By 1937 it reached 130 billion, a testament to hard times, stress, the addictive nature of smoking, and a slick, sophisticated, and knowledgeable ad campaign. In spite of a ten-cent pack of cheap Depression cigarettes called Wings turned out by two smaller companies, net earnings for the big four, Liggett and Meyers, Reynolds, Lorillard, and American, grew from $86 million in 1929 to $111 million in 1931. Lower tobacco prices, the advent of poorer mixtures into the market, and cheaper advertising rates led to a reduction in the prices of cigarettes and increased consumption despite the fast-burning ten-cent bargain. Tobacco companies had little incentive to agree to codes to regulate prices and production. While the Supreme Court busied itself with declaring key parts of the original National Industrial Recovery Act unconstitutional in the spring of 1935, representatives from Washington and the major tobacco companies in North Carolina still had not reached agreement upon industrywide codes. They never would.

In addition to government-supported prices, wages, and production quotas, all useless to the tobacco industry, the NRA offered a suspension from antitrust laws, especially those centering on combinations in restraint of trade. Already operating as a cartel, the four major companies found the antitrust provision not only unappealing and unnecessary but also menacing. Since the beginning of the Depression, the number of tobacco factories had dipped from sixty-one to fourteen, a decline that favored larger, more concentrated operations principally in three states, North Carolina, Virginia, and Kentucky. In 1933 the big four produced approximately 85 percent of all cigarettes and almost all smokeless tobacco products, perhaps 60 percent of that total from North Carolina alone. Operating in a secretive, highly competitive market where Camels and Lucky Strikes were not only successful marketing tools but also jealously guarded product formulations, tobacco officials did not want to divulge information to the government in order to come up with an industrywide code. Moreover, smaller companies, already moving into the market with an inferior yet attractive ten-cent pack, might learn about the undisclosed operations and formulations of the big four under NRA codes.

Like its sister textile industry, tobacco and its officials regarded the NRA's right-to-bargain clause for unions as a life-threatening sentence. Along with the ideas of cooperation, codes, and confessions of secretive operations, tobacco management found the concept of worker's organizations repellent. Certainly, tobacco workers, the lowest paid and most chronically underemployed in all the industries in North Carolina, could have benefited from government advocacy and aid. At the beginning of the Depression in 1930, North Carolina had perhaps twenty thousand workers in its tobacco factories, 75 percent of whom were African American, the majority of those women working as unskilled stemmers. Concentrated almost exclusively in three cities, Winston-Salem, Reidsville, and Durham, tobacco workers' average pay of $10.60 per week in 1929 made them the lowest paid all of industrial workers in the state and put them on the bottom-rung of wage earners in the South. The relative wealth of the industry, its growing influence in North Carolina and the nation, and the largely black workforce presented special problems for the NRA.

Even on the job, laborers in tobacco factories in the 1930s worked in segregated rooms and buildings, adhering closely to a Jim Crow system now a generation old. Moreover, African Americans, particularly women, overwhelmingly could be found in the most menial and unskilled positions, while whites dominated management, trades, and crafts jobs. In looking at the codes and at a segregated and gendered workplace, tobacco officials assumed that a wage differential between whites and blacks would be instituted according to southern customs and mores—that is, white workers would earn more than black workers. Yet the NRA pushed for equal pay for comparable work. In the end, stemmers received a minimum of thirty cents per hour, all others forty cents per hour, but the increasing prosperity of the tobacco companies allowed them gradually to raise the minimum wage to almost forty cents per hour by the end of the 1930s. Throughout the decade, over one-fourth of tobacco workers, a majority of them African American women, received relief payments from the federal government to remain above the subsistence level. Segregation, prosperity, and the plantation mentality of tobacco mills eventually deflected the threat of unionization and the impact of the NRA in the tobacco industry.

Facing a highly competitive market like textiles, the furniture industry readily cooperated with the NRA to develop a systematic code governing wages, hours, prices, and production. By the mid-1920s, North Carolina led the nation in the production of wooden furniture yet never approached the near monopoly of the state's tobacco industries. In 1931, the state manufactured over 10 percent of all the country's furniture, second only to New York and far above any other southern state, including Virginia. High Point became headquarters for the Southern Furniture Manufacturing Association and the point of convergence for southern factories, a majority of which operated within two hundred miles of the city.

Sen. Josiah W. Bailey (1873–1946), who consistently opposed Roosevelt's New Deal policies.
North Carolina Collection, University of North Carolina at Chapel Hill.

Unlike textiles, furniture manufacturing in North Carolina, although hurt by the continuing economic crisis of the 1930s, emerged from the Depression in a competitively strengthened position. Between 1929 and 1933, the number of plants declined by one-third and employment fell by one-fourth in the state overall. Yet for the eleven major furniture manufacturing states nationwide, the number of establishments and workers shrank by 50 percent. By 1937 southern furniture manufactures in general had regained their 1929 levels, while North Carolina in particular had shown even more growth in the number of workers, productivity, and overall total value of its products. The leadership and direction provided by the NRA, the collapse of competitors in other states during the Depression, a general economic recovery nationally, and a business boomlet in North Carolina effectively helped a foundering industry recover and reform its practices.

In general, the progressive plutocracy centered in the Democratic Party that had governed North Carolina for almost three decades welcomed federal efforts to help its industries and agriculture recover. Still, Democratic leaders balked at another mainstay of the New Deal, that of relief, especially if administered from Washington and not Raleigh. The state's responses to the plethora of federal relief measures such as the Federal Emergency Relief Act (FERA), the Civil Works Administration (CWA), the Civilian Conservation Corps (CCC), the Emergency Relief Appropriations Act (ERA), the Works Progress Administration (WPA), the National Youth Administration (NYA), and, of course, Social Security, made plain the limits of its Democratic liberalism and of its political and philosophical divergence from that of Roosevelt.

The Federal Emergency Relief Act came to North Carolina in May 1933. A major federal program, it provided grants, not loans, to states based upon projects submitted for approval. In the Senate, Josiah Bailey voted against the measure, in part because he thought it discriminated against North Carolina, a poor state that would have trouble with the required one-third matching funds. A staunch fiscal conservative, Bailey was appalled by the idea of spending more than a million dollars a month in North Carolina or any state for direct relief. To his pro-business friends, he confided that once poor southerners went on the federal dole, they would never want to work again. The federal government essentially took over the job of relief from local and state agencies, administering the funds through the North Carolina Emergency Relief Administration, a separate agency overseen by the FERA.

In the three years that it operated within the state, the NCERA distributed more than $40 million in federal funds and more than $700,000 in state funds, hardly a one-third match. Over 75 percent of the money went to direct relief, the rest to fund public works taken over from the Public Works Administration, including education projects, attempts

An example of harsh life in the mountains of North Carolina in the Depression.
North Carolina Collection, University of North Carolina at Chapel Hill.

to resettle rural farmers, and the distribution of surplus commodities such as flour and sugar. In the main, work relief replaced direct payments. Within eighteen months, the works division had provided funds for sixty-one schools, thirty grandstands for football and baseball games, seven airports, five hospitals, twenty public stadiums, six amphitheaters, 104 miles of sewers, 309 miles of roads, 150 new homes, more than 53,000 trees, and fourteen fish hatcheries and ponds. Additionally, more than ten thousand farm families, more than 65 percent of whom were black, received aid from the NCERA for resettlement loans.

For the first time since the Civil War and Reconstruction, a federal agency directly had given aid and assistance to blacks as well as to whites. Harry Hopkins, the director of the FERA, insisted on equal treatment for them within the agency, a stand that did not endear him and his liberalism to Senator Bailey. At its inception, the FERA estimated that blacks, 25 percent of North Carolina's population, comprised perhaps 50 percent of the state's unemployed but as much as 80 percent of its relief rolls. The FERA and the NCERA recruited and hired blacks and tried to see to the equal distribution of its funds as well. Mostly accustomed to menial, semiskilled jobs such as picking cotton, tenant farming, general maintenance work, and stemming tobacco, blacks found that working on the FERA projects with a living wage improved their standard of living. Forester B. Washington, director of the Negro Division of the FERA, thought the agency a godsend to his race, especially in the South. Generally disregarded by local and state agencies that had little money for relief, blacks in the New Deal instead looked to Washington for their welfare. They did not trust North Carolina to take care of them. In spite of the FERA's efforts, a stubborn figure of 10 percent of the state's population, half of that black, remained on relief throughout most of the decade of the 1930s.

The Civil Works Administration (CWA) had a short but productive life in North Carolina. From the middle of November 1933 until April 1934, almost six months, the agency built three hundred new schoolrooms, renovated four thousand more that had been neglected because of a shortage of funds, erected one hundred new gyms and repaired forty, and, looking to improve the overall health of North Carolinians, constructed more than fifty thousand outdoor toilets, "sanitary privies," in CWA terms. The CWA also initiated efforts to control mosquitoes and malaria along the coast. Senator Bailey outspokenly criticized the CWA, calling many of its projects boondoggles and its high wages unnecessary. In fact, he openly disliked "that pack of northern liberals," Hopkins; Lorena Hickock, Hopkins's southern representative and a close friend of Eleanor Roosevelt; and especially Secretary of Labor Frances Perkins. When she heard of Bailey's remark that he would vote for relief only to prevent a revolution, Perkins, the first woman appointed to a cabinet position, caustically observed that a social and not a class revolution would occur in the South if only all southerners would start wearing shoes. Bailey was not amused.

Of all the New Deal programs, the Civilian Conservation Corps (CCC) became the most successful and overly romanticized, the object of sentiment and nostalgia to those who served in it and who later studied it. The idea of putting young men eighteen to twenty-five years of age together in an emerald green forest to do conservation work under army supervision proved popular with many North Carolinians during the 1930s. The CCC gave each enrollee room and board and an additional thirty dollars per month, at least twenty-two of which had to be sent home to families. Since the young men originally came from relief rolls, the overall effect not only lessened the burdens of poor families but also provided for valuable vocational and educational training as well. Youth in the CCC constructed hiking trails in national and private forests, developed extensive recreational facilities in parks, helped with erosion and flood control projects, and landscaped and improved forest lands. In North Carolina, they fathered the state's park system, an enduring monument to federal and state cooperation. Much of the Great Smoky Mountains National Park and the Blue Ridge Parkway, as well as most state park facilities in North Carolina, derived from CCC projects and efforts.

Within six months, North Carolina, under the supervision of the NCERA, had set up thirty-one camps with approximately 6,200 enrollees. In the next two years the CCC reached its zenith in North Carolina with eighty-one camps and 16,200 enrollees. Once again, the views of liberal Democrats in Washington clashed with those who were more conservative in Raleigh and, once more, they involved the issue of race. Local officials in towns such as Butters, Laurinburg, and Washington protested first to Ehringhaus and then to Bailey that black camps had been located near them. Still, black camps located in the overwhelmingly white region of western North Carolina near mountain towns such as Bryson City and Franklin encountered little objection and had excellent interactions with local communities. Although Robert Fencher, the national CCC director from Tennessee, consulted with Ehringhaus and Bailey about the location of camps in general, the two preferred to blame Fencher and his quota system of enrolling blacks when protests occurred. In North Carolina and in the South in general, such complaints quickly ended, never approaching in number or intensity those from outside the region who objected to the location of black camps in their communities.

In the first hundred days of his administration, Roosevelt launched another deal for the nation and for North Carolina, aimed not at reform or relief but at recovery. In this case, the Agricultural Adjustment Act (AAA) sought to limit production of certain yields while giving direct benefit payments to farmers, a crucial element for North Carolinians. As its goal, the AAA wanted to raise prices for agricultural crops, and, in a heavily rural state such as North Carolina, the program, at first glance, seemed a bonanza for stricken and impoverished tobacco and cotton farmers. Its impact would be determinant to the survival of a rural way of life for the state.

Two statistics mirrored North Carolina's dilemma in agriculture. First, by 1930 it had the second largest number of farmers in the nation while it ranked dead last in cultivated acres per farm. In a sector of the economy where mechanization and scale had increased, North Carolina had gone backward. Throughout the 1920s, the number of farms rose perhaps 4 percent while acreage decreased as much as 10 percent. A great many farmers simply divided their acreage among family members who chose to live nearby. Unmistakably, North Carolina's ruralness lay in its small farms of less than sixty-five acres each. Its two major crops, tobacco and cotton, required little land and capital but intensive labor. Not surprisingly, the state also led the nation in the increase in farm tenancy in the decade before the Depression, as workers, particularly in the eastern region, continued to divide and subdivide land into smaller and smaller plots. By 1929 agriculture had become North Carolina's number one economic problem.

The AAA introduced a new glossary of words and terms into North Carolina's vocabulary. After 1933, "crop allotment," "adjustment," "crop controls," and "benefit payments" became permanently associated with the state's economy. To Senator Bailey, such terms described a form of government that violated not only a farmer's but also an individual's basic liberty. By "liberty," he had in mind the shift from voluntary to compulsory crop reductions, all controlled and planned by a central agency that smacked of socialism and communism. When Congress passed the Bankhead Act a year later mandating compulsory rather than voluntary crop controls, Bailey, in spite of overwhelming support among North Carolina farmers, voted against it. He balked when it came to giving the federal government power over central planning for the economy and also allowing Secretary of Agriculture Henry Wallace, whom he detested, to impose a processing tax upon textile manufactures to help subsidize farmers. "I wasn't built that way," he explained of his opposition to the bill. Instead, he wanted voluntary reductions and the federal government to pay a subsidy or else give a bounty for cotton and tobacco production to help exports overseas. Sen. Robert Reynolds and Congressman Lindsay Warren, more liberal than Bailey, broke with the more conservative North Carolina representatives and voted for the bill.

Within two years the AAA realized its goal of raising cotton prices by plowing under acreage, controlling crops as they came into production and giving benefit payments to farmers. As production declined from 13 million to 10.6 million bales from 1932 to 1935, prices rose from 6.5 cents to 11.1 cents per pound. With benefit payments from AAA programs came a doubling of income for cotton farmers in just three years. While the AAA temporarily resuscitated prices for cotton, it could do little for the basic long-term problems troubling the industry as a whole. By the end of the decade, North Carolina's cotton farmers, despite the respite afforded by the New Deal, still faced the enduring problems of overproduction, mechanization, increased costs for materials such as tools, seed, and fertilizer, growing competition from abroad, and a shrinking world market. When the U.S. Supreme Court declared the processing tax unconstitutional in 1936 in *United States v. Butler,* thus temporarily ending the benefit payments, the decision little affected the declining prospects of the state's cotton farmers.

Another basic commodity, tobacco, fared better under the AAA. With approximately 40 percent of the nation's crop grown in the state and with a healthy domestic market, tobacco, perhaps more than any other major crop, stood to benefit from an adjustment program. Unlike textile mills and manufactures, tobacco companies found little fault with the processing tax used to finance benefits for farmers. Indeed, with a secret system of grading tobacco, an auction warehousing procedure, the tendency of farmers to overproduce, and a near monopoly of four corporations in production, tobacco companies did not fear minor adjustments and reductions by the AAA. Still, one part of the program, the raising of prices for bright leaf, flue-cured, and burley tobacco and the subsequent empowerment of growers worried Liggett and Myers, Reynolds, Lorillard, and American.

As the Depression entered its third year in 1932, North Carolina's tobacco farmers could barely hide their bitterness and hostility toward the big four. When John Hutson, a chief executive of the AAA, met with North Carolina's tobacco companies and buyers, he found them to be as arrogant as any industry leaders in the United States, uncaring and unsympathetic to the plight of growers. When company officials graded the 1932 flue crop, of an unusually fine quality, as satisfactory and offered only ten cents per pound, tobacco growers in eastern North Carolina rioted, and, increasingly dissatisfied, held mass meetings in Wilmington and Raleigh. On the steps of the state capitol, tobacco farmers called for parity based on 1909–14 prices, an across-the-board acreage reduction, and, most telling of all, the use of government tobacco graders to replace secretive company ones. Governor Ehringhaus, an easterner himself, surprised everyone not only by agreeing with the growers but also by suspending market sales and operations until parity could be arranged through the federal government. With mounting pressure from growers, governor Ehringhaus, and AAA officials in Washington, tobacco companies finally agreed to a settlement that included a price of seventeen cents per pound for the same acreage produced in 1932, in effect an allotment to growers in the previous season. For their part, tobacco companies gradually raised cigarette prices over the next two years to cover their increased costs and profits.

While the AAA helped agriculture in North Carolina to recover in the 1930s, it did so at a price, namely, the gradual displacement and eventual disappearance of a majority of black farmers in the state. In terms of farm cash income and also crop values, the state ranked either first in the South or second only to Texas from 1932 to 1939. Because of the federal government's intervention in tobacco and cotton production and prices, by the end of the second New Deal both crops had recovered such that their values more than doubled from 1932 totals. Yet in the same period the number of black-owned or -operated farms declined by 15 percent, a historic reversal from the prior decade, when the state led the nation in the increase in black farmers. During the same period the number of white farmers increased by 14 percent, the largest jump since the 1880s. The acreage reductions usually displaced black tenants since most landlords paid under the AAA preferred to keep

A woman scrubbing the floor in Northampton County in 1939.
North Carolina Collection, University of North Carolina at Chapel Hill.

whites as tenants and move African Americans to wage labor. Blacks constituted perhaps 60 percent of the more than twenty thousand farm families displaced under New Deal policies, a large number of whom began the process of the Great Migration that would continue for forty years, first to southern and then to northern cities.

The clash of North Carolina's old politics with Roosevelt's New Deal produced a watershed in the state's history. The reactions of Gardner, Ehringhaus, Bailey, and Reynolds toward Roosevelt's program revealed the limits of the pro-business progressives who had ruled the state since 1898. New Deal legislation such as the NRA and AAA allowed conservative North Carolina politicians to cooperate with Roosevelt in revitalizing the state's economy while many of the deals also promoted the roles of farmers, unions, and blacks, much to the dislike of the same politicians. Thus, events of the 1930s tended to divide southern Democrats from their more liberal party members nationwide and to lay the foundations for the shift to Republicanism two decades later. Indeed, after World War II, some southern Democrats, unhappy with Roosevelt and Truman's liberalism, especially on civil rights, seceded from the Democrats altogether and established their own Dixiecrat Party in 1948.

The hostility of North Carolina's progressive plutocracy toward the overall philosophy of the New Deal produced paradoxical results. On one hand, the state ranked very low, forty-third nationally, in the per capita allocation of New Deal funds. Ehringhaus and his successor, Gov. Clyde R. Hoey (1937–41), restricted state matching funds for relief activities, in effect limiting projects and grants. In Congress, Senator Bailey openly attacked the NRA and voted against the AAA and FERA. On some programs, the state simply dragged its feet. It would take North Carolina two years to comply with the provisions of the Social Security Act, reluctantly beginning benefit payments only when the federal government threatened action. Textile company officials intensely disliked the provisions of the NRA allowing the formation of unions while tobacco officials stalled against the codes until the very last. When offered electrification for rural areas, the state instead created its own Rural Electrification Agency and cooperated with state-sponsored power companies instead of the federal agency, thus bypassing the Tennessee Valley Authority just across the state line in Tennessee and keeping many North Carolinians, especially in western counties, unnecessarily in the dark for years to come.

Yet on the other hand the New Deal brought substantial if not reconstructional change to North Carolina. It ushered in better times for many in the state. By 1940, North Carolina had the highest increase in per capita net income of any state, although it still reached only 55 percent of the national average. Alone among all the southern states, North Carolina's industries prospered overall and its percentage of the region's workers increased from 15 to nearly 20 percent. Between 1932 and 1940, federal aid to the state totaled more than $480 million. The AAA alone accounted for $78 million, the CCC more than $50 million, the FERA $40 million, and the WPA almost $38 million. By the end of the decade, farm products once more reached 1929 levels while the national figure tallied less than 75 percent of that total.

Most revolutionary of all, North Carolina for the first time abandoned its centuries-old tradition of disregarding the welfare of its citizens and, with the federal government, established a permanent state welfare agency to handle social security, especially for dependent children, the unemployed, and the elderly. By the spring of 1940, less than 9 percent of North Carolinians remained on relief rolls, the best figure in the nation and far below the national average of 15 percent. Through public works programs such as the Works Progress Administration, Public Works Administration, and Civil Works Administration, much of the state's infrastructure of schools and public buildings was either maintained or rebuilt. Lastly, the CCC and NYA offered not only opportunity but also hope for a generation of the state's young.

North Carolina also learned more about itself as a state and a polity during the Great Depression and the New Deal. Governor Gardner correctly pointed to the revolutionary legislation passed during the 1930s without the nudging of the federal government. The state took over control of roads and many public buildings from counties and local municipalities, instituted guidelines and rules for auditing the fiscal affairs of local government units, and, for the first time, passed a state sales tax of 3 percent to make up for lost revenues and to get itself out of debt. The consolidation and binding together of state agencies such as the university system eliminated many duplicate programs and aided overall efficiency. Yet the revolution, really a form of forced modernization, stopped short of direct aid to citizens and instituting any programs that smacked of social change and upheaval. In the end, North Carolina rejected any little new deal of its own, preferring instead its time-honored practice of hesitant radicalism instead of outright reform.

ADDITIONAL READING

Abrams, Douglas C. *Conservative Constraints: North Carolina and the New Deal.* Jackson: University Press of Mississippi, 1992.

———. "Irony of Reform: North Carolina Blacks and the New Deal." *North Carolina Historical Review* 66 (April 1989): 149–78.

Badger, Anthony J. *North Carolina and the New Deal.* Raleigh: Department of Archives and History, 1981.

———. *Prosperity Road: The New Deal, Tobacco and North Carolina.* Chapel Hill: University of North Carolina Press, 1980.

Beal, Fred E. "I Was a Communist Martyr." *American Mercury* 42 (September 1937): 33–45.

Bell, John L., Jr. *Hard Times: Beginnings of the Great Depression in North Carolina.* Raleigh: Department of Archives and History, 1982.

———. "Urban Problems in North Carolina during the Depression, 1929–33." In *Urban Affairs Conference of the University of North Carolina, Charlotte.* Charlotte: University of North Carolina, 1981.

Betters, Paul V., ed. *State Centralization in North Carolina.* Washington, D.C.: Brookings Institution, 1932.

Biles, Roger. *The South and the New Deal.* Lexington: University of Kentucky Press, 1994.

Bond, J. Percy, ed. *The Negro in the NYA for North Carolina.* Raleigh: National Youth Administration, 1939.

Brookings Institution. *Report on a Survey of the Organization and Administration of County Government in North Carolina . . . .* Washington, D.C.: Brookings Institution, 1931.

Carlton, David, and Peter A. Coclanis, eds. *Confronting Southern Poverty in the Great Depression: The Report on Economic Conditions in the South with Related Documents.* New York: St. Martin's Press, 1996.

Civil Works Administration Program in North Carolina, November 15, 1933, to March 31, 1934. Raleigh: State of North Carolina, 1934.

Corbett, David L., ed. *Addresses, Letters and Papers of Clayde Roark Hoey, Governor of North Carolina, 1937–41.* Raleigh: Council of State, 1944.

Crowell, Ruth W. "Administration of the National Labor Relations Act in North Carolina." Master's thesis, University of North Carolina, 1940.

Daniel, James C. "North Carolina Tobacco Marketing Crisis of 1933." *North Carolina Historical Review* (July 1964): 370–82.

Doughton, Josephine L. "Passage of the Sales Tax Law in North Carolina, 1931–1933." Master's thesis, University of North Carolina, 1949.

Draper, Theodore. "Gastonia Revisited." *Social Research* 38 (Spring 1971): 3–29.

Ebert, Charles H. "Furniture Making in High Point." *North Carolina Historical Review* 36 (July 1959): 330–39.

Ehringhaus, John C. B. *Addresses, Letters, and Papers.* Raleigh: Council of State, 1950.

Eskew, Glenn T., ed. *Labor in the Modern South.* Athens: University of Georgia Press, 2001.

Fink, Gary M., and Merl E. Reed, eds. *Race, Class, and Community in Southern Labor History.* Tuscaloosa: University of Alabama Press, 1993.

Gatewood, Willard B. "North Carolina's Role in the Establishment of the Great Smoky Mountains National Park." *North Carolina Historical Review* 37 (April 1960): 165–84.

Gill, Edwin, and David L. Corbett, comp. and ed. *Public Papers and Letters of Oliver Max Gardner, Governor of North Carolina, 1929–1933.* Raleigh: Council of State, 1937.

Hackett, David G. "The Prince Hall Masons and the African American Church: The Labors of Grand Master and Bishop James Walker Hood, 1831–1918." *Church History* 69 (2000): 770–802.

Hodges, James A. *New Deal Labor Policy and the Southern Cotton Textile Industry, 1933–1941.* Knoxville: University of Tennessee Press, 1986.

Hunter, Robert F. "AAA between Neighbors, Virginia, North Carolina, and the New Deal Farm Program." *Journal of Southern History* 44 (November 1978): 537–70.

Kirk, J. S., Walter A. Cutter, and Thomas W. Morse, eds. *Emergency Relief in North Carolina: A Record of the Development and the Activities of the North Carolina Emergency Relief Administration, 1932–1935.* Raleigh: Edwards and Broughton, 1936.

Marcello, Ronald E. "Selection of North Carolina's WPA Chief, 1935: A Dispute over Political Patronage." *North Carolina Historical Review* 52 (January 1975): 59–76.

Mitchell, Anne V. "Culture, History, and the Development on the Qualla Boundary: The Eastern Cherokees and the Blue Ridge Parkway, 1935–40." *Appalachian Journal* 24 (1996): 144–91.

Moore, John R. "Senator Josiah W. Bailey and the 'Conservative Manifesto' of 1937." *Journal of Southern History* 31 (February 1965): 21–39.

Morgan, Thomas S., Jr. "'Folly . . . manifest to everyone': The Movement to Enact Unemployment Insurance Legislation in North Carolina, 1935–1936." *North Carolina Historical Review* 52 (July 1975): 283–302.

National Youth Administration of North Carolina. "Final Report." Typescript. North Carolina Collection, University of North Carolina, 1943.

———. *Final Report of the National Youth Administration, Fiscal Years 1936–1943.* Washington, D.C.: Government Printing Office, 1944.

Pleasants, Julian M. "Senatorial Career of Robert Rice Reynolds." Ph.D. diss., Duke University, 1971.

Prior, John P. "From Community to National Unionism: North Carolina Textile Labor Organizations: July, 1932–September, 1934." Master's thesis, University of North Carolina, 1972.

Puryear, Elmer L. *Democratic Party Dissension in North Carolina, 1928–1936.* Chapel Hill: University of North Carolina Press, 1962.

Salmond, John A. "'The Burlington Dynamite Plot': The 1934 Textile Strike and Its Aftermath in Burlington, North Carolina." *North Carolina Historical Review* 75 (October 1998): 398–434.

Selby, John G. "'Better to Starve in the Shade than in the Factory': Labor Protest in High Point, North Carolina, in the 1930s." *North Carolina Historical Review* 64 (January 1987): 43–64.

Simon, Bryant. "Review Essay: Why There Are So Few Unions in the South." *Georgia Historical Quarterly* 81 (Summer 1997): 334–55.

Sumner, Jim L. "The Civilian Conservation Corps and the Development of North Carolina's Park System." *Carolina Comments* 40 (July 1992): 98–107.

Weeks, Charles J. "Eastern Cherokee and the New Deal." *North Carolina Historical Review* 53 (July 1976): 303–19.

Whalen, Robert W. "Recollecting the Cotton Mill Wars: Proletarian Literature of the 1929–1931 Southern Textile Strikes." *North Carolina Historical Review* 75 (October 1998): 370–97.

Wolfe, Audra J. "'How Not to Electrocute the Farmer': Assessing Attitudes Towards Electrification on American Farms, 1920–1040." *Agricultural History* 74 (2000): 515–29.

Zieger, Robert H., ed. *Southern Labor in Transition, 1940–1955.* Knoxville: University of Tennessee Press, 1997.

Civil Rights and Conservative Reactions in North Carolina

On the first day of February in 1960, four freshmen students from North Carolina Agricultural and Technical College sat down to a menu of ostracism and bigotry, North Carolina style, at a Woolworth's department store in downtown Greensboro. Led by Ezell Blair Jr., Joseph McNeil, Franklin McCain, and David Richmond, students occupied sixty-three of the available sixty-five seats within two days. By the fourth day, they had taken over not only the downtown Woolworth store but also several others that served food as well. Led mostly by students, sit-ins managed to seize control of the entire civil rights movement in less than six months, not only across North Carolina but the nation as well. Greensboro's sit-in, regarded as an outgrowth of earlier civil rights efforts by such notables as Rosa Parks and Martin Luther King Jr., in actuality indicated a much more significant shift in the postwar civil rights movement. The Greensboro sit-in marked a change in leadership, from King to a younger group led by students like John Lewis of the newly formed Student Non-Violent Coordinating Committee (SNCC) in Raleigh. Greensboro also signaled a change in protest tactics, from litigation and civil nonviolence to public demonstrations and student-led boycotts. Within the next fifteen years, North Carolina, from Greensboro to Charlotte, Weldon, Williamston, and Chapel Hill, provided precedents that defined not only civil rights within the state but also race relations in the nation as a whole.

The Greensboro sit-in did not come about in a vacuum. Indeed, it emerged as a natural evolution of a long tradition of agitation and protest within African American communities throughout the state. Moreover, the idea that many white North Carolinians had of themselves as citizens of a progressive southern state and thus liberal in race relations helped pave the way for change. Thus, the way that North Carolina reacted to the crisis precipitated by the *Brown v. Board of Education* ruling in 1954 set it apart from its sister southern states while it also provided a model for race relations and integration nationally. Moreover, North Carolina's response, in part, set in motion a series of events that propelled the state from a down-home disposition into the idea of modernity, of viewing itself in terms of a newer, more radical departure from its past. Still, the steps came gradually, through local elections, changing school board policies, meetings of chambers of commerce, and the actions of interracial committees and groups that met across the state. Yet in almost all instances the actions of blacks and not whites triggered concessions and change.

Civil rights demonstration at Chapel Hill in January 1964.
North Carolina Collection, University of North Carolina at Chapel Hill.

The first struggle for African Americans in North Carolina came for freedom. After 1865 the struggle was for equal opportunity. From the beginning of slavery in the 1670s to its end in 1865, rights seekers among slaves spoke out against the institution by running away, forming their own invisible institutions, and adopting attitudes of resistance toward white masters. Lunsford Lane, a slave of the Haywood family in Raleigh, made enough money by merchandising, buying and selling seed and supplies on his time off, so that he purchased his own freedom and eventually that of his entire family. After the American Revolution, a significant and growing number of free, well-educated blacks, perhaps thirty thousand by 1860, lived in North Carolina, primarily in the rural areas of the eastern counties but also in towns such as Wilmington and New Bern. A free cabinetmaker from Milton in Caswell County, Thomas Day paid careful attention to his craft, which allowed him to build one of the largest and most successful furniture factories in the state in the decade prior to the Civil War. So notable had the presence of free blacks become that, in the 1835 constitutional convention, the delegates, fearful of even so small an impact, stripped them of their first civil rights. Yet the end of the Civil War and the beginning of the initial Great Migration to towns such as Wilmington, Greensboro, Winston, Raleigh, and Charlotte provided the first enlarged opportunity for African Americans to practice their newly amended civil as well as economic rights.

Between 1865 and 1900 the institutions of family and church, hidden and invisible under slavery, flourished and grew while others such as education and politics, never deeply rooted, struggled for definition and clarity of their roles within both black and white communities. When the Greensboro students sat down at the Woolworth's lunch counter in 1960, they reflected long traditions of protests, demonstrations, rallies, and meetings dating back almost a century. Firmly established in Sunday school meetings and Baptist conventions, in teacher's protests and petitions, in political caucuses of both the Republican and Populist parties, and in a bewildering array of social and fraternal societies, these practices became embedded in communities that flourished both in an open and a segregated society. Sarah Dudley Pettey of New Bern belonged to that generation of African Americans born in freedom who nourished the idea that black accomplishments eventually would be recognized by whites and that class consciousness would someday extend across racial barriers to help end discrimination and prejudice. A well-educated teacher, she married Charles C. Pettey, a bishop of the African Methodist Episcopal Church, frequently using the pulpit and pew to speak out for civil rights and for opportunities for women.

Not surprisingly, the Greensboro freshmen four came from the same background as Sarah Dudley Pettey. North Carolina Agricultural and Technical College, established in 1891 along with Elizabeth City Colored Normal School, Shaw University, and Saint Augustine's College, which began in Raleigh just after the Civil War, furnished much of the student support for the demonstrations. Indeed, Bennett College, a women's institution in Greensboro, sent not only students but also its president, Willa Player, and one of its faculty leaders, Elizabeth "Lizzie" Laizner, to coordinate much of the behind-the-scenes activities of the sit-ins. Since the founding of Fayetteville Colored Normal College in 1877, the first African American school to train teachers in the South, North Carolina had by 1900 not only an extensive number of historically black colleges but also thousands of active alumni. The tradition of educating and training African Americans, formally established after the Civil War in primary, secondary, and higher education, had produced generations of black leaders, both men and women, who became the leaders of civil rights movements in the 1880s, 1920s, and especially after World War II.

Formal education for black North Carolinians began even before the end of the Civil War and within two decades had taken hold throughout the state. Between 1863 and 1898, the Freedmen's Bureau, Peabody Fund, American Missionary Association, African Methodist Episcopal Church, African Methodist Episcopal Zion Church, American Baptist Home Missionary Society, Christian Missionary Alliance, and Society of Friends (Quakers), had set up an extensive system of private schools, few of which survive today. Schools such as the Thompson Institute in Lumberton, Shiloh Institute in Warrenton, New Bern Eastern Institute in Brownsville, Johnston Academy in Smithfield, Scotland Neck Institute in Scotland Neck, Wharton Institute in Charlotte, the Allen School in Asheville, and the Girls Training School in Franklinton became community centers where blacks came together to discuss common problems and concerns. Located on the boundary of Nash and Halifax counties, one such institution, appropriately called the "old brick school," served several rural counties not only as an educational center but as a place where African American families lived while they learned about new farming techniques and how to cooperate together to form credit unions, loan money, purchase homes and supplies, set up markets, and, in general, take care of their own problems. Similar schools in Tyrrell and other counties likewise set up their own self-help programs.

If schools nourished one part of a century-old tradition of overt and covert opposition to discrimination within North Carolina's black communities, then churches formed the rock of conviction that kept dreams of justice and equality alive in the face of disfranchisement,

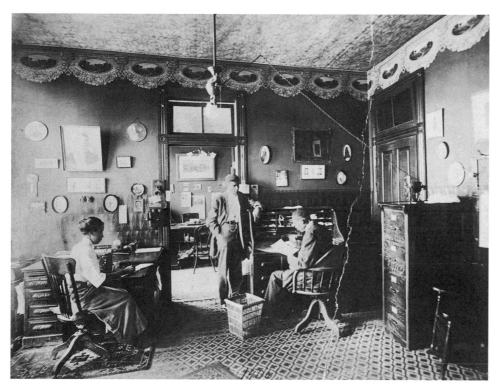

Susan V. Gillie Norfleet, C. C. Spaulding Sr., and John Merrick of the North Carolina Mutual Life Insurance Company in Durham, 1906. North Carolina Collection, University of North Carolina at Chapel Hill.

ostracism, lynching, intimidation, and segregation. As early as 1865, James W. Hood of Connecticut, speaking at one of the sacraria of the early civil rights movement in North Carolina, Saint Paul's African Methodist Episcopal Church in Raleigh, outlined the triangle of rights that African Americans must "contend for . . . and by the help of God we will have." First, Hood maintained, blacks should have "the right to testify in courts of justice," then "to be tried by a jury of his peers. I claim that the black man is my peer and so I am not tried by my peers unless there be one or more black man in the jury box," and lastly "the black man should have the right to carry his ballot to the ballot box." Ministers such as Hood became outspoken in the movement toward full civil rights.

As in much of the South, black churches in North Carolina operated as much more than religious organizations. Often members of regional or national associations, they published newsletters, invited speakers from outside the region, and even sponsored schools, burial associations, and insurance companies. Burial societies exemplified the mix of religious, altruistic, communal, and practical motives of African American cooperative associations. Frequently operating through local churches and auxiliary organizations, burial societies sold insurance against sickness and death, built homes for the elderly, founded orphanages, and even functioned as credit unions and banks. Born of such a cooperative movement in Durham, the North Carolina Mutual Life Insurance Company became one of the largest black-owned businesses in the nation and firmly established the triangle region of Raleigh, Durham, and Chapel Hill as a center of African American enterprise and

A black baptism at New Bern, ca. 1910.
North Carolina Collection, University of North Carolina at Chapel Hill.

culture. C. C. Spaulding, president of Carolina Mutual, headed the Durham Committee on Negro Affairs in 1935 and led the fight against segregation and disfranchisement with the slogan "A voteless people is a hopeless people." When Warren C. Coleman opened the only black-owned and -operated textile mill in the nation in Concord in 1901, much of his capital and support came from nickel-and-dime investors in Sunday schools in black Baptist churches throughout the region. A member of the general assembly for ten years, Henry Eppes, a Methodist minister, embodied the religious ties of the majority of the more than fifteen hundred African American officials elected to office between 1867 and 1901. More than places of worship and prayer, black churches promoted symbolic activities that for over a century united communities and collectively developed a public consciousness that recognized and fought against discrimination and racism.

Between the end of the Civil War in 1865 and the *Brown v. Board of Education* decision in 1954, African Americans in North Carolina also had developed a vocal, spirited, and assertive free press. Although spread throughout the state, newspapers and journals such as the Charlotte *Star of Zion* and *Africo-American Presbyterian,* the Raleigh *Gazette* and *Banner Enterprise,* the Durham *Reformer* and *Carolina Times,* the Weldon *North Carolina Republican* and *Civil Right Advocate,* and the Asheville *Colored Enterprise* actively informed and promoted civil rights causes while they reported on larger movements such as the formation of the National Association for the Advancement of Colored People in 1911. Louis Austin, founder and publisher of the *Carolina Times,* bitterly observed that, in the midst of a war against Hitler and tyranny in Europe in 1942, North Carolinians practiced their own form of racial superiority. "You notice," he editorialized, "that a white woman will ride next to her child's nurse in a private automobile, but when the Negro rides the bus he has to ride in the back of the bus." For blacks in North Carolina, Alexander Manly, the editor of the *Daily Record* in Wilmington who spoke out against white charges of rapes by African American males and whose presses were smashed and offices burned by a riotous mob in 1898, stood for the freedom of the black press not only in North Carolina but throughout the nation as well.

In an eloquent speech, Congressman George White of North Carolina called forth the 347 sense of history he felt for himself and all African Americans in 1901. An era had ended and a new one, that of segregation, had taken hold in America. White represented a tradition of black leadership and political participation that had come to an end at the turn of the century. Lynching and mob violence especially threatened the integrity of African Americans, and White, knowing that his bill in Congress giving the federal government jurisdiction over all such cases by removing them from state control would fail, nonetheless pleaded with Congress to end the racial hatred and prejudice that had overswept the nation. "This is," he predicted, "perhaps the Negroes' temporary farewell to the American Congress; but, let me say, Phoenix-like he will rise up some day and come again. These parting words are in behalf of an outraged, heartbroken, bruised and bleeding but God-fearing people." Still, he noted, African Americans politically remained a "rising people of potential force." No African American congressman from the South would be elected again until 1964.

From 1901 until the end of World War II, many black political organizations either disappeared altogether or else went underground. One underground group, the Twentieth-Century Voters Club in Raleigh, actually increased its membership in the 1920s, quietly encouraging blacks in Wake County to vote through nonpartisan and nonaffiliated clubs. Recalling the days of repression and slavery, many African Americans feared that after voting rights had been taken away many of their other hard-won freedoms, particularly those involving the use of their property and labor, would be either restricted or removed altogether.

From 1901 until 1945, African Americans practiced another form of protest, that of voluntary withdrawal and deliberate isolation from a white society they considered corrupted and debased by the virus of racism. Psychologically as well as physically, blacks masked themselves from their white neighbors and turned inward to develop their own

Meeting of the National Negro Business League in 1910. Front row, fourth from left: C. C. Spaulding. Second row, left to right: John J. Washington (second), Emmett J. Scott (fourth), Booker T. Washington (fifth), and John Merrick (seventh). North Carolina Collection, University of North Carolina at Chapel Hill.

communities, schools, churches, fraternal and mutual-aid societies, even banks, grocery stores, credit unions, and entrepreneurs. L. B. Capehart, an African American attorney and licensed physician in Raleigh, looked upon segregation as a blessing in disguise. By encouraging black-owned businesses and the formation of schools taught by well-educated black men and women, discrimination and prejudice unwittingly had promoted a consciousness of the distinctiveness of "a race with a common cause, a common purpose, [and] a common interest." Yet distinction came with a price.

The new assertion of an awareness by African Americans that they could control many of their own institutions manifested itself in the 1920s in a series of student-led rebellions and protests throughout the state against the administration of black colleges and universities. At Livingstone College in Salisbury in 1923, Johnson C. Smith University in Charlotte in 1926, and Saint Augustine's College in Raleigh in 1927 students struck against white-dominated administrations and boards of trustees that meted out harsh punishments for trivial incidents such as hazing and minor rules infractions involving curfew and conduct. Convinced that after sixty years of higher education in North Carolina for blacks, enough competent educators of their race had been produced to "man and manage their own institutions," students wanted self-determination and governance from their own race. Thus, two generations of black North Carolinians grew up under segregation, building their own institutions and nurturing a social and political consciousness largely without significant interaction with whites. World War II changed that perspective, and after 1945 African Americans began to define themselves in larger communities and terms.

World War II galvanized African Americans in North Carolina and throughout the nation. With veterans returning after fighting the Nazis and their ideas of racial superiority in Europe and also from the Pacific theater as well, black veterans came back to a southern culture that still seemed to promote white supremacy and not the ideal of universal democracy articulated by such allied leaders as Winston Churchill and Franklin Delano Roosevelt. Little had changed in North Carolina while an entire liberation movement had swept across Africa and Asia in the wake of the chaos and disorder at the end of the war. Even before the war ended, David Jones, president of Bennett College in Greensboro, predicted that minorities in America, especially blacks, would "furnish a close-at-hand test for the world to see . . . whether the American ideal that 'all men are created equal and are endowed by their creator with certain unalienable rights' shall become a reality or shall remain an ideal to which we pay mere lip service." No statement so clearly articulated the underlying principle of the coming civil rights movement in North Carolina and across the nation.

Noting the changed walk and talk of black veterans, J. W. Seabrook of Fayetteville State Teachers College predicted that they would "return seeking a large stake in the democracy" for which they fought. Black veterans now would expect jobs at living wages, sanitary and comfortable homes, protection for their families, opportunities for their children, and the right of participating in their government. From the vantage point of his long service to Durham and the rest of the state, C. C. Spaulding acknowledged that times had indeed changed. "I've been accused of being too easy-going and we failed," he mused. "A hint to the wise is sufficient. I am willing, if need be, to take a back seat and to permit others to use other methods, . . . I'm no longer going to be an Uncle Tom."

Although the basic tenets of North Carolina society had not changed before 1945, a somewhat more subtle transformation had taken place that presaged the larger one to come. Between the Great Depression and the end of World War II, perhaps as many as fifty thousand African Americans had left North Carolina, as part of a black out that did not end until the early 1970s. Many who stayed instead left their farms, moving to cities such as Charlotte, Winston-Salem, Greensboro, and Raleigh. In rural areas, entire black communities and towns stagnated or disappeared altogether. The subsequent rise of large blocs of black voters in cities such as Charlotte, Greensboro, and Raleigh in turn created political pressures that either persuaded or else forced North Carolinians to reconsider and even dismantle many of the worst social and institutional barriers to racial equality. All this occurred at a time when North Carolina, poised on the edge of a decades-long economic boom, could not afford prolonged racial strife. Indeed, the progressive plutocracy of businessmen and politicians who long had dominated politics now sought to accommodate African American demands as not only just and long overdue but also helpful in ensuring the state's future prosperity and well-being. Henry Grady's New South attitude had reemerged in the twentieth century in more modern, open-minded terms. Without such a reorientation of the state's thinking toward segregation and racial equality, many business leaders thought, prospects for research parks, for a nationally known university system, and for the attraction of new businesses and industry to the state would disappear or else diminish significantly.

Three events triggered the civil rights movement of the 1960s, the second civil rights reconstruction of the state, in North Carolina. The first came about because of the state and nation's participation in World War II. Although the walk and talk of returning black veterans gave momentum to the crusade, the war affected everyone else as well. As George Orwell put it, "if the war didn't kill you, it was bound to start you thinking," and, in North Carolina, a great many began to envision changing the state's racial status quo. The *Brown v. Board of Education* decision in 1954 additionally compelled the state to take action, and, from that, the passage of the Pearsall Plan in 1956, North Carolina's answer to the Supreme Court's mandate to end segregation with all deliberate speed, aroused all sides to take action. *Brown v. Board* allowed each state to desegregate in its own separate but equal way, and North Carolina chose a stubbornly conservative strategy that eventually satisfied no one. Named after Thomas J. Pearsall of Rocky Mount, chairman of the Special Advisory Committee of the general assembly, the Pearsall Plan provided for the payment of educational expenses in the form of grants for the private schooling of students assigned against the wishes of their parents or guardians to an integrated school. Moreover, under the law local school boards could suspend the operations of public schools if conditions became violent because of forced integration. The plan exemplified North Carolina's hesitant, stumbling stance toward desegregation in 1956. Reluctant to act on its own on such a divisive issue, the general assembly instead sent the plan to the public in the form of a constitutional amendment. Passed by an overwhelming margin of more than four to one, the Pearsall Plan did not so much reflect North Carolinians' racial views as it did their fear of radical change that might precipitate violence between the races, a distinct possibility in the turbulent years ahead. A poll conducted by Reed Sarrat of the Winston-Salem *Journal-Sentinel* found that a majority within the state favored full compliance with the *Brown* decision, and, in cities from Raleigh to Asheville, local officials stood ready to desegregate their schools. Integration proved far different. Never implemented, the Pearsall Plan stood as a sentinel to the reluctant radicalism of North Carolina in 1956. Declared unconstitutional in 1966, it had, within a decade, already been supplanted not only by events but also by other laws as well.

On 23 June 1957, the cities of Winston-Salem, Greensboro, and Charlotte voted to end segregation and to register twelve black students at formerly all white schools. While the tokenness of the numbers should not be overlooked, another potentially far-reaching significance of the decision to desegregate lay in the fact that the same school systems also limited any objections to a single response at a board meeting, effectively controlling the process and pace of change while paving the way for future actions. One year later the Women's College in Greensboro, now the University of North Carolina at Greensboro, graduated its first African American student, and by 1959 local school boards in Craven County, Wayne County, Durham, and High Point admitted blacks to formerly all-white schools. Within two years, eleven school districts, including Asheville, Chapel Hill, Raleigh, and Yancey County, had enrolled approximately two hundred black students. North Carolina had emerged as the first state in the South to move voluntarily toward integration yet in a painfully slow and cautious manner, all the while watching federal actions in other southern states such as Arkansas and Georgia.

Not surprisingly, North Carolina's attitude toward desegregation in its public schools mirrored the changes that had taken place within the state since the end of World War II. After the Supreme Court's 1954 decision, the passage and nonenactment of the Pearsall Plan, and the Greensboro sit-ins, the demands by African Americans for equal and integrated schools sparked reactions by white North Carolinians that divided them along class and geographic fault lines. The decision to allow African American students in schools in Winston-Salem and Greensboro, for example, elicited demonstrations from groups such as the Ku Klux Klan and White Patriots, all die-hard rural segregationists who insisted that an unwavering defense of racial caste took precedence over maintaining public schools. At the same time middle-class moderates in cities such as Charlotte, Raleigh, Greensboro, Winston-Salem, and Asheville led a limited revolt aimed at repoliticizing and preserving public education in the state by a greater inclusion of African Americans. Within five years, a growing number of grassroots organizations of ordinary parents, both black and white, along with a plethora of existing groups, forged a new desegregation consensus of legal, minimal compliance that eventually led to the famous Charlotte-Mecklenburg school ruling in 1969.

In Raleigh, for example, the Raleigh-Wake Citizens Association (RWCA), an African American political organization, emerged in 1958 as a reaction to the Pearsall Plan and the go-slow tactics of city leaders. Supported by active chapters of the National Association for the Advancement of Colored People (NAACP) and the Congress of Racial Equality (CORE), as well as students from Shaw University and Saint Augustine's College, two historically black institutions, RWCA aimed its protests at segregated hotels, restaurants, theaters, and two high schools, Needham Broughton and Enloe. Community-based groups in Chavis Heights and Walnut Terrace, two low-income housing projects, joined RWCA to give numbers and weight to the street marches and demonstrations. White sympathizers

A civil rights protest at Fowler's Food Store in Chapel Hill in 1964.
North Carolina Collection, University of North Carolina at Chapel Hill

from North Carolina State, the University of North Carolina, and several other colleges in the region frequently joined RWCA in its actions. In the summer of 1963, Raleigh's mayor, W. G. Enloe, formed a biracial Committee of One Hundred to find ways to deal with the demands of the RWCA, and by the end of the summer almost all of Raleigh's downtown restaurants, hotels and motels, theaters, and businesses voluntarily had opened their facilities to African Americans. Within six weeks, the demonstrations ended peacefully. All of downtown Raleigh had quietly given up segregation. In rapid succession, city recreational facilities, swimming pools, and the public library system integrated. That fall, black students enrolled in Needham Broughton, in Enloe, and in classes throughout the school system. Additionally, the city made the biracial committee permanent and appointed more than twenty African Americans to advisory and commission boards. One member of the Committee of One Hundred became a city councilman in 1964. With the aid of grassroots organizations, coalitions of moderate whites and blacks, and middle-class businessmen and ordinary citizens, an emerging consensus effectively desegregated Raleigh in six weeks.

The same pattern developed in cities and communities throughout the state between 1961 and 1973. By appeals to self-interest such as economic growth rather than by debating the moral considerations of integration and equality, businessmen, white moderates, and new suburbanites successfully deflected the massive demonstrations and violence that characterized desegregation and integration throughout much of the South. Still, the new desegregation consensus guaranteed only the repoliticization and not the depoliticization of public education, and, with such plodding progress within the state overall, blacks in North Carolina and elsewhere increasingly turned to the federal courts to have the promise of the *Brown* decision fulfilled.

In rural areas outside the larger cities, desegregation and the push for equality encountered a more implacable face of North Carolina. The story of desegregation in Monroe, a small town eighteen miles southeast of Charlotte and also just a few miles from the South Carolina border, portrayed a more malevolent attitude of North Carolinians toward desegregation. It involved a segregated local swimming pool; one of the South's most galvanic race rebels, Robert Williams; the town's police chief, A. A. Mauney; and, eventually, even Fidel Castro, the Cuban revolution, China, and communism. In sum, Monroe became a microcosm of many of the issues of the time. A Monroe NAACP leader whose admiration of Castro estranged him from the national organization, Williams invited the Cuban leader to visit North Carolina and the South when Castro attended the United Nations General Assembly in New York in 1960. In his letter of invitation, published openly, Williams maintained that he had experienced his "first freedom as a human being in revolutionary Cuba and I feel very much indebted to the people who gave me the human dignity of being accepted in the human race." Castro never came to Monroe, but much of the civil rights revolution did.

In the summer of 1961, while picketing the segregated swimming pool in Monroe, demonstrators had shots fired at them in broad daylight while Chief Mauney watched. Mauney ignored the gunfire. Apparently angry at Williams and the protests, Monroe's police chief personified the denial of one of the rights African Americans sought after World War II, the equal protection of the law, as well as the arbitrary manner in which law enforcement agencies applied it. By the middle of the summer, Monroe had divided into armed camps. Parades by the Ku Klux Klan, reputed kidnapings, sporadic shooting, and mounting tensions became part of everyday life. Citizens in Newtown, the segregated black community, collected guns and weapons and prepared to defend themselves. Events in Monroe soon caught the eye of the SNCC in Raleigh, the Southern Christian Leadership Conference (SCLC) in Atlanta, and the Freedom Council in Chicago, all of whom sent representatives to Monroe. The Chicago Council sent several Freedom Riders as well. On the evening of 27 August, a small civil war between whites and blacks broke out in the center of the city. Afterward, Williams and his family, fearful for their lives, fled first to New York, then to Cuba, and eventually to China. He quickly became an anti-American propagandist, broadcasting his *Radio Free Dixie* from Cuba and writing polemical pamphlets on the struggle against oppression and racism in the United States. His book *Negroes with Guns,* complete with a Chinese edition, told the story of the Monroe civil rights protests between 1957 and his departure. Williams's appeal to armed self-reliance attracted admirers in the mid- and late 1960s from the Black Power movement and also from the Nation of Islam, which saw in him an alternative to Martin Luther King's nonviolent strategy, which they saw as plodding. Monroe effectively remained segregated and defiant as late as 1972.

Dissatisfied with the unevenness and gradualism of desegregation and also with the even more frustrating inchmeal progress toward full equality, African Americans after 1965 increasingly turned toward the courts and not elected representatives for action. From Williamston to Wilmington, the Legal Defense Fund of the NAACP filed lawsuits across the state to fulfill the pledge they found in the *Brown* decision. In 1969 one such case came before the federal court in Mecklenburg County. There, Judge James B. McMillan ordered Mecklenburg to use "any and all known ways of desegregation, including busing," to implement the *Brown* decision. Julius Chambers, one of only a few African American graduates from the University of North Carolina law school since its reluctant desegregation, argued the case against Mecklenburg County. In McMillan he found an unexpected ally. An adherent of a southern intellectual liberal tradition that had flourished in Chapel Hill since the

1920s, McMillan, also a Chapel Hill law graduate, sought to end North Carolina's gradualism through a radical plan.

The Charlotte-Mecklenburg decree constitutionally reconceptualized the *Brown* decision of 1954. Instead of desegregation, the process of allowing minorities where they formerly faced exclusion, the emphasis now shifted to full integration using majority/minority ratios that reflected the racial mix of a school district. The distinction proved crucial for North Carolinians. Integration posed a far greater threat. It brought basic institutions built around schools, families, neighborhoods, and politics into play in a society effectively desegregated and kept apart for more than three generations. Integration posited a new concept of equality, of neighborliness, of hierarchy, and of politics to a society exasperatingly disinclined to change its ways. Moreover, integration forced North Carolinians who thought themselves to be moderate and even liberal to confront the idea they had that most African Americans preferred segregation, albeit on an equal basis, because it allowed them to develop their own institutions and even succeed within their own culture. Charlotte proved a litmus test for that belief. In the Charlotte-Mecklenburg case, McMillan mandated a 71 percent white to 29 percent black ratio for each school in the district, the same racial mix of the city and county. To achieve this, he also ordered mandatory busing, an inflammatory idea not only for North Carolinians but also for the entire nation. The *Washington Post* soon described school busing as the country's most volatile domestic political issue. In 1971, in a deeply divided decision, the Supreme Court upheld McMillan's ruling, and terms such as "quotas" and "school busing" entered the lexicon of racial adjustment. Prodded by sit-ins and consensus, by court decisions and cooperation, and by a sense of its own progressive past and emerging future, North Carolina, perhaps more nonviolently than other southern states, accepted a broader understanding of civil rights for all its citizens. Still, the hesitant embrace of an enlarged concept of civil rights in North Carolina triggered the conservative mummies and ghosts of the state's past. In the 1970s, they in turn haunted the state's new political consensus.

As he surveyed the contours of a changing southern landscape in 1961, Barry Goldwater, an Arizona senator and subsequent 1964 Republican presidential candidate, saw in the upheaval over segregation an opportunity for the Republican Party. "We're not going to get the Negro vote," he mused, so "we ought to go hunting where the ducks are." For the Republicans, the ducks lined up neatly in tiers of states on a southern pond stretching from Virginia to Texas. As the South moved from racial segregation to integration in its public schools and from a rural and urban setting into an increasingly middle-class suburban one, Republican strategists saw a favorable set of circumstances that would allow them to get more ducks. They at last had an opportunity to move from the solid Democratic control of the South to a two-party competition. For Goldwater, whose convictions formed much of the basis of modern Republicanism, the eruptions in the South over integration gave his party a second chance to reconstruct the solid South politically, only this time the Republicans and not the Democrats would emerge as the states' rights party. Goldwater believed that Democrats in the South longed for a change, and he wanted the Republican Party to be the vehicle for their frustrations.

North Carolinians and many southerners' problems with liberal Democrats began in the 1930s with Franklin Delano Roosevelt and continued with his successor, Harry S. Truman.

A broadside depicting Frank Graham as
liberal on the issue of racial mingling.
North Carolina Collection, University of North
Carolina at Chapel Hill.

Responding to continued lynchings, especially of black veterans in Georgia, Truman appointed a Committee on Civil Rights in December 1946. One year later it published its findings in a report, *To Secure These Rights,* which became the basis for many later civil rights enactments. In July 1948 Truman by executive order banned discrimination in the armed forces, thus allowing for full integration of the army, navy, marine corps, coast guard, and air force. At Truman's insistence, the Democratic Party's national platform in 1948 included a strong civil rights plank. So incensed were southerners at Truman's policies on civil rights and labor that many bolted the convention and formed their own independent party, the Dixiecrats, which was led by J. Strom Thurmond, the governor of South Carolina. This southern heresy almost cost Truman the election. The North Carolina electorate continued to support Truman, yet Democratic factions in the state severely criticized him and his liberal policies. Southern ducks no longer habitually flocked to the Democrats.

North Carolina's simmering resentment against Roosevelt, Truman, and the liberals in the White House, especially concerning the issue of race, surfaced in the senatorial election of 1950. It presaged a tectonic shift in the politics of the South but not necessarily of North Carolina. As the 1950 election unfolded in North Carolina, a young journalist, Jesse Helms, pointed the way for Republicans in future campaigns. In the primary, Helms, working for Willis Smith, orchestrated an attack against Frank Porter Graham, an overwhelming favorite, casting him as an ultraliberal, especially on the issue of race. Coming as it did in the beginning of the cold war, Helms's assault cleverly incorporated not just the question of race but also the idea that an entire southern way of life was threatened by liberal ideas. Already besieged by "Godless Communism" and "international conspiracies," Helms proposed that southerners should defend their values, especially moral ones centered around religion, patriarchy, order, and family against the mongrelization of the white race that liberals seemed to want. Willis Smith won the primary and went on to become the state's next senator. Crudely racist in its appeal in 1950, the message became more sophisticated in the next decades until, by the 1980s, it had all but disappeared in a sea of abstractions that nonetheless had racism as its invocation. Graham went down to a surprising defeat in 1950, one of the first of scores of similar political results in the 1950s that more and more became less extraordinary. Increasingly, Jesse Helms's position came to personify the far right wing of the Republican Party nationally but not of the majority of traditionally moderate Republicans in North Carolina.

The events from the *Brown* decision in 1954 until the passage of the Civil Rights Act of 1964 forever changed politics in North Carolina and the South. Increasingly, many of those who now lived in suburbia and who thought of themselves as middle-class moderates felt themselves to be a silent majority, left out of national issues and alienated from mainstream politics in the push for integration and, later, affirmative action. Moreover, many who lived in rural areas, especially white males, felt powerless and dispossessed in the face of civil rights legislation they thought all but ignored their own issues and concerns. After 1954, symbols of rebellion, some taken from the Civil War and the Old South such as the Confederate battle flag, began to appear on bumper stickers on trucks and recreational vehicles as well as on state flags. North Carolina kept its colors intact without the addition of the rebel battle flag, preferring instead to choose one day to honor its Confederate dead by running up the stars and bars. With pretensions to treat the South fairly and to let it become a full part of the nation again, Republican strategists, indulging in subtle ways the everyday segregationist leanings of white southern voters, invoked a strategy to bring powerful swing voters from the South into state, regional, and national politics.

In its most basic form, the southern strategy of the Republicans after 1964 aimed at convincing worried and anxious whites that they had a friend in the Republican Party. Eventually, a new Republican coalition, seeking Goldwater's ducks, brought together the silent, alienated majority of states' rights advocates, economic conservatives, and elements from the old-time gospel hour, the religious right that subsequently underwrote the self-styled movement toward values of the 1980s, into a new coalition. In Charlotte, Jim and Tammy Bakker and the Praise the Lord Club (PTL) personified, at least briefly, the emphasis on family values of North and South Carolinians who recently had moved to suburbia. Within twenty years, the Grand Old Party of Lincoln and abolitionism, Yankees, carpetbaggers, scalawags, and freedmen emerged in a new form in the South. Within a century after Reconstruction, political parricide in North Carolina had come full circle.

Sophisticated racial and segregationist appeals underwrote much of the modern Republican Party's appeal in the South after 1964. Indeed, the question of race intrinsically became part of the new strategy even as it took on a more abstract form. A newer vocabulary of code words replaced the older, more blunt vernacular of segregation and white supremacy. Instead of segregation, threats from police authorities, and even crude referrals to color, the more specious racialism of the 1970s encapsulated appeals against forced busing, quotas, affirmative action, and distributive welfare. Many of the newer strategies came wrapped in such terms as local control, vouchers, charter schools, tax cuts, distributive welfare, and limited government interference in the private affairs of ordinary citizens. Still, Jesse Helms helped sway the senatorial race in North Carolina against Harvey Gantt by cleverly and transparently appealing to race in his notorious "white hands" commercial depicting a voter tearing up a job application for a position denied to him because of affirmative action.

The fight over taxes uniquely embodied the new abstraction of race in the South. As one Reagan campaign official explained it in 1980, "You're getting abstract now . . . you're talking about cutting taxes." To him, the "totally economic things" about arguing taxes, particularly changing the "breaks" given to each class, meant that "blacks get hurt worse than whites. And subconsciously maybe that is a part of it." The southern strategy for the Republicans after 1964 clearly meant more hostility not only to civil rights but to their enforcement as well. In 1964 Barry Goldwater won four southern states, forever breaking the Democrat's solid South. Richard Nixon swept all the states in the South, and it was the first time North Carolina had voted Republican since 1928. Except for Jimmy Carter's win in his home state of Georgia and in North Carolina in 1976, the South has remained a Republican presidential stronghold ever since. In 1984 and again in 1988, two Republicans, Ronald Reagan and George Bush, once again carried the now solid Republican South. Indeed, much of the South retained a healthy disregard for the Democrats in 1992, 1996, 2000, and 2004, largely disdaining one of their own in the process. In the razor-thin election of 2000, the Republican George W. Bush narrowly won over Al Gore, the Democratic candidate from Tennessee, primarily because of the southern strategy that had built up a solid party base in the South, especially in Florida, Georgia, and South Carolina. Still, the top-down strategy of the Republicans, aiming to build a successful presidential coalition and then use its new-found strength to go after state houses, senate and congressional seats, and, afterward, concentrate on local mayoral, commission, and council races, largely stalled. Two figures, Jesse Helms and Jim Hunt, illustrated the effects of the Republican's southern strategy in North Carolina after 1964 while they also incarnated the state's changed polity as well. The two dominated the state's politics for the last three decades of the century.

The reemergence of the Republican Party in North Carolina began in earnest in 1972 with the reelection of Richard Nixon and, along with him, Jesse Helms. Nixon's landslide victory in North Carolina also swept into office two newcomers, James E. Holshouser, a lifelong Republican from the mountain bastion of the party, as governor, and Jesse Helms, a former Democrat and born-again Republican, as senator. Conservative and restrained, Holshouser brought to Raleigh the traditional concerns of old-style Republicans within the state. Helms, on the other hand, used his television experience and personality to concentrate more on national issues. Using bytes and bits of sound and sight from the media, Helms painted all Democrats as tired old liberals who only wanted to tax, tax, and tax, so they could spend, spend, spend the hard-earned money of working-class, everyday people. The Populism of Our Bob Reynolds of the 1930s had reemerged in the appeal of "Good ol' Jesse" in the 1970s. Helms received support from both Nixon and Reagan, who, in televised speeches, challenged a North Carolina initiative, court-ordered busing designed to achieve racial quotas in schools. Both Republican presidents made it clear that the Justice Department would pursue a very limited interpretation of civil rights cases in the courts, a stance that appealed to many North Carolinians. By 1964 a majority within the state had accepted the idea that African Americans could and would now vote, eat in restaurants, and, in general, use public accommodations freely. Yet they still exhibited a great deal of anxiety about what the courts would do to integrate blacks and whites publicly in housing, schools, and the workplace, as well as in the private sphere of social clubs and organizations. Because of their western backgrounds, seemingly far removed from southern prejudices, Nixon and Reagan helped create in North Carolina and in the rest of the nation an atmosphere where it became respectable to oppose many of the later issues of integration such as forced busing and affirmative action.

Helms recognized that the national Republican Party's strategy of promoting the idea of less government intervention in the economy and of doing away with overweening bureaucracies also meant less government intrusion into micromanaging race relations and private affairs, two appeals that underwrote the southern strategy. They became siren calls for the North Carolina Republican Party. When he won reelection in 1978, Jesse Helms extended his control over the Republican Party in North Carolina. In 1980, once again riding the top-down wave of Reagan's victory, Helms's protégé, John East, won election as the state's other senator. Yet the weakness of the Republican strategy in North Carolina manifested itself in 1984 when Helms narrowly won over former Democratic governor James Hunt, while Terry Sanford, another ex-Democratic governor, was elected in 1986 to fill the vacated seat of John East, who died while in office. In 1990 and 1996, Helms won reelection over Harvey Gantt, the former mayor of Charlotte who had led sit-ins in Charleston and had become the first African American to graduate from Clemson University.

Through his political action committee, the National Congressional Club, Jesse Helms effectively controlled the North Carolina GOP since 1978. An ultraconservative who appealed to many New Southerners in the urban triangles around Raleigh and Charlotte, Helms also attracted rural voters who felt left out of the new prosperity of the 1980s, as well as suburban evangelical Christians. An early high point of Republican success came in 1980 when the GOP won four of the state's eleven congressional seats. They would win even more in the years to come. Still, in districts such as the fourth and sixth in the heart of the state and in the eleventh in the western mountains, Republicans have found it somewhat difficult to sustain their triumphs.

James B. Hunt represented the Achilles heel of the Republican strategy in North Carolina. A Kennedyesque Democrat who redefined the role of the governor in the 1980s, Hunt's strength derived from the historical mistrust North Carolinians had of Republicans on the local level. Helms's invocation of conservative issues, especially those built around race, polarized a significant minority within the state but did not lead to the white backlash predicted by the southern strategy. Except in a landslide victory such as that by Nixon in 1972 or by Reagan in 1980, no significant broadening of the Republican Party appeared. In fact, North Carolinians continued to elect Hunt as governor for another decade, and, except in 1994 and 1996, they usually sent a majority of Democrats to the general assembly. Using a black-white coalition, Hunt remodeled the Democratic Party to broaden its base and to appeal to the silent majority on ecumenical issues such as education and cleaning up the environment. Moreover, the success of the Voting Rights Act of 1965 meant that perhaps 15–20 percent of the electorate was now African American, an important constraint at the local level in many areas within the state. Yet as urban areas continued their growth and the state's demographics changed, the Republican Party continued to have more ducks to hunt on larger and larger ponds in North Carolina and the South. As it had in the first reconstruction of North Carolina a century before, an era of increased civil rights for all had provoked a conservative reaction by many.

On 3 November 1979, almost twenty years after the original sit-ins, Greensboro once more took center stage in state and national affairs. In a housing project known as Morningside Homes, a group of Klansmen and neo-Nazis opened fire on a "Death to the Klan" rally sponsored by the Communist Workers' Party. Nine demonstrators were wounded, while five others, physicians James Waller and Michael Nathan, along with Sandra Neely Smith, William Evan Sampson, and Cuban exile Caesar Vincent Cause, died in the melee. One year later, an all-white jury found the defendants not guilty by reason of self-defense. After twenty years of racial strife and progress in North Carolina, it seemed, as Alphonse Karr once said, "Plus ça change, plus c'est la même chose" (the more things change, the more they remain the same). Yet despite the Greensboro riot in 1979, things in North Carolina had undergone a fundamental change.

ADDITIONAL READINGS

Aistrup, Joseph A. "Southern Strategy and the Development of the Southern Republican Parties." Ph.D. diss., Indiana University, 1989.

Bagwell, William. *School Desegregation in the Carolinas: Two Case Studies.* Columbia: University of South Carolina Press, 1972.

Barksdale, Marcellus C. "Indigenous Civil Rights Movement and Cultural Change in North Carolina: Weldon, Chapel Hill, and Monroe." Ph.D. diss., Duke University, 1977.

Barnes, Melody C. "Reciprocal Impact: Bennett College and the Civil Rights Movement." Honors essay, University of North Carolina, 1986.

Bartley, Numan V., and Hugh D. Graham. *Southern Politics and the Second Reconstruction.* Baltimore: Johns Hopkins University Press, 1975.

Black, Earl, and Merle Black. *The Rise of Southern Republicans.* Harvard: Harvard University Press, 2002.

Bovard, Timothy L. "Republican Campaigns in North Carolina: What Is the Right Strategy for the Right?" Master's thesis, University of North Carolina, 1987.

Chafe, William. *Civilities and Civil Rights: Greensboro, North Carolina and the Black Struggle for Freedom.* New York: Oxford University Press, 1980.

———. "Greensboro Sit-Ins." *Southern Exposure* 6 (1978): 78–87.

Cohen, Robert C. *Black Crusader: A Biography of Robert Franklin Williams.* Secaucus: N.J.: Lyle Stuart, 1972.

Coogan, William H. "School Board Decisions on Desegregation in North Carolina." Ph.D. diss., University of North Carolina, 1971.

Dunston, Aingred G. "Black Struggle for Freedom in Winston-Salem, North Carolina, 1946–1977." Ph.D. diss., Duke University, 1981.

Edds, Margaret. *Free at Last: What Really Happened When Civil Rights Came to Southern Politics.* Bethesda: Adler and Adler, 1987.

Goldfield, David R. *Black, White, and Southern: Race Relations and Southern Culture, 1940 to the Present.* Baton Rouge: Louisiana State University Press, 1990.

Hodges, Luther H. *Businessman in the Statehouse: Six Years as Governor of North Carolina.* Chapel Hill: University of North Carolina Press, 1962.

Hunt, James B. *Addresses and Public Papers of James Baxter Hunt, Jr., Governor of North Carolina.* 2 vols. Edited by Memory F. Mitchell. Raleigh: Department of Archives and History, 1982.

Korstad, Robert R. *Civil Rights Unionism: Tobacco Workers and the Struggle for Democracy in the Mid-Twentieth Century.* Chapel Hill: University of North Carolina Press, 2003.

———. "Opportunities Found and Lost, and the Early Civil Rights Movement." *Journal of American History* 75 (December 1988): 786–811.

Luebke, Paul. *Tar Heel Politics: Myths and Realities.* Chapel Hill: University of North Carolina Press, 1990.

———. *Tar Heel Politics 2000.* Chapel Hill: University of North Carolina Press, 1998.

Minchin, Timothy J. "'Color Means Something': Black Pioneers, White Resistance, and Interracial Unionism in the Southern Textile Industry, 1957–1980." *Labor History* 39 (1998): 109–33.

Mohr, Clarence L. "Schooling, Modernization, and Race: The Continuing Dilemma of the American South." *American Journal of Education* 106 (1998): 439–50.

Parker, Gail, and Marlin Smith. "Bibliography on School Desegregation and the South, 1954–1979." *Southern Exposure* 7 (1979): 156–60.

Peebles, Wilma C. "School Desegregation in Raleigh, North Carolina, 1954–1964." Ph.D. diss., University of North Carolina, 1984.

Schoen, Johanna. "Between Choice and Coercion: Women and the Politics of Sterilization in North Carolina, 1929–1975." *Journal of Women's History* 13 (2001): 132–56.

Schwartz, Bernard. *Swann's Way: The School Busing Case and the Supreme Court.* New York: Oxford University Press, 1986.

Shoemaker, Don, ed. *With All Deliberate Speed: Segregation, Desegregation in Southern Schools.* New York: Harper and Co., 1957.

Snider, William D. *Helms and Hunt: The North Carolina Senate Race, 1984.* Chapel Hill: University of North Carolina Press, 1985.

Steed, Robert P., Tod A. Baker, and Laurence W. Moreland. "Forgotten but Not Gone: Mountain Republicans and Contemporary Southern Party Politics." *Journal of Political Science* 23 (1995): 5–27.

Thompson, Cleon F., Jr. "Comparison of Black and White Public Institutions of Higher Education in North Carolina." Ph.D. diss., Duke University, 1977.

University of North Carolina, Chapel Hill. *School Desegregation Decision: A Report to the Governor of North Carolina on the Decision of the Supreme Court of the United States on the 17th of May, 1954.* Chapel Hill: Institute of Government, 1954.

Wehr, Paul E. "Sit-down Protests: A Study of a Passive Resistance Movement in North Carolina." Master's thesis, University of North Carolina, 1961.

Williams, Eddie C. "Racial Tolerance in North Carolina: A Note on the Importance of Region." Master's thesis, University of North Carolina, 1976.

Williams, Robert F. *Negroes with Guns.* Edited by Marc Schliefer. Chicago: Third World Press, 1973.

Triads, Triangles, and Parks

TWENTY-ONE

The Urbanization of North Carolina

As he addressed the first annual urban affairs conference held in 1979 in Chapel Hill, the Research Triangle Institute president George R. Herbert wryly observed that he found it "exceedingly difficult to establish any single, clear meaning for the word 'urban,'" especially in a North Carolina context. Indeed, he noted that the state's "population-settlement pattern always has been something of an enigma to development economists at the national level, particularly the fact that such a large population base could be supported by such a dispersed population." The enigma remained throughout the rest of the twentieth century.

When Louis Wirth, a Chicago sociologist of the 1930s, wrote his defining essay on "Urbanism as a Way of Life," he had in mind as a model for urbanization the teeming industrial cities of the Northeast, not the mill towns of the South. At best, urban growth models like the concentric zone theory, wedge or sector theory, and multiple nuclei attempt to describe but not satisfactorily explain what has happened in North Carolina in terms of urbanization. Even the new urbanism of the 1980s, personified in developments like Southern Village, located on the edge of Chapel Hill, seem more metropolitan in trying to blur the lines between urban and rural, recalling the villages of two centuries ago and the communities they supported. Indeed, the new urbanism projected for the next century smacks of the old towns that personified life in North Carolina for centuries. In the end, sociologists and economists, more by default than by analysis, have characterized the state's population settlement pattern as a series of multinucleated urban crescents, Metrolina with Charlotte as its center, the triad of Greensboro, Winston-Salem, and High Point in the Piedmont, and Centralina, clustered around Raleigh, Durham, and Chapel Hill.

As Herbert pointed out, the concepts of urban and urbanization, fuzzy at best, seemed even more indistinct when talking about North Carolina. After all, this is a state of un-cities, unpolluted air, uncongested highways, and, unlike almost any other area in the South, it is without a dominant cultural and political center such as Charleston, Atlanta, Richmond, or Birmingham. Even today, Charlotte, the state's largest city with over 550,000 in its metropolitan district, still has less than 7 percent of the state's population, ranking North Carolina forty-ninth in the nation in that ratio. Smallness and not largeness, dispersion and not concentration, towns and not cities have always defined North Carolina. Still, in the last decades of the twentieth-century, it nonetheless became an urban state but with a continuing distinct pattern of development.

Urbanization in North Carolina followed a pattern similar to that of its latent, almost unapparent growth. The nineteenth-century depiction of North Carolina as a Rip van

Winkle state, a sleepy habitat peopled by laggards and lazylegs not unlike those in Lubberland, described centuries ago by Virginian William Byrd, had never sufficiently or adequately explained the state's development. Indeed, in the accounts of many historians and chroniclers of the state's past, North Carolina had snoozed while other, more ambitious southern states such as Virginia and Georgia progressed by them. Both regionally and nationally, North Carolina looked like a perennial tortoise to northern and southern hares. Yet North Carolina never lay dormant. It only developed in a way that, as Herbert noted, did not fit neatly prescribed formulas worked out by developmental economists. The enigma existed only in the minds and formal models of outsiders, never in the experience and history of those who dwelt here. Thus, much of North Carolina's urban history should be understood within the context of a state that stubbornly wanted to remain townless and cityless while it grew only incrementally.

361

North Carolina's geography predestined its urban development. An east to west axis, a north to south orientation to Virginia and South Carolina, a series of rivers flowing north to south, a lack of world-class deposits of minerals such as coal, copper, and gold, and the barrier islands all foreordained its gradual unfolding. In describing urbanization in the South after the Civil War, William J. Cooper pointed to the clustering of people and services, "first at sea and river ports, then more along the network of rails that covered the cotton belt." Gradually, these clusters followed a "stair-step pattern of small towns to large towns to small cities to large cities. Logically, metropolises came next," but not in North Carolina. Indeed, North Carolina stepped off the developmental ladder in the 1880s and, until the last two decades of the twentieth century, preferred to spread itself horizontally in a series of large towns and small cities and not vertically into sprawling metropolitan areas like Atlanta and Houston.

The lords proprietors who first envisioned the colony in 1663 thought not in terms of a dispersed rural populace living on small farms and plantations but rather of congested commercial and social centers such as London and Paris. For them, Carolina would evolve into a New York, Boston, Annapolis, or Philadelphia, and not into myriad isolated communities sprawling uncontrolled in a boundaryless New World setting. How could the proprietors effectively dominate such a large and dispersed population without urban centers? How could they govern or benefit commercially? Outside the towns and cities lay only barbarism and rebellion. Extolling the virtues of Annapolis in 1694, only five years after its founding, a pleased Londoner described it as a pretty town of "forty dwelling houses . . . a State House and a free school built with brick . . . and the foundation of a church laid." Clearly, towns represented organized religion, education, government, civility, good manners and civic mindedness. Outside them, yahoos and savagery ruled.

When he wrote Carolina's organic law, the Fundamental Constitutions, in 1689, John Locke, almost with Lord Shaftesbury looking over his shoulder, planted the idea of towns in three of the basic articles. For more than two decades afterward, instructions from the proprietors to Carolina's governors elaborated on the necessity of establishing towns and not allowing a dispersed pattern of settlement. Writing in 1674, even before Locke revised the Carolina charter of 1663, Shaftesbury carpingly reminded the colony's officials to "be very punctual in observing the instructions you receive from us amongst which there is none of more consequence [to] the security and thriving of our settlement than that of planting towns." When settlers asked for funds to purchase cattle and to give up their small plots of land in and around towns, Shaftesbury's patience ended. Noting that the proprietors had never been paid for tools, clothes, and supplies, he asked why they should give " a greater charge in cattle? . . . especially it being our design to have planters there and not grazers, for if our intentions were to stock Carolina at that rate, we could do better by . . . servants of our own, who would be more observant of our orders than you have been" and "plant in towns where we direct, take up no more lands than they had use for nor by a scattered and large tracts of ground taken up not like to be planted these many years." With or without the permission of the lords proprietors, early settlers in North Carolina easily fanned out in search of new land and opportunity.

To implement the proprietor's plans for the laying out of towns, the first general assemblies passed myriad laws regulating everything from public to private spaces. Town limits, sizes of lots, commons for the community and for grazing, street widths, fences, the necessity of public building and lots, construction of chimneys, the keeping of livestock, the drainage of streets and lots, and the collection of trash and feces all came under the scrutiny of the assemblymen and proprietors. While many of North Carolina's early towns reflected the gridiron and public square pattern of development, only Salem and New Bern, both settled by Moravians, Germans, and Swiss, attempted to enforce these early zoning regulations. Nonetheless, when Christoph von Graffenried laid out New Bern in the form of a triangle, he had in mind the Swiss cantonments of his homeland and not the urban ideals of the proprietors. Regardless of these attempts, early North Carolinians opposed any restrictions upon the use of their property, whether in a town or outside.

The proprietors' ideas of towns, urban centers, and closely knit communities did not die in America as did the dreams of so many castle builders in faraway London. Indeed, to a remarkable degree, their vision succeeded, yet in a way that from the very first separated and distinguished the two Carolinas, north and south, from each other, and, eventually, North Carolina from the rest of the nation. In North Carolina, towns held a special place in the polity that allowed them an equal vote with counties, a rare stipulation that remained until 1835 and the advent of Jacksonian democracy. In South Carolina, Charleston emerged as a dominant city, one of the great trading and cultural centers of the British empire, a development that surely would have pleased even the irascible Shaftesbury. South Carolina became a city-state while North Carolina remained a cityless province. Once again, North Carolina, while seemingly asleep and backward, went its own hermetic way, avoiding the developmental pattern and subsequent misconstructions of other colonies while steadily expanding westward in its own nucleated way.

Almost from its founding, North Carolina pioneered a growth pattern of scattered clumps of interconnected towns, crossroads, farms, and plantations that resembled woodlands and chaos rather than civilization and order. Indeed, early travelers such as Robert Beveridge and William Byrd from Virginia, the haughty Janet Schaw from England and Scotland, and royalty such as Francisco de Miranda from Venezuela, wondered if the colony had a center at all, much less any towns and culture. Yet in two areas, the Albemarle Sound and Lower Cape Fear region, a series of countrified towns sprang up, becoming focal points for North Carolina's early urban development.

Wilmington, Edenton, New Bern, Bath, Beaufort, and Brunswick never developed into a Charleston or an Annapolis, yet they functioned as keys to a labyrinth of communal activities that snaked their way along the rivers, roads, and streams that led into the interior. The pattern would be repeated as towns moved inland, roads and transportation improved, railroads, mills, and industries sprang up, and interstate highways and airports made the state even more interconnected yet still different. Rustic on the surface, North Carolina's development prototype almost from the first emphasized low-density settlements clustered around towns and, much later, cities. For over three hundred years, the state's settlers preferred to live within a day's ride of their towns and cities, either on the goodness of little horses and strong mules or on the wheels of more massive suburban utility vehicles. The idea that towns did not matter became a subject of much concern to all but North Carolinians.

Surveying the landscape of early North Carolina, the absence of commercial, cultural, and political centers obscured the fact that by the time of the Revolution the province ranked fourth in population among all the colonies in North America, whether British, French, or Spanish. Although perhaps as much as two-thirds of its trade went through Chesapeake ports and Charleston, North Carolina's total production, with those additions to the balance, made it one of England's most prolific and valuable colonies. Still, North Carolina never developed a commercial or planter elite, as did other southern colonies, nor did it have an enriching staple commercial crop such as tobacco, indigo, or rice, all dismissive factors to those who studied progress in the development of large towns and cities. Nonetheless, even by early American standards, it could be described as a megacolony.

A century later, North Carolina had duplicated the earlier pattern originally established in and around coastal towns in another tier of settlements further inland. Just before the American Revolution, a series of backcountry towns emerged, once again surrounding themselves with crossroads, settlements, farms, and villages. The newer backcountry towns, Halifax, Campbelltown, Cross Creek (now Fayetteville), Tarboro, Salisbury, Hillsborough, Charlotte, and Salem typically served as political and local administrative centers and also as loci for trade, skilled services, and mercantile centers. A traveler to Halifax before the Revolution described it as a place of "about fifty houses, stores are kept here to supply the country round with European and West Indian commodities for which pork, tobacco, Indian corn, wheat and lumber" were exchanged in trade. Even in their pubescence, North Carolina towns not only furnished goods and services for an expanding population of frontier immigrants but also maintained contacts with overseas merchants and entrepôts as well. As she traveled through rural North Carolina just prior to the Revolution, the snobbish Janet Schaw found that several women in the countryside, instead of offering her soap made from ashes and oils presented her with sweet-smelling Irish soap, purchased from stores at a monstrous price. Sitting on the edge of the frontier on the Great Wagon Road, Salem's Moravians operated a thriving trade and postal service that pushed northward into Pennsylvania and New York and southward into Charlotte and Charleston. Hardly isolated even by modern standards, North Carolinians enjoyed their space while they avoided the forces of centralization that drew other colonists into ever larger units.

North Carolina's early prosperity, although rudimentary and formative, its occupational and economic diversification, and its nucleated settlements supported a large population base that remained spatially separated. To the colony's first settlers, towns did not matter, nor did the cultural diversity they brought. While towns and cities in other colonies pulled settlers into crowded centers, North Carolinians instead preferred a less gravitational approach, usually stopping at town limits. Maps showing the distribution of population in 1740, 1790, and 1830, represented by black dots spread over the state, never show them coming together in larger blobs or masses. Only after World War II did the population droplets strung throughout the state become swollen tearlike formations representing larger groupings, and then only in the Piedmont.

Between the American Revolution and the Civil War, towns in North Carolina developed sectionally, seemingly without links to each other or to larger communities in the antebellum South. Travelers through the area inevitably stressed the absence of large towns, the abundance of primitive taverns in isolated locales, the pervasiveness of tobacco culture, and the lack of refinement of its inhabitants. In fact, North Carolina's first real capital, Raleigh, was chosen almost precisely because of those factors. The large number of small and large towns in the 1830s reflected not only the expansion into the Piedmont and western mountains but also a future urban configuration that set North Carolina apart from the rest of the South.

Without a Richmond or a Charleston and with its relatively slow development, especially in education, North Carolina paid a heavy price for its participation in the Civil War. As a state, its soldiers, mostly from small farms and crossroads towns, became cannon fodder for Lee's campaigns in Virginia and Pennsylvania and also for keeping Sherman at bay in Tennessee and Georgia. The absence of a large seaport such as Mobile or New Orleans eventually made the much smaller port of Wilmington, the state's largest city, a major player in the blockade that kept the Confederacy alive. The state's nascent railroad system, principally the Wilmington to Weldon line, shuffled troops and supplies between South Carolina, Georgia, and Virginia, mainly for Lee's Army of Northern Virginia. Without major educational institutions such as the Universities of Virginia and South Carolina or military academies like Virginia Military Institute, North Carolina produced an oversupply of colonels for its long regimental lines but a dearth of field generals to decide where and when they fought and died.

In Richmond, the Tredegar Iron Works exemplified the newer technical competencies needed in the nation's first industrially advanced iron age war, skills noticeably absent in North Carolina, where production and processing lagged behind manufacturing. In both the Confederate and Federal Congresses, North Carolina, while large in population and production, had lessened influence politically. Without a large city or an elite class of planters, merchants, politicians, or first families linked to each other and to communities throughout the nation, North Carolina had fewer Jefferson Davises and Wade Hamptons to help decide policy. For his part, Zebulon Vance, North Carolina's Civil War governor, could get Richmond's attention only by threatening to withhold troops and warehoused supplies, never by negotiating as a political confidant of Jefferson Davis or through the state's Confederate cabinet or congressional representation. Of course, when the Civil War ended, North Carolina also did not have burnt-out hulks of cities and factories to rebuild, no Atlantas or Columbias or Richmonds to resurrect, as did other, more devastated southern states. Cities like Raleigh, Greensboro, and Charlotte emerged relatively intact.

A small county seat in 1850 with a population of just around one thousand, Charlotte developed rapidly before the Civil War when the Charlotte and South Carolina Railroad linked it with Columbia. With its marketing facilities and railroad line virtually intact at the end of the war, Charlotte quickly blossomed into the Queen City of the New South, surrounded by new cotton and textile mills. When Sherman turned into North Carolina after leaving the infamous burned-over district through Georgia and South Carolina, North Carolinians and historians took little notice. With no cities to raze and only one or two small armories to burn, Sherman's hike into the Piedmont resembled more a training exercise through the woods than a punitive war-is-hell campaign.

After the Civil War, North Carolina eagerly embraced the New South philosophy of urbanization, industrialization, and agricultural diversification but with differing results. As post–Civil War towns and cities began to build their economies around manufacturing and industry, North Carolina once again lagged behind. Richmond, an industrial center before the Civil War, quickly emerged as the South's leader with more than one hundred factories churning out tobacco and flour products as well as iron and steel foundries and mills producing goods for its southern hinterland. Six railroads terminated in Richmond while steamboats connected it to the Chesapeake cities of Baltimore and Norfolk and northward to Philadelphia and New York. Richmond justly deserved its designation as a terminus for southern industry. After 1886, Birmingham and the towns of Sheffield, Bessemer, and Anniston became the Pittsburgh of the South, producing one-tenth of the nation's pig iron. Nonexistent before the Civil War, Birmingham had seven-thousand workers in its mills by 1900 and perhaps forty thousand in its environs. To the west, Memphis, a small transshipping town on the Mississippi, quadrupled its value of manufactured products from 1880 to 1890, from more than four million to over thirteen million in products and from thirty-eight thousand to sixty-four thousand in population. Nashville, Little Rock, Atlanta, New Orleans, Mobile, Tampa, and, Galveston, Texas, experienced similar surges caused by the coming of the railroads and industry. Not surprisingly, the list of the South's largest cities from 1880 to 1900 did not contain any names from North Carolina. Once again, the state's development took a different turn.

Yet by 1900, the state nonetheless had emerged as the region's industrial leader. By 1920, it clearly dominated southern manufacturing in numbers of workers, plants, mills, and the value of its products, surpassing Texas, Tennessee, and Alabama as its closest rivals. By 1895 a string of new tobacco towns in North Carolina had replaced Richmond as the nation's tobacco center, using that city's own newer technologies to roll their cigarettes faster and better. With the appeal of national advertising, tobacco manufacturing became a lucky strike for the Dukes of Durham. Indeed, as late as 1870 the town of Durham did not even appear on the census or on regional maps, but by 1895 its population had reached eight thousand. In the Piedmont, Winston, really a sister town to the thriving but smaller industrial and manufacturing center at Salem, had less than five hundred inhabitants in 1880 but a decade later more than 10,000 people lived within two miles of downtown Elm and Market streets. The same pattern emerged in the west, where Hickory gradually replaced Danville as the nation's furniture center, and, in the Piedmont, a string of textile mills in towns like Concord, Gastonia, and Charlotte eventually gave the state not only the regional but also the national textile leadership. In the mountains, Asheville, discovered by the throngs of tourists who came on the newly laid railroad after 1880, ballooned from 2,616 in 1880 to 10,235 in 1890. Yet, while they moved to and near towns, North Carolinians avoided many of the significant centralizing forces that caused large cities to emerge throughout the nation. Textile, tobacco, and furniture mills preferred to operate in smaller towns and to avoid concentrating in any one area. Overall, the state still had only modest urban pretensions.

Almost all traditional histories of urbanization, whether in the South or in other regions, usually chronicled the rise of cities after the Civil War, commonly as a product of railroads and industries, then ignored them until after World War II. Within this lacuna, as historians tell us, cities, both in the North and the South, began to deal with the ills of rapid urbanization, slum housing, prostitution, inadequate sewer and water systems, electrification, and, most important of all, the impact of automobiles. Yet in this hiatus from 1890 until the end of World War II, North Carolina continued the same pattern of incremental development of its towns and cities while still expanding its overall population. The ills of concentrated urbanization would wait another half century to emerge in North Carolina.

When Sallie Southall Cotten attended the Chicago World's Fair of 1893, the experience not only inspired her latent feminism, it also quickened her aesthetic sensibilities. For her and for others at the turn of the century, Chicago offered a vision of the future, a "Great White City" of beautiful parks and Venice-like lagoons. The congruence of classical architecture, well-planned footpaths, landscaped parks, and planned commercial districts and neighborhoods, all hallmarks of Chicago at the turn of the century, inspired a "City Beautiful" movement across America. Yet in North Carolina, urban beautification instead took the form of a "City Parks" or a "Village Green" spirit. Since the state had no large cities, nor did it possess many of the ills associated with early urbanization, the focus of reformers centered around cleaning up cities and making them parklike in appearance. Mill villages elicited a similar pastoral response.

Women's clubs such as the Woman's Association for the Betterment of Public Schools quickly expanded their civic interest beyond schools to include the cities that nurtured them. While maintaining an interest in rural education as well, women's clubs, located mainly in towns and cities, drew their membership primarily from white, middle-class women who found that city beautification projects were not only popular with women but also seemed inoffensive to men and outside their criticism of "women's work." For many men, women's involvement in beautification programs simply seemed an extension of traditional roles they had come to accept. When the North Carolina Federation of Women's Clubs organized in 1902, village beautification became one of its founding departments. For many women, the shift from the private sphere to the larger community, in this case municipal housekeeping, seemed not only logical but natural.

Frederick Law Olmsted, the landscape architect of the Chicago World's Fair and New York's Central Park, came to North Carolina, where he created a model village on the edge of George Washington Vanderbilt's vast estate. Called Biltmore Village, it incorporated many of the ideas that reformers had of an ideal community at the turn of the century.

John Singer Sargent's portrait of Frederick Law Olmsted, America's finest landscape designer of the nineteenth century, painted on the Biltmore Estate in Asheville in 1893.
Used with permission of the Biltmore Company, Asheville, North Carolina.

The Biltmore House in Asheville. Planned and constructed by George Washington Vanderbilt and finished in 1891, it remains one of the "finest castles in America."
Used with permission of the Biltmore Company, Asheville, North Carolina.

Budgett Meakin, a British socialist who toured the United States at the turn of the century, thought it to be the most pleasant village to be found in either Europe or America. Biltmore had one hundred houses, an impressive Episcopal church, a hospital, a gym, a restaurant, gently curving roads for wagons and carriages, trees planted among grassy strips throughout, a commons area for recreation and community get-togethers, walking paths, and a schoolhouse surrounded by large trees and plantings. Attuned to the new technologies brought about by electricity and railroads, Olmsted ordered all wiring to be buried and the railroad station to be built apart from the village, separated by a wide space that accommodated four carriages side-by-side. Olmsted used natural barriers such as the Swannanoa River and the surrounding forests to insulate Biltmore from Asheville, its sprawling urban neighbor to the north.

Until 1880, Asheville, like many towns in the state, existed primarily as a rural county seat, a crossroads village with hogs running wild in the street and wagons loaded with corn and wood mired in the mud around Pack Square, its legal and cultural center. Describing it in 1870 as a pretty country town, a visitor remarked that the chief occupation seemed to be the manufacture of illicit corn whiskey and its sale on the square. Two decades later, Asheville had more than 10,500 people and a healthy reputation as a wide-open city. As mayor from 1889 to 1893, Charles Blanton, inspired by two activists, Mrs. W. F. Cocke and Helen Lewis, determined to reform Asheville and make it the most progressive city in the state. Blanton closed twelve brothels and gaming establishments, licensed saloons, and set up a board of health, added paved sidewalks around the square, helped bring streetcars to the city, gave funds for a public library, and promoted the establishment of universal public education for whites and blacks alike. With brothels and prostitution gone, a new public sanitation system in place, paved streets, and a landscaped downtown, Blanton hoped that Asheville would retain its parklike appearance in the midst of its unprecedented growth. By the turn of the century, North Carolina had several Charles Blantons in its bustling new cities.

In 1911 John Nolen, perhaps one of the finest city planners and developers of the early twentieth century, built Myers Park, a gardenlike subdivision outside Charlotte. Nolen's description of the setting, "a gently rolling countryside covered here and there with beautiful groves of oak and pine," echoed the sentiments of North Carolinians as they moved from farms to towns to cities. They took the countryside with them, a process that the historian C. Vann Woodward labeled "rurbanization." A comprehensive plan of wide boulevards, parks, homes, and stores, Myers Park avoided the crowding of row houses and tenements of older northeastern cities. North Carolinians transplanted their gardens, flowers, spacious lots, and, more than anything, trees to their new places in the city. An instant success, Myers Park became a model for early subdivisions. For his part, Nolen, a native of Cambridge, Massachusetts, went to Asheville, where he took Blanton's ideas and made them into still another "City Beautiful" plan.

Mill villages came in for special scrutiny from turn-of-the-century reformers. When the railroad came to all parts of North Carolina after 1880 and the textile industry mushroomed, mill owners, many of them with local roots, sought to recruit labor from surrounding farms and to house them in a nearby central village. For forty years, mill villages sprouted across North Carolina, many of them still visible today. Frequently hastily constructed, jerry-built from local materials and imperfectly planned, the villages had little to offer esthetically. Monotonous in their same paint and building schemes, dull in their rows of homes creeping up hills and gullies, and frequently without sidewalks and water or sewer systems, mill towns nonetheless offered most North Carolinians a better place to live than they had previously known. Mill workers set about planting gardens and flowers between their equidistant homes, bringing in chickens, cows, pigs, and livestock from their farming past, fixing up front and back porches, and customizing their new dwellings with rural-like accoutrements. Space, gardens, trees, flowers, and the barnyard, all fixtures in the country, followed North Carolinians into mills, towns, and cities.

Within a decade, first-generation mill owners, many from North Carolina or elsewhere in the South, began to encourage their managers and foremen to give prizes for

Howard W. Odum (1884–1954).
North Carolina Collection, University
of North Carolina at Chapel Hill.

home-grown vegetables, gardens, flowers, and, to the amazement of many mill workers, the best kept yard, now called a lawn, in each village. Beautification was catching. In similar fashion, mills themselves began to take on pleasant appearances, with increased plantings, flowers, and landscaping. In Greensboro, Budgett Meakin, still traveling through the South but thinking about England, called the aptly named Proximity Village, with its neatly painted white homes trimmed in green and blue, each with its own garden and landscaping, the best mill village he had come across in any southern state.

While the automobile gave birth to modern southern cities after 1900 and allowed them to expand horizontally instead of vertically, North Carolinians had initiated a good-roads movement after World War I that, while it enhanced automobility, did not alter their tendency to remain spatially dispersed. By 1920 the census counted sixty-nine towns with populations over 2,500, an urban boundary then, and three with more than 25,000 residents. Even in the Depression years of the 1930s, the tendency toward gradualism continued. By the beginning of World War II, Charlotte at last had attained a population of 100,000.

If anything, the New Deal and World War II, while they promoted urbanization in a great many southern states such as Louisiana and Georgia, did little to change North Carolina's slow shift from a predominantly rural to an industrial-urban economy. Although Wilmington benefited from shipbuilding contracts while training camps in Butner and Fayetteville boosted local economies, World War II did not bring large-scale government industries into the state, as it did in Texas, Alabama, and Louisiana. Government ordnance plants in Fayetteville and Durham, as well as other specialized industries such as manufacturing parachutes, did not easily convert into peacetime uses. Still, in the Piedmont, clothing, textile, and tobacco plants profited from increased demand. In addition, the war exposed North Carolina to the nation as a relatively underdeveloped region and encouraged the migration of capital, both human and fiscal, into the state. It also accentuated the continuing shift of population from rural areas to cities in triads, crescents, and in surprising new research parks.

Before he died in 1954, Howard W. Odum, perhaps the state's greatest social scientist and visionary of the early twentieth century, had done much to convince politicians and

University Day at the University of North Carolina at Chapel Hill, 12 October 1961.
Left to right: Terry Sanford, William C. Friday, John F. Kennedy, and William B. Aycock.
North Carolina Collection, University of North Carolina at Chapel Hill.

college officials of the necessity of bringing a new low-impact industrial park, a technology-oriented branch plant complex set in a beautiful village green, to North Carolina. In Odum's view, the enterprise would be overseen by a nonprofit but tax-paying corporation devoted to research and development, all affiliated with but separate from the University of North Carolina at Chapel Hill, Duke University, and North Carolina State University. Odum believed that if located within the groves of academia itself, the entrepreneurial impulses of such a corporate enterprise would be strangled by the ivy vines of traditionalism. Yet proximity to and long-term involvement with research institutions would only strengthen the complex overall.

In order to promote Odum's idea, Gov. Luther Hodges (1954–61) appointed a Research Triangle Committee to raise funds for the purchase and development of five thousand acres for the park and also to sell the idea not only to the public but also to the general assembly. The names of the committee members, all university presidents, officials, and representatives of industry, such as George Simpson Jr., Robert M. Hanes, William C. Friday, Hollis Edens, Karl Robbins, and Archie K. Davis, became famous as cultural icons in the new regionalism that swept over the South after World War II.

Howard Odum believed, as did Walter Hines Page before him, that North Carolina's phantoms that haunted its past—in this instance, segregation, lynching, religious fundamentalism, sharecropping, child labor, and undereducation—also doomed its future. Using his Institute for Research in Social Science and his journal, *Social Forces*, both located at the University of North Carolina at Chapel Hill, he set about to effect change in the South after World War II. For Odum, the early movement of some states toward desegregation and the end of World War II offered an unprecedented opportunity for his vision to take root. With the support of W. T. Couch, the editor of the University of North Carolina Press, who published much of his research, of the university's president, the much respected Frank Porter Graham, and of governor Luther Hodges, Odum attempted to convince outsiders that conditions in North Carolina had changed so much that they would do well to move here. After Odum's death, George Simpson, William Friday, Luther Hodges, and Terry Sanford carried on his work.

Between 1959 and 1961, the Research Triangle Park and, within it, the institute, struggled for an identity and survival. The purchase of a five-thousand-acre Research Park outside Durham, the move there of the Chemstrand Corporation, utilizing 200,000 square feet, and the displacement there of facilities of the U.S. Forestry Service all sustained the effort, but the park still had not emerged as a major technology-oriented industrial complex by the early 1960s. Two factors still slowed the growth and development of the park: North Carolina's old attitudes toward race and its own inhibiting statewide macroeconomic policies. In order to attract potential entrepreneurs and founders of new high-technology firms, most in their late thirties with advanced degrees, North Carolina had to prove that it had moved beyond its past to a new position of leadership in the South. That opportunity came with desegregation.

Although the struggle to eliminate segregated schools in North Carolina involved almost every town and county, it came to center on five cities with the largest African American communities, Winston-Salem, Greensboro, Durham, Raleigh, and Charlotte. One city in particular, Charlotte, became a national focal point as it pioneered the concept of school busing to desegregate the schools of urban America. Much like Durham and Chapel Hill, Charlotte also had a campus, a branch of the University of North Carolina system, and, equally significant, another research park modeled on the Research Triangle concept. Over the course of two decades, Charlotte had adapted itself to modified expectations in desegregating its schools, a change that came more easily than in most southern cities. With an organized and politically active black community, a white power elite that put aside its distaste for extensive busing and pupil mixing for larger economic goals, and a court system that guided the entire process against the backdrop of evolving and sometimes vague constitutional interpretations, Charlotte took a different view of segregation than much of the state and nation. When Judge James Bryan McMillan handed down his decision in the Swann case to bus students for racial mixing in 1969, Charlotte's leadership, both political and corporate, laid aside its personal opposition to racial mixing for the larger goals of community prosperity. Although seemingly a decision on schools and desegregation, the Swann case and its aftermath accelerated North Carolina's role in a burgeoning regional economy. When the University of North Carolina acquiesced in its battle with the Justice Department, the transformation seemed complete. After 1970 both technology-oriented industrial parks experienced phenomenal growth adjacent to metropolitan areas that increasingly became more diverse economically and socially.

Within two decades, a significant incidence of high-technology startups and spin-offs occurred in the Raleigh-Durham and Charlotte areas. Most began after 1980 in service-oriented industries and employed less than twenty to thirty people. The majority of the park's founders, just as Odum had hoped, had worked in the same or related businesses in other regions, had lived in North Carolina or the South only a short time, and had little entrepreneurial or small-business experience, but found the business climate, both micro and macro, to be exciting and potentially lucrative. More important, they sensed that North Carolina had changed, that it now provided a more conducive personal and social environment than other states in the region. In a fundamental way, the state's recruitment efforts for technology-oriented branch plants located in parks laid the foundation for a significant restructuring and reshaping of its economy. From 1970 to 2000, Wake and Mecklenburg counties grew by almost half a million people, the largest increase in the state. By 1997, 15 percent of North Carolina's population lived in the same two counties, now home to the state's two largest cities, Charlotte and Raleigh, and also to its two research triangle parks. By 2000, they accounted for perhaps 16 percent of the state's entire population.

At present, North Carolina has seventeen areas labeled as urbanized by the U.S. Census, a designation that makes them larger than cities of at least fifty thousand yet smaller than metropolitan areas, usually defined as counties that might share a larger city as well as other adjacent areas. Yet perhaps the easiest way to understand the new urbanism that has emerged in North Carolina since 1970 lies in another formulation. In 2000, almost 75 percent of all North Carolinians lived within fifteen miles of one of the state's interstate highways. One-third lived adjacent to Interstate 85 running from the Charlotte-Gastonia-Concord triangle in the South to the Raleigh-Durham-Chapel Hill triangle in the center of the state. To the east, Wilmington, and, to the west, Asheville, acted as anchors to other triads, triangles, and parks that today characterize urban North Carolina. Soon they, too, will form their own triangles around interstates that connect them to adjacent states.

Notwithstanding the enormous growth in the Raleigh-Durham and Charlotte-Gastonia areas, North Carolina still lacks a dominant city. Although Charlotte had more than 536,000 in population by 2000, that represented slightly less than 9 percent of the state's total, a figure that ranked the state next to last in the proportion of overall population contained in the largest urbanized area. Even West Virginia had a larger percentage of its population in one city, Morganton, than did North Carolina. Moreover, each of the state's largest ten cities, from Charlotte to Asheville, had carved out a niche for itself either in terms of a specific industrial, mercantile, cultural, or political distinctiveness. From banking in Charlotte to tourism in Asheville, North Carolina's new cities complement more than compete with each other in the state's new economy.

Yet even in the year 2000 urbanization in North Carolina still did not fit theoretical paradigms. Anthropologists such as Robert Redfield and Milton B. Singer classified the process of urbanization as proceeding in two stages, the first, or primary one, where cities simply reflected the folkways of those who moved there, and the second, where cities reversed the flow of assimilation, altered the dominant culture and diffused it back into the surrounding countryside. Redfield and Singer called the initial, or primary cities, orthogenetic in nature, and the secondary cities heterogenetic in their effect. In North Carolina, the process of urbanization, not surprisingly, has taken a different tack, not orthogenetic or heterogenetic but protean instead. In looking for its identity in a growing complex of metropolitan areas, North Carolina has managed to retain much of its love of dispersion, of space and land with its new growth and development. In so doing, it has become an attractive prototype for urbanization in the nation's future, all the while bedeviling economists and urban studies specialists who stubbornly have predicted its consolidation and high-density concentrations for the past three decades.

In describing the process of urbanization in North Carolina, Gerald L. Ingalls, a professor of geography at the University of North Carolina at Charlotte, expressed his disdain for Gov. James Hunt's balanced-growth policy of the late twentieth century. For Ingalls and many other urban policy analysts, the balanced-growth initiative represented a throwback to "what remains of the old courthouse crowd" in politics, to a group that wanted to protect "the economic interests of small-town and rural North Carolina, the textile industry, and tobacco" capitalists who helped make up an outdated progressive plutocracy of the past. Indeed, to urban analysts, frequently frustrated by North Carolina politics and its practitioners, such short-sighted schemes would "take increasingly scarce state resources . . . and allocate them by a formula that is highly favorable to rural areas." Ingalls referred to a 1992 formula in which state leaders suggested that "transportation funds be used to pave every road in the state that carries more than fifty cars per day" as an example of North Carolina's shortsightedness. Although Hunt's policy embodied sound county seat politics from a good old boys' perspective, Ingalls maintained that it instead should allocate funds "to the needs of the more competitive, largely urban, economic core of the state." Such an outlay of monies would better prepare North Carolina "for participation in the global economy of the future," the holy grail of urban planners and economists. Once more, an urban planner had misconstructed North Carolina's gradual unfolding.

North Carolina's prototype development into triangles, triads, and parks happened as much by accident as by design. When North Carolinians began moving to larger towns and cities after 1970, they took their love of place and space with them. "It's the land," mused Robert Bridwell, a planning director in Nash County in the late 1970s, "it gives them a sense of security. Even if they don't live on farms anymore, they prefer to live in subdivisions" away from freeways and cities. After Luther Hodges, Governors Terry Sanford and James Hunt worked to keep new industries and growth scattered. From 1961 to 1998, the state deliberately built good roads into even the most rural of communities, decentralized the state university system with its sixteen campuses over all three regions, set up a system of fifty-eight widely dispersed community colleges, and preplanned vocational education programs attuned to the needs of local industries. State policy, so derided by urban planners, sought, along with the new growth, to keep North Carolina a place where everyone could find a quiet corner or a busy triangle. Although most North Carolinians today live within fifteen miles of a major interstate or four-lane thoroughfare, they find their way to work on well-constructed smaller roads that lead to those freeways and interstates, all built by state planners. By "paving every road in the state that carries more than fifty cars per day," North Carolina has created an interconnected complex of highways that allowed most to commute not only to their jobs but also to their families within thirty to forty minutes. As high-density megacities characterized the transition of other states from rural to town to urban life, North Carolina instead established a slow-growth, low-density urbanization that, while it inevitably will consolidate into larger triangles and triads, still is spreading and broadening the sense of place that most who reside in the state traditionally have enjoyed.

Almost any explanation of urbanization in North Carolina emerges from the perspective of an increasingly congested Independence Boulevard in Charlotte, the gridlock of Crabtree Valley Mall in Raleigh, or a packed High Point Road in Greensboro. The products of high technology parks, of a new city-driven economy, of interstates, thoroughfares, and freeways, and of triads of midsize cities, Charlotte, Raleigh, and Greensboro, on the surface, seem ideal models to explain the process of concentration, consolidation, centralization, and urbanization in North Carolina. Still, another perhaps more appropriate interpretation emerges from the vantage point of Trust, a small crossroads town at the intersection of state highways 63 and 209 in western North Carolina. Located in the minuscule triad of Joe, Luck, and Pleasant Creek in Madison County, the state's most rural, the prosperous General Store at Trust serves seven different kinds of salads as well as veggie burgers not only to locals but also to tourists, businessmen from nearby Asheville and Waynesville, and recreational bikers and rafters from several states. At Stoney Knob, a small restaurant in Weaverville not more than twenty miles from Trust, a Mediterranean salmon dish complete with an excellent Chardonnay and a Greek baklava dessert awaits diners from three or more counties and states. Examples such as this abound in contemporary North Carolina.

Both Trust and Weaverville share the same characteristics, as do similar places near Southport and Beaufort. Located just off well-paved state roads, with easy access to interstates, local colleges, small and large towns, dispersed industrial sites, and new developments that include reasonable and spacious lots and homes, they personify North Carolina's idea of urbanization. Living in Trust, Weaverville, Eden, Supply, or almost any small town in North Carolina, residents easily can commute to their jobs, their families, and recreation areas in under forty minutes, which is quite reasonable compared to travel times in other regions. As much as Charlotte and Raleigh-Durham, smaller entities such as Trust have characterized North Carolina's urbanization, a process of slow growth and low-density settlement that makes the state distinct among its southern and northern sisters. Indeed, a larger understanding and even a prototype of future development in North Carolina and the nation can be found not in Charlotte, Raleigh, or Greensboro, but in Trust.

ADDITIONAL READINGS

Bishir, Catherine W., Charlotte V. Brown, Carl R. Lounsbury, and Ernest H. Wood III. *Architects and Builders in North Carolina: A History of the Practice of Building.* Chapel Hill: University of North Carolina Press, 1990.

Bishir, Catherine W., and Lawrence S. Earley. *Early Twentieth-Century Suburbs in North Carolina: Essays on History, Architecture, and Planning.* Raleigh: Division of Archives and History, 1985.

Chang, Jane. "Intermediate Socio-Economic Development Region: A Case Study of North Carolina." Master's thesis, Appalachian State University, 1990.

Clay, James W., and Douglas M. Orr Jr., eds. *Metrolina Atlas.* Chapel Hill: University of North Carolina Press, 1972.

Clay, James W., Douglas M. Orr Jr., and Alfred W. Stuart, eds. *North Carolina Urban Regions: An Economic Atlas.* Charlotte: University of North Carolina, 1983.

Clay, James W., and Alfred W. Stuart, eds. *Charlotte: Patterns and Trends of a Dynamic City.* Charlotte: University of North Carolina, 1987.

Colvard, Dean W., Douglas Orr Jr., and Mary Bailey. *University Research Park: The First Twenty Years.* Charlotte: University of North Carolina, 1988.

Escott, Paul D., and David R. Goldfield, eds. *The South for New Southerners*. Chapel Hill: University of North Carolina Press, 1987.

Fields, Ernest L. "State-Level Collaboration among Government, Education, and Private Industry for Economic Development in North Carolina and Ohio: An Ecological Perspective." Ph.D. diss., Ohio State University, 1984.

Franco, Michael R. "Key Success Factors for University-Affiliated Research Parks: A Comparative Analysis." Ph.D. diss., University of Rochester, 1985.

Goldfield, David R. *Cotton Fields and Skyscrapers: Southern City and Region, 1607–1980*. Baton Rouge: Louisiana State University Press, 1982.

Hamilton, William B. "Research Triangle of North Carolina: A Study in Leadership for the Common Weal." *South Atlantic Quarterly* 65 (Spring 1966): 254–78.

Hanchett, T. W. *Sorting out the New South City: Race, Class, and Urban Development in Charlotte*. Chapel Hill: University of North Carolina Press, 1998.

Harris, Linda L. *Early Raleigh Neighborhoods and Buildings*. Raleigh: Raleigh City Council, 1983.

Hobbs, Samuel H., Jr. *North Carolina: An Economic and Social Profile*. Chapel Hill: University of North Carolina Press, 1958.

Hoffman, Carolyn F. "Development of Town and Country: Charlotte and Mecklenburg County, 1850–1880." Ph.D. diss., University of Maryland, 1988.

Huggins, Kay H. "City Planning in North Carolina, 1900–1929." *North Carolina Historical Review* 46 (October 1969): 377–97.

———. "Evolution of City and Regional Planning in North Carolina, 1900–1950." Ph.D. diss., Duke University, 1967.

Kratt, Mary N. *Charlotte, Spirit of the New South*. Winston-Salem: John F. Blair, 1992.

Larsen, L. *The Urban South: A History*. Lexington: University of Kentucky Press, 1990.

Lemmon, Sarah M. "Raleigh—An Example of the 'New South'?" *North Carolina Historical Review* 43 (July 1966): 261–85.

Little, William F. "Research Triangle Park." *World & I* 3 (November 1988): 178–85.

McLain, Geraldine. "Economic Impact of North Carolina's Research Triangle Park on Its Tri-county Area." Master's thesis, University of North Carolina, 1966.

Moye, William T. "Charlotte-Mecklenburg Consolidation: Metrolina in Motion." Ph.D. diss., University of North Carolina, 1975.

Murray, Elizabeth R. *Wake, Capital County of North Carolina*. Vol. 1. Raleigh: Capital County Publishing Co., 1983.

Odum, Howard W. *Southern Regions of the United States*. Chapel Hill: University of North Carolina Press, 1943.

Odum, Howard W., and Katharine Jocher, eds. In *Search of the Regional Balance of America*. Chapel Hill: University of North Carolina Press, 1945.

Pathak, Chittaranjan. "Growth Patterns of Raleigh, North Carolina." Ph.D. diss., University of North Carolina, 1964.

Ready, Milton L. *Asheville, Land of the Sky: An Illustrated History*. Northridge, Calif.: Windsor Publications, 1986.

Russell, James Michael. "Regional and National Perspectives on American Urban History." *Canadian Review of American Studies* 21 (1990): 265–74.

Vickers, James. *Raleigh, City of Oaks: An Illustrated History*. Woodland Hills, Calif.: Windsor Publications, 1982.

Whittington, Dale. High Hopes for High Tech: Microelectronics Policy in North Carolina. Chapel Hill: University of North Carolina Press, 1985.

A Modern Megastate

The North Carolina Office of State Planning projected that by the year 2020 population would reach 9.3 million, up from the 6.6 million who lived in the state only a generation ago in 1990. In the two decades from 1980 to 2000, the state's population grew by 37 percent. Soon more people will live in North Carolina than in all of the first three centuries of the state's history. Yet the census of 2000 has moved those estimates still upward. In 2020, the state perhaps will have 10 million residents. In the next few decades, regardless of the accuracy of the predictions, millions more will likely be calling North Carolina home.

In 2000 North Carolina ranked as the tenth most populous state in the nation, one whose growth has been so significant since 1980 that it, instead of Utah, gained a precious new seat in Congress. Between 1990 and 2000 perhaps as many as 700,000 new residents came to North Carolina, which, along with a natural increase of those living here, made it one of the nation's high-growth states. The new immigrants solidified North Carolina's role as a modern megastate, adding not only jobs and skills but also diversity to its population. The most dramatic rise has been in the number of Latinos and Asians moving into the state. Now a magnet state for Latinos, North Carolina has replaced more well-known and traditional destinations in the Southwest and West in the last two decades. Indeed, within every major city and in towns large and small throughout the state, an entire Latin American world has materialized since 1990.

As late as 1980, the appearance of a microcosmic Latin society in North Carolina seemed unlikely. Yet the influx of significant numbers of Latinos since then has added to the shift in the state's demographics. For example, in 1790 whites comprised 73 percent of the state's population. In 1970 the percentage peaked at 77. African Americans made up almost all the nonwhite proportion from 1790 to 1970. Historically a biracial society dominated by whites with African Americans as the most significant minority, North Carolina ethnically became a different state altogether after 1980. Moreover, the demographic change that occurred after 1970, the movement of Latinos into North Carolina, has been as dramatic as the migration of the Scots-Irish who made their way from Virginia and Pennsylvania in the eighteenth century as well as the out-migration of African Americans after World War II.

Since 1990 North Carolina's Latino population has increased by approximately 150 percent, the fifth-largest growth rate of that group in any state. Between 1990 and 2000, North Carolina experienced the highest rate of Latino population growth in the country, more than 393 percent, compared to 58 percent nationwide. Out of the nation's thirty fastest growing counties in Latino population in 2000, North Carolina had five, Wake, Mecklenburg, Guilford, Forsyth, and Durham. Even the mountainous far western counties saw an increase in Latino residents. In Buncombe County the number jumped by 389 percent between 1990 and 2000, from 1,173 to 5,730 Latinos. Officials of the Diocese of the Catholic Church and some local community activists suggest that the total might be closer to 15,000.

In 1998 Gov. James Hunt announced the creation of a special Office of Hispanic/Latino Affairs to focus on the state's newest immigrants. In 2000, record keepers in Raleigh reported that more than 378,963 Latinos made North Carolina their home. In 1980, only 56,667 lived in the state. The impact has been felt statewide, especially in rural areas. For example, Chatham County had only 510 Latino residents in 1990. A decade later it had perhaps 6,000, prompting one pundit to call Siler City "the Mexico City of North Carolina." Forsyth County had 22,000 Latinos, Robeson County more than 3,000 by 2000. Charlotte, dubbed Metrolina because its growth across the two Carolinas, numbered more than 65,000 Latinos, officially and unofficially, among its 536,000 residents. In Mecklenburg County, Charlotte's yellow pages soon had a Spanish-language edition. *La Noticia,* a Spanish-language newspaper in Charlotte, was only one of twelve statewide. In Asheville, Latinos read the aptly named *El Eco de las Montanas.* A majority of the new parishioners in the Catholic diocese of Charlotte, one of the fastest growing in the nation, speak Spanish as well as English.

As North Carolina's Latino population has increased, so have Hispanic businesses and enterprises. In 1987 the state listed 918 Hispanic-owned businesses, but by 2000 the number had mushroomed to 2,802. Over 40 percent of Latino businesses fell into service spheres, primarily restaurants, while 17 percent centered around construction, and 13 percent retail, usually small import groceries and shops. Typically run by one person or members of a family, most Latino businesses catered to a Spanish market, but, in the last few years, several have expanded and now serve the majority population as well. Since 1990 Latino migration also has affected working and school-age populations as well. In 2000, they made up as much as 10 percent of the workforce and 9 percent of those attending primary and secondary schools, statistics certain to increase in the years ahead. In some districts and counties the numbers are much larger.

Historically, North Carolina's Latino population generally comprised migrant farmworkers, usually from Cuba or other Central American countries. No more. Most now come from Mexico along interstate corridors, particularly around I-95, I-40, and I-85. The latest influx of Latinos has led to settlement not only in urban centers like Charlotte and Raleigh but also in rural areas as well. In fact, Latinos now make up between 10 and 15 percent of the populations of Chatham, Duplin, Lee, Montgomery, and Sampson counties. Now employed primarily in nonagricultural jobs, Latinos, like other immigrants to the state in the last twenty years, have come to stay. They, too, like calling North Carolina home.

Two other groups, Asians and Native Americans, have similar histories in modern North Carolina. Resident long before whites arrived, and at their lowest point in the 1930s, Native Americans, principally the Cherokees and Lumbees, have experienced a growth rate exceeding 54 percent since 1980. Along with other tribes such as the Catawba, the Cherokees and Lumbees combine to give North Carolina the largest Amerindian population on the east coast, the fifth largest in the nation. From 1990 to 2000, the number of Asians more

North Carolina Population Growth, 1980–2000

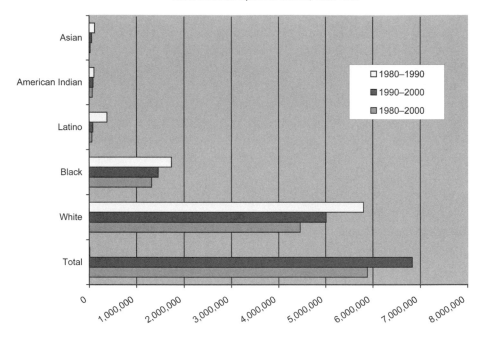

North Carolina Population Change in Percentages, 1980–2000

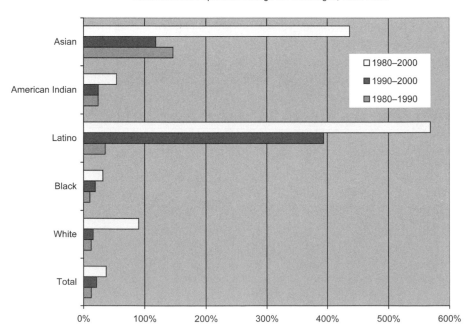

Source: U.S. Bureau of Census, Washington, D.C.

than doubled, from 53,000 to slightly over 100,000. Since 1980 Asian population overall has grown by 437 percent. By 2020 the number of Latinos and Asians likely will also double. Because of the in-migration of Latinos and Asians, almost every large town and city in the state now has an ethnically diverse population, the largest concentrations predictably occurring in cities such as Charlotte, Raleigh, and Greensboro. Although whites represented a diminished 71 percent of the total population in 2000, they nevertheless dominated one of the fastest-growing statistical groups, that of persons over sixty-five. Lured by the state's natural beauty and quality of living, more and more retirees, principally from Florida and New York, have chosen North Carolina over Florida, California, and Arizona. Along with older natives, they likely will be 20 to 22 percent of the population by 2020.

North Carolina's last economic renaissance prior to the one that began in the 1980s occurred in the 1920s. Much of the boom of that decade came from the state's liberal banking laws, a curse as well as a blessing by the time of the Great Depression, when banks failed statewide. In 1929 the general assembly passed a law that allowed branch banking, in essence permitting banks to build offices at new sites or else to acquire and merge with others statewide. One of only nine states to allow branch banking before the New Deal, North Carolina's relatively unrestricted banking legislation led to larger banks statewide and also to the accumulation of considerable capital and deposits. While localized smaller banks continued to do business in the state, larger firms soon dominated. The disasters of the Great Depression led to stricter federal legislation, such as the Glass-Stegall Act of 1933 and its later modification, the Douglas amendment of 1956, that effectively limited banks to state boundaries, a restriction that all but stopped interstate expansion. Nonetheless, when the Reagan administration looked disapprovingly at the Douglas amendment in the early 1980s, North Carolina and its banks, with their experience in mergers and acquisitions, enjoyed a competitive advantage in the geographic deregulation of that decade. By the end of the century, North Carolina had become the headquarters for sixteen of the nation's one hundred largest banks, a boggling statistic for a relatively poor state. The total deposits of these bank holding companies approached $480 billion by 2000, 80 percent from outside the state, the largest volume of deposits controlled by any state in the nation. North Carolina banks oversaw 35 to 40 percent of the total deposits in such states as California, Virginia, and Georgia. Located in Charlotte, Bank of America, formerly NationsBank, emerged as either the first or second largest bank in the nation by 2000, while First Union ranked fifth. Along with other investment and banking firms, Bank of America and First Union combined to stamp Charlotte as second only to New York City as a national banking center, well ahead of larger cities such as Chicago, Los Angeles, and Atlanta. Even now, Bank of America has sought to expand its markets in the Northeast corridor around Boston and New York. Winston-Salem, a much smaller city, still has headquarters for the sixth largest bank, Wachovia, and the sixteenth, BB and T, while Raleigh has First Citizens, ranked sixty-first in the nation. In 2000, First Union and Wachovia combined to create yet another prominent and even larger banking partnership. Surprisingly, Rocky Mount, assuredly not a large metropolitan area, served as the center of operations for Centura, the nation's sixty-second largest bank. With acquisitions of other insurance and banking-related companies, along with branches throughout the nation, North Carolina's banks helped fuel the state's second economic renaissance.

While the enormous growth of banks and investment capital has provided the funds for development since 1970, North Carolina's economy has changed little at the top. Indeed, of the state's top one hundred private companies, the ones that have been around the longest seem always to emerge as leaders. Textile manufacturing, furniture, food chains, distribution companies, and agriculture remain the bedrock of North Carolina's economy. As it has since the mid-1990s, Raleigh's General Parts, Inc., a distributor of replacement parts for automobiles and trucks, has remained the state's largest private company. Few high-tech companies even made the list in 2000.

The prominence of Raleigh's General Parts veils one of the state's lesser-known economic statistics. Automobiles, SUVs, vans, and trucks together accounted for 20 percent of the state's retail sales taxes in 1998. A $15 billion enterprise then, it has only increased in the last few years. Not only does Charlotte act as a distribution center for new cars throughout the region, it also serves as a giant parts warehouse for the Southeast. An estimated five hundred new vehicles joined the river of automobiles, trucks, and vans each day from 1995 to 1999 on the state's highways, most of them preowned. Indeed, North Carolina ranks ninth nationally in the number of car dealerships, a remarkable feat since, in the last fifty years, the national total declined dramatically from fifty thousand to slightly less than twenty thousand by 1999. From repair and collision garages to NASCAR shops and automobile dealerships, small businesses built around cars flourish in North Carolina.

Remarkable for its ongoing agricultural output, North Carolina continues to be second in the nation in the production of hogs, trout, peanuts, broiler hatching eggs, and chickens. Indeed, most "Virginia peanuts" come from North Carolina, especially around the Bertie County area. In 1913, Philip Lance of Charlotte took five hundred pounds of peanuts and sold them for five cents a bag. Soon Lance began combining peanut butter with crackers, and by 2001 his Toastchees and Cheese on Wheats had helped accumulate revenues of more than $583 million. Today, Lance products can be found in thirty-seven states, competing with Frito Lay and other companies for the "snack-attack" crowd. Bojangles did for North Carolina's brand of fried chicken what Colonel Sanders once accomplished for Kentucky's.

In the health and wellness craze that swept over America at the end of the nineteenth century, a New Bern druggist, Caleb D. Bradham, came up with a soft drink that would help with dyspepsia, a rather formal name for an upset stomach. Combined with large amounts of meat and potatoes, hard drinks such as liquor and alcohol only seemed to exacerbate the horrible symptoms of dyspepsia. At first called "Brad's drink," it took advantage of the reputation of the cola nut as a snake-oil remedy for its appeal. Bradham had Bayard Wooten, one of the state's best-known photographers who had a studio in New Bern, design the red, white, and blue trademark logo that soon came to represent Pepsi-Cola.

Although Caleb Bradham died penniless in 1923, Pepsi-Cola went on to become one of the South's best-selling soft drinks. Depending heavily on catchy phrases and advertising aimed at countering the appeal of Coca-Cola, Pepsi soon found a niche in a growing, fast-paced, commodity-driven society. At first, Pepsi emphasized its healthful attributes, principally its lack of narcotics and impurities, a sneer at its drugged, fizzy competitor from Georgia. After World War II, Pepsi sent planes over southeastern cities with sky-written mile-high letters six miles long with its unmistakable, patriotic red, white, and blue logo prominently featured. In a thrice-told tale, one lady supposedly rushed into an Atlanta grocery and asked for a Pepsi-Cola because "God told her to drink Pepsi." An entire generation grew up in the 1950s humming the Pepsi commercial, "Pepsi-Cola hits the spot, twelve full ounces, that's a lot." At the time, Coca-Cola had only eight ounces. In celebration of its centennial, the company gave one share of its stock to the first new year's baby born in every hospital and clinic in the Carolinas on the first day of January 1996.

The list of private companies and corporations that underlay much of the state's later twentieth-century success also included Cheerwine, Texas Pete sauce, and the goodliest doughnut of them all, Krispy Kreme. Cheerwine began in L. D. Peeler's grocery store in Salisbury, and within a decade it became not only a tangy soft drink but also a staple ingredient in many barbecue sauces, pies, and punches throughout the southeast. Indeed, Cheerwine added but one ingredient to North Carolina's sweetish, distinctive, and beloved barbecue pulled at pig pickings throughout the state. In Winston-Salem, the T. W. Garner Food Company, regionally known for its sauces, additives, jams, and jellies, found a niche in the competitive barbecue and hot spice sauce market with Mexican Joe, or, as it later came to be known, Texas Pete. In 1937 Vernon Rudolph and the "dough boys" from Salem College pooled together twenty-five dollars in the hardest of Depression times and started a hot doughnut called Krispy Kreme. Originally begun in Paducah, Kentucky, four years earlier, Krispy Kreme remained one of the state's best-kept secrets until 1966, when it expanded out of its sweetened southern market. Soon Krispy Kreme doughnuts and boxes conspicuously appeared in popular television shows such as *NYPD Blue* and *ER.* Sold from New York to Los Angeles, Krispy Kreme has now explored European markets for its doughnuts.

Given its agricultural past and continuing production, North Carolina naturally expanded into the retail grocery market after World War II. In 1957 Ralph Ketner and two other grocers in Salisbury successfully moved their operations into the Piedmont. Within two decades, Ketner and his company operated fifty-two stores throughout the state. Soon after, he moved into the Southeast and Mid-Atlantic regions. His store, Food Lion, quickly emerged as one of the nation's top ten supermarket chains. Concentrating on smaller towns and edge cities, Food Lion found a niche for itself along with its western North Carolina competitor, Ingles, in the fiercely competitive supermarket industry. Despite a devastating *Nightline* report on its sanitation standards, Food Lion nonetheless managed more than 1,120 stores in fourteen states by 1998. Along with Food Lion and Ingles, at least a half dozen other large retail chains have headquarters in North Carolina, among them Family Dollar, an inexpensive variety store, Pic N' Pay Shoes, and Belk's, one of the largest department store chains in the Southeast.

Given its exponential growth and prosperity of the last three decades, North Carolina did not escape the megamall craze of the 1980s. By national standards, shopping malls such as Hanes Mall in Winston-Salem, Crabtree Valley in Raleigh, South Park Mall in Charlotte, and the recently opened Concord Mill rank as megastate or regional centers. In fact, only eight other metropolitan areas in the nation have more per capita shopping space than the Raleigh-Durham-Chapel Hill triangle. In all, North Carolina had as many as 1,550 shopping centers in 2000, giving it twenty-two square feet per capita, well above the national average of twenty square feet. Carolinians and their neighbors love to shop.

"If you build it, they will come." That cliché of development particularly applied to one of the keys to North Carolina's economic success, the rapid expansion of transportation across the state since the early 1970s. In reality, North Carolina, known as a bad roads state for much of its history, has emerged with one of the most thoroughly interconnected systems of interstate highways, beltways, and state roads in the Southeast. Always thought of as a corridor state whose roads and transportation systems connected better to Virginia, South Carolina, Georgia, and Tennessee than they did to Manteo or Murphy, North Carolina emerged with more than 100,000 miles of highway in 2000. With over 80,000 of those under state control, North Carolina possesses the second-largest state-owned system of roads in the nation. Two singularities explain not only the state's high ownership of roads but also its viewpoint toward the role of highways in development.

First, Raleigh took over road construction and maintenance from counties during the Great Depression. Thus, counties have only marginal responsibilities, usually that of consultation and advising, in state roadway matters. Yet counties have retained a viable civic voice in Raleigh, and thus highway construction and placement became as much a political as an economic consideration. Much to the chagrin of city planners and think-tank bureaucrats, North Carolina deliberately began planning and constructing a network of secondary roads in the early 1970s connecting smaller towns and communities to interstates, beltways, loops, and even to local and regional airports. Convinced that cities and not small towns were the engines of North Carolina's burgeoning economy, regional planners, particularly in the Raleigh-Durham-Chapel Hill and Charlotte areas, lamented the state's "backward, county-seat" planning for future development. Even so, counties, with no ability to construct roads on their own, understood that they, too, could be involved in the planning and arranging of highway systems that would allow them to participate in the new wealth and prosperity that came to the state in the last three decades. In 1990 the general assembly affirmed its commitment by passing a program to put in place a 3,100–mile intrastate highway system that would place 90 percent of the population within ten minutes of a four-lane highway. Equally significant, North Carolina began paving 20,000 miles of dirt roads that would permit all but the most isolated residents access to a major highway. By building good roads connecting to interstates and loops, the state helped ensure that prosperity would come to a majority of North Carolinians.

North Carolina currently has seventy-five public airports, perhaps representing the next stage of its transportation odyssey since its founding in the seventeenth century. Fifteen offer air passenger service. Six passenger hubs operate within the state, the largest two in Charlotte and Raleigh-Durham, along with four smaller regional airports in Asheville, Fayetteville, Greensboro, and Wilmington. Two airports, Raleigh-Durham and Charlotte, offer international as well as continental service. Together, they accounted for perhaps as much as 75 percent of the twenty million airline passengers in North Carolina in 2000. Charlotte currently ranks seventh among the nation's top fifty airports; Raleigh-Durham, twenty-eighth.

Since the 1970s, sports, both at the college and professional level, have grown into an important economic development tool. While the state always has produced its share of well-known athletes such as Charlie "Choo-Choo" Justice of Asheville in football, Jim "Catfish" Hunter from Hertford in baseball, and Michael Jordan from Wilmington in

Charlie "Choo-Choo" Justice, of Asheville, an All-American at the University of North Carolina, with coach Marvin Bass.
North Carolina Collection, University of North Carolina at Chapel Hill.

basketball, sports has become a source of not only pride but also big business. From 1957 until 2001, basketball teams from Tobacco Road, Duke in Durham, North Carolina State in Raleigh, and North Carolina at Chapel Hill, consistently have been among the top-ranked teams in the nation. Duke, the University of North Carolina, North Carolina State, and Wake Forest regularly appeared on national television in featured games. No other state since John Wooden's UCLA teams of the late 1960s and early 1970s has won as many NCAA basketball titles as has North Carolina since 1982. Moreover, huge coliseums in Greensboro, Charlotte, and Winston-Salem regularly host regional finals in NCAA basketball.

By the year 2000, football and basketball programs at Duke, the University of North Carolina at Chapel Hill, and North Carolina State had become more valuable than many professional franchises. Frequent appearances not only on television but also in the NCAA basketball tournament have brought in significant revenues as well as recognition nationwide. Licensing a university's name for commercial products in the Carolinas as well as elsewhere has become a significant source of revenue. At Duke, outerwear and tee shirts fly off the racks while at North Carolina State a musical toilet seat that plays the Wolfpack fight song when raised sells well during football season.

As they have emerged as regional and even national centers, cities such as Raleigh, Charlotte, and even Greensboro actively have recruited professional sports teams not only as status symbols but also as unlimited profit potential. Before the team moved to New Orleans, a typical Charlotte Hornets game sold 10,000 hot dogs, 12,000 beers, 9,000 soft drinks, 2,300 programs, and 5,000 tee shirts, caps, and pennants, all grossing perhaps $520,000, or $7 per fan. A sold-out Carolina Panthers game generates more than three times that revenue. Raleigh and Greensboro actively recruited professional baseball and hockey teams in the 1990s, with the Carolina Hurricanes, a highly sought-after professional hockey team, eventually moving to Raleigh. Charlotte, sitting astride the Carolinas, still has a national football league franchise, the Carolina Panthers, while it seeks to fill the vacuum left by the removal of the Hornets to New Orleans. Developers look upon both professional and collegiate sports in North Carolina as highly marketable business enterprises if not as certain cash cows.

New Bern High School's female basketball team in 1914.
North Carolina Collection, University of North Carolina at Chapel Hill.

The location of Raycom Creative Sports Marketing and Jefferson-Pilot Sports in North Carolina, both nationally recognized syndicators of collegiate sports programs, enormously has aided the appeal of collegiate as well as professional sports throughout the region. Together, Raycom and Jefferson-Pilot produce more than eight hundred football and basketball broadcasts each year, selling them to be broadcast to local stations nationwide. In football and particularly in basketball, North Carolina teams frequently are highlighted.

North Carolina's long love affair with ordinary automobiles, stock cars, has paid significant dividends since the 1970s. With primary races in Rockingham, North Wilkesboro, and Charlotte, NASCAR, which legitimately could claim its origins in North Carolina with Junior Johnson, Lee Petty, and Richard Petty, annually has more than 500,000 fans in attendance at these three locations. Unofficially, Bruton Smith has made Charlotte and its raceway the home to auto shops for racing cars across the nation. On weekends during the racing season, hundreds of trucks loaded with racing cars and paraphernalia make their way back to their Charlotte garages.

The rapid transformation of North Carolina into a megastate has brought with it problems attendant with that status. The Garden of Eden feeling that many Carolinians have always had about the state in which they live has changed into one where there also are visions of beer cans and decaying refuse in the southern part of heaven. The romance of North Carolina as a picturesque paradise, as a mythical Mayberry of small towns and friendly people, has given way to a reality of a state of sprawling suburbs, commutes, and bustling, brusque, businesslike attitudes toward work and play. Early botanists and travelers to Carolina, such as the Virginian George Chicken and naturalists William Bartram and André Michaux, thought they had found a wilderness utopia beneath the green canopy of trees that stretched to the horizon. Indeed, early accounts spoke of the refreshing and champagnelike exhilaration and sweetness of the air and the pristine vistas.

Today, prevailing winds from polluted urban areas, acid rains from industrial states to the north, contaminated groundwater from agricultural bonanza and hog farms primarily in the eastern counties, and emissions from the hundreds of cars added to the state's highways each week threaten the very quality of life that has attracted and kept so many people over the centuries. In urban areas like Charlotte and Raleigh, unhealthy summer ozone occurrences have become common. One of the earth's most poisonous substances, mercury, has been detected in such quantities along the coast that, in 2000, the state advised against eating fish from ten eastern streams and one species of fish offshore in the Atlantic Ocean.

Since the 1980s, visitors to the mountains of western North Carolina and to the Great Smoky Mountains National Park, the most visited in the nation, rarely have had a clear day between April and October. For five years in a row in the 1990s, the Great Smoky Mountains National Park has been declared the most polluted in the nation, its vistas increasingly less clear, its ozone levels unhealthy, its trees killed and stunted by acid precipitation. Much of the unending canopy of trees that always has characterized North Carolina has disappeared in the last three decades, the result of modular and mobile chip mills, logging in publicly owned national forests, and increasing demand for recreational outlets. Shrunken forests have been replaced by pine plantations and quick-growth trees, but wildlife populations have been adversely affected. Each year, the National Forest Service and state wildlife officials release elk, bear, trout, and foxes into the state's forests and streams in an effort to restore original and endangered species to their natural habitats, now largely surrounded by development.

Overspreading particles of sulfur dioxide, carbon monoxide, and nitrogen dioxide together with ground-level ozone now penetrate every corner of the state. In the summer months, cities such as Charlotte have become fire islands of coughing, allergic, choking, and increasingly irritated North Carolinians. In fact, Charlotte has smog and pollution, though not as frequent nor as toxic as its Latin American counterpart, Mexico City. Because of the concentration of chemicals in the Mecklenburg-Gaston-Cabarrus area, contaminants from photochemical oxidants endanger not only people but also crops and animals. Perhaps twenty of North Carolina's counties suffer serious problems of air and water pollution as well as of deteriorating ecosystems. Not surprisingly, Mecklenburg-Gaston, Durham-Wake Forest, and Guilford-Forsyth head the list. In the Raleigh-Durham-Chapel Hill triangle between 1987 and 1997, rapid development, primarily of suburbs and smaller business parks, consumed more than 190,000 acres. Conservation efforts preserved only 8,500. The prosperous Boom Belt of the last twenty years could well turn into a noxious Doom Belt in the next decades.

The unprecedented growth of the last decades of the twentieth century has made available more privately produced consumer goods for North Carolinians than ever before, frequently at the impoverishment of the public good. As John Kenneth Galbraith pointed out in 1958, newly affluent societies sometimes floundered in "an atmosphere of private opulence and public squalor." In 2001 North Carolinians, happy with low taxes and good jobs, have allowed schools to become overcrowded, teachers to be reluctantly paid a national wage, and hospitals, mental institutions, and prisons to be understaffed and overfilled.

With state environmental laws lax and largely unenforced by a token staff, much of the air in the Piedmont has become unbearable at times. Despite the problem of too many cars and trucks on the state's highways, particularly along the I-85 corridor, mass transit remains a fantasy in the state's planning. Indeed, mass transit plans were abandoned in the Raleigh area, one of the most crucial, when the Triangle Transit Authority broke off negotiations with the U.S. Department of Transportation. Only reluctantly has the Triangle Transit Authority agreed to a compromise with the federal government with the first road segment to be completed by 2007. When Hurricane Floyd flooded many of the state's rivers in 1999, many eastern towns and communities became open sewers and fetid bogs. The state's public agencies, despite centuries of hurricanes and storms, were unprepared and understaffed. Large outlays of public funds either went into holding accounts for months or else overwhelmed inadequate public agencies ill suited to deal with the "public squalor" caused by Floyd. The devastation of Hurricane Isabel in the summer of 2003 only added to the state's economic woes.

Traditionally a green state, much of North Carolina's vast canopy of trees so noted by early travelers and naturalists, has disappeared under the bulldozers of developers as have farmland, wetlands, and marshes. Beaches from Virginia to South Carolina's borders have been dangerously overdeveloped and overbuilt despite the omnipresent threat of hurricanes and storms. The endless number of new cars, a majority sold and headquartered in the Charlotte area, and new suburbs in edge cities such as Cary and Concord have caused a paralysis of accompanying public services. Well-maintained highways, safe bridges, adequate parking facilities, traffic controls, state and local policing, hospitals, and other related needs point to the deterioration of public services. Many towns and cities in the state have decaying infrastructures, inadequate sanitation systems, strained power grids, and obsolete codes for builders and developers. Desperately needed public services such as these do not bring a profit for the state, nor do they come without new taxes and greater authority for government agencies, traditionally a greater curse to North Carolinians than poor roads and inadequate medical services.

The mantra for North Carolina's future echoes its past. Slow, sustained, and planned development mirrored the state's first three centuries. Indeed, the last three decades of the twentieth century seemed more a departure than a continuation of its history. As the Pandora's box of rapid urbanization and growth reveals still more conundrums, North Carolinians now must question whether some of their most basic values—a sense of place and community, a close relationship with nature and the environment, and a newly won prosperity—will be passed on to the next generation. More and more, planners and politicians are apprehensive that "sustainable development and smart growth" will not be enough to maintain and to restore the state's natural beauty and balance in the future. In Asheville, Charlotte, Salisbury, and Winston-Salem, as well as in a number of smaller towns and cities, groups and committees of concerned citizens and public officials have engaged in a visioning process of what they would like to see happen in their communities in the next ten, twenty, and even fifty years. Modern North Carolina also has its Archibald Murpheys and John Motley Moreheads who want a different state in the future. For example, in 1997 Salisbury won a prestigious national award for its "Park Avenue Neighborhood Plan," a blueprint that successfully sought ways to improve and enrich the quality of life for an entire community. In western North Carolina near the Tennessee border, Wolf Laurel, a mountain resort, has managed to combine North Carolina's sense of place with its need to expand. Set in an Edenic region sprawling across the Appalachian Trail, Wolf Laurel, unlike nearby developments, has allowed its residents to see nature more than each other's adjacent homes. North Carolina needs more John Nolens and Sallie Southall Cottens in the twenty-first century to build its new neighborhoods and developments.

Traditionally a state of fiercely independent property holders who have resisted zoning and planning in and across counties and regions, many, but assuredly not all, North Carolinians have abandoned their romantic and sometimes sentimental attachment to land and realty in favor of a more pragmatic and realistic approach to large developers and companies. Grassroots environmental and community groups have come together to raise concerns about the stewardship of the land and the social inequities that have emerged with accelerated economic growth. Livability, quality of life, and smart growth have become embedded issues in planning for land use, state standards for protection of the environment, the disposal of solid wastes, and the cleanliness needed for water and air to sustain a growing population. Historically, development and conservation have always believed the other to be the feral animal, forever waiting predatorily to devour each other. In the past, North Carolinians have always opted for jobs at the expense of the environment, chronically to keep the tigers of poverty and want at bay. In the future, that option, never a dichotomous one, will be made broader and less Manichean. In many parts of present-day North Carolina, property and development now lie down quietly with planning and conservation. Out of the dialectic between the two, the good state of the future likely will be made and maintained.

When the lords proprietors first envisioned Carolina in 1663, they saw an American Avalon of towns, mercantile centers, and bustling, contented villagers, all going about their business of creating a New World utopia. More than three centuries later, North Carolina, the northern part of the Carolina colony, has developed into a modern megastate never imagined by its founders. The original plan for Carolina contained within itself its own dystopian elements, endemic flaws such as class distinctions, slavery and racism, and restrictions upon freedom of religion and land ownership that bounded the vision. Even the Bishop of Durham clause that guaranteed all the rights of Englishmen to Carolinians had only a limited application in the beginning. Yet the flawed model of the proprietors also put forth ideals, that, while circumscribed by the context of cultures and centuries, grew to be a part of the modern state of North Carolina. The new modern megastate that has emerged in the latter part of the twentieth-century also contains the seeds of its own destruction. While appropriate to the smart growth of the last quarter of the twentieth century, the tendency to pave every winding path in the state in the belief that "if you build it, they will come" seems to have run its opportune course. North Carolina critically needs to find better ways of moving people both in towns and cities. Moreover, the millions of dollars now devoted to the highway department could be better used for the state's overall welfare. The natural limits of interstates and highways now threaten the good life they helped create. Perhaps Gerald Ingalls, the professor of geography at the University of North Carolina at Charlotte who decried the county seat politics of building roads, was right after all, if for the wrong reasons. The research triangle parks, so much an economic dynamo of growth for the last part of the twentieth century, have now become just another cylinder in the state's overall engine. Besides, almost every state and even smaller communities now have one. Although environmentalists and conservationists correctly point to the necessity of restoring the economic and environmental vitality of river basins, of protecting imperiled species throughout the state, of meeting the challenges and opportunities of protecting the quality of the air we breathe, of achieving a balance in managing our forests, and of protecting the state's natural heritage, they sometimes overstate and exaggerate the circumstantial dangers. After all, the first North Carolinians, whether Native or Anglo-Americans, hardly lived in balance or harmony with natural forces. Additionally, natural systems have always adapted and changed to meet new circumstances, even if newer technologies have a larger impact. North Carolina should not have a neutron-bomb vision of its future where most buildings, highways, and factories have been destroyed and only a few mortals are admitted into its natural, organic landscape. All the messy market vitality of modern North Carolina surely can be maintained in a less intrusive manner. As the new millennium drifted through North Carolina, the state had every appearance of ending one historical period of growth without knowing how to welcome another. Hesitant to change in the past, reluctant to embrace new ideas, North Carolinians endured both revolution and civil war before they abandoned many of the reactionary elements in their past. Modern North Carolinians seem equally reluctant to want to change from their transient, transparently prosperous present.

Walter Hines Page referred to the "mummies" that haunted North Carolina's past and shadowed its future—religious orthodoxy, slavery, and the failed legacy of the Confederacy—yet new ghosts have replaced the old. The first settlers brought such phantasms and contradictions with them, and they have remained, albeit in modern guises, ever since. For example, early colonists passionately believed in representative government but also just as zealously embraced slavery. Moreover, the early diaries and journals of explorers and colonists looked upon Carolina as a Garden of Eden waiting to be civilized and settled. Yet Europeans brought with them an exploitative concept of nature, one that looked upon forests, rivers, and land as individual grants from nature with which to do as they wished. Property rights became a holy grail of liberty itself. Still residual today, such ruggedly individualistic attitudes toward land and property sometimes mitigate against the larger idea of progress in an increasingly polluted and globalized society. North Carolina began as a heterogeneous, multicultural mixture of Native Americans, Englishmen, Scots and Scots-Irish, Welsh, Germans, Swiss, Africans, Creoles, and mulattoes who spoke a cacophony of languages and who brought with them a bewildering number of customs and beliefs. Only after the Civil War did North Carolinians insist upon a biracial society with an overriding Anglo-Saxon culture. Today, North Carolina somewhat reluctantly has gone back to its roots as a diverse multicultural and multiracial society, all the while forgetting the conflicts and problems of those first interactions.

Stubbornly anti-intellectual in its beginning and early history, the state today still manifests an ambivalent attitude toward education. Overall, the state's system of educating its youth has been described as "rife with mediocrity yet riddled with excellence." Only South Carolina, Georgia, or Mississippi consistently ranks lower than North Carolina on national test scores. One bumper sticker succinctly summarized the state's attitude toward education by declaring that North Carolina was "number two in hog production, number forty-seven in teacher's salaries." In 2000, more than one million North Carolinians could not read or write, or do basic calculations necessary to hold many jobs. Between 15 to 20 percent of high school students dropped out before graduation. In the increasingly sophisticated workplace of the twenty-first century, only a minority of North Carolinians will have the necessary competitive skills and education.

For over three centuries, the shadow of "poor Carolina," of a ragged, destitute, unfortunate, and unhealthy populace has stalked the state's steady but uneven progress. As measured in 2000, North Carolina has one of the highest rates of poverty in the nation, an estimated 28 percent who lived below that perniciously sustainable level. Sadly, children constitute the largest group living in poverty. As the new millennium began, many North Carolinians breathed some of the most toxic air in the nation and lived in relatively poor health. For two weeks in the summer of 2001, black clouds from brush and forest fires, a product of drought and mismanagement, turned day into night in Asheville and the surrounding mountains and made any outdoor activities untenable and unhealthy. Charlotte and Raleigh have experienced similar episodes of toxicity. Almost one in five North Carolinians lacked health insurance of any kind in 2001. Indeed, in comparative terms, North Carolina still seems to be as poor as it was when Janet Schaw described the province on a visit more than two centuries ago.

Lastly, the figure of Nathaniel Macon, not Thomas Jefferson or Andrew Jackson, looms over an enduring yet limited vision of what state government can and should do. Frugal to the point of cheapness, Macon believed that the state should not only govern sparingly but also tax and spend grudgingly, and then only in public and not private spheres. Reluctant to spend in education, for example, North Carolina, on a per capita basis, spent less for education in 2000 than it did in 1920. In an increasingly prosperous and developing state, a new proactive concept of governance has emerged, one that nonetheless reluctantly confronts North Carolina's new ghosts. Still, a lingering Maconite suspicion of what government should do exists. In the end, the state's motto, *esse quam videri* (to be rather than to seem), appropriately describes its past and present as well as its future intentions. What North Carolina has become and what it wants to be continue to live in a mutually dependent uncertainty.

Yet another perspective suggests itself from North Carolina's past. Where I am writing today in Asheville, mountain peaks once soared thousands of feet above my head. If I hike the Appalachian Trail meandering through western North Carolina, I can still see the roots of that huge billion-year-old range, remainders and reminders of which exist as far away as Newfoundland to the north and Georgia to the south. On the rim of the exquisitely beautiful Bay of Naples, the world's most notorious volcano, Vesuvius, huffs and puffs and threatens the entire region. Only a mile or two beneath the bay, the relentless pressure of the African tectonic plate, growing at the fingernail-rate of an inch a year, relentlessly pushes and plunges below the entire Neapolitan landscape. Off Cape Hatteras to the north and south, the barrier islands roll toward the mainland each year, the product of widening mid-ocean ridges that produce the forces that lead to a continual overwashing of the islands. The ancient supercontinent of Pangaea, still breaking apart, daily pushes North Carolina away from its European and African puzzle pieces. From Wrightsville Beach to

Nags Head, North Carolinians, despite the risks of erosion and hurricanes, still cling to fragile homes along the beach because of the siren beauty of the ocean.

390 North Carolina has another biography, that of its geology, as well as its people. Both furnish eyes that provide a far-reaching glimpse into its past and present. As the Dutch cartographer Abraham Ortelius said in 1570 on the eve of North Carolina's colonization, both the people who have lived in North Carolina for over four centuries and its geology give insight into the state's history. In all this, there is something obscurely heartening about the process of history through both eyes. In North Carolina, as in much of the world, we live on a globe we continually despoil with an ever-increasing technological efficiency and rapidity. We have genuine cause for concern and imperative action. Yet that is the living, man-made world we treat as if we were not a part of it or a participant. Eventually, nature will take its own revenge.

North Carolina's solid crust of seashore, Piedmont, and mountains floats on a mantle underlaid by pyretic fluids generating vast convection currents that drive the movement of tectonic plates far beneath us. The vast, majestic rocks on which we live and the equally marvelous and magnificent mechanism that makes them over time dwarfs us all. Little that we can inflict on the earth itself amounts to more than an impermanent pinprick. There is something reassuring and gratifying in the thought that North Carolina, geologically speaking, surely will survive us all for yet another four hundred years.

ADDITIONAL READINGS

Barrier, Smith. *On Tobacco Road: Basketball in North Carolina.* New York: Leisure Press, 1983.

Bledsoe, Jerry. *World's Number One, Flat-Out, All-Time Great, Stock Car Racing Book.* New York: Bantam Press, 1976.

Brook, David Louis Sterrett. *A Lasting Gift of Heritage: A History of the North Carolina Society for the Preservation of Antiquities, 1939–1974.* Raleigh: Division of Archives and History, 1997.

Buford, Elizabeth F., comp. *Private Lives/Public Roles: A Symposium of North Carolina Women's History: Abstracts of Papers.* Raleigh: Department of Archives and History, 1990.

Burrough, Bryan, and John Helyar. *Barbarians at the Gates: The Fall of RJR Nabisco.* New York: Harper Perennial, 1991.

Campbell, H., and A. Stuart. "Foreign Direct Investment in North Carolina." *North Carolina Geographer* 6 (Summer 1998): 37–49.

Corrigan, Thomas J. "For Better or Worse? The Switch to Chain Ownership in North Carolina." Master's thesis, University of North Carolina, 1989.

"Counting by County." *Business North Carolina* 21 (February 2001): 106–12.

Covington, Howard E., Jr. *Belk, a Century of Retail Leadership.* Chapel Hill: University of North Carolina Press, 1988.

Cowdrey, Albert E. *This Land, This South: An Environmental History.* Lexington: University Press of Kentucky, 1983.

Drape, Joe. *In the Hornet's Nest: Charlotte and Its First Year in the NBA.* New York: St. Martin's Press, 1989.

Dunn, James A. C. "History of Piedmont Airlines." *Pace* 15 (December 1988): 51–78.

Fox, William P. *Golfing in the Carolinas.* Winston-Salem: John F. Blair, 1990.

Geary, Bob. "The Trail Less Traveled." *Independent* 17 (May 2000): 20–25.

Gibbs, Stephanie. "Hispanic Hustle." *North Carolina* 58 (June 2000): 12–17.

Gilmore, Voit. "Pigeon River of Western North Carolina: Economic Exploitation vs. Environmental Quality." Master's thesis, University of North Carolina, 1984.

Golenbock, Peter. *Personal Fouls.* New York: Carroll and Graf, 1989.

Green, Ron. *From Tobacco Road to Amen Corner: On Sports and Life.* Asheboro, N.C.: Down Home Press, 1990.

Grundy, Pamela. "From Amazons to Glamazons: The Rise and Fall of North Carolina Women's Basketball, 1920–1960." *Journal of American History* 87 (2000): 12–46.

Haas, S., and B. Williams. *A Profile of North Carolina: Indicators of Sustainability.* Chapel Hill: University of North Carolina Environmental Resource Program, 1995.

Hawkin, P. *The Ecology of Commerce.* New York: Harper Business, 1993.

Heinzl, Toni J. "Fowl Business: The Other Side of the Poultry Boom in North Carolina." Master's thesis, University of North Carolina, 1991.

Herget, J. B., and Mike McLaughlin. "Not Just Fun and Games Anymore: Pro Sports as an Economic Development Tool." *North Carolina Insight* 14 (September 1992): 2–25.

Hirsch, Jerrold. "Grassroots Environmental History: The Southern Federal Writers' Project Life Histories as a Source." *Southern Cultures* 2 (1995): 129–36.

Hunter, Jim, and Armen Keteyian. *Catfish: My Life in Baseball.* New York: McGraw-Hill Book Co., 1988.

Jones, Matt. "Tienda Time in the Triangle." *Independent* 17 (October 2000): 44, 45.

Lakshimarayan, Chandrika. "Asian-Americans in the Triangle." Master's thesis, University of North Carolina, 1990.

Luger, Michael I., and Harvey A. Goldstein. *Technology in the Garden: Research Parks.* Chapel Hill: University of North Carolina Press, 1991.

Manuel, John. "Timber Tantrums." *Friends of Wildlife* 48 (Summer 2000): 2–7.

Martin, Edward. "The Snack Attack." *Business North Carolina* 58 (June 1996): 26–40.

Martin, Milward W. *Twelve Full Ounces.* New York: Holt, Rinehart, and Winston, 1962.

Maxwell, Tracey J. "Plant, Pick and Persevere: The Migrant Experience in North Carolina." Master's thesis, University of North Carolina, 1989.

Napoli, Lisa. "In the Media Jungle, the Lion Weeps Tonight." *Business North Carolina* 13 (March 1993): 16–19.

Nomiya, Akiko K. "The North Carolina Korean Church and the Korean Immigrants." Master's thesis, University of North Carolina, 1992.

Orr, Douglas M., Jr., and Alfred W. Stuart, eds. *The North Carolina Atlas: Portrait for a New Century.* Chapel Hill: University of North Carolina Press, 2000.

Perkins, Harvey C. "Bulldozers in the Southern Part of Heaven: Defending Place Against Sudden Growth." Ph.D. diss., University of North Carolina, 1986.

Quincy, Robert G., and Julian Scheer. *Choo-Choo: The Charlie Justice Story.* Chapel Hill: Bentley Publishing Co., 1958.

Reed, John Shelton. *The Enduring South.* Chapel Hill: University of North Carolina Press, 1986.

———. "Life and Leisure in the New South." *North Carolina Historical Review* 60 (April 1983): 172–82.

Setzer, Lynn. "Hot Doughnuts Now." *Our State* 68 (December 2000): 68–82.

Silcox-Jarrett, Diane. "Too Much of a Good Thing?" *Our State* 68 (February 2001): 49, 50.

Smith, Margaret Supplee. "North Carolina Women Making History." *Historian* 58 (1995): 101–6.

Speizer, Irwin. "To Be Rather Than to Seem." *Business North Carolina* 20 (October 2000): 42–55.

"Tar Heel Cities and Towns Share in Growth." *Southern City* 50 (March 2000): 1–15.

Thompson, Charles D., Jr. "The Great Deluge: A Chronicle of the Aftermath of Hurricane Floyd." *Southern Cultures* 7 (2001): 65–82.

Towle, Lisa. "Driving the Economy." *North Carolina* 67 (November 1998): 29, 30, 32, 37–40.

Turner, Walter R. "The Quest to Build a Great Airport in Winston-Salem." *American Aviation Historical Society* 41 (1996): 288–95.

Tuttle, S. "Clearing the Air." *North Carolina* 56 (February 1998): 37, 39–41, 43.

Wilkinson, Sylvia. *Dirt Tracks to Glory: The Early Days of Stock Car Racing as Told by the Participants.* Chapel Hill: Algonquin Books, 1983.

Wineka, Mark, and Jason Lesley. *Lion's Share: How Three Small-Town Grocers Created America's Fastest-Growing Supermarket Chain and Made Millionaires of Scores of Their North Carolina Friends.* Asheboro, N.C.: Down Home Press, 1991.

Woody, Stephen W. "Branch Banking in North Carolina: Its History, Economic Contribution, and Future." Ph.D. diss., Rutgers University, 1972.

Zellenko, Laura. "Finding Gold in the Games." *North Carolina* 50 (May 1992): 16–21.

INDEX